# The Concerto

# THE CONCERTO

## A Listener's Guide

MICHAEL STEINBERG

New York    Oxford
OXFORD UNIVERSITY PRESS
1998

Oxford University Press

Oxford   New York
Athens   Auckland   Bangkok   Bogotá   Buenos Aires
Calcutta   Cape Town   Chennai   Dar es Salaam   Delhi
Florence   Hong Kong   Istanbul   Karachi   Kuala Lumpur
Madrid   Melbourne   Mexico City   Mumbai
Nairobi   Paris   São Paulo   Singapore
Taipei   Tokyo   Toronto   Warsaw

and associated companies in
Berlin   Ibadan

Copyright © 1998 by Michael Steinberg

Published by Oxford University Press, Inc.
198 Madison Avenue, New York, New York 10016

Oxford is a registered trademark of Oxford University Press

Library of Congress Cataloging-in-Publication Data
Steinberg, Michael, 1928–
The concerto : a listener's guide / Michael Steinberg.
p.   cm.
ISBN 0-19-510330-0
1. Concerto.   I. Title.
ML1263.S74   1998
784.2'3'015—dc21   97-42678

9 8 7 6 5 4 3 2 1

Printed in the United States of America
on acid-free paper

*To Katja Andy*

# Introduction

I begin with silent thanks to all those who, across many years, have helped me to become a writer and have in various ways made it possible for me to be one. They are named in my book *The Symphony: A Listener's Guide*, and if I do not repeat that long recital here, it is not for lack of gratitude. Names I cannot omit, however, are those of my colleagues and collaborators with whom I have worked and without whose generous help and understanding none of this work could have been accomplished: Marc Mandel and Jean Miller Mackenzie at the Boston Symphony; Susan Feder, David Bowman, Laurence Rothe, and Katherine Cummins at the San Francisco Symphony; and James Keller at the New York Philharmonic. To Katherine Cummins I am especially indebted once again, not only for seventeen years of support, loyalty, and friendship, but also for reading the entire book in proof. To Debra Podjed, another San Francisco Symphony colleague and friend, go my warm thanks for her careful preparation of the musical examples. And once more, I am grateful to the librarians at the San Francisco Symphony, John Van Winkle, John Campbell, and Margo Kieser, and, at the Minnesota Orchestra, to Paul Gunther, Eric Sjostrom, and Carole Keller, all of whom have been immensely generous and helpful.

Most of these essays began as program notes for concerts. All have been revised and rewritten, some slightly, many almost beyond recognition. The following originally appeared in some form in the program book of the Boston Symphony, whose program annotator I was from 1976 to 1979: Bach, Brandenburg Concertos; Bartók, Violin Concerto No. 2; Beethoven, Piano Concertos Nos. 1, 4, and 5, and Violin Concerto; Berg, Violin Concerto; Brahms, Piano Concertos Nos. 1 and 2, and Violin Concerto; Martin, Concerto for Seven Winds; Mozart, Clarinet Concerto, Piano Concertos Nos. 9, 17, 19, 23, and 25, and Violin Concerto No. 5; Rachmaninoff, Piano Concerto No. 3; Saint-Saëns, Piano Concerto No. 2; Schoenberg, Piano Concerto; Schumann, Cello Concerto and Piano Concerto; Strauss, *Burleske*; Stravinsky, Violin Concerto; and Tchaikovsky, Piano Concerto No. 1, Violin Concerto, and *Variations on a Rococo Theme*.

The following notes first appeared in some form in the program book of the San Francisco Symphony, whose program annotator I have been since

1979: Bach, Harpsichord Concerto in D minor; Bartók, Piano Concertos Nos. 1, 2, and 3; Beethoven, Piano Concertos Nos. 2 and 3, and Triple Concerto; Brahms, Double Concerto; Britten, Symphony for Cello and Orchestra; Bruch, Violin Concerto No. 1 and *Scottish* Fantasy; Carter, Oboe Concerto, Violin Concerto, and Double Concerto; Chausson, *Poème;* Dvořák, Cello Concerto; Elgar, Cello Concerto and Violin Concerto; Grieg, Piano Concerto; Hindemith, *Der Schwanendreher* and *Trauermusik;* Korngold, Violin Concerto; Liszt, Piano Concertos Nos. 1 and 2; Mendelssohn, Piano Concerto No. 1 and Violin Concerto; Mozart, Horn Concerto No. 3, Piano Concertos Nos. 11, 12, 13, 14, 18, 20, 22, 24, and 27, Violin Concertos Nos. 3 and 4, and *Sinfonia concertante;* Nielsen, Flute Concerto; Perle, Piano Concerto No. 1; Prokofiev, Piano Concerto No. 2 and Violin Concerto No. 1; Rachmaninoff, Piano Concerto No. 2 and *Rhapsody on a Theme of Paganini;* Ravel, Left-Hand Concerto; Saint-Saëns, Piano Concerto No. 4; Schuman, Violin Concerto; Schumann, *Concertstück* for Four Horns; Sessions, Violin Concerto; Shostakovich, Cello Concerto No. 1 and Violin Concerto No. 1; Sibelius, Violin Concerto; Strauss, Oboe Concerto; Stravinsky, Piano Concerto; Tchaikovsky, Piano Concerto No. 2; and Walton, Cello Concerto, Viola Concerto, and Violin Concerto.

The essay on the Barber Violin Concerto first appeared in the program book of the New York Philharmonic, whose program annotator I have been since 1995.

I am deeply grateful to these orchestras, who hold the copyrights for the original versions, for their permission to use this material. In addition, the notes on the Adams Violin Concerto, the Britten Violin Concerto, and the Schoenberg Violin Concerto originally appeared in different form in the program book of the Minnesota Orchestra.

The musical excerpts from Bartók's Violin Concerto No. 2, copyright ©1946 by Hawkes & Son (London) Ltd., copyright renewed, are used by permission of Boosey & Hawkes, Inc. The excerpts from Berg's Violin Concerto, copyright © 1936 by Universal Edition, copyright renewed, all rights reserved, are used by permission of European-American Music Distributors Corporation, sole U.S. and Canadian agent for Universal Edition. The excerpts from Schoenberg's Violin Concerto, copyright © 1939 by G. Schirmer, Inc., Schoenberg's Piano Concerto, copyright © 1944 by G. Schirmer, Inc., and Shostakovich's Violin Concerto No.1, copyright 1956 by G. Schirmer Inc., are used by permission of G. Schirmer, Inc.

Many other people have helped with loans of scores, recordings, or other materials, by coming up with bits of information or stimulating ideas at just the right moments, and in countless other ways. For their contributions I warmly thank Styra Avins, Michael Beckerman, William Bennett (San Francisco Symphony), Alfred Brendel, George Class (European-American Music), Christine Dahl (Saint Paul Chamber Orchestra), Mary Ann Feldman

(Minnesota Orchestra), Lynn Harrell, Barbara Heyman, Angelika Hoffmann (Edition Schott), Michael Kennedy, Katherine Kolb, William Kraft, David Neumeyer (Indiana University), Garrick Ohlsson, Bruce Phillips (Oxford University Press, Oxford), David Robertson, Asadour Santourian (Minnesota Orchestra), Giselher Schubert (Paul-Hindemith-Institut, Frankfurt), Peter Serkin, Miranda Sielaff, Caroline Szylowicz (Kolb-Proust Archive, University of Illinois), and Simon Wright (Oxford University Press, Oxford). George Perle was hugely generous with his time, sharing his unparalleled store of information about Alban Berg and going through my essay on Berg's Violin Concerto with a fine-tooth comb. To George go not only my special thanks but also my apologies for using up hours that should have been his for composing.

Two other dear friends must be mentioned here. Robert P. Guter read part of the book in manuscript, and his comments, queries, and suggestions were wonderfully useful and welcome. Anne Hadley Montague brought her sharp eyes, ears, and mind to bear on nearly the entire manuscript. Turning many a muddle into clarity, she made a real difference, and I thank her from the bottom of my heart (a cliché from which she would probably have wanted to save me).

At Oxford University Press, I thank my editor, Sheldon Meyer, for his encouragement, advice, patience, and friendship. I am also grateful to Paul Schlotthauer for his careful and caring copy-editing and to the ever calm and unfailingly helpful Joellyn Ausanka, as well as to Susan Day and all the other people at OUP who turned a pile of manuscript pages into a book.

My wife, Jorja Fleezanis, answered questions about string technique, got a refractory paginating machine to work, fought for clarity of diction, and was always there with encouragement and love. Altogether, without her, this book would not exist.

Katja Andy, with her deep love and understanding of music, her blessed lack of solemnity, and her wry and cleansing humor, has been an inspiration for the more than three decades I have had the joy of knowing her. The dedication of this book is a small token of thanks for an unpayable debt as well as a belated ninety-first-birthday present.

Edina, Minnesota                                                     Michael Steinberg
January 1998

# Contents

# The Concerto

# John Adams

John Coolidge Adams was born in Worcester, Massachusetts, on February 15, 1947, and now lives in Berkeley, California.

## Violin Concerto

1. —
2. Chaconne: "Body through which the dream flows"
3. Toccare

Adams began his Violin Concerto on 7 January 1993. The official completion date of the score was 1 November 1993, although some changes of detail continued to arrive for two or three weeks after that and a few were made during rehearsal. The work was a joint commission by the Minnesota Orchestra, the London Symphony, and the New York City Ballet. The first performance was given in Minneapolis on 19 January 1994 by Jorja Fleezanis with Edo de Waart and the Minnesota Orchestra. Partly in collaboration with the violinist Gidon Kremer, who had been chosen to give the first performance with the London Symphony, Adams made some further revisions after the first performance. Adams dedicated the work to the late David Huntley of the publishing firm Boosey & Hawkes: American composers in recent years had no better friend. Adams has written: "[David Huntley] died not long after the premiere. . . . An arduous trip from New York to Minneapolis to attend the premiere during one of the coldest winters on record turned out to be the last of his many travels, a labor of love that I hope was at least partially rewarded by this dedication and by this piece."


Solo violin, two flutes (two doubling piccolo and alto flute), two oboes (two doubling English horn), two clarinets (two doubling bass clarinet), two bassoons, two horns, trumpet, marimba, two low tom-toms, five roto toms, tubular bells, three bongos, two congas, two bass drums, suspended cymbal, tambourine, three high timbales, guiro, vibraphone (bowed), claves, high cowbell, timpani, two synthesizers (Yamaha SY-99 and Kurzweil K-2000), and strings.


John Adams's father was a good amateur clarinetist and saxophonist. The clarinet was John's first instrument, too, though he chose to hone his skills to professional level: my first awareness of him was as a member of Sarah Caldwell's opera orchestra in Boston and as an occasional substitute in the Boston Symphony. He was then a student at Harvard. His principal mentor there was Leon Kirchner, for whose teaching, charged with imagination and intellectual vigor, Adams still feels profound gratitude. As a graduation present, his parents gave him John Cage's Silence, a collection of lectures and writings of which Jill Johnston said when it appeared in 1962 that "those who read [it] should find it difficult to curl up inside any comfortable box made before picking up the book." It certainly called into question everything that his musical experiences so far stood for. "I don't think my parents knew what they were giving," Adams reflected years later. He found "the seductiveness of Cage's reasoning "irresistible," a condition hardly disturbed by his finding the holes in Cage's arguments. Something that particularly stirred him was Cage's emphasis on the importance of sound itself as a physical entity as distinct from the emphasis, standard in teaching and criticism, on the organization of sound.

Harvard graduates tended typically to think about going to Europe on a Fulbright or a Paine Travelling Fellowship, but Adams now wanted to remove himself from that world. His response was to go 3,000 miles in the opposite direction, to California. At first he worked in an Oakland warehouse; then, in 1972, he joined the faculty of the San Francisco Conservatory, where he taught composition, founded a new-music ensemble, conducted the orchestra, and ran a graduate program in analysis and history.

When Edo de Waart became the San Francisco Symphony's music director in 1977, he let it be known that he would be glad of some help in guiding him through the unfamiliar territory of current American music. Someone proposed John Adams, and a warm professional and personal friendship was born. Adams's work as de Waart's new-music adviser was so effective that the relationship became the model for the composer-in-residence program established at many American orchestras in the 1980s. Adams himself became the San Francisco Symphony's first composer-in-residence, serving in that capacity for four years.

De Waart arranged for the Symphony to tender Adams a commission, and Adams responded with *Harmonium*, choral settings of John Donne and Emily Dickinson. At the time, Adams was known in the profession, although not very widely, and in the Bay Area's new-music community. At the premiere of *Harmonium*, Adams was cheered no less than the distinguished pianist who played the *Emperor* Concerto, and after that his life was never the same. His next San Francisco commission, *Grand Pianola Music,* got him entrée with the New York Philharmonic and the Royal Concertgebouw Orchestra of Amsterdam. In 1985 de Waart introduced an enormously difficult and ambitious score, *Harmonielehre,* named for Arnold Schoenberg's searching treatise of 1911, which Adams has described as a sort of Talmud of Western music theory. Orchestras everywhere, as far afield as Japan, Australia, and the Soviet Union, took up *Harmonielehre,* and the extraordinary success of that dauntingly difficult thirty-eight-minute work gave the lie to the received wisdom according to which only short and easy new pieces were admitted into the working repertory.

*Harmonielehre,* particularly in its powerful slow movement (called "The Anfortas Wound"), also showed that Adams had a lyric and expressive gift that singled him out among his colleagues of no matter what compositional school. This component of Adams's artistic personality was further stretched and developed in his opera *Nixon in China,* a remarkable amalgam of wit and emotional poignancy. Just as "The Anfortas Wound" was the departure strip for the most deeply touching portions of *Nixon in China* (Pat Nixon's aria in Act II and all of the introspective closing scene), so *Nixon* became the launching place for Adams's second opera, *The Death of Klinghoffer,* whose subject is the hijacking of the *Achille Lauro.* Since then, he has expanded his language and consolidated his position with such works as *The Wound-Dresser* (after Whitman), *El Dorado, Fearful Symmetries,* the Chamber Symphony, and the "song play" for pop singers and rock band, *I Was Looking at the Ceiling and Then I Saw the Sky.*

When he first went to California, Adams was deeply involved with the work of John Cage and some of the younger figures of the then avant-garde, Robert Ashley, Alvin Lucier, and Christian Wolff. During a three-year immersion with electronic music he built his own synthesizer. Paradoxically it was that immersion and his involvement with technical points of tuning that led to what he called his "diatonic conversion. It made me realize the *resonant* power of consonance. There's such a lack of resonance in atonal music with all the upper partials clashing against each other. There's seldom a sense of depth or of sympathetic vibration. The composers that mean the most to me are those whose music is music of sustained resonance." Adams's own purest essay in consonant minimalism is an orchestral work named *Common Tones in Simple Time* (1980), music that still leaves me dazzled with the lustre of its sound, enchanted by the purr of its engine, delightfully jolted by its powerful lifts into new harmonies, and happy in its deep calm.

At the time of *Harmonium*, the examples he cited were Beethoven, Sibelius "for sure" (particularly the Seventh Symphony), "the orchestral Wagner," early Stravinsky, Steve Reich. By the time he wrote *Harmonielehre*, he was ready to add early Schoenberg, particularly *Gurrelieder*. But even then, Adams voiced reservations about the relentlessly consonant, low-metabolism way of composing that was then coming to be known as minimalism: "[It] really can be a bore. You get those Great Prairies of non-event, but that highly polished, perfectly resonant sound is wonderful." In the years since *Common Tones in Simple Times*, Adams has sought—and found—a world of richer harmonic possibilities and has dared ventures into a language "of greater synthesis and ambiguity. The territory . . . is far more dangerous, but also more fertile, more capable of expressive depth and emotional flexibility." Adams's mature music is a celebration of this stretching, a celebration of event, of wonderfully satisfying, room-filling sonority, of energy born of the force of harmonic movement.

The idea that there should be an Adams violin concerto was born in Jorja Fleezanis's mind on Tuesday evening, 26 March 1985, when she heard John Adams's *Harmonielehre* on the radio. The week before, Edo de Waart and the San Francisco Symphony, where Fleezanis was then associate concertmaster, had given the first performances of that remarkable score. *Harmonielehre* is an exceedingly difficult piece to play, and during the rehearsals, performances, and the recording sessions that followed, Fleezanis had been too busy counting to get a coherent impression of the work. At that time, San Francisco Symphony broadcasts were heard locally on the Tuesday after the previous week's concerts. When Fleezanis had a chance to experience *Harmonielehre* from the outside, she found it a knockout. The moment the broadcast was over, she picked up the telephone, called Adams, and asked him to write her a violin concerto.

Much happened over the following eight years. De Waart, Adams's first champion among major conductors, left San Francisco for Minneapolis. San Francisco was still interested in commissioning the Violin Concerto, but naturally enough, when Fleezanis became concertmaster of the Minnesota Orchestra, San Francisco's plans for an Adams commission changed. (The work Adams wrote for San Francisco instead was *El Dorado*.) De Waart, however, reopened the question of the Violin Concerto at his new post, and eventually a triple commission from the Minnesota Orchestra, the New York City Ballet (for choreography by Peter Martins), and the London Symphony Orchestra was arranged.

On 7 January 1993, at 8:19 P.M., Fleezanis received a fax from Adams with the words "Wir haben es angefangen" (We have begun it) and an A-minor chord about five octaves deep. (Adams had previously told her that the work would be in A minor and had promised it would be "drenchingly beautiful.") In March 1993, by way of a preview, Adams sent Fleezanis the score and tape of his Chamber Symphony, which is full of virtuoso solos for the concertmaster. She got her first look at the Concerto a month later when she visited Adams in Berkeley.

Although 7 January 1993 was the date the first notes went down on paper, Adams had had the Violin Concerto steadily in his mind since completing his second opera, *The Death of Klinghoffer*, and *El Dorado* in 1991. In part, the virtuoso violin writing in the Chamber Symphony, written in 1992, can be seen as the composer's limbering-up exercise for the Concerto. In no way did Adams approach the task lightly; indeed, to begin with he found it quite intimidating. For one thing, so many composers—Beethoven, Mendelssohn, Schumann, Brahms, Tchaikovsky, Sibelius, Elgar, Stravinsky, Berg, Schoenberg, just to begin a list—had written just one violin concerto. "These," Adams remarks, "tend to be among their greatest works, so unless one is completely historically indifferent, which I can't say I am, one tends to tread lightly."

At the same time, Adams was excited by the challenge: "The violin commands incredible lyric intensity and has a fantastic capacity to deliver a white-hot message." He himself is not a violinist, and for a time he made use of an ingenious device patented by the composer Donald Martino, a T-square that corresponds to a violin's fingerboard, with lines to represent the four strings and with the positions of all the notes marked on those lines.

The Martino T-square is a great help—up to a point. It can help you determine, for example, whether a certain chord can be reached at all by a violinist with the normal quota of four fingers and a thumb.[1] But it is one thing to be able to reach a chord and quite another to play it in the middle of a rapid and active passage. Nor does the T-square help you with the fact that some chords, though theoretically possible, simply do not "sound" and would come across as colorless or feeble. At some point the composer has to come to terms with the violin as it really is.

In this instance, Fleezanis eventually came to replace the T-square, and in so doing, she—and later, Gidon Kremer—became part of the succession of violinist collaborators that began when Ferdinand David worked with Mendelssohn on his concerto.[2] Adams wanted to write a truly violinistic

---

[1]Schoenberg reinforced the reputation of his own Violin Concerto for extreme difficulty when he said that it would require a new and special brand of fiddler with six fingers on the left hand, but many five-fingered players have brilliantly proved him wrong.

[2]Facsimiles of the manuscripts of the Mendelssohn and Brahms violin concertos are published (by

piece. Suggestions, emendations, counter-suggestions flew back and forth by phone and fax between Berkeley and Edina, Minnesota. Sometimes three alternative new versions of a passage would arrive by fax, and Fleezanis would play the various solutions back over the phone, sometimes into Adams's answering machine.

To begin with, Adams had imagined a two-movement concerto lasting a little over twenty minutes, something on the scale of the Stravinsky Concerto. The idea was to have a highly energetic first movement and then a contrasting slow movement, a chaconne, a set of variations over a repeated bass or harmonic pattern. Adams, thinking of Bach's great chaconne for solo violin and the finale of the Brahms Fourth Symphony, imagined a movement that would begin quietly but get "wilder and wilder and more ornate. It was a grand idea, but somehow I never found the right material to justify the form." Musical material always makes its desires known, makes its own laws, and controls its own destiny. Thus the chaconne became, as Adams has said, "a more enclosed piece, a kind of dreamy, filmy, almost diaphanous slow movement" in the middle of the work, which, in its final form, has the familiar shape of fast-slow-fast. Partly for that reason, the Concerto also came to be a larger work than Adams had originally foreseen: "I was trying at first to avoid a collision with destiny; nevertheless it came out big." It also turned out to be an important contribution to the repertory: just three years after the premiere, it had entered the repertory of more than a dozen violinists.

The first music we hear is a figuration in the orchestra—eight notes rising, to begin with—whose presence is constant enough to give us a sense of regularity, but whose details keep changing. The solo violin lays a wonderfully free melody across this pattern. "Composed rhapsodizing," Fleezanis calls it, and this sense of freedom, of something being invented on the spot and born out of the very spirit of the violin, the contrast between this and the firm dance floor provided by the orchestra, is characteristic of the Concerto throughout. From time to time a clarinet or some other instrument will step forward with a solo, but essentially the show is in the endlessly inventive and evolving violin part. (As well as endlessly inventive, the violin part is virtually non-stop in all three movements.) It is wave motion enormously magnified; just three or four great surges define the flow of the whole movement. There are occasional changes of speed, and near the end, Adams winds the rhythmic coil tighter by changing from four beats in a measure to just three. This switch occurs in the orchestra; the violin sets up a spicy rhythmic dissonance by staying firmly in four. This friction of three against four is one of the simplest of the cross-rhythms that enliven this Concerto.

With a brilliant passage for the flute, the orchestra makes its exit, and

Garland and Harvard University Press, respectively), and there you can see David's and Joachim's emendations as well as Mendelssohn's and Brahms's various acceptances and rejections of them.

the violin begins a cadenza. After a brief coda at a more spacious tempo and with the solo instrument now muted, the music flows directly into the second movement. This has a title: Chaconne: "Body through which the dream flows," a phrase taken from a poem by Robert Hass. A chaconne is, as Adams puts it, "a highly identifiable musical artifact"—the Pachelbel Canon is probably the most familiar example to most people—and the recognition factor is definitely part of Adams's plan.

Chaconne and passacaglia basses in Baroque and earlier music were generally clichés that outlined basic harmonic progressions. Adams's six-measure repeated bass is likewise a cliché (he found it in the article on ground bass in *The New Grove Dictionary of Music and Musicians*): virtually a quotation of the bass Pachelbel used. In Pachelbel's day—and also in 1993 for Adams—the point was to show what fresh things could be done on ground trod so often before. (The literary critic Harry Levin has remarked that quotation, allusion, and collage are of the essence of twentieth-century art.)

But while in Baroque music these basses usually stayed at the same pitch and kept their rhythmic shape (as usual, Bach is the exception, at least with respect to constancy of pitch), this bass begins to travel after the third variation. At first the rhythm changes, and the pattern which took six measures to traverse when we first heard it is now expanded to nine. Later it will, for example, be compressed to four. Part of what makes this fresh and delightful is that these augmentations and diminutions, instead of being managed by simple devices such as doubling or halving, involve unusual arithmetic proportions such as 4:5. Adams owes some of these rhythmic ideas to his study of the music of one of the great American eccentrics, Conlon Nancarrow, who died in 1997.

In this movement, too, there is contrast between firmness and freedom (the body and the dream) as the familiar bass is beautifully disturbed by the violin melodies that float and soar freely across it, by changes in meter and harmony, and by the softly shimmering sound of the synthesizers in the orchestra. Something comparable happens in the harmony as well. The bass, at first, outlines the simplest imaginable major-key harmonies, but later, though it always remains recognizable, it moves into other, less familiar modes. (Computer technology now allows a composer to "translate" a melody from major into minor or into any other mode with a single keystroke.) The Chaconne is the movement that underwent the biggest changes in the course of composition. In its original form—and this probably goes back to the stage when Adams thought of it as the finale—the solo violin part was extraordinarily active, all luxuriant tendrils and coils, like something from an Ornette Coleman solo; the revisions allow much more room for expressive lyric melody.

The finale is titled "Toccare." This is an Italian verb meaning both to touch and to play a keyboard instrument—the French *toucher* does similar double duty—and we are more familiar with *toccata*, the noun derived from it. In post-Baroque music, a toccata is usually a brilliant display piece with a steady rat-tat of sixteenth-notes, and this Toccare is a finale in that spirit. Part of Adams's preparation for the writing of the Violin Concerto had involved intense listening to performances of bowed stringed instruments outside the Western classical tradition, such as the work of the extraordinary Indian virtuoso, Dr. L. Subramaniam, and here we find inventive and daring fiddle pyrotechnics on that order. Adams's wife, the photographer Deborah O'Grady, referred to the fast movements of the Chamber Symphony as "caffeine music"—one of the most characteristic features of the Adams-O'Grady house is the aroma of fresh and strong coffee—and this heady, high-spirited finale is definitely of that ilk. And no nonsense about decaf, either.[3]

---

[3]As this book goes to press, I learn from John Adams that he has given up caffeine.

# Johann Sebastian Bach

Johann Sebastian Bach was born in Eisenach, Thuringia, on 21
March 1685 and died in Leipzig, Saxony, on 28 July 1750.

## The Brandenburg Concertos, BWV 1046-1051

**B**ach wrote these works about 1720, and presumably led and took
part in their first performances at the court of Cöthen soon after
their composition. They were almost certainly introduced singly, not
as a set. Bach played the harpsichord in the Concerto No. 5, and probably
played violin in the first four concertos and viola in No. 6. The scoring is
discussed in the notes on the individual works.

When Bach assumed the post of Capellmeister to His Most Serene Highness
Leopold, Prince of Anhalt-Cöthen, in 1717, he made that move in the hope
of spending the rest of his life there. The court was Calvinist and thus required no church music, and Bach enjoyed the change of not being primarily
an organist and the challenge of providing great quantities of solo, chamber,
and orchestral music. His new patron, just twenty-three, loved music and
played the violin, the viola da gamba, and keyboards skillfully. But the idyll
was spoiled when Bach's wife died suddenly in the summer of 1720, and the
next year the professional scene darkened when the prince married. His musical interests, Bach recalled later, became "somewhat lukewarm, the more
so since the new Princess seemed to be alien to the muses." In fact the *Amusa*,
as Bach called her, soon died, and Leopold's second wife was a sympathetic
and sensitive patron, but by then Bach was restless and determined to leave.

In 1723 he moved to Leipzig, where he was the City Council's reluctant third choice as director of music at the churches of Saint Thomas and Saint Nicholas, and there he remained until his death in 1750.

Bach was looking around for greener pastures as early as March 1721, when, along with a suitably servile letter, he sent the Margrave of Brandenburg a handsome presentation copy of six concertos he had composed over the last year or so for performance at Cöthen. Bach had met the margrave and played for him in 1719 when he went to Berlin to collect a new harpsichord. (Brandenburg is the Prussian province immediately west and south of Berlin; its capital was Potsdam.) The margrave never replied to Bach, nor did he ever use or perhaps even open the score. We are lucky that at least he kept it, because his copy is our only source for these forever vernal concertos, which have been called "the most entertaining music in the world."

Whenever Bach assembled a collection of pieces, he always took pains to make it as diverse as possible. Musicians have always delighted in the wonderful timbral variety of the Brandenburgs. Bach wanted to impress his prospective patron—as he had already impressed his present employer—with the coloristic possibilities a composer on his plane of imagination and technique could draw from a band of only eighteen players. Variety for the sake of entertainment and charm must have been at the forefront of Bach's mind, but as he worked he must have become more and more fascinated with the compositional possibilities his varied instrumentations suggested. He constantly defines and articulates the succession of musical events by textural-timbral means: the Brandenburg Concertos are, so to speak, about their textures and their color.

**Concerto No. 1 in F major**, BWV 1046, for two horns, three oboes, and violino piccolo, with bassoon, strings, and harpsichord. In sound and form, this is the most complex concerto in the set. The violino piccolo, tuned a minor third higher than a normal violin, is the primary solo instrument. One oboe joins it in duet in the Adagio, but in general the wind players together form something like a secondary solo group. In the Adagio, the bass entrance of the melody leads to a famous harmonic collision, the most emphatic example of Bach's expressive play with the magic of what theorists used to call "false relations," here the appearance of A-natural and A-flat in different voices and adjacent beats.

The orchestral possibilities frequently lead Bach into a nine-layered polyphony. Nowhere is his concern with color more explicitly manifest than in the Adagio's last measures with their separation on successive beats into bass, oboes, and unsupported high strings. Bach's original version consists of three movements in the normal manner, but in its final form the Concerto gets an unexpected extension in the form of a minuet with three contrasting interludes: a true trio for oboes and bassoon, a polonaise for strings only and in a quicker tempo, and then, in a new meter, a virtuosic passage for two horns playing against all the oboes in unison. Thus the work crystallizes in this closing divertissement those fastidiously structured timbral sequences that are its most basic and serious compositional concern.

**Concerto No. 2 in F major**, BWV 1047, for trumpet, recorder, oboe, and violin, with strings and harpsichord. In the two concertos for strings alone, Bach sets himself the challenge of creating contrast where none explicitly exists. Here he has the opposite task, to integrate his most heterogeneous consort of instruments. No wonder that the dynamics are marked in unprecedented detail. The Andante is for the three gentler-voiced soloists with figured bass. What is best remembered about this Concerto is the trumpet part, the zenith of the clarino tradition, and one of the most spectacular sounds in all of Baroque music. Since Bach specifies a *traversière*, or transverse flute, in No. 5, he presumably means a recorder when, as here, he just says *flauto*; however, in most modern-instrument performances in large halls, the part is played on a regular flute.

**Concerto No. 3 in G major**, BWV 1048, for three violins, three violas, and three cellos, with bass and harpsichord. This Concerto has no players specifically and consistently designated as soloists, but Bach can arrange his seven voices—three violins and three violas, with everybody else working on the bass line—to get more different combinations than any orthodox solo concertino could provide. All the violin and viola parts become soloistic at some point and all contribute to the tutti in what is texturally the most inventive of the Brandenburgs.

Bach's concertos normally have three movements. Brandenburg No. 1, as we have seen, is an exception in that it adds a minuet; Brandenburg No. 3 is another in that it lacks a slow movement. Between the two allegros there is only a pair of chords marked "adagio." We cannot know for sure what Bach intended, and many solutions (including some absurd ones) have been tried. The simplest, most elegant, and most sensible is to have the first violinist play a flourish over each of the two chords (or at least over the first one).

**Concerto No. 4 in G major**, BWV 1049, for violin and two recorders, with strings and harpsichord. This Concerto has interesting solo-tutti combinations. In the first movement the solo violin dominates, and the recorders (whose parts are also played on flutes in most performances in large halls) are secondary. In the Andante, the flutes dominate, while the violin provides their bass in a vigorous dialogue with full orchestra, which is used in only this one of the Brandenburg slow movements. The orchestra then plays its largest role in the fugal finale, though no violinist negotiating Bach's scales at about a dozen notes per second will feel that the composer has neglected his soloists.

**Concerto No. 5 in D major,** BWV 1050, for flute, violin, and solo harpsichord, with strings and harpsichord. The solo harpsichord usually does double duty as continuo harpsichord. Bach himself must have played this Concerto on the harpsichord he fetched from Berlin in 1719. This is the first concerto ever written with a solo keyboard part, and the keyboard's new dominance is asserted in a spectacular cadenza at the end of the first movement. And no vague rhapsody, this: there is not a more powerfully built coda in the literature.

During the second movement the orchestra remains silent, but the concerto contrast continues. Sometimes the keyboard is soloistic (usually in duet with flute or violin), but at the beginning and end, and three times between, it adds a quasi-tutti effect with its figured-bass accompaniments. In performance at Cöthen, the second violinist would have taken over the viola stand where Bach normally played—hence there is no second violin part in this piece.

Bach would have played the solo keyboard part on the harpsichord, but it works fabulously as a piano piece, and such artists as Cortot, Schnabel, Furtwängler, Rudolf and Peter Serkin, Lukas Foss, Eugene Istomin, James Levine, and Angela Hewitt have rejoiced in its brilliance.

**Concerto No. 6 in B-flat major,** BWV 1051, for two violas and two violas da gamba, with cello, bass, and harpsichord. For Bach's audience the new sound in this Concerto would have been the contrast of the gambas—one of them played by Prince Leopold—with their modern replacement, the violoncello. The Adagio is an impassioned vocal duet, like the Adagio in No. 1; the finale is a gigue, like that of the Concerto No. 5. But how different these duets and gigues are, how varied Bach is even when the same labels must serve. The first movement's closely woven canon is one of Bach's most dazzling tours de force. In its violinless darkness, this Concerto is proto-Brahms.

# Concerto in D minor for Harpsichord (or Violin) and String Orchestra, BWV 1052

*Allegro*
*Adagio*
*Allegro*

In its final form, this work is part of a collection of keyboard concertos assembled by Bach around 1739. It is most likely that he himself led the first performance from the harpsichord at a Collegium Musicum concert at Zimmermann's Coffee House in Leipzig.

**In the version for solo violin, Bach would have had a harpsichord to fill out the harmony. In the keyboard version, his solo instrument would have been a harpsichord, but like most of Bach's harpsichord music, this concerto works wonderfully on a modern piano.**

It has long been assumed this fiery and expressive keyboard concerto is a transcription of a lost violin concerto and, as Donald Tovey rightly maintained, "the greatest and most difficult violin concerto before the time of Beethoven." It is the nature of the figurations in the solo part that has suggested this, especially the prevalence of passages rotating about a single note on an open string—for example, the one that corresponds to the violin's A-string.[1] Several transcriptions backwards, so to speak, have been made of this and of Bach's other concertos for one or more keyboard instruments for which the same origin is presumed.

Bach also used this music in two church cantatas. The finale served as the Sinfonia before *Ich habe meine Zuversicht* (I Have My Trust in God), BWV 188, probably composed in 1728. The first movement was used for the same purpose in *Wir müssen durch viel Trübsal in das Reich Gottes eingehen* (We Must Pass Through Much Tribulation to Enter God's Kingdom), BWV 146, dated somewhere between 1726 and 1728. In that same cantata, in one of Bach's most amazing strokes of transformation, the Concerto's Adagio becomes the opening chorus, the parts for a four-part chorus simply (!) being added to the existing movement. In both cantatas the solo keyboard part is

---

[1]The technical term for this kind of string writing is *bariolage*, literally a mixture of colors. Picking them up straight from Bach's D-minor Keyboard Concerto with no thought of the violin behind them, Stravinsky found these passages a useful model in his Concerto for Piano and Winds.

assigned to the organ. The cantata movements give us this music in slightly less developed and thus presumably earlier form. Most likely Bach prepared the final form of the Concerto for the Leipzig University Collegium Musicum concerts that Georg Philipp Telemann had started during his student days at Leipzig and which Bach ran from 1739 to 1741.

We don't know when Bach composed the lost violin concerto, but the most plausible assumption is that it was between 1717 and 1723, when he was Capellmeister at the court of Anhalt-Cöthen. The court there was Calvinist, which meant that music in church was restricted to unaccompanied hymns, and Bach's main responsibility was to compose instrumental music and to see to its performance. These were the years of the Brandenburgs and other concertos, of the first book of The Well-Tempered Clavier and the English and French suites, and of his sonatas and suites for string instruments.

Some scholars have proposed that the D-minor Keyboard Concerto was a transcription of a lost original by someone other than Bach. Tovey, doubting that any predecessor or contemporary of Bach's "could have designed the whole of a single paragraph of this concerto," speaks to this point: "My disrespect is unparliamentary for a musicology that has no sense of composition. The only composer who could have planned this concerto is John Sebastian Bach." Attributions on the basis of style can be notoriously treacherous, and Tovey's argument is not calculated to convince a historian looking for criteria other than—or, perhaps better, as well as—excellence. But in this instance, this view has prevailed. Current scholarly consensus credits Bach with this composition, and the scholarly new complete Bach edition (Neue Bach-Ausgabe) even includes a reconstruction of the putative violin original.

And an amazing composition this is, from the muscular, fiercely terse first tutti on. We can sense the presence of the Baroque concerto tradition in which the initial tutti several times reappears as a marker separating excursions for the soloist, but Bach has fused the two worlds into an organic and powerful discourse that is not to be found in the music of any of his contemporaries. Bach made this movement for a player, presumably himself, in whose rhetorical command he had immense confidence. Twice he creates space for a cadenza, one free, as the soloist breaks loose in a great flourish from an expectant diminished chord in the orchestra, the other in tempo and built up over a dramatically insistent pedal point in the bass.

The Adagio begins with thirteen grave measures for the orchestra, a single line, unharmonized. Its close is carefully lapped with the first note of an impassioned aria for the soloist, an aria of vast range and import. Immediately, the strings resume their opening music, while the violins and violas engage in quiet dialogue with the soloist. We expect the movement to turn into a gigantic passacaglia over that thirteen-measure ground bass, and we turn out to be both right and wrong. Bach hews to the principle of a repeated ground—there is not a single measure from which it is absent—but he presents it with powerful elasticity and at an incandescent level of invention, now repeated literally, now shortened or lengthened, made to modulate into new harmonic territories, or given simply in fragments, until another magnificently serpentine cadenza—a brief one—returns the music to its opening bars. Responding to this Adagio's effect of driving inexorably toward a destination of tragic significance, the pianist Zoltán Kocsis has called it a *Via Crucis*.

The finale reverts to the energy and the intensity of the first movement. It is on a grand scale, brilliant in its violinistic keyboard style and the unique instance of a Bach finale equal to a first movement in expressive thrust and virtuosic effulgence.

## Concerto in D minor for Two Violins and String Orchestra, BWV 1043

> *Vivace*
> *Largo ma non tanto*
> *Allegro*

Bach composed this Concerto between 1717 and 1723 while he was Capellmeister at the court of Anhalt-Cöthen. For more on that situation, see my essay on Bach's Brandenburg Concertos. About 1739, in Leipzig, Bach made a version of this work in C minor for two solo harpsichords and strings, BWV 1062. We do not know the dates of the first performances; we can safely assume, though, that Bach would have led them at Cöthen, either as one of the solo violinists or from the harpsichord, and as one of the harpsichordists at a University Collegium Musicum concert at Zimmermann's Coffee House in Leipzig.

**In the original version for two violins, Bach would have had a harpsichord fill out the harmony.**

If we step back and take a clinical look at Bach's two great D-minor Concertos, this one and the one for solo keyboard (or solo violin), BWV 1052, we might summarize the difference by saying that the enormous impact of the latter has everything to do with the composer's powerful command of form, while the magic of the Two-Violin Concerto lies primarily in the endlessly fascinating beauty of its fabric, its counterpoint. Together with a few movements in the Brandenburgs, this concerto is the one of Bach's that offers us the most joyously intricate play of voice against voice. Listening to it, I always imagine what pleasure it must have given Bach to accomplish this without the richly equipped Brandenburg paintbox. (Of the two Brandenburg Concertos for strings only, No. 3 is written for a seven-part ensemble that allows for a special, kaleidoscopic sort of variety, while No. 6, dominated by two violas and with its contrast of cello versus viola da gamba tone, uses a unique palette of colors.)

In 1940, George Balanchine made a ballet on this music, calling it *Concerto Barocco*. It is no surprise that the lively interplay of musical lines in this work was especially attractive to him. A fairly early instance of a ballet whose only subject was the music itself, and not always understood when it was new, *Concerto Barocco* is a luminous example of dance that adds new strands of counterpoint to those that Bach has already composed and, in doing so, illuminates and enhances the play of Bach's mind and spirit.

Reviewing a performance of *Concerto Barocco* in 1945, Edwin Denby, America's best dance writer (then or since), wrote: "The excitement is that of a constant impetus of dance invention and figuration, now rapid and brilliant, now sustained, outspread, and slow. The emotion is now one of gradually gathered and released weight, now one of a free and even outpouring of energy. Its emotional changes are like those of the music, all contained in a wonderfully serene, limpid, and spontaneous flow." Returning to the subject a week later, Denby, responding to some particularly intense images in the slow movement, added: "But these 'emotional' figures are strictly formal as dance inventions. They require no miming to make them expressive, just as the violin parts call for no special schmaltz." Denby's description also turns out to be one of the best accounts of Bach's music I know.[2]

The electrifyingly energetic first movement opens in a quasi-fugal way, the second violins, solo and tutti, leading off, the first violins joining in four measures later. It is not an uncommon procedure in Baroque concertos in general, but it is very rare in Bach. The first tutti is twenty-one measures long; then the two violins, this time with the first in the lead, separate themselves from the orchestra with a new theme whose chief characteristics are its leaps of tenths and its running passages of sixteenth-notes. The tutti reap-

[2]It is a pity that the Nonesuch Balanchine Library collection of videos does not include a performance of *Concerto Barocco*; however, Anne Belle's film *Dancing for Mr. B.*, which is part of that series, offers a couple of tantalizing glimpses of that ballet, danced with wit and spirit by Diana Adams and Tanaquil LeClercq.

pears several times, abbreviated and transformed; the solos continue in an unceasing flow of fresh invention.

In the slow movement—but not too broad, Bach warns—it is again the second violin that begins. Here the orchestra is strictly the accompanist for the two violins as they spin out their rapturous cantilena, exchanging musical lines and vying in quietly passionate avowals. It is a movement that wondrously blends tranquillity with intensity of feeling.

The finale is tempestuous. It is full of imitations, but they follow upon one another in an extraordinarily tight and compact way. The contrapuntal duetting is more inventive than ever and the writing for the violins is captivatingly virtuosic.[3]

---

[3]If you have a taste for the bizarre, you might want to check out the 1928 recording by Arnold and Alma Rosé (Biddulph). Twenty measures before the end, the music screeches to a halt, whereupon there follows a nearly two-minute cadenza by the famous nineteenth-century quartet-leader Joseph Hellmesberger. Its general clumsiness and one howling grammatical indiscretion are perfect examples of the sort of thing Mozart was sending up in his *Musical Joke*, K. 522.

# Samuel Barber

Samuel Osmond Barber II was born in West Chester, Pennsylvania, on 9 March 1910 and died in New York on 23 January 1981.

One morning when he was eight or nine, the future inventor of the Adagio for Strings, that concord of a solemn and archaic polyphony with melancholy Romantic passion at high tide, the man who would touch us with *Knoxville: Summer of 1915* and *Andromache's Farewell*, stir us with his evocation of Medea's fury, excite us with his Piano Sonata, give us *Sure on this shining night* (and who, having heard the song, can imagine James Agee's poem otherwise?), and make us smile with *Souvenirs, Promiscuity* and the feline cameo of *Pangur, White Pangur*, left this almost impeccably spelled message on his desk before he went to school:

Notice to *Mother* and *nobody else*

Dear Mother: I have written this to tell you my worrying secret. Now don't cry when you read this because it is neither yours nor my fault. I suppose I will have to tell it now without any nonsense. To begin with, I was not meant to be an athlet. I was meant to be a composer, and will be I'm sure. I'll ask you one more thing.—Don't ask me to try to forget this unpleasant thing and go and play football.—*Please*—Sometimes I've been worrying about this so much that it makes me mad (not very). Love, SAM BARBER II.[1]

---

[1]Quoted in Barbara Heyman, *Samuel Barber* (New York: Oxford University Press, 1992), and other sources.

He had started writing songs at seven, and only a year after so urgently declaring his life intentions to Daisy Barber, he set *Mother Goose* verses to music and composed one act of an opera, *The Rose Tree*, with a libretto by Annie Sullivan, the family's well-read cook. At fourteen, he was enrolled in the first class at the newly opened Curtis Institute in Philadelphia. As well as becoming a composer, he turned out to be a good singer and a fine pianist: his recording, made at twenty-five, of his own setting of Matthew Arnold's *Dover Beach* is a classic monument in phonographic history, and the one with Leontyne Price of his *Hermit Songs* attests to his finely honed skill at the keyboard.

His music was taken up not only by such champions of the new as Rodzinski, Koussevitzky, and Ormandy, but by such notable non-friends of modern music as Toscanini, who conducted the Adagio for Strings and the Essay for Orchestra in 1938; Bruno Walter, who conducted the Symphony No. 1 in 1944 and made the first recording of it; and Vladimir Horowitz, who introduced the Piano Sonata in 1950. Barber was not one of those composers, like Schoenberg, Stravinsky, and Carter, to whom it was given to change our world of music or our perception of it, but, working with craft and generous sentiment within the definitions and standards he inherited, he made that world a more civilized place with his finely executed monuments and ornaments. Barber's stock went down in his later years—the turning point was the premiere of *Antony and Cleopatra*, written for the opening of the Metropolitan Opera House in 1966, an event described by Gary Schmidgall as "the most famously dreadful night at the opera in the history of the American (if not the Roman) republic"—but ten years or so after his death, his work began to be re-examined and rediscovered.


## Concerto for Piano and Orchestra, Opus 38

> *Allegro appassionato*
> *Canzone: Moderato*
> *Allegro molto*

Barber's piano concerto was commissioned in 1959 by his publisher, G. Schirmer, Inc., to celebrate the 100th anniversary of that firm. The second movement was composed in another form in 1959. After that, Barber took up the concerto in March 1960 but did not complete the finale until 9 September

1962.[2] The first performance was given two weeks later, on 24 September 1962, during the opening week of the Lincoln Center for the Performing Arts in New York. Changes in details of the percussion part were being made as late as the eve of the premiere. John Browning was the soloist, and Erich Leinsdorf conducted the Boston Symphony Orchestra. The score is dedicated to Manfred Ibel.

**Solo piano, two flutes and piccolo, two oboes and English horn, two clarinets and bass clarinet, two bassoons, four horns, three trumpets, three trombones, timpani, snare drum, bass drum, cymbals, suspended cymbal, antique cymbals, tam-tam, low tom-tom, triangle, xylophone, whip, harp, and strings.**

Being taken on by a good publisher is a major landmark in the life of a young composer. For Barber, this came about in 1936, when Schirmer published three of his songs as Opus 2. (Opus 1 is a Serenade for String Quartet, written 1928 but not published until 1944.) It was a partnership that endured for the rest of Barber's life, bringing satisfaction to both parties; for Schirmer and the Barber estate it is still a gold mine.

Carl Engel, the musicologist who was president of Schirmer in 1936 and had served as head of the Music Division of the Library of Congress, could see he was on to a good thing when he signed the twenty-six-year-old composer. When he graduated from the Curtis Institute in 1933, Barber had no luck making a living as a singer, but he traveled as much as he could and did what he could to avoid the dread possibility of a career teaching "history of music at Mudlevel College, Ark.," though he did teach some composition and theory privately. But not many weeks after his graduation, the Philadelphia Orchestra under Alexander Smallens played his *School for Scandal* Overture, a piece that held its place as *the* short American concert-opener until Bernstein's *Candide* Overture came along, and by the time he signed his Schirmer contract, Barber had also written, among other works, a setting for baritone and string quartet of Matthew Arnold's *Dover Beach*, a sonata for cello and piano, *Music for a Scene from Shelley* (inspired by *Prometheus Unbound*), some settings of James Joyce poems, and his First Symphony. Right after the symphony came the String Quartet, Opus 11, whose slow movement, transcribed for string orchestra, went on to lead an independent life as the Adagio for Strings. Half a century later, when it was used in the film

[2]One of Barber's student compositions, written in 1929–1930, was a piano concerto, an ambitious work, for which Barber had prepared himself by detailed study of Beethoven's Fifth and Brahms's Second Concertos. Leopold Stokowski looked at it and turned it down for performance with the Philadelphia Orchestra, and the score was subsequently lost or destroyed. In an interview in 1964, Barber described the 1962 work as his "first [piano] concerto."

*Platoon*, it reached thousands who would never dream of darkening the doors of a concert hall.

In her biography of the composer, Barbara Heyman writes that "spring of 1935 . . . was a time of windfalls for Barber." NBC put on two one-hour broadcasts of his music (someone had persuaded Toscanini to listen, and he would introduce both the Adagio for Strings and the First Essay for Orchestra on an NBC Symphony broadcast in 1938), Werner Janssen and the New York Philharmonic-Symphony gave the first performance of *Music for a Scene from Shelley*, RCA Victor recorded him singing *Dover Beach* with the Curtis Quartet, he was awarded a Pulitzer travel grant of $1,500, and, having submitted his cello sonata and the *Shelley Scene* in support of his application, he won the Prix de Rome "as the most talented and deserving student of music in America."[3]

By 1962 the year of his Piano Concerto, Barber had added to his catalogue, among other works, the Violin Concerto; *A Stopwatch and an Ordnance Map*; the Second Essay for Orchestra, which became his most-played orchestral work after the Adagio for Strings; the *Capricorn* Concerto; *Excursions for Piano*; the Cello Concerto; *Medea* (for Martha Graham); *Knoxville: Summer of 1915*; the Piano Sonata (for Horowitz); the *Hermit Songs*; *Prayers of Kierkegaard*; *Summer Music*; *Vanessa* (for the Metropolitan Opera); and the *Toccata festiva*. Roger Sessions and Elliott Carter were more highly regarded in some parts of the music community, but Barber and Copland were much more performed, enough for them actually to make a good living composing without taking a university position. Clearly, they were the two composers who above all had come to represent contemporary American classical music to the general concert-going, music-loving public, and still do. Since Copland was with Boosey & Hawkes and Barber was clearly the star of the Schirmer stable, it was natural that the publisher's principal commemorative commission should go to him. Moreover, the Lincoln Center for the Performing Arts was scheduled to open its doors in September 1962, with several of America's major orchestras giving concerts during the inaugural week, and that would provide a gratifyingly visible occasion for the first performance.

Barber approached the task with confidence, not least because, as an excellent pianist himself, he felt sure about being able to write effectively for the instrument. He also relished the idea of writing for the twenty-eight-year-old John Browning, whose New York Philharmonic debut in Rachmaninoff's Paganini Rhapsody he had heard in 1956 because Dimitri Mitropoulos was conducting the premiere of Barber's *Medea's Meditation and Dance of Vengeance* on the same program. Barbara Heyman writes:

[3]Heyman notes that the year before, Barber had submitted the same two works with his Prix de Rome application to the same jury—Deems Taylor, Carl Engel, Leo Sowerby, and Walter Damrosch—but had been turned down. There must be a moral to that story somewhere.

[Barber] had always admired the Russian style of pianism and Browning, who had studied with Rosina Lhévinne, had been rigorously trained in that style. . . . Almost as soon as he began thinking about the work he invited [Browning] to Capricorn [his and Gian Carlo Menotti's house near Mount Kisco, New York], where for three days he had him play through virtually all his repertory. . . . Barber profited from Browning's stories about Madame Lhévinne, her insistence that he practice double sixths, her use of the term "flutter pedal"—keeping a "wet" pedal but shifting it rapidly so the sound does not become too thick—and her "old Russian trick" of effecting a brilliant sound by placing a run of parallel octaves two octaves apart. Much of this technical *sagesse* came to be incorporated into the Concerto.[4]

Barber began with the middle movement. This actually existed already as an Elegy for Flute and Piano that Barber had written in 1959 for Manfred Ibel, a German art student and amateur flutist whom he had met in Munich the year before and with whom he shared a house on Martha's Vineyard that summer. Ibel, who eventually received the dedication of the Piano Concerto, was an important figure for the rest of Barber's life. Among other things (and I quote Heyman again), he

> created many miles of walking trails through the fifty-three acres of woodland [at Capricorn]. . . . Because from the early 1950s Menotti [Barber's lover since 1928] was drawn more and more into the public arena and the demands of his and Barber's professional lives limited their time together, Barber welcomed having an available companion with whom he could travel and talk about music and literature. What seemed to draw him to the charismatic Ibel was [what Ibel called] "their mutual affinity for the spirit of German Romanticism and culture". . . . Their friendship long outlasted a romantic relationship. [5]

The Elegy, Barber's gift to Ibel, became one of his loveliest inspirations.

Barber achieved both the transformation of the Elegy into the Concerto's Canzone and the composition of the first movement in 1960. The finale, however, gave him trouble. First depression brought on by the death of his sister Sara, then a trip to the Soviet Union, a rare opportunity in those days, caused major delays. Meanwhile, September 1962 was not as far away as it had once been, and Browning, facing a task for which one would ideally like to have year, was looking at a rapidly diminishing number of weeks. Copland firmly told Barber: "You cannot treat a soloist like this!" That seems to have done the trick. "So I suddenly thought of something the next morning," Barber recalled. "I was terrorized into thinking of something which became the last movement." In the event, Browning achieved the near-

[4]Heyman, op. cit.
[5]Heyman, op. cit.

impossible and played brilliantly. His 1964 recording with George Szell and the Cleveland Orchestra still sets the standard. For Barber, the concerto earned both a Pulitzer Prize and the New York Music Critics' Circle Award.

The piano gets the Concerto off to a forceful start all by itself. This cadenza begins with a declamatory phrase (marked *quasi recitativo*) and goes on to phrases of distinct rhythmic profile and of which Barber will make much in the rest of the movement. At the *forte* return of the first of these rhythmic figures, which consists of three-note spasms, the orchestra punctuates its repetitions with a series of chords that firmly propel the music toward the first unambiguous arrival on the tonic, E minor. This introductory paragraph is handsome both in its harmonic shape and its commanding rhetoric. The piano sound is indeed very much "Russian style," and this superb opening as well as the heated melody for the orchestra that follows have often made me think that this concerto is the perfect gift for all who wish there were one more Rachmaninoff concerto.[6]

The orchestra's E-minor melody has splendid sweep: there is real passion to that tune. The piano picks it up, more quietly, and then moves into a long sequence of Madame Lhévinne's double sixths while the woodwinds continue the song. When the piano momentarily interrupts this lyricism with the three-note rhythmic spasms we first heard in the cadenza, Barber's direction to the player is "arrogant." At a slower tempo, the oboe introduces a new theme, one that swings up and down through a great range and is very free in rhythm. The rest of the orchestra is induced to join in and leads the music to a quiet chapter-ending.

A breath, and the orchestra jolts us with *fortissimo* sequences of the three-note spasms; this time it is the piano that supplies the punctuations. And more, it launches into another cadenza, brief but imposing with its fierce thunder of double octaves. This marks the beginning of the development. The three-note figure is the most prominent feature of the next phase; the oboe theme is also revisited, surrounded by brilliant piano figurations. A further episode is of scherzo character. Then a huge crescendo—it feels as if one were being swept along by a mighty wind—leads to yet another cadenza, a wonderful festivity of pianistic derring-do; Rachmaninoff himself could not have been more expert. A six-octave chromatic scale—the two hands an octave apart as the Lhévinne recipe recommends—sweeps us into the recapitulation.

This, although compressed, proceeds as expected. The music calms

---

[6]Invoking the name of Rachmaninoff raises the issue of Barber's musical conservatism, much lauded and much reviled. Of course Barber was conservative in that he composed to familiar designs, used immediately intelligible expressive gestures, and stayed with tonal harmony, but, as the first movement of the Piano Concerto demonstrates with considerable force, within those confines his musical language could be wonderfully personal and fresh.

down, as it did at the end of the exposition, and the piano, now in distant B-flat minor, revisits the first theme. This first part of the coda, all suppressed excitement and a kaleidoscopic shifting of colors, suggests that the movement is heading toward a quiet ending; at the last minute, however, a sudden rush of energy takes us to one more outburst of octaves and a thunderous final cadence.[7]

The Canzone is a beautiful movement, notable for its touching melody and even more for its delicate scoring. Its original version, the Elegy, must have been some of the last music Barber heard, for the flutist Ransom Wilson came to play it for him during his last hospital stay shortly before Barber returned to his apartment to die. The translation into a concerto movement is elegantly done, and Barber devises appealing conversations for the piano with solo woodwinds. He also uses to great effect the trick, invented by the nineteenth-century virtuoso Sigismond Thalberg, of creating the illusion that a three-handed pianist is at work, the melody being played in the middle range by the thumbs, with different figurations added above and below. (An example Barber would have known and enjoyed is Horowitz's celebrated solo piano arrangement of *The Stars and Stripes Forever*.) In this movement, the atmosphere is sometimes more French than Russian, a return to a musical language Barber had visited in 1950 when he had written *Mélodies passagères*, settings of some of Rilke's French poems, for Pierre Bernac and Francis Poulenc.

All three movements of Barber's Piano Concerto are in minor, the keynotes descending by thirds from E to C-sharp and then to B-flat minor. The beginning of the finale does suggest that when the dilatory Barber, called to order by Copland, "suddenly thought of something the next morning," what he thought of was to go to his cabinet of piano music and pull out the score of Prokofiev's Seventh Sonata. Never mind: writing down something closely akin to the ostinato in Prokofiev's finale, on the same keynote and also in an odd meter—Barber in B-flat minor and 5/8, Prokofiev in B-flat major and 7/8—got the machinery moving. And Barber's finale, it must be said, is not only the more varied but in every way the more interestingly composed of the two. An accelerando—*con frenesia*, Barber exhorts—heightens the excitement of the last half-minute. The final, crunching cadence owes between something and everything to Ravel's *La Valse*.

---

[7]Having never been convinced by this rather shallow ending, I was interested to read in Heyman's biography that Erich Leinsdorf, who heard Browning play the first two movements at Capricorn in 1960, "believed that the *pianissimo* ending Barber had written for the first movement did not offer enough contrast to the beginning of the slow movement. Within two days Barber responded to his suggestion with a new *fortissimo* ending so that the second movement, in contrast, could seem to 'emerge from nowhere.'" Leinsdorf was an extraordinarily intelligent and erudite man, but was committed to knowing everything better than everybody else; in this instance he was wrong, and I am sorry Barber took his advice.

# Concerto for Violin and Orchestra, Opus 14

> *Allegro*
> *Andante*
> *Presto in moto perpetuo*

Barber began his Violin Concerto at Sils Maria, Switzerland, in the summer of 1939, continued work on it in Paris, and completed it at Pocono Lake Preserve, Pennsylvania, and in Philadelphia in July 1940. In March 1940 Oscar Shumsky and the composer gave a private reading of the not yet orchestrated but otherwise complete work at the New York apartment of the critic Gama Gilbert; later that year there was a read-through in Philadelphia by Herbert Baumel with the orchestra of the Curtis Institute of Music, Fritz Reiner conducting. The first public performance with orchestra was given on 7 February 1941 by Albert Spalding with Eugene Ormandy and the Philadelphia Orchestra. In 1948 Barber undertook some revisions, and the definitive version was played for the first time on 7 January 1949 by Ruth Posselt with the Boston Symphony under Serge Koussevitzky.

**Solo violin, two flutes, two oboes, two clarinets, two bassoons, two horns, two trumpets, timpani, snare drum, piano, and strings.**

During the winter of 1938–1939, it occurred to Samuel Fels, who had made a fortune from Fels Naphtha soap, to commission a violin concerto for Iso Briselli, his adopted son. Briselli was born in Odessa, that amazing breeding-ground of violinists that also produced Elisaveta Gilels, Nathan Milstein, David and Igor Oistrakh, Josef Roisman, Toscha Seidel, and Yulian and Dmitry Sitkovetsky, and he had come to America at the age of twelve when his teacher, the eminent Carl Flesch, went to head the violin department at the newly founded Curtis Institute in 1924.[8] Gama Gilbert, a former Flesch student who had become an interesting music critic at the *New York Times*, suggested to Fels that Barber, a good friend of his, would be the right composer for his project. And with that, the complicated and interesting story of the Barber Violin Concerto begins.

Fels offered Barber a $1,000 commission for a concerto, $500 down,

---

[8]In his memoirs, Flesch recounts that he had changed the boy's name from Isaak to Iso because he feared it would be difficult to find accommodations at the German Baltic resort of Sellin for someone with such an unmistakably Jewish name.

$500 on delivery. It was Barber's first major commission and a generous one for a composer early in his career: $1,000 was exactly what the Koussevitzky Foundation paid Bartók for his concerto for orchestra a few years later. (In 1930 the immeasurably more famous Stravinsky had received $3,000 from the Boston Symphony for the *Symphony of Psalms*.) When the contract came through, Barber and his lover Gian Carlo Menotti were in Switzerland in the galactic company of Toscanini, Adolf Busch, Rudolf Serkin, Bernardino Molinari, Erika Mann, and Friedelind Wagner. The luminaries were involved in or hanging about the Lucerne Festival, just founded as the anti-Nazi answer to Salzburg, and the young composers from America were living at Sils Maria, where Nietzsche had written *Also sprach Zarathustra* in the 1880s. There Barber began his Concerto, continuing it in Paris but having to hurry home to Pennsylvania as Europe stumbled toward war near the end of the summer of 1939. Serkin and John Barbirolli, then conductor of the New York Philharmonic, were among their companions on the S.S. *Champlain*.

Trouble began as soon as the "concertino," as Barber called it in his journal, was written (though not yet orchestrated): Briselli was not happy with the finale and Fels wanted his $500 advance back. In his 1956 biography of Barber, the first book-length study of the composer, Nathan Broder, a highly regarded scholar, critic, and editor, wrote: "When the movement was submitted, the violinist declared it too difficult . . . and Barber, who had already spent [his advance] in Europe, called in another violinist . . . who performed the work for the merchant and his protégé, to prove that the finale was not unplayable."[9] Broder, by the way, does not identify Fels or Briselli by name. Barbara Heyman, author of what is now *the* Barber biography (1992), reasonably suggests that "Broder's account is probably the version Barber presented to his publisher": when he wrote this book, Broder was manager of the Publications Department at Schirmer, Barber's publisher.

This story has been repeated by countless program-note writers, and it went uncontradicted, at least in public, for twenty-six years. Then, in 1982, Briselli, who had long since given up the violin in order to devote himself to running the Fels business, offered Barbara Heyman, already at work on her book, a revisionist account. I quote from Heyman: "[Briselli] professes that although he believed the first two movements of the concerto were beautiful and eagerly awaited the finale, he was disappointed with the third movement as 'too lightweight' compared to the rest of the concerto. He suggested that the middle section be expanded to develop the movement into a sonata-rondo form, but Barber would not consider it."[10]

Part of what happened in 1939 is clear. Barber wanted someone to perform the controversial finale to demonstrate that it was playable, and one

[9]Nathan Broder, *Samuel Barber* (New York: G. Schirmer, 1956).
[10]Heyman, op. cit.

afternoon Herbert Baumel, a Curtis student, was buttonholed by the pianist Ralph Berkowitz, given the pencil manuscript of the first half of the movement, told he had two hours in which to learn it and that it should be played "very fast," and instructed to appear at the proper time, "dressed up," in the studio of the great Josef Hofmann, then director of the Institute. Berkowitz would accompany him. (Broder mistakenly identifies Oscar Shumsky, another Curtis alumnus and by then a member of the NBC Symphony, as the violinist who gave this demonstration.) This shotgun audition went brilliantly, and the assembled company, which included Hofmann; Mary Louise Curtis Bok, the founder of the Curtis Institute; the composer and pianist Edith Evans Braun; Menotti; and Barber himself, decided, as Heyman writes (citing Baumel), "that Barber was to be paid the full commission and Briselli had to relinquish his right to the first performance." Contrary to Broder's account, Briselli was not present and probably not invited.

Presumably the enforcement of the jury's verdict was managed discreetly behind the scenes. Mrs. Bok's fortune came from her father, Cyrus Curtis, publisher of, among other periodicals, the *Saturday Evening Post* and *Ladies' Home Journal;* her husband, a remarkable figure in the history of American journalism and author of one of the great autobiographies, *The Americanization of Edward Bok,* was editor of *Ladies' Home Journal.* Samuel Fels was on the board of the Curtis Institute. The Felses, being Jewish, were not "in society" in quite the same way as Mrs. Bok; however, Jenny Fels and Mary Louise Bok were friends, and it was in fact Mrs. Fels who had gotten Mrs. Bok interested in music education and had persuaded her to put her enormous resources behind founding a music school. And yes, Barber did get the other $500 due him.[11]

The question remains: Was Briselli's displeasure with the finale a technical issue, as the Broder (or Barber-Broder) story has it, or was it a musical issue, as Briselli put it to Heyman forty-three years after the event?[12] Heyman writes that it is unlikely Briselli would have found Barber's finale "too diffi-

---

[11]Herbert Baumel benefited from this episode. When the premiere of the concerto approached, Eugene Ormandy got him to play the solo part at the preliminary rehearsal, which the actual soloist, Albert Spalding, did not attend; on the strength of Baumel's showing on that occasion, Ormandy offered him a permanent position in the orchestra.

[12]Why, for that matter, did Briselli wait so long to dispute Broder's account? In any event, it is understandable that he did not wish to be remembered as the man who had declared the Barber Concerto unplayable. Stories of "unplayability" abound: Leopold Auer, whom Briselli must have known at Curtis, had said that Tchaikovsky's Concerto could only be performed if rewritten by himself; Albert Spalding, who would eventually be the one to introduce Barber's Concerto, had declared the Violin Concerto by Roger Sessions "unplayable" after he had been engaged to give its first performance with Koussevitzky and the Boston Symphony; Heifetz stated that the Schoenberg Concerto could only be played when violinists grew a sixth finger. All three were wrong, but all three had plenty of accomplishments for which they would be remembered. For Briselli, whose moment in the violinistic limelight was brief and who was going to be remembered only for his role in the Barber brouhaha, the situation was different.

cult": he was an excellent violinist, consistently praised in reviews for "immaculate, facile technique, poetic expressiveness, and rich tone," and his repertory included, along with such classics as the Beethoven Concerto, which he played at his Philadelphia Orchestra debut, taxing bravura pieces by Paganini, Sarasate, Wieniawski, Ysaÿe, et al. But if playability was not the issue, as Briselli maintained in his 1982 interview with Heyman, why was this demonstration necessary?

And what about the musical issue? Almost everyone who listens to the Barber Concerto is struck by a split that separates the first two movements from the third: the Allegro and Andante are lyric and almost entirely lacking in brilliant passagework, the Presto is a crackling virtuoso number whose harmonic language is also noticeably more biting. Briselli thought this split a blemish: he is not alone in this, but by no means will every listener agree with him on that point, either.

I want to propose a third possibility. As I sought to understand this mysterious and fascinating story, it occurred to me that perhaps Briselli was musically unhappy with the finale not just in its relation to the first two movements, but per se. Even in 1939 this was relatively conservative and accessible music—the ovation at the premiere attests to that—but such concepts as "reactionary," "conservative," "advanced," and "radical" are in the ear of the beholder. I can easily imagine how Barber's metrical oddities and the rapidly shifting chromatics would be daunting to a performer who had not been trained even in mild twentieth-century music—Flesch played virtually none—and most of whose experience was in nineteenth-century music. In the course of their conversation, Briselli told Heyman that around the same time, someone had suggested he learn Prokofiev's Concerto No. 2, another piece most of us would regard as standing at the conservative end of the musical spectrum in the 1930s, but that he had not done so because he found the idiom strange.

All musical experience begins with the ear: what we cannot hear we cannot play. Barber's finale requires what has been called "virtuosity of the ear" as well as virtuosity on the fingerboard and with the bow-arm, and the latter will not kick in unless the former is present. As a purely mechanical challenge, Briselli could of course have managed Barber's flying triplets, rocketing ninths, and chromatic zigzags, but it was *not* a purely mechanical challenge—it was the application of technique to a musical purpose, and in this instance a musical purpose with which the player may not have been at home. In sum, I propose that it was not a question of technical *or* musical unhappiness so much as of a conjunction of the two.

The collapse of the Briselli scheme left Barber free to find another soloist for what he came occasionally to call his *concerto da sapone* (soap concerto). Having heard that Albert Spalding was looking for an attractive American concerto, Barber went to see him in August 1940 and, as he told the conductor William Strickland, "he took [it] on the spot." Spalding was a solid, respected player, not of the first rank—as Barber remarked, "He's no Heifetz, but we shall see"—but his performance of the Barber won praise and brought the composer great acclaim. Strangely, given its initial success, the concerto as good as vanished from the scene, and by the 1980s it was not in the active repertory of any major violinist. Only the end of that decade brought the flood of attention that has made this one of the most popular of all concertos.

The opening is magical. Does any other violin concerto begin with such immediacy and with so sweet and elegant a melody? A rolled G-major chord on the piano ushers it in.[13] The melody itself belongs to the solo violin, and it stretches its deliciously unpredictable way through twenty-four measures. If you go along with the idea that some composers are essentially vocal composers (Mozart) and some essentially instrumental (Beethoven), allowing room for the possibility that some are both (Bach), then Barber was as surely a vocal composer by nature—and here, like Mozart, he is composing vocal music for an instrument. Barber himself, I should add, thought of himself as musically "bisexual" (his adjective): "I do both." Two more themes appear, both introduced by the violin: one is lightly touched by melancholia, the other is *grazioso e scherzando*. The development begins with a surprising darkening of the scene. Toward the end, Barber gives us at least a hint of a cadenza, which is more effectively introduced in the revised version than in the original.

Next comes the slow movement, and it must be said that performances too often give the impression that the concerto begins with two slow movements in a row. In his 1948 revision, Barber in fact changed the tempo mark for the first movement from *Allegro molto moderato* to plain *Allegro*, probably because violinists, loving that first melody and longing to linger on it dragged. Alas, they still tend to, and this has a bearing on the Briselli question: when the first movement is Allegro ($\phantom{}= 100$) rather than a lachrymose Andante, the finale, as the closing element in a fairly fast/very fast design, sounds much more connected to the rest of the concerto.

The Andante begins with another inspired melody, this one given to the oboe. With touching tact, Barber lets the oboist bask in that glory, for the violin enters and occupies itself with quite different, more rhapsodic material; only at the recapitulation does the violin take the oboe theme,

---

[13]If I could ask Barber one question about the Violin Concerto, it would be, why the piano? Most of what the piano does here sounds as though it belongs on the harp; the piano has an odd makeshift sound, as though the pianist were pinch-hitting for the harpist, who had got stuck in traffic and hadn't made it to the concert. If I could ask a second question it would be why, in his revision, he did not make the orchestration more transparent. Both in the Concerto's first page and in much of the finale it is difficult for the solo violin to cut through because the orchestra is so much in the same register.

singing it *molto espressivo* low on the G-string. The coda, one of Barber's most beautiful pages, is one of the products of the revision.

The finale starts with a hushed tattoo on muted timpani; the violin enters almost immediately and plays nonstop for 102 measures. The soloist gets nine measures of respite here and another sixteen a little later; otherwise it is unremitting up-tempo motion. In the coda, Barber increases our sense of speed both by shortening the measures and shifting from triplet eighth-notes to sixteenths. Three measures before the end, an arpeggio in two keys at once (the ghost of Petrushka?) slews the music over to E-flat minor, about as far from the home key of A minor as you can get. For a moment the solo violin seems to embrace this wild idea, but it is cut off by a *fortissimo* A-minor chord that unmistakably says, "That's it!"

# Béla Bartók

Béla Victor János Bartók was born in Nagyszentmiklós, Hungary (now Sânmiclăusulmare, Romania),[1] on 25 March 1881 and died in New York City on 26 September 1945.

Bartók's first and last compositions were for his own instrument, the piano: a waltz he wrote as a boy of nine in Nagyszöllös (now Vinogradov in Ukraine), and the concerto he was struggling to complete for his wife and former student, Ditta Pásztory-Bartók, as he lay dying of leukemia in New York's West Side Hospital. His father, Béla Bartók, Sr., ran an agricultural college but was an able and versatile amateur musician; his mother, Paula Voit, who was widowed young, supported herself most of her life by teaching piano, and it was from her that the young Béla had his first lessons. These began on his fifth birthday, though by then he was already an old hand at picking out folk songs with one finger.

Another five years and it was evident that his case was serious. On 1 May 1892—he had just turned eleven—Bartók made his public debut as pianist and composer, offering his audience in Nagyszöllös, where the family had moved in 1889, the first movement of Beethoven's *Waldstein* Sonata as well as his own *A Duna folyása* (The Course of the Danube). As Paula Bartók moved about in search of economic security with young Béla and still younger Erzsébet, Béla worked with teachers of varying worth, except for their year

[1]Variously spelled: Sânmiclăuşulmare (Halsey Stevens), Sânnicolaul-Mare (*Webster's New Geographical Dictionary* and *Hammond World Atlas*), Sânnicolaul Mare (Serge Moreux, who says this is what Bartók called it), Sînnicolau Mare (*The New Grove Dictionary of Music and Musicians*), Sînnicolaul-Mare (Démeny edition of Bartók's letters), and Sinmiclausu (U.S. Board on Geographic Names).

in Beszterce (Bisţrita, Romania), where it turned out that the twelve-year-old boy was himself the best pianist in town. It looked as though he would go to Vienna, but on the advice of a school friend four years older than himself, Ernö Dohnányi, who was already embarked on a distinguished career as a composer and pianist, he decided on Budapest instead, specifically to work with Dohnányi's teacher István Thomán. In Thomán, who had studied with Liszt, Bartók found a superb teacher as well as something like a surrogate father, a friend, and the generous owner of an ample library. It was from Thomán that Bartók derived the ethical stance and uncompromising probity that informed his entire musical life. Bartók also studied with Dohnányi for a summer.

In 1905 Bartók suffered a setback when he failed to take a prize at the Anton Rubinstein Competition in Paris, though he acknowledged that the winner, the twenty-one-year-old Wilhelm Backhaus, was "a truly fine pianist." Bartók was less inclined now to think of playing the piano as his primary career, though he continued to make public appearances into the 1940s. In 1907 he was appointed professor of piano at the Budapest Conservatory, something he welcomed because it provided a steady income that allowed him to compose and to pursue his ever more absorbing studies in Hungarian and Balkan folk music. He had little interest in teaching composition and had few students in that subject.

If his failure to impress the Rubinstein jury as a pianist disappointed him, his rejection as a composer at the same competition enraged him. No one was in fact awarded a prize in composition, but even in the vote on honorable mentions, he came in behind a certain Attilio Brugnoli, later a teacher at Parma and Florence, whose pieces Bartók described to his mother as "absolutely worthless conglomerations." (In the same letter he vowed that the moment he received it he would send his "diploma of (dis)honorable mention" back to Leopold Auer, the chairman of the jury of "empty-headed Saint Petersburg cattle.")[2]

In any event, Bartók's career as a composer had developed impressively since the days of *The Course of the Danube*. The earliest pieces by Bartók now in general circulation are the Violin Concerto No. 1, composed 1907–1908, though not performed for another fifty years, and the String Quartet No. 1, completed in 1909. But Bartók had composed prolifically before that: specifically, 1902 had been the crisis year in the development of his artistic personality. It was then that he had heard Strauss's *Also sprach Zarathustra*, and the encounter with that brilliant score, so different not only from the classics on which he had been brought up but even from Liszt, the one composer he then ranked with "the big four" (Bach, Beethoven, Schubert, Wag-

[2]For more on Auer, see my essay on Tchaikovsky's Violin Concerto.

ner), awakened him from torpor and shocked him into an awareness of his own possibilities. A year later he responded with a symphonic portrait of Lajos Kossuth, the revolutionary leader under whom Hungary had made a heroic strike for independence from Austria in 1848. Bartók's compositional and pianistic concerns overlap interestingly at this time: one of his dazzling party pieces for some years was his own transcription of Strauss's *Ein Helden-leben*.

The Waldbauer Quartet introduced Bartók's Quartet No. 1 at the group's debut in Budapest in 1910 (it had actually been founded for that purpose), and over the next few years, Europe's major cities came to know the Quartet No. 2, the ballet *The Wooden Prince*, the opera *Bluebeard's Castle*, the Études for Piano, and the two violin sonatas. With the premiere of the *Dance Suite* in Budapest in 1923 he had his first huge success—within a year there were fifty performances of it in Germany alone—and with that of the sexually shocking *The Miraculous Mandarin* in Cologne he enjoyed his first major *scandale*. (His chief opponent in that collision was the devoutly Catholic and conservative mayor of Cologne, Konrad Adenauer.)

To many who love Bartók's music, the years from 1918 to 1931, which are also the years of the Études for Piano; the piano suite, *Out of Doors;* the first two piano concertos; the Third and Fourth Quartets; and the *Cantata profana,* are those of his greatest achievements as a composer, the years in which invention was incomparably charged with an electrifying energy, boldness, individuality, and spirit. Like many of his contemporaries, Bartók softened his style in midlife, but continued to compose with no diminution in elegance, craft, color, and communicativeness.

Bartók had a good contract with a major publisher ("This is a splendid thing . . . [it] counts as my greatest success as a composer so far"), and his music was performed widely and, more often than not, well. His fortieth birthday was the occasion for important studies in *Die Musikblätter des Anbruch* (Vienna) and *La Revue musicale* (Paris), and in 1928 he made his first recordings.

Bartók traveled extensively, coming to America for the first time in 1927. Most of his journeys were occasioned by appearances as a pianist, sometimes in solo recital, sometimes with orchestras, most often in his own music, and frequently as partner to distinguished Hungarian violinists, among them Jenö Hubay, Imre Waldbauer, Joseph Szigeti, Zoltán Székely (leader of the Hungarian Quartet and the man for whom Bartók would write his Violin Concerto No. 2), Jelly d'Arányi (Bartók wrote both his violin sonatas for her), and André Gertler.

From time to time, Bartók became embroiled in the political scene at home, though not always by design. For several years after World War I, *The Wooden Prince* and *Bluebeard's Castle* could not be produced in Hungary because their librettist, Béla Balázs, was a Communist.[3] The Hungarian government also questioned Bartók's patriotism because of his interest in Romanian folk music. This was especially ironic because Bartók was the most fervent of patriots, who for years wore national costume and used to write hectoring letters to his mother and sister because they often spoke German at home rather than Hungarian. He protested Fascist attacks on Toscanini in 1931,[4] refused to play in Germany after Hitler came to power, forbade broadcasts of his music in Germany and Italy, and after the Anschluss changed from his Viennese publisher, Universal, to Boosey & Hawkes in London.

In the 1930s, Hungarian politics also became increasingly polluted by Fascism, and Bartók, a fervent democrat, loathed what was brewing both at home and nearby. In October 1938, a few weeks after the Munich Pact in which Czechoslovakia was sold down the river, he wrote a charmingly polyglot letter to the wife of his friend Zoltán Székely to congratulate her on the birth of her son, but in one of his English paragraphs he strayed to the pressing and darker topic:

> Meantime, so much trouble has broken out all over the world, such unrest, such upheavals—and now this shocking change of front on the part of the Western countries. One ought to get away from here, from the neighborhood of that pestilential country, far, far away, but where: to Greenland, Cape Colony, the Tierra del Fuego, the Fiji Islands, or somewhere even the Almighty has not heard of![5]

Actually, Bartók was reluctant to abandon Hungary as long as his mother was alive. Her death in December 1939 left him emotionally free to take the plunge. In October 1940 he emigrated to the United States with his wife and their sixteen-year-old son, Peter. I tell something of that story in the essay on the Piano Concerto No. 3.

## Bartók's Piano Concertos

There are six works by Bartók for piano and orchestra: the Rhapsody, Opus 1 (1904), arranged from the Rhapsody for solo piano and full of Richard Strauss; the Scherzo (*Burlesque*), Opus 2 (1904), which has quite an infusion

---

[3]In 1930 Balázs removed this obstacle by renouncing the use of his name and the payment of royalties in connection with these two works. Bartók used to pay him the appropriate fees in cash when they met abroad.

[4]Four years later, Stravinsky was still being received by Mussolini and saying laudatory things about Il Duce at press conferences.

[5]Claude Kenneson: *Székely and Bartók: The Story of a Friendship* (Portland, Ore.: Amadeus Press, 1994).

of Liszt; the three concertos of 1926, 1931, and 1945; and the transcription of the Sonata for Two Pianos and Percussion (1937/1940). Bartók retained a soft spot for the Rhapsody and played it often in Europe.

Bartók the pianist is present in this music, much as the performing personalities of Mozart, Beethoven, Brahms, Rachmaninoff, and Copland are in their works for piano. Writing for himself, Bartók made tremendous demands on his own technical resources in matters of color, marksmanship, and stretch.[6] His playing was firmly rooted in the nineteenth century: after all, his most celebrated repertory pieces were Liszt's Sonata in B minor, *Spanish Rhapsody*, and *Totentanz*. Much of the playing of Bartók's piano music in the first decades after his death was driving and percussive; however, Bartók's own pianism, of which there is extensive recorded documentation, was flexible, colorful, and witty, and sometimes the hands of this contemporary of Rachmaninoff, Hofmann, Friedman, and Nyiregyházi are not quite together. More recently, some members of what is now the middle generation of pianists, including Peter Serkin, Garrick Ohlsson, Zoltán Kocsis, Yefim Bronfman, and András Schiff, among others, have rediscovered the possibilities of the composer's own not so aggressively "modern" approach.

## Concerto No. 1 for Piano and Orchestra

*Allegro moderato*
*Andante*
*Allegro molto*

Bartók began his Piano Concerto No. 1 in August 1926 and completed it on 12 November that year. He himself was the soloist at the first performance, which Wilhelm Furtwängler conducted and which took place on 1 July 1927 at the Festival of the International Society for Contemporary Music in Frankfurt.

**Solo piano, two flutes and piccolo, two oboes and English horn, two clarinets and bass clarinet, two bassoons, four horns, two trumpets, three trombones,**

---

[6]Like Carl Maria von Weber, another brilliant composer-pianist, Bartók had unusually long thumbs, allowing stretches difficult for most pianists to encompass. Apropos special piano effects, the first movement of the Concerto No. 1 abounds in tone clusters, a device the American composer Henry Cowell is usually credited with inventing. Bartók heard them for the first time in 1923 when he and Cowell were houseguests together in London. He was fascinated, got Cowell many concerts in Europe, and the next year wrote to him, politely requesting permission to use clusters himself.

timpani, one snare drum with snares and one without, triangle, cymbals, bass drum, tam-tam, ten each of first and second violins, and six each of violas, cellos, and basses.

Bartók's Piano Concerto No. 1 displays in more elaborately developed form some of the compositional and pianistic concepts he had explored in the just completed Piano Sonata and *Out of Doors*, a suite of five pieces. Drawing, as always, on a fascinating mixture of sources—folk music, Beethoven, Liszt, and Debussy—and gifted with an amazing and fantastical delight in the sheerly sensuous side of music, Bartók created a composition that speaks with compelling urgency and in his own unmistakably pungent voice.

Bartók begins his First Concerto with a conversation in percussion. Piano and timpani are the principal participants, but horn and trombone in their extreme low registers also join in. The subject of the conversation appears to be pitch, and the piano soon decides that the A in the brasses has more validity than the timpani's B. Meanwhile the horns, seconded more timidly by the bassoons, propose a melody that consists of a very few notes in constantly changing permutations and rhythmic patterns. You often find such melodies in Stravinsky's most "Russian" works; here, indeed, is another reminder of how wide a swath *Le Sacre du printemps* cut (and still cuts). Clearly, though, all this is preparatory, and it is with the piano's triumphant twenty-five-fold assertion of A and the arrival of a somewhat quicker tempo that the movement properly begins. (Repeated notes and chords are a prominent feature of this work.) The music is characterized by fierce forward drive: as Bartók's biographer Halsey Stevens so succinctly puts it, "the eighth-note is king," and these eighths are arranged in joltingly nervous, shifting designs.

The Andante, in which the strings are silent throughout, also begins as a conversation of piano and percussion; this one, however, is all quiet and mystery. This is a realm Bartók would explore again a decade later in the *Music for Strings, Percussion, and Celesta*, and even more, the Sonata for Two Pianos and Percussion, two of his finest scores of the 1930s. Bartók asks that the percussion group be placed directly behind the piano and he devises an unprecedentedly detailed notation for the many kinds of touch, attack, and color he wants from his four percussionists. A clear pattern quickly emerges, three eighth-notes in major seconds followed by a long chord of piled-up fourths. The piano proposes this, and the percussion instruments—or, if you like, the other percussion instruments—assent at various rates of speed and with varying delays. The piano soon asserts itself as an instrument that can also produce polyphony, an idea that the woodwind soloists pick up and extend for the movement's middle section. The piano accompaniment to this episode of superimposed wind solos grows thick to the point where each hand is playing five-note chords, then recedes again to transparency.

A sudden spurt forward and a piano glissando through five and a half octaves propel us into the last movement. The transition brings some wonderfully dirty sounds right out of the brothel world of *The Miraculous Mandarin*. With its alternations of ostinato and polyphony, this finale resembles the first movement in style. The voltage is high and the sense of drive tremendous, giving the Concerto a rousing conclusion.

## Concerto No. 2 for Piano and Orchestra

> *Allegro*
> *Adagio—Presto—Adagio*
> *Allegro molto*

Bartók began his Piano Concerto No. 2 in October 1930 and completed the score on 9 October 1931. The first performance took place in Frankfurt on 23 January 1933 with the composer at the piano and Hans Rosbaud conducting. Hitler came to power a week later, so Bartók made this his last appearance in Germany.

**Solo piano, two flutes and piccolo (doubling third flute), two oboes, two clarinets, two bassoons and contrabassoon (doubling third bassoon), four horns, three trumpets, three trombones, bass tuba, timpani, snare drum, triangle, bass drum, cymbals, and strings.**

In a program note he wrote for a concert in Lausanne in 1937, Bartók stated: "I think [my First Piano Concerto] is a good work in spite of the slight or even considerable difficulties it presents to both orchestra and audience. For this reason, I wanted my Second Concerto . . . to be a kind of antithesis to the First, easier in its orchestral part and more lucid in structure. This is the purpose and at the same time the reason for the more conventional and simpler treatment of most of the themes."

Bartók enjoyed symmetrical structures, and here is a remarkable example that benefits from the sturdiness of the design and which sounds entirely fresh and unmechanical.[7] He has, in sum, the best of both worlds. Here is how it works over all:

First movement (Allegro)
Second movement, part 1 (Adagio)
Second movement, part 2 (Presto)
Second movement, part 3 (Adagio, variation of part 1)
Third movement (Allegro molto, variation of first movement)

A piano scale propels the first Allegro into energetic motion, and while the piano continues with hammered trills, the orchestra plays the first theme—or, perhaps better, first thematic group—which consists of three distinct ideas, all very short: one, down and up, part scale and part broken chord, played by the trumpet; another, mainly scalar, played by the piano; and finally, a zigzag of thirds, also in the piano. Those three elements suffice for a considerable amount of vigorous conversation. A transition with swirling triplets leads to a new idea made up of piano chords, those in the right hand rolled upward and those in the left hand rolled down, and punctuated by pings on the triangle. Here the character is changed to *tranquillo* and the tempo reduced somewhat; however, this quieter and playful mood does not stay with us long, and the exposition ends with a return to the first, hyper-energized manner.

Sometimes it pleases Bartók to reduce one of his spiky themes to something harmless and entirely tonal, and here he begins the development by giving us the second of his original three in a thoroughly innocent-sounding D-flat major. The first phase of the development builds to a pair of rhetorical halts. Then the clattering eighth-notes resume, and this time they suddenly remind Bartók of something: Bach. And now, in an amusing passage, the zigzag motif is given in the manner of a Bach invention. (It sounds like a Glenn Gould parody thirty years ahead of its time.) The scale with which the movement began now returns, extended in duration and expanded in gamut, and this marks the recapitulation. Bartók gives this section a new twist by presenting the themes upside down; in fact, in the coda we will hear them played backwards. A two-handed scale across six octaves brings the movement to a crashing close. The final cadence confirms what has been broadly hinted at throughout, namely that the tonal center is G. We have, by the way, heard no strings yet—just woodwinds, brass, and percussion.

After nine minutes or so of an unremitting athletic high, Bartók now gives us what we need: a slow pace, a sense of deep calm, string tone, and *pianissimo*. Muted strings, played without vibrato, sound what one might de-

---

[7]Bartók's Fourth and Fifth quartets (1928 and 1934 respectively), which chronologically straddle the Second Concerto, are built to similar designs.

scribe as an abstract chorale, chordal in a way that suggests hymn style, but with the intervals of the melody very compressed. Within the texture, the violins and the other strings are like reflections in the water, rising lines in the one group being mirrored by falling ones in the other and vice versa.

A timpani roll introduces the piano. It is a wonderful thought, to use the drum as mediator between strings and keyboard; Brahms would have nodded admiringly. The piano enters with a grave melody in octaves, accompanied by timpani glissandos. Two of these piano statements are enclosed within three chorale passages for the muted strings. Then another soft drum roll takes us into the second movement's quick middle sections. Bartók said we could hear this as "a scherzo within an adagio, or, if you prefer, an adagio containing a scherzo." The scherzo is witty, culminating in trills in tone clusters which embody both the pianistic brilliance and the harmonic adventurousness of this fantastical movement. The return of the Adagio is fascinatingly varied: in the first statement of the chorale, for example, the long notes are broken up into thirty-second-note tremolandos to be played at the bridge so that the sound is very glassy, and the piano superimposes a long trill.

The first movement was for winds and percussion only, the chorale of the second movement for strings and timpani, and the scherzo section for strings with a few winds and lighter percussion. The finale brings in the full orchestra for the first time. Here arpeggios function much as scales did in the first movement. The form is a kind of rondo—one could represent it as ABA-CADA with an introduction and a coda—in which many of the ideas are variants of material from the first movement, a plan Bartók would pursue again in his Violin Concerto No. 2. In the middle of the movement, Bartók gives us a most magical section in which the bass lies still for long periods, where the colors are all shimmering mystery, and in which our pulse and breathing are invited to slow down. With an outburst of busy brass playing, Bartók rouses us for the brilliant coda, with everything resolved on a bright chord of G.

## Concerto No. 3 for Piano and Orchestra

*Allegretto*
*Adagio religioso*
*Allegro vivace*

Bartók worked on his Third Piano Concerto during the summer of 1945. According to the preface to the published score, "he was able to finish the score with the exception of the last seventeen bars, which he noted in a kind of musical shorthand. These last bars were deciphered and scored by his friend and pupil Tibor Serly. Only a few expression marks and tempo indications, and no metronome marks were found in Bartók's score. . . . In order to give a complete picture of the work, such markings as were deemed necessary have been added by Tibor Serly; by Eugene Ormandy, who conducted the first performance; by Louis Kentner [Hungarian-born British pianist and composer]; and by Erwin Stein [Austrian-born British writer and editor]." György Sándor gave the first performance on 8 February 1946 with Ormandy and the Philadelphia Orchestra.

**Solo piano, two flutes, two oboes, two clarinets, two bassoons, four horns, two trumpets, three trombones, bass tuba, timpani, xylophone, triangle, snare drum, cymbals, bass drum, tam-tam, and strings.**

When Bartók arrived in America in October 1940, he hurried straight to Washington, where he and his old friend Joseph Szigeti gave a recital at the Library of Congress. The recording of that event is one of the great monuments of phonographic history. Over all, though, Bartók's American years were a wretched time of bad health, economic hardship, cultural dislocation, and scant artistic satisfaction. Few conductors would touch his music (the notable exception was Fritz Reiner, then conductor of the Pittsburgh Symphony), his string quartets did not become standard repertory until after his death, and there were virtually no engagements for Bartók or his wife, Ditta Pásztory-Bartók, as pianists.[8]

For a couple of years, Bartók stopped composing and worked primarily at his ethnomusicological studies, though these too brought him disappointment when publishing his transcriptions of Romanian and Turkish folk songs proved financially unfeasible. His tendency toward self-absorption increased and he became bitter. And all this time, he was very ill. By the summer of 1941, at latest, he had contracted leukemia, though he never learned that this was the cause of his persistent fever and general physical misery. From the spring of 1942 on, he never felt well again.

The last two years brought some rays of light as a few important musicians began to step forward with commissions. In June 1943, Serge Kousse-

---

[8]Bartók's compatriot Fritz (originally Frigyes) Reiner had served the composer's cause in America as early as 1928, when he invited him to play his Piano Concerto No. 1 with the Cincinnati Symphony after Willem Mengelberg canceled the scheduled American premiere with the New York Philharmonic. Reiner was also responsible for Bartók's last appearance as a pianist; that was when he and Ditta introduced the Concerto for Two Pianos, a reworking of the 1937 Sonata for Two Pianos and Percussion, at a New York Philharmonic concert in January 1943.

vitzky, who had been spurred on by Reiner and Szigeti, went to see Bartók in the hospital and offered a commission for what turned out to be the Concerto for Orchestra. The visit had a miraculous effect: Bartók's appetite for life and work returned. Even his appetite for food came back: in the fall of 1943, while working on Koussevitzky's concerto, he told Szigeti that his weight had risen from 87 pounds to 105: "I grow fat. I bulge. I explode."

Yehudi Menuhin asked for a sonata for solo violin; William Primrose, who had been turned down by Stravinsky, wanted a viola concerto; and in Hollywood, Nathaniel Shilkret requested a five-minute contribution to a composite cantata on the book of Genesis. Menuhin got his sonata, and Bartók left just enough by way of coherent sketches for the Viola Concerto to enable Tibor Serly to assemble (not very well) a "performing version." But with characteristic conscientiousness, Bartók returned the advance on Shilkret's commission when he realized he would not be able to produce the work, and he would not even discuss a request from Ethel Bartlett and Rae Robertson for a two-piano concerto.[9]

As Bartók began the Viola Concerto, he nurtured another plan, not on commission, but for love: a piano concerto for Ditta. It was to be a surprise present for her forty-second birthday on 31 October 1945, and Bartók cherished the idea that its performances by her might provide a source of income after his death.[10] In his more optimistic moments he also hoped that after completing the two concertos he would write another string quartet.

Bartók's physical condition was manageable at the beginning of the summer of 1945, but became very bad around 10 August. He continued to work, dividing his waning energies between the Viola Concerto and the Piano Concerto No. 3. On 8 September he wrote to Primrose that the Viola Concerto was "ready in draft," but eighteen days later he was dead. He had been taken to the West Side Hospital on 22 September; until the evening before, he had worked desperately to complete his labor of love, the concerto for Ditta, and he had in fact achieved all but the last seventeen bars of orchestration.

Bartók's first two piano concertos get off to aggressive starts; the Third, however, begins gently, with the piano unwinding a ruminating melody over a

---

[9]Two notable pieces came out of Shilkret's scheme, Schoenberg's *Genesis* Prelude and Stravinsky's mini-cantata *Babel*.

[10]In the event, it was György Sándor who gave the first performance, four and a half months after Bartók's death. Mrs. Bartók, embittered by her own and her husband's American experience, moved back to Hungary in 1946. Malcolm Gillies writes in *Bartók Remembered* that "she lived [there] in seclusion for many years. During the 1960s, however, she began to perform again, even recording" the Third Piano Concerto with Tibor Serly. That recording was not issued in this country, and I have never come across it. Béla's present to her, even though she herself played it only a couple of times, has been a steady moneymaker for the Bartók estate and for Boosey & Hawkes. Ditta Pásztory-Bartók died in 1982.

murmuring accompaniment. Here, free of the constraints of writing for a public eminence like Koussevitzky or Menuhin, Bartók allowed his fantasy to travel back to Hungary with unabashed nostalgia. There is contrasting material of lighter weight, a brief development, a recapitulation more regular than any he had ever written in Budapest, and a magical coda in which the music dissolves in a touchingly intimate exchange between flute and piano.

In 1825 Beethoven had celebrated recovery from illness in the "Sacred Hymn of Thanksgiving from a Convalescent to the Deity" that forms the slow movement of his A-minor Quartet, Opus 132. Bartók's own illness in at least modest remission, his spirits cheered by the end of the war and by the news that his sister and his son Béla and their families were safe, that his oldest friend and colleague Zoltán Kodály was well, and that his younger son Peter was discharged from the U.S. Navy, he was now ready to sing his own hymn. It is closely modeled on Beethoven's: the piano intones the chorale and the strings provide the connecting tissue.

For contrast, Bartók returns for the last time to one of his most personal genres, a restlessly buzzing, twittering, chattering, chirruping "night music." He had written the first one of these nineteen years before in the piano suite *Out of Doors*, and that, too, had been dedicated to Ditta. Only now the birds are American—the Baltimore oriole and the various warblers whose songs Bartók had notated the previous spring in Asheville, North Carolina, where he had gone to work on the sonata for Menuhin and to seek health. The insects and birds disappear, and the chorale returns in one of Bartók's most beautifully fresh reprises, the song now in the orchestra, with a crescendo of rhapsodic commentary in the piano.[11]

The finale is cheerily fugal and generously virtuosic. To help speed the work for his father, Peter Bartók had ruled the barlines on the manuscript paper. The last seventeen measures were still blank on the twenty-sixth day of September, but under the final double bar the composer had written *vége*— The End.

---

[11]One could say that Bartók's model here was the Adagio of his own Piano Concerto No. 2, which begins with orchestra and piano alternating in contrasting material and which has a livelier middle section. For that matter, Beethoven in Opus 132 also has a livelier section ("Feeling new strength") to set against the slow hymn.

# Concerto No. 2 for Violin and Orchestra

*Allegro non troppo*
*Andante tranquillo*
*Allegro molto*

Bartók seems to have had in mind the idea of writing a violin concerto in September 1936; that month, at any rate, he asked his publisher to send scores of some recent examples (they sent him Szymanowski, Weill, and the brand-new Alban Berg). Bartók did not, however, begin this concerto until August 1937. He completed it in September 1938. Zoltán Székely, who had asked Bartók for the work, requested a more brilliant ending, which the composer provided by the end of the year. This is the first of the two alternative endings in the printed score and the one played at most performances. Székely introduced the Concerto on 23 March 1939 with Willem Mengelberg and the Amsterdam Concertgebouw Orchestra.[12]

**Solo violin, two flutes (second doubling piccolo), two oboes (second doubling English horn), two clarinets (second doubling bass clarinet), two bassoons (second doubling contrabassoon), four horns, two trumpets, three trombones, timpani, two snare drums, bass drum, cymbals, triangle, tam-tam, celesta, harp, and strings.**

Béla Bartók and Zoltán Székely, nearly twenty-three years his junior, became friends about 1925.[13] Székely's principal teachers—Zoltán Kodály in composition and Jenő Hubay for violin—were friends of Bartók's, and Bartók was impressed by the young man's cultivated, responsible musicianship and elegantly brilliant violin playing. In 1928 Bartók wrote his Second Rhapsody for Székely, and the two often gave sonata recitals together. In 1935 Székely founded the Hungarian String Quartet, which was to give countless performances of Bartók's quartets and make memorable and authoritative recordings of them. For a time, though, Székely was interested in furthering his solo career, and so it came about that in 1937 he asked Bartók to write him a concerto.

[12]In 1928 Mengelberg canceled the scheduled American premiere of Bartók's Piano Concerto No. 1 when he found himself unable to cope with its rhythmic difficulties; however, he did a good and certainly very spirited job preparing and conducting the Violin Concerto. A radio recording of the premiere has been sporadically available on Philips.

[13]As of May 1998, Székely, at ninety-four, is active as a teacher and coach in Banff, Alberta.

Bartók had written a violin concerto thirty years earlier, but that work, whose genesis was tied to a long-gone romance with the violinist Stefi Geyer, was neither published nor performed until nearly thirteen years after his death. Bartók recycled the first movement in his Two Portraits for Orchestra, Opus 5, but Székely had no idea of the existence of the 1907–1908 concerto. As far as everyone except Bartók and Stefi Geyer-Schulthess (still, or again, a good friend) was aware, the new concerto would be Bartók's first for the violin. Some Bartók scholars in fact do not acknowledge the legitimacy of the earlier work inasmuch as the composer himself kept its existence a secret, and therefore object to calling the 1937–1938 work Concerto No. 2. But the attractive 1907–1908 Concerto has found a place in the repertory—there have been recordings by more than a dozen violinists—so it makes sense to bow to that reality and refer to the two works as No. 1 and No. 2.

What Bartók really wanted to do in response to Székely's request was to write a set of variations for violin and orchestra, but Székely insisted on a full-dress, three-movement concerto. Bartók amused himself by contriving a means to please both himself and his friend: his three-movement concerto includes a formal set of variations as its slow movement, and the principal themes of the finale are all variations of their first-movement counterparts.

Bartók did not play the violin. Few composers, though, have understood the instrument so fully, and perhaps it is in his music for strings—the six quartets, the two sonatas for violin and piano, the Sonata for Solo Violin, the *Music for Strings, Percussion, and Celesta*, this present concerto, and even the forty-four little *Duets*—that he is at his most unfailingly inventive and gloriously characteristic.

He did not, of course, hesitate to ask for advice on technical details, and Székely clearly left his mark on "his" concerto. He and Bartók spent a lot of hours together while the work was in progress, but because of commitments for an American tour, the composer, to his disappointment, could not attend the premiere in Amsterdam. He heard the work for the first time in October 1943 when Tossy Spivakovsky played it with Artur Rodzinski and the New York Philharmonic-Symphony, and with obvious relief he reported to Szigeti: "I was most happy that there is nothing wrong with the scoring; nothing needs to be changed, even though orchestral 'accompaniment' of the violin is a very delicate business." The letter continues with an outburst against the "brutishness" of the New York critic who "doesn't believe that this work will ever *displace* the Beeth. Mendel. Brahms concerti. How is it possible to write such an idiotic thing: what fool fit for a madhouse would want to displace these works with his own?"[14]

---

[14]*Béla Bartók's Letters*, ed. János Demény (New York: St. Martin's Press, 1971).

Bartók begins with gentle preluding on the harp, which is soon joined by lower strings, also plucked. It is against this background that the soloist enters with a melody at once rhapsodic and elegant. Some sense of rhapsody, of quasi-improvisation, is always present in this Concerto, whether in the expansive and always unpredictable flights of lyric song or in the scrubbings and rushings of Bartók's fiercely energetic bravura style. Paula Kennedy has pointed out that the opening theme has some touch of the swagger associated with the style called *verbunkos*. In eighteenth-century Hungary, army recruits were enlisted in a ceremony in which a group of hussars, led by their sergeant and accompanied by Gypsy musicians, performed an impressively macho dance that came to be called a *verbunkos*. This was replaced in 1849, less picturesquely, by universal conscription, but the musical traditions and gestures of the *verbunkos* were here to stay. The word, by the way, comes from the German *Werbung*, meaning recruiting, courtship, and, nowadays, advertising.

A couple of minutes into the movement, the solo violin introduces a new melody, one that floats serenely across the trill fragments in the lower strings. This theme has given commentators much to chew on because it presents, one after another, all twelve notes of the chromatic scale as though it were a twelve-note row in a piece by Schoenberg or one of his school. The notion, proposed by some writers, that he intended this as a parody is absurd: the theme is beautiful and in no way suggests anything parodic. Perhaps looking at the score of the Berg Concerto had reminded Bartók that twelve-note rows do not dictate style. Berg's music is strikingly different from Schoenberg's, and that of Schoenberg's other famous student, Webern, goes off on a still more individual path; it may have occurred to Bartók to show to anyone who cared to listen and look in such detail that a twelve-note melody by him would be yet another thing. His, for example, is firmly anchored to one note, A, which is both its beginning and its end, and which sounds as a pedal through its entire length. Then again, Bartók may have just liked his melody, and its being "twelve-note" is incidental.

The development begins with a clear reminder of the opening, harp chords and all. What follows includes music both sweeter and more agitated than any we have heard so far. In the former category there is an especially magical passage in which the solo violin plays the opening theme, but upside down, while celesta, harp, and orchestral violins surround it with a delicious, starry-bright aura. In the latter, there is a moment when the solo swoops down a scale, to be met at the bottom by a terrific crash in the orchestra. I remember so vividly my first hearing of this measure—it was the Menuhin/Dorati/Dallas recording in the listening booth of a record store—and my instant and unbidden reaction of "Air raid!" It may be nonsense; yet Bartók must in those years have seen newsreels of the bombings of Addis Ababa,

Nanking and Shanghai, and Barcelona, and I cannot rule out the idea that these hateful images may have left a mark here.

Near the end of the movement, Bartók builds in a forceful cadenza. As this begins, and before the soloist has induced the orchestra to keep quiet, Bartók introduces quarter-tones in the violin part (as he would do again in the solo Sonata of 1944).

The second movement is based on a delicate theme of a haunting "speaking" character, exquisitely accompanied by just second violins, violas, and cellos, plus timpani and harp. In Variation 1, the violin part is elaborated in quicker figurations, and the accompaniment, just timpani and plucked basses to begin with, is more delicate still. In Variation 2, the violin is less shy, becoming more sonorous and covering a greater range. Woodwinds participate, while the harp remains fascinated by the running sixteenth-notes of the previous variation. Snarling horns add dissonance to Variation 3, the violin playing with sharp accents and in a deliberately "rough" style. Variation 4 is the magic center of this movement: the theme, now in cellos and basses, is shorn of ornament, but the solo violin hangs garlands of trills and scales. To this variation Bartók adds a mysterious close with many canonic imitations. Variation 5 is a perkily scored scherzo. Variation 6 presents new fantasies in embellishment, texture, and counterpoint, and leads to a coda in which the movement quietly dissolves.

The hush of that *pianississimo* close is dispelled by the rambunctious, dancelike opening of the finale. This is a rich and vibrant movement whose structure and themes, as I mentioned earlier, all have connections to the first movement. Here, for example, are the opening themes of the first and third movements:

Ex. 1

It is as though the finale, full of whimsy and play, were one gigantic and essentially comic variation on the first movement. Bartók's original close had the soloist bow out twenty-six measures before the end. Székely was of course quite right to ask that the work finish "like a concerto, not like a symphony," and Bartók did oblige with a new and properly effective ending. Very few soloists have been so self-sacrificing as to go for the original ending in concert, but at least you can hear it on the Tetztlaff/Gielen and Zukerman/Slatkin recordings. With its nine bars of trombone glissandos, followed by similar wildness from the trumpets and horns, it is, however inappropriate for its context, one of Bartók's most imaginatively colorful orchestral passages.

# Ludwig van Beethoven

Ludwig van Beethoven was born in Bonn, then an independent electorate, probably on 16 December 1770 (he was baptized on the 17th), and died in Vienna on 26 March 1827.

## The Piano Concertos

Primarily, Beethoven was a pianist, although in his young years in Bonn he contributed to the family income by giving violin lessons and playing viola in the court and theater orchestras. He first played the piano in public when he was seven; by the time he was eleven he was something of a local celebrity who had, among other things, mastered *The Well-Tempered Clavier*. (Bach was to be a presence, a beneficent spirit, all his life.) When he moved to Vienna in November 1792, just before his twenty-second birthday, he first made his mark as a pianist, and it was then that he wrote the cadenzas to Mozart's D-minor Concerto that pianists still play more than any others.

By all accounts he was a thrilling performer, at least while he could still hear: in reports of his playing we read such phrases as "tremendous power, character, unheard-of bravura and facility," "great finger velocity united with extreme delicacy of touch and intense feeling," and, in a comparison with Abbé Vogler, "in addition to astonishing execution [Beethoven offers] greater clarity and weight of idea as well as more expression—in short, he is more for the heart—equally great, therefore, as an adagio or allegro player."

In 1814, too deaf to hear that the instrument was desperately out of tune, let alone to judge dynamics properly, he made his last public appearance as a pianist in the first performance of the *Archduke* Trio. In later years, he would sometimes improvise for friends and visitors on the Broadwood that the London builder presented to him in 1818; even then, contact with the keyboard could transform him. Sir John Russell, an observant traveler and celebrity-hound who called on Beethoven in 1821, the year he worked on his last two sonatas, wrote: "The moment he is seated at the piano, he is evidently unconscious that there is anything in existence but himself and his instrument."

The first time Beethoven sat down to compose a piano concerto he was a boy of thirteen; what he produced then was a competent but faceless work that survives only in piano score, though with enough hints about the orchestration to make a reasonable reconstruction possible. The last time was in 1815, when he was forty-four: then he began but soon abandoned a promising first movement in D major. He had already decided not to take on the challenge of performing the hugely demanding Concerto No. 5, presumably because the state of his hearing would have made coordination between himself and the orchestra too dicey. I imagine him, in 1815, torn between the desire to tackle once more a genre he had commanded so potently and the realization that he himself could not be the protagonist on stage. We should also remember that Beethoven's start on the unfinished D-major Concerto occurred in the middle of a fallow decade for him: between the E-minor Piano Sonata, Opus 90, completed in August 1814, and the song cycle *An die ferne Geliebte* (To the Distant Beloved) in April 1816, he composed no major work. After putting the drafts of his D-major fragment away, Beethoven never returned to the concerto.

Between the little piano concerto from Bonn and the unfinished D-major come the canonical five, three from his bold youth, two from his towering maturity. Two other works involving solo piano must be mentioned. In 1803–1804, between the Third and Fourth concertos, Beethoven wrote a Triple Concerto for Piano, Violin, and Cello, a beautiful piece and one of his sunniest. Of the other he might have said, with Fiorello La Guardia, "When I make a mistake it's a beaut." Beethoven's mistake in this instance was to allow himself to be induced by Muzio Clementi, the Italian-born English composer, pianist, publisher, and piano manufacturer, to make a keyboard transcription of the Violin Concerto. (It was part of an extensive publishing deal favorable to both parties.) It sounds feeble and just doesn't work; even so, it has a point of acute interest, namely the extraordinary cadenzas with timpani obbligato Beethoven invented for the first movement.

Apropos cadenzas: In the Piano Concerto No. 5, the cadenzas are built in. Beethoven left cadenzas for the other four concertos.

# Concerto No. 1 in C major for Piano and Orchestra, Opus 15

*Allegro con brio*
*Largo*
*Rondo: Allegro*

The most recent research on this hard-to-pin-down concerto suggests that Beethoven wrote it in 1795 and played it in Vienna on 18 December that year at a concert organized by his teacher, Joseph Haydn, for the primary purpose of presenting three of the symphonies Haydn had composed for his recent visit to London. It is also likely that Beethoven considerably revised the work before its publication by the Viennese firm of T. Mollo & Co. in 1801. The dedication is to Princess Barbara Odescalchi, née Countess Babette von Keglevics, a gifted amateur who took piano lessons from Beethoven; this Concerto is one of four piano compositions inscribed to her.

**Solo piano, one flute, two oboes, two clarinets, two bassoons, two horns, two trumpets, timpani, and strings.**

Virtually every discussion of this Concerto begins by explaining that it was written after the piece we know as No. 2 in B-flat. This one is no exception. As the more ambitious and impressive of the two, Beethoven chose it to be published first, and that is how it came to be No. 1. Brilliant concertos were a likely road to success, and in this work, with its grand scale—it would have been the longest concerto his audience had ever heard—its splendid orchestral style, and its difficult *and* impressive piano writing, Beethoven gave the Viennese a humdinger, something to make them sit up and take notice.

He scored the work in the festive trumpet-and-drums mode of Mozart's C-major concertos, and its first movement shares something of the marchlike character of those works. Beethoven thinks and plans broadly, and his initial exposition for the orchestra covers an astonishing lot of territory. After the first theme, which we hear both in conspiratorial *pianissimo* and lights-on *fortissimo*, we meet a lyric theme that begins, startlingly, in faraway E-flat major. (In the earlier "Concerto No. 2" in B-flat, Beethoven had done something similar at the parallel place by presenting a new theme in D-flat: the key relationship is the same, although in the C-major Concerto Beethoven slightly softens the shock by preparing the appearance of the new theme with two measures of vamp-till-ready accompaniment.)

Actually—and this is typical for the bigness of Beethoven's design—we hear only the first half of the new theme: for its complete presentation we have to be patient for more than 100 measures and the entrance of the solo piano. But even this beginning leads us on quite a tour, one involving a surprising amount of time in minor, before the music finds its way back to C major. There Beethoven ushers in his last theme (for the time being, anyway), a captivating march in what D. F. Tovey calls "Beethoven's best British Grenadiers style."

From Mozart, Beethoven learned the effectiveness of having the soloist enter with a completely new idea, but unlike Mozart—for that matter, unlike himself in the B-flat Concerto—he never returns to the pianist's first tune.[1] As the piano continues the exposition, we experience some more minor-mode shadows before the contrasting theme, the one Beethoven had so startlingly placed in E-flat, returns in its "rightful" key of G, the dominant. The British Grenadiers theme returns as well in a charming new scoring for piano and orchestra together, after which, by way of some highly colored harmonies, the music makes a grandly emphatic affirmation of G major. And there the exposition comes to an end.

In the B-flat Concerto, Beethoven had managed his startling excursion to D-flat simply by lifting the music a half-step from C to D-flat without the formality—or propriety—of a modulation. Here, in the C-major Concerto, he uses the same device for the quietly dramatic start of the development. He has brought his exposition to a close with a grand series of cadential chords in G major, the sort that Wagner objected to as "the rattling of dishes at a banquet." Now Beethoven gives us another measure of G, played by strings alone, in the rhythm of his opening march—and *pianissimo!* The oboe picks up the last G and hangs on to it, and underneath, in dissonance against the oboe, the strings repeat their phrase a half-step higher, on A-flat. This gives the orchestra a bold idea, and in a handful of confidently *fortissimo* bars it swings the music around into E-flat major. Now the development can really begin. The music is new, but the key is one we know from its unexpected appearance in the middle of the opening tutti: it is a happy combination of freshness and consolidation.[2]

The development itself is one of Beethoven's most magical chapters. Except for the first beat and the final two measures of transition into the recapitulation, all of it is *piano* and excitingly held-in *pianissimo.* With its descending parallel chords and scales, it is a kind of dream interlude, undis-

---

[1] I recall an interesting cadenza for this movement by Tonu Kalam in which the pianist's first phrase made a surprise return, played by a solo string quartet.

[2] Beethoven remained fond of this kind of play with half-steps, as listening to his last two piano concertos will reveal. We also find dramatic examples of it even in works as late as the *Hammerklavier* Sonata (the transition from the third movement to the fourth), the Ninth Symphony (the entrance into the first movement's development), and the C-sharp-minor String Quartet, Opus 131 (the shift from the first to the second movement).

turbed by ghostly visitations of the movement's opening theme, many of them involving the same dissonantly overlapping semitones that initiated the development. It is, as Alfred Brendel has remarked, "a piece within a piece," and the pianist must not be afraid to hear it that way. The corresponding sections of the Third and Fourth Concertos and of the Violin Concerto have their astonishing moments of *Träumerei* as well, but this is the only instance of Beethoven's giving over an entire development to this state.

It is told of Beethoven that sometimes, when he had moved listeners to tears with his improvisations, he would shock them by bursting into loud laughter. Here he wakes us with similar rudeness, recalling us to the world of public music with a *fortissimo* right-hand scale in octaves, and by this means he effects his triumphant return to C major. This is the most explicit instance of the bravura style so characteristic of this concerto.[3] The recapitulation then consolidates the primacy of the home key, though this does not keep Beethoven from delighting us with many colorful harmonic touches along the way.

In the usual way, near the end Beethoven provides a spot for a cadenza, which he would have improvised (not without advance thought and preparation), and brilliantly. Some years after the first performance—the keyboard range tells us it must have been at least 1804, and it may well have been as late as 1809—Beethoven wrote two cadenzas for this movement and began a third. Of the two he completed, one is modest, the other huge. Most pianists choose the latter, which is as fantastical as it is immense. It revisits much of the music we have heard in the previous fifteen minutes or so, and one of its finest and subtlest touches is the reappearance of the lyric E-flat-major theme, now in D-flat and thus—D-flat being a half-step away from the home key of C—reminding us one more time of the importance of semitone connections in this movement. As in the no less outsize and wild cadenza he wrote around the same time for the Concerto No. 2, Beethoven eschews the customary return to the tutti by way of a preparatory trill on the dominant: his invention here is an instance of his most deliciously crazy humor.

Beethoven's pupil Carl Czerny points out in his valuable book about the performance of his teacher's piano music that the second movement, although marked *Largo*, is notated *alla breve*, that is, with the half-note rather than the quarter as the rhythmic unit. This means there are two rhythmic pulses in each measure, not four, and the piece should thus be taken "as a tranquil Andante," not too slowly. It is in the distant key of A-flat major—perhaps hinted at by those touches of E-flat major in the first movement—

---

[3]Beethoven intended this scale to be played as a glissando. This was quite manageable with the relatively light action and shallow keys of an 1800 piano, but on a modern concert grand it is quite another matter. Occasionally a pianist dares the octave glissando, but most players turn to one of several possible compromise solutions. The *Waldstein* Sonata presents a similar problem.

and its inflections, just on the dark side of wistful, set a tone that was quite new in 1795. The Adagio (in the same key) of the *Pathétique* Sonata of 1798–1799 mines the same vein. The scoring is delicate and beautifully varied, and the orchestra's solo clarinet is an important secondary hero.

The finale—a touch of polka here?—is full of rambunctious humor, just on the edge of acceptable manners. The central interlude is an irresistible bit of country dance music—probably most listeners' favorite moment in this movement—and Beethoven is nicely generous in letting us enjoy our fill of it. (It can also bring Carmen Miranda and *Tico-Tico* to mind.) He does not lose his delight in jumping into odd keys: one momentary return of the principal theme is in B major, and so you see that semitones are not forgotten either. The ending, in which the soloist seems to want to sidle off the stage unnoticed, is quite a surprise, and Czerny recommends that the conductor wait as long as he dare before unleashing the final *fortissimo*.[4]

## Concerto No. 2 in B-flat major for Piano and Orchestra, Opus 19

*Allegro con brio*
*Adagio*
*Rondo: Molto allegro*

What the American musicologist Geoffrey Block has called "the arduous odyssey" of this concerto began in 1790. Beethoven may have played it in Vienna on 29 March, by which time the work had already been revised twice; 18 December of that year is also a possible date for the first performance, but it seems more likely that what he played on that occasion was the Concerto No. 1 in C. He definitely played this one in Prague in 1798, although in rather different form. After a few more fairly slight revisions, the concerto attained its final form in 1801, and Beethoven offered it to the Leipzig publisher Franz Anton Hoffmeister that year at a bargain price. The work is dedicated to Carl Nicklas von Nickelsberg, an official in the Austrian Imperial Commerce Department about whose connection to the composer nothing is known.

**Solo piano, one flute, two oboes, two bassoons, two horns, and strings.**

---

[4]He also mentions that Beethoven showed him his own way of rearranging the main theme so as to make it sound more brilliant; unfortunately he does not pass the secret on.

To the distress of the tidy, Beethoven's Second Piano Concerto is an earlier work than his First. In his day, opus numbers usually reflected dates of publication (March 1801 for the Concerto in C, December 1801 for the B-flat), not of composition, and Beethoven chose the C major as his first concerto to go into print because it was the more ambitious, brilliant, and impressive of the two. For that matter, inasmuch as it is preceded by a concerto he had written as a boy of thirteen, the Second is not even Beethoven's first. He himself seems to have forgotten about his baby piece from Bonn (it was not published until 1890), even though in his early years in Vienna, when new scores from him were much in demand, he did occasionally dip into the stack of material he had brought with him from his home town. The Concerto No. 2 is in fact an example of that practice.

The genesis of the Concerto No. 2 has never been completely established—the most exhaustive investigation of the problem, an article by Geoffrey Block in the Elliot Forbes Festschrift, is titled "Some Gray Areas in the Evolution of Beethoven's Piano Concerto in B-flat Major, Opus 19"—but it does seem clear that the origins of the work antedate Beethoven's move to Vienna.[5] The sketches and other traces of the pre-1801 versions suggest that Beethoven was troubled by the question of how far-reaching his revisions should be. It is as if he felt caught between the desire to make improvements on the basis of his rapidly growing experience and skill and, on the other hand, some unease at the thought of moving too far from his original concept. Not entirely convinced by the outcome, he let the publisher, Hoffmeister, have it for only half the price he asked for his Septet and the Symphony No. 1 because "I don't consider it as one of my best works."

Modest it may be both in dimensions and demeanor when we compare it to the expansive and original Concerto in C, but the B-flat Concerto is a joy nonetheless, fresh, personal, and crackling with invention. The young Beethoven is one of the most undervalued composers we have. Of charm and good humor there is no lack in the Concerto No. 2, and such details as the *pianissimo* sneak into distant D-flat when Beethoven has just deposited us on the doorstep of F major with such ceremony must have served notice to the musically awake Viennese that the slender young Rhinelander with the coal-black thatch and the rough complexion would turn out to be someone to reckon with.

The opening tutti is eventful and, for a cheery comedy, surprisingly full of minor harmonies. The piano enters with something new and lyric that, with a delightful sense of leisure, initiates a transition to the return of the orchestra's alert opening theme. So at least it seems, but already in the second measure we discover that the soloist has no intention of repeating the first

---

[5]Block's title embodies a pun inasmuch as it deals in part with what can be learned from Beethoven's use of a particular kind of gray ink in part of the manuscript.

idea as the orchestra had given it to us: the continuation is quite different and it leads us to another new and graceful theme. Courteously, the soloist allows the orchestra to introduce it before taking off with it in a version full of inventive new touches.

Arriving on a trill on F, he stops as though to look about him; then, with a move that combines magic with seeming nonchalance, he turns to D-flat major with yet another lyric idea. D-flat was the strange key with which Beethoven had startled us in the opening tutti, and this return to that distant world is placed as though to reassure us that the bold young composer, for all his fondness for caprice, knows just what he is doing and is of no mind to wander randomly off-track. It takes just a few bars of D-flat to accomplish this; then Beethoven quickly gets back to his main mission, which is to bring the exposition to a firm close in the dominant, F major. This he manages with engaging originality and, for himself as pianist, a happy display of virtuosity.

This is a lot of action, and almost as though wanting to offer a quiet counterpoise, Beethoven begins the development by going back to something familiar, the first solo entrance. And now, as one should in a development, he begins to travel. His first move is to the lyric theme that had first appeared so oddly in D-flat. Then he had gotten into D-flat, not by modulating, but by simply lifting the music a half-step from C to D-flat; now, to tighten the connection between development and exposition, he uses the same economical means of a simple half-step ascent to land in a new key, E-flat.[6] Further moves take us across considerable patches of ground, with some time allowed for contemplation of another previously unvisited key, B-flat minor. In due course we arrive at the recapitulation, which begins with some felicitous redistribution of material between piano and orchestra and then proceeds regularly.

Just before the end of the first movement, in accordance to custom, Beethoven allows space for a cadenza, which he would have improvised in his own performances. Some years after the composition of this concerto, however, he wrote out a cadenza that both in compositional style and pianistic manner goes far beyond the movement into which it is placed. It is hugely irruptive, forward-looking even for its presumed date of 1809 or so, and wonderful: Beethoven was utterly free of scruples when it came to mixing vintages. Not the least remarkable thing about this cadenza is the way it ends. "Normal" Classical cadenzas—for example, all of Mozart's—end on a suspenseful dominant so that the re-entrance of the orchestra can then provide the relief of a firm landing on the tonic. Here, against strange dissonances in the treble, the bass settles on an extended measured trill on

[6]Half-steps play a big role in the First, Fourth, and Fifth concertos as well in many of Beethoven's later works.

B-flat: in other words, Beethoven has come back to the tonic long before he is done with the cadenza. And now he puts us to bed in the home key, fluffs up the pillow, straightens the covers, turns out the light, and softly closes the door. Except of course there is the little question, Whatever became of the orchestra? I would rather not reveal here how he resolves this situation.

Beethoven's pupil Carl Czerny, he of the thousand finger exercises, wrote an illuminating and authoritative book on the performance of his teacher's piano music, and of the deeply plumbing slow movement of the Second Concerto he says it might be compared to a dramatic vocal scene. Here is music that offers us a glimpse of Beethoven the great Adagio player. The orchestra leads off with music whose meditative lyricism is soon ruptured by impassioned outbursts, and it is at the height of one of these that the piano enters with an unforgettably eloquent gesture. These sixteen notes tell you everything about the difference between walking into a room and making an entrance. The piano begins by repeating the orchestra's opening phrase, but then goes on to a nobly ornamented melody that seems suspended across a great space. The pianist is the principal singer; nonetheless, the movement as a whole is an intense dialogue between piano and orchestra. Beethoven's new and original voice is everywhere manifest: nowhere in Mozart, for example, will you find anything like the passage in which, against pizzicato strings, woodwinds carry the melody while the piano adds a rapid flicker of thirty-second-note triplets.

Here, too, Beethoven does something utterly astonishing with the cadenza convention. The orchestra draws up to a halt, *fortissimo*, on the usual six-four chord used to introduce a cadenza. A moment of silence—then the piano, right hand alone, *con gran espressione*, begins a tender recitative, softly blurred in a delicate wash of pedal. Three times the orchestra punctuates this with *pianissimo* recollections of its opening theme. With utmost pathos, the piano ends its plea, but inconclusively, stopping on a question mark, so that the orchestra must complete the phrase. To these last bars the flute adds its gently worded condolence.

The bouncy finale is a captivating, high-spirited comedy. It was a late-comer to this score, and very likely what is now the stand-alone Rondo in B-flat, WoO6, was the original finale.[7] The rhythmic double-dealing in the very first phrase is neatly gauged, and Beethoven nicely exploits the comic potential of the ambiguity about where the accent falls. One of the episodes in this enchanting rondo has something of Gypsy flavor. At the last moment, this time clearly taking a leaf out of Mozart's book, Beethoven treats us to a

[7]WoO, an abbreviation used in the Kinsky-Halm thematic catalogue of Beethoven's music, stands for "Werk ohne Opus" (work without opus number). Pronounce it "woo."

graceful and entirely new phrase as well as concocting something quite special by way of a neat exit for the soloist.

## Concerto No. 3 in C minor for Piano and Orchestra, Opus 37

*Allegro con brio*
*Largo*
*Rondo: Allegro*

Sketches for this concerto appear as early as 1796, but the main work on the score was done in 1800. Probably Beethoven made some revisions late in 1802. He was the soloist at the first performance, which took place in Vienna on 5 April 1803, the Symphony No. 2 and the oratorio *Christ on the Mount of Olives* being introduced on the same occasion. The Symphony No. 1 was also on the program, giving critics an opportunity to point out how much better it was than the Second. The Concerto is dedicated to Prince Louis Ferdinand of Prussia, who, like his uncle, Frederick the Great, was a culti- vated amateur musician. Beethoven had met the Prince when, on a visit to Vienna, he had attended one of the early performances of the *Eroica* Sym- phony at the *palais* of Prince Franz Joseph von Lobkowitz.

**Solo piano, two flutes, two oboes, two clarinets, two bassoons, two horns, two trumpets, timpani, and strings.**

The concert at the Theater an der Wien at which Beethoven introduced this concerto is alarming to read about. That day there was a rehearsal that went nonstop from eight in the morning until three in the afternoon, by which time everyone was dotty with fatigue and more than ready to stop. At this point, Beethoven's patron Prince Carl von Lichnowsky sent out for cold cuts and wine to stoke up the exhausted musicians, then asked them to run through *Christ on the Mount of Olives* "just one more time." Beethoven him- self had been awake since before five that morning, when his pupil Ferdinand Ries discovered him in bed copying out trombone parts for the oratorio. The concert itself began as scheduled at six o'clock but, Ries tells us, "was so long that a few pieces that had been planned were not performed."

Ignaz von Seyfried, the newly appointed young conductor at the Theater an der Wien, was recruited to turn pages for Beethoven during the Concerto, but heaven help me!—that was easier said than done. I saw almost nothing but empty leaves; at the most, on one page or another a few Egyptian hieroglyphs wholly unintelligible to me were scribbled down to serve as clues for him; for he played nearly all of the solo part from memory since, as was so often the case, he had not had time to set it all down on paper. He gave me a secret glance whenever he was at the end of one of the invisible passages, and my scarcely concealable anxiety not to miss the decisive moment amused him greatly and he laughed heartily at the jovial supper which we ate afterwards.[8]

Well might it have been a jovial supper. The reviews, which would be very mixed, were not yet in; the box office, at double and triple normal prices, had been terrific.

The opus number of the C-minor Piano Concerto—37—reflects the date of publication, which was 1804, the year in which Beethoven completed the *Waldstein* Sonata as well as the short and ever-astounding Sonata in F major, Opus 54, and in which he began the *Appassionata*. The Concerto itself belongs more to the world of the Opus 18 string quartets, the Septet, and the Symphony No. 1. Insofar as it rarely gets the patronizing treatment sometimes accorded to "early Beethoven," it has benefited from this misunderstanding.

Although not much time had elapsed since Beethoven's preceding concerto, the C major, Opus 15, this one does suggest an advance, especially in the sense of a specific and vivid human and musical presence. There are voices other than Beethoven's behind these works, of course. H. C. Robbins Landon speaks of Beethoven's desire to "out-Mozart Mozart" in these concertos—the great C-major pieces, K. 415, K. 467, and K. 503 in Beethoven's Concerto No. 1, and the C-minor, K. 491, in the Third.[9]

Mozart's C-minor Concerto is one Beethoven particularly admired; once, when he heard it in the company of the English pianist and composer J. B. Cràmer, he sighed, "Ah, dear Cramer, we shall never be able to do anything like that." But doing "anything like that" was not really his agenda anyway; he had business of his own to attend to, and that he did superbly. While you can hear that Beethoven knew and admired Haydn and Mozart— and what other composer has had such daunting parental figures to contend with?—you would have a hard time finding a dozen consecutive measures in any of his compositions that would fit plausibly into any work by his great models. Even in Beethoven's most demure and mannerly pieces of the 1790s, attentive listening reveals detail after detail, strategy after strategy, that attest to the presence of a personality not at all like Haydn's or Mozart's. The

[8]In Thayer's *Life of Beethoven*, rev. and ed. Elliot Forbes (Princeton: Princeton University Press. 1964).
[9]The Mozart concerto Beethoven played most often, the D-minor, K. 466, for which he wrote some dramatic—and disruptive—cadenzas, is one he does not emulate so directly, although in some ways it left its mark on Beethoven's sonata in the same key, Opus 31, no. 2, the *Tempest*.

composer of the first three piano concertos was an assured young man, very much ready to set out on his own, and to give voice to his personality he quickly developed a correspondingly and constantly expanding musical vocabulary.

A composer much less known than Mozart who made a difference to the young Beethoven was Abbé Johann F. X. Sterkel (1750–1817), active chiefly in Mainz and in his native city of Würzburg. The British musicologist Basil Deane pointed out a startling similarity of the second theme of the C-minor Concerto's first movement to one from a sonata by Sterkel.

Ex. 1 Sterkel

Ex. 2 Beethoven

It is not surprising that Beethoven's version is more fluid. Sterkel's piano style made an impression, too, when Beethoven visited him at Aschaffenburg in 1801. Not that his playing was to everyone's taste: Mozart found him too inclined to sacrifice expressiveness to speed, while Franz Ries, Beethoven's first violin teacher and father of his pupil Ferdinand Ries, complained of its being excessively "ladylike." Beethoven, however, was fascinated by the delicacy of Sterkel's touch and manner, and the elegant passages in thirds in the Largo of this Concerto are a new element added to his pianistic vocabulary by Sterkel.

The C-minor Concerto is and feels tight compared to its expansive predecessor in C major. Lean and spare, it has moments of severity that sometimes bring Gluck to mind, and Alfred Brendel has remarked on a kinship "to the austere Josephinian classicism one finds in Viennese architecture around 1800." The first movement's gestures, the stark octaves, the sharply profiled rhythms, are those of a tensely dramatic music, something also supported by Beethoven's demand that the Allegro be fiery (*con brio*). For some reason, Carl Reinecke, the composer, pianist, and conductor who edited the piano concertos for the mid-nineteenth-century complete edition of Beethoven, changed the meter of the first movement from c to ¢, and all editions since 1862 have perpetuated this error. Perhaps Reinecke meant well, thinking that two beats to the bar rather than four would promote more *brio;* it has not worked out that way, though, and Brendel observes that with only two beats to the bar "the eighth-notes of the opening theme lose their rhythmical footing. A chair that needs four legs is made to stand on two." (For good writing about meddlers, well-meaning and otherwise, read Milan Kundera's *Testaments Betrayed*.)

The gestures are taut, but even so, the orchestral exposition of the first movement is markedly spacious. Beethoven soon modulates out of his home key into the relative major, E-flat—this is for the lyric "Sterkel" theme—and then has to make a quick recovery from that indiscretion so that the piano entrance can be properly placed in the tonic (compare his excursions to E-flat and D-flat in the first movements of the concertos No. 1 and No. 2, respectively). This recovery itself is by no means simple, for Beethoven first goes to C major, switching back to the minor just in the nick of time. The piano enters with three explosive C-minor scales and then plays its own version, at once elegant and forceful, of the opening theme. Solo and orchestra together discourse on this, their discussion taking them into E-flat minor. The contrasting lyric theme reappears as well. Brilliant keyboard writing plays an increasingly prominent role, and the solo brings its part of this chapter to a flashy conclusion with a spectacular scale through four and a half octaves. The orchestra is caught up in the momentum and carries the exposition to its conclusion, though without a formal full close.

The development begins with something familiar, the three explosive piano scales, now in D major. We quickly hear, however, that Beethoven intends D not as a key in its own right, but as a preparation for G minor, and that is where conversation about the first theme begins. From there, Beethoven carries us into the still darker region of F minor, after which his lyric bent insists on its privileges in a beautiful and dreamy passage with graceful octave triplets in the piano and beginning in the soft warmth of D-flat major. But Beethoven does not indulge himself—nor us—very long, and soon, in one of his most intense and powerful pages, sets about making his way back to C minor and the recapitulation.

For this movement, as for the first movements of the two preceding concertos, we have a cadenza by Beethoven, but from a later date, possibly 1809, and an assertive and pianistically brilliant affair it is. Even more remarkable is Beethoven's way of bringing the orchestra back in after the cadenza: here we sense one of his periodic stirrings to question the conventional ways of handling major points of demarcation. Ever since 1803, many a listener must have thought that the punctuating C's and G's in this movement's third and fourth measures sounded like a timpani figure and wondered why Beethoven did not give it to the timpani. This is a touch he holds in reserve for a moment at which audiences often stop listening, i.e., the close of the movement right after the cadenza. There always tends to be a drop of tension after the razzle-dazzle of the cadenza; Beethoven, however, is anxious to keep the audience with him and so takes pains to make sure that this moment is arresting and not conventional. His poetic exits from the cadenzas in the Piano Concerto No. 4 and the Violin Concerto are examples, just as the idiosyncratic closes of his cadenzas for the first two piano concertos are clear wake-up calls. In the C-minor Concerto, in lieu of the normal cadenza-ending with a trill on the dominant and a *forte* orchestral re-entry, he gives us something mysterious and tension-laden which, in a completely unexpected way, also at last brings together the timpani figure with the timpani themselves.

Like Haydn, from whom he learned so little in composition lessons and so much in real life, Beethoven sometimes set his slow movements in remote keys. Here he chooses E major, and the sound of that first hushed chord on the piano is a shock that does not lose its magic. This Largo is a movement of immeasurable depth, beautiful melodies, and wonderful sounds. The sheerly sensuous element is manifest with special magic in the quietly suspended transition passages in which the dialogue of flute and bassoon is accompanied by plucked strings and wide-ranging, delicate piano arpeggios.

The look of the printed page can surprise. The time signature is 3/8, which means that the quickest notes among the prolific embellishments come out to be 128th-notes—and there are many of them! The effect of what the performer sees on how he plays is an interesting topic but too far-ranging for discussion here. In brief, I should suppose that Beethoven chose 3/8 rather than the more obvious and easier to read 3/4 (less ink on the page) to remind conductor and pianist, aware not only of the Largo heading but also of the need to convey a sense of depth, that there must also be a compensating fluency to keep the music from bogging down in its largo-ness. Just before the close, which is itself a surprise, Beethoven gives a brief, written-out cadenza to be played *sempre con gran espressione*.

Both the Largo's principal melodies begin on G-sharp, the third note of the E-major scale. The first accented note of the finale's main theme is an A-flat. This is the same as G-sharp on the piano, but now, as A-flat, it functions as the sixth note in the scale of C minor: thus Beethoven starts with a pun that is also a retroactive explanation of the strange harmonic relationship between the first two movements. Later in this vigorous rondo, he makes the pun more obvious and actually brings back the main key in what is now no longer the drastically remote key of E major. And with admirable surefootedness, he introduces a fugued interlude just when a change of pace and texture is needed. This movement, too, has a cadenza near the end, and, like Mozart in *his* concerto in the same key, Beethoven has the music emerge from that cadenza with a rush to the finish in a new key (C major), a new meter (6/8), and a new tempo (Presto).

## Concerto No. 4 in G major for Piano and Orchestra, Opus 58

*Allegro moderato*
*Andante con moto*
*Rondo: Vivace*

Beethoven began this Concerto in 1805, completed the score early the following year, and was at the piano for a private performance in March 1807 at one of two all-Beethoven programs at the town house of his patron Prince Franz Joseph von Lobkowitz. Beethoven made his last appearance as a concerto soloist in the first public performance of this work, which was part of the famous Akademie on 22 December 1808 in the Theater an der Wien—whose heating system had broken down—when the Fifth and *Pastoral* Symphonies and the Choral Fantasy also had their premieres along with the first hearings in Vienna of three movements of the Mass in C and the concert aria *Ah! perfido,* not to forget one of Beethoven's remarkable solo improvisations. Beethoven's student Carl Czerny tells us that his teacher's performance on this occasion was very playful (*mutwillig*), and it seems likely that it incorporated many or all of the virtuosic, capricious, and sometimes witty variants he entered into the corrected copy of a professional copyist's manuscript score, but which have not yet found their way into any printed edition. They are described in detail and given in musical notation in Barry Cooper's article, "Beethoven's Revisions to his Fourth Piano Concerto" in *Performing Beethoven,* edited by Robin Stowell (Cambridge University Press, 1994). (Not all pianists find these emendations persuasive.) This concerto is one of the many compositions that Beethoven dedicated to his patron, student, and friend, Archduke Rudolph.

**Solo piano, one flute, two oboes, two clarinets, two bassoons, two horns, two trumpets, timpani, and strings.**

Charles Rosen remarks in *The Classical Style* that "the most important fact about the concerto form is that the audience waits for the soloist to enter, and when he stops playing they wait for him to begin again." Experienced listeners in the audience at the Lobkowitz *palais* or at the marathon in the freezing Theater an der Wien would have expected to wait for the soloist to make his first entrance after a substantial tutti lasting a couple of minutes and introducing several themes. That is how concertos began. They were in for a shock.

Concerto is a form of theater. Commanding pianist and experienced performer that he was, Beethoven had a keen feeling for that, and his first three piano concertos (not counting the one he wrote as a boy in Bonn) and his Violin Concerto, all of which had been heard in Vienna by the end of 1806, make something quite striking of the first solo entrance. And the older Beethoven grew, the more imaginative he became. In the beautiful Triple Concerto, the solo cello enters repeating the first theme, but a breath later than you expect and with a magical transformation of character. In the Violin Concerto, the solo, with wonderful and quiet authority, rises spaciously from the receding orchestra. After that comes the great Piano Concerto No. 5, where right at the beginning three plain chords in the orchestra provoke three grand fountains of arpeggios, trills, and scales. For the unfinished D-major Piano Concerto of 1815, Beethoven planned a cadenzalike irruption in the eleventh measure.

But it is here, in this most gently spoken and poetic of his concertos, that Beethoven offers his most radical response to Rosen's Law—to begin with the soloist alone. (Perhaps one or another among those first listeners recalled hearing Mozart play his Piano Concerto in E-flat, K. 271, in which the soloist surprises us by interrupting the orchestra in the second bar.) It was a move without precedent, and it is also remarkable how rarely Beethoven, imitated so often and in so many things, has been copied in this stroke: Rachmaninoff's Piano Concerto No. 2; Bartók's First Violin Concerto, Prokofiev's Second, and Schoenberg's; the Bernstein Serenade; the piano concertos of Schoenberg, Barber, and Carter, as well as Wuorinen's Third; the Shostakovich Cello Concerto No. 2—the examples are few and they all come from the twentieth century.[10]

What the piano says is as remarkable as its saying anything at all so early. D. F. Tovey recalled Sir George Henschel "happening to glance at a score of the *Missa solemnis*, open at its first page, putting his finger upon the first chord and saying, 'Isn't it extraordinary how you can recognize any single common chord scored by Beethoven?' " The orchestra's exordial chord in the Fifth Piano Concerto is an example, and so, no less, is the soft, densely voiced, *dolce* chord with which the piano begins this Concerto in G major. Czerny, by the way, appears to recommend rolling the first chord; at least he prints it with an indication to do so in his book *On the Proper Performance of All of Beethoven's Works for the Pianoforte*, and indeed, if the roll is executed with delicacy and exquisite timing, the effect is lovely.[11]

The whole brief opening phrase—five measures long—is arresting in its

---

[10]One near-exception is Schumann's Fantasia in A minor, the original version of the first movement of his Piano Concerto; Schumann soon changed it, however, so that a five-octave *forte* E in the orchestra sets up the piano entrance, and even in the original, the orchestra enters less than a second after the piano's two opening chords.

[11]Angela Hewitt is the only pianist I have heard do this.

subtle rhythmic imbalance; the still greater wonder is the orchestra's hushed, sensitive and far-seeing, harmonically remote response. That response is a chord of B major and it seems to come from another world; at the same time, it is connected to the piano's opening phrase in that both have B as their top melodic note and sound out the same rhythmic pattern. Except in his cadenzas and improvisations, Beethoven was not interested in pursuing the irrational.[12] The distance between the pianist's opening bars and the orchestra's reply is something we can't help hearing; our awareness, no less essential, of the connection between the statement and the response requires both that the pianist not be too narcissistically "poetic" and slow in the first five measures, and that the conductor not hurry the orchestra's entrance. A sensitive conductor will ask the string players to have instruments and bows in playing position before the music begins so that there is no visual commotion to disturb the piano's opening statement.

The strange B-major chord—and the shock and strangeness are the greater for the *pianissimo*—tells us that we have entered a world of poetry and of mystery. It also tells us something about the size of the space we have entered. Unless we really want to assume that this chord, which in effect lasts for two measures, is an inconsequential excursion—literally inconsequential, without consequences—it also tells us that we are at the beginning of a big work. Imagine a surveyor plotting out a building site. He has laid down a marker for G major right at our feet and then another for B major far, very far, over there: it is going to take a considerable structure to connect the two. Or to put it another way, it will take a lot of space to "explain" so bold a departure less than fifteen seconds into a piece.

Beethoven is not going to stay in—or even *on*—B major long: to do so would create the impression that the G-major beginning was caprice, and that would be silly. In fact it takes him only a few seconds to gently shift the harmony so that in measure 14 we are back on G-major terra firma. (You could actually make a cut from the middle of measure 5, where the piano leaves off, to the middle of measure 14: you would lose all the poetry, but the passage would still make grammatical sense.) We might say that now, back on terra firma, it feels as though we have never been away, but of course this is not true: we may have pushed the B-major shock to the back of our mind, but that experience remains alive in our memory and demands further exploration, demands making sense of. Beethoven will not let us down.

---

[12]What we know about Beethoven's improvisations is only what we can guess from descriptions; there is, however, good reason to believe that the quite mad Fantasy, Opus 77, might be a written-down recollection of what he extemporized at the December 1808 Akademie.

Ex. 1

    The persistently present three-note upbeat makes this music tender cousin to the Fifth Symphony (in progress at the same time, though not completed until two years later). The rhythmic elasticity of the first solo-and-orchestra statement-and-response foreshadows an uncommon sense of pace: the allegro is *moderato* and motion is leisurely to begin with, but later we sometimes feel as many as eight urgent beats per measure and are dazzled by the brilliance of the passagework. (There was comment in 1808 about the tremendous speed of Beethoven's playing.)

    With the piano fallen silent after setting the music into motion, the orchestra generously expands the first paragraph, carries it briefly to *fortissimo*, then introduces a new theme, gentle but full of melancholy passion. Its harmonies are restless. It starts as though it were going to be in A minor (an odd choice of key for a second theme in a movement in G major), but as it moves about it remembers—with a striking *pianissimo* hush—to pay a call on B, though this time it is the less remote B *minor*. That touch of B releases the pent-up tension, and a joyous passage for the full orchestra prepares the next entrance of the soloist. Beethoven manages this crucial moment with a device he has learned from Mozart. The rhythm and the harmony make it quite clear when the soloist is supposed to come in. But he doesn't: the orchestra continues, and *then* the solo enters unexpectedly, possibly with something unexpected, and in this instance at an unexpected angle. Rosen's Law again.

    Here the piano begins with an elaboration of the three-note upbeat, and this leads to an orchestral entrance that corresponds to the terra firma landing in measures 14-15. Now the second part of the exposition—the part involving solo and orchestra together—is properly under way. It is not long, however, before Beethoven produces an amazing surprise—a dream episode of just a few measures, *pianissimo* and *espressivo*, and in a completely strange key (B-flat), which he enters almost without preparation. It is also scored with the pianist's hands very far apart, so that the sound itself is unlike any other we have heard to this point. But Beethoven quickly returns to the main track. A new theme is introduced, one with much emphasis on B, and the harmonically restless, somewhat dark one from the orchestral exposition returns as well.

The development begins as the second part of the exposition did, with the three-note upbeat, but heard this time at an even stranger angle and prepared to travel much farther. For the most part, the development is active and pianistically brilliant rather than contemplative. The exception is another fleeting dream episode, *pianissimo* and *dolce*, and again in a most unexpected key (C-sharp minor). The recapitulation enters in grandly rhetorical style, and it brings a third dream episode, *pianissimo* and *espressivo*, and in yet another strange key (E-flat).

Of the two cadenzas Beethoven wrote for this movement, the overwhelming majority of pianists prefers the first.[13] When someone remarked to Beethoven that his Seventh Symphony was so much more popular than his Eighth, the composer growled that this was because the Eighth was so much better. I am tempted to apply this to this virtually unknown second cadenza, which the composer, aware of its musical and pianistic land-mines and never one to deny himself a pun, headed *Cadenza ma senza cadere* (cadenza, but without falling down). It also exemplifies to perfection Alfred Brendel's characterization of Beethoven the cadenza composer as "the architect [turned] into a genius running amok." Nowhere is this more true than here, and most audiences usually don't believe it is really by Beethoven. Calculated to scare an audience into a state of extreme wakefulness, it begins with a violent version of what Beethoven does so poetically at the concerto's beginning— an excursion into a blatantly "wrong" key. This game continues to give him pleasure, and in what appears to be a peace-making gesture he returns to the piano's first statement, *dolce*. But this, too, is in a completely irrelevant key (A major), and recovery from this carefully planted gaffe turns into quite an odyssey.

Nor does the adventure end when the cadenza does. Audiences tend to stop listening as the tension of an exciting cadenza is released by the re-entry of the orchestra, and so Beethoven likes to do something special at this point. In the Piano Concerto No. 3 he had made something highly dramatic and

---

[13]Some other cadenzas, tentatively attributed to Beethoven, but of uncertain pedigree, have come to light in recent years.

mysterious of this moment; here, as he would in the Violin Concerto later in the same year, he makes it a moment of supreme poetry. Usually, the end of a cadenza is a dominant-to-tonic cadence, the most common one in classical music, writ large and so arranged that the entrance of the orchestra marks the appearance of the "releasing" tonic chord. Here, the suspenseful dominant continues even after the orchestra has come back in, and the music goes on for nearly half a minute before Beethoven sets us down on the tonic.

The second movement is the most famous. D. F. Tovey wrote in his essay on the work: "If I am not mistaken, it was Liszt who compared the slow movement of this concerto to Orpheus taming the wild beasts with his music." Tovey was in fact mistaken, though countless writers, including this one, have ignored his caveat and attributed the Orpheus analogy to Liszt. But in an article in the Spring 1985 issue of *Nineteenth-Century Music*, Owen Jander reminded us that it was the German theorist A. B. Marx "who first began to bring the Orpheus program of the Fourth Piano Concerto into focus" in his Beethoven biography of 1859.[14] Even earlier than that, in his 1842 book on Beethoven performance I mentioned earlier, Czerny had suggested that "in this movement (which, like the entire concerto, belongs to the finest and most poetic of Beethoven's creations) one cannot help thinking of an antique dramatic and tragic scene, and the player must feel with what movingly lamenting expression his solo must be played in order to contrast with the powerful and austere orchestral passages."

Marx proposed, not altogether convincingly, a tie to Gluck's *Orfeo ed Euridice*. Jander has pursued the matter further and offers a connection with an Orpheus opera by Beethoven's friend Friedrich August Kanne, linking the music to Kanne's libretto and its source in Ovid's *Metamorphoses*; indeed, he goes so far as to maintain that "to analyze this work without [reference to this] program misses the point of the form." Jander's provocative article is worth reading, as are the sharp critical responses it drew from Edward T. Cone ("Beethoven's Orpheus—or Jander's" in the same issue of *Nineteenth-Century Music*) and Joseph Kerman ("Representing a Relationship: Notes on a Beethoven Concerto" in *Representations 39*), as well as Jander's further thoughts on the subject in the Summer 1995 issue of *Nineteenth-Century Music*. The Spring 1996 issue of that journal brought a further exchange between Kerman and Jander, but by then the conversation was beginning to get cranky.[15]

---

[14]Discussion of this point does not begin with Jander. In Joseph Horowitz's *Conversations With Arrau* (New York: Knopf, 1982), the Chilean pianist stated that "there is a tradition in Germany that gives the atmosphere for the *first and second movements* as the legend of Orpheus and Eurydice" (emphasis added), citing specific examples of musical gestures in the first movement that supposedly represent the pleading of Orpheus.

[15]In any case it is a delight to read Ovid. There are many fine translations, and I suggest finding a bookstore or library with a good selection and doing some taste-testing. As a supplement I recommend

In this movement the orchestra is loud, staccato, declamatory, in stark octaves; it must be fierce and frightening. The marking is *Andante con moto* and the meter is 2/4, both indicators that the tempo must not be slow. The music for the piano is soft, legato, songful, and richly harmonized. At the end, after a truly Orphic cadenza—and Beethoven almost persuades us that he invented the trill expressly for this moment—the orchestra has learned the piano's way. One wants to amend Czerny: it is not just a question of the "movingly lamenting" piano *contrasting* with "the powerful and austere" orchestra; the piano, soft-spoken though it is save for one wild and anguished outburst in the cadenza, *subdues* the orchestra.

But the music itself holds us captive no less than the poetry and the drama. Beethoven steadily compacts the dialogue: we would, after all, go mad with impatience if each exchange took thirteen measures, as the first one does. The orchestra interrupts the piano, and the piano sings across the orchestra's peremptory phrases: think of the poetic suggestiveness of those elisions. The phrases of both orchestra and piano become shorter and shorter until their essences are distilled in a single pizzicato and a single diminished chord.

How dramatically that drastic distillation sets off the piano's grandly spreading, reticently confident cadenza! This begins as a supremely eloquent melody, which dissolves in highly colored harmonic sequences. These in turn lead to a chain of fierce trills, violently punctuated by fragments of chromatic scales. Gradually the music becomes quiet, Beethoven directing the pianist gradually to depress the soft pedal so as to go from three strings to two to one. The orchestra re-enters, playing full chords of harmony now, but *pianississimo*. Across its last chord, the piano breathes one final, poignant, long, softly dissonant appoggiatura.

Pathos? Grief for the lost Eurydice? Orpheus? Virgil? Ovid? Gluck? I don't know. The confrontation of stern orchestra and pleading, persuasive piano fits the Orpheus legend well, and the idea that Beethoven might have had this scene in mind is not implausible: he did, after all, tell his friend Karl Amenda that the slow movement of his Quartet, Opus 18, no. 1, depicted the tomb scene in *Romeo and Juliet*. But Jander becomes problematic for me in his insistence on tying so much musical detail in all three movements to details in Ovid and Gluck's *Orfeo*, breaching the boundary between imagery and literalism.[16]

Until the end of this sublime Andante, this is a quietly scored concerto; now, in the finale, trumpets and drums appear for the first time. Not that this

---

*After Ovid*, a brilliant collection of translations/paraphrases by forty-two contemporary poets, edited by Michael Hofmann and James Lasdun (New York: Farrar, Straus and Giroux, 1995).

[16]Kathleen Norris has wise words on the mixing of imagery and literalism in *The Cloister Walk* (New York: Riverhead, 1996).

music is in any way grand: its domain is lyricism and wit. Beethoven takes a charmingly oblique, Haydnesque approach to the question of how to resume after the evocative scene just played. The second movement has ended with a chord of E minor with E on top. Still *pianissimo*, the strings play a series of chords that also have E on top, but now they are chords of C major, and they dance. That is how Beethoven makes his way into this beguiling finale. He pulls a lot of amusing surprises in the matter of when and how solo and orchestra take over from each other. The finale also has moments that remind us of the first movement's dream interludes and, with its two sections of violas, it is also given to outrageously lush sounds—one more unexpected element in this most subtle, suggestive, and multifaceted of Beethoven's concertos. He allows room for a cadenza but warns that it "must be short": his own thirty-second outburst gets it just right.

## Concerto No. 5 in E-Flat major for Piano and Orchestra, Opus 73

> *Allegro*
> *Adagio un poco mosso*
> *Rondo: Allegro ma non troppo*

In English-speaking countries, this Concerto is called the *Emperor*—to Beethoven's "profound if posthumous disgust," as D. F. Tovey put it. The origins of the name are obscure, although there is a story, unauthenticated and unlikely, that at the first Vienna performance a French officer exclaimed at some point, "C'est l'Empereur!" The Concerto was written in 1809, and the first performance was given in Leipzig on 28 November 1811 by Friedrich Schneider, Johann Philipp Christian Schulz conducting the Gewandhaus Orchestra. Vienna got to hear it only on 12 February 1812, when the soloist was Beethoven's student Carl Czerny. Like the Concerto No. 4, this is one of many compositions that Beethoven dedicated to his patron, student, and friend, Archduke Rudolph.

**Solo piano, two flutes, two oboes, two clarinets, two bassoons, two horns, two trumpets, timpani, and strings.**

"Nothing but drums, cannons, human misery of every sort!" Thus Beethoven on 26 July 1809 to Gottfried Christoph Härtel, his publisher in Leipzig. The

Fifth Concerto is a magnificent affirmation asserted in terrible times. Alfred Brendel has described it as imbued with "a grand and radiant vision, a noble vision of freedom." This quality does not endear it to all—not, for example, to those who, following the philosopher Herbert Marcuse, deplore the idea of "affirmative" music that fails to rebel against the ills of oppression.

In 1809 Austria was at war with France for the fourth time in eighteen years. In 1792 the Girondists had come to power, the Parisian mob stormed the Tuileries, the royal family was arrested and the Republic proclaimed, Louis XVI was brought to trial, and an efficient new decapitation machine— popularly known as Louisette or Louison and only later named for its chief propagandist, Dr. Joseph-Ignace Guillotin—began its bloody work. The conservative forces of Austria, Prussia, Spain, Portugal, and Sardinia formed a coalition to fight the spirit of the French Revolution. In 1795, the Prussians, the strongest of the Allies, had deserted the cause in order to attend to business of their own in Poland. The following spring, the ill-fed, ill-equipped, ill-shod French army, led by the twenty-six-year-old Napoleon Bonaparte, inflicted on the Austrians the first in a series of defeats that led them to sue for an armistice a year later. It was the beginning of the destruction of the Habsburg Empire as a major power, a process whose completion was accomplished and acknowledged in 1806, when Francis II abdicated the ancient title of Holy Roman Emperor.[17] Having returned to the fray after the 1797 armistice, Austria was defeated for a second time in 1800 and again in 1805, when French troops actually occupied Vienna. (The unrest caused by their arrival ruined the chances for Beethoven's opera *Fidelio*.) Each peace brought Austria new humiliations, new territorial losses, new economic chaos.

In the midst of this crescendo of civic wretchedness, Beethoven had been working with phenomenal intensity. Between 1802 and 1808 he wrote the five symphonies from the Second through the *Pastoral*; the three *Rasumovsky* string quartets and the two trios, Opus 70; four sonatas for violin, including the *Kreutzer*, and the Cello Sonata, Opus 69; six piano sonatas, among them the *Waldstein* and the *Appassionata*; the Third and Fourth piano concertos, the Violin Concerto, and the Triple Concerto; *Fidelio* in its original form and its first revision; the oratorio *Christ on the Mount of Olives*, the C-major Mass, and the Choral Fantasy—to mention only the large-scale works. Even so, one can understand why he was seriously tempted late in

---

[17]In the 1760s, Voltaire rightly remarked that the Holy Roman Empire was "neither holy, nor Roman, nor an empire." But from 800, when the title of *imperator augustus* was conferred on Charlemagne by Pope Leo III, until the end of the Thirty Years' War in 1648, the Empire was a real political force. It comprised chiefly German lands and from the fifteenth century on was known as the Holy Roman Empire of German Nations. By way of claiming historical legitimacy, Germans often called the Empire of 1871–1918 the Second Reich, and it was with the same motivation that Hitler called his enterprise the Third Reich.

1808 to accept the offer of a post as court composer to Jerome Bonaparte, puppet king of Westphalia. That gave the Viennese another cause for alarm, and three wealthy patrons banded together to guarantee Beethoven an income for life provided that he stay in Vienna or some other city within the Austrian Empire.

Beethoven entered into this unprecedented agreement on 1 March 1809 and must have regretted it many a day and night during the subsequent months. On 9 April Austria once again declared war on France, this time with Britain and Spain as allies. One month later, Napoleon's army was in the suburbs of Vienna. The empress left the capital with most of her family and household.[18] The French artillery began its terrifying assault. On the worst night of all, that of 11 May, Beethoven made his way through the broken glass, the collapsed masonry, the fires, the din, to find refuge in the cellar of the house of his brother Caspar. There he covered his head with pillows, hoping thus to protect the remaining shreds of his hearing.

Toward the end of the summer, Beethoven regained his ability to concentrate, and by year's end he had completed, besides this Concerto, the String Quartet, Opus 74, and the *Farewell* Sonata, both also in E-flat; and two smaller piano sonatas, the wonderfully lyric F-sharp major, Opus 78, and its snappy companion in G major, Opus 79. Excellence is, to say the least, undiminished, but in productivity, 1809 is a slender year compared to the previous seven. Perhaps the contract with the princes was a symbol of acceptance and arrival that allowed Beethoven to push himself less fiercely than before, although in hard reality, because of the prevailing fiscal chaos the promised moneys did not arrive punctually and dependably. Whatever the reasons, Beethoven never again composed as prolifically as he had between 1802 and 1808, the period his biographer Maynard Solomon calls his "heroic decade." The *Sinfonia eroica* (1803–1804) most forcefully defined the new manner; the Fifth Piano Concerto marks both its summit and its termination.

Beethoven had begun his Fourth Piano Concerto in an unprecedented way, with an unaccompanied lyric phrase for the soloist, and only after that bringing in the "normal" exposition of material by the orchestra. Starting to sketch the Fifth Concerto, he again turned his mind to the question of how one might begin a concerto in an original and striking manner. Here, too,

---

[18]Among those who accompanied the empress was her brother-in-law—and Beethoven's pupil—the twenty-year-old Archduke Rudolph, whose departure and return the following year are commemorated in one of Beethoven's most beautiful piano sonatas, the *Lebewohl* (Farewell), Opus 81a. It was for Rudolph's installation as Archbishop of Olmütz (Olomouc) that Beethoven later composed his *Missa solemnis*; the list of important works that Beethoven dedicated to him includes, besides this E-flat Concerto, the Piano Concerto No. 4, the Violin Sonata, Opus 96, the *Archduke* Trio, the *Hammerklavier* Sonata, Opus 106, and the Sonata, Opus 111. With the princes Lobkowitz and Kinsky, the archduke was one of the three guarantors of Beethoven's life income.

he introduces the piano sooner than an audience 185 years ago expected to hear it—not, however, with a lyric or indeed any sort of thematic statement, but in a series of cadenzalike flourishes.

A cadenza is a cadence—an extended, elaborated, and usually brilliant one, but a cadence nonetheless. The *Harvard Dictionary of Music* has a good definition: "A melodic or harmonic formula that occurs at the end of a composition, a section, or a phrase, conveying the impression of permanent or momentary conclusion." A cadence is an odd thing, therefore, to find at the beginning of a composition; nonetheless, it is what we do find here.[19]

In three sonorous chords, the orchestra outlines the components of the most basic and familiar cadential formula in tonal music. The opening E-flat chord, besides being magnificently imposing, is also instantly recognizable as belonging to this work and no other. Beethoven had an extraordinary gift for investing such basic materials as common chords with individual character, and this particular chord sounds so "specific" because it consists only of E-flats and G's; not until the piano comes in do we hear the B-flats that complete the triad.

The piano responds to each of the three chords with fountains and cascades of arpeggios, trills, and scales. Splashy as this is, it is also totally organic.[20] In no other concerto by Beethoven, in no other classical concerto at all, are figurations so much of the compositional essence as here: thus perhaps the opening cadenza is "thematic" after all. Each of the three fountains brings in new pianistic possibilities, and the entire first movement—the longest Beethoven ever wrote—is continually and prodigiously inventive in this department. The climax of the third fountain briefly introduces the tension of a triplet cutting across the basic two-by-two. That also foreshadows what is to come: the simultaneous presentation of different rhythmic versions of the same idea is a specialty of this Concerto, as is, in a more general way, the play of two against three (or patterns that are rhythmically even more dissonant).[21] Indeed, the crescendo of excitement that Beethoven builds during this movement depends crucially on the increase in dissonance, both the cross-rhythms themselves and the actual harmonic dissonances produced by these collisions of two against three, three against four, four against five, and

[19]This is not without precedent. With less rhetorical splash, but still with remarkable effect, Haydn begins his C-major Quartet, Opus 74, no. 1, with a dominant-tonic cadence, and he uses the same device, this time as a joke, in the finale of his D-major Quartet, Opus 76, no. 5. In his unfinished D-major Piano Concerto of 1815, Beethoven, interested in further exploring what he had done in the Concerto No. 5, had the soloist enter in measure 11 with a cadenza that then leads to an expansive tutti.

[20]Apropos splashy, I learned from Alfred Brendel that Hans von Bülow proudly told his pupils that he always got special applause from the audience for this cadenza.

[21]A subtle and delicious example: the chromatic scale in sixteenth-notes with which the piano re-enters after the first tutti and which occurs at several other important junctures in this movement makes its last appearance in triplets.

so on. Worth noting as well is the blending of brilliance with quiet, another characteristic foreshadowed in the dramatic exordium. Throughout, Beethoven tempers the virtuosic writing with the instruction *dolce* (literally, "sweet"), which invites a more inward manner than is implied by *espressivo*.

The first thing to be said about the slow movement is that it should not be too slow. As early as 1842, Czerny warned that "it must not drag." Beethoven himself makes this quite clear, qualifying *Adagio* with *un poco mosso* (moving a bit) and, even more significantly, giving ¢ as the time signature, meaning that players and listeners should feel two principal pulses in each measure of four quarter-notes. In the complete edition of Beethoven that came out in the middle of the nineteenth century, the same Mr. Reinecke who messed up the first movement of the Concerto No. 3 by changing the time signature from ¢ to ¢ again committed a foul, but this time changing Beethoven's two beats per bar to a plodding four. All editions—and most performances—have perpetuated this destructive interference.

B major, the key of this Adagio un poco mosso, comes across as both interestingly fresh and reassuringly tied to where we have been. Its five sharps look foreign after the three flats of the first movement, but if Beethoven had notated this movement in its "real" key of C-flat major, we would be looking at a key signature of seven flats and not be a bit grateful for it. Beethoven affirms the connection of the Adagio to the preceding Allegro by beginning its melody on D-sharp, which is for practical purposes the same as E-flat, the key of the first movement and the concerto as a whole. The chief music here is a hymn introduced by muted strings, to which the piano's first response is a quietly rapturous aria, *pianissimo, espressivo,* and mostly in triplets. Beethoven gives us two variations on the chorale, the first played by the pianist, the second by the orchestra with the piano accompanying (but the accompaniment contains the melody, rhythmically "off" by a fraction and thus another instance of rhythmic dissonance).

The music subsides into stillness. Then Beethoven makes one of his characteristically drastic shifts, simply dropping the pitch by a semitone from B-natural to B-flat (bassoons, horns, pizzicato strings, all *pianissimo*). This puts us right on the doorstep of E-flat major, the Concerto's home key. That move accomplished, but still in the tempo of the slow movement and still *pianissimo*, Beethoven projects the outlines of a new theme, made, like all the others in this Concerto, of the simplest stuff imaginable. Suddenly this new idea bursts forth in its proper tempo, that of a robust German dance, and *fortissimo*: the finale has begun.[22] The dance theme is elaborately and excit-

---

[22]This is most often marked *Allegro*, but Charles Rosen has pointed out that Beethoven modified this, first with *non tanto*, later with the more common *ma non troppo*, both meaning "not too much." Breitkopf & Härtel, the publishers of the first edition (1811), omitted this modification, which found its way into print only in the 1840s. ("Mistakes! Mistakes! You yourself are just one big mistake!"

ingly syncopated. Beethoven works out the movement with his very own—
and ample—sense of space. Nor is his sense of humor absent. Just before the
end, the timpani attain unexpected prominence in a passage of equally unexpected quiet. But this descent into adagio and *pianissimo* is undone in a
coda as lively as it is brief.

## Triple Concerto in C major for Piano, Violin, and Cello, Opus 56

> *Allegro*
> *Largo*
> *Rondo alla Polacca*

In 1802 Beethoven made some sketches for a concerto in D major for this
combination, but abandoned them when the concert at which he had
planned to play it was canceled. In October 1803 there is mention of a triple
concerto in a letter from the composer's brother Carl to the publishers Breitkopf & Härtel, and Beethoven probably began work on the present score
fairly soon after that, the piece then being completed in the summer of 1804.
Anton Schindler, who became Beethoven's amanuensis much later, in 1822,
maintained that the solo parts were intended for Archduke Rudolph, the
violinist Ferdinand August Seidler, and the çellist Anton Kraft. Schindler
was a forger and one of the world's most uninhibited liars, and as Susan
Kagan, the archduke's biographer, remarks, "although he would seem to have
little reason to fabricate this particular assertion, one must approach all his
statements with caution." If Schindler is in fact correct, the Triple Concerto
may have been privately performed by the archduke's orchestra in 1804 or
so. The first public performance of the work was given in Leipzig early in
April 1808; the soloists, we learn from a review in the 27 April issue of the
*Allgemeine musikalische Zeitung*, were "Mad. Müller, Herr Matthäi, and Herr
Dozzauer." Neither this nor a performance in Vienna in May of that year
was a success, and one gathers from the reports in the *AmZ* that on both
occasions the soloists, not identified for the Vienna concert, were not good.

**Solo piano, violin, and cello, two flutes, two oboes, two clarinets, two bassoons,
two horns, two trumpets, timpani, and strings.**

---

wrote Beethoven to Härtel about this and other typos in the first edition.) Modern editions have
tended to repeat the error of 1811.

It is a pity we have so little information about the background of this work: it would be fascinating to know what moved Beethoven, on the verge of completing the *Eroica*, to tackle an unprecedented concerto combination—one, for that matter, rarely tried again and not, so far, impressively.

Two things possibly speak for the idea that Beethoven wrote the Triple Concerto for Archduke Rudolph, though we are on somewhat shaky ground with both. One is the date. Alexander Wheelock Thayer, the great nineteenth-century Beethoven biographer, suggested that the winter of 1803–1804, the time of the Triple Concerto, was when the then fifteen-year-old archduke began to study piano, composition, and theory with Beethoven; Thayer had to point out, though, that no one, including "the indefatigable Köchel," had succeeded in establishing the date precisely. If, however, this *is* when Rudolph began those lessons, it is believable that Beethoven, either on his own or at his pupil's request, wrote this work for him. "Believable," however, is hedged with question marks: there are no letters, firsthand reports, court financial records, or anything else to provide tangible support for this attractive theory.

Then there is the piano writing, which, by Beethoven's standards for 1803–1804, is easy. It requires fluency with basic scales and arpeggios, but it comes nowhere near the technical demands of other Beethoven works of this time, such as the *Kreutzer*, *Waldstein*, and *Appassionata* sonatas. Of course, a good pianist with a chamber-music sense and a cultivated coloristic imagination can make it sound quite brilliant. It might well have been within the range of what Rudolph could do; he was never a fire-eating virtuoso, but even when you allow a discount for some flattery due a Habsburg archduke, it is clear that his playing was well thought of.

In time, Rudolph became his teacher's greatest patron and one of his most constant friends. My essay on the Piano Concerto No. 5 includes the remarkable list of the works Beethoven dedicated to the archduke. Notably missing from this list, however, is the Triple Concerto, which is inscribed to Prince Franz Joseph von Lobkowitz, Beethoven's most generous patron next to the archduke, and himself the recipient of many important Beethoven dedications. The archduke and Prince Lobkowitz were on excellent terms, and the former often played at private concerts at the latter's Viennese *palais*.

On the other hand, the association of the Triple Concerto with Anton Kraft is completely believable. Kraft was probably the finest cellist of his generation, and the taxing cello part, with its high-register flights, is something that might well have been composed with his virtuosity in mind. Kraft was born in 1749 in what is now Rokycany in the Czech Republic and, before making up his mind to devote himself entirely to music, studied philosophy and jurisprudence at the University of Prague. He joined the Esterházy orchestra in 1778 and took composition lessons from Haydn for a time; Haydn wrote his (also very difficult) D-major Concerto for him, and he was the cellist in the first performance of Mozart's great Divertimento in E-flat for String Trio, K. 563. After the disbanding of the Esterházy orchestra in 1790, Kraft settled in Vienna. In 1796 he became the principal cellist in Prince Lobkowitz's orchestra, which means he would have sat at the front desk for the premieres of Beethoven's *Eroica* and Fourth symphonies. Kraft also toured extensively as a soloist admired as much for his deeply expressive playing as for a fabled technique. (His son, Nicolaus, was hardly less renowned as a superb cellist.) He died in 1820.

Little is known about Ferdinand August Seidler except that he was a Berliner who settled in Vienna, where he joined Archduke Rudolph's musical household. The composer and excellent writer on music Johann Friedrich Reichardt heard him and the archduke three times while visiting Vienna in 1810 and reported that Seidler distinguished himself both "with his own concerto movements and with his excellent manner of accompanying the Archduke in the difficult Trios of Beethoven and Prince Louis Ferdinand [of Prussia]." Reichardt described Rudolph's playing as characterized by "much skill, precision, feeling . . . self-possession, repose, and accuracy."

Criticism has sometimes been condescending toward the Triple Concerto, but as D. F. Tovey wrote in his searching examination of the work, "If [it] were not by Beethoven, but by some mysterious composer who had written nothing else and who had the romantic good sense to die before it came to performance, the very people who most blame Beethoven for writing below his full powers would be the first to acclaim it as the work of a still greater composer."[23] The Triple Concerto, a wonderful work, is formal, at times reserved in manner, spacious, and rich in themes. Some of these themes are characterized by that certain studied neutrality we find in Beethoven from time to time when it seems he just wants to show the unexpected possibilities of material that many people might find unpromising. But as I have pointed out elsewhere, the ability to make powerful—and original—statements with the plainest chord sequences and figurations is amazing in Beethoven.

The hushed, stalking opening—cellos and basses alone—generates a mysterious, suspenseful atmosphere both with its silences and its odd phrasing (4 + 5 + 1 measures). Beethoven works this up in an electrifying crescendo that carries us to G major and a new, genial theme. This ends less innocently than it begins, for Beethoven diverts its cadence into what almost becomes a softly cushioned landing in faraway A-flat major: this is what Tovey likes to call a "purple patch." But the bass finds its way back to G in the nick of time, and for ten measures, no less, over which Beethoven gives us another and irresistibly swinging theme. If this were a symphony, Beethoven would want to turn that G into the tonic of a new key and thus bring the exposition

---

[23]D. F. Tovey, *Essays in Musical Analysis*, Vol. 3 (Oxford: Oxford University Press, 1936).

to a close. Here he comes perilously close to G as a key, and only at the last moment, with four beautifully gauged measures of bare octaves (two for woodwinds, two for strings), does he slew the music back into C major. It is a nice touch that the exposition ends as well as begins with quiet music in unharmonized octaves.

The first violins continue to keep the pulse quietly going on C, and their repeated eighth-notes constitute the screen against which the cello begins the solo half of the exposition by playing the first theme. It is the only instance in Beethoven's seven concertos where a soloist begins that way, without any introductory or transitional material, but Beethoven makes something special even of this most familiar way of introducing a soloist, surprising us by having the cello start a breath later than our sense of the rhythm leads us to expect. (Cellists have told me that the temptation to come in a bar early is dangerously strong.) The theme itself has also undergone a magical transformation of character in that the silences that were such a striking feature at the beginning are now filled in by the softly ticking eighth-note C's. The violin joins in eight measures later and the piano arrives after a few measures of passagework for the two strings. This illustrates one of the challenges Beethoven faced in writing a concerto for this combination: the necessity of a design that allows each solo instrument its own presentation of every idea but avoids becoming mechanical or simply too long. Beethoven is unfailingly ingenious about inventing overlaps and fresh orderings.

Soon a buoyant new theme is introduced, a march begun by the full orchestra and transformed by the solo cello into something lyric. This leads to an A-minor melody that is full of pathos; the piano offers it and the cello continues. The genial theme from the orchestral exposition returns in the cello's high register, *dolce*, musing, and in a place that is harmonically very remote (A major). Passing through another *pianissimo* "purple patch," Beethoven arrives at yet another theme he has held in reserve, this one a gruff minor-mode affair in the cello's low range, and followed immediately by two variations. The buildup to the exposition's closing chord, first dreamy, then moving through masses of scales and trills to a gloriously startling deceptive cadence, is expansive and wondrously fantastical.

Like the solo exposition, the development begins with the cello playing the first theme, *dolce*, again in remote A major, and prefaced by five measures of delicate poetry.[24] It is this first theme that most occupies Beethoven in the development; much of the time fragments of it are surrounded by forceful contrary-motion arpeggios for the solo instruments. Once—and who knows what private matter Beethoven had in mind—we hear a

[24]For all the energy of this Concerto, the prevalence of quiet dynamics and actual *pianissimo* is one of its notable features; only when this is realized in performance can the shape of the work and the variety of detail be perceived.

fleeting quotation of the Piano Concerto No. 3, and in its original key of C minor. The retransition to the recapitulation is elaborate and brilliant, and when the recapitulation itself arrives, we hear the opening theme *fortissimo* and in the full orchestra for the first time. Further events bring new reshufflings of themes and keys, another astonishing moment of poesy at the beginning of the brief coda, and two more breath-stopping deceptive cadences.

It really will not do to say, as Tovey's hypothetical listener says, that Beethoven is "writing below his full powers" in the Triple Concerto. It takes the full powers of a first-class mind and imagination to compose music so beautifully laid out and marked by so sure a sense of how to make sweet reverie and exuberant athleticism live happily side by side.

In his later years, Beethoven returned to his early practice of writing slow movements on a grand scale. Here, as in the final version of the *Waldstein* Sonata and the Fourth Piano Concerto, he presents a slow movement that is short, intense, non-developmental, and preludial to the finale. This one is an eloquent Largo, beautifully scored, with an accompaniment confined to muted strings and just a few carefully chosen notes for clarinets, bassoons, and horns, and in a key—A-flat major—untouched since the first movement's first "purple patch." Once again Beethoven chooses the cello to lead, *molto cantabile,* the violin taking charge when the noble melody is repeated. The pianist is an accompanist throughout, although an inventive and expressive one. Beethoven writes this music in 3/8, which means that the fastest subdivisions are actually 128th-notes; as in the Piano Concerto No. 3, he makes this choice rather than 3/4 in order to indicate that the tempo must not be *too* slow.

Without break but after a suspenseful transition, the Largo spills into the Rondo alla polacca, a polonaise-finale of enchanting elegance.[25] Beethoven's immediate order of business is to reconquer the harmonic territories of the first movement, something he accomplishes with felicity and wit in the opening sixteen-measure paragraph. This is one of Beethoven's sunniest finales: the returns to the main theme are managed with Haydnesque teasing, and the middle of the movements brings an exuberant Gypsy tune which, once you know the piece, you wait for much as you look forward to the *Tico-Tico* episode in the finale of the Piano Concerto No. 1.

Near the end, Beethoven speeds the music up by switching from the spacious 3/4 measures of the polonaise to a real Allegro in 2/4. The first movement has no cadenza, but Beethoven does give us one here, fully written out and including some orchestral punctuation. To conclude the Concerto, Beethoven reverts to the polonaise meter and tempo, and this return is the

---

[25]This is one of only three polonaises by Beethoven. The first occurs in the Serenade, Opus 8, for string trio (c. 1797); the last is a free-standing piano piece, Opus 89 (1814).

occasion for one of his most delicious inventions: the theme, with new variants in the melody, is divided among the three soloists, each of whom steps forward as though taking a solo bow. Even in the formality of the closing cadence, Beethoven finds room for a personal touch, his final pedaling instruction being designed so that in the last two measures the sound of the piano rings across the silence of the other two soloists and the orchestra.

## Concerto in D major for Violin and Orchestra, Opus 61

> *Allegro ma non troppo*
> *Larghetto*
> *Rondo*

Beethoven wrote this Concerto in the second half of 1806. It was first played on 23 December that year at a concert put on at the Theater an der Wien, Vienna, by Franz Clement, music director and concertmaster of the orchestra there, and it seems that Beethoven had completed the score only two days before, on 21 December. We owe its existence to a request from Clement, whose artistic personality is reflected throughout the work and to whom the autograph score is dedicated in a punning inscription: "Concerto par Clemenza pour Clement primo Violino e direttore al theatro a vienna Dal L v. Bthvn 1806." Clement was of course the soloist at the first performance, and the composer conducted. The legend persists that Clement performed a set of variations of his own with the violin held upside down between the first two movements of Beethoven's Concerto; he did indeed play such a piece, but it came, decently, at the end of the program, which also included works by Méhul, Mozart, Cherubini, and Handel.

In 1807, persuaded by an excellent contract from the Italian-born English publisher, composer, pianist, teacher, and instrument manufacturer Muzio Clementi, Beethoven transcribed the Violin Concerto for piano and orchestra. (Clementi acquired the English rights to the three *Razumovsky* Quartets, the Piano Concerto No. 4, the *Coriolan* Overture, and the Violin Concerto in its original form at the same time.) It is possible, perhaps even likely, that Beethoven merely authorized this transcription rather than undertaking it himself, but if that is so, he would probably have contributed some suggestions of his own anyway. No question, though—Beethoven (or whoever) did a perfunctory, ineffectual job with what may have been an impossible task to begin with; the one thing of value in this version is the cadenza—with timpani!—for the first movement, and this is undoubtedly Beethoven's own. Wolfgang Schneiderhan and Christian Tetzlaff have both transcribed this odd and remarkable invention for violin, Beethoven having left no cadenza for the Violin Concerto in its original form. In the earlier part of the twentieth century, Joseph Joachim's cadenza was the one most often played; the ingenious one by the nineteen-year-old Fritz Kreisler has by now surpassed it in popularity. There are of course many more: the Russian composer Alfred Schnittke composed a stimulating cadenza for Gidon Kremer that includes quotations from Bartók and Berg among others, and several violinists, including Leopold Auer, Adolf Busch, Váša Příhoda, Nathan Milstein, Joseph Silverstein, and Stephanie Chase have written interesting ones as well.

The inscription to Clement on the autograph notwithstanding, the first edition, which came out in August 1808 under the imprint of the Bureau des Arts et d'Industrie in Vienna and Pest, was dedicated to Beethoven's old friend from Bonn, Stephan von Breuning. The piano transcription, issued by the same publisher at the same time, was dedicated to Julie von Breuning, Stephan's wife and an excellent pianist with whom Beethoven enjoyed playing duets. The English scholar Alan Tyson surmises that the double dedication was a wedding present to the von Breunings, who had been married in April.[26]

**Solo violin, one flute, two oboes, two clarinets, two bassoons, two horns, two trumpets, timpani, and strings.**

Beethoven took his first stab at composing a violin concerto about 1790–1792, shortly before he moved to Vienna. All we have is 259 measures of the first movement, but scholars have inferred from the appearance of the autograph that the remainder of this movement is lost, not that it was never written. We have no idea about any further movements. Around the turn of the century, Beethoven wrote two Romances for violin and orchestra that were published in 1803 and 1805 as Opus 40 and 50, slight works not without some charm. The D-major Violin Concerto followed in 1806, and Beethoven's most sublime invention for solo violin with orchestra came into being fourteen years later, in the winter of 1820–1821: the Benedictus in the *Missa solemnis*, which the English scholar Martin Cooper aptly called "a celestial Romance."[27]

Beethoven and Franz Clement met in 1794, when the composer added

[26]This story has a sad ending: Julie von Breuning died in March 1809 at the age of seventeen.
[27]The *Kreutzer* Sonata of 1802–1803 can almost be counted as an honorary concerto; at any rate, Beethoven noted on his draft title page that it was "scritta in uno stilo molto concertante quasi come d'un Concerto [written in a very concertolike style, almost like that of an actual concerto]." These words appear in the first edition, issued by Simrock in Bonn and Paris in 1805.

his signature to the thirteen-year-old prodigy's 415-page book of souvenirs "dedicated to the eternal remembrance of his travels." By the time of his encounter with Beethoven, whom he must then have thought not nearly as famous as himself, Clement had already covered many a mile of Europe's highways in the company of his father. One of his trophies from those journeys was another autograph—"Joseph Haydn, your true friend"—garnered in 1791 when, aged ten, Clement played a concerto of his own at one of Haydn's concerts in London. Clement also took part in the concert at the Sheldonian Theatre when Oxford University awarded Haydn an honorary doctorate, and he sat concertmaster the last time Haydn heard one of his own works in public, a performance of *The Creation* led by Antonio Salieri in Vienna in March 1808. In later years, Clement returned to the life of a traveling virtuoso, conducted in Prague for a time, and died in Vienna in 1842, his career and his finances in disarray.

At the time he introduced Beethoven's Concerto, Clement was widely regarded as one of the outstanding violinists in Europe. An article that appeared in 1805 in the *Allgemeine musikalische Zeitung,* the most influential musical periodical of its day, described his style: his performances, the writer observed, were marked not by "the vigorous, bold, powerful playing, the affecting, compelling Adagio, the power of bow and tone that characterize the school of Rode and Viotti; rather, an indescribable delicacy, neatness, and elegance, an extremely delightful tenderness and purity, are the qualities that indisputably place Clement among the most perfect violinists."[28] Invariably, he was praised for perfect intonation and dazzlingly dexterous bowing.

As well as being a superb instrumentalist, Clement was a formidable musician with an extraordinary memory. In April 1805 he conducted the first performance of the *Eroica,* and in December of that year he was part of the ad hoc "committee" that assembled at the *palais* of Prince Carl von Lichnowsky to discuss the revision of Beethoven's opera *Fidelio,* whose premiere the month before had not gone well. While Princess Lichnowsky read through the opera at the piano, Clement, who had been concertmaster at the first performances, sat in a corner by himself with no music before him

---

[28]Giovanni Battista Viotti (1755–1824) spread his gifts as composer, performer, teacher, and administrator thinly over a wide patch of ground, and his career as a solo violinist was brief, but he was one of the most admired and influential players of his time. In his entry on Viotti in *The New Grove Dictionary of Music and Musicians,* Chappell White quotes an article from the *Allgemeine musikalische Zeitung* that "describes the principles of Viotti's 'school': 'A large, strong, full tone is the first; the combination of this with a powerful, penetrating, singing legato is the second; as the third, variety, charm, shadow, and light must be brought into play through the greatest diversity of bowing.' " Pierre Rode (1774–1830), a student of Viotti's, was one of the most renowned players of his day, adding, as Boris Schwarz wrote in *The New Grove,* "characteristically French verve, piquancy, and a kind of nervous bravura" to Viotti's style. Beethoven wrote his last violin sonata, Opus 96 in G major, for Rode but was disappointed in his performance of it. The Viotti concertos and Rode's Caprices are still very much alive in violin teachers' studios, and Viotti's Concerto No. 22 in A minor still clings to a place at the fringes of the repertory (see also my essay on the Brahms Double Concerto).

and played along from memory—principal vocal lines, orchestral solos, and all. With nothing but a libretto to remind him, he made a piano reduction of *The Creation*, again on the basis of having sat concertmaster, leaving the alarmed Haydn convinced that Clement must have had access to a stolen score. Louis Spohr testifies that Clement, after hearing two rehearsals and one performance of Spohr's oratorio *The Last Judgment*, could play several movements of it on the piano without leaving out a note and with all the harmonies intact.

His prodigious musical mechanism stood him in good stead at his December 1806 concert. In Alexander Wheelock Thayer's *Life of Beethoven* we read that one contemporary, not named, "notes that Clement played the solo *a vista*, without previous rehearsal." Even if this is a slight exaggeration—and we do not actually know—these are harrowing conditions for the first performance of an extraordinarily difficult and novel concerto; no wonder something was wanting in the matter of clear projection and articulation of what was, aside from its enormous technical challenges, music with a new sense of motion and form.

Under those circumstances it is always the composer who gets blamed: more than a hundred years later, Arnold Schoenberg would remark wryly about his own music that it was not modern, just badly performed. This event was typical. Long afterward, in 1842, Beethoven's pupil Carl Czerny recalled that Clement had played the new work "with very great effect" and that there had been much applause for soloist and composer, including some "noisy bravos" for the former. Czerny was nothing if not honest, but at least one contemporary report paints a different picture: the highly regarded Johann Nepomuk Möser in the Viennese *Zeitung für Theater, Musik und Poesie* tells us that "*cognoscenti* are unanimous in agreeing that, while there are beautiful things in the concerto, the sequence of events often seems incoherent and the endless repetition of some commonplace passages could easily prove fatiguing." "Beethhofen" was once again scolded for no longer writing in the manner of his earlier works, many of which had been reviewed unfavorably when they were new: "If [he] pursues his present path, it will go ill with him and the public alike."

In any event, although there were occasional performances over the next three or four decades, some by players as distinguished as Pierre Baillot, Jacob Dont, and Henri Vieuxtemps, the Beethoven Concerto did not really catch on. The first violinist to make a success of it was the twelve-year-old Joseph Joachim, who played it in London in 1844 with Mendelssohn conducting, the Philharmonic Society setting aside for the occasion its rule barring the appearance of child prodigies. Mendelssohn reported that the first movement was interrupted by applause several times. Joachim came pretty much to own the work, and it was mainly through his persuasive advocacy that it took its place as an indispensable item in the repertory. As Robert Schumann wrote, "[Joachim] is the magician and necromancer whose skillful hand led us through the heights and depths of that marvelous structure which the majority explore in vain."

The music begins with five soft beats on the kettledrum: how this must have amazed that first audience! Some of the people at the Theater an der Wien that night would have known the Haydn symphony that begins with a timpani roll, but they had never heard anything like this. On the fifth of those gently resonant taps, woodwinds begin a tranquil and *dolce* melody. We could, for a moment, take those beats to be a mere introduction to the melody, or, if we wanted to be a little bit fanciful about it, an invitation, but the violins' immediate imitation of the timpani notes on a strange pitch—D-sharp— quickly disposes of that idea. Time has blunted the strangeness of those D- sharps, but in San Francisco I heard a concert, the program ingeniously put together by the conductor David Robertson, in which they came back into startling life. The Beethoven Concerto was preceded by Bernd Alois Zim- mermann's *Stille und Umkehr* (Stillness and Return). D above middle-C sounds the whole length of that eight-minute bit of *pianissimo* magic, and even with the interruption of applause, a stage change, and more applause for the entrance of the soloist, that note worked like an immense prolonga- tion *backwards* of the Concerto's opening. And after that those D-sharps really did amaze.

The pattern of four knocks, sometimes with, sometimes without a re- solving fifth note, is more than a colorful incident: this entire, immensely expansive movement will be saturated with it. Rhythmic saturation like this is something we find often in Beethoven's music around this time: the first movement of the Fifth Symphony is the most famous instance, but the first movements of the *Appassionata*, the Piano Concerto No. 4, and the *Pastoral* Symphony, and the scherzo of the F-major Quartet, Opus 59, no. 1, are no less striking.

Ex. 1

Ex. 2

The dense knots of repeated sixteenth-notes that accompany the next idea, a scale melody for clarinet and bassoon, are a variant of the drumbeat motif, and so is the rhythmic pattern of the first *fortissimo* outburst.

Ex. 3

Ex. 4

When, presently, the woodwinds sing the Concerto's most famous and loved theme, the violins, with discreet support from horns, trumpets, and timpani, make sure we do not forget the pervasive tapping.

Ex. 5

Indeed, as that lyric paragraph expands so astonishingly, the drum rhythm becomes an integral part of the melody itself.

Ex. 6

As D. F. Tovey pointed out, these D-sharps "explain" or rationalize the violins' startling D-sharps right after the opening woodwind melody.

One more grandly sweeping melody is heard before the solo entrance. Then, when the long tutti has subsided from *fortissimo* to *piano*, the violin, with quiet authority, rises from the receding orchestra, and by way of a light-footed mini-cadenza leads us to the return of the first theme, including the five drum taps. This time the violin joins the woodwinds, but in a higher octave and adding embellishments to the melody—a little preparatory flourish and a series of dactyls in the third.

Ex. 7

These few measures tell us a lot about the violin-writing and the role of the solo instrument in this Concerto. Beethoven exploits the high register in a way that makes his violin language quite different from Mozart's, but, as Boris Schwarz pointed out in 1958 in a *Musical Quarterly* article on "Beethoven and the French Violin School," this is characteristic of the style of Viotti, Rode, Pierre Baillot, and Rodolphe Kreutzer (whose name lives on in the title of the Beethoven sonata and the Tolstoy novella, and whose studies are still essential teaching material). These measures also predict how much and how strikingly the function of the violin in Beethoven's Concerto is to be decorative, fanciful, capricious, more often a commentator on than an initiator of ideas. This has everything to do with the kind of player Franz Clement was. Beethoven, who obviously knew Clement's playing well, wrote to his strength, and this is music, therefore, for a violinist with a light hand, one of "an indescribable delicacy, neatness, and elegance, an extremely delightful tenderness and purity."

Solo and orchestra together now move through the succession of themes we have already heard, omitting only the assertive Example 4. All are wondrously transformed by the violin's charming and virtuosic embellishments. Then Example 4 comes into its own, *fortissimo* and, startlingly, in F major, initiating a long passage for orchestra that in effect brings back most of the opening tutti, which, at the last, Beethoven skews strangely and powerfully into C major.

It is there that the exposition comes to its formal close and it is also in that key, so distant from the worlds of D and A major where we expect these events to take place, that the solo violin returns, appropriately enough, with a variant of the improvisatory flight in which we first heard it. This now leads to a new version of the opening theme, in B minor and very high. It is also the first time the soloist is directed to play *espressivo*. (There have already been many requests for the very different, inward *dolce*.) The entry into this theme—the violin by itself on a long high F-natural, then joined by cellos and basses on G four and five octaves lower—is itself one of the most magical moments in Beethoven.

The two bassoons seize on the fourth measure of the theme (Example 1) and carry it across the harmonic landscape, the solo violin embroidering it with Clementian elegance and lightness, the orchestral strings adding constant reminders of the five-beat rhythmic figure. That pattern moves from the strings to the horns, setting an ominous and inescapable background against which the violin sings an impassioned plea. This begins in dark, dark G minor and in *pianissimo*. One of the most maddening of mindlessly accepted performance traditions has taken hold here, one of hugely slowing the tempo, which coarsens and sentimentalizes the violin melody and disrupts the relentless stabbing of the five-note figure. It is, after all, this obsessive knocking that integrates and imparts sense to a passage whose surface is so different from everything else in this movement.[29]

---

[29]Heifetz used to maintain some degree of coherence in this passage, though playing the melody in what Virgil Thomson described as his "silk underwear" style rather undid the good effect. Nathan

The music gathers energy as the five-note motif moves first to the bassoons, then to the trumpets and drums. The violin figurations become faster, their phrases shorter and more breathless. The orchestra stops on A, still *pianissimo*, and in suppressed excitement, with triplets rising against curt reminders of the drumming figure in pizzicato strings, the violin carries us into the recapitulation.

This time the opening repeated "drumming" D's and indeed the whole of the first phrase are given out *fortissimo* by the full orchestra. The solo violin joins in at the arrival of what was originally the scale melody for clarinet and bassoon, after which matters unfold much as they had in the exposition. Beethoven leaves space for a cadenza, which, given the dimensions of this movement, can afford to be quite grand. Just as he always sought fresh ways of introducing the solo instrument in his concertos, so did Beethoven rethink the question of the orchestral re-entry after the cadenza. He does it with drama and mystery in his Third Piano Concerto and exquisite poetry in the Fourth. Here Beethoven, again choosing poetry, gives us something we have (perhaps unconsciously) waited for but that he has withheld until now: the lyric theme played all the way through by the solo violin, and in its simplest form. Also, in this piece so given to high-altitude flight, we now hear it for the first time low, settled, and gentle on the D and G strings. The briefest and calmest of exchanges among bassoon, cellos, and solo violin lead to a quick crescendo which brings this movement to a firm close.

The slow movement—but only larghetto, not adagio—is the concerto's still point. The orchestral strings are muted and the motion of the harmonies is minimal, not only in detail but also in the larger strategy, there being no departure at all from G major. These pages, too, are a touching tribute to Clement's grace in the art of playing embellishments.

The movement is a set of variations on a ten-measure theme or, more accurately, an eight-measure theme rounded off with a two-measure benediction. The theme itself has something of the simplicity of a chorale. It is first played by muted strings, and when it is repeated by the clarinet in the first variation and the bassoon in the second, the violin adds its delicate ornaments. (It is essential for the player to understand that this is the violin's function here, and that all those "little notes" are secondary rather than primary matter.) Variation 3 again belongs to the orchestra alone.

Then comes something to stop the heart. It is not a fourth variation

---

Milstein and Adolf Busch keep an intelligible flow going, both with strong support from their conductors (Erich Leinsdorf and Fritz Busch), who get the horns to play with clear articulation. Interestingly, Wolfgang Schneiderhan plays the passage intelligibly in a 1954 concert performance with Sergiu Celibidache but is extremely slow in his 1953 studio recording with Wilhelm Furtwängler: I don't know whether Celibidache speeded him up or Furtwängler slowed him down. Among violinists currently active, Joseph Silverstein shows that he has a clear sense of what is happening in the music, and the performances I have heard by Christian Tetzlaff have been exemplary.

but, rather, a sixteen-measure episode—five measures of improvisatory lead-in, eight measures of lyric melody, and three measures of exit/transition. Between the winged introduction and exit, the lyric melody itself is a moment of sublime cessation. It lies low, on the G and D strings, but its cadential trill is repeated in a higher octave and so leads the violin line back to its accustomed heights.

Now Variation 4 can begin. It follows the pattern of the first two variations: the orchestra carries the melody while the soloist ornaments it. But it is also different from Variations 1 and 2. For one thing, the orchestral strings play the theme pizzicato, minimally, as it were (*sempre perdendosi*, Beethoven writes, "becoming ever fainter"). For another, the solo violin plays a sustained melody very different in character from the fine-spun, short-breathed arabesques it contributed earlier, both for contrast against the plucked notes in the orchestra and because it is still under the spell of the blissful dream episode. Then Variation 4 leads to a second episode, more elaborate than the first, but embracing the lyric melody, touchingly ornamented this time and beautifully accompanied in utmost simplicity by clarinets and bassoons.

Now the music loses itself in new improvisations and sinks to *pianississimo*. The orchestral strings declare that we have had enough of musing, the soloist responds with a brief cadenza (Beethoven wrote out only the trill that sets it in motion and the last six notes), and we move into the amiable, diverting finale. This is now a time for relaxation—for the listener, not for the soloist—and for simple games, one of the most delightful being Beethoven's way of introducing the only two pizzicato notes for the solo violin. In the midst of the merriment, Beethoven sets an episode in G minor, both the key and the prominence of the bassoon being designed to remind us of the first movement's development. In this Rondo, too, there is room for a cadenza, and once again Beethoven devises a striking re-entrance for the orchestra. He also diverts himself and us by inventing a coda far longer and more eventful than the tone of most of the finale would lead us to expect. The close is brilliant, nicely calculated to earn Clement those bravos Czerny tells us he was greeted with that December evening in 1806.

I have already commented on the tradition of slowing down the eloquent G-minor episode near the end of the development section in the first movement, and I pointed out that Beethoven's tempo marking for the second movement is larghetto, not adagio. I also believe that in most performances the base tempo is too slow in the first movement as well as in the second. Violinists and conductors misread Beethoven's direction of *Allegro ma non troppo*; that is, the emphasis is all on the qualifying *ma non troppo* and the basic *Allegro* is forgotten.

This happens because the concerto has become weighted down by the dread burdens of "greatness" and "depth," qualities many musicians feel can be realized only when the performance is suitably solemn, i.e., slow. This in turn has to do with the fact that this is Beethoven's only violin concerto, as well as with our feeling about the violin itself, one beautifully expressed by the thirteenth-century Persian mystical poet Djelal-Eddin-Rumi, who wrote that "the voice of the violin is the sound of the opening gate of paradise."[30] I want, however, to express a view not uniquely mine but nonetheless likely to strike some readers as heretical, namely, that Beethoven's beautiful Violin Concerto is an elegant, gracious, playful, and virtuosic work more than a "deep" one—except in the Larghetto's two dream episodes. (To paraphrase Justice John Paul Stevens's statement on pornography, I cannot define depth but I know it when I encounter it.)

I have also commented on the way the music of the Concerto reflects the style of its first interpreter, a style whose essential quality was lightness of touch. In choosing tempos for this work, we need to take that into account. Even more, we need to consider the music itself, its rhythm and the rate at which the harmonies change, and our sense of tempo for other Beethoven movements that are comparable in rhythmic and harmonic character. It is inconceivable that if the Violin Concerto had been lost since 1806 and was found today, anyone would choose the tempos you hear in most performances.

There reside in my memory some beautiful *and slow* performances that I am forever grateful to have heard: two I recall with special joy are Erica Morini's with Bruno Walter and the New York Philharmonic-Symphony in 1949 and Yehudi Menuhin's with Erich Leinsdorf and the Boston Symphony in 1967. Nonetheless, I also recall that in 1954 in Rome, when I heard the Schneiderhan-Celibidache performance I mentioned earlier (and which used to be available on a Melodram LP), I felt that for the first time I *understood* the Concerto as much as I loved it.

[30]E. M. Cioran quotes this in his *Tears and Saints,* trans. Ilinca Zarifopol-Johnston (Chicago: University of Chicago Press, 1995).

# Alban Berg

Albano Maria Johannes Berg was born on 9 February 1885 in Vienna and died there on 24 December 1935.

## Violin Concerto

*Andante and Allegretto*
*Allegro and Adagio*

Berg began work on his Violin Concerto at the end of April 1935; he had it ready in short score by mid-July (that is, with the instrumentation indicated but not fully written out) and in full score on 11 August. After private run-throughs with the pianist Rita Kurzmann in New York (for an audience that included Mischa Elman and Leopold Godowsky) and in Vienna, Louis Krasner, who had commissioned the work, gave the first performance on 19 April 1936 in Barcelona at the opening concert of that year's International Society for Contemporary Music Festival. Hermann Scherchen conducted the Orquesta Pau Casals; the Concerto shared the program with music by Roberto Gerhard, Ernst Křenek, and another work by Berg, Three Fragments from *Wozzeck*. The score bears a double dedication, "For Louis Krasner" and "To the Memory of an Angel."

Solo violin, two flutes (both doubling piccolo), two oboes (second doubling English horn), three clarinets (third doubling alto saxophone) and bass clarinet, two bassoons and contrabassoon, four horns, two trumpets, one tenor and one bass trombone, tuba, timpani, bass drum, cymbals, snare drum, low tam-tam, high gong, triangle, and strings.

Alban Berg's father, Conrad Berg, whom he resembled to an uncanny degree, was a book dealer and later a merchant in the import-export business who had moved to Vienna from Nuremberg in 1867, and the whole family crackled with literary, theatrical, musical, artistic, and commercial talent. Alban was one of two children who became professional musicians; his younger sister, Smaragda, was a much-sought-after opera coach, one of whose pupils was Frida Leider, the great Isolde and Brünnhilde of the pre-Flagstad years (and whom Alban did not admire). Musicality was part of Alban and Smaragda's heritage from their mother, Johanna Braun, but their tendency to depression and general psychological fragility came from their father's side. An older brother, Hermann, who emigrated to the United States and joined the New York firm of importers Geo. Borgfeldt & Co., was responsible for a creation that, if not more significant than *Wozzeck*, *Lulu*, the *Lyric Suite*, and the Violin Concerto, was certainly of wider circulation: the teddy bear.

On 8 October 1904, Smaragda spotted a newspaper advertisement announcing that Arnold Schoenberg would be teaching some night classes in harmony and counterpoint. The oldest of the four Berg siblings, Karl, called Charly, secretly took six of Alban's songs to the already celebrated—indeed, notorious—thirty-year-old composer for evaluation. Thus began Berg's trying, exceedingly dependent, but also nourishing connection with Schoenberg. Formal lessons came to an end when Schoenberg moved to Berlin in 1911, but the flavor of their relationship hardly changed over the years.

For a time after his father's death in 1900, Berg had had to support himself with a civil service job in the Imperial Department of Agriculture, but in 1906 an inheritance from an aunt made him modestly independent. In 1908 he finished his Piano Sonata, which was his official Opus 1 and the work he counted as marking his real start as a composer. There followed a string quartet in 1910, Five Songs with Orchestra on texts by Peter Altenberg in 1912, Three Pieces for Orchestra in 1913, and, in 1922, the completion of *Wozzeck*, which he had begun in 1914. That great opera entered the repertory of some thirty European theaters in a few years, and its success was a turning point in Berg's life.

In 1911 Berg had married Helene Nahowski, whom Altenberg, who was also in love with her, described as looking like "a tall, thin, ash-blond Russian student, only very tired from unfought battles." The conspicuously beautiful young couple moved into the apartment at Trauttmannsdorffgasse 27 where

Alban would live the rest of his life and which was still Helene Berg's home when she died in 1976. Berg served briefly in the army, wrote some criticism and analysis, and after the war assisted Schoenberg in setting up the Society for Private Musical Performances in Vienna. He traveled to places where his music was done, carried on a copious correspondence, and read voraciously (Balzac, Strindberg, Ibsen, Kafka, Karl Kraus, Adalbert Stifter, Gottfried Keller, Shakespeare, Goethe, Musil, and Thomas Mann were special favorites, but there was also room for Jack London and the Styrian poet Peter Rosegger). He played with his albino dachshunds, laughed at Buster Keaton and Laurel and Hardy movies, cheered himself hoarse at soccer games, was delighted to receive a visit from George Gershwin, and wished in vain that the Austrian government's tobacco monopoly, which had named its most luxurious grade of cigarette Heliane after an opera by Korngold, would call its cheapest brand Wozzeck in honor of his oppressed underclass antihero. Distinctions and awards began to come his way, but when the City of Vienna offered him the honorary title of Professor—and that is a big deal in Austria and Germany to this day—he turned it down: "Too late," he said. "Alban Berg is quite enough."

Berg also taught composition, his most famous pupil being that formidable polymath Theodor Wiesengrund Adorno, who eventually wrote a brilliant and characteristically idiosyncratic study of his master. On the other hand, the parents of a prodigiously gifted young Englishman refused, on the advice of authorities at his school, to allow him to study with Berg for fear the composer of Wozzeck would prove a corrupting influence: Benjamin Britten never got over his chagrin.

Berg spent as much time as he could at his country house, where he could concentrate so well on his work and which, with characteristic black humor, he called his concentration camp. (During his final illness he commended the choice of the Rudolf Hospital for its convenience in being already halfway to the Central Cemetery.)[1] After Wozzeck, Berg composed the Chamber Concerto for Violin, Piano, and Thirteen Winds, the concert aria Der Wein on a text by Baudelaire, and most of Lulu, a project whose first seed was planted in 1905, when he heard Karl Kraus, Frank Wedekind, and others in a reading of Wedekind's Pandora's Box, one of the two plays of his on which Lulu is based. And finally there was the Violin Concerto, for whose sake Berg had interrupted work on Lulu.

On 12 August 1909, Berg had written to his fiancée: "This morning a wasp stung me in my right hand, middle finger. It began to swell and has now become so thick that I can hardly move the fingers—quite painful. Well,

[1]Berg rests not with Beethoven, Schubert, Brahms, Wolf, the waltzing Strausses, and Schoenberg in the huge, celebrity-filled Central Cemetery, but in a small one in the southwestern suburb of Hietzing.

that's life in the country." In the next day's letter he writes, evidently from experience: "My hand is not better yet. I really ought to keep it very quiet so that the inflammation won't spread to the arm."[2]

Twenty-six years later, almost to the day—it was 11 August 1935—Berg drew the final double bar on the last page of his violin concerto. A few days after that, the wasps got to him again, and this time Berg, all his life a bundle of ailments, allergies, and hypochondriac fantasies, did not recover. Carbuncles developed, then boils, then an abscess on his back. It seems that, with Alban applauding her courage, Helene Berg took it upon herself to lance the abscess with a pair of scissors. Whether that operation or something else was the cause, general septicemia developed, for which, with the advent of sulfa drugs still a few years in the future, there was no help.[3]

On 23 December, after a week in the hospital, Berg said: "Today is the 23rd. It will be a decisive day." Since his first, terrifying attack of bronchial asthma on 23 July 1908—at age twenty-three—he had decided that 23 was a critical number for him. Helene Berg sought to convince her husband that the decisive day was past by moving the clocks ahead. In vain: Berg survived the critical 23d, but only by an hour and a quarter. He was two days older than his adored Gustav Mahler had been at the time of his death. Twelve days before, wracked by fever, Berg had nonetheless gone to a performance of the symphony he had extracted from *Lulu*. Except for two virtually unintelligible broadcasts of that Symphony, it was the only time he ever heard any of *Lulu*. It was also the last music he heard.

Of his Violin Concerto Berg never heard a note. After his death, the program committee of the International Society for Contemporary Music asked Louis Krasner to play the work at the festival scheduled in Barcelona for April 1936. Schoenberg's other famous pupil, Anton Webern, was to conduct, but, emotionally upset, unable to get along with the Catalan orchestra linguistically or in any other way, allowing himself to become hopelessly mired in detail, he withdrew at the last moment, and Hermann Scherchen, with minimal chance to study the score and with next to no rehearsal time left, came to the heroic rescue. During the next couple of years, Krasner played the Concerto all over Europe (except, of course, Germany) and North America with such conductors as Busch, Horenstein, Klemperer, Koussevitzky, Mitropoulos, Munch, Rodzinski, Stock, Stokowski, Wood, and even Webern (in London with the BBC Symphony). In Berg's own Vienna, most of the members of the Philharmonic expressed their hos-

---

[2]*Alban Berg: Letters to His Wife*, ed. and transl., Beruard Grun (New York: St. Martin's Press, 1971).
[3]The only source for the story of Helene's kitchen surgery is *Alban Berg und seine Idole* (Lüneburg: zu Klampen, 1995) by Soma Morgenstern, a writer who had been on terms of close friendship with the Bergs until Alban's death. Morgenstern also maintained that Helene Berg blamed the Jewish doctors at the Rudolf Hospital for her husband's death. Even though there is no corroboration, most scholars well versed in the facts of Berg's life find these stories believable.

tility to the music as well as their anti-Semitism (directed at Krasner and Klemperer) by ignoring the applause and leaving the stage the moment the performance was over.[4]

The earlier paragraph about the dachshunds, the soccer games, Gershwin, and so on, presents an idealized picture of Berg—the official one, so to speak. Everything in it is true, but it ignores the turbulence—political, financial, and amorous—that churned below the surface. (As though being a modernist and a member of the Schoenberg circle weren't enough.)

In the 1930s Berg became deeply depressed about the Nazi regime in Germany, which had driven Schoenberg and many others into exile. He was no less discouraged by the lurch to the right in Austrian politics, the anti-democratic current, and the rise of insurgent Nazi groups in his country, and he was personally hurt by ever louder imputations that, as a composer of twelve-tone music, he was un-Austrian, not *bodenständig* (truly attached to his native soil). The triumph of savagery in Germany also had a direct impact on Berg's livelihood: *Wozzeck* was labeled "degenerate art" and "cultural Bolshevism," and its performance in German theaters was forbidden. Losing what had become a substantial source of royalties caused him severe financial hardship, and he had to think seriously about selling his country house and the little Ford convertible he had proudly bought in 1930 with his *Wozzeck* earnings. Furthermore, with German opera houses closed to him and Austrian ones equally inhospitable, *Lulu*, whose composition had consumed him since 1929, had no prospect for performance, not a nibble from anywhere.

Berg's emotional life was also in perpetual turmoil, despite the image of his marriage as one of untroubled bliss, an image he and Helene connived at keeping polished. According to Adorno, who was close to him, Berg left a trail of love affairs, all of which ended badly. One of these matters to us, and to this I shall return.

Two summonses called Berg's Concerto into being. First, in February 1935 the Russian-born American violinist Louis Krasner approached Berg with the offer of a $1,500 commission for a concerto.[5] Krasner liked Berg's early Piano Sonata and had been overwhelmed by *Wozzeck* when he heard Stokowski conduct it in New York in 1931. Then, in Vienna early in 1935, he heard the Galimir Quartet play the *Lyric Suite*. Not only was he impressed by the music, he also fell in love with, proposed to, and married Adrienne Galimir, the second violinist of this all-sibling quartet.

Berg, anxious to finish *Lulu*, was reluctant to take on the concerto; just

---

[4]By the end of the 1950s, the Berg Concerto had become standard repertory. Not surprisingly, Joseph Szigeti, always a pioneer, was the first internationally celebrated soloist to take it up.

[5]This amount would be equivalent to about $30,000 in 1998. Today, a commission for a major work from a composer as famous as Berg was in 1935 might run to $50,000.

recently, and in spite of his financial straits, he had refused a string quartet commission from the Library of Congress, which Schoenberg had arranged for him. Berg told Krasner that the world of Wieniawski and Vieuxtemps was not his world, a silly attempt at evasion to which Krasner sensibly replied that Mozart and Beethoven had written violin concertos too. Still more persuasive was Krasner's argument that Berg was the man to demonstrate the lyric and expressive potential of twelve-tone music and to release it from the stigma of "all brain, no heart." Berg stuck to his guarded position a while longer, but then he accepted the commission, and friends observed that he had lately acquired the habit of attending violin recitals.

The second summons was a tragic one: the death on 22 April 1935 of Manon Gropius, the eighteen-year-old daughter of Alma Mahler by her second husband, the architect Walter Gropius. Manon, gifted, gentle, vivacious, beautiful, and apparently loved by everyone who met her (Ernst Křenek, briefly Manon's half-sister's husband, seems to have been the one exception), was studying to be an actress when she was struck down by polio. Paralysis and death followed a year later. While Berg was fond of Manon, he was deeply attached to Alma, not only because of a close friendship of long standing but, without doubt, also because she was the relict of the great Mahler.

And since 1977 we have known of yet another crucial connection between Alma and the Violin Concerto. That year, the American composer, theorist, and Berg scholar George Perle tracked down and found the miniature score of the *Lyric Suite* that had belonged to Hanna Fuchs-Robettin. The wife of a Prague paper manufacturer, Hanna was also the sister of the novelist Franz Werfel, who was Alma Mahler's lover (and eventually husband). Berg had elaborately annotated this copy for Hanna so as to decode most of the musical ciphers in which he had declared his love and in effect secretly dedicated that fiercely passionate work to her.

Their affair, which had begun in 1925 and which ended only with his death, engaged Berg passionately (none of Frau Fuchs-Robettin's letters to Berg survive, so we have less direct knowledge of her feelings), but there is no reason to believe that the lovers ever considered ending their marriages. Hanna's daughter Dorothea, to whom the score of the *Lyric Suite* had passed when her mother died in 1964, told Perle that Hanna's decision about that was based on the realization that if she divorced her husband, her children would stay with him. Berg, for his part, had no thought of leaving the woman who understood him profoundly and on whom he had grown very dependent. One imagines Alban and Hanna caught in the voluptuousness of impossibility and—at least Alban—fantasizing about a Tristan and Isolde union *post mortem.*

Through her connection with Werfel, then, Alma Mahler was even further involved in Berg's emotional life, and it is not surprising that Berg's urge to make a musical response to her daughter's death was intense.[6] Suddenly he saw that he could combine his inner need to compose a Requiem with the commission for Krasner. At the top of the title page of the Violin Concerto Berg wrote *Für Louis Krasner* and at the bottom, *Dem Andenken eines Engels* (To the Memory of an Angel).[7] "Angel" carried special significance in that Max Reinhardt had planned to have Manon make her debut playing an angel in his Salzburg production of *Everyman*.

If the Requiem for Manon is the public program of the Violin Concerto, the work embodies other, private layers of meaning, ones that, like the connection of the *Lyric Suite* to Hanna, Berg took pains to conceal but which, once discovered, show that the Violin Concerto is as much about himself—or himself and Hanna—as it is about Manon Gropius. Berg was in mental agony in the summer of 1935: along with the stress of the political situation in Germany and Austria and its disastrous effect on his career went the tension caused by the relationship with Hanna.

Adorno writes that Berg made every effort to keep the affair secret, not so much for the obvious reasons but because he loved secrets for their own sake. In fact Helene Berg knew all about it, and Adorno, who was an occasional messenger for the lovers, reports that everything was managed so clumsily, by himself included, that Hanna's husband was aware of it as well. Berg himself was painfully riven by the contradiction between the public fiction of an idyllic home life and the truth: when he gave Adorno a score of the Three Fragments from *Wozzeck*, he changed the title page to read "Fragments of Alban Berg."[8]

But it is important to realize that Berg needed this tension. As Helene Berg, who understood accurately the nature of Hanna's place in Alban's life but just did not want anyone else to know about it, perceptively put it in a letter to Alma Mahler: "He himself created obstacles and thereby created the romanticism he required."

In a prosaic sense there was something unreal about Berg's liaison with Hanna Fuchs-Robettin; according to her daughter, it was never consummated. Like the equally idealized affair carried on at more or less the same time between Leoš Janáček and Kamila Stösslová, however, it lit a real fire that was miraculously stimulating to the creative juices. All of us who cherish *The*

---

[6]Alma was the person in whom Helene Berg confided about Alban and Hanna; Alma happened also to be the person who had brought the lovers together in the first place. For reasons that are not entirely clear, the friendship between Alma and Helene ended after Berg's death. The story of Helene Berg, whose suppression of Act 3 of *Lulu* became a cause célèbre in the operatic world, is fascinating, but it goes beyond the scope of this essay.

[7]In 1941 Werfel dedicated his novel *The Song of Bernadette*, aptly described by Thomas Mann as "a well-made bad book," to Manon's memory.

[8]While Berg was alive, Adorno was discreet to the point of not only concealing what he knew but actually laying down false trails. Before his death in 1969, he had made sure that his account of the affair would not be published until all the parties directly involved were dead.

*Cunning Little Vixen*, the Glagolitic Mass, the *Diary of One Who Vanished*, the *Kreutzer Sonata* and *Intimate Letters* quartets, the *Lyric Suite*, *Lulu*, and the Berg Violin Concerto must be forever grateful to Kamila Stösslová and Hanna Fuchs-Robettin.

The Violin Concerto swept through all this like a firestorm. Berg had always been one of the slowest of composers, and his catalogue, though rich, is small; the Violin Concerto, however—written with a gold fountain pen that was ostensibly a gift from Franz Werfel but was really from his sister Hanna—poured from him with a speed and a sense of compulsion totally and stunningly new to him.

That the Violin Concerto became a Requiem for Berg himself as well as for Manon Gropius is an observation often expressed since his death. Less familiar is the idea that Berg perhaps thought of it that way himself. Mozart and Mahler come to mind—Mozart in his final illness and depression growing convinced that the Requiem he was struggling to finish for the "mysterious stranger" was really for himself, and Mahler filling his Ninth Symphony, the last work he completed, with gestures and messages of farewell. But these are two very different stories. Mahler, for all his *gestures* of farewell and fantasies of death, was far from writing an *actual* valedictory, and in fact plunged into his next symphony with immense energy and as soon as he could; Mozart did indeed suffer from that tormenting delusion.

For Berg we have nothing as direct as Franz Xaver Niemetschek's account of Mozart's state of mind in the fall of 1791, but, recounting later what Helene Berg had told him, Louis Krasner wrote: "Refusing to stop for food or sleep, he drove his hand relentlessly and in fever. 'I must continue,' Berg responded to his wife's pleadings, 'I cannot stop—I do not have time.' "

In June 1935, Krasner visited Berg at his country house on the Wörthersee, and while Berg walked from room to room, talking with his wife, going about his ordinary business, Krasner improvised for hours at a stretch so that Berg might get to know the strengths and characteristics of his technique and style. (Berg was fond of pointing out that the house was just across the lake from Pörtschach, where Brahms had written his Violin Concerto.) Any time Krasner strayed into "real" music, Berg would call out from wherever in the house he happened to be, "Nein, bitte, keine Konzerte, nur spielen!" ("No, please, no concertos, just play!") On 16 July, Berg was able to write to Krasner that he had finished the composition of "our" concerto the day before: "I am perhaps even more astonished than you. I was, to be sure, industrious as never before in my life and must add that the work gave me more and more joy. I hope—no, I believe confidently—that I have succeeded."

Aside from the sinister urgency with which it was composed, there are clues in the Violin Concerto itself to its status as a Requiem for Berg himself. I have mentioned Berg's obsession with the number 23. Having arrived in-

dependently at the idea that this number was significant for him, he had been
excited to find confirmation in two books by the Berlin otolaryngologist
Wilhelm Fliess he read in 1914, *Der Ablauf des Lebens* (The Course of Life)
and *Vom Leben und Tod* (Of Life and Death). The English Berg scholar
Douglas Jarman discusses this at length in a fascinating essay, "Alban Berg,
Wilhelm Fliess, and the Secret Programme of the Violin Concerto," in *The
Berg Companion*, and I quote his summary of Fliess's idea:

> It was Fliess's contention that . . . "all life is controlled by a periodic rhythm
> through a mechanism that exists in the living substance itself—a mechanism
> that is exactly the same for human beings, for animals, and for plants; a mech-
> anism that informs the hour of our birth with the same certainty as that of our
> death." . . . Through his analysis of the dates of the menstrual and other peri-
> odic cycles, he had been able to discover that the whole of life was governed
> by two constants, the numbers 28, associated with women, and 23 with men.
> "These numbers," Fliess wrote, "were not invented by me but were discovered
> by me in nature."[9]

Cockamamie though this sounds, Berg was not alone in finding it persuasive: Einstein and Freud were among Fliess's adherents for many years.[10]
One who would not buy it was Schoenberg, even though he was deeply involved in numerology and number superstitions of his own. (His fateful
number was 13: he was born on 13 September 1874 and, convinced he
would die on a Friday the 13th, he did, on Friday, 13 July 1951.) In any
event, the metronome marks and the structural divisions of Berg's violin
concerto are completely wrapped up in the female 28 and multiples thereof
in the first movement and the male 23 and its multiples in the second.
Berg and Hanna Fuchs-Robettin had also established that 10 was her special number (we do not know why), and so that number plays a role in the
*Lyric Suite* and the Violin Concerto as well. In both those works, Berg also
uses his and Hanna Fuchs's initials. B in German is B-flat in English and H
in German is our B-natural; their musical initials therefore read A/B-flat
and B/F, and these appear individually, side by side, embraced, and intertwined.

As we shall see, Berg also brings in his first love, Marie Scheuchl, kitch-
en help in his parents' house, who gave birth to his daughter in 1902 when
he was seventeen. When Albine, as the girl was amazingly named in yet
another Bergian game of concealing and revealing, died in 1954, her par-
entage was still a secret from everyone except her mother and Alban and

---

[9]*The Berg Companion* (Boston: Northeastern University Press, 1990).
[10]So was my father, a physician, with the result that I knew about 23s and 28s long before I had ever
heard of Alban Berg or Wilhelm Fliess.

Helene Berg; Alban, however, had kept in touch with her, and she attended his funeral.[11] We also know that in 1930 he sent her a ticket for the first Vienna performance of *Wozzeck*. What must her reaction have been to this tragic story of a mother—named Marie—of an illegitimate child! With Marie Scheuchl at one end and Hanna Fuchs-Robettin at the other, as it were, the Violin Concerto spans the entire history of Berg's emotional life and is thus a commemorative *tombeau* to himself.

Berg casts his Concerto in two movements, each divided into two parts. The first movement's two tempi are somewhat slow and somewhat fast (Andante and Allegro); those of the second movement are distinctly energetic and very slow (Allegro and Adagio), so that the contrast is greatly intensified. On the public level, the two movements represent a portrait of Manon Gropius and a drama of "death and transfiguration." The music starts in utmost quiet, as harp and clarinets with the solo violin begin some exploratory preluding, gently drifting at first—the violin's entrance is just a soft touching of the four open strings from G up to E and down again—but gradually taking on a firmer sense of direction. Berg explicitly marks this opening as "Introduction (10 measures)"; this odd specificity remained puzzling until the connection between the number 10 and Hanna Fuchs-Robettin became known. These ten measures are a dedicatory epigraph: "This is for you." A clear cadence is reached and, with a simple accompanying figure to set the pace, the first movement proper begins.

At its next entrance, the solo violin again starts on the open G-string, but this time it climbs up into a high register. The pitches are these:

Ex. 1

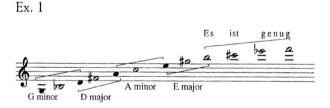

Most of the choices of pitch Berg makes in the Concerto are related to that particular ordering of the twelve notes of our chromatic scale. The black notes are the ones to which the four strings of a violin are tuned, and each bears a minor or a major triad: they are the scaffolding of Berg's chosen twelve-note series. The last four notes assume special meaning later on. It is

---

[11]Albine is an extraordinarily rare name, but by wild coincidence, another woman with that name was to enter Berg's life in the person of Hanna Fuchs-Robettin's mother, Albine Werfel.

clear from the outset that a place for traditional tonal harmonies and a specifically violinistic element are both built right into the material.

The Andante, which Berg thought of as a Praeludium, soon leads to a wistful Allegretto by way of a sweetly achieved transition.[12] This is music in the Austrian pastoral tradition of Beethoven and Schubert, Bruckner and Mahler, and full of pictorial reference: the honeyed thirds in the violin are to be played *wienerisch*, a more bumpkinlike passage is marked *rustico*, and we hear the hiccup of a yodel. After a couple of contrasting episodes—trios to this scherzo, really—a Carinthian folk song, whose entrance Berg wants to be imperceptible (*unmerklich*), is passed tenderly among horn, solo violin, and two trumpets.[13]

Ex. 2

Speaking to his biographer, Willi Reich, Berg referred to this theme as being "in the manner of a Carinthian folk song," but in the printed score it is actually marked as "Carinthian folk melody." And it is indeed a real song, in whose ribald text, unearthed many years after Berg's death, a young man remarks that he is thankful to have been awakened by a bird in the plum tree, "otherwise I would have overslept in Mitzi's bed." As we know from *Wozzeck*, *Lulu*, and the *Lyric Suite*, Berg never quotes just generically or for atmosphere, but always with a specific reference in mind. In that light, Douglas Jarman's suggestion that the appearance of this song refers to Mizzi Scheuchl—Mizzi or Mitzi being the common Austrian nickname for Marie—is convincing, and perhaps made more so by Berg's attempt to hide his tracks. Jarman also notes that "Berg probably enjoyed the play on words implied by the similarity between the song's 'Mizzi' and Manon's pet-name 'Mutzi.' "

After the Allegretto's gentle close, the second movement enters violently and with an intensity of dissonance Berg has avoided till now. This is a vision of catastrophe. The solo violin immediately asserts itself in a fiery accompanied cadenza whose first gesture is a wildly heightened variant of the quiet arpeggio with which it had begun the first movement—*fortissimo*, al-

---

[12]The metronome mark for the Andante is 56 (i.e., 2 x 28); for the Allegretto it is 112 (i.e., 4 x 28).
[13]Carinthia is the province in the southwest of Austria where Berg composed the Violin Concerto. Its German name is Kärnten, and the Kärntnerthor Theater in Vienna that one encounters so often in writings about Mozart and Beethoven was by the city gate through which one passed to take the road to Carinthia.

legro, and with the intervals stretched from G/D/A/E to G/D/B-flat/F-sharp.[14]
Berg sets up a powerful contrast between the freedom with which this opening must be projected and the strictly rhythmic style that takes over later on.
A dotted rhythm—it is first heard in measure 23—ominously bestrides this
scene.

Ex. 3

Another cadenza—mostly slow, in three- and four-part harmony, incredibly difficult, and with occasional contributions from strings in the orchestra—halts the forward thrust for a time. The orchestra re-enters at full
strength, pushing toward an immense climax. This is music of snarling brasses, and the dominant rhythm (Ex. 3) pounds unmercifully. Then the storm
subsides, and the solo violin quietly but decisively begins a Bach chorale.
Only a bassoon and a few of the orchestral strings accompany. The final
chapter has begun.

Berg knew early on that he wanted to introduce a chorale at the end of
his Requiem, but even when the first movement was far advanced and the
basic compositional material of the whole work long since determined, he
had still not found anything suitable. When at last he saw Bach's setting of
*Es ist genug!* (It Is Enough!) in a collection sent to him by Willi Reich, it
was so right he could hardly believe it: not only was the text perfectly apt,
but its first four notes were the last four of his own ordering of the twelve
notes (Ex. 1). This is, moreover, Bach's most adventurous, chromatic, "modern," tension-laden chorale harmonization, so that it fits uncannily with
Berg's own harmonic style. Many years later, Louis Krasner mused about this:
"One of the prayers I like to hear on Yom Kippur says that in the eyes of the
Lord, a thousand years is as if it were yesterday. That is why I believe Bach
wrote the chorale for Berg, 'only yesterday,' because he knew Berg would be
needing it."

The chorale comes from the Cantata No. 60, *O Ewigkeit, du Donnerwort*
(O Eternity, Thou Word of Thunder); the melody is by the seventeenth-

[14]The third and fourth measures of this cadenza are garbled in the printed score: there are wrong
notes, and the range is cut down by a full octave. You can hear it played correctly by Thomas
Zehetmair on his Teldec recording with Heinz Holliger and the Philharmonia Orchestra; once you
have experienced the forceful gesture Berg actually invented, it is hard to tolerate the hobbled
standard version.

century Mühlhausen church musician Johann Rudolf Ahle (1625–1673) and the words are by the Lüneburg poet Franz Joachim Burmeister (1633–1672).[15]

| | |
|---|---|
| Es ist genug! | It is enough! |
| Herr, wenn es dir gefällt, | Lord, if it please you, |
| So spanne mich doch aus! | Unyoke me now at last! |
| Mein Jesus kommt: | My Jesus comes: |
| Nun gute Nacht, o Welt! | Now good night, O world! |
| Ich fahr' ins Himmelshaus, | I travel to my heavenly home, |
| Ich fahre sicher hin mit Frieden, | I travel surely and in peace. |
| Mein großer Jammer bleibt darnieden. | My great distress remains below. |
| Es ist genug! Es ist genug! | It is enough! It is enough! |

Berg's and Bach's harmonizations of *Es ist genug!* alternate and subtly intersect. Berg presents each line in his own setting, the melody played by the violin, and follows that with Bach's version played by a quartet of clarinets, sounding like the organ in a village church. The Bach phrases do not completely exclude Berg, whose presence is felt in *pianissimo* comments in the orchestral strings. Berg marks the successive phrases of the chorale *deciso, doloroso, dolce,* and *risoluto;* then for the last phrase he writes *molto espressivo e amoroso,* which he follows immediately with his own signature in the first horn, that is, with the four letters in his name that are also the names of notes: B-flat/A/G/E. *Amoroso* is a strange, indeed out-and-out incongruous, direction in a chorale, but it will occur nine more times—ten in all. Clearly something is going on here beyond a Requiem for Manon Gropius. The presence of Berg's own signature and of various numerological clues once again leads to Hanna Fuchs-Robettin and to Berg himself. Perle likens it all to "a jigsaw puzzle whose pieces can be put together in different ways to make two completely different pictures."[16] And here it must be said: The point is not for you to count measures or be on the lookout for B's and F's but rather to understand how these concerns that burned at white heat in the composer's mind help account for the intensity of expression in this music.

I hear this double chorale as a sublime arrival and resolution, which is of course what Berg intended, but some critics have been bothered by the collision between 1723 and 1935. Ernest Newman, for example, who hated the piece because it showed the influence of Schoenberg, called it "falling between two stools," while the twenty-three-year-old Pierre Boulez, who despised it for not being modern enough, declared that Berg had "committed

---

[15]Another work that introduces *Es ist genug!* with shattering emotional impact is Bernd Alois Zimmermann's "ecclesiastical action," *Ich wandte mich und sahe an alles Unrecht, das geschah unter der Sonne* (So I returned, and considered all the oppressions that are done under the sun). Zimmermann, writing in 1970, was alluding to Berg as well as to Bach.

[16]Perle also cites Henry James's *The Turn of the Screw* as an instance of a story whose "facts" allow widely divergent interpretations.

a serious error" and that this "hybridization" caused the resulting structure to be "without justification and without stability."[17]

Two variations follow the first statement of the hymn, beginning with the melody in muted cellos and harp. The solo violin, also muted, joins in. A single violin from the orchestra adds its voice, then another, then more and more, and Berg asks that the soloist "audibly *and visibly*" assume leadership of the orchestral violins and violas.[18] Krasner tells us that for Berg this was "the real cadenza" of the Concerto and that he thought of this passage as one in which you seem to perceive the solo through an ever-stronger magnifying glass until one violin, grown to overwhelming dimensions, entirely fills the hall.

Then the process is reversed as, gradually, the orchestral strings drop away until only the soloist is left. Mizzi's Carinthian song is heard as though from a great distance—a distance of thirty-three years—but it is the chorale, garlanded with a filigree of solo strings, that leads the Concerto to its serene close: "My great distress remains below." The last music we hear is a scarcely audible recollection of that preluding on open strings where it all began.

[17]Newman, Boulez, and others are cited in Anthony Pople's valuable monograph on the Berg Concerto in the Cambridge Music Handbooks Series.
[18]Kennedy is the only violinist I have ever seen do this in the uninhibited, unembarrassed spirit Berg surely intended. The effect is very moving.

# Johannes Brahms

Johannes Brahms was born in the Free City of Hamburg on 7 May 1833 and died in Vienna on 3 April 1897.

## Concerto No. 1 in D minor for Piano and Orchestra, Opus 15

*Maestoso*
*Adagio*
*Rondo: Allegro non troppo*

Using some material that goes back to 1854 and was originally intended for other purposes and designs, Brahms completed his Piano Concerto No. 1 early in 1858, but continued to tinker with details of the first movement even after the first performances. With Joseph Joachim conducting the Hanover Court Orchestra, where he had a royal appointment as concertmaster, Brahms played a reading rehearsal on 30 March 1858 and gave the first public performance with the same partners on 22 January 1859. No one should be deprived of the pleasure of knowing that the first performance in England (apparently an excellent one) was by a Miss Baglehole (first name not given).

Solo piano, two flutes, two oboes, two clarinets, two bassoons, four horns, two trumpets, timpani, and strings.

Admit: When you think of Brahms, you probably see him as he appears in the famous von Beckerath drawing, seated at the piano, hands crossed (playing one of the two Rhapsodies, Opus 79, from the look of his hand position)—an older man with grey hair and flowing white beard, stout, sure to light a cigar the moment he has finished playing, then off to a pub called The Red Hedgehog for wine and smoke and conversation, gruff, sometimes outright rude, but still capable of turning on charm for the ladies, going for long walks, writing many letters, some of them distressingly arch, spending summers composing in places with such names as Pörtschach, Mürzzuschlag, and Bad Ischl, but unable to tolerate any of them more than three years in a row, and of course writing solid masterpiece after solid masterpiece. Right enough, but it has nothing to do with the D-minor Piano Concerto and the struggle of the twenty-four-year-old Brahms to bring that refractory score to completion.

"I have no judgment about this piece any more, nor any control over it," he wrote on 22 December 1857 to Joseph Joachim, violinist, composer, conductor, Brahms's senior by two years, and his chosen mentor.[1] Four years earlier, on 28 October 1853, Robert Schumann had closed his career as music critic with the celebrated, oft-invoked article "New Paths":

> I have always thought that some day, one would be bound suddenly to appear, one called to express in ideal form the spirit of his time, one whose mastery would not reveal itself to us step by step, but who, like Athene, would spring fully armed from the head of Zeus. And he is come, a young man over whose cradle graces and heroes have stood watch. His name is Johannes Brahms. . . . Even outwardly he bears all those signs that proclaim: here is one of the elect. [2]

That year, with Joachim having made the introduction, Brahms had come to the Schumanns in Düsseldorf as a shy, awkward, nearsighted young man, blond, delicate, almost wispy, boyish in appearance as well as in manner (the beard was still twenty-two years away), and with a voice whose high pitch was a constant embarrassment to him. His two longest, closest musical friendships began that year, those with Joachim and Clara Schumann. Both friendships went through turbulent, painful phases, the one with Joachim much later, that with Clara almost at once.

On 27 February 1854 Robert Schumann, whose conducting career had collapsed and who had begun to suffer from auditory and visual hallucinations, tried to drown himself in the Rhine; five days later he was committed to an asylum at Endenich just outside Bonn. Clara, pregnant with their seventh child, was desperate, and in the following weeks Brahms's kindliness,

---

[1] For more on Joachim, see the essays on the Brahms Violin Concerto and Double Concerto.
[2] Robert Schumann, *Gesammelte Schriften über Musik und Musiker*, (Leipzig: VEB Breitkopf & Härtel, 1985), my translation.

friendship, reverence, and gratitude were transmuted into a state of being passionately in love with this gifted, strong, captivatingly charming, and beautiful thirty-five-year-old woman. Moreover, in some way she returned his feeling. In their correspondence there is reference to "the unanswered question." Robert's death in July 1856 was a turning point in Brahms's relations with Clara, though not the one for which Brahms must have hoped. She seemed more married to Robert than ever. She and Brahms pulled apart, and it took some time before they settled into the loving, nourishing friendship that endured until her death in May 1896.[3]

All this time, the music we know as the D-minor Piano Concerto was in Brahms's head, occupying more and more pages of his notebooks, being tried out at one piano or two, sent to Joachim for criticism, discussed in letters. It is marked by the turmoil of those years, by Robert Schumann's madness and death, by Brahms's love for Clara Schumann and hers for him, by their confusion about how to live with their feelings and with their retreat from their passion. The process of composition was marked no less by purely musical troubles, by the mixed effect of the very young composer's originality, his ambition, his inexperience (particularly in writing for orchestra), his almost overpowering feeling for the past, his trembling sense of his own audacity at inserting himself into history as a successor of Bach and Handel, Haydn and Mozart, Beethoven (most daunting of all), Schubert, and Schumann.

In 1854 Brahms set out to compose a sonata for two pianos. By June of that year he was already uncertain about it and wrote to Joachim: "I'd really like to put my D-minor Sonata aside for a long time. I have often played the first three movements with Frau Schumann. (Improved.) Actually, not even two pianos are really enough for me. . . . I am in such a confused and indecisive frame of mind that I can't beg you enough for a good, firm response. Don't avoid a negative one either; it could only be useful to me."[4]

That March, he had traveled the few miles from Düsseldorf to Cologne to hear the Beethoven Ninth for the first time. More than twenty-two years would pass before he allowed himself to complete a symphony and have it performed, but still, from then on, the idea of writing such a work gave him no peace. Brahms may have considered turning the sonata for which two pianos were not enough into a symphony in the Beethoven-Ninth key of

[3]For an admirably calm, informed, informative, and sensitive summing up of the Johannes-Clara relationship see Appendix A to *Johannes Brahms: Life and Letters*, selected and annotated by Styra Avins (Oxford and New York: Oxford University Press, 1997). For another sensitive and beautifully expressed commentary on this subject, see Lisel Mueller's poem "The Romantics—Johannes Brahms and Clara Schumann" in her collection *Alive Together* (Baton Rouge: Louisiana State University Press, 1996).
[4]Excerpt from the correspondence with Joachim from *Letters From and To Joseph Joachim*, ed. and transl. Nora Bickley (New York: Vienna House, 1972), translations amended.

D minor—the history is not clear. To turn the music into a piano concerto seemed to be the answer, and by April 1856 he was sending drafts to Joachim: "You know how infinitely you could please me—if it's worth the effort at all—by looking at it very carefully and passing on to me even the most trivial of your thoughts and reservations."

Joachim to Brahms, 4 December 1856:

> I don't know whether you will be pleased by my penciled suggestions and wish you'd soon answer that unstated question, best of all by simply sending me the concerto's continuation. . . . I become more fond of the piece all the time, though certain things don't altogether convince me compositionally: from page 21 to 24 it's too fragmentary, not flowing enough—restless rather than impassioned—just as in general, after the significant opening, that wonderfully beautiful song in minor, I miss an appropriately magnificent second theme—I do realize that something commensurately elevated and beautiful in major, something that competes in breadth with the opening idea, must be hard to find—but even these reservations don't blind me to the many glories of the movement.

Brahms to Joachim, 12 December 1856:

> So here is the finale, just to be finally rid of it. Will it be good enough for you? I doubt it. The end was really meant to be good, but now it doesn't seem so to me. A thousand thanks for having looked over the first movement so benevolently and precisely. I have already learned a lot from your beautiful commentary. . . . Scold and cut all you want.

Brahms to Joachim, early January 1857:

> You're not embarrassed to make heavy and heavier cuts in the rondo, are you? I know very well that they're needed. Send it soon. Here's the first movement, copied over for a second—and, please, severe—going over. . . . Oddly enough, an Adagio is going along at the same time. If I could only rejoice over a successful Adagio! Write to me about it, and firmly. If you like it a little, show it to our dear friend [i.e., Clara Schumann], otherwise not. . . . I like the little alteration on page 19, line 2, but doesn't it remind me of Wagner? . . . Dear Joseph, I am so happy to be able to send you my things, it makes me feel doubly sure.

Joachim to Brahms, 12 January 1857:

> Your finale—all in all I find it really significant: the pithy, bold spirit of the first theme, the intimate and soft B-flat-major passage, and particularly the

solemn reawakening toward a majestic close after the cadenza—all that is rich enough to leave an uplifting impression if you absorb these principal features. In fact, I even believe that after the impassioned spaciousness of the first movement and the elevating reverence of the second it would make a satisfying close to the whole concerto—were it not for some uncertainties in the middle of the movement, which disturb the beauty and the total effect through a certain instability and stiffness. It sounds as though the themes themselves had been invented by the creative artist in the very heat of inspiration, but then you hadn't allowed them enough time to form proper crystals in the process of fermentation [there follow several pages of detailed criticism of the harmonic structure and some questions about the scoring]. . . . A conversation with Frau Schumann led me to think it would be well if you wrote another finale, revision often being more trouble than new invention. But that would be a waste of so much that is meaningful in the rondo, and perhaps you can bring yourself back to the point of working with your original impetuosity so as to make these few places over—I'd like that.

So it went for months more, with alterations, decisions to leave certain things alone ("I'm returning one passage still with the mark of Cain on its brow"), and inquiries about horn transpositions, the risk involved in assigning a solo to the third horn ("The players in Hamburg and Elberfeld are useless, and who knows about other orchestras?"), the advisability of omitting the piccolo altogether (Brahms did leave it out, settling on a contained and essentially Classical orchestra). In December 1857 he wrote, "Nothing sensible will ever come of it." To which Joachim wisely replied, "*Aber Mensch* [but I beg you, man], please, for God's sake let the copyist get at the concerto." "I made more changes in the first movement," Brahms reported in March 1858 and even risked *not* sending them to Joachim. That good friend made his orchestra in Hanover available for a reading rehearsal in April, and, bit by bit, Brahms came to face the inevitable—he must let the work go and perform it.

The official premiere in Hanover went well enough, but the performance in the more important city of Leipzig a few days later, with Julius Rietz and the Gewandhaus Orchestra, was a disaster. Brahms reported to Joachim:

No reaction at all to the first and second movements. At the end, three pairs of hands tried slowly to clap, whereupon a clear hissing from all sides quickly put an end to any such demonstration. . . . I think it's the best thing that could happen to one, it forces you to collect your thoughts and it raises your courage. After all, I'm still trying and groping. But the hissing was really too much, wasn't it? . . . For all that, one day, when I've improved its physical structure, this concerto will please, and a second one will sound very different.

He was right on both counts, though in fact he revised only some details. And he became a master.

Aside from the D-minor reference, we sense the impact of the Beethoven Ninth in the First Concerto's general demeanor, in its artistic and rhetorical ambition: it is weightier in content as well as simply much longer than any previous concerto. On the other hand, while the opening of Beethoven's last symphony, with its progression from the inchoate to the coherent, its representation of the act of becoming, irresistibly fascinated many later composers, most famously Bruckner, Brahms was not tempted to imitate something that had been done perfectly. Instead, he devises an opening that appears to be the diametric opposite of Beethoven's—an immediate and powerful assertion of D (including a D pedal on timpani and basses for ten broad measures) and a fiercely combative musical gesture of grandly striding arpeggios and trills. This could, however, be a reference to the tumultuous opening—with drum rolls on A and D—of the Beethoven Ninth finale.

At the same time, for all the aggressiveness of the gesture, one also has the sense—and this is certainly related to Beethoven—of *sound* struggling to emerge. Erich Leinsdorf, who had a particularly virulent form of that conductor's disease of always knowing better, extensively reorchestrated this Concerto so as to make it "sound," to make it "effective." The sound of Brahms-Leinsdorf—you can hear it on Van Cliburn's recording with Leinsdorf and the Boston Symphony—is indeed clear and forward and brilliant, but nothing could more surely have subverted Brahms's expressive intention.

The darkness of Brahms's sound here is emblematic of something else mysterious, or at least not straightforward, even in *fortissimo*. The harmonies built upon that long D are not what you would expect, not those of the tonic, of D minor; rather, the first chord is one of B-flat major, and the A-flat measures 4, 6, 8, and 10 push the harmony in the direction of E-flat, even farther removed from home. Referring to a "powerful assertion of D," I meant *the note D*, not yet *the key of D minor*. We shall have to wait nearly three minutes before Brahms gives us a clear landing on a D-minor chord. And so he has, after all, picked up Beethoven's strategy of delaying the unambiguous affirmation of the home key, but with a vocabulary and a metabolism that are all his own.

The orchestral exposition—and it is an exposition of essential themes, not an introduction—is spacious and full of event. The first tumultuous paragraph is succeeded by a lyric theme that seeks to appease.[5] The mystery deepens; then, in sudden *fortissimo*, the opening music returns, elaborated by

[5]I hear the rising fourth with which it begins as a reference to a theme in the first movement of the

canonic imitations and with echoes in the brass of its jabbing gestures. Only then does the harmony settle, with Brahms remembering from Mozart's D-minor Piano Concerto and *Don Giovanni* Overture the sound, coldly gleaming, of quiet drums together with trumpets on their lowest D.

During these last moments a new idea has come to the fore, and this is what the piano chooses for its entrance music. It was full of energy and thrust when we first heard it emerge from the chains of trills in the orchestra; now it is gentle and *espressivo*, and has something of the atmosphere of a Bach arioso. But the opening theme will not be kept at bay, and returning, it becomes big virtuoso stuff for the pianist. The lyric theme and its mysterious pendant follow, and then comes the "appropriately magnificent . . . commensurately elevated and beautiful" theme in major for which Joachim had begged. It is a long piano solo, sumptuous at first, then delicate. Characteristic of Brahms, even this very young Brahms, is his concern for integrating the new theme into the movement instead of having it just sit there being beautiful but unconnected. He accomplishes this by having it flow seamlessly into yet another version of the lyric/mysterious complex (with a solo for the third horn after all), and this, subsiding very slowly, brings the exposition to a close.

And there is the rich material for this huge movement. The development begins with an arresting display of octave-bravura—this concerto says much about the young Brahms as a pianist—and in its not very long course it touches on every theme except the noble one in major.[6] The piano's quiet entrance with the "appeasing" lyric theme is a special marvel. The dramatic re-entry into the recapitulation plays brilliantly on the harmonic ambiguity of the movement's beginning. After a tense buildup, Brahms arrives on his

------

Ninth whose expressive function is parallel; that is, it is mollifying in the midst of tumult, and it begins with the same interval.

Ex. 1

Ex. 2

[6]Fanny Davies, one of Clara Schumann's pupils, gives a lively and perceptive account of Brahms's piano-playing as an appendix to the Brahms entry in *Cobbett's Cyclopedic Survey of Chamber Music*.

thunderous D; this time, however, it is the piano that responds, and on a chord far stranger than the one of B-flat major we heard at the concerto's beginning.[7] The recapitulation itself brings a host of subtle and interesting transformations; the piano's Bachian entrance theme, for example, reappears in F-sharp minor, new harmonic territory for this movement. The coda is both sparkling and forceful.

For the solemn, sarabande-like music he had sketched as the slow movement of the two-piano sonata that never was, Brahms found a beautiful use when he set it to the words "For all flesh is as grass, and all the glory of man as the flower of grass" in his *German Requiem*. The Concerto has a solemn Adagio—also in D, but D major—over whose opening notes he once inscribed the words "Benedictus qui venit in nomine Domini." This music holds everything that, in his painful, Werther-like loyalty and love, he felt about Robert and Clara Schumann. Here, too, I sense the presence of Beethoven, specifically of the Benedictus and its rapt Praeludium in the *Missa solemnis*. But this movement also brings grave arabesques and even a Gypsy lament. When the arabesques come back near the end of the movement, they open out into a cadenza that is no less spellbinding for being *molto adagio* and *pianissimo*. The orchestra speaks the final blessing, and the first timpani entrance in the movement—on A, not on the keynote D—is another wonder and something to listen for.

As for the finale, Joachim characterizes its elements well when he writes about "the pithy, bold spirit of the first theme [and] the intimate and soft B-flat-major passage." Brahms adds another of his generous themes in major—mixed minor/major when it returns, with the further distinction (often glossed over by pianists) between *forte, con passione* the first time and *mezzo-forte* and *espressivo* the second. The coda, with its sequence of cadenzas and what Joachim called "awakenings," is one of the most inspired inventions in this daring and scarred and great concerto.[8]

---

[7]Brahms had already invented a similar, boldly aslant entrance into the recapitulation in the first movement of his C-major Piano Sonata, Opus 1.

[8]We hear echoes of these "awakenings" in the musing horn calls in *Es tönt ein voller Harfenklang*, the first of the Four Songs for Women's Chorus with two horns and harp, Opus 17, composed in February 1860. The opening of the slow movement of the Double Concerto is also part of this thematic-coloristic family.

## Concerto No. 2 in B-flat major for Piano and Orchestra, Opus 83

*Allegro non troppo*
*Allegro appassionato*
*Andante*
*Allegretto grazioso*

Brahms sketched this Concerto in the late spring of 1878 and completed the score at Pressbaum near Vienna on 7 July 1881. After a private tryout of the Concerto with Hans von Bülow and the Meiningen Orchestra, Brahms gave the first public performance on 9 November 1881 in Budapest, with Alexander Erkel conducting the orchestra of the National Theater. Brahms dedicated the score to his "dear friend and teacher Eduard Marxsen."

**Solo piano, two flutes (second doubling piccolo), two oboes, two clarinets, two bassoons, four horns, two trumpets, timpani, and strings.**

"[A]nd a second one will sound very different," wrote Brahms to Joseph Joachim, rendering a report on the disastrous reception in Leipzig of his Piano Concerto No. 1. More than twenty years would elapse before there was "a second one." They were full years. Brahms had settled in Vienna and given up conducting and playing the piano as regular activities and sources of income. Belly and beard date from those years—"clean-shaven they take you for an actor or a priest," he said. The compositions of those two decades include the variations on themes by Handel, Paganini, and Haydn; the string quartets and piano quartets (three of each), as well as both string sextets, the Piano Quintet, and the Horn Trio; a cello sonata and one for violin; the first two symphonies and the Violin Concerto; and, along with over a hundred songs and shorter choral pieces, a series of large-scale vocal works including *A German Requiem*, the *Song of Destiny*, and *Nänie*.

He was resigned to bachelorhood and to never composing an opera. He had even come to terms with the fact that at the beginning of the century there had been a giant called Beethoven whose thunderous footsteps made life terribly difficult for later composers. To the young Brahms, Beethoven had been an inspiration and a model, but also a source of daunting inhibition. Fully aware of what he was doing and what it meant, Brahms waited until he was in his forties before he sent into the world any string quartets or a first symphony, both being genres peculiarly associated with Beethoven. In sum, the Brahms of the Second Piano Concerto was a master, confident and altogether mature. The University of Breslau called him *artis musicae severioris in Germania nunc princeps* (now the leader in the field of serious music in Germany) when it awarded him an honorary doctorate in 1879. *Severioris* disposed of Wagner, and once that distinction was made, it was clear that Brahms had no rival in Germany to the title of *princeps*.

In April 1878 Brahms made what was to be the first of nine journeys to Italy and Sicily. His companion was another bearded and overweight North German who had settled in Vienna, Theodor Billroth, an accomplished and knowledgeable amateur musician and, by profession, a surgeon, a field in which he was even more indisputably *princeps* than Brahms was in his. Brahms came back from Italy elated and full of energy. His chief task for that summer was to compose a violin concerto for Joseph Joachim. He planned unconventionally to include a scherzo but dropped the idea at Joachim's suggestion. He had, however, made sketches for such a movement after his return from the south, and he retrieved them three years later, making them the starting point for his new piano concerto's second movement.

Eighteen-eighty-one began with the first performances of the *Academic Festival* and *Tragic* overtures, and there were professional trips to Holland and Hungary as well as another Italian vacation. In memory of his friend the painter Anselm Feuerbach, he made his setting of Schiller's *Nänie* and then set to work on the sketches that had been accumulating for the Piano Concerto No. 2. By this time Brahms had established a regular pattern for his year: concentrated compositional work was done during the summer in various Austrian or Swiss villages and small towns, each visited for two or three years in a row and then dropped, while winter was the season of sketches, proofreading, and concerts. On 7 July 1881 he reported to his friend Elisabet von Herzogenberg, perhaps his closest musical confidante of those years, that he had finished a "tiny, tiny piano concerto with a tiny, tiny wisp of a scherzo," and when Billroth was sent his copy of the score, it was with a remark about "a bunch of little piano pieces."

The measure of Brahms's sureness about the new Concerto can be found in his dedication of it to "his dear friend and teacher Eduard Marxsen." Marxsen, to whom Brahms had been sent by his first teacher, Otto Cossel, as a boy of seven, was born in 1806 and had studied with Carl Maria von Bocklet, the pianist who had played in the first performance of Schubert's E-flat Trio. An orchestral version by Marxsen of Beethoven's *Kreutzer* Sonata was widely performed in the nineteenth century. All of us who love Brahms's music have reason to be grateful to Marxsen: He never took a penny for the lessons he gave to Johannes and his brother Fritz, he gave both boys an education in music and life that went far beyond piano lessons, and even after Johannes left Hamburg he was unfailingly generous with financial support whenever anyone in the Brahms family was in difficulties. Brahms's devotion lasted until the end of Marxsen's life in 1887. The choice of the B-flat Concerto as occasion for the long-delayed formal tribute to his master is surely significant: Brahms must have felt that he had at last achieved what had eluded him in the wonderful D-minor Concerto, namely the perfect fusion of inspirational fire with that encompassing technique whose foundations were laid in those long-ago lessons in Hamburg.

The new Concerto was the last work Brahms added to his repertory as a pianist, and, for someone who had long ago given up regular practicing, to have gotten through it at all is amazing. Most pianists would name it as the most difficult of all the standard concertos; Alfred Brendel writes of its "unsurpassable pianistic perversions." After the premiere, Brahms took the work on an extensive tour of Germany with Hans von Bülow and the superb Meiningen Orchestra. Leipzig resisted once again, but the rest of the trip was one triumph after another. People tended to find the first movement harder to grasp than the rest, and almost universally a new relationship between piano and orchestra was noted, phrases such as "symphony with piano obbligato" being much bandied about. With respect to the latter question, it is mainly that Brahms knew the concertos of Mozart and Beethoven better than his critics did and was prepared to draw more imaginative and far-reaching conclusions from the subtle solo-tutti relationships propounded in those masterpieces of the Classical style.

"Dream, Mr. X.," I once heard a conductor say to his solo horn as they were about to begin a rehearsal of this Concerto. It turned out to be an unwise invitation: Mr. X. dreamed very, very slowly. Still, it is easy to understand why a conductor might say that. The music begins with a gentle phrase played solo by the horn, that most romantic of instruments, and it is a phrase that longs for an artist capable of dreaming, of musing. And before the phrase is even complete, the piano enters with its own rhythmically cunning variant of it.

This response is poetic and reticent; at the same time, there is something quietly assertive about the way the piano at once takes possession of five and a half octaves from the lowest B-flat on the keyboard to the F an octave above the top of the treble staff. When, after a complementary three-measure phrase, the woodwinds and then the strings have continued in this lyric vein, the piano enters with a cadenza that silences the orchestra altogether. But this cadenza, hugely sonorous, massive, and almost violent though it is, settles on a long dominant pedal, showing that its real function is to introduce, as dramatically as possible, an expansive and absolutely formal orchestral exposition. Among other things, this is a confident, almost competitive gloss on the opening of Beethoven's Fifth Piano Concerto.

The exposition begins with the horn theme (Example 1), now transmuted into a vigorous march for full orchestra. This does not last long, being soon succeeded by an intensely expressive violin melody in D minor. It, too, is quickly broken off to make way for an idea in sharply dotted rhythm, after which this phase of the movement concludes with a grandiose variant—still in minor—of the horn theme.

Now the piano enters with three richly scored, wide-spread chords (but, like so many of the "big" moments in this concerto, *forte*, not *fortissimo*) and, after a grand survey of the keyboard, embarks, together with the orchestra, on an expansive review of the horn theme. This part of the exposition is as spacious as the purely orchestral portion was terse. The themes we already know reappear, the expressive violin melody being imaginatively varied, and several new ideas make their appearance as well until the exposition ends in high drama. No small part of that drama resides in the immensely demanding piano writing with its huge leaps and stretches and what D. F. Tovey calls its "cataracts of trills."

Caught up in the momentum, the orchestra sweeps us into the development. The horn comes back to its first idea, but in melancholy F minor, the piano again adding its overlapping echo. But now there is a small but significant variant: what was originally

Ex. 1

has become

Ex. 2

The syncopated start adds new tension, but above all it is the little upbeat to the last note that makes a difference, for this tiny gesture will be an almost constant presence through the development. When this section, wide-ranging in harmony and mood, has run much of its course, the first three rising notes of the horn theme assert themselves *fortissimo* in the strings and clarinets. They retreat at once to *pianissimo*, but, exploding into *fortissimo* now and again, they insist on our attention. Clearly it is time to think about the return of the horn theme in full and thus to think about the recapitulation.

This arrival is a most magical moment. The horn call and its extensions on the piano are now gently embedded in a continuous and flowing texture. This tells us that the opening of the movement should be played not as an introduction in a slower tempo but as a real and organic beginning. In other words, dream, but dream in tempo (or close to it). When this soft dawning occurs, you remember the piano's eruption into the cadenza the first time around, and the contrast now of the entirely lyrical continuation is the more poignant for that memory. We tend to think of this Concerto as granitic and declamatory, the quintessential blockbuster, but the expression mark that occurs more often than any other is *dolce* (followed in frequency by *leggiero*).

For the rest, the recapitulation proceeds regularly, though it is of course full of freshening changes of detail. The coda begins in darkness, and here I quote Tovey once more: "Out of subdued mutterings the first theme arises and hovers, while the air seems full of whisperings and the beating of mighty wings." Suddenly the first theme reappears *fortissimo* in both piano and orchestra. It is, however, poised over F in the bass rather than the keynote, B-flat, and when the orchestra finally lands on a firm, definite B-flat, the piano insists on F in a four-octave scale and a long trill, and this tension is not resolved until two measures before the end.

Beethoven had had to answer tiresome questions about why there were only two movements in his last piano sonata, and now Brahms was constantly asked to explain the presence of his "extra" *Scherzerl*. He told Billroth that the first movement appeared to him "too simple" and that he "required something strongly passionate before the equally simple Andante." This answer half convinces: simplicity is not so much the issue as urgency and speed. Long-range harmonic strategy, particularly with respect to the Andante to come, must also have had a lot to do with Brahms's decision. In any case, the contrast is welcome, and the movement, in which one can still sense the biting double-stops of Joachim's violin, goes brilliantly. The mood of the main part of the movement, in D minor, is ferocious, with perhaps something of tragedy; a new section, something like a trio in the way it presents a new world of flavor and feeling, is in D major and joyous. The coda is enormous both in scope and in energy.

The first and second movements end in ways meant to produce the ovations they got at their early performances—and how priggish and out-and-out anti-musical our present custom that indiscriminately forbids such demonstrations between movements! From here on, Brahms reduces the physical scale of his utterance, trumpets and drums falling silent for the remainder of the concerto. Erich Leinsdorf often remarked about something he called "anti-emphasis" in Brahms and about which he felt that nothing was more deeply characteristic of him: here is a perfect example.

The Andante begins with a long and famous cello solo, which, like its oboe counterpart in the Adagio of the Violin Concerto, becomes increasingly and ever more subtly enmeshed in its surroundings (and thus less obviously soloistic). The cello and the horn, the two subsidiary solo voices in this Concerto, were the instruments besides the piano on which Brahms had been a proficient performer as a boy and a young man. Five years later, Brahms found a different and equally beautiful continuation of the same melodic germ in the song *Immer leiser wird mein Schlummer*. The piano does not undertake to compete with the cello as a singer of that kind of song. Its own melodies stand on either side of that style, being either more embellished or more skeletal. (Charles Rosen once remarked that this is the slow movement Rachmaninoff tried all his life to write.)

The key is B-flat, the Concerto's home key and thus an unusual choice for a slow movement; there are, however, some precedents in Beethoven, to say nothing of Brahms's own earlier piano concerto. The excursions from B-flat are bold and remarkable in their effect: to cite one especially striking example, it is its placement in the distant key of F-sharp that gives the return of the cello solo its magically soft radiance. For me, the most breathtaking page is the one just before that return, when, over slow-moving harmonies, two clarinets and the piano seem to forget that they are playing a concerto in a large concert hall and instead lose themselves in the intimate confidences of chamber music, *pianississimo, dolcissimo, molto espressivo*. In some of the harmonies we sense the presence of Schumann, and in this deeply melancholic and serene music, Brahms also alludes to one of his own songs, *Todessehnen* (Longing for Death).[9] The movement ends with a cadenzalike coda of small dimensions but immense emotional weight, the piano's closing chords alluding to the very opening of the Concerto.

The sweetly charming finale moves gently in that not-quite-fast gait that is so characteristic of Brahms. A touch of Gypsy music passes now and again, and just before the end, which occurs without much ado, Brahms spikes the texture with triplets.

[9]This was pointed out to me by Garrick Ohlsson, who had learned it from Claudio Arrau. Dillon Parmer writes in his interesting article "Brahms, Song Quotation, and Secret Programs," in the Fall 1995 issue of *Nineteenth-Century Music*, that "the allusion is noted in Max Friedlaender, *Brahms's Lieder, An Introduction to the Songs for One and Two Voices* (1922)."

## Concerto in D major for Violin and Orchestra, Opus 77

*Allegro non troppo*
*Adagio*
*Allegro giocoso, ma non troppo vivace—Poco più presto*

Brahms wrote his Violin Concerto in the summer and early fall of 1878, but the published score incorporates a few revisions made after the first performance, which was given on 1 January 1879 in Leipzig by Joseph Joachim, with the composer conducting the Gewandhaus Orchestra. The work is dedicated to Joachim.

**Solo violin, two flutes, two oboes, two clarinets, two bassoons, four horns, two trumpets, timpani, and strings.**

Faint phonograph recordings exist of Joseph Joachim playing two of Brahms's *Hungarian Dances*, some unaccompanied Bach, and a Romance of his own. Through the crackle and distance, one can hear that even in his seventies his bow-arm was surprisingly firm and the left hand sure. The records also convey a sense of the vitality of his playing and tell something about the style of a player who began performing in public while Mendelssohn, Schumann, Chopin, Cherubini, and Donizetti were still alive. In the end, though, they tell us less than we should like to know about this violinist whose debut at eight was hailed as the coming of "a second Vieuxtemps, Paganini, Ole Bull" and the musician whose name became, across the more than sixty years of his career, a byword for nobility and probity in art.

Joachim the violinist is remembered not only as a superb and commanding soloist but also as the leader of the most highly esteemed quartet of his day. In addition, he was an accomplished composer and conductor, and in the latter capacity he was also an unswerving and effective advocate for Brahms, in England no less than in Germany, also making his conservatory orchestra in Berlin available to Brahms for tryouts. Joachim became an eloquent spokesman on the Brahms side in the Holy War Against the Wicked Wagner (which Brahms himself disdained to join), but in his teens he had been Franz Liszt's concertmaster at Weimar and had played in the first performance of *Lohengrin*. His passionate identification with the musical past was productive: that Beethoven's Violin Concerto, which he performed for the first time in London just before his thirteenth birthday, took its place in the concert repertory was largely due to Joachim's persistence and to the persuasiveness of his interpretation. He was also the first to play Bach's solo sonatas and partitas without the piano accompaniments that even musicians as good as Schumann and Mendelssohn had thought necessary.

Brahms and Joseph Joachim, whom Brahms liked to call Jussuf, had been friends since May 1853, when Brahms had just turned twenty and Joachim would soon be twenty-two, and over the years they gave many concerts together with Brahms at the piano or on the podium. The gap, however, seemed far wider, for while Brahms was a desperately shy young man with great aspirations but as yet little confidence, Joachim was a celebrity as well as, at that stage, the more sure and technically solid composer. Brahms quickly acquired the habit of submitting work in progress to Joachim for stern, specific, practical, and carefully heeded criticism.[10]

The first mention of a violin concerto in the Brahms-Joachim correspondence occurs on 21 August 1878. Brahms was spending the summer at Pörtschach on Lake Wörth in southern Austria, where he had begun his Second Symphony the year before. It was a region, he once said, where melodies were so abundant one had to be careful not to step on them. As he worked, Brahms sent Joachim passages of his score, and Joachim offered his comments and suggestions. At last, plans were made for a trial reading with the orchestra of the Berlin Conservatory, for Joachim to compose a cadenza, and for the premiere either with the Vienna Philharmonic or at the Leipzig Gewandhaus.

On New Year's Day 1879, Joachim and Brahms introduced the new concerto in the same hall where, twenty years earlier, Brahms's First Piano Concerto had met with brutal rejection. Joachim had proposed a program beginning with Beethoven's Violin Concerto and closing with Brahms's, with songs, two movements of Bach's C-major unaccompanied Sonata, and an overture of his own in between. Brahms demurred: "Beethoven shouldn't come before mine—of course only because both are in D major. Perhaps the other way around—but it's a lot of D major—and not much else on the program," but in the event, Joachim's plan prevailed.

Brahms had not written a concerto since the debacle with the Piano Concerto in 1859. Since then, however, he had become a great eminence, and anticipation was keen, the more so because there were so few significant violin concertos; received opinion, indeed, had it that there were just two, Beethoven's and Mendelssohn's. The first movement puzzled the audience, the Adagio was greeted with some warmth, and the finale elicited real enthusiasm. (Brahms's forgetfulness about changing into dress trousers and his failure to attach his gray street pants to a pair of properly functioning suspenders also did not go unnoticed.) If not everyone took to the Concerto itself right away, there was no disagreement about the splendor of Joachim's

[10]For more on this, see the essay on Brahms's Piano Concerto No. 1.

playing, and his cadenza, which has virtually become a canonical part of the Concerto, was universally admired. In fact, after the Vienna premiere two weeks later, Brahms reported to his friend Elisabet von Herzogenberg that Joachim had played the cadenza "so magnificently that people clapped right into my coda."

On 6 March Joachim wrote from London that he had dared play the Concerto from memory for the first time, and he continued to champion it wherever he could. (England took to the work at once.) Of the early performances, the most moving for Brahms and Joachim was the one at the unveiling of the Schumann monument in Bonn on 2 May 1880: Brahms's Concerto was the only work chosen that was not by Schumann. Meanwhile, composer and violinist had continued to exchange opinions about the work well into the summer of 1879, Brahms urging Joachim to propose *ossias* (easier alternatives), Joachim responding with suggestions for where and how the orchestration might be usefully thinned out, with changes of violinistic figurations, and even with a considerable compositional emendation in the finale. Except for the last, Brahms accepted most of Joachim's proposals.[11]

In spite of Brahms's prestige at this point in his career, in spite of Joachim's ardent and effective sponsorship, the Concerto did not make its way easily, and as late as 1905, Brahms's devoted biographer, Florence May, was obliged to admit that "it would be too much to assert that it has yet entirely conquered the heart of the great public." It was thought terribly severe (a criticism often leveled at Brahms in his lifetime), and Hans von Bülow's quip about the difference between Max Bruch, who had written a concerto *for* the violin, and Brahms, who had written one *against* the violin, was widely repeated. Fritz Kreisler, who took it into his repertory about 1900 (and who would make the first recording of it—an enchanting one—in 1926), had as much to do with changing that as anyone. Brahms would be surprised to know that his Violin Concerto has come to equal Beethoven's in popularity (and that Mendelssohn's elegant essay is no longer thought of as being in that league at all).

To us it seems odd to think of playing the Beethoven and Brahms concertos on the same program. But then, the likenesses that make the idea questionable for us—as it was for Brahms—were probably the very aspects that made it attractive to Joachim. After all, he was not presenting two established masterpieces; he was presenting one classic and a new and demanding work by a composer with a reputation for being difficult. But Beethoven is present

[11]In 1979 the Library of Congress, together with Harvard University Press, published a beautiful facsimile of the manuscript, in which one can follow the fascinating process of Brahms's composing, Joachim's suggested amendments, and Brahms's acceptance or rejection of his friend's ideas. In fact, when you hear the Brahms Concerto, more than just a few of the notes are Joachim's.

in Brahms's choice of key, in the unhurried gait, in the proportions of the three movements, in the fondness for filigree in the high register, in having the soloist enter in an accompanied cadenza, and in leading the big cadenza near the end of the first movement not to a vigorous tutti but to a last unexpected and hushed reprise of a lyric theme.[12]

Brahms begins with a statement that is formal, almost neutral, and unharmonized except for the last two notes. But the sound itself is subtle—violas, cellos, and bassoons, joined in the fourth measure by two horns, with the other two horns and the basses coming in for the half-cadence. And the resumption of motion after the cadence—quietly, on a remote harmony, and with the new sound of the solo oboe—is altogether personal in tone. At the same time, it is a bow to Beethoven, inspired by the orchestra's first mysterious entrance in his Fourth Piano Concerto. So striking and so early a harmonic departure from the home key of D major will take some justifying, and thus the surprising C-major chord under the oboe melody also serves as a signal that this movement will cover much space. A moment later, the rhythm broadens—that is, the beats are still grouped by threes, but it is three half-notes rather than three quarters—and this too establishes a sense of immense breadth.

This music is full of rhythmic surprise and subtlety on every level: the aggressive theme for strings alone insists that the accents belong on the second beat, another idea dissolves order (and imposes a new order of its own) by moving in groups of five quarter-notes, the 3/4 versus 3/2 ambiguity returns again and again, and the musing and serene outcome of the cadenza is a matter not only of the *pianissimo* and *dolce* and *tranquillo* that Brahms writes in the score but also of the trancelike slow motion of the harmonies.

To return to the beginning, we have had the simple declaration of tempo and key, and the oboe's mysterious response. We quickly hear that the C-major chord does not represent an attempt at a C-major takeover: the harmony moves forward and sweeps us quickly to A, the dominant. The sturdy *forte* here and the grand measures of 3/2 also tell us that this is not just music about dreaming. More C-naturals and even B-flats confirm the implications of the earlier C-major harmony, but the true goal here is to confirm the real key, D major, and that is where the full orchestra makes a jubilant landing, playing a variant of the Concerto's opening three measures. We have experienced a lot of changes of temper in less than a minute, and this too is a signal—of the expressive richness of what Brahms plans to present.

Characteristically, Brahms goes immediately from his *fortissimo* D-major

---

[12]Like Beethoven's, if not as badly, Brahms's Concerto has suffered from a tradition of stuck-in-the-mire tempos and also inflexible ones in the first and second movements. See my essay on the Beethoven Violin Concerto.

affirmation into *piano*, *pianissimo*, then *pianississimo*. This is where the strange 5/4 groupings come in. Once again, he wakes us brusquely from dreaming. The strings give us a new theme, the one with the accents placed so incisively on the second beat. It is also a theme that smells of fiddle virtuosity, an impression that is heightened by the excited sixteenth-note scurrying for all the violins and violas. The sixteenths are the hotter for the tension created by the low string and woodwind syncopations behind them. And there is another signal: this is, after all, a concerto, and it is time for the soloist to make an entrance—not just to come in—and for brilliant solo style to assert itself. Brahms cared deeply—and consciously—about organic transitions, and so we often find him subtly anticipating some aspect of the event to come or allowing some trace of what has just passed to remain. These measures of solo style but without the soloist's actual presence are a striking example.

The soloist's entrance itself is as magnificent as any ever invented in a concerto: the violin has picked up the energy of the orchestra's sixteenth-notes and now announces its arrival in a fiery recitative redolent with the aroma of paprika—and in D *minor*.[13] It sounds at first like something entirely new, but as we listen, we hear that these bold gestures are in fact a variant of the opening theme and that the orchestra's punctuations come from the string theme with the second-beat accents.

---

[13]Ever since his early experience of giving recitals with the Hungarian violinist Ede Reményi, Brahms had been fond of spicing his music with Gypsy elements. In this instance, the tzigane solo entrance can be read as an homage to Joachim, also of Hungarian birth and the composer of a Violin Concerto in the Hungarian Style. As Bartók never tired of pointing out, "Hungarian" as used in titles such as that of Joachim's concerto, Brahms's dances, and Liszt's rhapsodies is a misnomer, the idiom in those pieces being Gypsy, not Hungarian.

Ex. 1

comes from mm.1-3

comes from mm. 78-79

In other words, Brahms gives us something that is at once arresting in its newness, yet organic and anchored in the movement's most central musical idea. Moreover, the sense of being anchored is furthered by the way two horns and the timpani glue themselves to the keynote, D. This D in fact persists quietly through thirty measures, which are followed by sixteen more that are tied to the dominant, A. In other words, these two passages with the D- and A-pedals amount to an immense magnification of measures 7 and 8 of the movement, the half-cadence with which the movement's opening phrase ends. Eight very plain measures have turned into forty-six elaborate and adventurous ones.

The adventure of these forty-six measures of the solo entrance unfolds in two phases, which, by the way, do not correspond to the thirty- and sixteen-measure divisions of the bass line—Brahms is not that mechanical. The first phase consists of the dramatic and virtuosic violin recitative with the string orchestra punctuations: this lasts twelve measures. Then comes a change of climate. The violin continues with brilliant figurations, but it withdraws from *forte* to *piano*, becoming accompanist to the orchestra. And what is the orchestra doing here? One by one, different instruments or combinations of them—first oboe, then clarinet and bassoon, flute, bassoon, and finally strings—meditate dreamily on the fragments of the principal theme, their phrases spinning slowly downward like the last leaves of autumn falling to the ground. And then, in a beautifully curved line—down, then up—the solo violin leads us back to the main theme, richly accompanied by bassoons and violas with horns and cellos. The viola figurations are also derived from the theme, and the orchestral sonority—low strings with bassoons and horns—is the one with which the movement began, though the texture is much more elaborate now and, most important, the gleaming sound of the solo violin has been added. We are back with the first theme, and now the second part of the exposition, that part involving solo together with orchestra, can begin.

Elements by now familiar are brought back, but always in a fresh presentation, and a new, rapturously lyric theme is inserted before the ethereal passage in 5/4 (*pianissimo* followed by *diminuendo*).[14] This is worked up to a brilliant climax and a grand landing on C major, a fulfillment of the hint of C major by the oboe at the very beginning of the movement. Or almost a grand landing on C major: a deceptive cadence beautifully frustrates the firm close because what Brahms needs here is something that is a beginning (or continuation) as well as a stop.

As the development gets going, we first hear the rapturous lyric melody, followed by the 5/4 theme with the solo violin adding its voice in low, juicy double-stops. Then Brahms straightens out or "normalizes" the 5/4 idea by stretching each group of five into two measures of 3/4, expanding it, that is, from five beats to six, while the solo violin decorates it with graceful anapests. But the mood changes when the violin suddenly switches to furious chains of trills, to which the orchestra adds hints of the string theme with the second-beat accents. This leads to the moment of highest temperature, a proudly athletic and exciting series of leaps of ninths across almost four octaves, and from there, with unceasing energy, the music heads for D major and the return in blazing *fortissimo* of the first theme.[15]

We have reached the recapitulation, and this too is richly inventive in

[14]Neither here nor earlier nor later does Brahms actually change the meter and notate this idea in 5/4, but that is what we hear.

[15]The twelve measures with the ninth-leaps are a moment violinists both dread and rejoice in. They are terribly difficult for the left hand because of the big shifts in position, but no less so for the ear, both because the two-note phrases are all syncopated across the beat and because the harmonies, more dissonant than anything else in this work, are not easy to hear.

its reconsiderations of familiar themes. I believe this is the last concerto in which the composer leaves a blank space in the old Classical manner for the performer to provide a cadenza. I have mentioned Joachim's cadenza; great though this is, it would be a pleasure—and also reassuring about the willingness of violinists to think freshly about masterpieces—if someone would occasionally play one of the many others that are available. I especially recommend those by Ferruccio Busoni (very dramatic, and with participation by the orchestra), Enescu, Kreisler, D. F. Tovey, Nathan Milstein (as elegant as his playing), and Joshua Bell. I have already described the miraculous exit from the cadenza. It is the ultimate transformation and fulfillment of the movement's first and principal theme.

When the renowned Pablo de Sarasate was asked whether he had yet played or intended to learn the new Brahms Concerto, he replied: "I don't deny that it is very good music, but do you think I could fall so low as to stand, violin in hand, and listen to the oboe play the only proper tune in the work?" What the oboe plays at the beginning of the Adagio is indeed one of the most beautiful melodies ever to come to Brahms. It is part of a long passage for winds alone, subtly voiced and anything other than a mere accompanied solo for the oboe, and it makes a most wonderful preparation for the entrance of the solo violin. The passage is, I am sure, inspired by the profoundly spiritual *O Gott! Welch ein Augenblick* ensemble—also in F major and with oboe solo—just before the end of *Fidelio*. Here is a characteristic detail, another instance of Brahms's subtle ties of past to present, present to future: the oboe melody is preceded by two measures of an F-major chord for bassoons and horns; the violin entrance, which is an urgently ecstatic variant of the oboe tune, is preceded by the same two measures, but this time they are given to the orchestral strings as they make their first appearance under the dissolving and receding wind-band music.

As the critic Jean-Jacques Normand charmingly put it, "Le hautbois propose, le violon dispose." It is sad that Sarasate did not relish the opportunity to transmute the oboe's chastely beautiful melody into enraptured, super-violinistic rhapsodies. A new and agitated music in minor intervenes, music that could be a study for the inspired flights—Gypsy visions again— in the slow movement of the clarinet quintet Brahms would write thirteen years later. In the recapitulation, the violin tries out the role of sensitive, imaginative accompanist to the rich-sounding orchestra; it is of course essential for violinists and recording producers to understand this change in the hierarchy. It is music that calls to mind the words of Hermann Hesse set so beautifully by Strauss in *Beim Schlafengehn*, words in which the poet describes how the unguarded soul is freed when the body sinks into sleep, "afloat, so as to live deeply and a thousandfold in the magic circles of night."

Then, for the confidently energetic finale, Brahms returns to his love of

Gypsy music, fascinatingly and inventively laid out. And the turn, just before the end, to a variant in 6/8 (heard, but not so notated), with the accents all falling on the weak beats, is an unmistakable Brahms signature.

## Concerto in A minor for Violin, Cello, and Orchestra, Opus 102

*Allegro*
*Andante*
*Vivace non troppo*

Brahms wrote his Double Concerto (as it is generally called) in the summer of 1887 at Thun, Switzerland. On 21 and 22 September that year at Baden-Baden, the violinist Joseph Joachim and the cellist Robert Hausmann tried the work with Brahms at the piano, and two days later the two string players ventured a reading with the Baden-Baden Spa Orchestra, Brahms conducting. The official first performance took place on 18 October 1887, again with Joachim, Hausmann, and the composer, this time with the Gürzenich Orchestra, Cologne.

**Solo violin and cello, two flutes, two oboes, two clarinets, two bassoons, four horns, two trumpets, timpani, and strings.**

Robert Hausmann, the cellist of the Joachim Quartet, liked to recount how Brahms, hearing him play Dvořák's Cello Concerto for him at his apartment shortly before his death, had said with some chagrin that had he known it was possible to write such a good cello concerto, he himself would have done it long ago. (See also my essay on the Dvořák, page 184.) In 1884, Hausmann had in fact urged Brahms to do just that, "or at least [to produce] a companion piece" to the E-minor Cello Sonata. Brahms did not write a concerto for Hausmann, but in 1886 he offered some consolation in the form of the F-major Sonata and being his keyboard partner at its first performance, the Double Concerto for him and Joachim coming along a year later.

To be sure, for both musical and personal reasons Joachim was the more urgent cause behind this project. Brahms and Joachim had become friends in 1853, and as a young man, Brahms had relied heavily on Joachim's advice in compositional questions. Even the middle-aged composer of the greatest of violin concertos submitted happily to his friend's violinistic expertise: more than just a few notes in the solo part of that work are Joachim's. (Albeit to a far smaller extent, Joachim also contributed some of the violinistic detail in the Double Concerto.) Not least, Joachim, over the years, had given the first performance of the Violin Concerto and about half of Brahms's chamber works.

But the long friendship was clouded in 1884 by the divorce proceedings between Joachim and his wife, the contralto Amalie Weiss. Joachim had always been madly jealous, even though his wife's behavior gave him no reason to be, and now he suspected her of having an affair with Brahms's publisher, Fritz Simrock. Brahms, sure of Amalie's innocence, sympathized with her and wrote her a long letter to say so. Amalie produced this letter in court, and it proved crucial in convincing the judge of her innocence. Joachim, hurt and enraged by what he regarded as Brahms's treachery, broke off relations. The Italians have a sensible proverb, imprinted these days on ashtrays and tea towels, that advises, "Fra moglie e marito, non mettere dito"—Don't put even one finger between husband and wife.

Brahms worked hard to repair the friendship, and the most significant of his efforts was to tender this Double Concerto as a peace offering. It is of course odd—but then this is Brahms, which means the situation could not be uncomplicated—that a composer should write a double concerto as an irenicon for a violinist but make the cello part the more prominent and rewarding. In any event, he told Joachim in a letter that he had been unable to resist composing the work, that nothing about it really mattered to him except Joachim's attitude toward it, but he urged him simply to write the two words "I decline" on a postcard if that is what he felt like doing. "If not," Brahms went on, "my questions begin. Would you like to see a sample? I am now copying the solo parts. Do you feel like getting together with Hausmann to check them for playability? Could you think about trying the piece with Hausmann and with me at the piano, and eventually with the three of us with orchestra in some town or other? I won't say out loud and specifically what I quietly hope and wish. . . ."[16]

For three and a half strained years, Brahms had been writing to Joachim and sending him scores, and Joachim had continued to play Brahms's music but refused to resume the friendship. This time, however, the poor *cocu imaginaire* succumbed. He, Hausmann, and Brahms met in Baden-Baden, where they read the work both on Clara Schumann's piano and with the spa orchestra, going on from there to plan the official premiere in Cologne. The friendship was at least functionally restored, with both men reverting to the intimate *du* and complete cordiality, but their old closeness was gone for good.

As for the concerto itself, it met with only a *succès d'estime* at its early performances, and even many members of the Brahms circle were markedly reserved in their response to what turned out to be the composer's last or-chestral work. Musicians love it, and audiences can be persuaded by the right performance. It lacks what seems to us the captivating brilliance of the Violin Concerto and the two piano concertos, although brilliance was a quality that many of Brahms's contemporaries failed to discern in those great works too. It is worth remembering that Brahms wrote the Double Concerto for two musicians who had been the twin anchors of a great string quartet for eight years: it takes a chamber-music approach to make the piece really work. To get it together is more like preparing one of Brahms's trios than another of the concertos. It is not by chance, nor only because of the extraordinary musicianship of the three performers, that the still-unsurpassed recording of the work was made by members of a trio who were profoundly attuned to one another even though they did not play together often—Pau Casals and Jacques Thibaud as the soloists, with the pianist Alfred Cortot confirming his reputation as a skilled conductor.

With its muscular, sometimes stern first movement, tender and subtly lyric Andante, and flavorful finale, the Double Concerto offers rich rewards. In his first two concertos, the D-minor for piano and the one for violin, Brahms had followed the Classical procedure of beginning with a long ex-position for the orchestra. In the Piano Concerto No. 2, he preceded this orchestral exposition with an introduction in which music for piano and music for orchestra are folded into one another, a poetic variant of the grand opening of Beethoven's Piano Concerto No. 5. In the Double Concerto, Brahms again does something on this order, but something more dramatic, both in the sense of making sharply profiled gestures and of establishing his two soloists as distinct personalities.

The orchestra begins forcefully but on an odd harmonic slant, and it stops very quickly, as though choked off in mid-phrase. The cello, directed to play "in the manner of a recitative but always in tempo" (a paradox not entirely easy to work out in performance), picks up the orchestra's last three notes and uses them as a springboard from which to launch a powerfully assertive twenty-two-measure solo.[17] The orchestra responds with a musing phrase for woodwinds, and the solo violin, when it enters, continues to spin out that dream. (Using woodwinds to set off a poetic violin entrance is a device Brahms had employed magically once before, in the Adagio of the Violin Concerto.) A triplet passage descending through two octaves awakens the cello's attention, and from here the solo becomes an increasingly excited duet.

The four bars with which the orchestra begins the Concerto pose a

---

[17]Brahms took his tempo and character direction for the cello solo from Beethoven's Ninth Sym-phony, specifically the first of the six declamatory passages for cellos and basses at the beginning of the finale, where the composer writes "Selon le caractère d'un Récitatif, mais in Tempo." Conductors mostly deal with Beethoven's paradoxical challenge by ignoring it.

conflict between the basic duple meter (the first two measures) and rhythmically dissonant triplets (the next two). This tension is an important feature throughout the work. In the double cadenza, triplets gradually give way to multiples of two, and this emergence from rhythmic dissonance into clarity is a crucial part of what gives this page its energy. Urged in by a series of thrusting chords in multiple stops, the orchestra returns, playing the same phrase with which it had begun but now firmly placed in A minor. This is our first sense of an unmistakable downbeat. Introductory gestures are over.

The exposition, firmly articulated, is based for the most part on material we have already heard—the forceful opening theme and the more yielding one that introduced the violin. When the soloists enter again, the cello once more takes the lead, this time with a lyric variant of the opening theme. The development is active indeed. It is also virtuosic (the orchestral writing is as difficult as any in Brahms), with wide-ranging arpeggiated passages and a sequence of the maddest trills since Beethoven's *Hammerklavier* Sonata. The recapitulation, this too heralded by a series of hugely sonorous seven- and eight-note chords for the two soloists, is, as always in Brahms, full of new inventions and new perspectives. One detail in this movement should get special mention, and that is Brahms's use of the two solo instruments in octaves. He is aware of its effectiveness, as any composer would be, but unlike most composers he is possessed by an almost fanatic sense of economy in such things; the octave passages therefore are few and brief and, as a result, hair-raising. Since Brahms began with a cadenza, he does not make room for an additional one near the end; this is also his strategy in the Piano Concerto No. 2.

After the storms of the Allegro, the slow movement—in D major—is gentle. A romantic horn-call and its woodwind echo, cousin to similar calls in the Piano Concerto No. 1 and the first of the *Four Songs for Women's Chorus*, Opus 17, cue a glorious, subtly limned melody. It is first played not just by the two soloists in octaves, but, much of the way, with the orchestra joining in as well. The refinement with which Brahms maneuvers the orchestra in and out of that melody is one of its loveliest features. The song itself is folklike, but later both melody and texture become more elaborate. Harmonies range widely, and an extraordinarily difficult—and quite unshowy—double cadenza brings us back to another journey through the opening melody. The orchestration is amazingly inventive and diverse throughout—there is no repetition that is not a variation—and the movement ends in a reminiscing coda that is a moment of exquisite poetry.

The finale is another in Brahms's Gypsy vein. It is also full of humor; for instance, in the violin's inclination to disrupt the cello's attempt to bring back the opening tune. Toward the end, with the tempo momentarily slowed, the music becomes surprisingly delicate and lyric, with closely worked filigree passages for the soloists, but the final page is all strength and energy.

# Frank Bridge

Frank Bridge was born in Brighton, England, on 26 February 1879 and died in Eastbourne on 10 January 1941.

## *Oration (Concerto elegiaco)* for Cello and Orchestra

*Poco lento—Allegro—Ben moderato (poco lento)—Allegro giusto—
Ben moderato mesto e tranquillo—Cadenza—Allegro—Lento—
Epilogue: Andante tranquillo*

Bridge began work on his *Concerto elegiaco* in the fall of 1929, completed the score on 25 May 1930, and was done with all revisions on 29 June that year. One of those revisions had to do with the title: to strengthen the point that he wished this composition to be understood as a protest against war, Bridge decided to call it *Oration*, with *Concerto elegiaco* to follow as subtitle in parentheses. The first performance was given in London on 16 January 1936 by Florence Hooton, with the composer conducting the BBC Symphony Orchestra.

Solo cello, two flutes and piccolo, two oboes, two clarinets, two bassoons, four horns, two trumpets, three trombones, tuba, timpani, snare drum, triangle, harp, and strings.

Frank Bridge, neglected in his lifetime, is still one of the forgotten men of twentieth-century music. Mention of his name is most likely to conjure up the brilliant *Variations on a Theme of Frank Bridge*, composed in 1937 by his former student Benjamin Britten for a concert at the Salzburg Festival. For Britten, the grown man as well as the boy who began lessons with him at thirteen, "Mr. B." was an awesome model of what an artist might be; as late as 1963, when Britten, the celebrated composer of *Peter Grimes*, the *War Requiem*, and a raft of other masterly works, was about to turn fifty, he could still write with chagrin, "I am enormously aware that I haven't yet come up to the technical standards Bridge set me." Britten did everything he could to make the world know about Frank Bridge—bringing his music and his name into the first piece he wrote for an international audience, later through performance and recordings, persuading Rostropovich and Menuhin to play Bridge's music too—but, as Anthony Payne observed in his monograph on Bridge, "the effect, ironically, was merely to remind us who Britten's teacher was."

Bridge studied at the Royal College of Music with Sir Charles Villiers Stanford, who was also professor of music at Cambridge and had a formidable reputation as a teacher. Stanford's symphonies and concertos display a livelier and more charming musical personality than one might expect from a composer so routinely placed as one of those academics in contrast to whom Elgar, Vaughan Williams, and Holst represented a vital rebirth in English music. On the other hand, he despised the new music being written on the Continent by Strauss, Debussy, and Ravel, regarding it as an ephemeral aberration eventually to be erased by a "return to sanity." For students of an exploratory turn of mind—Vaughan Williams, Holst, Bridge, Ireland, and Bliss most prominent among them—he was an oppressive master, quick to quash dangerous, non-Brahmsian impulses, and they learned little from him.

These young men found their own voices, of course—Vaughan Williams and Holst through their love for folk music, Ireland by gritting his teeth at Stanford's abuse, the rather younger Bliss by stimulation from Paris (Vaughan Williams also went to Ravel for a while). Bridge, who was to travel much the farthest of these as a composer, was the slowest to emancipate himself from Stanford's Brahms-based Weltanschauung, and his early music is definitely late Romantic in character. He quickly found a place as an outstanding and sought-after violist, playing briefly in the Joachim Quartet in its last days and for a longer period in the highly regarded English String Quartet. He was a first-rate conductor, uncompromising and considered difficult; that part of his reputation cost him the chance of appointment as the BBC Symphony's first conductor in 1930.

In 1905 W. W. Cobbett, head of a profitable business concern called Scandinavia Belting, Ltd., amateur violinist and collector of string instruments, generous and intelligent patron, and possessed by a consuming passion for chamber music, instituted an annual prize for a chamber composition in the old English "phantasy" style.[1] What Cobbett had in mind was music outside the multi-movement sonata tradition, which had come to represent *the* respectable way to compose; he wanted music akin to the Elizabethan viol "fancies" and Purcell's string fantasias, single movements but with many sections in contrasting rhythms and tempos. It makes me think of Verdi's "Torniamo all'antico; sarà un progresso." Bridge, who had submitted a Phantasie String Quartet in 1905, won the Cobbett Prize the following year with his Phantasie Piano Trio. The new formal challenge of the Cobbett phantasies was stimulating and liberating to Bridge, and the arch form he devised for his Cobbett entries—a design one can represent schematically in its simplest form as ABCBA—was one he came back to again and again. We shall encounter it in *Oration*.

The high points of the first large chapter of Bridge's career, a chapter filled with fresh and poetic music, are *The Sea* (1911), a resplendent four-movement suite about which the ten-year-old Britten said it had "knocked [him] sideways" when he heard the composer conduct it in 1924; the tone poem *Summer* (1914); and the Cello Sonata (1917), of which Rostropovich and Britten made a superb recording. But the Piano Sonata (1924) gave notice that Bridge had left that still-comfortable world: this is music in some ways more compacted than any he had written before, and certainly in a more complex harmonic language. He was a pacifist (something else he passed on to Britten), and the horrors of 1914–1918 had changed him.

In the years that followed, Bridge took further steps in the direction defined by the Piano Sonata with four of the finest—and least-known—pieces of chamber music written in the twentieth century: the Third and Fourth string quartets (1926 and 1937), the Piano Trio No. 2 (1929), and the Violin Sonata (1932). In his outstanding book *The English Musical Renaissance*, Peter J. Pirie places Bridge's musical language of the 1920s and beyond as akin especially to the earlier music of Alban Berg, specifically the works from the String Quartet, Opus 3 (1910), to *Wozzeck* (1922), communications of blistering intensity in a highly chromatic, often highly dissonant idiom.[2]

*Oration* is one of two works for solo instrument and orchestra that Bridge wrote in quick succession; the other is *Phantasm for Piano and Orchestra* (1931). By then, Bridge existed in near-total obscurity. The English musical climate was implacably hostile to anything that smacked of modernism, particularly Viennese-tinged chromatic modernism; even responses to Mahler

---

[1]Aside from being godfather to some fine pieces inspired over the years by his competition, Cobbett is gratefully remembered as editor and part-author of the *Cyclopaedia of Chamber Music*, a reference work almost as entertaining as it is informative. Cobbett's little postscripts when he disagrees with his distinguished contributors are especially delightful.

[2]Bridge warmly encouraged Britten's ultimately unfulfilled desire to study with Berg.

were obtuse and often out-and-out vicious. Moreover, Bridge's pacifism continued to earn him a lot of resentment; later, having been the teacher of the quasi-modernist, pacifist, *and* homosexual Britten was another demerit.

As Anthony Payne suggests, Bridge's life span was unhappily timed. When, after World War II, there grew up in Britain a generation of composers suited by temperament, training, and experience to be Bridge's disciples, Bridge was dead, his reputation eclipsed, his very name hardly known to most musicians. It is symptomatic that he is barely mentioned in such books as Eric Blom's *Music in England* (1942) and Humphrey Searle and Robert Layton's *Twentieth Century Composers: Britain, Scandinavia and the Netherlands* (1972), and is passed over without a word in W. J. Turner's *English Music* (1941); on the other hand, the fifth edition (1954) of *Grove's Dictionary of Music and Musicians* has an informative and sympathetic entry by Edwin Evans, a cosmopolitan Englishman who had served as president of the International Society for Contemporary Music in the late 1930s. Evans also found a few friendly words for Bridge in A. L. Bacharach's *A Musical Companion* (1934). The 1970s brought the first, slight stirrings of a Bridge revival; one of the most significant markers in that revival was the beautiful recording of *Oration* in 1987 by Steven Isserlis with Richard Hickox and the City of London Sinfonia.[3]

It took Bridge nearly six years to get a performance for *Oration*. His first choice of soloist was Felix Salmond, who had given the first performance of Elgar's Cello Concerto and had played the Bridge Sonata. After much hesitation and even exploration of a premiere with the Chicago Symphony, Salmond turned the piece down, as did Guilhermina Suggia, renowned almost as much for having been the lover of Casals (even calling herself Suggia-Casals) and the subject of a powerful portrait by Augustus John as for her dramatic style as a cellist. Lauri Kennedy, an Australian musician who had settled in London as first cello of the BBC Symphony, agreed to play *Oration* in 1931, but withdrew at the last moment when the work was already in rehearsal. At this point, Bridge, who was in any event becoming more and more discouraged by the lack of sympathy for his music, gave up. Three years later, the young cellist in a performance of his Piano Trio No. 2 struck him as a musician who understood what he was about; he approached Florence Hooton with *Oration*, and so it came about that she had the honor of introducing the work. There was only one other performance of *Oration* in Bridge's lifetime—also in 1936 and also with Hooton, this time with Adrian Boult conducting. The score of *Oration* was not published until 1979!

[3]Inspired by the Isserlis recording, the principal cellist of one of the best orchestras in the United States wanted to play *Oration* at his annual concerto outing. The orchestra's music director was not interested, but an attempt was made to have a European guest conductor program the piece. When approached, the conductor replied, "I do not conduct music by third-rate American composers."

Peter J. Pirie described Bridge as a man "rewarded [at the end] with a unique vision, the vision of one who looked, like Blake, not with but through the eyes." The eloquent *Oration* is one of Frank Bridge's Blakean visions. It was not his first "war requiem": In 1915, he had written a *Lament for Strings*, which was a *tombeau* for a nine-year-old girl named Catherine who was drowned when the *Lusitania* was torpedoed, and his Piano Sonata was dedicated to the memory of Ernest Farrar, a promising composer who was killed in action a few weeks before the Armistice.

*Oration* is an arch:

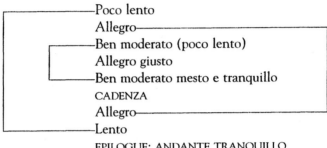

Poco lento
Allegro
Ben moderato (poco lento)
Allegro giusto
Ben moderato mesto e tranquillo
CADENZA
Allegro
Lento
EPILOGUE: ANDANTE TRANQUILLO

More precisely, it is an ABCDCBA arch with two extra components— the Cadenza (after the second C) and the Epilogue, both of which I have given in small capital letters in the diagram—thus ABCDC^BA^. Also, Bridge's realization of this design is by no means mechanical, and not only because of the extra sections: the second Allegro is distinctly shorter than the first, and the second Ben moderato is very much shorter than the first.

The music begins with the sound of low strings set on a timpani roll. Flutes and clarinets play soft chords, each one of which is in itself consonant, but whose sequence suggests dissonance. Their effect is that of a distant, transfigured fanfare. The solo cello enters with a cry, which devolves into an urgent recitation. Chords flutter down, evoking the descent of a wounded bird, and then this Introduction arrives at its destination, a solemn cortege in the manner of one of Mahler's funeral marches.

The cello keens its grief in the tumultuous Allegro; again, its music is like a vocal declamation. Constantly, we are reminded that this is an oration in music. An oboe solo emerges to engage in dialogue with the cello. Then the tempo slows for the third section, Ben moderato (poco lento). Here is where Bridge is closest to Berg. Once again, the music is that of a cortege, the cello adding an obbligato of agitated commentary.

The central section of *Oration* (Allegro giusto) is a scherzo, but a grim sort of jest indeed, music for the Horsemen of the Apocalypse. The march element is very present, painfully present. Fanfares cut through the texture;

the cello hardly dares speak; an unyielding pedal point glues everything to the ground as in a nightmare. Two years after *Oration*, the cinema brought the visual counterpart of this scene: William Cameron Menzies's shattering sequences in *Cavalcade* of wave after wave of World War I soldiers moving into hailstorms of bullets.

When the third section (Ben moderato) returns, it is a ghost of its original self: this time Bridge asks that it be "mesto e tranquillo," mournful and calm. The flute, followed by the oboe, puts a spiky counterpoint to the cello line. The Cadenza is dramatic, not brilliant. From it emerges the last Allegro. It too is now saturated in march music, ruthless music of trumpets and drums, of cannons. For a long time the solo cello is silenced, as decency and truth are silenced by war. When the solo returns, its music is very slow, and slow music finally gives way to total stillness. After a pause, horn and a luminously clear harp begin the Epilogue. High violins with distant remnants in horns and woodwinds of march rhythms and the harmonic jolts of the introduction lead the music to its close. The last sound is that of a radiant D-major triad, a reminder of at least the possibility of a world better than the one the kings and emperors and statesmen had made in 1914.

Payne writes of *Oration* that "while appearing to be public in its rhetoric and sense of solemn celebration, it belongs in a deeper sense to a private world, and the opposition of cello—that most speaking and, at times, inward of instruments—and orchestra perfectly embodies this concept. . . . It is by implication a passionate indictment." As such, it is a painful work to come to terms with, much as Berg's prophetic *Three Pieces for Orchestra* (written on the eve of the 1914 war), Hartmann's *Concerto funebre*, and Britten's Violin Concerto are painful, and more so than Britten's not-so-raw *War Requiem*. Listening many times to *Oration* made me think of Elgar's Symphony No. 2 and its rejection by the English public in 1911. A politely eloquent response to the death of King Edward VII would have been welcomed; Elgar's pitiless exposure of vulnerability and grief was an outrage. Some music is, like some of life, almost too much to bear. The great cry of *Oration* is an example.

# Benjamin Britten

Edward Benjamin Britten was born at Lowestoft, Suffolk, England on Saint Cecilia's Day, 22 November 1913, and died at Aldeburgh Suffolk, on 4 December 1976. On 12 June 1976 he had been created Lord Britten of Aldeburgh in the Queen's Birthday Honours, the first musician to be elevated to the peerage. Many members of the musical community felt that this distinction was rather devalued when the composer of *Jesus Christ Superstar* and *Phantom of the Opera* was similarly made a life peer in the New Year's Honours of 1997.

### Concerto for Violin and Orchestra, Opus 15

*Moderato con moto*
*Vivace*
*Passacaglia*

B ritten began his Violin Concerto in November 1938; in a letter dated 29 September 1939, he referred to it as "just completed." The first performance was given on 28 March 1940 by Antonio Brosa, with John Barbirolli conducting the New York Philharmonic-Symphony. Britten twice revised the score, in 1950 and again in 1958, one of his principal objectives being to prune some of the virtuoso luxuriance he had admitted into the score at Brosa's urging. (When Britten heard Brosa play the Tchaikovsky Concerto in London in 1935, he had noted in his diary that while much of the performance was "marvellous" and "the slow movement . . . a miracle of beauty . . . excessive virtuosity & speed robbed the music of something in places.") Britten dedicated the Concerto to Henry Boys, teacher, critic, old friend, and, after the war, one of Britten's musical associates in the English Opera Group.

**Solo violin, three flutes (second and third doubling piccolo), two oboes (second doubling English horn), two clarinets, two bassoons, four horns, three trumpets, three trombones, tuba, timpani, glockenspiel, triangle, snare drum, tenor drum, bass drum, cymbals, harp, and strings.**

What an amazing explosion of violin concertos—masterpieces, nearly all of them—there was in the 1930s! It began with Stravinsky's in 1931, after which came Szymanowski's No. 2 in 1933, the Berg, the Prokofiev No. 2, and the Sessions in 1935, the Schoenberg in 1936, the Bartók No. 2 and the Bloch in 1938, and the Barber, the Britten, the Hindemith, Piston's No. 1, the Walton, and Hartmann's *Concerto funebre*, all in 1939. Of the fourteen, six were written by Europeans who lived or later came to live in North America, at least for a time. Britten was one of those, and it was in St. Jovite, Quebec, that he finished his Violin Concerto just as, to his deep despair, war engulfed Europe.

Britten had come to the United States in 1939. "A discouraged young composer—muddled, fed-up, and looking for work, longing to be used"— that is how he described himself later. Under the guidance of Frank Bridge, a fascinating maverick among English composers, he had acquired a superlative technique to support his astounding gifts of invention and ear. He had also become a superb pianist. In 1934 he heard a broadcast of Alban Berg's opera *Wozzeck* and knew at once that he wanted to study with Berg, a plan encouraged by Bridge; however, in a perfect exemplification of British insularity, Sir Hugh Allen, director of the Royal College of Music, where Britten was a student, advised his parents not to permit a move that could only lead to musical corruption.

In his twenties, Britten began to attract attention with his scores for the documentary films *Night Mail* and *Coal Face*, whose verse scripts were by W. H. Auden; the cantata *Our Hunting Fathers*, another Auden collaboration and one that infuriated some of its hunting audience at the Norwich Festival; the *Variations on a Theme of Frank Bridge*, written for the Boyd Neel Orchestra to take to the last pre-Anschluss Salzburg Festival in 1937; and the Piano Concerto, in which he was soloist in the 1938 Promenade Concerts. Critics at home, however, were generally hostile to anyone outside the English pastoral tradition. The foreign influences on Britten's music—notably Mahler and Shostakovich—did not help his position. Neither did his brilliance: "Too clever by half" was the consensus.

Britten's loyalty to left-wing causes, his homosexuality, and his ties to such openly openly homosexual writers as Auden and Isherwood also made him a suspect figure. His discouragement was political as well as musical. The appeasement policies of successive Tory governments vis-à-vis Hitler and Mussolini enraged and depressed him. When Auden and Isherwood moved to the United States in January 1939, Britten, feeling politically as well as artistically out of place in England, made arrangements to follow suit. He took two unfinished scores, the Rimbaud song cycle *Les Illuminations* and the Violin Concerto. Britten's companion on the journey—and for life, as it turned out—was the tenor Peter Pears, whom he had met three years before when they had given a benefit recital for the Republican side in the Spanish Civil War.

That tragic conflict, in which 600,000 died, has a bearing on the Violin Concerto. The Republicans were defeated by General Franco, with Fascist aid, in March 1939. (The British government, to Britten's disgust, had recognized the Franco government a month before.) Britten had friends among the British volunteers who went to fight on the Republican side, and his diaries and letters from that time reflect constant preoccupation with and despair over the war. In April 1936, shortly before the outbreak of hostilities, Britten had been to Barcelona with the Spanish violinist Antonio Brosa, another musician in the Frank Bridge circle, to play his own Suite for Violin and Piano at the International Society for Contemporary Music Festival. In Barcelona Britten had heard Louis Krasner and Hermann Scherchen (whose son Wulff was a sometime-lover of Britten's around this time) give the first performance of the Berg Violin Concerto, a work he was, not long after, able to hear again on a BBC broadcast. It made an immense impression and, specifically, it provided a model for the idea of violin-concerto-as-requiem. Britten's grippingly eloquent work became a *concerto funebre*, a "war requiem," closely related to the *Sinfonia da Requiem* that followed it in 1940.

It was to Brosa that Britten decided to entrust the first performance and the editing of his Violin Concerto.[1] After approaches to Serge Koussevitzky in Boston and Eugene Goossens in Cincinnati had led nowhere, the English

[1]Brosa, who also gave the premiere of Roberto Gerhard's beautiful Violin Concerto and the first performance in England of the Schoenberg Concerto, was a doughty champion of new music both as a soloist and as quartet leader; he was also a formidable virtuoso. Reports of the premiere of Britten's Concerto, which Heifetz had pronounced unplayable, all stress the brilliance of Brosa's performance. Unfortunately, he made hardly any recordings, and none of major pieces, but you can hear him play parts of the Beethoven and Tchaikovsky concertos in Elisabeth Bergner's 1936 film *Dreaming Lips* (with Raymond Massey as the arm-synching violinist).

piano duo of Ethel Bartlett and Rae Robertson, for whom Britten would compose his Introduction and Rondo alla Burlesca in 1941, provided the connection to Barbirolli, then conductor of the New York Philharmonic-Symphony, which led to the premiere with that orchestra. When that occasion arrived, the Concerto, cushioned between Rossini's *Semiramide* Overture and the Beethoven Fifth, was warmly received.

Writing to Ralph Hawkes, his publisher, Britten said: "So far it is without question my best piece. It's rather serious, I'm afraid—but it's got some tunes in it!" The concerto is in three movements, but, as in Prokofiev's Violin Concerto No. 1, which impressed Britten when Szigeti and Beecham played it in London in 1935, and in Walton's Viola Concerto, which had already taken on something of the status of an English classic, the design is the familiar fast-slow-fast plan turned inside out. There is no actual slow movement, but an extremely quick and virtuosic scherzo is bracketed by two movements in varying tempos that range from fairly slow to fairly fast.

Brosa attested that the first music in the Violin Concerto—the quiet five-note timpani figure with cymbal punctuation—is in a specifically Spanish rhythm. Britten sets this figure for drums and cymbal. Its third statement releases a series of sighs in the orchestra, and, while the Spanish figure continues, more elaborately scored now, the solo violin enters with a long paragraph of lyric melody. A striking feature of that melody is the way it sways back and forth between major and minor, and this conflict will be an issue throughout the Concerto. (The major-minor question is central in the work of three composers whose music Britten loved most intensely: Mozart, Schubert, and Mahler.) After the orchestral winds extend and vary this melody, the violin in percussive triple-stops and backed by timpani introduces another Spanish dance rhythm. This passage opens up into a march that you had best enjoy now, for it will not return. After a brief and agitated development, Britten makes a poignant transition into the recapitulation: the solo violin plays rhapsodic figurations against a background of slow chords for just a few strings, with woodwinds recalling fragments of the march and muffled drums dropping in a single sinister reminder of the Spanish dance rhythm.

Britten has saved the harp for this moment of homecoming, and for some time the mysterious blur of its low glissandos marks the beginning of each of its measures. Britten's orchestral imagination is amazing, and this early work by the future composer of scores as uninhibitedly colorful as *The Prince of the Pagodas* or as austere as the Symphony for Cello and Orchestra shows that the mastery was there from the beginning. The recapitulation also marks the arrival at the Concerto's true harmonic home, D, which at this moment is a luminous D major. The melody, *espressivo* but *pianissimo*, is sung by the orchestral violins and violas, while the solo violin, basses, bass drum, and harp fiercely add the Spanish figure that began the movement. Contin-

uing the reversal of roles, the solo violin extends the melody. Slowly, with
one or another of the Spanish rhythms inescapably present, this impassioned
elegy sinks into silence.

From this silence, the sardonic scherzo springs into life. The violin slash-
es percussive chords *con tutta forza* against swirling figures and trills in the
orchestra. But all this is preparation and upbeat, and the theme proper, a
melody that describes a large curve up and down across two octaves, is finally
introduced by the soloist. Contrast comes in the form of a violin tune with
a strong near-Eastern tinge. Then we hear what in the matter of sheer color
is the most amazing music in the Concerto: while muted strings play tremolando, the scherzo theme is transformed into a solo for the tuba with two
piccolos dancing a giddy round in the stratosphere. Eventually the orchestra
proposes a return to the near-Eastern tune. But the wheels spin frantically in
place, and when the orchestra stops, the soloist continues the crazed gyra-
tions.

This is in fact the beginning of a cadenza, which is also the bridge to
the finale. The cadenza begins by bringing back music we already know, the
Spanish figures and rhythms as well as the lyric melody of the first movement,
and it ends by adumbrating music we are about to get to know, the passacaglia
theme of the finale. This movement, *in memoriam* the British volunteers who
fell in Spain, is the first of Britten's many passacaglias, a set of variations over
a reiterated bass, a form he would use tellingly throughout his life. Its use
calls to mind another of Britten's passionate and formative musical loves, his
great seventeenth-century predecessor, Henry Purcell.

It is for this moment that Britten has saved the trombones, who quietly
cut across the end of the cadenza with the passacaglia theme (Andante
lento). This theme consists of a scale ascending and descending in alternating
whole- and half-steps, that pattern symbolizing another aspect of the major-
minor ambivalence. Britten begins with a series of overlapped statements of
this scale. Then come nine variations, several of which also encompass more
than one statement of the theme: 1. (con moto) "speaking" violin figurations
over tremolando strings; 2. (pesante) the theme in the winds with more
elaborate violin commentary, the whole anchored to a pedal C; 3. (tranquillo) oboe solo, orchestra alone; 4. (con moto) a rhythmically free violin
melody over a clear 3/4 accompaniment; 5. inversion of the theme by the
violin, which then picks up the decorative scales begun by the woodwinds,
all on a pedal F; 6. a march over a pedal C; 7. (molto animato) a pedal E,
the theme in the bassoon, and swift, featherweight violin figurations; 8. (lar-
gamente) a grand statement for orchestra alone.

The final variation (lento e solenne) is the keening lament toward
which the whole Concerto has led. I think of Thomas Mann's phrase about
"that speaking unspeakingness that is given to music alone." Various orchestral groups play sequences of grave chords, and over these the violin sings

out its anguish. At the close, Britten achieves extraordinary intensity by having the violin climb to great altitudes, but on the lowest string. The orchestra, *pianissimo*, comes to rest on an empty D-chord, one without either the F-sharp or the F-natural that would fix major or minor. It is on just those two notes that the violin sobs its final trill.

## Symphony for Cello and Orchestra, Opus 68

*Allegro maestoso*
*Presto inquieto*
*Adagio*
*Passacaglia: Andante allegro*

Britten completed the Symphony for Cello and Orchestra on 3 May 1963 and conducted the Moscow Philharmonic in the first performance at the Great Hall of the Moscow Conservatory on 12 March 1964. The soloist was Mstislav Rostropovich, to whom the work is dedicated.

**Solo cello, two flutes (second doubling piccolo), two oboes, two clarinets (second doubling bass clarinet), bassoon, contrabassoon, two horns, two trumpets, trombone, tuba, timpani, bass drum, gong, cymbals, tenor drum, side drum, tambourine, tam-tam, slapstick, vibraphone, and strings.**

The composer Nicolas Nabokov, cousin of the famous Vladimir, recounts watching Stravinsky work on the score of *Orpheus* and constantly asking George Balanchine exactly how many seconds of music would be needed to cover a dancer's traversal of the stage. The more precise the stipulation, the happier he was. Benjamin Britten was that sort of composer too, one who reveled in prescriptions, limitations (no one ever wrote better music for amateurs and children), and specific challenges. Much of his music was written with a specific interpreter in mind. Most famous are the more than thirty works, chiefly songs and operatic roles, for that stupendous artist Peter Pears, who was Britten's lover, most essential friend, and closest professional associate for forty years. Next in importance and sheer quantity comes the astonishing series of compositions written for Mstislav Rostropovich and his wife, Galina Vishnevskaya.

Rostropovich first visited England and the United States in 1956. Then twenty-nine, he was not yet the electrifying superstar he soon became; surprising as this now sounds, he was thought a bit on the dry side, though musicians were quick to recognize that his technical command and his musical understanding were truly uncommon. Glière, Khachaturian, Miaskovsky, and Prokofiev had already composed works for him, and in 1959 Dmitri Shostakovich made important contributions to the cello repertory with two concertos for Rostropovich. Dutilleux, Foss, Lutosławski, Piston, and Prokofiev are among the many composers who have written for him since.

In September 1960, Rostropovich introduced the Concerto No. 1 by Shostakovich in London, the composer going along on the trip. Britten had known and admired Shostakovich's music since 1936, when he heard a concert performance of *Lady Macbeth of Mtsensk* and noted in his diary that he found it "tremendous." He was delighted when Shostakovich invited him to share his box at the Royal Festival Hall, and not less so when the ebullient cellist, to whom he was introduced by Shostakovich afterward, immediately asked that he write something for him. They discussed the project the following morning, and Britten left Rostropovich's hotel having agreed to compose a sonata. This was accomplished by January 1961 and, with Britten at the piano, the work was introduced at the Aldeburgh Festival in July. This completed an interesting chain of events in that Shostakovich had decided to write his concerto upon hearing Rostropovich play the Symphony-Concerto that Prokofiev had decided to write upon hearing the cellist play the sonata that Miaskovsky had composed for him.

By then Britten, Pears, Rostropovich, and Vishnevskaya were fast friends, increasingly adept at getting along in a makeshift patois they called Aldeburgh Deutsch, and the Cello Sonata which quickly became an indispensable repertory item, was just the beginning of their various musical collaborations. There followed the *War Requiem* (1961), with its soprano part for Vishnevskaya, but for whose premiere the Soviet government would not let her travel to England; the Symphony for Cello and Orchestra (1963), which is Britten's finest composition for orchestra; three Suites for Solo Cello (1964, 1967, 1971); and *The Poet's Echo*, a Pushkin song cycle for Vishnevskaya to sing and Rostropovich to play at the piano (1965).[2]

---

[2]The story of how the cello suites came to be written is charming and characteristic. In 1964 Britten and Pears took Rostropovich to visit Princess Mary, the Princess Royal, daughter of King George V, aunt to Queen Elizabeth II, and one of the few musical members of the British royal family. Rostropovich, to whom princesses were fairy-tale creatures, thought that the Princess Royal ought to be approached with a certain flamboyance, which he demonstrated by leaping from Britten's car, pirouetting in the air, and landing on his knees. Britten and the exceedingly proper Pears became worried that Rostropovich might really make such a scandalous entrance at Harewood House, the princess's residence, and finally Britten offered any price at all if Rostropovich would promise to behave. Rostropovich at once wrote a contract on the menu of the restaurant where they had stopped for lunch: "I, Benjamin Britten, promise to write six major works for cello in recompense for which Slava Rostropovich will agree not to perform his pirouette in front of Princess Mary." Britten happily signed, though he died before completely fulfilling the agreement.

Rostropovich and Vishnevskaya were able to record "their" pieces with Britten at the piano for the Cello Sonata and on the podium for the *War Requiem* and the Cello Symphony; Rostropovich and Britten also made wonderful recordings of Haydn, Schumann, Debussy, and Britten's teacher, Frank Bridge. Both Russians participated more than once in the Britten-Pears Aldeburgh Festival. Moreover, the last performances of the *War Requiem* Pears sang were memorable ones with the National Symphony under Rostropovich (and again with Vishnevskaya) in Washington and New York, after Britten's death.

By 1963, the year of the Cello Symphony, Britten was an exceedingly famous man, even though the Gold Medal of the Royal Philharmonic Society, the Order of Merit, and the peerage were yet to come. Twice in his life, public awareness of him and his work had advanced explosively. The first time was in 1945 when *Peter Grimes* was produced for the postwar reopening of the Sadler's Wells Theatre in London. The triumph of that opera not only marked the confirmation of a prodigious talent, but also gave grounds for hope that England had produced a composer of international stature, something it had not done since the death of Henry Purcell 250 years before. The second time followed the premiere in Coventry Cathedral in 1962 of the *War Requiem*. Its impact was still greater.

Britten, approaching fifty, had become, since *Grimes,* the composer of several more operas, including *The Rape of Lucretia, Albert Herring, Billy Budd, Gloriana, The Turn of the Screw,* and *A Midsummer Night's Dream;* of the *Spring Symphony, Saint Nicolas,* and *Noye's Fludde;* and of song cycles on texts by Donne, Hardy, and Hölderlin. He had become an artist whose every new utterance was awaited with the most lively interest and the highest expectations. The *War Requiem,* moreover, was tied to a pair of events—the destruction of Coventry Cathedral in an air raid in 1940 and its reconsecration twenty-one years later—that were heavily freighted with history and emotion. The work itself was a statement both weighty and poignant on a subject of piercingly urgent concern to much of humankind. To remind, 1961 was the year of the Bay of Pigs and of the construction of the Berlin Wall, and in that year and the next, U.S. involvement in Vietnam escalated frighteningly.

Britten himself was uneasy with the immense success of the *War Requiem,* the flood of performances worldwide, the sale of 200,000 record albums in less than half a year, the near-universal acclaim. His biographer Michael Kennedy suggests that perhaps he thought of some words of Gustav Holst: "Every artist ought to pray that he may not be a 'success.' Woe to you when all men speak well of you." Certain it is that in November 1963, a few days before his fiftieth birthday, Britten wrote: "People sometimes seem to think that with a number of works now lying behind, one must be bursting with confidence. It is not so at all. I haven't yet achieved the simplicity I should like to in my music, and am enormously aware that I haven't yet come up to the technical standards Bridge set me.[3]

In any event, Britten never again wrote a piece so "public" as the *War Requiem*, and the best of the works that followed—the Cello Symphony, the three church parables (*Curlew River*, *The Burning Fiery Furnace*, *The Prodigal Son*), the Blake and Pushkin cycles, the cello suites, the last two canticles (*Journey of the Magi*, *The Death of Saint Narcissus*), *Death in Venice*, *Phaedra*, the String Quartet No. 3—all attest to his quest for simplicity, for a more austere, pared-down manner. The Cello Symphony represents, if not quite a U-turn (as one might say about Sibelius's Third Symphony, for example), surely the first veering off into the new direction.

That clear-headed, no-nonsense musician Pierre Monteux once said of Debussy's *Pelléas et Mélisande* that it "was never meant to be a success." Doubtless one goes too far in applying Monteux's shrewd witticism to Britten's Cello Symphony; nonetheless, it is a work that, for all its fearsome demands on the soloist's virtuosity and its generously sonorous closing pages, disdains to make an obvious appeal for public approval. I recall Rostropovich's saying some thirty years ago, in the course of expressing disappointment that so few orchestras asked him to play what he considered one of the most phenomenal works in the entire cello repertory, that the time for this complex and subtle work had not yet come, and I see him quoted to the same effect in Alan Blyth's *Remembering Britten*, published in 1981. And a great work it is, this Cello Symphony.

Before one has heard a note, one has looked at the strange title: Symphony for Cello and Orchestra. A hundred years ago there were those who snorted that the Piano Concerto No. 2 of Brahms was not a concerto at all but a symphony with piano obbligato. Similar cases include Berlioz's *Harold in Italy*, with its viola-as-Byronic-hero soloist (and which its composer classified as a symphony), Vincent d'Indy's charming *Symphonie cévenole* (Symphony on a French Mountain Air) for Piano and Orchestra, and Falla's *Nights in the Gardens of Spain*.

But what did Britten have in mind? A comparison with his Piano Concerto (1938, revised 1945), Violin Concerto (1939/1950), *Diversions* for piano left-hand and orchestra (1940/1954), and *Scottish Ballad* for two pianos and orchestra (1941) helps make it clear. In all these, the solo-orchestra relationship is based on the familiar concept of a partnership between not-quite equals, the soloist(s) finally enjoying some sort of triumph over the orchestra and being carried aloft in victory. In fact, when Britten introduced his Piano Concerto at the London Proms in 1938, he wrote in his program note that he had conceived it "with the idea of exploiting various important

---

[3]One of the truly wonderful pianists of his time, Britten suffered hellish torment before each concert, and, Pears told me, could usually be coaxed onto the stage only with the help of a shot of brandy.

characteristics of the pianoforte, such as its enormous compass, its percus-sive quality, and its suitability for figuration; so that it is not by any means a Symphony with pianoforte, but rather a bravura Concerto with orchestral ac-companiment."[4] To say that you are writing "a bravura Concerto with or-chestral accompaniment" is not remarkable, but Britten's formulation about "a Symphony with pianoforte" sounds almost as though he already had the idea of a symphony for solo and orchestra at the back of his mind, the program note being a statement, as much to himself as to his readers, of "not yet."

In the Cello Symphony, the partnership is like that of cellist and pianist in a sonata, a well-written sonata of course. No one "wins." Perhaps Britten was thinking of the literal meaning of *symphony*, a sounding together. Given his practical turn of mind, I would guess that primarily he meant to simply go along with that tradition of nomenclature according to which we say *sonata* when we mean a work for one or two instruments but *trio, quartet, quintet*, and so on, all the way up to *symphony* when we refer to a similar piece for more than two players. Britten's Symphony for Cello and Orchestra, then, is closer in spirit and technique to the sonata he wrote for Rostropovich and himself than to any of his concertos.[5]

Predominantly, the mood and sound of the Symphony are dark: Yo-Yo Ma has spoken of the "claustrophobic" atmosphere of the first three move-ments. The first of these, which begins Allegro maestoso in broad 3/2 mea-sures, is the biggest; it is in fact as big an instrumental movement as Britten ever wrote. Over a soft bass drum roll, tuba and basses begin a descending scale, with the contrabassoon fleshing out the cadences with a sinuous worm figure, and against this backdrop the cello plays a rhetorical theme in double- and triple-stop chords. The tempo suddenly becomes fast, and the cello plays an intensely agitated theme which continues the descending-scale idea. In the recapitulation, cello and orchestra exchange their previous roles. The coda, expansive and intense, combines these materials. Throughout, the scor-ing is astonishing, not only for the immediate effect of its often sinister colors, but equally for the ease with which Britten solves one of the most difficult of technical problems, that of allowing the cello always to be heard while keeping the orchestral texture very much alive. Britten's Mahlerian palette, with its emphasis on extremes of high and low, thus staying out of the registers that the cello mostly inhabits, has much to do with that achievement.

[4]Another early work, the engaging and lightweight *Young Apollo* for piano, string quartet, and string orchestra (composed in 1939, subsequently withdrawn by Britten but resurrected after his death), has a solo part that is very showy indeed, but it seems not so much like a concerto as like a string orchestra piece to which an extremely assertive pianist adds masses of ornate decoration.

[5]One finds the odd sonata for large ensemble—for example, the wind sonatinas of Richard Strauss and the *Saint Michael* Sonata by Peter Maxwell Davies. In this connection it is also worth noting that Britten wrote no "normal" symphony. Both the Sinfonietta for chamber orchestra (1932) and the powerful *Sinfonia da Requiem* (1940) are unusual in layout, while the *Spring Symphony* (1949) is a song cycle for soprano, alto, tenor, chorus, boys' chorus, and orchestra.

The image the Scherzo brings to mind is the one conjured up by T. S. Eliot's line about "rats' feet over broken glass." The cello, muted and barely audible, plays six scurrying notes, three up, three down, before being stopped by the solid wall of a three-note chord for trumpets and trombone. The effect of this is the greater for the fact that these brasses, too, are muted and *pianissimo*. It takes only three notes to generate this, for the cello's second three notes are the same pattern as the first, only upside down, and the brass chord also has the same content, only played simultaneously rather than in sequence. And, very nearly, that is all there is to this ghostly, horrific music: permutations, constantly changing, of these notes set in different registers, rhythms, and colors. In the brief trio, which comes twice, the cello wails rather than scurries.

The Adagio begins as pure rhythm, on timpani alone. When the cello enters, it does so with an eloquent theme made almost entirely of thirds, the interval that dominated the Scherzo, here descending more often than not. Later, against trills and harmonics in the string orchestra, there comes a smoother theme of which we shall hear rather more. A development, with much speedy and agitated work by the cellist, leads into a recapitulation. This is interrupted after the first theme by an enormous cello cadenza in which the timpanist, on the single note G, as at the beginning of the movement, participates for a long time. This cadenza, which virtually amounts to a second development, gradually becomes tranquil and finally spills without break into the finale.

Now we discover why the recapitulation in the Adagio never reached the second theme: Britten brings it back now, played on the trumpet, *mezzoforte* but *brillante*, and sounding pleasantly Coplandish in that color, as the theme of the last movement. This finale is a passacaglia, a set of variations over a repeated bass or reiterated set of harmonies. This, part of his inheritance from his beloved Purcell, is a favorite Britten form, one we find in many of his works including the Violin Concerto (where he approaches it similarly, by way of a big cadenza), the revised version of the Piano Concerto, the String Quartet No. 2, and, most famously, *Peter Grimes*. Here the spell of darkness is at last broken. Britten gives us six variations. The fourth of these is a homage to the scherzo in Elgar's Cello Concerto, and the fifth, free and rhapsodic, leaves out the by-now familiar ground. At the last, cello and orchestra join in a sonorous and harmonious coda.

# Max Bruch

Max Karl August Bruch was born in Cologne in the Rhine Province of Prussia on 6 January 1838 and died in Friedenau, a suburb of Berlin, on 2 October 1920.

Bruch's mother, a soprano, was his first teacher; his father was a civil servant. The first musical training he received outside his home was from Heinrich Carl Breidenstein, a jurist and philosopher (a pupil of Hegel) as well as a musician. Later he worked with Ferdinand Hiller and Carl Reinecke. This all amounted to indoctrination in the conservative Mendelssohn-Schumann-Brahms faction as against the progressive Liszt-Wagner wing. At twenty, Bruch settled down to teach in Cologne, where his first opera *Scherz, List und Rache* (Jest, Cunning, and Revenge), after Goethe, was staged the same year. He had composed prodigiously since boyhood. He took up conducting and over the years held a succession of appointments in Koblenz, Sonderhausen, Liverpool (for whose Jewish community he wrote his *Kol Nidrei* for cello and orchestra), and Breslau (now Wrocław, Poland).[1]

In the 1870s, in part because of the phenomenal success of the G-minor

[1]Because of the *Kol Nidrei*, whose melody is part of the Yom Kippur liturgy, it is often but erroneously assumed that Bruch was Jewish. The Bruchs had in fact been Lutherans since 1560, when Thomas Bruch, the first of many clergymen in the family, became a convert to that new faith. In his 1988 biography of the composer, Christopher Fifield records some of the anti-Semitic remarks that the dyed-in-the-wool nationalist and conservative Bruch made as the German Empire was collapsing in 1918; I imagine this topic has given him and Wagner and other colleagues something to talk about wherever they are now. In his lifetime, Bruch owed much to Joseph Joachim and Hermann Levi, and posthumously he has been mightily indebted to violinists named Elman, Heifetz, Kogan, Menuhin, Milstein, Mintz, Oistrakh, Perlman, Zukerman, et al., not to forget Haendel, Kreisler, and Morini, whose names do not obviously signal their Jewishness. Note, however, the presence of the name of Ferdinand David and Hermann Levi in the last paragraph of this introductory note.

Violin Concerto, Bruch enjoyed some patches of prosperity and independence that allowed him to devote himself entirely to composition. In the early 1890s he was granted the titles without which no self-respecting German can go to his reward in peace: a professorship (at the Berlin Academy of Fine Arts) and a doctorate (from Cambridge, received in the distinguished company of Grieg, Saint-Saëns, and Tchaikovsky). From 1891 until his retirement in 1910, Bruch taught in Berlin. In 1893 his travels brought him to America, where he conducted his oratorio *Arminius* with the Handel and Haydn Society in Boston. His contemporaries knew him chiefly as a composer of choral music, and I hope that his vocal works have not disappeared from view for good. Certainly his oratorio *Odysseus*, the cantata *Frithjof* (much admired by Brahms and Clara Schumann, and the work that first made a reputation for Bruch when he was twenty-six), and his early opera *Loreley* merit study and the occasional revival.

As Bruch lived in comfortable retirement in his Berlin villa, the world around him changed nearly beyond recognition from the days of his sometimes uneasy friendships with Brahms, Joachim, Ferdinand David, and Hermann Levi. Although the popularity of his Violin Concerto No. 1 remained a reassuring constant, when he died at eighty-two many who read the respectful obituaries must have been astonished to learn that he had been alive until the day before.

## Concerto No. 1 in G minor for Violin and Orchestra, Opus 26

*Prelude: Allegro moderato*
*Adagio*
*Finale: Allegro energico*

Bruch's G-minor Concerto, part of whose music goes back to 1857, was completed in 1866 and first performed on 24 April that year by Otto von Königslow, with the composer conducting. Bruch substantially revised the Concerto with the help of Joseph Joachim, who reintroduced it in its present form on 5 January 1868 in Bremen, Karl Martin Rheinthaler conducting.

**Solo violin, two flutes, two oboes, two clarinets, two bassoons, four horns, two trumpets, timpani, and strings.**

Bruch comes perilously close to being a one-work composer, this G-minor Concerto being the one work. In his day, however, he was a most substantial figure on the musical landscape, an artist who consistently won respect for his command of craft and affection for his devotion to euphony.

Assessing the four most famous German violin concertos—the Beethoven, the Mendelssohn, the Bruch G-minor, and the Brahms—Joseph Joachim, who was intimately connected with all four, called Bruch's "the richest, the most seductive." If you take "richest" to refer to immediate sensuous impressions, Joachim is exactly on target, and it takes less than a minute to find that out. Bruch had originally called the first movement *Introduzione-Fantasia*, but changed the title to the more prosaic *Vorspiel* (Prelude). Orchestral flourishes alternate with solo flourishes: it is a dreamy variant of the opening of Beethoven's Fifth Piano Concerto. Bruch finds—or makes—room for two expansive and memorable melodies. It could be a "real" first movement up to the point where a development seems due. Then Bruch brings back his opening chords and flourishes, using them this time to prepare the soft sinking into the Adagio. This design caused him considerable concern, and he asked Joachim whether he ought not to call the whole work a Fantasy rather than a Concerto. "The designation 'concerto' is completely apt," replied the Elder Statesman. "Indeed, the second and third movements are too fully developed for a Fantasy. The separate sections of the work cohere in a lovely relationship, and yet—and this is the most important thing—there is sufficient contrast."[2]

It is in the Adagio that the soul of this perennially fresh and touching Concerto resides, lyric rapture being heightened by Bruch's artfully cultivated way with form, proportion, and sequence. As for the crackling, Gypsy-tinged finale, having paid no attention to the date of composition, I had always assumed that Bruch had borrowed a notion or two from his slightly older colleague Johannes Brahms. It turns out that Bruch got there first and, always inclined to be jealous of Brahms, he would have found my mistake very annoying.

[2]Christopher Fifield, *Max Bruch: His Life and Works* (New York: George Bragiller, 1988).

## Fantasy for Violin with Orchestra and Harp, with Free Use of Scottish Folk Melodies, Opus 46

> *Prelude: Grave—Adagio cantabile*
> *Allegro*
> *Andante sostenuto*
> *Finale: Allegro guerriero*

Bruch composed his *Scottish* Fantasy, as it is more handily known, in the winter of 1879–1880. Bruch himself referred to it as a concerto on several occasions, and in his lifetime it was sometimes listed that way on concert programs. The work was first played in Liverpool on 22 February 1881 by Joseph Joachim—"carelessly, with no modesty, very nervously, and with altogether insufficient technique," according to Bruch, who conducted. The score is dedicated to Joachim's great rival, Pablo de Sarasate.

**Solo violin, two flutes, two oboes, two clarinets, two bassoons, four horns, two trumpets, three trombones, tuba, timpani, bass drum, cymbals, harp, and strings.**

As I note in my essay on his Violin Concerto No. 1, Bruch comes perilously close to being a one-work composer; the other piece that has most nearly stayed consistently before the public is his *Kol Nidrei* for cello and orchestra. (It is a favorite of violinists, too.) A few other musicians—Hans Pfitzner and Kurt Masur prominent among them—have gone to bat on behalf of Bruch's Other Works, among which the most serious contender for a place in the repertory has been the *Scottish* Fantasy. Jascha Heifetz's 1947 recording, in spite of his damaging and unnecessary cuts, accomplished much in winning friends for this beguiling composition.

Interest in folk music and its use in concert music were widespread in the second half of the nineteenth century—for some composers in central Europe and Russia this issue virtually became a fetish—and Bruch's oeuvre reaches into the music of many cultures. When the *Scottish* Fantasy was new, Bruch was subjected to some criticism for "getting the tunes wrong," but as William Foster Apthorp, the Boston Symphony's first program annotator, pointed out in 1896, "it is important to remember one item in [the] title: the 'free use' of Scotch songs."[3] There is nothing of the professional folklorist's technique in Bruch's approach. He loved Scottish songs, and as far back as 1864 he had made arrangements of twelve (including two that turn up again in the Fantasy). They were, for him, chiefly the stuff of atmosphere and romance—in this respect the Fantasy is a direct descendant of Mendelssohn's *Hebrides* Overture and *Scotch* Symphony—and the prominent role of the harp is part of that atmosphere, part of a desire to convey a sense of something bardic. Surely it is also the spirit of Bruch's times that makes his Scots distillate smooth and sweet rather than smoky and untamed—more Johnnie Walker Black than Laphroaig.

What strikes one particularly about the *Scottish* Fantasy, aside from the beauty of the melodies themselves and the lucidity of form, is Bruch's cultivated sense of orchestral euphony. The voicing is rich and right—for an example, you need go no further than the opening with its combination of horns, trombones, and harp, softly accented by drums and lightly brushed cymbals—and the placement of the solo violin into the orchestral texture is uncannily skilled and graceful.

Bruch begins the Fantasy with a solemn Prelude to which the uncommon key of E-flat minor lends a special darkness. The musicologist and critic Wilhelm Altmann reported that Bruch had told him this music was intended to evoke "an old bard who contemplates a ruined castle and laments the glorious days of old." (Altmann also noted that the works of Walter Scott, already explored by Bruch in his cantata *Das Feuerkreuz*, based on *The Lady of the Lake*, helped inspire the *Scottish* Fantasy.) This melancholy opening recitative leads into the first movement proper, whose main material is the song *Auld Robb Morris*, which is given in two stanzas.

The second movement is a dance, with low strings and horns making bagpipe drones. The energetic tune is called *The Dusty Miller*, and the solo violin hangs some elegant decorations on it. When it is over, the violas suddenly remember the gentle strains of *Auld Robb Morris*. With four peremptory, bright G-major chords, the orchestra attempts to restore the jolly atmosphere of the dance; however, the soloist prefers melancholy, and he prevails. His reminiscence of *Auld Robb Morris* is in fact darker still, and through a rhapsodic flight it prepares the path into the third movement. This is slow music again, and the touching song that provides its material is called *I'm Down for Lack of Johnnie*.

The finale's tempo and character designation is *Allegro guerriero*, meaning a warlike allegro. Bruch picked up this unusual marking from Mendelssohn, who used it for the finale of his *Scotch* Symphony, though in the preface of the score only, not in the score itself. Bruch's finale is an energetic stomp,

---

[3] The "rule" that "Scotch" is for whiskey (or whisky) and that for people the proper word is "Scottish" or "Scots" is a twentieth-century invention.

based chiefly on *Scots wha hae*, the song sung by the Scots in 1314 when, 10,000 strong, they beat the tar out of 23,000 Englishmen at the battle of Bannockburn. Just before the close, in one of those wonderful, sentimental gestures that a nineteenth-century artist could bring off without inhibition, the solo violin interrupts this bare-kneed athleticism with one last nostalgic remembrance of *Auld Robb Morris*.

# Elliott Carter

Elliott Cook Carter, Jr., was born on 11 December 1908 in New York City and now lives there and in Southbury, Connecticut.

We have Mozart, Schubert, Mendelssohn, Richard Strauss, the prodigies, and we have the slow starters, such as Haydn, Wagner, and Janáček, of whose existence only specialists would be aware had they died as young as Mozart or Schubert. Elliott Carter was one of the slow ones. Nobody could have discerned the future composer in the boy whose second-grade report card marked him "Good" in music but "Excellent" for all other subjects. He was midway through his forties when he found an audience, when the first performance of his String Quartet No. 1 in 1953 compelled the attention of the music world and put abroad the idea that Carter's was a singularly original voice on the American scene.

Of course, as an upper-middle-class boy in New York, Carter "took" piano, hating Chopin, scales, and the rest of it; not until high school did he really make contact with music. The music teacher at the Horace Mann school was Clifton Furness, whose classes dealt with the three B's, but who after hours and on weekends took his bright, Beethoven-hating student to concerts of modern music as well as to meet his friend Charles Ives. Carter sometimes went as Ives's guest to the Boston Symphony's Saturday matinees at Carnegie Hall, was feverishly excited by Stravinsky's *Le Sacre du printemps*, practiced Scriabin on the piano, heard Stokowski conduct Varèse, and attended the Sunday afternoon sessions in the 14th Street loft of Katherine Ruth Heyman, mystic, theosophist, and pianist who played Scriabin, Schoenberg, Ives, and Griffes. He listened to Middle Eastern, Indian, and Balinese music, went to the Chinese opera, looked at the paintings of modernists such as Picasso and Duchamp, saw the films of Eisenstein and Pudovkin, heard

Mayakovsky recite, and went to the Moscow Opera's *Carmencita and the Soldier*.

With his father, a well-to-do lace importer, he traveled to Europe several times, buying scores and sheet music—particularly the works of Schoenberg, Berg, and Webern because Paul Rosenfeld, a critic he admired, said they were important—and also texts on theory and analysis. When it came time to go to college, he chose Harvard "because of all the advanced musical activity that was then going on [at the Boston Symphony] under Koussevitzky."

But when Carter actually got to Harvard he discovered that most of the music faculty hated contemporary music and were scandalized by Koussevitzky's fervent advocacy. Carter had hoped that someone would explain to him why Stravinsky, Schoenberg, and Bartók wrote as they did, but no such help was forthcoming; nor could anyone explain convincingly why it was useful for him to write harmony exercises in the style of Mendelssohn. Disappointed and angry, Carter decided not to major in music as an undergraduate; he did, however, return to it as a graduate student, studying for a time with Gustav Holst, who had come in as an exchange professor. As for the rest, Carter found that the one sympathetic person on the music faculty was Walter Piston, who had just returned from studying with Nadia Boulanger in Paris.

On the other hand, there was Koussevitzky; there was the experience of singing Bach in a cantata club and Stravinsky's new *Oedipus Rex* in the Glee Club with the Boston Symphony; the Boston Pops concerts, then under the direction of that remarkable Italian composer, conductor, and pianist Alfredo Casella (and a box office failure for precisely the reasons that made them appealing to Carter); the visits to the Cambridge house of the composer Henry F. Gilbert; the guest engagement of the Chicago Opera with Mary Garden in Debussy's *Pelléas et Mélisande*; the books and lectures of Alfred North Whitehead; Carter's independent reading of William Carlos Williams, Marianne Moore, Eliot, e. e. cummings, Joyce, D. H. Lawrence, and Gertrude Stein (the Harvard English department stopped at Tennyson); talk with his own contemporaries such as James Agee, Harry Levin, and Lincoln Kirstein.

After Harvard, and in emulation of Piston and Aaron Copland, Carter went to Paris to study with Boulanger, who had been a pupil of Gabriel Fauré and was a magnet to three generations of American musicians, sharpening their ear, shoring up their technique, and forming their taste. From her, at last, Carter received the technical and analytical grounding for which he had hungered. It is also true that she gave him a technique for what, by the time of the First Quartet at least, he no longer wanted to say, but it was the strong foundation he gained in his studies with her that has enabled him so confidently to work out the solutions to the problems to which his fantasy has led him. Carter undertook the move to Paris with virtually no support from home: his father was appalled by and implacably opposed to the frivolity of a career as a composer, and neither parent ever came to take an interest in Carter's work or to gather any sense of its worth.

When Carter returned to America, he wrote criticism for *Modern Music* and other periodicals; served as music director for Ballet Caravan, the first of several companies his Harvard friend Lincoln Kirstein started for George Balanchine; and joined the faculty of Saint John's College in Annapolis, where he taught mathematics and Greek as well as music. It was hard for him to find time for composition in the midst of all this, and he was already beginning to discover he was a slow writer.

In 1942 he took time off for composition exclusively and, by the end of that year, had completed his Symphony No. 1. An open and lovely American pastoral, it seems unconnected to *Le Sacre du printemps* and the other modern music that had excited Carter in the twenties, but during the Depression, he recalled later, "the musical world here had taken a new turn, towards a kind of populism which became the dominating tone of the entire musical life." His decision to write something "many people could presumably grasp and easily enjoy at a time of social emergency" was, then, an act of social consciousness more than an aesthetic choice. It was a decision he came, in retrospect, to view with some doubt. Audiences, he realized, still

> just wanted to hear Beethoven and Brahms and Mozart. . . . When it comes to modern music they aren't able to distinguish very much . . . they just know new music doesn't sound very much like Brahms, and that's about all, as far as I can see. In fact, I should have known better than to try writing works like my First Symphony and *Holiday* Overture in a deliberately restricted idiom—that is, in an effort to produce works that meant something to me as music and yet might, I hoped, be understandable to the general musical public.[1]

The irony of Carter's career is that his first work to make an immense impact, the Quartet No. 1, was one he wrote absolutely and only to please himself. At that moment, the present and the past were connected in his life. This, at last, was the music that grew directly out of his electrifying experiences in the 1920s. Elliott Carter had hatched unmistakably as Elliott Carter.

I recall, many years ago, putting on a record of a Bach aria—it was "Mein teurer Heiland" in the *Saint John Passion*—and having Carter, who was present but engaged in a conversation with someone else, look up and say, "Why, that's just like my music." He meant the intricately layered texture of Bach's aria: voice, cello obbligato, bass line, and chorale. The feature of style that has developed most richly in Carter's music is the layered sound,

---

[1]Allen Edwards, *Flawed Words and Stubborn Sounds: A Converstaion With Elliott Carter* (New York: W. W. Norton , Inc., 1971).

the effect of a conversation (or sometimes simultaneous monologues) carried on by speakers of sharply differentiated manner and tone of voice. You can hear this clearly in his Cello Sonata (1948), which begins by establishing the contrast between the rhapsodic, always just off-the-beat singing of the cello and the detached, metronomic clicks of the piano.

In later works, Carter began to turn these differences to dramatic account. He has never written an opera, but he is a composer of dramatic music, one who has said that he regards his scores as "auditory scenarios" for players to act out with their instruments. Even in a piece like the *Riconoscenza* Carter wrote in 1984 for the eightieth birthday of his friend the Italian composer Goffredo Petrassi—and here we are talking about a three-minute album leaf for one violin alone—the player, projecting the kaleidoscope of moods, does well to imagine himself as a quick-change virtuoso of voices and faces on the order of Charles Laughton or Robin Williams. In the tumultuous Concerto for Orchestra, written for the New York Philharmonic in 1969, the movements are intercut in the manner, for example, of the four plots of D. W. Griffith's 1916 film epic *Intolerance,* something Carter went on to explore still more fully in his String Quartet No. 3 (1971) and A *Symphony of Three Orchestras* (1976).

David Schiff begins his book *The Music of Elliott Carter* this way:[2]

> Elliott Carter makes music out of simultaneous opposition. A piano accelerates to a flickering tremolo as a harpsichord slows to silence. Second violin and viola, half of a quartet, sound cold, mechanical pulses, while first violin and cello, the remaining duo, play with intense expressive passion. Two, three, four orchestras superimpose clashing, unrelated sounds. A bass lyrically declaims classical Greek against a mezzo-soprano's American patter.[3] These surface oppositions point to profound structural and aesthetic polarities. The music is often Apollonian and Dionysian at the same time. This is not because different aspects of the music belong to one category or the other, as when we say that Brahms's melodies are Romantic and his structures Classical, but because every aspect of the composition articulates opposed values. The music is often at once highly structured and improvisatory; fragmented yet unbroken.

Schiff writes about Carter's "appetite for opposites" and remarks that "highly charged contrasts provoke his imagination." Given that, it is not surprising that Carter has several times been drawn to the concerto, the genre that is all about contrast, about conversation, competition, virtuosity, about

[2]*The Music of Elliott Carter* (London: Eulenburg, 1983),.
[3]The Double Concerto (1961), the String Quartet No. 3 (1971), the Concerto for Orchestra (1969) and A *Symphony of Three Orchestras* (1976), and *Syringa* (1978).

pitting sounds of different weights, colors, characters, degrees of rhetorical and expressive significance against one another.[4]

Carter's music is difficult but always rewarding to play, and it is very difficult to read (mainly because our notation is designed for music whose flow is more predictable and whose rhythm is not so independent of beat). Because the detail in it is prodigiously abundant as well as fine, it can also be difficult to hear, but my experience has always been that even when one of his works is new to me and I do not follow all (or even most of) the detail, it is overwhelming in its dramatic sweep. Carter is one of the few composers whose music reaches white heat. Demanding and sensuous, pure and theatrical, Carter's music involves head and heart, passion and fun, the long line and delicious detail, and it provides some of the richest of listening pleasures.

## Concerto for Oboe and Orchestra

Carter began his Oboe Concerto in 1986 and completed it on 10 October 1987. Heinz Holliger gave the first performance—actually the first two performances: the work was played twice at the same concert—in Zurich on 17 June 1988, with John Carewe conducting the Zurich Collegium Musicum. The work is dedicated to Paul Sacher, who commissioned it for Holliger. In an introductory note to the score, Carter writes: "I am deeply grateful to Paul Sacher for having proposed and commissioned this concerto and to Heinz Holliger . . . for his advice about the instrument, and his wonderful performances."

The ensemble is divided into a concertino consisting of the solo oboe, four violas, and percussion (timpani, vibraphone, glockenspiel, low and high metal blocks, low and high wood blocks, four temple blocks, low and high cowbells, four bongos, low and high tom-toms, medium suspended cymbal, and guiro), and an orchestra consisting of flute (doubling alto flute and piccolo), clarinet (doubling bass clarinet), horn, tenor trombone (doubling bass trombone), percussion (marimba, xylophone, large bass drum, large tam-tam, military drum

---

[4]Making music out of simultaneous opposition brings Charles Ives to mind, and that has been a complicated issue for Carter. Ives was an important figure in Carter's early life, and Ives's music, with its own fascinating counterpoints and simultaneities, obviously influenced the younger composer. At some point—it was around 1939, when John Kirkpatrick's landmark performance of the *Concord* Sonata brought about public awareness of Ives's significance (or even his existence)—Carter turned away from Ives. I will leave the Oedipal issues to others, but I have no difficulty understanding a deep incompatibility between the ultra-precise Carter and the sometimes recklessly exuberant al fresco composer of the *Concord* Sonata and the Fourth Symphony.

with detachable snares, tenor and soprano snare drums with detachable snares, and bass and soprano suspended cymbals), and strings.

The score includes a brief introductory note by the composer:

> In this Oboe Concerto, which is in one continuous movement, the [soloist] is accompanied in his widely varying, mercurial moods by a percussionist and four violas. The main orchestra opposes their flighty changes with a more regular series of ideas, usually on the serious side, sometimes bursting out dramatically. Each of the two groups uses different musical materials which they develop throughout the work.

In 1975 Carter wrote a song cycle on poems by Elizabeth Bishop, *A Mirror on Which to Dwell*. The third of the six songs is a setting of Bishop's *Sandpiper*, whose five four-line stanzas paint a portrait of the obsessed and jittery bird, "finical, awkward, in a state of controlled panic," in the midst of hissing sand and "interrupting water," hoping "to see a World in a Grain of Sand." "A student of Blake," she calls him. The composer translates that vision into a duet for soprano and oboe (the instrument he himself had played in his undergraduate days), lightly and colorfully accompanied by piano and four solo strings. The oboe plays the part of the sandpiper; the singer, sympathetic and amused, fits the words where she can into the spaces on a musical surface that shifts as rapidly as the grains on the beach.

I thought of *Sandpiper* the first time I heard Carter's Oboe Concerto. The Concerto is of course on a bigger scale—it runs about twenty minutes— and capable, therefore, of accommodating a far wider expressive and technical gamut; nor, obviously, is it bound to a single and specific poetic idea. It is full, though, of sandpiping of dizzying brilliance and enchanting humor, and at a level of virtuosity that goes beyond even the considerable demands of the earlier song. What you also hear—and which is not in the *Sandpiper* vocabulary—is a series of seamless lines of immense breadth and vertical range. Both of Carter's demands, for anti-gravitational agility and magisterial calm, are tributes to Heinz Holliger, aptly characterized by Alfred Brendel as one of the few "who really matter."

The Oboe Concerto begins with sustained chords in the orchestra and nervous drumming in the concertino, all *pianissimo* except for the initial accent in the cellos and basses. (Having a concertino function as a kind of middle ground between solo and orchestra is a plan Carter first used in his Piano Concerto.) The first of the oboe's widely varying moods we encounter—and that is very soon—is one of magnificent calm, as the oboe sings a spacious melody that swings with ease across nearly three octaves, from high A to the B-flat below middle C. Hearing Holliger play this Concerto, one would not guess what a risk it is to ask the soloist to make his first entrance on that high A. This opening melody also contains a double-stop for the oboe, and quite soon Carter calls for a triple-stop.[5]

The Concerto has not been going long before a trombone attempts the first in a series of rowdy coups d'états to establish itself as a kind of secondary soloist. (A trombone misbehaves similarly in Nielsen's Flute Concerto.) The orchestral music becomes more frenzied, an infection that spreads to the concertino as well, but the oboe glides along in sovereign indifference. The basic tempo at this stage is fairly slow, though the measures are most variously filled in, sometimes with very few notes, sometimes with flurries of wildly excited activity. In this opening section we also become acquainted with the oboe's other, "sandpiper" personality. There is a dramatic episode in which the orchestra makes one attempt after another to move forward at high speed but is seven times called to order by a loud chord from the violas in the concertino and a forceful low B-flat, also fiercely *fortissimo*, from the oboe.[6]

The middle of the Concerto is a kind of scherzo; the change of mood is first effected within the original, fairly spacious tempo, but then moves into a new and fast tempo. The most remarkable episode in the Concerto, both as drama and as virtuoso display, is the brief cadenza, in which the oboe, accompanied by barely audible percussion, demonstrates its possibilities as a polyphonic instrument: a high-voiced, agitated, complaining personage is repeatedly brushed off with curt, monosyllabic responses in a harsh, low voice. This is of course yet another tribute to Holliger's astonishing and pioneering virtuosity. After a dramatic double climax and one more recrudescence of the trombone, the music returns to the gentle tempo and the long, lyric lines of the opening.

[5]Multiple stops or multiphonics for wind instruments, whose accidental intrusion often plagues students and unskilled players, became part of the virtuoso vocabulary of avant-garde music in the 1960s. Looking up this topic in *Oboe* by Leon Goossens and Edwin Roxburgh, I see that in his *Ecclissi* for solo oboe, Roxburgh asks for a quadruple-stop.

[6]That B-flat below middle C is the oboe's lowest note; in fact, many orchestration manuals give B-natural as the lowest note and counsel against the casual use of even that. The low B-flat is not a sound you will hear often, and once you have heard it, especially as it is so baldly presented in Carter's concerto, you will not forget it.

# Concerto for Violin and Orchestra

$$\left\{\begin{array}{l} \textit{Impulsivo} \\ \textit{Tranquillo (orchestra)} \\ \textit{Angosciato (solo)} \\ \textit{Scherzando} \end{array}\right.$$

Carter composed his Violin Concerto in Waccabuc, New York, and New York City in 1989–1990, completing it on 26 February 1990, some revisions of detail being accomplished after that date. The work was written in response to a joint commission from the violinist Ole Böhn and the San Francisco Symphony, whose participation in the project was made possible by a gift from Mrs. Ralph I. Dorfman. The score is dedicated to Ole Böhn and Herbert Blomstedt, then the San Francisco Symphony's music director. The first performance was given on 2 May 1990 by the two dedicatees with the San Francisco Symphony.

**Solo violin, two flutes and piccolo (second flute also doubling piccolo), two oboes and English horn, clarinet in B-flat, clarinet in E-flat (doubling clarinet in B-flat and bass clarinet), bass clarinet, two bassoons and contrabassoon, four horns, three trumpets, three trombones, tuba, timpani, glockenspiel, crotales, vibraphone, small and large suspended cymbals, small and large snare drums, tam-tam, bass drum, and strings.**

The idea that there should be a Carter Violin Concerto came from one of the composer's European champions, the Norwegian violinist Ole Böhn, who had often played the Duo for Violin and Piano—to the very great satisfaction of the composer, who characterizes Böhn's performances as "very dramatic"— and who longed for another major Carter piece to play.

The first question that engaged Carter when he began to think about his Violin Concerto was how the soloist should make his first entrance. With that came the corollary question of how to arrange his final exit. In the Piano Concerto and the Double Concerto the soloists play non-orchestral instruments; thus their entrances are striking almost by definition. In the Oboe Concerto the solo stands apart because Carter did not include an oboe, nor for that matter any other double reed woodwind, in the orchestra. But the violin is *the* quintessential orchestral instrument—it is strings, after all, that make an orchestra not a band—and Carter did not choose to follow the example of the Sessions Violin Concerto, a work he admires very much, and write for an orchestra without violins. He decided, therefore, to make the most of the fact that there are thirty or so other violins on stage and to turn the first solo entrance into a gradual emergence from the orchestral texture.

The first thing we hear, then, is a fairly quiet but agitated orchestral hubbub—"a great sort of confusion," Carter calls it—in which the solo violin joins in the sixth measure. The orchestra backs off at the soloist's entrance and, in a few measures, clears a path that allows the violin to propose quite a different sort of music, broader and in the general realm of *espressivo*.

Not only are the violin's musical gestures different from those of the orchestra, so are the details of rhythmic and pitch vocabulary of their respective languages. This idea of assigning distinct vocabularies to the various performers in a particular piece is something Carter first explored in that sometimes amusing, sometimes fraught, and always arresting four-way conversation, the Second String Quartet, where each of the characters speaks a language that is his and his alone. The same plan is pursued in the Double Concerto.

In the Violin Concerto we find three strands of music. The solo violin almost always moves in triplets, and its favored intervals are the minor second (e.g., C to C-sharp), the minor third (e.g., C to E-flat), the perfect fifth (e.g., C to G), and the minor seventh (e.g., C to B-flat). The orchestra plays duples, and among its characteristic intervals are the major second (e.g., C to D), the perfect fourth (e.g., C to F), the major sixth (e.g., C to A), and the major seventh (e.g. C to B). Musicians will notice that the orchestra's intervals are the inversions of the violin's intervals: if, for instance, you turn a minor second (C to C-sharp) upside down, you have a major seventh (C-sharp to C-natural). The orchestra sometimes picks up the soloist's vocabulary, but not the other way around: the soloist is, after all, the dominant personality. Finally there is an intermediate strand that combines the intervallic characteristics of both the others and whose primary rhythmic division is the quintuplet.

The concerto is in three movements, a familiar enough design, but here, too, we find surprises. The question of the division of a large work into movements is also one that has long fascinated Carter. In the Quartet No. 1, for example, the differentiation of the movements is perfectly clear; however, the actual stopping points for tuning and coughing and all that occur not at these boundary markers, but before or after them.[7] In the Concerto

---

[7] When Carter first saw Balanchine's *Serenade* (to Tchaikovsky's Serenade for Strings) in the 1930s, he was delighted by how when "one movement ends the people who are to dance the next one are already onstage."

for Orchestra, the movements are intercut like the four plots of D. W. Griffith's silent film epic, *Intolerance*. In the String Quartet No. 3 and in *A Symphony of Three Orchestras*, movements overlap and proceed simultaneously.

Carter's music of the 1980s is no less intricate in facture than most of his work of the '60s and '70s; it is, however, more transparent, and in that same spirit the formal design of the Violin Concerto is not especially daunting. But there are two unusual features to point out. One is that the three movements, varied though they feel in pace, and differently though the spaces between the barlines are filled in, are bound together by a common pulse; the other is the way the middle movement will turn out to be two movements in one.

In the first movement, which is marked *Impulsivo*, the violin's manner is predominantly lyric. Carter treats the violin as a singing instrument and, while the solo part is exceedingly challenging, he did not choose to follow the path of virtually reinventing the instrument as charted by Schoenberg in his great concerto. "No fiddle effects," he says. As a lyric singer, the violin plays with almost constant rubato, though these deviations from the beat are in fact written out in a characteristic Carter placement of events just to one side or the other of the beat. By contrast, the orchestra is strict and straight, without rhythmic caprice. At the same time, something in the orchestra yearns to share the soloist's freedom, but though it is constantly trying to catch up with its mercurial partner, it never manages to do so.

The first movement arrives at its close with a passionate rising solo, but the music does not stop. Instead, Carter gives us a precisely measured silence, broken first by a single violin note (the open-A string, almost as though the violinist wanted to tune between movements), then by a *pianissimo* chord that combines extremes of high and low, and finally by another "tuning" touch from the soloist.[8] With that, the bridge is crossed and the second movement can begin.

Low-pitched orchestral chords slowly succeed one another; all is indeed, as the marking tells us, *tranquillo*. But when the violin comes in, soon and "to the fore," it is unable to enter this mood. Each of its notes has a crescendo or decrescendo or a combination of the two, and the character is unmistakably *angosciato* and *esitando*, anguished and hesitant. The violin's task here is to spin a long line, one that comes across as continuous even though it is broken by pauses—the violinist must think and feel across those gaps—and even though the orchestra creates what Carter calls "waves of sound," some big, some small, which threaten sometimes to engulf the solo's impassioned discourse.

In the finale, marked *scherzando*, solo and orchestra once again find

---

[8] Alban Berg incorporated the "tuning" effect into his Violin Concerto, and so did Henri Dutilleux in his *L'Arbre des songes* (1985).

common purpose. The rhythmic divisions of the solo part look like threes and nines on the page, but the jazz-touched syncopations keep the music from sounding like triplets. Here, too, the solo part is an exercise in focus for the violinist, a constant striving for continuity across breaks, a persistent picking up of the thread as though no disturbing interruption had occurred. The play of the contrasting vocabularies of intervals becomes more intense. To Carter, the difference between a major and a minor interval is most striking in major and minor seconds, and that is now the pair of intervals on which Carter increasingly concentrates. The movement rises to one last climax. Then comes a brief solo, almost like a cadenza, and a good bang that could be the end of the movement and of the Concerto. But no. The notes continue to swirl, and only then does the Concerto quickly disappear in a vapor of *pianissimo*. "And that," says the composer with combined amusement and rue, "is not really what you should do."

## Double Concerto for Harpsichord and Piano with Two Chamber Orchestras

> *Introduction*
> *Cadenza for Harpsichord*
> *Allegro scherzando*
> *Adagio*
> *Presto*
> *Cadenzas for Piano*
> *Coda*

Carter completed his Double Concerto in August 1961. The work was commissioned by the Fromm Music Foundation and is dedicated to its founder, Paul Fromm. It was first performed in New York on 6 September that year at a concert given for the Eighth Congress of the International Musicological Society; the soloists were Ralph Kirkpatrick and Charles Rosen, with Gustav Meier conducting.

**Each of the two solo instruments is accompanied by its own orchestra. Orchestra I, situated stage right with the harpsichord, consists of flute (doubling piccolo), horn, trumpet, tenor trombone (doubling bass trombone), viola, and bass. Orchestra II, at stage left with the piano, consists of oboe, clarinet (doubling E-flat clarinet), bassoon, horn, violin, and cello. Carter asks that the two wind groups be as far apart as the stage allows. Evenly spaced in an embrace**

around the two orchestras is an array of percussion instruments, requiring four players. This, beginning on the harpsichord side, consists of slapstick, anvil, high and low cowbells, high and low wood blocks, alto triangle, soprano and mezzo-soprano cymbals, soprano tambourine, medium gong, and contrabass tam-tam (Percussion 1); five temple blocks, soprano triangle, alto cymbal, mezzo-soprano snare drum, alto tambourine, alto military drum, bass tam-tam (Percussion 2); crotales, claves, maracas, tenor cymbal, soprano and alto snare drums, tenor military drum, and medium bass drum (Percussion 3); crotales, four bongos, alto and tenor tom-toms, bass cymbal, contralto snare drum, guiro, and very large bass drum (Percussion 4).

In 1956 the harpsichordist, scholar, teacher, and editor Ralph Kirkpatrick, who was a younger contemporary of Carter's at Harvard, suggested to Carter that he write a piece for harpsichord and piano. Carter was interested and stored the idea in the back of his head; however, the first order of business was to write a work that had been commissioned by the Stanley String Quartet, and only when that score was completed, on 19 March 1959, was he free to think about Kirkpatrick's proposal.[9] With its advantages of dynamic flexibility and just plain loudness, the piano supplanted the harpsichord as the preferred stringed keyboard instrument, public and domestic, during the second half of the eighteenth century. In 1788 Carl Philipp Emanuel Bach wrote a double concerto for the two instruments, but that ingenious composer disappoints us here: he does not assign distinctive material to the two instruments and thus makes only the not very interesting point that a given theme sounds like *this* on the harpsichord and like *that* on the piano. Neither while the harpsichord was still around in the eighteenth century nor since its revival at the beginning of the twentieth have composers shown much interest in the harpsichord-piano contrast. They may also have been baffled by what to do with it. Frank Martin's *Petite Symphonie concertante* for Harp, Harpsichord, Piano, and Double String Orchestra (1945), for example, has some pretty music, but it seems chiefly to demonstrate that harpsichord and piano mix about as well as oil and water.

Carter thus had no model or even a good precedent, but that was not a situation to bother him. What Kirkpatrick had in mind when he approached Carter was a duo, but what began to take shape in the composer's imagination was an enhanced duo, a conversation for harpsichord and piano, but with each instrument seconded by its own mini-orchestra, the whole bound to-

[9]When the Stanley Quartet received the score of Carter's Quartet No. 2, they soon saw that it was beyond their ability. Carter returned his $500 commission fee, and the first performance was given in 1960 by the Juilliard Quartet. The Second Quartet is one of Carter's most admired and most played works, has been recorded five times, and was awarded the Pulitzer Prize, the New York Music Critics Circle Award, and the UNESCO Prize.

gether by a semi-circular lineup of percussion. It is not going too far to say that it was the imagined presence of other instruments that made it possible for the harpsichord and piano to be brought together within a single aural context.

Also, as Carter began to think about Kirkpatrick's request, the seeming incompatibility of the two instruments became a primary stimulus, a liability to be turned into an advantage.[10] As he planned his Double Concerto, Carter thought first about the tactile difference between managing plucked strings and hammered strings, and, as he later wrote: "There was a desire to get to the physical origins of musical sound and to take off from there." From this beginning, he found his way to the idea of surrounding each keyboard with its own instrumental court that would seize on its characteristic color, pick it up, play with it, make the most of it, offer variations upon it. It works like the mutual sympathy of skin and perfume. Finally he thought of adding the richly equipped percussion group, partaking of both color camps, yet adding something independent and new. For the most part, metallophones (triangles, anvil, cymbals, etc.) and lignophones (maracas, wood blocks, temple blocks, etc.) are allied with the harpsichord and membranophones (tambourines, snare drums, bass drums, etc.) with the piano.

The stage placement—harpsichord group on the left as you look at the stage, piano group on the right—is more than a matter of tidy housekeeping. Where the music comes from is important in the Double Concerto, not only for the left-right dialogue and contrast, but also for the way the ripples, thunders, and tidal waves of sound travel along the percussion belt, and most excitingly when Carter sets crescendos and decrescendos going in alternating clockwise and counterclockwise spirals.

As for taking off from "the physical origins of sound," Carter writes that "the Double Concerto, in fact, has a shape that parallels this attitude, starting . . . by presenting gradually changing percussion sounds that first 'give birth' to a few musical pitches that in turn bring on the sound of the piano and then the harpsichord, which in their turn become more and more differentiated, only to sink back eventually to a more chaotic, undifferentiated state near the end."

Carter's feelings about music and text have changed over the years. As a young man, he wrote some songs and choruses, but between Allen Tate's *Emblems* in 1947 and the Elizabeth Bishop song cycle *A Mirror on Which to Dwell*, composed in 1975, he set no texts to music at all. Becoming aware that a generation of singers had grown up who performed his music not only

---

[10]It is characteristic of Carter to think about such questions of color and texture thoroughly before beginning to make any compositional sketches. I recall a conversation in the early 1960s in which he mentioned that the Philadelphia Orchestra had asked him for a concerto for string quartet and orchestra. He decided to turn it down "because I couldn't think of what to do with the second violin." The commission eventually went to Benjamin Lees.

competently but joyously, he began to give vocal compositions an important role in his later music. Most astonishing: in his ninetieth year, Carter began to think about writing an opera. On the other hand, his instrumental music is often informed by literary models: for example, the *Ethical Characters* of the Peripatetic philosopher Theophrastus in the Variations for Orchestra (1956), the great transcontinental winds evoked by Saint-John Perse's *Vents* in the Concerto for Orchestra (1969), and Hart Crane's inspired fantasies about the Brooklyn Bridge in *A Symphony of Three Orchestras* (1976). The design of the String Quartet No. 1 is based on an image in Cocteau's film *Le Sang d'un poète*.

As Carter worked on the Double Concerto, with its chaos-to-order-back-to-chaos scenario, he discovered—and then explored and used—parallels, first with *De rerum natura,* the unfinished poem in which the first-century B.C.E. writer Lucretius expounded his theory of the creation of the universe (including the gods) through the indeterminate and unpredictable swervings of atoms through infinite space. Sensations and perceptions, Lucretius writes, reflect the images created by the motion of these atoms.[11] Bit by bit, Carter wrote, a parody of Lucretius in Alexander Pope's *Dunciad* "took over in my thoughts." He cites these lines as an example:

> All sudden, Gorgons hiss, and Dragons glare
> And ten-horn'd Fiends and Giants rush to war;
> Hell rises, Heav'n descends, and dance on earth;
> Gods, imps, and monsters, music, rage, and mirth
> A fire, a jig, a battle, and a ball
> Till one wide conflagration swallows all.

The Double Concerto is in seven connected movements:

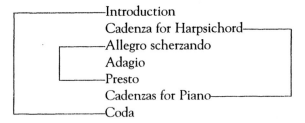

As you can see in the diagram, the form is chiastic, with correspondences between Introduction and Coda; between the Cadenza for Harpsichord and

---

[11]Sometimes the correspondences with Lucretius are quite specific, and David Schiff spells them out in detail in *The Music of Elliott Carter* (London: Eulenburg, 1983).

the two for piano; and between the two quick movements. We can think of the correspondence of Introduction and Coda as one between units that are each other's mirror images, the Introduction being music of becoming, the Coda music of disintegration. The Adagio is the Concerto's central panel. Parallel to the movement from chaos to order and back, there is an overall movement from "comparative unity with slight character differences to greater and greater diversity of material and character and a return to unity."

Just as each of the two ensembles has its characteristic timbre, so does each have its own vocabulary of melodic intervals, chords, rhythms, and speed: for the harpsichord group, minor seconds, minor thirds, perfect fourths, augmented fourths, minor sixths, minor sevenths, and minor ninths, with polyrhythms based on four against seven (and multiples and other derivatives thereof); for the piano group, major seconds, major thirds, perfect fifths, major sixths, major sevenths, and major ninths, with polyrhythms based on five against three (and their multiples and derivatives). This may sound fearsome; the point is, however, that you will hear how different the two ensembles sound as they converse in distinctive tempers and tones of voice, and for those who are curious about such matters, the list of intervals gives some indication how those differences are achieved and how the musical personalities are defined.[12]

The Introduction "breaks the silence" with noises of unpitched percussion, simultaneously accelerating and decelerating, and quickly rising to *fortissimo*.[13] As the Lucretian atoms swirl and swerve, this section introduces the two solo instruments and, gradually, all the characteristic speeds, colors, and intervals that make up the vocabulary for the entire Concerto.

"The Cadenza for Harpsichord presents, in condensed form, all the salient characteristics, rhythms, and intervals of its ensemble." That ensemble cheers its soloist with a little fanfare, but the piano group draws attention away. The music fades to nothing, dissolving into the first of the Concerto's two major silences.

Movement breaks in Carter are rarely clean; that is, we are likely to hear the next movement prefigured before the break and elements of the previous one lingering on afterward. And so in this spot, the interruption of the end of the harpsichord cadenza by the piano group alerts us to the fact that the next movement, the Allegro scherzando, belongs primarily to the piano side. Both here and in the corresponding Presto, "the featured instrument and its orchestra are frequently interrupted by the other instrument and *its* orchestra playing at a dynamic level [and speed] opposite to that of

[12]Unattributed quotations in what follows are drawn from the composer's several descriptions of the Double Concerto.
[13]These simultaneous accelerations and decelerations as well as those in the Adagio reflect another interest of Carter's, namely in the ingenious and giddily delightful *Studies for Player Piano* by one of America's great musical explorers, Conlon Nancarrow.

the main group." Allegro scherzando is the piano group's tempo; the interruptions are slow and somber. These interruptions also become more assertive as the movement progresses.

In the central Adagio, what Carter calls the "choreography" changes. The two wind sections play slow music, while in the background the two soloists, the strings, and the four percussionists surround the winds with accelerating and decelerating patterns that move alternately clockwise and counterclockwise. Here the two keyboards are silent for some time. Somber drumbeats prepare the return of the harpsichord and the piano, whose music—patterns of quick broken chords—seems for a time to amalgamate them into a single instrument. But gradually they diverge again, and the disappearance of the music—the harpsichord slowing, the piano spinning into a whir of repeated notes—is celebrated by angelic pings from the anvil, the crotales, and the triangle.

The Presto, the counterpart of the Allegro scherzando, is for harpsichord and all orchestral instruments except percussion (who have their one moment of rest here). As in the Allegro scherzando, the principal group is "frequently interrupted by the other instrument and *its* orchestra playing at [the opposite] dynamic level [and speed]." This time, therefore, it is the piano that does the interrupting, bringing back fragments of the Adagio.

Then follow two Cadenzas for Piano, both brief. A huge crescendo leads to a silence, a great indrawing of breath, followed by—nothing. This blankness, the second of the two silences that interrupt the whirlwind of Carter's musical atoms, is broken by an immense crash. Then the Coda, "like a large gong, dies away over many measures in wavelike patterns, with many diverse tone colors fading out and returning—each time slightly different and with less energy—until the work subsides to a quiet close.

"The beautiful end of Pope's [Dunciad] seemed to articulate in words the work I had already composed:

> ". . . the all-encompassing hour
> Resistless galls; the Muse obeys the power.
> She comes! She comes! the sable throne behold
> Of Night primeval, and of Chaos old!
> Before her Fancy's gilded clouds decay,
> And all its varying rainbows die away.
> Wit shoots in vain its momentary fires,
> The meteor drops and in a flash expires.
>
> Nor public flame, nor private, dares to shine;
> Nor human spark is left, nor glimpse divine!
> Lo! thy dread empire, Chaos! is restor'd;
> Light dies before thy uncreating word:
> Thy hand, great Anarch! lets the curtain fall;
> And universal Darkness buries all."

# Ernest Chausson

Amédée-Ernest Chausson was born in Paris on 20 January 1855 and died at Limay, near Mantes in the Department of Seine-et-Oise, on 10 June 1899.

## *Poème*, for Violin and Orchestra, Opus 25

Chausson began the *Poème* in April 1896 and completed it on 29 June that year. In November, Eugène Ysaÿe, to whom the score is dedicated, sight-read it at an all-day-and-most-of-the-night musicale at the house of the Catalan painter Santiago Rusinal in Sitgès, Spain. Ysaÿe gave the first public performance on 27 December 1896 at Nancy; the conductor was Guy Ropartz, who like Chausson, was a pupil of César Franck.

**Solo violin, two flutes, two oboes, two clarinets, two bassoons, four horns, two trumpets, three trombones, tuba, timpani, harp, and strings.**

"To have to one's credit the dedication of works like the Chausson *Poème* and the César Franck Sonata—can there be greater proof of the impact of Ysaÿe's interpretive genius on his creative contemporaries?" asks Joseph Szigeti in his memoirs, *With Strings Attached*. "And to have been entrusted by Debussy with the first performance of his Quartet is not a negligible episode in *any* interpreter's life, even an Ysaÿe's. Less generally known is the fact that Debussy originally conceived his Nocturnes as a violin solo for his friend Ysaÿe."[1]

---

[1]Joseph Szigeti: *With Strings Attached* (New York: Alfred A. Knopf, 1967). What may be Chausson's

For Szigeti—and by no means for Szigeti alone—Ysaÿe was "perhaps the last representative of the truly grand manner of violin-playing." He made a few records, but of trivial pieces and at a point when he was ill and far beyond his prime: he is one of those artists whose playing has its memorial in the music written, as the French say, *à son intention*. Szigeti suggests that Ysaÿe's six inventive and highly cultivated sonatas for unaccompanied violin were "a subconscious attempt on [his] part to perpetuate his own elusive *playing* style." But the *Poème* and Franck's ardent Sonata, a wedding present to the twenty-eight-year-old violinist, are the two truly living monuments to Ysaÿe's noble art.[2]

Ysaÿe was one of the artists and intellectuals who met regularly at Chausson's house at 22 Boulevard de Courcelles in Paris. Among Chausson's friends—and this is restricting the name-dropping to the headiest level—were Manet, Odilon Redon, Degas, Vuillard, Rodin, Mallarmé, Gide, Colette, his fellow-Franckist Vincent d'Indy, Franck himself, Duparc, Fauré, Dukas, Chabrier, Debussy, Albéniz, Satie, Charles Koechlin, Jacques Thibaud, Alfred Cortot, Raoul Pugno, Claire Croiza, and Ernest van Dyck. Degas, Manet, Redon, and Vuillard also had the pleasure of seeing their work on the walls, sharing space with Bonnard, Corot, Courbet, Delacroix, Gauguin, Berthe Morisot, Puvis de Chavannes, Renoir, and Signac.

Chausson was a gentle and cultured man, born to privilege—his father was a contractor who had become wealthy in the wake of Baron Haussmann's rebuilding of Paris during the Second Empire—and unoppressively generous. He was also blessed in being a richly happy husband and father. The well-named Prosper Chausson had insisted that his son equip himself for a life of respectability and financial security; it was, therefore, not until he was twenty-four and had completed his law degree that Chausson enrolled at the Paris Conservatory in order to study with Franck and Jules Massenet. After the first year he worked with Franck exclusively. From Massenet he acquired a strong foundation in craft and some encouragement of his congenital sweet tooth; Franck gave him a language and a Weltanschauung.

Like Franck, Chausson was innocent of any skill at making the great public music machine work on his behalf. His work was occasionally abused and more often simply ignored. But the year 1897 was a turning point. When

---

finest instrumental work, the Concerto for Violin, Piano, and String Quartet, was also written for and first played by Ysaÿe.

[2] To quote Szigeti once more: "There can be no doubt in the mind of any violinist who had the good fortune to hear Ysaÿe in his great days that the solo exposition in Chausson's *Poème* with those typically Ysaÿean sinuous double-stop passages across the strings could never have been written but for the inspiration—and probably the collaboration—of Ysaÿe. I was confirmed in this feeling when by chance I met David Holguin, a pupil of Ysaÿe's. He told me how, one morning in class in Cincinnati, André de Ribeaupierre asked Ysaÿe about the genesis of this particular passage, saying: 'It sounds as if you had written it yourself.' To which Ysaÿe replied with a smile: 'Mais oui, that is precisely what I did—on Chausson's framework.' "

Ysaÿe introduced the *Poème* in Paris that April, the applause rang on and on. Chausson's friend the novelist Camille Mauclair recalled that the bewildered composer kept repeating, "I can't get over it." That success was surpassed six weeks later by the acclaim that greeted his Symphony in B-flat when the Berlin Philharmonic under the charismatic Arthur Nikisch brought Chausson's symphony to the French capital. It had been played in Paris before, but the endorsement of a foreign conductor and orchestra made the Parisians sit up and take notice.

During the next two years, Chausson composed some of his finest music, including the Piano Quartet, the atmospheric tone poem *Soir de fête*, and the *Chanson perpétuelle*. Suddenly it was over. The forty-four-year-old composer lost control of his bicycle and smashed into the wall next to the gate of a country villa he had rented for the summer. With his daughter Étiennette, he had been on the way to the railway station to meet the rest of the family who were coming in from Paris. He was killed instantly.

In his biography of Chausson, Jean Gallois points out that the *Poème* originally bore a subtitle, *Le Chant de l'amour triomphant* (also that it was at first called *Poème symphonique*). *The Song of Love Triumphant* is the title of a short story by Ivan Turgenev, one of Chausson's favorite authors. Turgenev's fascinating story, set in the sixteenth century, is about two young men from Ferrara, the closest of friends, one a blond painter, the other a swarthy musician, who are in love with the same pale and repressed young woman. They agree to abide by her decision. She makes what she supposes to be the less complicated choice, and the rejected dark Muzio sets out to spend many years traveling in India and the Orient. He returns with new skills, many of them on the shady side, among them the performance on an Indian stringed instrument of the strangely compelling *Song of Love Triumphant*. This piece of music then takes on a crucial role in the sinister unfolding of the tale.

Gallois suggest correspondences between musical themes and the characters and events in Turgenev's story. He really does suggest rather than impose, and one is grateful for his tact. He is not, in the end, convincing. It is best, perhaps, to take the presence of Turgenev's story in the background as support for the idea that the *Poème* is more than just another pretty face.[3]

The introduction, which Chausson marks *lento e misterioso*, is dark in harmony and color. The violas and cellos are divided into multiple sections, and the first time we hear violin tone is when the solo instrument begins. Its entrance causes the orchestra to fall silent, and the violin alone plays an expansive melody. The muted orchestral strings repeat it, whereupon the

---

[3]Antony Tudor movingly played upon the dark side of the *Poème* when he used it for his 1936 ballet *Jardin aux lilas* (brought to America in 1940 by Ballet Theatre as *Lilac Garden*). The subject is the series of encounters at a garden party of a woman about to marry a man she does not love, her fiancé, her lover, and her fiancé's mistress. Tudor's title has Chaussonian overtones in that *Le Temps de lilas* is a Chausson song and also the closing portion of his beautiful cycle *Poème de l'amour et de la mer*.

soloist elaborates on it with the "Ysaÿean sinuous double-stop passages" to which Szigeti refers. This material forms the beginning, middle, and end of the *Poème;* its second appearance is much abbreviated, but the final one rises to a searing climax. These chapters are separated by the double occurrence of an episode of intensely impassioned music in a faster tempo, and so arranged that the second of these passages is the fulfillment of what the first had promised. Reviewing a performance of the *Poème* in 1913, Debussy wrote about the quiet close that nothing could be "more touching than [this] gentle dreaminess . . . where, casting aside any ideas of description or narrative, the music itself is the sentiment that commands our feelings. . . . Fine music, this, and full of ardor."

# Aaron Copland

Aaron Copland was born in Brooklyn, New York, on 14 November 1900 and died in Peekskill, New York, on 2 December 1990.

## Concerto for Clarinet and String Orchestra, with Harp and Piano

*Slowly and expressively—Cadenza—Rather fast—Trifle faster—Tempo I (rather fast)*

Drawing on material he had sketched fairly fully between December 1945 and February 1946, Copland began his Clarinet Concerto, commissioned by Benny Goodman, while on a lecture tour of Latin America in the fall of 1947. He interrupted work on it because a request from Republic Pictures for a score for Lewis Milestone's *The Red Pony* was "too good to turn down," and then wrote *Four Piano Blues*, finally coming back to the Concerto in August 1948 after his summer teaching stint at Tanglewood. The first performance, on 6 November 1950, was a broadcast by Benny Goodman with Fritz Reiner and the NBC Symphony; the first public concert performance was given on 28 November 1950 by Ralph McLane, with Eugene Ormandy conducting the Philadelphia Orchestra. The score is dedicated to Goodman.

**Solo clarinet, harp, piano, and strings.**

The King of Swing had an uneasy relationship with classical music. His first important teacher, Franz Schoepp, was a classically trained musician, but, as Richard Wang observes in *The New Grove Dictionary of American Music*, in the early 1920s Goodman, just getting into his teens, was absorbing the influence of such musicians as Ted Lewis, Leon Roppolo, King Oliver, Louis Armstrong, Johnny Dodds, Buster Bailey, and Bix Beiderbecke. In sum, he had made a clear commitment to what Stravinsky called "the other fraternity." By 1936, having organized his first big band, his trio with Teddy Wilson and Gene Krupa, and his quartet with Wilson, Krupa, and Lionel Hampton, Goodman was the best-known musician in America. The famous and, at the time, controversial Carnegie Hall concert, when his quartet was joined by Harry James, Ziggy Elman, Jess Stacy, and musicians from the Duke Ellington and Count Basie bands, happened in January 1938.

About this time, Goodman moved to secure a place in the classical world as well. He took lessons from Reginald Kell, the English artist who revolutionized classical clarinet playing by introducing the virtually constant use of rubato (much as Kreisler had done in violin playing at the beginning of the century); he performed and recorded the Mozart Clarinet Quintet with the Budapest Quartet; and he gave a non-jazz solo recital at Town Hall, New York. More important were his commissions to Bartók (*Contrasts*, 1939), Milhaud (Clarinet Concerto, 1941), Copland, Hindemith (Clarinet Concerto, 1947), and Morton Gould (*Derivations*, 1954)—important because at least two of these works, *Contrasts* and the Copland Concerto, have become indispensable to the repertory.

The sad side of all this is that Goodman never learned to be at ease with any of this music: his recordings of Mozart's Quintet and Concerto, the Nielsen and Copland concertos, *Contrasts*, and various pieces by Beethoven, Brahms, and Weber reveal playing that is stiff, uninflected, devoid of enthusiasm—lifeless stuff impossible to associate with the captivating artistry you hear on his records from the early thirties with such colleagues as Wilson, Krupa, and Jack Teagarden.

*Copland: Since 1943*, by Copland and Vivian Perlis, yields an interesting anecdote. Not long after the premiere, Goodman played the Concerto at the American Academy in Rome with the composer Harold Shapero at the piano. Shapero felt compelled to tell Goodman to loosen up: "You're supposed to swing it," and Goodman, whom Shapero remembered as "very resistant to criticism of any kind," replied "Yeah? You think so?" Coming to this Concerto from a jazz background is not necessarily an advantage, although Copland himself had "always thought that it would help if a player had some feeling and knowledge of jazz, yet when jazz clarinetist Johnny Dankworth attempted [it] in concert, he ran into difficulty."[1]

[1]Aaron Copland and Vivian Perlis, *Copland: Since 1943* (New York: St. Martin's Press, 1989). All the Copland quotes come from this source.

In *Copland: Since 1943*, the composer recounts that in their original form, the Concerto's closing flourishes took the clarinet up to high B-flat: "I knew Benny could reach that high because I had listened to his recordings. He explained that although he could comfortably reach that high note when playing jazz for an audience, he might not be able to if he had to read it from a score or for a recording. Therefore, we changed it."[2]

The initial reaction to the Clarinet Concerto was not hostile, as it had been to the Piano Concerto twenty-four years earlier, but it was by no means enthusiastic—I recall it falling quite flat at the performance by McLane and Ormandy I heard in 1950—and it was the persistence of grateful clarinetists that established it. Interestingly, Copland recalled that European audiences were much more receptive than American ones at first.

One musician who had an intriguing mixed reaction was Serge Koussevitzky, a steadfast supporter of Copland's since he had become the Boston Symphony's conductor in 1924. Clearly, Koussevitzky loved something about this music, because he tried to persuade Copland to arrange the first movement for full orchestra and call it *Elegy*, even setting a performance date for December 1950. Koussevitzky could be very persuasive and, over the phone, Copland agreed; however, on thinking it over, he begged off: "I am convinced that it takes away from the integrity of the concerto as I originally conceived it, and I am basically unwilling to do that—at least until the work has had a chance through several seasons to make its way as a complete concerto." The other side of Koussevitzky's reaction was that he flatly refused to allow a performance at Tanglewood with Goodman and Leonard Bernstein, who wrote to Copland: "I fought with Kouss valiantly over the Clarinet Concerto, to no avail. Benny and 'Tanglevood' don't mix in his mind."

Copland's concerto did, however, take on another incarnation in December 1951, when the New York City Ballet gave the premiere of *The Pied Piper*, a ballet Jerome Robbins set to this score with, as Lincoln Kirstein put it, his "genius for improvised comedy, his canny instinct for the artificed use of the apparently accidental." The curtain was up before anything began, and the almost dark stage was open to the back wall of the theater, bare of scenery, and with just a few unused flats and ladders standing around. (Kirstein also mentions how Robbins "proved himself a wizard in the virtues of necessity, the surprising richness of poverty.") A clarinetist, casually dressed, wandered onto the stage, tried a couple of reeds, blew a few experimental notes, and then, from the dark orchestra pit, came a sequence of simple chords. The

[2]A footnote by Vivian Perlis tells us "the first version of the 'coda' cadenza is at the Library of Congress, with a memo by Copland, 'too difficult for Benny Goodman.' " It would be valuable if Boosey & Hawkes, Copland's publisher, would print this first version as an *ossia* in some future edition of the concerto. Goodman never played Milhaud's concerto at all, and Copland's made him sufficiently nervous that he postponed the premiere by a year and a half from its original date. Gould's *Derivations* had to wait six years until Goodman felt ready to play it.

lyric song of the first movement drew dancers to the stage, and gradually a ballet evolved, tender at first, wildly ebullient at the end. *The Pied Piper* was a charmer, and it has never left the repertory for long.[3]

In *Copland: Since 1943*, the composer Philip Ramey, who in later years often accompanied and assisted Copland on his travels, writes words that illuminate the concerto's first movement: "I never once saw Aaron indulge in sentimentality; but he has a sad core that is perhaps responsible for the wonderful bittersweet lyricism heard from time to time in his music (I think especially of the opening of the Clarinet Concerto and some of the exposed woodwind writing in *Inscape*)." In that quality—sadness without sentimentality—we can perhaps find the essential reason Copland was reluctant to turn the first movement of the Concerto into the *Elegy* requested by Koussevitzky, a conductor to whom understatement was an unknown and probably incomprehensible concept.

For the rest, I give, with a couple of interpolations in brackets, Copland's own description of the music:

> The first movement . . . is a languid song form composed in 3/4 time, rather unusual for me, but the theme seemed to call for it. [The spacing of those first few notes for low strings and harps is a marvel of simplicity and beautiful sound; like Robbins, Copland understood "the surprising richness of poverty." And the way the accompaniment echoes or subtly duplicates the melody recalls some of Mahler's delicate accompaniments in *Das Lied von der Erde*, Mahler being a composer loved, understood, and mined by Copland long before Mahler's vast popularity began in the 1960s.] The second movement, a free rondo form, is a contrast in style—stark, severe, and jazzy. The movements are connected by a cadenza, which gives the soloist considerable opportunity to demonstrate his prowess, while at the same time [it] introduces fragments of the melodic material to be heard in the second movement. [Cadenzas most often sum up and thus look backward rather than forward; therefore, having a cadenza propose material yet to come is an original and happy touch.] The cadenza is written fairly close to the way I wanted it, but it is free within reason—after all, it and the movement that follows are in the jazz idiom. It is not ad lib as in cadenzas of many traditional concertos; I always felt there was enough room for interpretation even when everything was written out.
>
> Some of the second movement material represents an unconscious fusion of elements obviously related to North and South American popular music:

[3]Apropos issues about classical and jazz competencies, it is interesting to turn to the review by Edwin Denby, the most perceptive American dance critic at that time: "I was mortified to see [the company] dancing in the style of *Swan Lake*, dancing the piece wrong and looking as square as a covey of suburbanites down in the rumpus room. All but one dancer, [Tanaquil] LeClercq, who does the style right, and looks witty and graceful and adolescent as they all so easily might have by nature. The piece has a Robbins-built surefire finale, and the public doesn't even guess at the groovy grace it is missing." Edwin Denby, *Dance Writings* (New York: Alfred A. Knopf, 1986).

Charleston rhythms, boogie woogie, and Brazilian folk tunes. The instrumentation being clarinet with strings, harp, and piano, I did not have a large battery of percussion to achieve jazzy effects, so I used slapping basses and whacking harp sounds to simulate them. The Clarinet Concerto ends with a fairly elaborate coda in C major that finishes off with a clarinet glissando—or "smear" in jazz lingo.

# Antonín Dvořák

---

Antonín Leopold Dvořák was born at Mühlhausen (Nelahoz-
eves), Bohemia, on 8 September 1841 and died in Prague on
1 May 1904. His name has only two syllables, with the D at
the beginning folded into the V, i.e. not "de Vořák."

---

## Concerto in B minor for Cello and Orchestra, Opus 104

*Allegro*
*Adagio ma non troppo*
*Finale: Allegro moderato*

Dvořák began the first movement of his Cello Concerto in New
York on 8 November 1894. Unusually for him, he worked on
sketches and the full score simultaneously, beginning the latter on
18 November. He completed the work "Thanks be to God on 9 February
1895, on the day of our [son] Otářek's birthday, Saturday in the morning at
half past eleven." On the last page of the autograph there is a note in Dvořák's
hand: "I finished the Concerto in New York, but when I returned to Bohemia
I changed the end completely to the way it stands here now. Písek, 11 June
1895." His wife's sister, Josefina Kaunitzová, with whom he had once been
deeply in love, had died, and the new sixty-measure coda, of which more
below, was his response to her death. Dvořák intended his Cello Concerto
for Hanuš Wihan and dedicated it to him, but the first performance was given
by Leo Stern with the London Philharmonic Society at Queen's Hall, London, under the composer's direction on 19 March 1896.

Solo cello, two flutes (second doubling piccolo), two oboes, two clarinets, two bassoons, three horns, two trumpets, three trombones, tuba, timpani, triangle (in the finale only), and strings.


In the spring of 1891, Dvořák, in Prague, received a letter from Jeannette Thurber in New York, inviting him to assume the directorship of the National Conservatory of Music, which she had founded in 1885. Dvořák was far from sure whether New York was a good idea for him, but Mrs. Thurber was a determined woman. She was an idealist who wanted the National Conservatory to be an institution where gifted students of all races might study, and she imagined Dvořák founding an American school of composition. Married to a wholesale grocer, Mrs. Thurber also had some money, even after she and her husband had lost $1.5 million dollars in an attempt to start an English-language opera company in competition with the newly established Metropolitan Opera.

She was persuasive, and on 27 September 1892, Dvořák, his wife, and their eldest daughter and eldest son arrived in Hoboken on the S.S. *Saale*. Within a few days they were installed in an apartment on East 17th Street, and three weeks later Dvořák conducted his three concert overtures, *In Nature's Realm*, *Carnival*, and *Othello*, in Mr. Carnegie's Music Hall that had been opened absurdly far uptown on 57th Street a year and a half before. Dvořák had already begun his teaching, coaching, and conducting duties at the Conservatory.

America was a mixed experience for Dvořák. He was homesick, and sometimes, because the Thurbers were still in recovery from their National Opera Company debacle, the salary checks did not come in punctually. But he had some serious students, enjoyed being lionized, had great pleasure conducting his music with excellent orchestras in Chicago and New York, and made some interesting new friends, including the conductor Anton Seidl and the composer and cellist Victor Herbert. He quickly figured out where to watch trains, always an important delight to him, though not entirely easy because in New York you could not get on a station platform without a ticket; he also learned where to look at pigeons to remind him of those he had raised at home. And he added a new hobby: watching the great steamers depart for Europe, something that must have both stimulated and assuaged his homesickness.

Best of all was the long summer vacation in 1893 at the Bohemian colony at Spillville in northeast Iowa, where the father of his assistant and secretary, Joseph Kovařík, was schoolteacher, organist, and choirmaster. (The cemetery behind Saint Wenceslas's Church in the little town is full of Kovaříks.) The four younger children joined the family for this adventure. Dvořák delighted in hearing Czech spoken all around him and partaking of the familiar food and games. He was refreshed by his early morning walks along the

Turkey River, loved hearing birds again—he once declared that he had "studied with the birds, flowers, trees, God, and myself"—and enjoyed taking over Kovařík's organist duties. According to local legend, the summer was, at its end, troubled for the strict paterfamilias when his eldest daughter, Otilie, called Otilka, fell in love with Big Moon, a Native American, but in every other way it was a happy and productive time in which Dvořák composed the *American* Quartet, Opus 96, and the E-flat-major Quintet, Opus 97.

Dvořák was already under contract to stay in New York for 1893–1894; after that, not without some difficulty, Mrs. Thurber persuaded him to return for a third year. When he sailed to Europe in April 1895, on the same *Saale* that had brought him the first time, it was for good and without regret, though as late as August 1897 Mrs. Thurber was still trying to get him back. Her conservatory survived some years into the new century.

Aside from the two masterpieces of chamber music he composed in Spillville, the principal works of this American sojourn of Dvořák's were the Symphony *From the New World*, the once-immensely popular Violin Sonatina in G, and the *Biblical Songs*, Opus 99. A second stay in New York yielded the Cello Concerto, like the *New World* Symphony a work of dark and troubling eloquence.

On 9 March 1894, Dvořák went to Brooklyn to hear Victor Herbert, then principal cellist at the Metropolitan Opera, give the first performance of his own Cello Concerto No. 2 with Anton Seidl and the New York Philharmonic.[1] Herbert had been first cellist at the memorable premiere of the *New World* Symphony in December 1893, which Seidl had conducted. Reminiscing in 1922, Herbert wrote that "after I had played my (2nd) Cello-Concerto in one of the Philh. Concerts—Dr. Dvořák came back to the 'Stimm-Zimmer' [tuning room]—threw his arms around me, saying before many members of the orchestra: famos! [splendid] famos! ganz famos!"[2]

Several times, Dvořák had been asked for a concerto by his friend Hanuš Wihan, founder and cellist of the Czech String Quartet.[3] Hearing Herbert's Concerto nudged Dvořák into thinking seriously about that project. The warmhearted, melodious, and beautifully composed piece appealed to him immediately, and, having always been distrustful of the cello's upper range, which he found thin and nasal, he was impressed when Herbert, who managed high-flying passages elegantly and wrote plenty of them for himself, showed Dvořák that he had been wrong on that point.

---

[1]Lynn Harrell and Yo-Yo Ma have been advocates of this engaging concerto, but Herbert's name lives on chiefly thanks to his operettas *Babes in Toyland* and *Naughty Marietta*. He was a skilled and refined composer, a first-rate cellist, and the conductor who made the Pittsburgh Symphony into a front-ranking orchestra.

[2]Claire Lee Purdy, *Victor Herbert : American Music-Master* (New York: Julian Messner, 1944).

[3]Before leaving for America in September 1892, Dvořák went on a farewell tour of thirty-nine Czech cities and towns with Wihan and the violinist Ferdinand Lachner. The mainstay of their programs was Dvořák's *Dumky* Trio.

It was eight months before Dvořák began his own Concerto, a period that included five months at home in Prague. In 1865 he had written a Cello Concerto in A major but had never bothered to orchestrate that unsatisfactory piece. (It is occasionally heard in a high-handed performing edition made in the 1920s by the German composer Günther Raphael.) Now, just as Dvořák had encouraged Joseph Joachim to give him advice and to suggest and even make revisions in his Violin Concerto in 1879, he now leaned on Wihan for technical assistance. He was, however, less docile now than fifteen years before, and there was some friction, particularly concerning a fifty-nine-measure cadenza Wihan inserted into the finale. Writing to his publisher, Fritz Simrock, Dvořák allowed for the addition of easier alternatives for certain passages, but otherwise made it clear that he would give Simrock this work "only if you promise not to allow *anybody* to make changes—Friend Wihan not excepted—without my *knowledge* and *consent*—and also not the cadenza Wihan has added to the last movement."[4]

A reconciliation was achieved easily enough, but a series of misunderstandings over dates between Dvořák and the Secretary of the Philharmonic Society of London made it impossible for Wihan to undertake the premiere of the concerto, which had meanwhile been dedicated to him. Wihan played the work for the first time in 1899 with the Amsterdam Concertgebouw Orchestra under Willem Mengelberg and later performed it on several occasions under the composer's direction.

The Cello Concerto is not so much a greeting from America, like the *New World* Symphony, as a look homeward. The first movement includes two of Dvořák's most memorable themes. The one at the beginning bears some of the characteristics of funeral music—the heavy, dotted rhythm and the somber colors of low clarinet, joined by bassoons, with a penumbral accompaniment of violas, cellos, and bassess—and so anticipates the elegiac mood of the close of the finale. Michael Beckerman believes that the theme deliberately alludes to the third movement of Brahms's *German Requiem*, "Lord, teach me to know the number of my days." This melody lends itself to a wonderful series of oblique, multifaceted harmonizations. The other, more lyrical, is as beautiful a French horn solo as exists in the repertory. Dvořák admitted that he himself could not hear it without emotion.

The solo cello makes a commanding entrance—hair-raising in the 1937 Casals recording—in a passage Dvořák marks *quasi improvvisando* and sets over strangely mixed major and minor harmonies. The cello gets its turn at the horn theme, the soloist all too often demonstrating that he has less taste than the horn player. That great melody is not something for development, and so it is the first theme that furnishes the material for the quite short but densely composed central section of the movement. The most wondrous moment comes

---

[4]John Clapham, *Antonín Dvořák: Musician and Craftsman* (New York: St. Martin's Press, 1966).

when the cello, now in a very remote key (A-flat minor), muses over the first theme and, together with the flute, transforms it into a song of ecstatic and deeply sad lyricism. Since we have been given so much of the first theme in the development, Dvořák launches the recapitulation with the horn theme, now begun *fortissimo* by the violins and woodwinds but immediately taken over by the solo cello. A technically terrifying scale in octaves introduces this triumphal homecoming. The movement ends with jubilant fanfares.

The Adagio begins in tranquillity, but this mood is soon broken by an orchestral outburst that introduces a quotation from one of Dvořák's own songs, sung by the cello in its high register and with tearing intensity. The song, the first of a set of *Four Songs*, Opus 82, composed in 1887–1888, is *Kéž duch m°uj sám* (Leave me alone). It was a special favorite of Dvořák's sister-in-law, Josefina Kaunitzová. Thirty years earlier, Dvořák had been deeply in love with the then sixteen-year-old Josefina Čermáková, an aspiring actress to whom he gave piano lessons. The love was not returned, and Dvořák eventually married Josefina's younger sister Anna.[5] Something of the old feeling remained, and the song intruded on the Concerto when the news of Josefina's illness reached Dvořák in New York. Josefina died on 27 May 1895, a month after the Dvořáks' return to Prague, and it was in her memory that Dvořák added the coda—elegiac and agonized—to which he did not want Wihan to add his cadenza. Here is how Dvořák described this passage: "The Finale closes gradually diminuendo, like a sigh, with reminiscences of the first and second movements—the solo dies down to *pp*, then swells again, and the last bars are taken up by the orchestra and the whole concludes in a stormy mood. That is my idea, and I cannot depart from it."[6]

Dvořák had been skeptical about writing a concerto for cello, but thanks at least in part to Victor Herbert, he had overcome his inhibition—fortunately, since it remains the most beautiful one we have. Robert Hausmann, the cellist of the Joachim Quartet, played Dvořák's Concerto for Brahms at his apartment in 1897 and told both D. F. Tovey and Brahms's occasional piano student and future biographer, Florence May, that the dying composer had said, "Why on earth didn't I know one could write a cello concerto like this? If I'd only known, I'd have written one long ago!" By then, Brahms had actually known the Concerto for a good year, having done the proofreading on it for his and Dvořák's publisher, Fritz Simrock, early in 1896, and he had written to Simrock then that "cellists can be grateful to your Dvořák for bestowing on them such a great and skillful work."

---

[5]This was parallel to Mozart's love for Aloysia Weber, her indifference to him, and his eventual marriage to Aloysia's younger sister Constanze.
[6]Clapham, op. cit.

# Edward Elgar

Edward William Elgar—Sir Edward after being knighted by King Edward VII on 4 July 1904—was born at Broadheath, Worcestershire on 2 June 1857 and died in Worcester on 23 February 1934.

## Concerto in E minor for Cello and Orchestra, Opus 85

*Adagio—Moderato*
*Allegro molto*
*Adagio*
*Allegro, ma non troppo*

Elgar wrote the *moderato* theme of the first movement on 23 March 1918, immediately after returning home from the hospital, where he had undergone a tonsillectomy. He began concentrated work on the score that July and completed it on 3 August 1919. The first performance took place in Queen's Hall, London, on 26 October 1919, the composer conducting the London Symphony and with Felix Salmond as soloist. The score is dedicated to two dear friends of Elgar's, Sidney and Frances (misprinted Francis in the Novello score) Colvin, Sir Sidney then being Keeper of Prints and Drawings at the British Museum. Elgar authorized the violist Lionel Tertis to make a transcription of this work for viola and orchestra.

**Solo cello, two flutes, piccolo (*ad lib.*), two oboes, two clarinets, two bassoons, four horns, two trumpets, three trombones, tuba (*ad lib.*), timpani, and strings.**

Elgar's was a strangely paced career. He was a few weeks short of forty when he first drew attention with an *Imperial March* for Queen Victoria's Diamond Jubilee, he composed all the music on which his fame rests between the ages of forty-two and sixty-two, and he lived to be seventy-six. Once on his way, he quickly achieved an eminence of which few artists dare dream, the first performances of his Symphony No. 1 in 1908 and the Violin Concerto (with Kreisler) in 1910 marking the zenith of his fame. But at the premiere of his Symphony No. 2 in 1911 it was clear that the tide had turned. By 1919, the year of the Cello Concerto, he had become a monument. He commanded some respect and provoked occasional ridicule, especially among those swept up in the excitement of the new music of Stravinsky, Schoenberg, and others, but for the most part he was an object simply of indifference.

Elgar had a keen sense of his own "irrelevance." More was at stake for him than the purely musical issues that, for example, made Rachmaninoff, for example, feel for some years after 1918 that the work of Schoenberg, Bartók, and Stravinsky had rendered his kind of music obsolete. The 1914–1918 War had depressed Elgar utterly. The slaughter of men and horses (the latter almost more devastating to him than the former) caused him unquenchable anguish, and he saw clearly that a whole world—*his* world—was being swept away. Not that his relationship to that world was ever anything other than uneasy. He was poor, he was self-taught and had not been to one of the great universities, he was Catholic in a land of often uninhibited anti-Roman sentiment, and he felt (although he probably exaggerated) the disapproval of his Worcestershire neighbors for having married "above his station." He never learned to be at peace with these differences.

Elgar's *Pomp and Circumstance* marches celebrate the prewar Empire without reservation, but the composer of the two symphonies, *The Dream of Gerontius*, the Violin Concerto, and *Falstaff* is far removed from the world of Empire. There is a great "imperial" tune in the First Symphony, and it does triumph—but only by the skin of its teeth; in the other works—resigned, melancholy, moody, introspective, even tormented—triumph is not in the picture at all. Even though he himself constantly questioned *Pomp and Circumstance* heroics, especially once the Great War had begun, Elgar also loved what he questioned and needed it as something to play against. And, no less, he needed the opulence, the sumptuousness, and the spaciousness of Edwardian upper-crust culture. The guns of August blasted away the context for his music.

For four years after the completion of *Falstaff* in July 1913, Elgar wrote only minor and occasional pieces. In 1918 and 1919 he wrote, almost as postscript, a series of compositions whose chamber-musical intimacy was new in his work: the Violin Sonata, the String Quartet, the Piano Quintet, and the slightly—but only slightly—more "public" Cello Concerto.

The prospect of the first major Elgar score since *Falstaff* was not enough to fill Queen's Hall when the Cello Concerto was introduced; no one, moreover, bothered to protest on the composer's behalf when Albert Coates, the conductor of the rest of the program, usurped much of Elgar's rehearsal time to work on Borodin's Symphony No. 2 and Scriabin's *Poem of Ecstasy*. Only consideration for the soloist kept Elgar from withdrawing his Concerto. The performance itself, underrehearsed, was a near disaster.

A week after the premiere of the Cello Concerto, Alice Elgar, eight years older than her husband (something else for the Worcestershire gentry to gossip about), entered her final illness. She died five months later, in April 1920. Elgar had numerous emotional attachments to other women, but he was totally devoted and faithful to Alice, who had been no less devoted to her "Edu" and who had steadied him as much as he could be steadied. Losing her depressed him profoundly and, except for minor scores, he stopped composing for many years.

Futile though it is to do so, I nonetheless wonder what might have happened had Alice Elgar not died when she did. Because they were in effect the end, we think of the Violin Sonata, the String Quartet, the Piano Quintet, and the Cello Concerto as Elgar's "farewell," as though they were intentionally final. Perhaps Elgar even thought of them that way at the time or in the immediate aftermath, but as a result of the composer Anthony Payne's investigation of the sketches for the Symphony No. 3, we now know that in 1932 Elgar's creative powers came once again to blazing life when, at the urging of George Bernard Shaw, the BBC tendered him a commission for a symphony. When he died in February 1934, Elgar had made far more progress on the work than was previously supposed, and Payne was able to make a realization of the sketches that was given its first public performance in London by Andrew Davis and the BBC Symphony on 15 February 1998, with a recording on the NMC label following immediately.

Sir Adrian Boult, as deeply perceptive an interpreter as Elgar's music ever had, once observed that in the Cello Concerto Elgar had "struck a new kind of music, with a more economical line, terser in every way." Boult was surprised that Elgar had not been "bitten by the new style." Elgar-Payne No. 3, though laid out on a grand scale, tells us that he in fact had been.[1] But cellists, a sentimental lot, lay upon the concerto the burden of their sense of

---

[1] As a composer who also went through a phase of feeling depressed, outdated, obsolete, "irrelevant," Rachmaninoff presents an interesting parallel to Elgar, but after a time he certainly did to some degree get bitten by *his* new and leaner style, for example in the *Rhapsody on a Theme of Paganini*, the Symphony No. 3, and the *Symphonic Dances*.

"farewell" and therefore deny the "economical line," the terse utterance, the lean textures of this music. It will be interesting to see whether the awareness of the Third Symphony will have an effect on the performance tradition of the Cello Concerto. I am not holding my breath.

The soloist begins the Concerto with a sentence of recitative that is spacious, extroverted, noble, and tinged by melancholy. What happens in the orchestra, a few notes of accompaniment and a brief woodwind echo of the first phrase, is a miracle of unostentatious mastery. Picking up the cello's last sound, the violas begin a gentle, ambling theme; this was the first idea Elgar had jotted down for this work. It descends beyond the violas' range, is carried on by the cellos, and is then reiterated and expanded by the soloist. Unaccompanied at first, it gets a lovely series of subtly oblique harmonizations once the soloist has taken it on. Clarinets and bassoon propose a lilting new theme, on which the cello makes sweetly tristful comment—which does not, however, keep the tune from moving into warm E major. The first section is recapitulated with ever more beautiful scoring: enjoy, for example, the delicately placed notes for the timpani.

The first movement subsides on a low E, plucked by the solo cello, bowed in the orchestra. The sound of that note in the orchestral cellos and basses seems to remind the soloist of the way the Concerto began. It is enough, at any rate, to start the cello on reminiscences, still in pizzicato, about the recitative. The orchestra is quick to discourage any such sentimental musings and urges the soloist to get going. The scherzo, when it is finally under way, is a virtuosic study in repeated notes, full of rhythmic surprises, and the orchestra accompanies with the utmost deftness. A new theme with a delightful touch of swagger makes a few visitations, but the dominant style of the movement is lighter-than-air.

Now the stage is darkened. The songful Adagio is a great page by a great composer of slow movements. Brief and simple, a wistful Schumann romance rather than an outburst of Mahlerian anguish, it tends to bring out the worst in cellists. (Just look at Elgar's metronome marking of $\flat = 50$ and of his choice to write the music in 3/8 rather than 3/4.)[2] For only a moment, the music rises to an urgent climax, sinking then to a close on a question mark (that, too, a Schumannesque touch).

The orchestra takes the hint and begins a distant marchlike music to rouse the solo cello from its Adagio musings, at the same time modulating rapidly so as to bring things back to the main key of E minor. The effect,

---

[2]Beatrice Harrison's beautiful 1928 performance, with the composer conducting, is an illuminating document that tells us how Elgar wanted cellists to give voice to this tender confession. The 1973 recording by Paul Tortelier with Boult is the only other one I know that attains deep feeling without sentimentality.

however, is to send the solo cello into its recitative mood again. The brief unaccompanied cadenza done, the march takes off and the finale is under way. Up to a point it seems to be a cheery, uncomplicated rondo. Then a newer and slower theme in a broader meter and rich chromatic harmony changes the mood. That new and somber atmosphere established, another change of meter, now to 3/4, brings the music to its most impassioned climax. We catch just a ghost of the Adagio, followed by one more recollection of the opening recitative, and then the Concerto hurries to its close.

## Concerto in B minor for Violin and Orchestra, Opus 61

*Allegro*
*Andante*
*Allegro molto*

In 1891 and again in 1901, Elgar made a start at writing a violin concerto, but it is not known whether any part of either project survives in the present score. The Violin Concerto includes material sketched as early as October 1905, but the main work on the score was done between April 1909 and 5 August 1910. On 12 May 1910, Elgar, at the piano, read the first movement in private performance with Leonora von Stosch (Lady Speyer) and considerably revised it in the light of that experience. After the work was completed, there were two private hearings during the 1910 Three Choirs Festival at Gloucester, both with the composer at the piano, one on 4 September with W. H. Reed, who had assisted the composer with many of the violinistic details, and another on 8 September with Fritz Kreisler, whose request in 1906 had prompted Elgar to write the Concerto and who would give the first public performance. That event took place in London at a concert of the Philharmonic Society on 10 November 1910, with Elgar conducting. The score is dedicated "To Fritz Kreisler" but also carries an epigraph in Spanish, "Aquí está encerrada el alma de . . . . . ", which Elgar translated in a letter to his friend the conductor Nicholas Kilburn as "Here, or more emphatically *In here* is enshrined or (simply) enclosed—*buried* is perhaps too definite—*the soul of?* the final 'de' leaves it indefinite as to sex or rather gender." This epigraph comes from Alain-René Lesage's picaresque novel *Gil Blas* (1715–1735); however, Elgar's biographer Jerrold Northrop Moore surmises that the composer got it at second hand from *Echoes* by the Victorian poet William Ernest Henley.

Solo violin, two flutes, two oboes, two clarinets, two bassoons with contrabassoon (*ad lib.*), four horns, two trumpets, three trombones, tuba (*ad lib.*), timpani, and strings.

> *I have written out my soul in the concerto, Sym. II & the Ode [The Music Makers] &*
> *you know it . . . in these three works I have shewn myself.*
>                                         Elgar to Alice Stuart-Wortley, 29 August 1912

At forty, in 1897, Elgar was just beginning the breakthrough from a provincial reputation to a cosmopolitan one, thanks largely to the *Imperial March* he wrote for Queen Victoria's Diamond Jubilee that year. Ten years later he was the renowned composer of the *Enigma* Variations, the song cycle *Sea Pictures*, the three oratorios *The Dream of Gerontius*, *The Apostles*, and *The Kingdom*, the first four *Pomp and Circumstance* marches (the famous No. 1 got a double encore at its premiere in 1901 and as *Land of Hope and Glory* had become a second, unofficial national anthem), the *Cockaigne* Overture, the Introduction and Allegro for Strings, and the first *Wand of Youth* Suite. After a spell as Dr. Elgar (*honoris causa* at Cambridge in 1900), he became Sir Edward. With the exception only of the singer to whom he referred in a letter as that "battered old w—e . . . Melba," he was the most prominent, the most popular musician in the British Empire, and he looked it, every inch.

It was *The Dream of Gerontius* that had established Elgar's considerable prewar reputation on the Continent. In England it took some time for that work to recover from the debacle of a bad first performance in Birmingham in 1900; however, Julius Buths, the music director in Düsseldorf, was present and immediately perceived the oratorio's quality, giving it excellent representation with his own forces in December 1901 and to even better effect in May 1902. The day after this second German performance, Richard Strauss, in a widely publicized gesture, toasted "the welfare and success of the first English progressivist, Meister Edward Elgar, and of the young progressive school of English composers."

One of the musicians to get caught up in the subsequent Continental Elgar boom—along with Arthur Nikisch, Fritz Steinbach, Felix Weingartner, Wilhelm Backhaus, Ferruccio Busoni, Ignace Jan Paderewski, Alexander Siloti, and Adolph Brodsky—was Fritz Kreisler, still in his twenties but an international celebrity since his Berlin Philharmonic debut in 1899. In June 1904, Henry Ettling, a German conductor and wine merchant, wrote to Elgar, with whom he had been friendly for some years, that he had just visited Kreisler and found him at the piano "deep in *The Dream of Gerontius*, he told me full of enthusiasm for you, whether it is true you once wrote a violin concerto & if so, he would feel happy if you would trust it to him."

That October, Kreisler played the Brahms Concerto at the Leeds Festival as part of a program on which Elgar conducted his *In the South* Overture.
The idea of getting a concerto out of Elgar grew in the violinist's mind, and
when he returned to England to play Bach at the Norwich Festival in October
1905, where Elgar conducted his Introduction and Allegro and *The Apostles*,
he said some strong things to an interviewer from the *Hereford Times*:

> If you want to know whom I consider to be the greatest living composer, I say
> without hesitation, Elgar. Russia, Scandinavia, my own Fatherland, or any oth-
> er nation can produce nothing like him. I say this to please no one; it is my
> own conviction. Elgar will overshadow everybody. He is on a different level.
> . . . His invention, his orchestration, his harmony, his grandeur, it is wonderful.
> And it is all pure, unaffected music. I wish Elgar would write something for
> violin. He could do so, and it would certainly be something effective.[3]

Elgar took the bait. Back home from Norwich, he sketched some themes,
two of which

Ex. 1

Ex. 2

"Allegro Orch"

made their way into the first movement of the Concerto. A third, a portrait
of Hans Richter, the conductor who had introduced the *Enigma* Variations
and, less fortunately, *Gerontius*, found a place in the finale of the Symphony
No. 2. The following year, Kreisler formally requested a concerto from Elgar.
First, though, the composer had to deal with the consequences of a melody
that had come to him in Rome at the beginning of 1907, and it was not until
September 1908 that his Symphony No. 1 was completed. After its triumphant premiere that December (again under Richter), Elgar went into a winter depression, but a stay in Italy and the exercise of keeping his hand in by

---

[3]Jerrold Northrop Moore, *Edward Elgar: A Creative Life* (Oxford: Oxford University Press, 1984).
Later quotations except where otherwise identified, come from Moore's book.

writing some part-songs revived him. By April 1909 he was seriously at work on the Kreisler project, and in August Lady Elgar noted in her diary, "E. possessed with his music for the Vl. Concerto."

As he worked—first on the Andante, proceeding then to the first Allegro, and after that to the finale—Elgar's spirits swung up and down. The success of the First Symphony in 1909 and 1910 was amazing, with more than a hundred performances in nine countries; on the other hand, there were saddening deaths—of two of the friends pictured in the *Enigma* Variations (one of them "Nimrod," August Jaeger of the publishing firm of Novello, who had done more than anyone to encourage Elgar and make him feel like a professional); the soprano Olga Ouroussoff Wood, wife of the conductor Henry J. Wood; Professor Samuel Sanford at Yale, who had organized Elgar's first visit to America; and Edward VII ("that dear sweet-tempered King-Man").

Elgar's letters tell some of the story of his pregnancy. 7 February 1910: "I am not sure about that Andante and shall put it away for a long time before I decide its fate." 29 April: "It is so dreary to-day & the tunes stick." 8 May: "I have the Concerto well in hand & have played (?) it thro' on the p.f. & it's *good!* awfully emotional! too emotional but I love it: 1st movement finished & the IIIrd well on—these *are* times for composition." 16 June: "I have made the end serious & grand I hope & have brought in the real inspired themes from the 1st movemt. . . . I did it this morning . . . the music sings of memories & hope." 23 June: "I am appalled at the last movement & cannot get on—it is growing so large—too large, I fear." 29 June: "This Concerto is *full* of romantic feeling—I should have been a philanthropist if I had been a rich man—I *know* the feeling is human & right—vainglory!" 7 July: "That last movement is good stuff! Kreisler saw it on Friday & is delighted. . . . He said at one passage, 'I will shake Queen's Hall!' "

A happy event occurred on 27 May 1910 when Elgar, walking along Regent Street, met W. H. (Billy) Reed, a young violinist about to begin a twenty-three-year reign as the London Symphony's concertmaster. Reed was astonished and flattered not merely to be recognized but to be asked whether he had any spare time and would be willing to help "settle some questions of bowing and certain intricacies of violin technique." (As a young man, Elgar had played and taught the violin, but had never come near commanding the virtuosity needed to play what he was concocting for Kreisler.) Reed, who many years later wrote two books about Elgar, described going the next day to the composer's *pied-à-terre* in New Cavendish Street, where he found

> Sir Edward striding about with a number of loose pieces of MSS. which he was arranging in different parts of the room. Some were already pinned to the backs of chairs, or fixed up on the mantelpiece ready for me to play, so we started without any loss of time. I discovered then that what we were playing was a

sketchy version of what is now the Violin Concerto. The main ideas were written out, and, to use one of his own pet expressions, he had "japed them up" to make a coherent piece.[4]

Reed worked with Elgar into the summer, thus taking his place in the ranks of violinist-helpers to the great concerto composers.

That Kreisler would give the first performance was sure, but an inconvenient number of orchestras, conductors, and impresarios wanted to get into the act, and the politics of it all caused Elgar much annoyance. It was resolved in favor of the Philharmonic Society, with Elgar himself conducting. Kreisler, asked by the *Christian Science Monitor* whether he thought the work ranked with the Beethoven and Brahms concertos, said firmly: "Yes, we have not had a romantic concerto of this value. . . . From a player's point of view it is perhaps the most difficult of all concertos for endurance, and it is the first to have all the intricacies of modern scoring. . . ."[5]

More important, Kreisler, though nervous and "white as a sheet," played magnificently and was handsomely partnered by Elgar. A storm of applause greeted each of the three movements, and afterwards, according to the *Daily Mail,* "the huge audience went wild with pride and delight. For a quarter of an hour they called and recalled [Elgar], who had achieved a triumph not only for himself but for England, and hailed him with wonder and submission as master and hero." The premieres of the First Symphony and the Violin Concerto were the double apogee of public appreciation of Elgar during his lifetime; the Violin Concerto was the last new work of his to enjoy unambiguous success.

Kreisler gave many more performances of the Concerto during the next few years but caused Elgar distress when he began to make cuts in the finale. (A few famous violinists have emulated Kreisler in this, always with the effect of making the movement sound badly composed.) His Master's Voice made repeated efforts to organize a recording with Kreisler and Elgar, but Kreisler evaded the challenge. In 1932 Fred Gaisberg of HMV then got Yehudi Menuhin to learn and record the work; the resulting collaboration of the sixteen-year-old violinist with the seventy-five-year-old composer is one of the great monuments in the history of recorded sound. Menuhin's playing in the studio as well as at concerts in London and Paris made Elgar entirely happy, and to the words "To Fritz Kreisler" on the title page he added "and to my dear Yehudi Menuhin."

[4]W. H. Reed, *Elgar as I Knew Him* (Oxford: Oxford University Press, 1989).
[5]Elgar was surely aware that the opus number he gave his Violin Concerto—61—was also that of Beethoven's. Nimrod, who had had many impassioned conversations with Elgar about Beethoven, would have loved that touch. Had Elgar wished to avoid this coincidence he could easily have traded numbers with the *Eastern European Folk-Song Paraphrases,* Opus 60, or the *Romance for Bassoon and Orchestra,* Opus 62, which was composed during work on the Violin Concerto, using related material, and which was finished many months before the larger work.

Other notable early interpreters of the Elgar Concerto were the great Eugène Ysaÿe, who carried the work all over Europe until he quarreled with Novello over performance fees; Adolph Brodsky, who had given the premiere of Tchaikovsky's Concerto in 1881; and that finest of English violinists, Albert Sammons, who made the first complete recording of the work in 1929 with Sir Henry Wood conducting. One who displeased Elgar was the nineteen-year-old Heifetz (one of the cutters): "Yes, it was a tremendous display—not exactly our own Concerto: as to the noise afterwards—none of it was for me or my music—the people simply wanted Heifetz to play some small things with piano—the latter instrument being dextrously provided by his agent."

When Elgar translated "Aquí está encerrada el alma de . . . . ." for Kilburn, he added, "Now guess." The favorite candidate of the guessers has been Alice Stuart-Wortley (later Lady Stuart of Wortley), in Jerrold Northrop Moore's words "a brilliant and deeply sympathetic woman with a fine understanding of artists"; she was the daughter of Sir John Millais, whose *Pot of Basil* was Elgar's favorite painting, wife of the Member of Parliament for Sheffield, and a friend since 1897. She shared a first name with Elgar's wife and, after about 1906 when the Elgars and the Stuart-Wortleys came to be on first-name terms, the composer found that hard to deal with: Alice S-W therefore became "the Windflower." It was to her that he wrote of "our concerto" and "your concerto." He thought of certain phrases in the work as "Windflower themes," and he was particularly anxious that she like and "approve" it. Most telling of all, in September 1910 he wrote out the Spanish quotation for her on a sheet of her own notepaper. Another of the composer's biographers, Michael Kennedy, also cites as evidence the *five* dots (for the five letters of the name "Alice") at the end of the quotation, since typographical convention, which Elgar knew well, would call for three or four.

Five dots could also point to another friend, Julia Worthington (nicknamed Pippa), whom the Elgars had met in America in 1905 and whom they saw frequently on their visits to Italy where she had a villa. Mrs. Worthington's candidacy as "el alma" was first advanced by Mrs. Richard Powell, the Dorabella of the *Enigma* Variations, and it is endorsed by two important Elgar scholars and biographers, Percy M. Young and Diana McVeagh; the weight of evidence, however, is surely with the Windflower. Moore, a daringly speculative as well as perceptive observer, imagines a trio of living "souls," each with a "ghost" standing behind: for the first movement, the Windflower and Helen Weaver, a Worcester neighbor who was briefly Elgar's fiancée in 1883–1884; for the second, Alice Elgar and Ann Elgar, his mother; for the third, Billy Reed and the physically so similar Nimrod.[6] We remember also that

---

[6]*Gerontius* by James Hamilton-Paterson is a wonderful novel with deep insights into Elgar's creative life and his life with his "souls."

Elgar told Alice Stuart-Wortley he had "written out my soul in the concerto," and indeed, in spite of its size and brilliance and "publicness," this is music of almost painful intimacy, a work of "self-communing," to borrow a term from Michael Kennedy. Then, too, few violinists would wish to quarrel with Kennedy when he writes that "no matter whose soul [the Concerto] enshrines, it enshrines the soul of the violin."

This must be the last great concerto to open with a long orchestral exposition in the manner of the great Classical concertos and of Brahms's. (Elgar's Cello Concerto of 1919 does without.) Elgar begins with the first idea he had jotted down in October 1905 and had then marked *Allegro Orch* (Example 2, page 191). Short ideas, often with a close family likeness, come thick and fast, coalescing into grand, richly varied paragraphs. The forceful, thrusting beginning yields to a new, descending theme, begun in second violins and violas, and full of pathos—conceived "in dejection," Elgar told the Windflower:

Ex. 3

When he sketched it, he noted not only the day but the hour: "Feb 7 1910 630 p.m." Of its passionate continuation, however, he wrote: "This is going to be good! 'When Love and Faith meet there will be Light.' "

The "dejection" idea is one of the Windflower themes. The clarinet sings the second of these, which is also the second of those that Elgar had noted in 1905, but this moment of quiet is succeeded by the stir of anticipation that heralds the entrance of the soloist. We might expect him to begin as the orchestra did; indeed, the orchestra itself hints strongly that he should. But Elgar has something more poetic in mind. The excitement subsides, the orchestral violins restate the two opening bars (*piano* this time rather than *mezzo-forte*, and more softly accompanied), and only then does the soloist step forward to complete the sentence—broadly and *nobilmente*—leading us at the same time to the first fully settled cadence in the home key of B minor. Adrian Boult, who would become one of the great Elgar conductors, attended the first performance as a twenty-one-year-old Oxford undergraduate: he never forgot "the thrill of first hearing the tone of Fritz Kreisler's G-string unobtrusively carrying on the line."

Ex. 4

In fact the solo violin never plays those first two measures, and Reed recalled that "several times we played the opening to [Elgar's] great satisfaction at the novelty of the idea."

A quietly eloquent recitative inaugurates a second exposition, whose character, to use Moore's evocative term, is the translation of "orchestra 'fact'" to "solo 'fantasy.'" The development is stormy, and for thirty-six critical and impassioned measures the solo violin withdraws altogether. It returns only with the recapitulation, once again completing the orchestra's sentence, but now leading their conversation into a different, more melancholy strain. The two Windflower themes reappear soon, extended, transformed, fantastically decorated, combined with other themes. Elgar builds the coda on what he described to Reed as an "affliction" of the opening phrase, and the movement is driven to a powerful conclusion.

The Andante is set far away, in B-flat major. The music is gentle. As the orchestra repeats its opening strain, the violin adds a melody to the middle of the texture. With the entrance of the soloist, the temperature rises, even though the dynamics stay generally quiet, and the music swiftly traverses new harmonic territories, eventually to land in a sensual D-flat major. The violin bursts melodic bounds with a wild and virtuosic phrase whose working out gave Elgar and Reed special pleasure, particularly the discovery that when it returns in the recapitulation, the great twelfth-leap from the low A-flat - should be negotiated riskily on the G-string rather than in some safer fingering:

Ex. 5

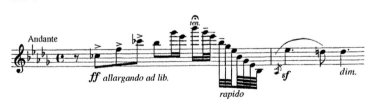

An intense climax is reached—and is swiftly left. The music subsides for a collected and regular recapitulation. But there is a remarkable change, so quietly and unobtrusively, so privately placed that one could almost believe it is addressed only to the players: this time a slightly different chord introduces the solo violin's wild phrase with the virtuoso leap, and it is that most unmistakable "*Tristan* chord." It even returns, still in utmost softness and brevity, three measures later.

I cannot offer a specific interpretation of the allusion. Elgar first heard the Prelude and *Liebestod* at a memorial concert at the Crystal Palace on 3 March 1883 (Wagner had died on 13 February) and noted then, "This is the finest thing of W.'s that I have heard up to the present. I shall never forget this." He saw *Tristan* several times in London, Bayreuth, and Munich, always in the company of his wife, always with a most intense response. Rosa Burley, headmistress at the girls' school where Elgar taught violin, accompanied the Elgars to Bayreuth in 1893 and wrote in her recollections of the composer: "*Tristan* was a shattering experience. . . . On all of us the heavily erotic melodies worked such a spell as to make sleep impossible for the whole night."

Altogether, the Violin Concerto is a work full of allusions, most of them kept more private still in the form of notations scribbled in the sketches. It is well to remember that the musical gestures were brimming with personal meaning for the composer. It is easy to succumb to the temptation to give these gestures biographical significance (as Moore so persuasively does and Donald Tovey so persuasively warns us not to). We must, in the end, also remember that what Elgar chose to give us was not an autobiography but a violin concerto, and it is to the music that we must attend.

The coda is tranquil and hushed. The themes, their passion spent, converse quietly in the final bars. In September 1932, Elgar invited a few friends to Marl Bank, his Worcester house, to hear the test pressing of the Menuhin recording. Among them were George Bernard Shaw and his wife; T. E. Lawrence ("Lawrence of Arabia"); and Vera Hockman, a young violinist from London and the last in the succession of women to whom Elgar formed a strong emotional attachment. It was Miss Hockman who recorded Elgar's words as Menuhin "lovingly lingered over the last melting phrase . . . : 'This is where two souls merge and melt into one another.' "

The swirling sixteenths that propel the finale into being crackle with suppressed tension, but the brilliant figurations deceive us if they lead us to expect that, like the finales of the Beethoven and Brahms concertos, this will be the lightest of the three movements. There is more unabashed virtuosity here than before.[7] Many and varied themes pass by; one of them, played

---

[7]Dialogue, 1932, between Sir Edward and the future Lord Menuhin concerning the scales in measures 9–11: E. E.: "No rallentando, the music must rush on." Y. M.: "Then why did you put it into octaves?"

against a constantly descending accompaniment in strings and bassoon, is distinctly "Windflowery":

Ex. 6

As in the first movement, the music grows tempestuous, with solo and orchestra often at loggerheads. The recapitulation brings the themes in re-verse order, a device used now and again by composers since Mozart. The music goes by swiftly, and then we understand: all this is preparation for the extraordinary event that will become the Concerto's emotional and structural focal point.

Neither the first movement nor the second made room for a cadenza, but now the music slows down for one. We see or hear the word cadenza and we think first of technical brilliance. But a cadenza—literally a cadence, a fanciful expansion of the concluding harmonic steps of a composition—is also a summing up, a gathering in, a last moment in which to recall what we have experienced. In this cadenza, virtuosity is, to be sure, an indispensable element, but it is unobtrusive. Recalling the past and reflecting on it is every-thing, as is hardly surprising in music that carries so much emotional freight.

"How excited he was about the cadenza!" Reed recalls. Usually the orchestra is mute at this point, but here, strings, clarinets, bassoons, horns, and timpani participate, sometimes to accompany, sometimes to contribute to the conversation. It is in fact the orchestra of the Concerto's opening bars, now ghostly, barely audible. Once again the violin steps in at the third mea-sure to complete the sentence, but this time it does so by playing sadly (mesto) a variant of the "dejection" theme. The solo violin, Elgar wrote to a friend, "sadly *thinks over* the 1st movemt." This was the passage he described to Windflower in the words quoted earlier: "[I] have brought in the real inspired themes from the 1st movemt . . . the music sings of memories & hope."

The violin plays quick and soaring figurations against the screen of a new orchestral sound. *Pizzicato tremolando* is what Elgar writes, explaining in the score that this should be " 'thrummed' with the soft part of three or four fingers across the strings." Writing to Nicholas Kilburn, he elaborated: "*Rustle* 3 or even 4 fingers *flatly* (not hooked) over the strings. Reserve the plucking & let the sound be sustained, soft & harmonious." For a moment the or-chestra falls silent as the violin spins a series of gently descending triplet figures. This, Reed tells us, "nearly moved him to tears as he repeated it again and yet again, dwelling on certain notes and marking them 'tenuto,' 'espress.,' 'animato,' or 'molto accel.' as he realized step by step exactly what he sought to express."

The music dissolves in a trill. Cadenzas traditionally end in trills, but the end is not yet. Not quite. The orchestra finds a phrase from the Andante, then falls silent again for the soloist to recall one of the Windflower phrases. Then the great circle of the cadenza is closed. As at its beginning, we hear the orchestra play the Concerto's opening bars, but this time the violin gives them their proper completion—*lento, espressivo, nobilmente*. And so we wake from the dream, from the play of memory, as violin and orchestra carry the Concerto to a swift, brilliant conclusion. And the last word—in the horns—is also the first:

Ex. 7

# Edvard Grieg

---

Edvard Hagerup Grieg was born on 15 June 1843 in Bergen, Norway, then part of Sweden, and died there on 4 September 1907.

---

## Concerto in A minor for Piano and Orchestra, Opus 16

*Allegro molto moderato*
*Adagio*
*Allegro moderato molto e marcato—Quasi presto—Andante maestoso*

Grieg began his Piano Concerto in June 1868 and completed the score early the following year. Edmund Neupert was the soloist at the first performance, which took place in Copenhagen on 3 April 1869, with Holger Simon Paulli conducting the orchestra of the Royal Theater. Grieg revised the Concerto many times, in 1872, 1882, 1890, and 1895, sending his last set of changes (including the addition of third and fourth horns) to his publisher on 21 July 1907, six weeks before his death. What is generally heard nowadays is an edition prepared in 1917 by the Australian composer and pianist Percy Grainger that includes still further changes Grainger said had been authorized by Grieg; Grainger had studied the Concerto with Grieg, who declared that Grainger would play it better than anyone.[1] Most of these revisions affect the orchestration and details of performance directions rather than the work's shape or thematic material.

---

[1]In 1919 Grainger recorded the solo portions of Grieg's concerto with the "orchestral accompaniment

The orchestra in Grieg's final version consists of two flutes and piccolo, two oboes, two clarinets, two bassoons, four horns, two trumpets, three trombones, timpani, and strings.

The Griegs were originally Scottish and spelled their name Greig; the composer's great-grandfather emigrated to Bergen in 1746. The romantic explanation for Alexander Greig's emigration is that it occurred right after the Battle of Culloden, the final defeat by the English of Stuart claimants to the throne; the more realistic one is that the young man saw a good opportunity for economic betterment. In any event, the connection with Britain stayed alive, for Edvard's father, a merchant, was the British consul in Bergen. Edvard grew up with music, his mother being a cultivated amateur player who also sang pleasingly; he himself was only five when he became enchanted with the possibilities of sounding two or three, even four or five notes on the family piano all at the same time. When he was fifteen he played for the renowned violinist Ole Bull, also from Bergen and in fact a distant relative, who urged Edvard's parents to send him to the Leipzig Conservatory, the training ground for so many young men and women from the musical hinterlands on both sides of the Atlantic, and it was really only then that it occurred to the boy to become a musician rather than a pastor.

Grieg found his teachers at Leipzig rigid and stuffy, but some welcome light was provided by his piano teacher, Ernst Ferdinand Wenzel, who had been a good friend of Mendelssohn and Schumann. Wenzel instilled in him a lifelong love for the music of Schumann, a feeling Grieg shared with his classmate Arthur Sullivan; one of Grieg's happiest memories of Leipzig was hearing Clara Schumann play her late husband's piano concerto at a Gewandhaus concert. After his return home, Grieg established himself as a respected pianist—there are piano-roll recordings that attest to his skill—but he still felt far from adequately prepared as a composer.

He went to Copenhagen, where he was encouraged by the composer Niels Gade (another Schumannite), became acquainted with many figures in Danish cultural life, including Hans Christian Andersen, and met a young singer, Nina Hagerup, who also happened to be his first cousin and who would become his wife four years later.[2] In the winter of 1864–1865 Grieg came under the spell of Rikard Nordraak, a composer just a year older than himself and possessed by the belief that Norwegian composers must participate in

adapted and added" by himself on Duo-Art piano rolls; in 1978 RCA combined the solo parts with a performance of the orchestral portion played by the Sydney Symphony under John Hopkins. The recording shows that Grainger played the work superbly—if not "better than anyone," certainly as well as anyone. A recording of a 1945 performance at the Hollywood Bowl with Leopold Stokowski conducting confirms this impression.

[2]Norway had been part of Denmark from 1397 until 1814, when it was ceded to Sweden; thus cultural ties with Denmark were still close in Grieg's young years.

the formation of a specifically Norwegian style, although it took a while before, in Grieg's case, this ideal became reality. (Nordraak himself died at twenty-three and so did not live to see the realization of his ideal nor the flowering of his friend's talent.)

A concert in Oslo (then called Christiania) in 1866, at which he introduced some of his songs and his first two violin sonatas, gave Grieg a name in his own country; the immensely popular Piano Concerto, presented in Copenhagen in 1869, started his international reputation. Eventually he came to be not only Norway's most important composer but a beloved figure whose major anniversaries were celebrated as national holidays. Abroad, he received recognition and awards wherever he went, among them honorary doctorates from Oxford and Cambridge, to say nothing of many performances and a dependable flow of royalty checks, and he was on friendly terms with some of the greatest musical and literary eminences of his day.

The composer of the Piano Concerto, however, was a young man of twenty-five with all that before him. Even if we did not otherwise know of the pleasure Grieg took in Schumann's Piano Concerto, we might well infer it from the way Grieg's begins in obvious emulation of it—an orchestral bang (which Grieg makes more dramatic with his preparatory drumroll), a cascade of piano chords, then a surprisingly hushed theme in the orchestra that is at once taken up by the soloist.[3]

Grieg's variant, we might also note, has just a touch of harmonic and melodic piquancy, which we are likely to find delightful but which the critic of the *Musical Times* assailed as "uncouth" after one of its early London performances. Once, however, that obeisance to Schumann has been rendered, what is far more impressive is the originality with which Grieg proceeds as well as the freshness of his voice. His themes have a deliciously personal cut—the A/G-sharp/E shape with which the piano enters would become very much of a Grieg signature—and they are strikingly presented. As in Schumann's concerto, the energies of the first movement progress toward a splendid gathering-in cadenza, though Grieg's is more virtuosic, indeed Lisztian. At the first performance, Neupert created such a firestorm of excitement with this cadenza that the audience burst into applause right in the middle of the movement.

The slow movement, with its wonderful sonorities (those muted strings!)

---

[3]In the first version of Grieg's Concerto, the drumroll is set in motion by a pizzicato chord for all the strings, and the tuba (which Grieg later dropped from the score) and two horns make a crescendo on A together with the timpani. To anyone listening to the original version, now available on an excellent recording by Love Derwinger with Jun'ichi Hirokami and the Norrköping Symphony, the most startling detail is likely to be the appearance of the second, gorgeously lyric theme in the first movement as the sweetest of trumpet solos. The first movement of Schumann's concerto in its original form also began differently from the now familiar version (see my essay on that work).

and its alternations of deeply felt song with melancholy arabesque, is of compelling lyric fervor. Certainly it left its mark on Rachmaninoff.[4]

The finale, music full of sapid, sometimes very Norwegian, boldly contrasted themes, is fresh in design and colorful in detail. The device of the grand peroration has become so familiar to us thanks to the concertos of Tchaikovsky and Rachmaninoff that we too easily forget its origination is right here. Tchaikovsky, by the way, was unstinting in expressing his admiration of Grieg: "What charm, what inimitable and rich musical imagery! What warmth and passion in his melodic phrases, what teeming vitality in his harmony, what originality and beauty in the turn of his piquant and ingenious modulations and rhythms, and in all the rest what interest, novelty, and independence."

More familiar is the story of Liszt's excitement about the Concerto. He had already been taken with one of Grieg's violin sonatas, and that is how he came to invite the young composer to visit him. He dazzled Grieg by playing the Concerto at sight. The melodic and harmonic transformation—by just one note—when the flute theme in the finale returns in grand style in the coda especially pleased him, and above the roar of his own playing he shouted his pleasure: "G-natural, G-natural, not G-sharp! G-natural!" Awed by the warmth and generosity of so senior a master, Grieg adopted some of Liszt's suggestions with respect to scoring; it seems, though, that these emendations eventually disappeared in the course of Grieg's own numerous later revisions.

Tchaikovsky's and Liszt's enthusiasm is easy to understand, as is the delight of the countless pianists who have brought audiences to their feet with this work. It has made its way with its singular and charming personality as well as with another characteristic that Tchaikovsky praised, "that rarest of qualities, perfect simplicity."

---

[4]Rachmaninoff never played the Grieg concerto, but he conducted it when his cousin Alexander Siloti played it at the Saint Petersburg concert at which Rachmaninoff introduced his own Second Symphony, and he also conducted a memorial program after Grieg's death. In the 1920s Rachmaninoff made glorious recordings of some of Grieg's *Lyric Pieces* for piano as well as of the C-minor Violin Sonata with his friend Fritz Kreisler.

# Paul Hindemith

Paul Hindemith (or Hindemitch, Hindemouth, Hintelmant, Hindismith, Heldeman, Hinder Mith, Hendrath, Hindemild, Algumuth, Hindemist, Hammermitt, Hairdemith, and Hundemith, to cite just a few of the variants the composer collected from letters, telegrams, bills, newspaper articles, concert programs, etc.) was born in Hanau, Hesse-Nassau, on 16 November 1895 and died in Frankfurt on 28 December 1963.

## Concerto for Cello and Orchestra

*Moderately fast/Moderato*
*Quietly moving/Andante con moto*
*March: Lively/Allegro marciale*

Hindemith began this Concerto in the early summer of 1940 and completed its three movements on 30 June, 4 July, and 9 September that year, all at Lenox, Massachusetts. He was on the faculty of the Berkshire Music Center, which held its first session at Tanglewood that summer. With Serge Koussevitzky conducting the Boston Symphony, Gregor Piatigorsky gave the first performance at Sanders Theater, Cambridge, Massachusetts, on 6 February 1941.

**Solo cello, two flutes, two oboes, two clarinets and bass clarinet, two bassoons, four horns, two trumpets, three trombones, tuba, timpani, snare drum, cymbals, bass drum, triangle, tambourine, field drum, celesta, and strings.**

The two greatest cellists in America vied for the premiere of this Concerto. Like Hindemith, Emanuel Feuermann and Gregor Piatigorsky had come to this country in the process that pushed such an amazing crowd of artists, writers, scientists, and intellectuals out of Hitler-governed and Hitler-threatened central and western Europe. Unhandicapped in the exercise of their profession by a language problem, the musicians were on the whole the most fortunate of those who were exiled in paradise (to borrow the title of Anthony Heilbut's important study of refugee culture in America). Feuermann and Piatigorsky settled well into the musical life of the United States, and Hindemith was among the most fortunate of the composers: the virtuosos did not come running for Bartók's Violin Concerto or Schoenberg's Piano Concerto, nor would they have done so for a new concerto by Stravinsky, then at the nadir of his reputation.

But Hindemith's music was "user-friendly" (an adjective that sounds like a fractured refugee-German construction), and he himself was forever being lauded as "practical." He was an imposingly versatile musician, and he had energy to match. "Paul Hindemith has burst like fireworks over New York, scattering performances everywhere," reported Elliott Carter in *Modern Music* in the spring of 1939, and the wide circle of his admirers included so unlikely a figure as John Cage, who, reviewing the Chicago premiere of the Cello Concerto in 1942, wrote that he found it "one of the most deeply moving experiences" of that season. Even Stravinsky—and one could hardly imagine a more different artistic personality—was an admirer and friend.[1]

In 1938 Hindemith and his wife emigrated from Berlin to Switzerland, four months after he had been prominently featured, along with Schoenberg, Stravinsky, Weill, Irving Berlin, and Louis Armstrong, among others, in the German government's much publicized traveling exhibition of "Degenerate Music." Hindemith's wife was half-Jewish by birth but a Catholic convert since her youth; it was primarily Hindemith's conflict with the artistic policies of the Third Reich, however, that determined his decision to leave. In 1940 they moved to the United States, Paul in February, Gertrud in September. Colleagues and friends arranged teaching and lecturing appointments, and that fall, Hindemith joined the faculty at Yale. The Hindemiths became American citizens, but after the war they began to spend increasing amounts of time in Europe, settling in Switzerland in 1953.

Before he began at Yale, Hindemith spent the summer at a new institution, the Berkshire Music Center at Tanglewood (now the Tanglewood Center) in Lenox, Massachusetts. He and Aaron Copland were the compo-

---

[1]Of course Hindemith had his detractors too, and Virgil Thomson, then critic for the *New York Herald-Tribune*, was the most articulate of them. In "The Hindemith Case," a Sunday piece of February 1941, Thomson wrote: "Paul Hindemith's music is both mountainous and mouselike. The volume of it is enormous; its expressive content is minute and not easy to catch."

sition teachers, incredibly different in their aims and attitudes.[2] Tanglewood's combination of festival and school was the brainchild of Serge Koussevitzky, conductor of the Boston Symphony since 1924. Hindemith's English biographer, Geoffrey Skelton, remarks that Koussevitzky, Mitropoulos, Ormandy, Rodzinski, and the other conductors in America who performed Hindemith's music, new and old, were not personal friends of his in the way Furtwängler, Scherchen, Sacher, and Rosbaud had been in Europe.[3] Hindemith had, however, been on amiable terms with Koussevitzky since a Paris engagement in 1927, when they had performed the *Kammermusik* No. 5 for Viola and Large Orchestra. Koussevitzky had seen to it that one of the commissions in honor of the Boston Symphony's 50th Anniversary in 1931 went to Hindemith, and the conductor was rewarded with the *Concert Music for Brass and Strings*, one of the best of that fine group of commissioned works. In the 1939–1940 season, Koussevitzky not only invited Hindemith to Tanglewood but gave seven performances of the *Mathis der Maler* Symphony and conducted the American premiere of Hindemith's new Violin Concerto in Boston.

Hindemith, for his part, could not bear idleness. He went to Lenox two weeks before the start of the Tanglewood season to get some composing done and spent all available hours that summer on the Cello Concerto as well as beginning his Symphony in E-flat. He was very much of a presence that summer: Koussevitzky repeated *Mathis*, E. Power Biggs introduced a new organ sonata, students played many of the recent sonatas for various orchestral instruments, and the opera department produced the amusing 1927 skit *Hin und zurück* (There and Back).

It was not unusual for Koussevitzky, who was possessive as well as just curious, to look over Hindemith's shoulder as he wrote his music, and, as the composer put it in a letter to his wife, he "annexed the [Cello Concerto] immediately. Piatigorsky happened to come through here at the same time, and they both took the work over for a Boston performance and later performances in New York and everywhere else." Mrs. Hindemith must have mentioned Feuermann in one of her letters, because Hindemith wrote: "I had not thought of Feuermann—actually of no one in particular. I was only interested in trying to write a piece for cello like the Violin Concerto." That Feuermann himself, who had played and recorded chamber music with Hindemith as violist and the violinist Szymon Goldberg at the beginning of the 1930s, was desperately interested emerges clearly in S. W. Itzkoff's biography of that great artist; in the event, the Russian connection between Koussevitzky and Piatigorsky prevailed. Feuermann never did get a chance at

---

[2]Among their students were Leonard Bernstein and Lukas Foss, both of whom did well in the conducting seminar, too.
[3]Skelton also suggests that Hindemith, as a former orchestra player—he had become concertmaster at the Frankfurt Opera at nineteen—had a built-in and permanent suspicion of and resistance to star conductors, making an exception only for Furtwängler.

Hindemith's concerto—he died a little over a year after the premiere at the age of thirty-nine.[4]

Aiming to write "a piece for the cello like the Violin Concerto," Hindemith set himself a high goal, for his Violin Concerto is one of his most impressive achievements as a composer of orchestral music. Hindemith had included a Cello Concerto in his early *Kammermusiken*. Opus 36, no. 2, composed in 1925, is a delightful piece, ingeniously scored for an ensemble of ten solo instruments, and it embodies perfectly the quality that Donald Tovey called attention to in the title of his essay "The 'Lean, Athletic Style' of Hindemith." The composer of the 1940 Cello Concerto is clearly the same Hindemith—the artistic personality and aesthetic preferences through which that personality is manifested are remarkably consistent from about 1921 to the end of his life—but the later Hindemith, though still athletic by temperament, is not as lean. Like the 1939 Violin Concerto, the 1940 Cello Concerto is a work in a grand manner, expansive in gesture, ample in sound.

The first of its three movements is marked both *Mässig schnell* and *Allegro moderato*, the Italian translation, new in Hindemith's scores, being a concession to his emigrant status. It begins with a grand call to attention by the full orchestra, which prepares the way for a handsome cello melody. We soon discover not only that these two elements go nicely together but also that the initial fanfare makes good cello music. Virtuosic triplet passages for the soloist lead to a long and powerful development for the orchestra alone, but when the cello returns, it is to play a solo cadenza. The traditional place for a cadenza is at the end of a movement, where it functions literally as a highly elaborated cadence, but here Hindemith is thinking of such unconventional models as Beethoven's Piano Concerto No. 5 and the Mendelssohn Violin Concerto. After recapitulation—with further transformations of musical character—the movement comes to a firm G-major conclusion in the manner of the fanfarelike opening.

The second movement begins with a lyric cello melody, delicately accompanied by plucked and muted strings with low flutes.[5] Flute and horn

---

[4]Piatigorsky had a Berlin connection, too, having been principal cellist of the Philharmonic from 1924 to 1928, taken part in some of the early performances of Schoenberg's *Pierrot lunaire*, and played chamber music and recorded sonatas with Artur Schnabel.

Aside from their interest in the Hindemith Concerto, there was another link between Feuermann and Piatigorsky in that they were both members, with Arthur Rubinstein and Jascha Heifetz, of what was dubbed by RCA Victor as "The Million Dollar Trio," Piatigorsky succeeding Feuermann after the latter's death.

Early in 1941, there was some sort of quarrel between Hindemith and Koussevitzky. Hindemith was not invited to return to Tanglewood, and the Symphony in E-flat, intended for Koussevitzky, was introduced by Mitropoulos and the Minneapolis Symphony. Piatigorsky stayed loyal to Hindemith's Concerto and played it often and beautifully.

[5]One who was taken with this music was William Walton, whose Viola Concerto Hindemith had introduced in London in 1929, and who in 1962–1963 made this melody the basis of his *Variations on a Theme by Hindemith*, dedicated to the composer and his wife, to their deep pleasure.

repeat this melody, the solo cello together with violins and violas adding an embroidery of flowing triplets. Suddenly, as the clarinet takes off in a whirl, the pace is three times as fast. Eventually, the running triplets pull the cello into the action, but essentially this exuberant episode belongs to the orchestra—at least for the moment. A climax with crashing percussion brings back the original slow tempo and, rather in the manner of those Gilbert and Sullivan choruses in which it is revealed after a while that the gentlemen's slow music and the ladies' quick music make charming counterpoint, flute and clarinet, with sonorous pizzicato chords, sing the opening, while the cello continues to romp through the fast music of the middle section. Only in the last fourteen bars does the soloist rejoin the party of the slow tempo. Hindemith liked this way of combining slow movement and scherzo into one design: he had already done it in *Der Schwanendreher*, and he would do it again in the *Symphonia serena* of 1946 and the Symphony in B-flat for Concert Band of 1951.

The finale is marked *Marsch—Lebhaft* in German and *Allegro marciale* in Italian. (There is no such word as *marciale* in Italian; march is *marcia*, but the adjective is *marziale*.) I quote from John Cage's review:

> It is a concerto in which the soloist is not merely displaying virtuosity, but one in which the cello is an individual and the orchestra is the group and the musical relationships are also human relationships. This is particularly clear in the last movement in which the orchestra sets forth in martial character, the cello remaining distinct and apart, poetic and not marching, having, as it were, another point of view. The cello maintains this individual point of view with increasing intensity and up to the last possible moment. It is clear then that the choice is one between insanity and conformance. The latter course is followed and the cello becomes a subservient part of an overwhelming orchestra. [6]

The trio is an enchanting episode for whose character and sounds the word "cute" is not out of place. In the score, Hindemith says only that this is "*nach einem alten Marsch*" (after an old march) but, in a conversation in 1941 with John N. Burk, the Boston Symphony's program annotator, the composer revealed that the composer of the march was Princess Anna Amalia of Prussia, sister of Frederick the Great.[7] Hindemith's predilection for march-

[6]*John Cage*, ed. Richard Kostelanetz (New York: Praeger, 1970).
[7]Anna Amalia (1723–1787) was an interesting and important lady. She amassed an immensely valuable collection of printed and manuscript music, she was an excellent harpsichordist, and, under the tutelage of Bach's pupil Johann Philipp Kirnberger, she became a competent composer of extremely conservative inclinations. Her conservatism had weighty consequences, for it was in her salon that Baron Gottfried van Swieten, the Austrian ambassador to Prussia, learned to value the music of Johann Sebastian Bach, a taste—or rather, a passion—that he passed on to Haydn and Mozart, with crucial effect on the development of the Classical style.

es was of long standing: the finale of his 1927 *Kammermusik* is a set of variations on an eighteenth-century Bavarian march, and he quotes marches in the *Symphonia serena* (Beethoven), the 1948 Septet (a Swiss military march), and the 1949 Concerto for Woodwinds and Harp (Mendelssohn's "Wedding March," a surprise for Gertrud, for the first performance fell on their silver wedding anniversary). At the end of the Cello Concerto's finale, the main march music returns and, as Cage indicates, the soloist too becomes one of the cheery marchers in the exuberant progress to the finish line.

## *Der Schwanendreher*, Concerto on Old Folk Songs for Viola and Small Orchestra

Zwischen Berg und tiefem Tal: *Slow—Moderate speed, powerful*
Nun laube, Lindlein, laube: *Fugato*
*Variations on* Seid ihr nicht der Schwanendreher?: *Moderately fast*

Hindemith composed *Der Schwanendreher* in the summer and fall of 1935 and was the soloist in the first performance with Willem Mengelberg and the Amsterdam Concertgebouw Orchestra on 14 November that year.

**Solo viola, two flutes (second doubling piccolo), oboe, two clarinets, two bassoons, three horns, trumpet, trombone, timpani, harp, four cellos, and three basses.**

> *A musician [Spielmann] arrives at a merry gathering and displays what he has brought with him from afar: songs grave and gay, and a dance to end with. As the real musician he is, he expands and embellishes these tunes according to his ability and fancy, preluding and improvising.*
>
> Preface *to* Der Schwanendreher

To be a *Schwanendreher* is to engage in one of the most specialized of occupations: that mouthful of a German word means "swan-turner" and refers to the kitchen functionary who turns roasting swans on a spit. *Seid ihr nicht der Schwanendreher?* (Aren't You the Swan-Turner?) is an old German song, one of four songs that show up in this work. As a friend of mine remarked, that sounds like something from a Monty Python skit. With a nice nose for what would work, Hindemith chose this attention-catching title when he was pondering a name for his concerto.

Hindemith was fond of German folk songs. As a very young man he acquired a collection called *Altdeutsches Liederbuch*, edited by Franz Böhme and published in 1877. It served him all his life as a source for songs he used in contexts as diverse as his magnum opus, the opera *Mathis der Maler*; pieces for schoolchildren to sing; and classroom exercises in strict counterpoint.[8] All four songs in *Der Schwanendreher* are to be found in the Böhme book.

*Der Schwanendreher* is the most famous of more than a dozen works Hindemith wrote for himself to play on the viola and the viola d'amore.[9] Like most violists, he had begun as a violinist. He had performed since childhood, when he was in the Frankfurter Kindertrio with his sister as second violin and his brother on cello, their father accompanying them at the zither. At nineteen he was concertmaster of the Frankfurt Opera, and when he switched to viola around 1920 he soon came to be regarded, with Lionel Tertis and William Primrose, as one of the outstanding violists in the 1920s and 1930s.

At first, Hindemith resisted taking the threats represented by the Hitler regime seriously, even as he watched Jewish colleagues driven from Germany and some non-Jewish ones go into exile in disgust. And for a time, he himself seemed to be secure. The first performance in 1934 of his *Mathis der Maler* Symphony, composed concurrently with his opera of the same name, whose subject is the crisis of conscience of the painter Grünewald in the turmoil of the Lutheran Reformation—was a resounding success. But German *Kulturpolitik* was unpredictable. Hindemith's reputation as a dangerous modernist, based on some of his work in the 1920s, still clung to him, and only a month after the premiere of the *Mathis* Symphony, Hans Rosbaud was forbidden to conduct that work for the Frankfurt radio. Furtwängler, who had led the *Mathis* Symphony premiere, was dismissed (though not for long) from his posts at the Berlin Philharmonic and the State Opera—in part because he supported his Jewish concertmaster, Szymon Goldberg, but even more because of his stand on behalf of Hindemith. Dr. Goebbels himself addressed the Hindemith Case in a major speech. It is ironic that of all Hindemith's works, *Mathis* was the one that got him into real trouble with the Nazis, for

[8]When Hindemith taught at Yale in the 1940s he founded a Collegium Musicum for the study and performance of early music. He liked to make audiences work at the Collegium's concerts, not just listen, and I recall well how at one of those evenings he divided the audience into three groups and, with his irresistible energy and enthusiasm, got us to sing a round, *Der Gutzgauch auf dem Zaune sass* (The Cuckoo Sat on the Fence), the tune that becomes the theme of the fugue in the middle of *Der Schwanendreher*'s middle movement.

[9] I am counting the *Kammermusik* No. 6 for viola d'amore (1927) as well as the *Kammermusik* No. 5 for viola (1927) and the *Konzertmusik*, Opus 48 (1930). Just as Hindemith had hoped, *Der Schwanendreher* brought him much renown and many orchestral engagements. He also recorded the work in Boston with Arthur Fiedler and a group of Boston Symphony musicians who played together as the Fiedler Sinfonietta, and it is interesting to note that Hindemith found Fiedler by far the most congenial and satisfactory of his collaborators on this, his first visit to America.

it was intended at least in part as damage control, a move on the composer's part to establish himself as a good German artist. Finally, in September 1938, the Hindemiths left Germany for a new home in Switzerland, and it was partly for relaxation that the beleaguered composer turned his attention to writing something playful—the *Schwanendreher*.

Hindemith thought of himself as the Spielmann he describes in his little preface to the score: composer and performer in one, like the musicians of olden days, "expanding and embellishing the tunes he has found according to his ability and fancy," and of course in the language of his own day. One gets the feeling he had fun doing it, and from the beginning violists have enjoyed this sturdy addition to their repertory.

The first movement is based on a song called *Zwischen Berg und tiefem Tal* (Between the Mountain and the Deep Valley). The sentiment is simple: There is an open road between mountain and valley, and if you are tired of your lover, let him go. But before we get to hear the horns and trombone play it our Spielmann takes a solo bow in the form of an unaccompanied prelude. Hindemith's "expanding and embellishing" of the song is extensive and elaborate.

After the strenuous counterpoint and active orchestration of *Zwischen Berg und tiefem Tal*, the quiet beginning of the second movement comes as a lovely and even welcome contrast. The prelude is played by the violist, sparingly accompanied on the harp, and it is itself charmingly songlike. Then comes the simple song *Nun laube, Lindlein, laube* (Now Put Forth Your Leaves, Little Linden Tree), presented as a soft woodwind chorale. A bassoon changes the mood by intoning a cheery children's song, *Der Gutzgauch auf dem Zaune sass* (The Cuckoo Sat on the Fence): it rained, and the cuckoo got wet; then the sun came out again, and the happy (and dry) bird flew away. With a running bass in the low strings, this becomes a boisterous accompanied fugue. *Lindlein*, now accompanied by its own beautiful prelude, returns to close the movement.

The finale brings the *Schwanendreher* song, presented as a theme with eleven free and wide-ranging variations. The seventh and tenth of these are cadenzalike, and the last is expanded to become an energetic coda.[10]

---

[10]At a series of performances by the San Francisco Symphony in 1988, Herbert Blomstedt preceded Hindemith's work with instrumental arrangements of Renaissance settings of the four songs. It is a good idea and worth emulating.

# Trauermusik (Music of Mourning), for Viola and String Orchestra

> Slow
> Quietly moving
> Lively
> Chorale, Vor deinen Thron tret ich hiermit: Very slow

The score of the *Trauermusik* carries the following note: "This piece was written in London on 21 January 1936, the day after the death of King George V of England, and was performed for the first time on 22 January at a memorial concert by the English Radio (BBC), the composer appearing as soloist."

On 14 November 1935 Paul Hindemith was soloist in the first performance of *Der Schwanendreher* with Willem Mengelberg and the Amsterdam Concertgebouw Orchestra. On 19 January 1936 Hindemith traveled to London, intending to launch the international career of that work with a performance on the 22d at Queen's Hall with Dr. (not yet Sir) Adrian Boult and the BBC Symphony.

What the English had most urgently on their minds at that moment was that their seventy-year-old sovereign, King George V, was dying at Sandringham House, his Norfolk residence. He had seen them through some hard times—the 1914–1918 War, the General Strike of 1926, and the Depression—and the Silver Jubilee celebrations of 1935 had consolidated the nation's affection for this simple country gentleman whose chief interests, other than the welfare of his empire, were shooting and his stamp collection. On the afternoon of the 20th, Lord Dawson, physician to the royal family, issued a bulletin that has found a place in the history of verbal felicity— "The King's life is moving peacefully towards its close"—and at a few minutes before midnight, George V died, the end hastened by injections of morphia and cocaine so that the news could make the first edition of *The Times*.

For what happened next, let us turn to the letter that Hindemith wrote on the 23d to his publisher, Willy Strecker:

> Dear Willy,
>     You should learn right away what all happened. I don't know whether you had aimed your excellent radio in the direction of London last night. If you did, you will have noticed that for reason of dead King the swan could not be turned. The day before yesterday in the morning there was great despair at the BBC. Boult and Clark [Edward Clark, Supervisor of Music at the BBC]

wanted absolutely that I should take part in the concert—it took place in a studio, not at Queen's Hall—and because after hours of looking around no suitable piece had turned up, we decided that I should produce a "Trauer-musik."

As I read in the paper yesterday, I was assigned a studio, some copyists were stoked up, and then, from 11 to 5, I did some heavy mourning. It turned out a nice piece, in the general direction of *Mathis* [the opera *Mathis der Maler*] and the *Schwanendreher*, with a Bach chorale at the end (*Vor deinen Thron Tret ich hiermit*—very suitable for kings), which it turns out that every schoolchild in England knows, something I only found out afterwards. Maybe you know it too; it is called "the old hundred" or something like that.

We had a very good rehearsal yesterday and in the evening the orchestra played with great devotion and feeling. It was very moving. Boult was, by English and his own personal standards, quite beside himself and kept thanking me. My students are now writing articles about the affair; they were very proud that the old man can still do it so well and so quickly. The solo violist of the orchestra is going to repeat the piece several times.

Shouldn't we perhaps make use of this story? ... It is after all not an everyday thing for the BBC to get a foreigner to write a piece on the death of their king and to broadcast it over their entire network. I now want to specialize in corpses, perhaps there'll be some more opportunities.... The *Schwanen-dreher* will be done later, perhaps at the beginning of August.... I didn't see much of London this visit since I spent the whole time sitting behind viola and music paper....

P. H., Bespoke Tailor[11]

The same day, Hindemith wrote to his wife, more briefly and candidly, "[The *Trauermusik*] is not exactly highly original, but at that speed I couldn't set out on a voyage of discovery. You'll hear it. A bit of *Mathis*, a bit of 'Lindlein' [the second movement of *Der Schwanendreher*], and a chorale to finish.... So, enough for now, my paws hurt from writing all those notes."[12]

Werner Reinhart, the Swiss music patron, remarked later to Gertrud Hindemith that there was "something Mozartian" about the affair: "I know no one else today who could do that." Reinhart was probably right. It is indeed wonderful that Hindemith produced a piece so touching in its sim-plicity that it immediately entered the repertory, being taking over by cellists as well and even by the occasional violinist, but in any event, Hindemith would have thought that a composer was no composer who had not the craft to turn out at the very least a competent piece under such conditions.

The *Trauermusik*—it seems always to be called by its German title—is in four brief movements. The string orchestra sets the tone with very slow

[11]Heinrich Strobel, *Paul Hindemith* (Mainz: Schatt, 1948).
[12]Paul Hindemith, *Das private Logbuch: Briefe an seine Frau Gertrud* ed. Friederike Becker and Giselher Schubert (Munich: Piper, 1995).

music whose hesitant gestures recall "The Entombment" from *Mathis der Maler*. The soloist enters with a series of eloquently expressive phrases of commentary. The second section is a viola melody in a lilting 12/8 meter that is characteristic of Hindemith's music. The third part continues the 12/8 but steps up the tempo, and the expression becomes grave and stern. This leads to the last section. The chorale is played by the orchestra, and after each of its first three phrases the solo viola interjects a kind of recitative, each a little longer and more passionate than before. (Something almost exactly like it happens in the middle movement of *Der Schwanendreher*). The chorale Hindemith chose carries this text:

> Thus I stand before your throne
> O God, and humbly beg:
> Do not turn your merciful face
> Away from me, poor sinner.

The tune is by Louis Bourgeois from the Geneva Psalter of 1551, and we— and the British—know it as *All People That on Earth Do Dwell* and *Praise God from Whom All Blessings Flow*.[13]

King George would have hated the *Trauermusik*. In spite of his intensely musical grandparents, Victoria and Albert, musical genes have not done well in the House of Windsor. A notable current exception is George V's grandson, another George, the Earl of Harewood, who was for some years the remarkably innovative director of the English National Opera. (Prince Charles is another exception.) In his memoirs, *The Tongs and the Bones*, Lord Harewood recounts how the Duke of Windsor asked Topazia Markevitch, wife of the conductor Igor Markevitch, whether Harewood was competent at his job, at that time at Covent Garden, and "then could not resist saying: 'It's very odd about George [Harewood] and music. You know, his parents were quite normal—liked horses and dogs and the country!' " No biography of George V, Queen Mary, Edward VIII, or George VI mentions the *Trauermusik*; nor, for that matter, does Harewood.

---

[13]It is called "Old Hundredth" or sometimes "Old Hundred" because it was set to Psalm 100 in the Sternhold and Hopkins metrical psalter of 1562. At its original appearance in the Geneva Psalter it was associated with Psalm 134. Bach used it in his cantata for the feast of Saint Michael, *Herr Gott, dich loben alle wir* (Lord God, We All Praise You), BWV 130.

# Erich Wolfgang Korngold

Erich Wolfgang Korngold was born in Brünn, the capital of the Austrian crownland of Moravia (now Brno, Slovak Republic) on 29 May 1897 and died in Hollywood, California, on 29 November 1957.

## Concerto in D major for Violin and Orchestra, Opus 35

> *Moderato nobile*
> *Romance*
> *Finale: Allegro assai vivace*

At the urging of the great Polish violinist Bronislaw Huberman and drawing on material from his film scores for *Anthony Adverse* and *Another Dawn* (both 1936), *The Prince and the Pauper* (1937), and *Juarez* (1939), Korngold composed his Violin Concerto in the summer of 1945, completing the orchestration that October. The first performance was given on 15 February 1947 by Jascha Heifetz with Vladimir Golschmann and the Saint Louis Symphony. The work is dedicated to Alma Mahler-Werfel.

Solo violin, two flutes (second doubling piccolo), two oboes (second doubling English horn), two clarinets and bass clarinet, two bassoons (second doubling contrabassoon), four horns, two trumpets, trombone, timpani, glockenspiel, xylophone, vibraphone, cymbals, chimes, tam-tam, bass drum, harp, celesta, and strings.

" 'He will be a Meyerbeer, a Mozart, a——.' As no third name of equal signif-icance occurred to her, she confined herself to showering kisses on her neph-ew." "She" is Toni Buddenbrook Permaneder, marveling at her young neph-ew Hanno's prodigious performance at the piano of a fantasia of his own. Had Thomas Mann's lovable not-quite-heroine been exclaiming some forty years later, one name that might very well have occurred to her is that of Erich Wolfgang Korngold, who was making formidable waves as he entered his teens. Mahler, Strauss, Puccini, Nikisch, Schnabel, Kreisler, Cortot, Men-gelberg, and Bruno Walter were among those ready to salute him as a Mozart-sized genius.

The son of Julius Korngold, Vienna's most influential music critic after the death of Eduard Hanslick, the boy played the piano well by the time he was five and was composing large-scale works at ten. Walter was the pianist, joined by the concertmaster and solo cellist of the Vienna Philharmonic, in the first performance of the boy's Opus 1, a thirty-three-minute piano trio. At about the same time, with Erich barely past his bar-mitzvah, the Austrian Imperial Ballet staged his Snowman, and Artur Schnabel was playing his Piano Sonata, Opus 2, on his tours. The Court Opera in Munich produced two one-act operas he had composed at sixteen. Of course, there were always voices to say that these performers were eager to curry favor with the powerful critic of the Neue freie Presse; perhaps some of them were, but the important fact is that these early opuses are imposing accomplishments, serious pieces still worth hearing and, some of them, more impressive than what Mozart, Schubert, Mendelssohn, and Meyerbeer had to offer at that age.

Korngold's success continued into his twenties. His opera Die tote Stadt (The Dead City) was staged all over Europe after its simultaneous premieres in Cologne and Hamburg in 1920 and even came to the Metropolitan in New York with Maria Jeritza in the title role. It still gets revived, and sopranos still sing and record Marietta's sumptuously melancholic song, "Glück, das mir verblieb." The Austrian government's tobacco monopoly named its most luxurious cigarette Heliane in honor of another of Korngold's operas (see my essay on Alban Berg's Violin Concerto). A poll conducted by a Viennese newspaper in 1932 came up with the result that Korngold and Schoenberg were the two greatest living composers—which is utterly weird in every way.

Korngold did not turn out to be a second Mozart, but thanks to a twist of events no one could have foreseen at the time of his triumphs, his music came to be heard by uncounted millions. In 1934 the producer and director Max Reinhardt, with whom he had already collaborated in Vienna on a gussied-up version of Die Fledermaus titled Rosalinde, invited him to Hollywood to score his film version of *A Midsummer Night's Dream*. He was immediately asked to stay on and write the music for *Captain Blood*, the film that made Erroll Flynn a star. Even before this he had enjoyed an immense success on Broadway with a Straussian pastiche, *The Great Waltz*.

Having talked Warner Bros. into a very good contract, Korngold traveled back and forth between Vienna and California until the Anschluss in 1938. That year he moved his family, including his parents and brother, to Hollywood. His films won him two Oscars—for *Anthony Adverse* and *The Adventures of Robin Hood*—as well as Academy Award nominations for *The Private Lives of Elizabeth and Essex* and *The Sea Hawk*. His last movie, from 1946, was that still-stirring drama *Deception*, and the Cello Concerto that Paul Henreid plays in the film became a concert piece in its own right; by then Korngold had already drawn his Violin Concerto from four other film scores.

The Hollywood years brought Korngold ample material success but not much happiness otherwise. He decided to give up composing other than the film music with which he supported himself and his family until Hitler was defeated. He was also hurt by the assumption that a successful film composer had necessarily sold out, just as he had been hurt in Europe by the imputation that he was performed only because of his father's position. Even now it is all too easy to encounter dismissive commentary along the lines of "Korngold's scores were lush and melodious imitations of Brahms, not to say Rachmaninoff" (Otto Friedrich in *City of Nets*—it being understood of course that "Rachmaninoff" is a pejorative of the worst sort) and "In Hollywood, Erich Korngold . . . joined the ranks of such glorified hacks as Max Steiner, Alfred Newman, and Franz Waxman" (Anthony Heilbut in *Exiled in Paradise*).[1] The advocacy of a few conductors, especially Charles Gerhardt and John Mauceri, has demonstrated the vitality and superb craftsmanship of Korngold's film scores even when they are heard apart from the movies for which they were written, and the composer's centenary in 1997 brought about new and overdue attention to his concert music.

After the war, Korngold gave up his work in the studios and came back to composing for the concert hall. The Violin Concerto was the work that marked his return, and in 1950, Furtwängler and the Berlin Philharmonic gave the premiere of his *Symphonic Serenade*. In 1952, Korngold attained the summit of his artistic life when he completed the work that most eloquently fulfills his early promise, the imposing, often powerfully original fifty-minute Symphony in F-sharp major, dedicated to the memory of Franklin D. Roosevelt. Korngold was never to hear this music properly done: rehearsals in Vienna in 1954 for the premiere went so badly that the composer tried, in

[1]Korngold and Waxman were united at the premiere of the Violin Concerto in that Heifetz also played one of the most famous of his party pieces, Waxman's *Carmen* Fantasy.

vain, to have the performance canceled. For a long time after that, no conductor could be interested in a symphony so long by a composer so unfash-
ionable. In 1959, two years after Korngold's death, Dimitri Mitropoulos, very
ill and without an orchestra of his own, declared that in Korngold's symphony
he had found "the perfect modern work" and undertook to perform it the
following season. But Mitropoulos died in 1960—on the podium at La Scala,
rehearsing Mahler's Symphony No.3—and it was not until November 1972
that Rudolf Kempe reintroduced and recorded the score.

Nor did Huberman ever have a chance to play the concerto he had
urged Korngold to write. He returned to Europe as soon as possible after the
war, and in any case, though he was not far into his sixties, that idealistic
artist had so worn himself out in the cause of a Pan-European Union and
with the founding of the Palestine Orchestra (now the Israel Philharmonic)
that his playing had come to be quite shaky. In the event, Heifetz became
an ideal champion for the work—as you can hear on the recording he made
in 1953 with Alfred Wallenstein and the Los Angeles Philharmonic. Korngold wrote a touching tribute: "In spite of the demand for virtuosity in the
finale, the work with its many melodic and lyric episodes was contemplated
rather for a Caruso than for a Paganini. It is needless to say how delighted I
am to have my concerto performed by Caruso and Paganini in one person:
Jascha Heifetz."

The solo violin is immediately present, and with a glorious, eloquent theme
that rises through almost two octaves in just five notes. Korngold rescued it
from his score for *Another Dawn*, a film, as the composer's son George tells
it, made by Warner Bros. because they didn't want their "elaborate and ex-
pensive standing sets" for *The Charge of the Light Brigade* to go to waste. Seeing
that in a world without the censoring Hays Office, the love scenes between
Erroll Flynn and Kay Francis would go rather farther than they in fact do—
this also according to George Korngold—the composer amused himself by
composing the second half of this rapturous episode to his own unsung text,
"Maybe I'll get a baby." After a transition of quicker music, a new theme
arrives, no less lyric than the first, and beautifully supported in the orchestra.
This one is taken from *Juarez*, one in the long series of Warner biopics star-
ring Paul Muni. One of the sources of *Juarez*, by the way, is the novel *Maximilian and Carlota* by Franz Werfel, late husband of the concerto's dedicatee.
A brief development and a businesslike cadenza lead to the recapitulation,
in which all the material is imaginatively rescored.

The second movement is titled "Romance." Its principal theme comes
from *Anthony Adverse*, a movie with Frederick March and Olivia de Havil-
land, and based on a Hervey Allen novel whose vast popularity in the 1930s
now seems quite incomprehensible. Korngold, along with Gale Sondergaard
(best supporting actress) and Tony Gaudio (photographer), won Oscars for

this one. In its demand for an elegantly poised cantabile and with its pages of suave noodling, this Romance gives a perfect picture of what Heifetz was all about.

The finale is a playful rondo, whose second theme—the first one we hear when the music emerges from its giguelike beginning—is the title music for *The Prince and the Pauper*. And no question about it, Korngold knows how to write a bring-the-house-down ending.

# Edouard Lalo

Edouard-Victor-Antoine Lalo was born in Lille, France, on 27 January 1823 and died in Paris on 22 April 1892.

## *Symphonie espagnole*, for Violin and Orchestra, Opus 21

*Allegro non troppo*
*Scherzando: Allegro molto*
*Intermezzo: Allegretto non troppo*
*Andante*
*Rondo: Allegro*

Lalo wrote the *Symphonie espagnole* in 1874 for Pablo de Sarasate, who introduced the work in Paris on 7 February 1875, with Edouard Colonne conducting.

Solo violin, two flutes and piccolo, two oboes, two clarinets, two bassoons, four horns, two trumpets, three trombones, timpani, triangle, snare drum, harp, and strings.

Lalo's family had been military people ever since moving from Spain to Flanders in the seventeenth century, and Désiré-Joseph Lalo, who was decorated for bravery at the battle of Lützen in 1813, was firmly against such nonsense as having his firstborn become a professional musician. Edouard was allowed violin and cello lessons at the Lille Conservatory—his cello teacher, Peter Baumann, had often played under Beethoven in Vienna—but that was all. He was without means of support, but he was determined and took himself to Paris. There he studied violin with François-Antoine Habeneck, remembered as the conductor who gave Paris its first serious performances of the Beethoven symphonies, and composition with the brilliant Julius Schulhoff, who had been a protégé of Chopin's and had for a time enjoyed an enviable career as composer and pianist. Another of Lalo's teachers was a musician (and lace manufacturer) by name of Crèvecoeur.

Lalo did well enough to take second place in the Prix de Rome competition of 1847 (the winner was the forgotten Pierre-Louis Deffès). He paid the rent by playing viola and later second violin in the Armingaud Quartet, an admired group that specialized in the Viennese classics and was joined from time to time by such eminent pianists as Camille Saint-Saëns, Clara Schumann, and Anton Rubinstein. Interestingly enough, Lalo married into a military family: his wife, who had been one of his students, was the daughter of a brigadier general. More important, Victoire Besnier de Moligny was also an excellent contralto, and it is to her presence in Lalo's life that we owe the existence of his fine songs.

But public recognition of his gifts stubbornly refused to come. He was in his fifties when he first got a large-scale work published (it was his unperformed opera *Fiesque*, based on Schiller) and when Sarasate finally brought him fame by his eloquent championing of the Violin Concerto in F minor and the *Symphonie espagnole*. Not even the support of Charles Gounod, undisputed monarch of the Parisian opera world since the triumph of *Faust* in 1859 and *Roméo et Juliette* eight years later, could get a hearing for Lalo's opera *Le Roi d'Ys*, whose overture still shows up on concert programs now and again. The best that came Lalo's way was the sop thrown him by Auguste-Emmanuel Vaucorbeil, director of the Opéra, who commissioned the ballet *Namouna*. (Debussy liked to recall how, at nineteen, he had been thrown out of the Opéra by Vaucorbeil personally for displaying excessive enthusiasm at a performance of *Namouna*.) It took many more years of maneuvering before *Le Roi d'Ys* was accepted, not by the Opéra, but by the less illustrious Opéra-Comique. At that point everyone wondered what the hesitation had been about, for the Opéra-Comique found itself with an enormous success on its hands, selling out a hundred performances within thirteen months of the premiere.

Lalo's F-minor Violin Concerto is forgotten, but cellists, who do need to give the Schumann and the Dvořák a rest now and again, are grateful for the existence of his D-minor Concerto, a piece that is especially attractive in its lighter pages. Primarily, though, Lalo's reputation rests on the *Symphonie espagnole*. It is a difficult piece, and not only in the obvious, technical sense: it is hard to get the manner just right. Most performances are either effortful or flashy, and the latter is almost as wrong as the former. This is music that asks for nonchalance. It wants a virtuoso who has plenty to show off but who disdains showing off, the violinistic counterpart of one of those too-cool people evoked by the verbiage in the J. Peterman catalogue. Charles Rosen observed this quality in the way such pianists as Rachmaninoff, Rosenthal, Godowsky, Levitzki, and Friedman presented the barn burners in their repertory: they played, Rosen said, "like gentlemen." Sarasate was that kind of player, and in his *Encyclopedia of the Violin* Alberto Bachmann, a sharp observer, maintains that no one had "been able to play with so prodigious an artistry as Sarasate, combining grace, clean-cut brilliancy, and bewildering vitality in so remarkable a degree." It is a pity that Sarasate's few records include nothing from the *Symphonie espagnole*. The great and unsurpassed classic among recordings of the work is Bronislaw Huberman's from 1934.

Lalo sometimes set himself the trap of making like a great composer, and in the first movement of the *Symphonie espagnole* he teeters on the edge of that pit. This music has sternly forceful intentions, but the effort of deriving nearly everything in it "symphonically" from the opening two-measure fanfare seems just a bit undernourished. An arresting feature of those first two measures is the rhythmic distinction between them: the pitches are the same—D and A—but the first has duplet D's and the second a triplet. The two-plus-three pattern, sometimes varied as three-plus-two, is prevalent throughout the movement. The more relaxed and very attractive contrasting theme is of unmistakably Iberian coloration.

Now Lalo takes his coat and tie off, and the piece really gets good. Charm and lyricism are Lalo's strengths, and that is mostly what he gives us from here on. The second movement is a scherzo with an imaginative middle section of considerable seriousness. The dominant style is that of a seguidilla, a lively dance from the south of Spain and in triple meter. The orchestra lays down the framework, with pizzicato strings and harp suggesting the sound of guitars, and the solo violin speeds across it all in weightless and fanciful flight.

It used to be the custom to omit the Intermezzo. I don't know when this began, or why, but this cut was observed at least as early as 1887, the date of the first American performance, in which the soloist was that estimable composer Charles Martin Loeffler, then the Boston Symphony's assistant concertmaster. Yehudi Menuhin seems to have been the first violinist to restore the movement, and he included it as early as 1933 in the first (and best) of his four recordings of the work. Most performances in the postwar period have been of the full five-movement version.

In any event, this Intermezzo, with its pleasingly nervous changes of register and the demands it makes on the soloist's virtuosity, actually the most taxing in the entire work, is an interesting and appealing episode. To leave it out is a pity. Some of it might make us think, "Aha! *Carmen*," but in fact the *Symphonie espagnole* came first. It is, however, entirely possible that Sébastien Yradier's *El arreglito*, the source of Carmen's Habañera, was as familiar to Lalo as it was to Bizet.

The Andante opens with portentous proclamations whose sound—clarinets and bassoons, brass, cellos, and basses, all in their low registers—is impressive. Then it finds what is perhaps its more authentic voice in the dark and impassioned song of the solo violin, which for Bachman "seems to evoke that Berber Africa where the Moors of Spain took refuge after having been driven from their terrestrial paradise in Grenada." At some moments this music comes surprisingly close to Bruch's *Kol Nidrei*. Didn't Schoenberg say that in the end all folk music is alike?

To begin the peppy closing Rondo, repeated *pianississimo* chords on high woodwinds and harp harmonics with percussion introduce an ostinato tune that the bassoon begins and which gradually spreads to the whole orchestra. The solo violin responds with a delightful variant of this idea. For a moment the music relaxes into the slower pace and more impassioned manner of a malagueña, but for the most part this finale is a feast of offhand bravura.

# György Ligeti

György Sándor Ligeti—the accent falls on the first syllable—
was born on 28 May 1923 in Dicsöszentmárton (now Tîrnăv-
eni), Romania, and now lives in Hamburg, Germany.

L igeti became known to the international music community in 1960,
when his *Apparitions* was performed under Ernest Bour at the International Society for Contemporary Music Festival in Cologne. A
year later, Ligeti composed *Atmosphères* for the Southwest German Radio;
no piece of avant-garde concert music has been heard by more people than
*Atmosphères*, which, without the composer's knowledge and to his immense
annoyance, was hijacked in 1968 by Stanley Kubrick for *2001: A Space Odyssey*. Only an infinitesimal percentage of the millions who saw that movie
(which Ligeti loathed, all but the last twenty minutes) or bought the record
of the soundtrack would recognize Ligeti's name. (His *Lux aeterna* for *a cappella* mixed chorus is also used in *2001*.) Ligeti's treatment by Kubrick and
MGM, then and in later litigation, does them no honor, but you have to
give Kubrick credit for having made some inspired musical choices.[1]

   *Atmosphères* is a long way from the first music Ligeti knew: the operetta
numbers his mother loved to sing, the Beethoven and Schubert his father
loved to listen to. There was also a record at home of the Magic Fire Music
from *Die Walküre*, but for Ligeti's father, Wagner was no longer "real music."
The jazz records, whose muted trumpets mightily attracted young György,

---

[1]Those choices include *The Blue Danube* and the opening of *Also sprach Zarathustra*, both aptly used;
Ligeti, however, hated being yoked to the two Strausses (and Khachaturian), and he wrote pungent
comments on this subject for the San Francisco Symphony's program book (17–21 March 1971,
reprinted 9–12 January 1980). Paul Griffiths, today's leading expert on Ligeti, became interested in
the composer's music as a result of seeing *2001* when he was an undergraduate.

were "not for children." He was a good piano student, and Grieg's *Lyric Pieces* left their mark on his own first attempts at composition.[2] When he was sixteen, his Aunt Marcsi gave him the second volume of an orchestration textbook, whereupon he set out to write a titanic *Grand Symphony in A minor with Dynamite Explosion*, imagining how its success at the Hungarian Theater would arouse the girls at school to such a pitch of enthusiasm that they would be willing to overlook his adolescent acne.

Ligeti's formal training was traditional, and he received it at the conservatories of Cluj and Budapest. His principal teachers were two distinguished Hungarian composers, Sándor Veress, himself a pupil of Bartók and Kodály, and Ferenc Farkas, who had been taught by Leo Weiner and Respighi; and for a time, Ligeti shared Veress's, Bartók's, and Kodály's interest in folk music. His education was interrupted when, as a Jew, he was sent to a labor camp; his father and brother did not survive their imprisonment.

As a young man Ligeti made his living as a teacher of harmony, counterpoint, and analysis at the Budapest Academy. He was one of the many who left Hungary in 1956 after the Soviet occupation and the imposition of martial law, moving first to Cologne, where he worked at the electronic music studio of the West German Radio. Through most of the 1960s he lived in Vienna, later took up residence in Berlin, and has lived and taught in Hamburg since 1973. He has been much in demand as a teacher in European centers as far apart geographically and culturally as Stockholm and Madrid, and has also been composer-in-residence at Stanford University and at Tanglewood.

*Atmosphères*, like *Apparitions* just before and the organ piece *Volumina* just after, projects a series of sound "clouds" of changing density and color. One of the most interesting new ideas to have entered music early in the twentieth century is the elevation of texture and color to the status of primary compositional elements along with melody, harmony, and rhythm. Or as Ligeti put it: "*Matière*, the physical stuff of music . . . is liberated from form to become an independent entity." Debussy had much to do with this development, though the single most dramatic manifestation of it occurs in the third of Schoenberg's *Five Pieces for Orchestra*, Opus 16 (1909). Here Schoenberg begins with a soft five-note chord, and for three measures the only action is in the entry and withdrawal—both as nearly imperceptible as possible—of different instruments. The pitch content begins to change very gradually—new chords appear, though usually only one note is changed at a time—but the principal issue here is the subtle play of colors.

Beginning with *Requiem* (1963–1965), counterpoint became an essential part of Ligeti's music, and the textures became more active and less dense.

---

[2] Although he rarely played in public, Ligeti became a very good pianist indeed, and in his three books of études he has given us the finest piano music of the last half-century.

On either side of the *Requiem*, Ligeti composed two short theater pieces on wordless texts of his own, *Aventures* (1962) and *Nouvelles Aventures* (1965), with those vocal works, indebted, as Paul Griffiths has observed, to Beckett, silent movies, and comic strips, we become aware of Ligeti's sense of drama and of his humor. The humor came out as well in another work—and title: *Poème symphonique* (1962) for 100 metronomes (the old-fashioned, wind-up sort with wagging pendulum) plus ten operators; at the same time, the *Poème*, in which the multi-layered ticking subsides slowly into silence, is a serious study in contrapuntal rhythm. Something of the same mix of humor and seriousness can be heard in *Continuum* (1968), a harpsichord piece so fast that it sounds static ("the usual Ligeti effect," was the composer's own ironic comment). *Aventures, Nouvelles Aventures, Continuum,* and the *Ten Pieces for Wind Quintet* (1968) also display Ligeti's delight in virtuosity. Mystery is an element in the complex textures and enigmatic entrances and exits of his orchestral works *Lontano* (1967), *Melodien* (1971), and *San Francisco Polyphony* (1974).

Bit by bit, there had emerged those elements of Ligeti's artistic personality that delight us in his concertos: a fascinating tension between order and seeming chaos, refreshing transparency and simplicity, drama, humor, virtuosity, and, to go back to the wonders of *Apparitions* and *Atmosphères*, an endlessly resourceful sense of color. Writing about *San Francisco Polyphony*, Ligeti remarked on the "combination of order and disorder (which I like in daily life too)." Elsewhere, Ligeti has compared this to the hurling of individual objects into a drawer in wild confusion, "and yet the drawer itself has a clearly defined form: Chaos reigns inside it, but the drawer itself is well constructed."[3]

György Ligeti is a kind of Haydn for our time: an exhilaratingly and jubilantly inventive artist whose profundity and seriousness never weigh him down (nor us), an explorer, a humorist, a composer who rejoices in the skills of performers, a master who wears his own virtuosity lightly and with grace. He has been especially happy in his composing of concertos—and there he certainly differs from Haydn, in whose life the concerto was not central. Ligeti has written five concertos, of which I discuss the three for solo instruments, one each for cello (1966), piano (1988), and violin (1992). Between the Cello Concerto and the Piano Concerto come a Chamber Concerto for Thirteen Instruments (1970) and a Double Concerto for Flute and Oboe (1972).

As part of a note he once wrote about his piano concerto, Ligeti offered his

[3]Ligeti's comments on his own music, here and in the three essays that follow, are drawn from his liner notes for the Wergo record album WER 60095 (Mainz, 1984); *Ligeti in Conversation with Peter Varnai, Josef Hausler, Claude Samuel, and himself* (London: Eulenburg, 1983); and Paul Griffiths, *György Ligeti* (London: Robson Books, 1983).

artistic credo; my independence both from the criteria of the traditional avant-garde and from those of fashionable post-modernism. The musical illusions so important to me are not pursued as an end in themselves, but rather form the foundation of my aesthetic considerations. I favor musical forms that are less process-like and more object-like. Music as frozen time, as an object in an imaginary space that is evoked in our imaginations through music itself. Music as a structure that, despite its unfolding in the flux of time, is still synchronistically conceivable, simultaneously present in all its moments. To hold on to time, to suspend its disappearance, to confine it in the present moment, this is my primary goal in composition.

## Concerto for Cello and Orchestra

$$\text{♩} = 40$$
*Lo stesso tempo*

Ligeti composed his Cello Concerto in 1966 on commission from Radio Free Berlin. The first performance was given on 19 April 1967 by Siegfried Palm with the Berlin Radio Symphony conducted by Henryk Czyz. The score is dedicated to Siegfried Palm.

**Solo cello, flute (doubling piccolo), oboe (doubling English horn), two clarinets (second doubling bass clarinet), bassoon, horn, trumpet, trombone (doubling bass trombone), harp, and strings. Ligeti suggests a small-to-medium string orchestra, but the parts can also be taken by five solo strings.**

First there is silence. Then we think we hear something, music. It is one note, E above middle C, played by the solo cello alone. This entrance, Ligeti writes, should be inaudible, "as though coming out of nothingness." To make sure, he writes *pppppppp*, has the cello muted, and directs that there be no vibrato and that the bow be over the fingerboard (*sul tasto*), which further veils the sound. For nearly two minutes, we hear only this E. Gradually, though, it seems to step forward, to take on flesh: The orchestral strings join in (*ppppp* at first), then a flute, then a clarinet, then another clarinet. The while, the string color has changed: the players begin to use vibrato, which gradually becomes more intense; the bows move away from the fingerboard toward the bridge (*sul ponticello*), which produces a creepily glassy, sometimes raspy

sound; and the violins, violas, and orchestral cellos start to play dense tremolandos. And even within the confines of this single note, the pitch becomes more complicated: When the cello plays E as a harmonic on the C-
string and the bass plays E as a harmonic on the A-string, the two notes are
not perfectly in tune with each other, but Ligeti asks that the players not
correct the discrepancy, even though those clearly audible vibrations or
throbs called "beats" may result.[4]

Now the repertory of pitches expands: F is introduced against the E, still
very quietly and slowly, after which other chromatic neighbors come in: F-
sharp, E-flat, G, A-flat, A. Then comes B-flat, half an octave away from the
initial E. But what an entrance this is, when the dissonant wind chord (still
*ppp*) suddenly gives way to the sound of all the strings playing a *pppp* B-flat,
muted, without vibrato, *sul tasto*, and six octaves deep. The next stage, as
the pitches fan out from B-flat, is a variant of the opening, but with everything traversed much more rapidly, and rising quickly and just for a moment
to *fff* (for the harp, the direction is "*sffff*, snatched, very shrill, *con tutta
forza*").[5]

The cello climbs to the F-sharp two octaves above the top of the treble
staff, Ligeti acknowledging in the score that this sound is "dangerously thin,"
and even makes its way up to G-sharp. Six octaves below, the bass sustains
its deepest G, moving gradually from *sul ponticello* to *sul tasto*, and so reca-
pitulating in reverse and on a compressed time scale the modulation of tone
color with which the movement began. Speaking to the critic Péter Várnai
about this immense and empty space between violin and bass, Ligeti said that
he wanted "to create the impression of a vast soap-bubble that may burst at
any moment." In the same conversation, he remarks that a "danger zone" of
this kind can be found in almost all his works. Seven slow measures of silence
bring this astonishing conquest of musical space to an end.

In 1937–1938, Béla Bartók wanted to please both his friend Zoltán Székely, who had asked him for a set of variations for violin and orchestra, and
himself, who preferred to compose a full-length concerto; he found the solution by making the second movement a set of variations *and* making the
entire finale a huge variation of the first movement. In his Cello Concerto,

---

[4]In 1949–1950, Elliott Carter wrote *Eight Études and a Fantasy for Woodwind Quartet*. Étude No. 7
consists of a single note, G above middle C, which the players pass back and forth. (Another of the
études in the set consists, as pitch content, of a single D-major triad.) The *Études and Fantasy* were
performed at the Warsaw Musical Autumn of 1956, when many composers from central and eastern
Europe first encountered recent American music, and Carter's work made a considerable impact on
that occasion. Of course the aesthetic difference between Carter's witty, rhythmically complex game
and Ligeti's mysterious creation drama is wide.

[5]"Snatched" is the translation given in the glossary in the score for Ligeti's German word *gerissen*.
More literally, *gerissen* means "torn" (Mahler sometimes uses *abgerissen* or *abreissen*, "torn off" or
"tear off"), but the word also carries the quite different set of meanings of "artful, crafty, cunning,
shifty," and the like. In his book on Ligeti, Paul Griffiths translates *gerissen* as "wily."

Ligeti picks up the really ingenious part of Bartók's plan and makes his second movement a variation of the first. And another Bartókian parallel comes to mind: the *Two Portraits* (One Ideal, One Grotesque).

Ideal-Grotesque is not precisely the nature of the contrast between the two movements of Ligeti's Concerto, but we can certainly say that the second movement is the unruly sibling of the first. The genetic material is the same, so is the tempo, and so is the length (between seven and eight minutes each), but where the first movement holds everything in except for that one *fff* outburst, the second knows no restraint and, in the composer's own words, "attains the extremes of wild passion and rigid clockwork-like alienation." It is theater, and Ligeti himself has suggested that it is an instrumental counterpart to *Aventures*. Paul Griffiths writes: "To follow [the composer's] own description, the music spins on through twenty-six assorted episodes, sometimes moving continuously from one to another, sometimes having one interrupt another as if opening a window onto another landscape, but a landscape which turns out to be the same as the one it interrupts." And if that is not a Beckett idea . . .

In this second movement, then, we have overwrought outbursts of virtuosity, suggestions of the spooky frog pond in which Wozzeck drowns, affectless *pianississimo* mutterings, and a drily clicking music as though for an unsmiling version of Klee's *Twittering Machine*. There are some pretty overwrought performance directions, too—for example, *ferocissimo*, *virtuosissimo*, and my favorite, "Like a sudden eruption! Exaggerated! Even louder than possible!"

Of the close, Ligeti writes: "In the first movement, the end suggests being alone and lost. . . . The end of the second movement is formed by the whisper-cadence which seems to disappear into nothingness: It is a figured variant of the shattered harmonic [at the end of the first movement]." One of the episodes of colorless murmurs suddenly falls apart as the harp and a single bass *sul ponticello* skid downward toward their lowest notes. When they stop, the cello has already begun its "*Flüster-Kadenz*," whose pitches are not written out, but about which Ligeti specifies that it must be *prestissimo*, *quasi perpetuum mobile*, voiceless, and that it should last forty to fifty seconds. Bit by bit, the cellist stops using the bow, only drumming on the strings with the fingertips of the left hand. The sound recedes—there is a wonderful sense of near and far, downstage and upstage in this piece—and after a time, we can no longer tell whether we are really hearing anything anymore or not. After *niente* has been reached, Ligeti commands ten seconds of "*Absolute Stille*."[6]

---

[6]The Deutsche Grammophon recording of Ligeti's Cello Concerto, Piano Concerto, and Violin Concerto includes a photograph of Ligeti and Pierre Boulez, the conductor of the recording, looking at a score together, which is certainly intended to suggest that the composer was present for at least some of the sessions and that the recordings were approved by him. I bring this up because Jean-Guihen Queyras, the brilliant soloist in the Cello Concerto, begins and ends the cadenza in whispers,

## Concerto for Piano and Orchestra

*Vivace molto ritmico e preciso*
*Lento e deserto*
*Vivace cantabile*
*Allegro risoluto, molto ritmico*
*Presto luminoso: fluido, costante, sempre molto ritmico*

Ligeti writes:

I composed the Piano Concerto in two working periods: the first three movements in 1985–86, the last two in 1987, completing the full score of the last movement in mid-January 1988. In its initial three-movement state the premiere of the Concerto took place on 23 October 1986 [at the Styrian Autumn] in Graz, Austria, with Mario di Bonaventura [conducting members of the Vienna Philharmonic] and his brother Anthony di Bonaventura as soloist. The performance was repeated two days later at the Vienna Konzerthaus. Hearing the two performances led me to decide that the third movement was not an appropriate conclusion. My feeling for form required an extension and completion of the large formal design, so I came to compose two additional movements. The premiere of the completed work took place on 29 February 1988 [with the Austrian Radio and Television Symphony] and the same conductor and soloist.

The work is dedicated to Mario di Bonaventura.

**Solo piano, flute (doubling piccolo), oboe, clarinet, alto ocarina (played by a percussionist when two percussionists are available, otherwise by a clarinetist or violinist), bass, horn, trumpet, trombone, triangle, two pairs of crotales, two suspended cymbals (one small, one normal), four wood blocks, five temple blocks, tambourine, snare drum, three high rototoms (tuned a fourth apart and played with the hand, like bongos), four tom-toms, bass drum, guiro, castanets, slapstick, siren whistle, police whistle, slide whistle, flexatone, chromatic harmonica, glockenspiel, xylophone, and strings (either 8-6-6-4-3 or one on a part).**

but creates a tremendous uproar in the middle. It is very exciting and cellistically stunning, but not at all the whisper-cadenza (*Flüster-Kadenz*) that Ligeti asks for in the score, has referred to in his own comments on the work, and which you can hear on the recording by Siegfried Palm, the work's original soloist and dedicatee.

The first movement, marked *Vivace molto ritmico e preciso*, gets going in a manner that might make you suspect you had tuned in when it was already in progress. Piano and percussion are notated in 12/8, strings in 4/4. That would not in itself be an especially peculiar cross-rhythm; you can, in fact, find that very one in Bach. Nothing in the sound, however, is as reassuring as the sight of those two time signatures. After having taken just one measure to set a metrical context, in other words, playing one measure that is instantly intelligible as 12/8, the piano begins to displace all its accents, and the strings in fact, except for their very first pizzicato chord, start out displaced. Both the 12/8 and the 4/4 teams each have extended rhythmic patterns that they regularly repeat, a device Ligeti has borrowed from fourteenth- and early fifteenth-century motets. The main point is that the beginnings of these *taleas*, as they are called, never coincide, just as the accents of the two instrumental groups do not occur simultaneously. "The repetitive patterns . . . appear in constantly new kaleidoscopic combinations."[7]

Ligeti of course does not want us to try to sort all this out as though it were a kind of aural MRI; rather, he wants us to ride with and enjoy the rhythmic buzz. What he has imagined, and what is immensely difficult for pianist, orchestra, and conductor to realize, is something akin to the patterns in one of Conlon Nancarrow's *Studies for Player Piano*, music which, as we hear it, we cannot analyze or imagine how to notate or play (which is why it is written for player piano), but which fascinates and thoroughly tickles us. "When this music is properly performed, that is at the given speed and with the given accentuation within the separate levels, after a certain time it will 'lift off' like an aircraft: The rhythmic events, too complex to be perceived in detail, hang in a suspended state. This blossoming of isolated structural details into a transforming global structure is one of my basic compositional assumptions."

The second movement, *Lento e deserto*, is the concerto's only slow music, even in its expanded five-movement form. Ligeti still uses the *talea* idea, but there is none of the complex rhythmic counterpoint of the first movement. He has invented a particular scale for this movement, one that repeats a pattern of two minor seconds followed by a major second—for example, C, C-sharp, D, E, F, F-sharp, G-sharp, and so on, and with this he unrolls a series of plaintive two-note figures. The piccolo begins in its lowest register, the bassoon joins in on the E-flat *above* the notorious high C at the beginning of *Le Sacre du printemps*. The next instruments to join this lament are the slide whistle (played by one of the percussionists) and the piano, after which muted brass and various woodwinds, including the ocarina, enter the conversation. For a long time, a low double-bass F anchors all this in place.

---

[7]Unattributed quotations in this essay come from the composer's own remarks about his Piano Concerto.

The piano meditates alone. Ghostly string harmonics make sympathetic comment. Suddenly there is violence, a *ffff* outburst of low strings, woodwinds, horns, and guiro. The piano is undeterred, just as it is by a later crash and snarl, *sffffff*. When a third explosion occurs, the pianist smashes his palms down on the high end of the keyboard: It is as though the instrument had been compelled to contribute to its own destruction. Against a strident *fortissimo* of woodwinds, the strings start an irresistible crescendo, to whose crest the siren whistle and police whistle add their penetrating voices. Now the music is impassioned and declamatory, but at the close, the descent from *fffff* to *niente* takes but five measures.

In the third, rapid movement, *Vivace cantabile*, Ligeti plays with "inherent melodic patterns," a designation he has taken from "Gerhard Kubik with reference to sub-Saharan African music. When played at the correct tempo and with very clear accentuation, there appear . . . illusionary rhythmic-melodic shapes. These illusionary shapes are not directly performed, do not appear in the separate real parts, but rather appear only in our perception from the combination of the various voices." The overall design of this movement, in which the piano is continuously active in quick figurations, is that of a huge crescendo and decrescendo.

Ligeti regards the fourth movement, *Allegro risoluto, molto ritmico,* as the central one of the Concerto. If the first three movements celebrated continuity, this one goes in the opposite direction, the antithesis of a perpetual-motion machine. It is made of very short musical ideas—"rudimentary," Ligeti calls them—that constantly contradict one another. The opening—a three-note phrase for winds, set going by a snare-drum rim shot and "Bartók" pizzicato, in which the string is plucked so hard that it snaps back against the fingerboard; three barely sounded chords on violin harmonics; and two dry *fortissimo* chords on the piano—is a typical example.

> Without our realizing it at the beginning, a complex, gradually emerging *talea*-like rhythmic order secretly governs. . . . Very gradually, as the initial longer pauses are filled in with motivic fragments, we realize that we are in the middle of a rhythmic-melodic maelstrom. . . . All the motivic figures resemble previous motivic figures, without literally repeating any such figure, while the total structure is also self-similar. . . . This great self-similar maelstrom goes back—very indirectly—to musical associations that originated through the computer representations of the Julia- or Mandelbrot-sets. . . . These remarkable pictures of fractal structures have played an important role in my musical conceptions.

His "constructions," Ligeti stresses, are "not based on mathematical considerations, but [are] 'craftsman-construction, . . . It is a matter of intuitive, poetic, synaesthetic correspondences, not so much scientific thinking as poetic."

The finale, *Presto luminoso: fluido, costante, sempre molto ritmico,* is the

Concerto's shortest movement: Ligeti even puts a note on the last page of the score saying, "The right tempo was reached if the movement (without the final rest) lasts no longer than three minutes." Both in physical, forward-thrusting energy and in its full texture, it gives the impression of dense busyness. Running through it is a melancholy tune oddly suggestive of Kurt Weill. Ligeti's personal, often unconventional directions to his performers are always a source of delight: in this movement, he tells the trumpet and trombone that their playing must be *minaccioso, brutale, ma "jazzy"*; elsewhere, the horn player is told, "Please practice, it *is* possible! Thank you." At the end, piano and xylophone have a duet in which they must play at exactly the same volume so as to create the impression of being one new instrument. A single remark from the highest of the four wood blocks cuts this off, and after three seconds of silence, this adventurous, virtuosic, and exuberant Concerto is over.

## Concerto for Violin and Orchestra

> *Praeludium: Vivacissimo luminoso*
> *Aria, Hoquetus, Choral: Andante con moto—Solenne—Maestoso*
>     *misterioso*
> *Intermezzo: Presto fluido*
> *Passacaglia: Lento intenso*
> *Appassionato: Agitato molto*

In response to a joint commission from Saschko Gawriloff, to whom the score is dedicated, and the West German Radio, Cologne, Ligeti wrote his Violin Concerto between 1990 and 1992, beginning with the third and fourth movements. With Peter Eötvös conducting the Ensemble Modern, Gawriloff was the soloist at the first performance, which took place on 8 October 1992 in Cologne. In 1993 Ligeti somewhat revised the third and fourth movements.

**Solo violin, two flutes (first doubling alto flute and soprano recorder, second doubling piccolo), oboe (doubling soprano ocarina in C), two clarinets (first doubling E-flat clarinet and sopranino ocarina in high F, second doubling bass clarinet and alto ocarina in low G), bassoon (doubling soprano ocarina in C), two horns, trumpet, trombone, timpani, medium and low suspended cymbals, tam-tam, very high and low wood blocks, tambourine, snare drum, bass drum, crotales, chimes, gong, whip, glockenspiel, vibraphone, marimbaphone, xylo-**

phone, two slide whistles, five violins (one with scordatura), three violas (one with scordatura), two violas, two cellos, and one bass.

*Scordatura* (literally, "mistuning") is a term that refers to tuning strings to pitches other than the usual ones. In a preface to the score, Ligeti explains how to achieve the desired violin and viola scordaturas. The bass plays the seventh harmonic on the G-string, which yields a note thirty-one cents lower than the F at the top of the treble staff. The violin tunes the E-string to that slightly low F, then tunes the other three strings down by fifths from there, that is, to correspondingly low versions of B-flat, E-flat, and A-flat. For the viola, the bass plays the fifth harmonic on his A-string, which yields a note fourteen cents lower than the C-sharp above middle C. The viola tunes the D-string to that slightly low C-sharp, then tunes the other three strings by fifths from there, that is, to correspondingly low versions of G-sharp, F-sharp, and B-natural. In the second and third movements, Ligeti specifies that the horns play natural harmonics and that the players should not "correct" those pitches. Likewise, the ocarina players should not worry about deviations from tempered pitch in the second and fourth movements.

At the top of the first page of the score, Ligeti addresses a paragraph about string technique to the soloist and conductor. In much of the first part of the Praeludium, all the string players except the basses, but including the soloist, are called upon to use natural harmonics, sometimes called "flageolet tones." This means that, instead of producing the desired pitch in the normal way by pressing the string down onto the fingerboard, the player does so by touching it lightly over one of the nodal points where the string's overtones are to be found. The sound has a certain disembodied quality and also a hint of something hooty: hence the name "flageolet tones," flageolet being a term used for several types of flute. (As well as natural harmonics, there are also artificial harmonics, produced by both depressing the string in the ordinary way with one finger and, with a second finger, touching it lightly as in a natural harmonic.) Natural harmonics do not always speak with certainty, and this is the point Ligeti addresses. He writes that if the natural harmonics do not speak completely, the players should not use the more reliable artificial harmonics instead, "for the glassy-glittering character of this movement is based on natural harmonics, and the quality of 'not speaking with certainty' creates the impression of fragility and peril."

The first sounds of this Concerto are indeed of extreme fragility: a single violin oscillates rapidly, breathlessly, between its open A- and D-strings, the while negotiating a crescendo from *pppppp* to *ppppp*. A lot of overtones rise up, so that you actually hear more than just those two pitches.[8] A viola with scordatura joins in on C-sharp and F-sharp, a violin from the orchestra, also with scordatura, adds F and B-flat, and a bright whirring fills the air—bright but, because of the uncertainty of the way the harmonics speak, twinkling as stars do. This exploration of the possibilities and the range of instruments is traditionally preludial: Bach or Chopin with other notes and different sounds.

Against this vibration a halting tune emerges, consisting of accented notes picked out from the swirl of the soloist's figurations and highlighted by dabs of sound from the marimbaphone. After a time, the orchestra settles into a pattern of detached notes, while the solo violin steps to the foreground for the first time, taking off, *feroce,* in a forceful passage full of double-stops. Now this really sounds like a concerto. Fragments of agitated melody alternate with reminders of the initial buzzing, and the violin interrupts its own fierce outbursts with *pianissimo* passages in quarter-tones that are to be played "like a lament." Then the motor runs down, and the Praeludium vanishes in a rumble of distant thuds on the bass drum.

After the wildness of the Praeludium and the sense of fragility, vulnerability, imperilment, the second movement, with its elaborate title, could not be more different. It begins in utmost serenity, generating a sense of steadiness. Ligeti's Aria is sung, to begin with, by the violin alone, calmly and in long notes. Eventually a viola joins in, adding a bass line, and flute and alto flute try out their skills as singers of melody, and the texture becomes generally more elaborate.

We are now in the second phase of the movement, the Hoquetus. *Grove's Dictionary of Music and Musicians* tells us that hoquetus—"hocket" in English—is "related to English hickock, hicket, hiccup, and similar onomatopoeic word formations in Celtic, Breton, Dutch, etc., meaning bump, knock, shock, hitch, hiccup. . . . [It is] the medieval term for a contrapuntal technique . . . which effects the dovetailing of sounds and silences by means of the staggered arrangement of rests between two or more voices." The Irish musicologist Frank Ll. Harrison called it "a mutual stop-and-go device."

Then the violin is joined by the two horns, the players being directed to treat them as natural horns without valves, that is, to take the pitches from the instruments' own overtones and not to adjust them to equal temperament. And now we hear the ocarinas for the first time, these children's instruments—at least, that is how we best know them—whose sound is so vibrant, so delightfully out of tune and out of place according to Philharmonic standards, and so evocative. They play a melody that represents the Choral section of this movement. Against their sustained line, the solo violin

---

[8]Because of the speed and the extreme softness of the dynamics, it is hard to be sure, but it sounds as though, on his recording, Saschko Gawriloff plays the D on an open string but produces the A fingered on the same string, thus generating a still richer sound mix.

adds an emphatic commentary of sonorous four-note pizzicato chords.[9] The music speeds up, but in due course the Aria returns. This time the first horn plays it, with the violin adding a new counterpoint, after which the entire orchestra takes it up. The alto flute ends the movement with one more return to the principal melody.

The Intermezzo combines the characteristics of the first two movements. Some of the orchestral strings set up a nonstop whirling of chromatic scales, *pianissimo*, very fast, but clearly articulated; up above, the solo violin sings a marvel of a melody, ecstatic and free. The brasses enter threateningly. In self-defense, the ensemble rises to *ffffff*, and, as though the current had been cut, the music stops with disconcerting suddenness.

The fourth movement is all continuous sound, no empty spaces, and everything to be executed *legatissimo*. The ground bass, to whose presence the title Pasaacaglia alerts us, is a slowly climbing chromatic scale. The violin, muted, rides high above the accompanying wind instruments. Heated outbursts alternate with quiet sounds that seem to come from a great distance, and the ocarinas once again blur the intonation. Here we meet some typical Ligeti instructions: the violin, for example, is told to play "molto appassionato, vibrato, big tone, excessive!" and the bassoon is assured that the G, *fff possibile*, at the top of the treble staff really is possible and must not be transposed down on any account.

The finale begins the way the first movement did, with rapid oscillations in solo strings. Flute and oboe superimpose a sustained melody. But this movement, too, rises to ferocious explosions of sound—*ffffff possibile*. To this the violin responds *dolcissimo*, bringing peace. One more outburst from the orchestra introduces a cadenza for the soloist, bringing back material from all five movements, but allowing for great freedom in execution. Ligeti indicates that this cadenza, which is essentially by Gawriloff, should be hectic and played with "crazed virtuosity." It has no real ending: at some point, while the violinist is playing high and fast, the conductor must suddenly bring in the orchestra for a few measures of descent from deafening to inaudible. And that brings this fantastical Concerto to a close.

---

[9]On his recording, Gawriloff plays most of them arco rather than pizzicato.

# Franz Liszt

Franz (Ferenc) Liszt was born in Raiding, Hungary, on 22 October 1811 and died in Bayreuth on 31 July 1886.

## Concerto No. 1 in E-flat major for Piano and Orchestra

*Allegro maestoso: Tempo giusto*
*Quasi adagio*
*Allegretto vivace*
*Allegro marziale animato*

Sketches for this Concerto go back to about 1830, and Liszt worked on the score in the late 1840s and again in 1853. Still more revisions of detail followed the premiere, which took place at Weimar on 17 February 1855 with the composer at the pianist and Hector Berlioz conducting. Liszt dedicated the work to the pianist, composer, and publisher Henry Litolff.

Solo piano, two flutes and piccolo, two oboes, two clarinets, two bassoons, two horns, two trumpets, three trombones, timpani, triangle, cymbals, and strings.

The sudden spurt in physical growth achieved by Beethoven's *Eroica* Symphony presented composers with new problems in organization and form, problems that affected not only big pieces like Berlioz's fifty-minute *Symphonie fantastique*, which was on the program when the Liszt E-flat Concerto was heard for the first time, but also comparatively short ones like this Concerto. All his life, Liszt gave serious, imaginative, and productive thought to the issue of form. His quest was most extraordinarily, most richly rewarded in his B-minor Piano Sonata of 1852–1853, a work in which nobility of spirit, intellectual power, and fascinatingly virtuosic writing exist in perfect equipoise. If the E-flat Concerto has never shared the intellectual respectability of the sonata or even of Liszt's other piano concerto, the A major of 1857–1861, it is a piece pianists have always enjoyed playing and one that audiences love to hear.

It is said that Liszt and his son-in-law, the brilliant pianist and conductor Hans von Bülow, put words to the two opening measures: *"Das versteht ihr alle nicht, haha!"* (None of you understand this, ha-ha!).

Ex. 1

The story sounds believable. Certainly von Bülow never passed up an opportunity to express his sense of superiority. I cannot say what exactly he and Liszt had in mind. It is easy to be dazzled by the flying octaves in this Concerto (after all, that is what they are for) and to take note of the unusual prominence accorded the triangle (and for some to take umbrage as well), and perhaps the point that Liszt and von Bülow were trying to make, even if they were only talking to each other, is that there is more to the E-flat Concerto than that—more invention, more wit, and more poetry. Liszt may have been one of the nineteenth century's most exasperating underachievers, to say nothing of committing the unforgivable sin of success on a staggering scale, but he was a genius. This Concerto can remind us.

*"Das versteht ihr alle nicht"* is a simple and powerful phrase for strings in octaves (this was the first idea Liszt noted down around 1830); *"haha!"* is a firm punctuation mark added by woodwinds and brass. Liszt repeats the phrase

a step lower, leading to a startlingly different harmony. At this point, widening the harmonic horizons still further, the pianist makes his presence known in an imposing cadenza. And there we have, in essence, Liszt's method for this astonishing movement, which is filled with harmonic ambiguity. Again and again he returns to his opening phrase, and each time it leads to something new, to a recitative, to a lyric melody, to thundering octaves, and finally to weightlessly glittering passagework that ends the movement in a puff of smoke.

A word about the orchestra in all this: there is very little of the massive scoring we hear at the outset; rather, there are many delicate solos. The first extended lyric melody, for example, is a duet between solo clarinet and piano (perhaps learned from the Schumann Concerto?), which is then continued by the piano with two violins in unison. It seems that in the earlier stages of working on the Concerto, Liszt sought the advice of his pupil Joseph Joachim Raff in questions of scoring; in any event, Raff was not shy about claiming credit.

Liszt strings the second, third, and fourth movements together without pause. He does not specify *attacca* in the transition from the first movement to the second, but it is clear that this is what he means. The strings lead off and suggest a melody which the piano then sings for us in full. This is one of Liszt's most beautiful inspirations, full of passion and poetry. When this melody comes to its close, the orchestra restates its suggestive beginning, more urgently this time. Now the piano responds with a fervently declamatory recitative. When the passions have calmed, woodwind soloists present a new idea against a decorative background provided by piano and strings. But when the clarinet offers to bring back the great melody from the beginning of the movement, there is an interruption: silence, the ping of a triangle, and the dancing reply of plucked strings. Berlioz on the Weimar podium must have been delighted by this bow to his Faustian goblins.

This scherzo is another movement that is not concluded. Liszt breaks it off for a cadenza. The pianist recalls the beginning of the Concerto, and suddenly those pages loom large again in a dramatic and developing restatement, which in turn opens the way for the martial finale. And here there is really nothing new. All is transformation and recapitulation, which Liszt described with evident pleasure in a letter to his cousin:

> The fourth movement of the Concerto . . . is only an urgent recapitulation of the earlier material with quickened, livelier rhythm, and it contains no new motifs, as will be clear to you from a glance through the score. This kind of *binding together* and rounding off a piece at its close is somewhat my own, but it is quite organic and justified from the standpoint of musical form. The trombones and basses take up the second part of the motif of the Adagio. The pianoforte figure which follows is nothing other than the reappearance of the

motif which was played in the Adagio by flute and clarinet, just as the whole concluding passage is a variant and development in major of the scherzo's motif, until finally the very first theme of all comes in over a dominant B-flat pedal with a trill accompaniment and concludes the whole.[1]

## Concerto No. 2 in A major for Piano and Orchestra

*Adagio sostenuto assai—Allegro agitato assai—Allegro moderato— Allegro deciso—Marziale un poco meno allegro—Allegro animato*

Although Liszt drafted this Concerto in 1839 and put it away for ten years, he scrutinized and revised it repeatedly; the fourth and last time was in 1861. He dedicated it to his pupil Hans von Bronsart, who gave the first performance, Liszt conducting, at Weimar on 7 January 1857.

**Solo piano, three flutes (one doubling piccolo), two oboes, two clarinets, two bassoons, two horns, two trumpets, three trombones, tuba, timpani, cymbals, and strings.**

In manuscript, Liszt called this work *Concerto symphonique;* it only became *II. Konzert für Pianoforte und Orchester* in 1863, when it was published by Schott in Mainz. Liszt borrowed his original title from the *Concertos symphoniques* of Henry Litolff, an unclassifiably international composer, pianist, and publisher of Alsatian-Scots descent, English birth, and chiefly French and German residence.[2] Liszt admired his slightly younger colleague, took part in the festivals he organized at Braunschweig, corresponded with him, and dedicated his First Piano Concerto to him.

Liszt not only liked Litolff's *Concerto symphonique* designation, but was intensely interested in what it stood for. This was a way of composing that Liszt had already learned from an earlier and nobler source, Franz Schubert. Liszt's technique of symphonic or thematic metamorphosis—drawing themes of highly diverse character from a single melodic shape—is a much publicized affair, and I recall being given to understand long ago, in an undergraduate music appreciation class, that *Les Préludes*, a good example of the method,

---

[1]Frank Walker, *Franz Liszt: The Weimar Years, 1848–1861* (Ithaca: Lornall University Press, 1989).
[2]The delightful Scherzo from Litolff's *Concerto symphonique* No. 4 still gets played from time to time; otherwise the family names survives mainly through the publishing firm Litolff, which he acquired with his second marriage and which is now a subsidiary of Peters.

was an extraordinarily innovative work. I was left to find out on my own—
at a recital when Rudolf Serkin played the *Wanderer* Fantasy—that the dis-
coverer was Schubert, who wrote that great work not long before the eleven-
year-old Liszt met him in Vienna. A little later, browsing about the record
library, I came across Edward Kilenyi's recording of Liszt's version of the
*Wanderer* Fantasy for piano and orchestra, and began to put two and two
together.

One of the areas in which the ever inventive and exploring Liszt was
independent and ahead of his time was in his appreciation of Schubert, a
field that still has plenty of room for growth as I write in 1998. Schubert had
his defenders, the most eloquent and effective of them in Liszt's generation
being Robert Schumann, but the fashion of the time was to be patronizing
about him, to regard him as a confectioner and purveyor of Viennese charm
and *Gemütlichkeit* (*Gretchen am Spinnrade* and *Erlkönig* being unaccountable
descents into the abyss), a wonderful melodist and therefore a fine song writer,
but hopelessly garrulous and out of his depth when he attempted larger forms.
As the loving arrangement of dances that Liszt published under the title of
*Soirées de Vienne* show us, he was as susceptible as anyone to the seductive
caresses of Schubert the miniaturist; in the *Wanderer* Fantasy, which Liszt
turned into a concerto around 1850 after knowing it for many years, he
recognized both an extraordinarily powerful compositional command and the
presence of a spirit as innovative as his own.

In external appearance, the *Wanderer* Fantasy is a sonata, a large piece
in four movements, but all those sonatalike structures to which Schubert
gave the name of Fantasy, notably the great C-major work for violin and
piano and the powerful F-minor piano duet, embody special concerns attention to the process of linking their several movements. Schubert's bold concept of combining the functions and characteristics of a single-movement
work and a multi-movement sonata was fascinating and fruitful: among its
distinguished progeny one finds, besides many works by Liszt, the Chamber
Symphony No. 1 and the String Quartet No. 1 of Arnold Schoenberg, and
the Seventh Symphony of Jean Sibelius.

Liszt's two piano concertos are part of this heritage. Both are short,
pianistically brilliant pieces whose movements are connected. That said, they
are markedly different from each other. The Concerto No. 1 is an octaves-
and-glitter piece whose slow movement provides a moment of real poetry. It
is hard, as near to performer-proof as any concerto in the repertory, and,
within the range of its limited but delightful intentions, it hits home.

The Concerto No. 2 is another matter. One would not want to go so
far as to apply to it what Pierre Monteux said about Debussy's *Pelléas et
Mélisande*, that it was never meant to be a success; still, one notices how
sparing Liszt is with devices such as contrary-motion scales in octaves that
are guaranteed to bring the house down. There you have the influence of

Litolff, who sought in his *Concertos symphoniques* to integrate the piano parts with the orchestra rather than giving them an aggressively soloistic a presence. But beyond that, the Second Concerto is pervaded by a manner, a tone, that asks listeners for concentrated attention and delicacy of response. An expert keyboard athlete of little musical insight can make a go of the First Concerto, but the Second Concerto is for poets only.

The music begins quietly (*dolce, soave*, says the score), confidingly, with just half a dozen woodwinds, actually never more than five at one time. It also moves slowly so that the curious turn of the phrase may settle in our memories. Although the first sound, an A-major chord with the third (C-sharp) on top, could not be more ordinary, little could be more surprising than the chord that follows it, a dominant seventh on F-natural. The two chords share one note, A; otherwise the second opens windows onto a world undreamed of by the first. This chord sequence, so colorful and strange, yet so easily grasped and sounding so inevitable, is the key to the whole Concerto. That becomes evident later. For the moment, we hear it as the quietly arresting beginning of a short paragraph of wistful questions; the last of these, pronounced by the clarinet alone, leads us back to A major and to what we most wait for in a concerto, the entrance of the soloist.

Let us again remember the First Concerto, where, impressively set up by the orchestra's forceful opening gesture, the pianist begins with a cadenza of thundering octaves and clangorous chords—Beethoven's Fifth Concerto, but raised to the nth (or Lth) degree of mid-nineteenth-century wow-effect. In the Second Concerto, the soloist asserts his presence not with a display of power, but as a sweetly harmonious, sensitive, responsive accompanist to the woodwinds and muted strings, who play a newly and beautifully scored version of the opening bars. In fact we shall never hear the soloist play those measures in their plain form: his task is to invent—or seem to invent—ever fresh pianistic dress for them. He immediately suggests a new way of hearing the phrase, *marcato*, but in an easy *forte*, accompanied by full chords.

Another variant with wind and cello solos, garlanded by piano scales, leads to a brief cadenza, which is one of Liszt's ways of getting from one section to another in this Concerto, a work of many and distinct episodes that follow each other rapidly. In an essay titled "Liszt Misunderstood," Alfred Brendel writes imaginatively about this technique:

> There is something fragmentary about Liszt's work; its musical argument, perhaps by its nature, is often not brought to a conclusion. But is the fragment not the purest, the most legitimate form of Romanticism? When Utopia becomes the primary goal, when the attempt is made to contain the illimitable, then form will have to remain "open" in order that the illimitable may enter. It is the business of the interpreter to show us how a general pause may connect

rather than separate two paragraphs, how a transition may mysteriously transform the musical argument. This is a magical art. By some process incomprehensible to the intellect, organic unity becomes established, the "open form" reaches its conclusion in the infinite.

Anyone who does not know the allure of the fragmentary will remain a stranger to much of Liszt's music, and perhaps to Romanticism in general.[3]

Emerging from his brief cadenza, Liszt proceeds with his metamorphoses. A host of musical characters passes before us, including one where Liszt seems to remember the barking of three headed Cerberus in Gluck's *Orfeo*. The tempo gets faster, the harmonic range wider. F major and B-flat minor become primary issues before Liszt takes us to what ought to be his most obvious and urgent harmonic destination, E major, the dominant of A. Liszt's harmony is no less daring once he has reached his E-major goal in the gentle string music that comes so soothingly after some grand pianistic derring-do in octaves. We might say that he reaches E major only to leave it; or rather, that he uses it as a point of departure and return for a series of journeys to D-flat major, where he first gives us a lyric movement built around a gorgeous cello solo and then a forceful Allegro close.

Again the tempo and the harmonic changes become faster until, after a big building up of suspense, we come back to A major (really for the first time since the Concerto's opening) and to the last metamorphosis. Liszt now turns the opening music into a march, triple *forte* for full orchestra, with excited punctuation from the piano. Almost without exception, writers have attacked this as vulgar and as a betrayal of the theme's poetic essence. It is nonetheless, as the American musicologist Robert Winter has noted, "a masterstroke that demonstrates the full emotional range of thematic transformation"; it also has exactly the weight and force needed to re-establish the Concerto's proper key of A major, which has been subjected to a lot of assault and has retreated quite far in the course of the adventures of the last fifteen minutes. And let us not neglect something quite basic: the Marziale gets the blood going.

But Liszt has no intention of forgetting the poetry, for the march leads to the most imaginative and personal page in the work, a variation for piano, quietly seconded by a few orchestral instruments, and to be played *appassionato* and with subtle rubato. It is startling to realize that, except for a brief passage just after the first cello solo, this is the first music in the Concerto where the pianist is unambiguously dominant. The rest of this astonishingly original Romantic masterpiece is coda, excitingly paced, forcefully scored, and to the end very much a matter of tight partnership between solo and orchestra.

[3]In *Musical Thoughts and Afterthoughts* (Princeton N.J.: Princeton University Press, 1976).

# Witold Lutosławski

Witold Lutosławski was born on 25 January 1913 in Warsaw, Poland, then still a province of the Russian Empire, and died there on 7 February 1994.

## Concerto for Cello and Orchestra

Lutosławski wrote his Cello Concerto in 1970 on commission from the Royal Philharmonic Society of London and the Calouste Gulbenkian Foundation. On 14 October 1970, in London, Mstislav Rostropovich gave the first performance, with Edward Downes conducting the Bournemouth Symphony Orchestra. The Concerto is dedicated to Rostropovich.

Solo cello, three flutes (third doubling piccolo), three oboes, three clarinets (third doubling bass clarinet), three bassoons (third doubling contrabassoon), four horns, three trumpets, three trombones, tuba, timpani, xylophone, slapstick, five tom-toms, vibraphone without motor, suspended cymbal, tam-tam, wood block, bass drum, field drum, tenor drum without snares, chimes, tambourine, small cymbals, celesta, harp, piano, and strings.

Stravinsky's death in 1971 brought about a huge change in the musical landscape. It was a tremendous loss for us to come to terms with. He was the last survivor of the generation of Schoenberg, Ives, Ravel, Bartók, Webern, and Berg, and among those who made up the new constellation of senior composers, only one, Roger Sessions, was born in the nineteenth century. Of those who were born before World War I and who survived Stravinsky, there is a handful whose music will stand significant as their 100th and 150th birthdays come around: Sessions, Copland, Dallapiccola, Tippett, Shostakovich, Messiaen, Carter, Britten, belong on that list, and surely Lutosławski does. Lutosławski has the smallest catalogue among these, but on hearing the eight hours or so of music that constitute the work of the last forty years of his life, I am struck by how incredibly close his achievement comes to being unalloyed gold.

Lutosławski grew up in an intellectually and artistically rich environment, his father being a keen and informed musical amateur, his mother a physician, and his uncle one of Poland's most eminent philosophers. He played the piano at six, started on his own to write music at nine, and then began to study composition with Witold Maliszewski, who had been a pupil of Rimsky-Korsakov. Lutosławski also spent two years studying mathematics at the University of Warsaw. Under the guidance of Jerzy Lefeld he became an excellent pianist, also working on violin with Lidia Knitowa. His keyboard skills would provide him with a living for several years.

When he was still in his twenties, Lutosławski had become known in Polish musical circles thanks to the success of his *Variations for Orchestra*, introduced by Grzegorz Fitelberg in 1938. During the war, he spent a brief period in the Polish army and a rather longer one in German custody. After his release, he and his friend and fellow-composer Andrzej Panufnik began to give two-piano concerts, many of them underground: Lutosławski's most performed composition, his *Firebird*, so to speak, is the sparkling set of *Variations on a Theme of Paganini*—that same Twenty-Fourth Caprice treated so famously by Schumann, Liszt, Brahms, Rachmaninoff, Blacher, Rochberg, and others—which he wrote for himself and Panufnik to play on some of those dark evenings.

After the war, Lutosławski found himself in trouble again, this time with the Communists. In 1948 Shostakovich and other major figures in Soviet music were hounded by their government for the sin of writing "formalist" music too much in the thrall of Western influence. The monkey-see, monkey-do Polish government of those years took the same tack, and Lutosławski's Symphony No. 1 was the first composition to be banned in Poland. Later, Lutosławski came to construe that as an honor; at the time, it was a wretched setback for the thirty-five-year-old composer, who now had to limit himself to writing music for films and radio, and arranging folk songs.

In the 1950s the situation began to ease, and Lutosławski emerged on the international scene. His brilliant *Concerto for Orchestra*, first heard in 1954, attracted particular attention. In 1956 Khrushchev denounced the Stalin era in the Soviet Union; Poland, too, opened up correspondingly. Lutosławski was one of the founders that year of the Warsaw Musical Autumn, a festival that gave most Poles their first opportunity to catch up with what had been happening in western Europe and America since the end of the war, and which brought Poland into the mainstream of European music. It was soon after this that Lutosławski's younger colleagues Tadeusz Baird and Krzysztof Penderecki began to be heard from.

As for Lutosławski himself, the *Music of Mourning* in memory of Béla Bartók, first played in 1958, added further to his renown, and he began to be in demand as performer, teacher, or just distinguished guest. In 1962 he came to the United States to teach at Tanglewood. It was the first of many visits to this country. He conducted orchestras in Europe and America, and began a series of recordings of his major works. Honors and awards came and continued to come his way.

Among those who are classified—loosely—as being of the advance guard, Lutosławski is one of the few to have maintained contact with the world of star performers. Mstislav Rostropovich introduced, recorded, and vigorously sponsored his Cello Concerto, a work now in the repertory of most important cellists, and he commissioned and introduced the *Noveletten* for orchestra; song cycles by Lutosławski were given their premieres by Peter Pears (*Paroles tissées*) and Dietrich Fischer-Dieskau (*Les Espaces du sommeil*); and Anne-Sophie Mutter is the violinist for whom he composed *Chain 2*.

In 1957 Pierre Boulez published an article in the *Nouvelle Revue Française* with the title *Aléa* (from the Latin *alea*, "dice"). Ever since, the word *aleatory* has been a standard part of musical terminology, describing compositions in which some element of chance or unpredictability plays a significant role.[1] In his essay, Boulez discusses "the constant preoccupation, not to say obsession, with chance" that he finds "notable" among several of his contemporaries. He defends with passion this new road "toward that supreme conjunction with probability." Among other matters, he points out that composers were bringing the performer "back into the creative role after many years during which he has been asked merely to play the text as 'objectively' as possible" and transforming him again from "an interpreter-robot of bewildered precision [to] an involved interpreter freed to make his own choices." No doubt Boulez is tendentious here, and debatable. No doubt also that composers found these fresh possibilities more stimulating than most of the "freed" performers did. No question, though, that what he describes is a trend that had begun increasingly to attract composers since the appearance in 1951 of John Cage's *Music of Changes* for piano.

Cage got his chances and changes, which in this work affect rhythm but not pitch, from the *I-Ching*; his younger Greek-Romanian colleague Iannis Xenakis preferred to work with the mathematical laws of chance. Composers

---

[1]The word itself has been around a long time. The *Oxford English Dictionary* cites its use in Sir Thomas Urquhart's Rabelais translation of 1693 and gives an example dated 1581 of the now obsolete *alear*.

on both sides of the Atlantic were drawn to the new mode, allowing—according to their vastly different temperaments and the nature of the work in question—many degrees and kinds of license. Inevitably, the movement sometimes ran wild, with a few composers saying in effect, "Do anything you like but be sure to put my name on the program."

Lutosławski was one of the most accomplished, thoughtful, and responsible of the European musicians to be drawn into this new aleatory world. (It was a chance hearing of a broadcast of Cage's *Concert for Piano and Orchestra* that got him interested.) As Poland became a culturally more open society—one, moreover, with an almost Japanese knack for imitation, absorption, and assimilation—Lutosławski became the leader of a group of composers influenced by the explorations of such figures as Boulez, Cage, Karlheinz Stockhausen, Luigi Nono, and Earle Brown. Between 1958 and 1960, Lutosławski wrote *Three Postludes for Orchestra*. "These works," he told a lecture audience in Stockholm in March 1965, "were not named at random. The word 'postlude' is connected . . . with the conclusion of something, and this applies here. The Postludes for Orchestra are the last works in which I did not apply the element of chance."

Three years earlier, at Tanglewood, Lutosławski had told Alan Rich, then with the *New York Times*: "I have just made what I regard as a new beginning, or, at least, a new concretization of everything I believe about music. My new style dates from *Jeux vénitiens* [1961]. . . . That work makes considerable use of the techniques of chance, or aleatoric music, and now I am working solely in that direction. My early works I have now come to regard as *passé*."[2]

What Lutosławski had discovered in his *Venetian Games* he consolidated in the remarkable series of works that followed: *Trois Poèmes d'Henri Michaux* for chorus with winds, pianos, harps, and percussion (1963), the String Quartet (1964), *Paroles tissées*, the Symphony No. 2 (1967), and *Livre pour orchestre* (1968). Amplifying on his use of aleatory means in *Jeux vénitiens*, Lutosławski wrote:

> The loosening of time connections between sounds is not—as it may seem—a great innovation. And yet its consequences may have an enormous importance for the composer's work. I have in mind both the possibility of a great enrichment of the rhythmical side of the work without increasing the difficulty of performing, as well as facilitating free and individualized playing on the part of particular performers within the framework of an ensemble. These elements of aleatory technique have attracted me above all. They open up a way for me to realize quite a number of sound visions which otherwise would for ever have remained only in my imagination.

[2]*New York Times*, 22 July 1961.

On the other hand I am not interested in regarding the chance element as the leading one to determine the form of a composition, or the element of surprise for the listener, performer, and even the composer himself through every consecutive and unforeseeable version of the work. In my composition the composer still remains the leading factor, and the introduction of the chance element in a strictly fixed range is merely a way of proceeding and not an end in itself.[3]

In the introduction to his string quartet, Lutosławski made the point still more firmly:

The idea behind the "collective *ad libitum*" is to transfer the whole wealth of possibilities of solo playing to the field of ensemble playing. . . . I am not concerned with the differences between single performances or with moments of surprise or with freeing myself from a part of the responsibility for a work and transferring it to the performer. . . . When I was composing my piece I had to think in advance of all the possibilities that could arise within certain given limitations. And this in turn required that even the least desirable possibility in performance should be acceptable. In this way it is guaranteed that everything that happens within the bounds of my piece is a fulfillment of my intentions.

In the 1970s and '80s Lutosławski composed some of his most admired works, among them the Cello Concerto, the Prelude and Fugue for Thirteen Strings, *Les Espaces du sommeil*, *Mi-Parti* for Orchestra, the Symphony No. 3, and the three *Chains*. Some things changed over the years. Though the 1987 Piano Concerto includes some aleatory passages, Lutosławski was now less involved with the idea of the "collective *ad libitum*." Also, his later music is not as dissonant, dense, complicated, unpredictable, overtly adventure-seeking. In a word, it is easier. The Symphony No. 3, for example, completed in 1983 for the Chicago Symphony, has enjoyed considerable public success and won the handsome Grawemeyer Award. There is no way that either of these things could have happened to the powerful Symphony No. 2 of 1967. The parallel of Bartók comes to mind. Late works like the Concerto for Orchestra or the Piano Concerto No. 3 are beautiful music, and they contain pages that Bartók could not have dreamed up earlier in his life; at the same time, you will not find there that sense, so potently communicated in the Violin Sonata No. 2 and the Third and Fourth string quartets, that here a mind and an imagination are traveling on paths never explored before. At a

---

[3]Quoted from *Lutosławski*, ed. Ove Nordwall, transl. Christopher Gibbs (Stockholm: Wilhelm Hansen, 1968). The gist is clear even if the details are not. We are evidently dealing with a double translation, Christopher Gibbs's English being taken from a Swedish text, which in this passage presumably goes back to a Polish original. At some stage in these international travels the syntax became unraveled.

certain age you no longer set out to sail around the world alone. (The unique exception in Western classical music is Beethoven.)

In other ways, Lutosławski's music stayed consistent. He continued to explore the possibilities of a harmonic style that is richly chromatic and divorced from tonality but which has never had any connection with Schoenbergian serialism. (In this he resembled America's senior master, Elliott Carter.) He loved color and used it brilliantly whether writing for full orchestra or a single instrument. Walter Pater defined form as the life-history of an idea: Lutosławski had a powerfully developed concept of form in just that sense of knowing how to reveal the growth and unique character of each of his musical ideas. In his predilection for designs that proceed with a clear feeling of purpose and direction from loose to tight, sketchy to distinct, he remained steadfast.

Rostropovich had asked Lutosławski for a Cello Concerto as far back as the 1950s, but Lutosławski was hugely in demand, and he worked slowly. At last, Rostropovich's opportunity came when the Royal Philharmonic Society tendered a commission to Lutosławski. He had recently completed two large orchestral works, the Symphony No. 2 and the *Livre pour orchestre*, and writing a concerto beckoned as a welcome and refreshing change. And the idea of writing for an extraordinary musician whom Lutosławski admired immensely was an additional pleasure. The Society was agreeable, and so Rostropovich got what he had looked forward to for so many years. He told Lutosławski not to worry about cellistic problems—he would figure out how to play whatever the composer presented him with. Rostropovich said later that he had had to devise some fingerings that were utterly new to him even after thirty years of performing in public. What Lutosławski composed was a stunning work that asks for an instrumentalist of limitless resources, a consummate musician, a performer with a vivid dramatic imagination, and a larger-than-life personality.

Like many Russian musicians, Rostropovich welcomes extra-musical associations into his thinking about music.[4] "This is the Central Committee at full strength," he said about the spot in Lutosławski's Concerto where the brass brutally interrupt the soulful cantilena of all the strings. Of another place he said that it always made him cry "because here I die." Lutosławski enjoyed this in Rostropovich because it was part of the whole lovable, irresistible Rostropovich package. In general, though, he was leery of that sort of interpretation: in a book of conversations with the critic Tadeusz Kaczyński, the discussion of the Cello Concerto is full of replies from the composer along the lines of "None of this was in mind," or "I didn't in the least intend the analogy you mentioned," and finally, "I'm horrified to see how one can

---

[4]This is not an exclusively Russian thing; see, for example, my essay on Schoenberg's Piano Concerto.

be carried away by my careless mention of the dramatic conflict between the solo part and the orchestra. I must immediately use the reins on this galloping imagination which prompts you to interpret the work as an illustration to some macabre spectacle." But conflict there is, comic to begin with, grim and terrifying later on. Conflict or, at the very least, difference of stance and needs and resources is built into the very concept of concerto, and rarely has it been so compellingly presented as in this masterpiece of Lutosławski's.

The Concerto proceeds in four phases: a monologue for the cello, interrupted by brass; a series of four episodes, varied in instrumentation and character, each interrupted by brass; a cantilena for the solo cello, which is taken up by the orchestral strings and interrupted by brass; a finale and coda.

The opening music for the cello is not only unaccompanied but suggests the uncomposed, un–self-conscious actions and motions of someone who believes himself to be unobserved. The cello begins with a dry ticking on a single note, D: *piano indifferente* is the direction. Various figures emerge from this: trills, little scurries, wails, some resolute gestures (like someone rehearsing a speech to be made to the boss later), but always the music keeps coming back to that *indifferente* D. When the cello has arrived at a new idea, a cheery four-note micro-fanfare, it is interrupted by a blast from the three trumpets. Nonchalantly, the cello returns to its bland D's, but the trumpets reduce it to silence. The worst of it is the banality of those interruptions.

After the trumpets have indulged themselves in a bit of triumphant crowing, there begins the first episode: agitated cello music, surrounded by dabs of color from the clarinet, the harp, and the orchestral strings. The percussion joins in and the cello risks some cantabile, but the brass—this time two trumpets and a trombone—interrupt for the second time. The second episode adds flute, bass clarinet, percussion, and keyboards to the instrumentation of the first episode and is more densely composed. The cello, encouraged by percussion, ventures some dance music, only to be halted by brass interruption no. 3. This is achieved by the trombones, and now the quality of the discourse has really deteriorated.

Episode no. 3 features wonderful cascades of flute and clarinet sound, along with lively percussion, keyboards, and harp. The cello music is expansive and brings a touch of pathos. The trumpets interrupt again, very briefly this time, after which the music moves into the fourth episode, the busiest and most colorful yet.

The next brass interruption—trumpets and trombones together—elicits a different response. First, the cello reverts to its *indifferente* D, but as basses growl in the depths and more and more strings add clouds of changing color, the solo instrument finds its way into an intense, broad-spanned, rhythmically flexible, and, above all, grieving song. This most moving page becomes an inspiration to all the strings of the orchestra, who join the solo cello in its agonized lament. The aria is unharmonized, but keeps gaining in heat as it speeds up. A fearsomely dissonant chord from the orchestra chokes it off ("the Central Committee at full strength").

Now we are in the last part of the Concerto, with agitated cello music and ever more crushing detonations from the orchestra in order to beat that cello music down, arriving at a climactic chord of almost unbearable force. But still the cello is heard, *dolente* (lamenting), while the orchestral strings scurry in the background. Suddenly everything moves forward at a tempo faster than any we have heard so far. This music crests as the cello, alone for a moment, cries out on a series of high E-flats. But E-flat is not enough: the line rises to F, to G, to A, and the concerto ends on a series of high A's— spaced rhythmically as the D's were at the beginning, but far, far from *indifferente*.

# Frank Martin

Frank Martin was born in Geneva, Switzerland, on 15 September 1890 and died in Naarden, the Netherlands, on 21 November 1974.

Hearing Bach's *Saint Matthew Passion* was the first decisive musical experience in Frank Martin's life. At sixteen he began studies with Joseph Lauber, himself a student of Rheinberger and Massenet, among others, but it was another four years before this youngest of ten children of a Calvinist pastor made up his mind to dedicate his life to music, abandoning the study of mathematics and the natural sciences that had been urged on him by his parents. His musical horizons widened, coming to include early masters such as Monteverdi as well as recent ones such as Debussy and Schoenberg. After World War II, Martin moved to the Netherlands, the country of his third wife's birth, but maintained close contact with the musical life of his own country. He and Arthur Honegger were the first Swiss composers to gain international reputation since the days of Ludwig Senfl early in the sixteenth century. Early in his career, Martin was active as a performer, and he taught all his life, his pedagogic and theoretical interests including the eurhythmics of his compatriot Émile Jaques-Dalcroze, whose pupil he was for a time in the 1920s.

Martin's music was publicly performed as early as 1911, but the composer grew to maturity quietly and slowly, and not without some uncertainty. Throughout his life, Ernest Ansermet, the founder and conductor of the Orchestre de la Suisse Romande, was a steadfast supporter of Martin's, introducing works from *Les Dithyrambes* in 1918 to the *Psaumes de Genève* and the *Mystère de la nativité* in 1959, but also serving the composer as an intellectual sparring partner and whetstone. Martin became known to a wider audience only with the first performance of his secular oratorio *Le vin herbé*, completed in 1941 and based on Joseph Bédier's version of the Tristan story. Still more acclaim was brought him by the *Petite Symphonie concertante* for harpsichord, harp, and piano, with double string orchestra or full orchestra.

By temperament and intellectual heritage, Martin was drawn to order, orthodoxy, and discipline. The first encounter with what seemed to him the dangerously "free form" music of Debussy disturbed him, while later he was excited by the implications and possibilities of Schoenberg's serialism. But Martin also had a side deeply susceptible to the sheer sensuous beauty of Debussy and, like Stravinsky, he found the Expressionist tone of Schoenberg's work hopelessly alien, much as he admired and even loved the man's intellect and musicality. Out of his conflict, Martin eventually plucked a musical language of his own, one founded on the ideal of order that Schoenberg represented for him, but which in its aesthetic stance firmly faces Paris rather than Vienna or Berlin.

In 1944 Radio Geneva asked Martin for a work to be broadcast the day the war in Europe came to an end. He saw this as the most demanding task of his life so far and responded to the commission with a cantata on Biblical texts, *In terra pax*. It was a turning point for him, an act that released a series of works on sacred subjects, a world he had stayed away from except for a couple of scores in the 1920s.[1] Not that sacred music became an exclusive preoccupation, but this was territory in which he was singularly eloquent. In 1948 he completed his great passion oratorio *Golgotha*, and among Martin's later and most beautiful works we find *Le Mystère de la nativité* (1959), the cantata *Pilate* (1964), the Geneva Psalms (1958), the lovely *Maria-Triptychon*, which consists of settings of the Ave Maria, Magnificat, and Stabat Mater, designed as a kind of double concerto for the soprano Irmgard Seefried and the violinist Wolfgang Schneiderhan (1969), a Requiem, and the *Polyptyque* for violin with double string orchestra (1973).

---

[1] The 1943 *Jedermann* [Everyman] *Monologues*, settings of passages from von Hofmannsthal's version of the medieval morality play, are fringe-sacred.

Concerto for Seven Wind Instruments, Timpani, Percussion, and String Orchestra

> *Allegro*
> *Adagietto*
> *Allegro vivace*

The score of this Concerto is inscribed "Amsterdam-Genève, 1949" and the three movements were completed respectively on 29 March, 2 June, and 9 August that year. Martin wrote the work for the orchestra of the Bern Musikgesellschaft, which gave the first performance on 25 October 1949, Luc Balmer conducting.

**The solo instruments are flute, oboe, clarinet, bassoon, horn, trumpet, trombone, and timpani. The percussion in the score consists of cymbals, snare drum, and bass drum.**

It is possible to imagine this Concerto as the outcome of a liaison of Stravinsky with Ravel. "I set out to display the musical qualities of the various soloists in the wind and brass groups as well as their virtuosity," Martin wrote, "and so I made the music brilliant and technically difficult. But I also tried to make the most of the characters of sonority and expression of the seven instruments, which differ so greatly in the manner of producing sound and in their mechanism." Both the virtuosic element and the conversational manner lead to an engagingly playful, sportive music. This work comes from a time when the writing of concertos particularly interested Martin: the *Petite Symphonie concertante* for harp, harpsichord, piano, and two string orchestras dates from 1945, the Violin Concerto from 1951, and the Harpsichord Concerto from 1952.

The first movement most thoroughly explores the idea of seven soloists as seven individuals, each with a characteristic vocabulary.[2] The second movement is especially striking. Here Martin asks that the effect be *misterioso*

---

[2]This sort of talk may remind some readers of Elliott Carter. The music will not. It is not merely a matter of difference in harmonic styles (Martin being always tonal) or density. The concepts of conversation are quite different. In Martin, what one instrument says rarely touches or affects another. In Carter, whose archetypal model is the second movement of Beethoven's Fourth Piano Concerto, the crucial point is how the language and expressive manner of an individual is affected by the language, the manner, the force of personality of other individuals existing and "talking" in the same musical space.

*ed elegante.* He also specifies that the tempo must be "imperturbably even" until the retard that introduces the trombone solo a dozen measures from the end. Strings, some muted and some not, some playing with the bow and some pizzicato, set up a tick-tock accompaniment rather like that in the second movement of Haydn's *Clock* Symphony, and over this there moves a procession of melodies, "some elegant and serene, others somber and violent." And, Martin might have added, some Spanish. (His daughter Teresa was a proficient flamenco dancer.) Here the soloists appear in groups more often than alone, a tendency that is extended in the dance-like finale. In that movement the timpanist at last asserts himself as a soloist. His cadenza gives way to the sound of a distant march, an imperialist affair that obviously wants to take over the whole Concerto, but which nonetheless defers to the initial dance music.

## *Polyptyque,* Six Passiontide Images for Violin and Two Small String Orchestras

> Images des rameaux *(The Palm Branches)*
> Image de la chambre haute *(The Last Supper)*
> Image de Judas *(Judas)*
> Image de Gethsémané *(Gethsemane)*
> Image du jugement *(The Trial)*
> Image de la glorification *(Glorification)*

Martin composed *Polyptyque,* his last work for orchestra, in 1972–1973, completing it in June 1973. It was commissioned to celebrate the twenty-fifth anniversary of the founding of the International Music Council. The first performance was given in Lausanne, Switzerland, on 9 September 1973 by Yehudi Menuhin with Edmond de Stoutz conducting the Zurich Chamber Orchestra, the artists for whom Martin had written the work.

The story of this work begins in 1308, when Duccio di Boninsegna, then about fifty years old, signed a contract with the governors of the Siena Cathedral, undertaking "with all the skill and power granted him by God" to paint an altarpiece in honor of the Virgin Mary, promising as well to accept no other commissions that might distract him from his task. The Siena vestry could not have chosen better: with his slightly older contemporary Cimabue and his younger colleague Giotto, Duccio was one of the three supremely great Italian artists of his day. If there was any cause for worry it was because

Duccio was a temperamental and difficult man who had a rather friction-filled relationship with law and the authorities.

In the event, there was no problem. Duccio delivered, and on 9 June 1311, his work, which came to be known as the *Maestà*, was carried to the cathedral. That day was declared a public holiday in the city, with all stores closed, and the bearers of the huge picture—approximately twelve feet by fifteen—were escorted by church and civic officials, all carrying lighted candles, followed by men, women, and children from the general populace. The procession made its way from Duccio's workshop, circling the Campo and then arriving at the cathedral, with all the church bells "ringing in glory and veneration."

The *Maestà* was a stupendous achievement. The front shows the Madonna and Child, enthroned with saints and angels. Above, as a crown, is a set of eight panels whose subject is the life and death of the Virgin; the predella below consists of thirteen panels, seven of them depicting scenes from the early life of Jesus, the remainder being pictures of Solomon and various prophets. The reverse of the *Maestà* consists of forty-three panels of diverse shapes and sizes, depicting episodes from the public life of Jesus, including some that follow his death and resurrection.

That, at least, is what the Sienese saw hanging over the main altar of their glorious cathedral in 1311 and for 194 years thereafter. By the time the sixteenth century began, no one had much regard any more for Duccio, Giotto, and the other masters of their day. In 1505 the successors of the men who had commissioned Duccio and proudly paid out immense sums of money for labor and materials commissioned a new high altar from Baldassare Peruzzi, the magnificent Sienese architect who had just moved to Rome to work as Bramante's assistant on Saint Peter's; at the same time, they ordered that the *Maestà* be moved to the museum attached to the cathedral. In 1771 Duccio's masterpiece suffered a further degradation when the cathedral officials decided to break it up. Recto and verso were separated, and since Duccio had done a good job of gluing and nailing them together, some damage to the painting occurred in the process. Most of the *Maestà* remained in the cathedral museum, but some of the panels that made up the back were dispersed and are now in collections as far afield as London and Fort Worth, Texas; a few have vanished altogether.

On holiday in Italy, Frank Martin and his wife visited Siena, its nearly 700-year-old cathedral, and the museum that adjoins it at the east end of the choir. It was not the first time the composer had seen the *Maestà*; this time, however, he took it in with special emotion because it provided the answer to a troubling question. Yehudi Menuhin and Edmond de Stoutz, the conductor of the Zurich Chamber Orchestra, had asked him to write a concerto for solo violin with string orchestra, but he had felt, immediately and intensely, that since this implied the impossible challenge of living up to the

Bach concertos he should think of some other way of fulfilling the commission. He recalled later that he thought it might be "more appropriate to write a suite of relatively short pieces, a sequence of pictures relating to a subject not yet clear to me." The *Maestà* panels representing the Passion story gave him the scenario he was looking for.[3]

Martin continues:

> But music is not a representational art, and there could be no question of an actual representation of the scenes I had been absorbing. All I could do, therefore, was to imagine in my mind, as vividly as possible, the several scenes I wished to evoke. After that, I sought to transpose into music what these scenes stirred up in me. . . . Whether I have succeeded in translating my wholly private impressions into music is another question. Perhaps this music will help some people to recreate these Passion images within themselves; for others, they will be pieces for violin with two string orchestras, more or less interesting, more or less successful.[4]

Duccio's Passion paintings, so powerfully and sometimes even so stormily composed, so compact, often showing more than one moment within a single panel, the faces so distinctive, the body language so arresting, the colors, from the brilliance of the robes to the sinister black of the trees, still ablaze after more than six and a half centuries, draw us irresistibly into the action and involve us in the human situations set before us. I can only imagine what, in addition, they must say to the Christian believer. What is obvious, from a good performance of *Polyptyque*, is that Frank Martin was affected to the depths of his being.

The hard part came after that—turning his emotional and imaginative response into music, dealing with the process he called "sublimation" ("this sublimation which evokes in us a finished form and which is, I think, what is called 'beauty' "). While finishing *Golgotha*, Martin wrote about this in an article for the French journal *Polyphonie*:

> [The composer] has to imagine the end product, something that cannot be done with any degree of accuracy. It is a kind of premonition, a movement of the spirit that manifests itself in a hundred different ways before the music assumes final form—visual, tender, or passionate impressions like those sudden feelings of joy or sadness that come over us for no specific reason. . . . This first vision is quite inconstant. It cannot be expressed because only the finished

---

[3]This was not the first time Martin had found inspiration in visual art. *Golgotha* came to be what it is because Martin had been profoundly moved by Rembrandt's etching *The Three Crosses*; before that, in 1943, he had written a dance score based on the fifteenth-century *Dance of Death* series in the Dominican Cemetery in Basel.

[4]From the composer's program note for the Gallo recording (CD-713) of *Polyptyque* by Zbigniew Czapczynski with Edmond de Stoutz and the Zurich Chamber Orchestra.

work will express it. All volition, all powers of being are focussed on a goal that is entirely unknown. You know it only when you reach it.[5]

But what is a good performance of *Polyptyque?* One of the least showy of all works for solo violin, *Polyptyque* is more than a work with an obbligato violin, but not quite a concerto either. For one thing, the concerto mentality is fatal to the work. What is required from the violinist is complete instrumental command along with the ability to compel the audience through sheer concentration and conviction, but there can be no question of "this is all about me." It sounds paradoxical, but in no concerto are the orchestral passages, when the violinist is silent and *still*, such a crucial and expressive part of his presentation. Even the visual/physical picture of the violinist alone in the empty space between the two string orchestras is telling and powerfully eloquent. *Polyptyque* is for the violinist who can play the Cavatina in Beethoven's String Quartet, Opus 130, especially its naked, choked middle section, and when I evoke playing the Cavatina as, for example, Adolf Busch and Peter Cropper (leader of the Lindsay Quartet) have been able to play it, I refer both to the deep spirituality of the moment and of mastery of a vocal, "speaking" style. And I must add: knowing the Bible, knowing Duccio is essential.[6] Frank Martin never found success in the opera house, but *Polyptyque* is a consummate masterpiece of vividly evocative, dramatic music, an utterance to be set before the listener with an intensity equal to that of the images in the *Maestà* itself.

Martin set up his polyptych as a set of six panels, articulated as three pairs each consisting of a fast movement and a slow one. *Image des rameaux* (literally Picture of the Branches) refers to the palm branches that are part of the ceremonial for Palm Sunday, in French *dimanche des rameaux*, the Sunday before Easter and the day that commemorates Jesus' triumphal entry into Jerusalem. The tempo is *Allegro non troppo ma agitato*. The two orchestras start with busy, nervous, agitated music. The first solo entrance is like one of those sudden, startling, but beatific appearances that Christ makes after his death to the three Marys at the tomb, to Doubting Thomas, to the disciples on the road to Emmaus, to Peter on Lake Tiberias. Suddenly nothing is the same anymore. In this movement, by his own testimony, Martin imagined the swirling crowd pushing forward to see Jesus, mounted on a gray donkey, approach the city gates. Here the voice of the solo violin, sometimes speaking, sometimes singing forth in great hymnic phrases, is the voice of Jesus, lofty in thought, quietly dominating the tumult, and so aware of the human fragility of this moment. The violas already mourn: it is like one of

[5]Quoted in H. H. Stuckenschmidt, *Twentieth-Century Composers: Germany and Central Europe* (New York: Holt, Rinehart & Winston, 1971). I have slightly modified the translation.
[6]I recommend the same thing for listeners. The Library of Great Masters Series has an excellent volume on Duccio by Cecilia Jannella (Scala/Riverside, 1991).

those Nativity paintings in which the artist shows us the tree from which the cross will be hewn. In keeping with the spirit of this dramatic scene, the *Image des rameaux* culminates in a powerful closing gesture, a swift upward arpeggio, all uniting on an A-major chord with an added F-sharp. This first movement also introduces us to the beautiful sound of *Polyptyque*, the double orchestra miraculously rich, varied, and unfailingly transparent. Of course, another of the desiderata for a successful projection of the work is a conductor with an imaginative sense of string color.

*Image de la chambre haute* takes us to the "large upper room furnished" where Luke tells us the Last Supper was held. Here is one of the sublime slow movements in all of music. It brings us images of fear, of anguish, but above all of surpassing love. The music rises to a great crest, *fortissimo* and very high, but ends with a lonely descent to a calm, final chord of E major, the violin quiet, confident, and vibrant on its lowest B.

*Image de Judas*, handsome and tense in Duccio's portrayal, is a grim scherzo in jagged 7/8 time, much of it with mute for the solo violin. It is an uncanny portrait of a torn and sundered personality, one, as Martin sees him, "anguished and tormented, in the grip of an obsession and finally collapsing in despair." The music is uneasy in its breathing, all off-balance rhythms, *fortissimo* eruptions, dissonances, broken-off utterances. Using the mute is a marvellous touch: the contradiction between its thwarting and the violence expresses to perfection Judas's posture of concealment and devastating internal conflict. After the orchestra reaches the height of tension, there is one more violin cry—then an abrupt, growling, and dissonant close.

*Image de Géthsémane* is very slow music. The violin begins alone with an eloquent utterance in Bachian double-stops. It sings, dares a piercing climb, and returns to Bach. Then the violin begins to play slow arpeggios as though accompanying something, but in fact there is nothing to accompany except virtually incorporeal chords in the orchestra, *pianississimo*, and with the veiled sound that results from playing with the bow over the fingerboard, chords that themselves sound like accompaniments.[7] This *image* is the journey from "Father, if thou be willing, remove this cup from me" to "Not my will, but thine, be done." And perhaps we hear Jesus' infinitely sad and despairing appeals to the disciples.

*Image du jugement* evokes Jesus' appearances before Annas, Caiaphas, Pilate, and Herod, something Duccio covers in six different panels. Here is a picture of us at our worst and at our most naked and vulnerable. The music begins with orchestral chords that are tormented in rhythm and harmony alike. The brutal, driving orchestra, suggesting one of Shostakovich's nightmare visions, is interrupted by anguished cries from the solo violin. Whose

---

[7]In a performance by Jorja Fleezanis in Minneapolis in 1997, the conductor Claus Peter Flor achieved a haunting effect by having the orchestra play these chords without vibrato.

cries are these? Is it the anguish of the witnesses, the imagined characters who sing the arias and chorales in Bach's Passions? The close is fierce and tight-lipped. The *via crucis* has begun.

It is hard to survive this movement. Martin sensed that, writing: "Having arrived here, I felt there was no possible ending other than an *Image de la glorification.*" This is rescue and redemption. The music begins with chant or hymn in violas and cellos, unharmonized. (Many Protestant hymns are variants of Gregorian chants.) It is repeated, now with minimal harmony. The orchestral violins play it in faster notes, the solo violin energizes it a step further into to sixteenth-notes. The violin climbs upward, more slowly each time. When the violin begins its last ascent, the orchestra softly sounds the hymn-chorale-chant one again. Once more, the music speeds up, the solo violin adding a counterpoint in eighth-notes. Finally, as the orchestra breathes the hymn once more, the violin moves very slowly up to a high C-sharp that floats in serenity and quiet glory above the last, radiant chords of F-sharp major.

# Felix Mendelssohn-Bartholdy

Jakob Ludwig Felix Mendelssohn was born in Hamburg, then under French rule, on 3 February 1809 and died in Leipzig, Saxony, on 4 November 1847.

B artholdy was the name of Felix's maternal uncle Jakob, who had changed his own name from Salomon, taking Bartholdy from the previous owner of a piece of real estate he had bought in Berlin. It was he who most persistently urged the family's conversion to Lutheranism: the name Bartholdy was added to Mendelssohn—to distinguish the Protestant Mendelssohns from the ones who stayed with their Jewish faith—when Felix's father converted in 1822, the children having already been baptized in 1816. There is an interesting bit of historical background to this. In the 9 January 1997 issue of *The New York Review of Books*, the historian Gordon A. Craig pointed out that while "the 'philosopher-king' Frederick II of Prussia" was willing to work with Jewish financiers when it came to paying for the Seven Years War, his anti-Semitism was firmly in place with respect to Moses Mendelssohn, the composer's grandfather and a philosopher with a reputation that extended across Europe. "The King acted as if he did not exist and effectively blocked his election to the Royal Academy. Indeed, Mendelssohn had difficulty in acquiring the privilege of maintaining a residence of his own in Berlin and, when he sought to have it extended to his children, his request was refused. . . . Clearly, Moses Mendelssohn had chosen the wrong occupation."

## Concerto No. 1 in G minor for Piano and Orchestra, Opus 25

*Molto allegro con fuoco*
*Andante*
*Presto—Molto allegro e vivace*

Mendelssohn sketched his Piano Concerto No. 1 in Rome in November 1830 and completed the score the following year. He himself was the soloist at the premiere in Munich on 17 October 1831.

**Solo piano, two flutes, two oboes, two clarinets, two bassoons, two horns, two trumpets, timpani, and strings.**

Felix Mendelssohn was the cherished crown prince in his cultured, prosperous, and seemingly happy family.[1] It was the blessed lot of such well-to-do young men to be sent on an educational grand tour. Mendelssohn's lasted a year and took him via Munich and Vienna to Italy (Venice, Florence, Rome, Naples, Rome again, Florence again, and Milan), Switzerland, Munich for a second time, Paris, London, and so home to Berlin. Munich in October 1831 was a round of parties for the attractive young musician, but he also found time to play chamber music, to give a daily lesson in double counterpoint given to "little Mademoiselle L." ("Imagine a small, delicate-looking, pale girl with noble but not pretty features, so singular and interesting that it is difficult to turn your eyes from her . . ."), and to complete the piano concerto he had sketched earlier on his journey. [2]

Competing with Mlle. L. for Mendelssohn's attentions was a talented seventeen-year-old pianist by the name of Delphine von Schauroth. She was well connected: King Ludwig I himself spoke to Mendelssohn on her behalf, rather to the composer's annoyance. But Mendelssohn liked Delphine— "[she] is adored here (and deservedly)"—and she received the dedication of the concerto, which became one of her party pieces in her later career. Men-

[1]One who might not have been so happy, though she seems to have allowed herself no outward signs of discontent, was Felix's older and also immensely gifted sister, Fanny, the person to whom Felix was closest all his life and whose early death helped hasten his own. She is one of the lost women of nineteenth-century history. Her father would not countenance the thought of a musical career for her, and for all his awareness of and admiration for her talent, Felix also did his share when it came to squelching her, discouraging her from publishing her music and even publishing some of her songs under his name.
[2]Excerpt from Mendelssohn's letters from Felix Mendelssohn, *Letters*, ed. G. Selden-Goth (New York: Pantheon Books, 1945).

delssohn, however, played the premiere himself at a concert devoted entirely to his own music. Also included were his Symphony No. 1, the astounding Overture he had written at seventeen for Shakespeare's *Midsummer Night's Dream*, and some keyboard improvisations.

"I was received with loud and long applause," Mendelssohn wrote home, "but I was modest and would not reappear." The advocacy of both Clara Schumann and Franz Liszt helped further to establish the concerto's popularity; Mendelssohn himself, however, tended to view it disparagingly: "I wrote it in but a few days and almost carelessly; nonetheless, it always pleased people the most, but me very little." Berlioz, too, remarked on its extreme popularity, and in his collection *Evenings in the Orchestra* he described the fate of an Erard piano that had been through that inescapable piece once too often:

> M. Erard arrives, but try as he will, the piano, which is out of its mind, has no intention of paying him any heed either. He sends for holy water and sprinkles the keyboard with it, but in vain—proof that it wasn't witchcraft but merely the natural result of thirty performances of one concerto. They take the keyboard out of the instrument—the keys are still moving up and down by themselves—and they throw it into the middle of the courtyard next to the warehouse. There M. Erard, now in a fury, has it chopped up with an axe. You think that did it? It made matters worse. Each piece danced, jumped, frisked about separately—on the pavement, between our legs, against the wall, in all directions, until the warehouse locksmith picked up this bedeviled mechanism in one armful and flung it into the fire of his forge, finally putting an end to it. . . . Such a fine instrument! We were heartbroken, but what could we do?[3]

The audience at the Munich Odeon, which included the King, must have been astonished by the way the Concerto begins—not just by the tempestuous orchestral crescendo but even more by the entrance of the piano after only seven preparatory bars. In five concertos he had written in his teens, Mendelssohn had provided the full orchestral exposition listeners expected. True, Beethoven had introduced the piano startlingly early in his Fourth and Fifth concertos (in the first and second measures, respectively), but in both works a relatively brief solo is followed by a normal long tutti.

Although in the generation of composers including Weber, Berlioz, Chopin, Schumann, Liszt, and Wagner, Mendelssohn counts as a conservative, that turn of temperament did not keep him from having and cultivating an inquiring mind. The question of how pieces begin interested him, and so did the problem of how movements of large works might be connected. In the Piano Concerto No. 1, the drastic short-circuiting of formal conventions

[3]Hector Berlioz, *Evenings in the Orchestra*, transl. and ed. Jacques Barzun (Chicago: University of Chicago Press, 1956), translation amended.

consorts well with the urgent gestures of this music—*Sturm und Drang* revisited.

The piano enters not just soon and impetuously, but with an imposing display of bravura. Alone, it also begins a lyric second theme, to which the violins add just a touch of delicate commentary. This episode, a brief moment of relaxation, begins in B-flat major, which, as the relative major of the home key, G minor, is normal, although at the same time, Mendelssohn is careful not to stabilize B-flat too much, keeping his melody poised over a dominant pedal. Moreover, he almost immediately repeats its opening phrase in B-flat *minor*, then uses that change as a hinge to go into D-flat major, and by now he has moved very far away from home. Thunderous octave scales begin the development, which is full of pianistic and harmonic adventure.

At the end of the recapitulation, a series of fanfares commands quiet, cutting into the G-minor cadences with assertive and startling B-naturals; then, after an elegantly tactful introduction by the piano, cellos and violas sing the touching, lightly sentimental song-without-words of the Andante. (The violins are silent in this movement until it is more than four-fifths over.) In the middle comes a lovely opportunity for the pianist to show off her skill in filigree, while violas and cellos—each section is divided in two to make a gloriously rich crème caramel of a sound—continue the melodic flow. Finally, with violins adding their shimmer to the orchestral palette, the piano reclaims the melody.

Another fanfare rouses us from these dreams, and, with a more expansive imitation of the Concerto's opening—suspenseful crescendo in the orchestra and a bravura entrance for the soloist—Mendelssohn launches his headlong and glittering finale with its sparkling and dancing themes and decorative counter-themes. For a moment, he relaxes tempo and mood to bring the briefest of recollections of the first movement's lyric theme; then, the pianist having been given this chance to catch her breath, he launches his sure-to-bring-the-house-down coda.

## Concerto in E minor for Violin and Orchestra, Opus 64

> *Allegro molto appassionato*
> *Andante*
> *Allegretto ma non troppo—Allegro molto vivace*

Carrying out a plan that went back to 1838, Mendelssohn completed his Violin Concerto on 16 September 1844, and it was played for the first time on 13 March 1845 at the Leipzig Gewandhaus by Ferdinand David, concertmaster of the Gewandhaus Orchestra, and with the Danish composer Niels Gade conducting.

**Solo violin, two flutes, two oboes, two clarinets, two bassoons, two horns, two trumpets, timpani, and strings.**

At the celebration of his seventy-fifth birthday in June 1906, Joseph Joachim said: "The Germans have four violin concertos. The greatest, the most uncompromising, is Beethoven's. The one by Brahms vies with it in seriousness. The richest, the most seductive, was written by Max Bruch. But the most inward, the heart's jewel, is Mendelssohn's."

Joachim spoke from a position of singular authority. Not only had he been performing Beethoven's Concerto since just before his thirteenth birthday—the first time was with Mendelssohn conducting—but it was his advocacy that had turned it from an obscure and problematic work into the summit and cynosure of the violin concerto repertory. He had crucially helped Brahms with his Concerto, had been the first to play it, and wrote a mangificent cadenza for it. He had worked with Bruch on the revisions that put the popular G-minor Concerto into its final form and had given the premiere of that definitive edition. As for Mendelssohn, Joachim had become his protégé and intellectual ward when he was twelve. The two, man and boy, were partners in concert on many an occasion; Ferdinand David, who gave the first performance of the Mendelssohn Concerto, was Joachim's mentor, not only in violin playing but in composition, general musicianship, and concertmastering; and Joachim himself played Mendelssohn's Concerto more than 200 times in his long career, the first time having been in 1846 with the composer conducting.

Ferdinand David was more than the first violinist to play the Mendelssohn; the work was intended for him from the beginning. The two had been friends since 1825, when David, just fifteen, had given his first concerts in Berlin with his sister Louise. He had studied violin with Louis Spohr and theory with Moritz Hauptmann, worked in Berlin and Russia, and was appointed concertmaster in Leipzig in 1835. In 1843, when Mendelssohn founded the Leipzig Conservatory, which quickly became the most renowned institution of its kind in the world, David was one of the first people he appointed to his faculty (along with Hauptmann, Robert Schumann, and, soon after, Clara Schumann, Ferdinand Hiller, Niels Gade, and Ignaz Moscheles). David was held in highest regard as soloist, model concertmaster, quartet leader, and not least as teacher, his *Violinschule* holding a place as a basic pedagogical work until some way into the twentieth century. (His conducting met with less acclaim.)

"I would like to write a violin concerto for you for next winter," Mendelssohn, then conductor of the Gewandhaus Orchestra, wrote to his concertmaster on 30 July 1838. "There's one in E minor in my head, and its opening won't leave me in peace." David, delighted, promised to practice it "so that the angels in heaven will rejoice." "You want it brilliant," replied Mendelssohn, "but how is someone like me supposed to manage that?" And with that coy question, Mendelssohn drew back from his plan, kept busy as a conductor and pianist, and composed his Trio in D minor, two symphonies (the *Song of Praise* and the *Scotch*), the incidental music for A *Midsummer Night's Dream*, the Cello Sonata No. 2, the revised version of *The First Walpurgis Night*, and many piano pieces, including the *Variations sérieuses* and the splendid Prelude and Fugue in E minor. Only in the summer of 1844, at peace in Soden near Frankfurt, did he return to the long-deferred Concerto, immediately drawing David into the project.

David played a role parallel to that taken a generation later by Joachim with the Brahms Concerto. Mendelssohn's is in fact the first in the distinguished series of violin concertos written by non-violinist composers with the assistance, or at least the advice, of violinists. Bach and Mozart, although primarily keyboard players, were also able violinists, and Beethoven, besides having had some string experience in his youth was not of a mind to ask anyone's help, but after Mendelssohn-David we find the crucial partnerships of Bruch, Brahms, and Dvořák with Joachim, Tchaikovsky with Yosif Kotek; Elgar with W. H. Reed; Szymanowski with Paweł Kochański; Stravinsky with Samuel Dushkin; Bartók with Zoltán Székely; Shostakovich with David Oistrakh; and John Adams with Jorja Fleezanis and Gidon Kremer.

Even though at thirty-five Mendelssohn was an old hand at concertos, having written one for violin (when he was thirteen), three for piano, two for two pianos, and one for violin and piano, he was nervous about this project. On 17 December 1844 Mendelssohn wrote David a long letter full of detailed questions about changes he had just made in the solo part (many of them, it seems, specifically to please the violinist) and seeking his approval, or at least his views. Is the new and longer cadenza all right, and is it "written correctly and smoothly?" Are all the alterations playable? Is the balance better now? And so it goes, with question after question about specific measures.

What does David think of using pizzicato to accompany the theme of the slow movement?

> I had intended to write it this way originally but was dissuaded later, I really don't know why. Actually the problem is NOT how the pizzicato sounds because that I know, but how it sounds together with the *coll'arco* [with the bow] of the basses and the solo violin. Won't these accents make a confused effect because of the combination of arco and pizzicato? Please ask Gade to have a

look at this too, and let me know his opinion. Don't laugh at me too much, I'm ashamed already, but I can't help it, I'm just groping here. [This has remained arco, either because David or Gade talked Mendelssohn out of the pizzicato or because for some other reason the alteration never made it into the published score.] Thank God the fellow is through with his concerto, you will say. . . ."[4]

Mendelssohn's letter illuminates both the nature of his specific concerns and the precision and clarity—the articulateness, one might say—of his compositions in general. One hears and reads so much of these aspects of Mendelssohn, the master of poised music-making—this has even been at the core of a century and a half of (more or less veiled) anti-Semitic attacks on him: the Jew as resourceful but rootless and soulless imitator and manufacturer of simulacra, etc., etc. But Mendelssohn was in fact exceedingly vulnerable to passion and to the signals of his sensibility, and to the listener not distracted by his exquisite manners, he reveals himself in his best work as an inspired musician of a singularly fresh turn of mind. He was not far into his teens when he found his own unmistakable voice unmistakably, and his classicism is a brace, not a muzzle or a mask.

In his G-minor and D-minor piano concertos, Mendelssohn gives us just enough of an orchestral exordium to propel the soloist into action; excited and theatrical in the former work, brooding in the latter, it amounts to less than ten seconds of music in either case. In the Violin Concerto—and "the Mendelssohn Violin Concerto" *tout court* always means the great E-minor work under discussion here—he reduces the orchestra's participation still further: a backdrop for not as much as two seconds of E minor, given an *appassionato* character by the quietly pulsating drums and plucked basses. Across this the violin sings its melody. At once urgent and elegant, stunningly economical in harmony, it sounds like something that must have come to Mendelssohn in a single rush of inspiration: in fact it cost him enormous trouble to find precisely the contours and the rhythmic balance that so eloquently and now so inevitably give voice to feeling.

The first extended passage for the orchestra is dramatically introduced by upward-thrusting octaves of the violin. It soon gives way to the next solo, a new melody, full of verve, and barely begun by the orchestra before the soloist makes it his own. As in all concertos between Beethoven and Brahms, the orchestra here is not so much partner or rival in dialectic discussion as provider of accompaniment, punctuation, scaffolding, and a bit of cheerleading. Nonetheless, we should not make the mistake of thinking that Men-

[4]Felix Mendelssohn, *Letters*, op. cit.

delssohn's attention to his orchestra is in any way perfunctory: the work-manship, the sonorous fantasy, the delight in detail are exquisite. The violin dazzles us with brilliant passagework, which is what Mendelssohn really means us to pay attention to, but at almost any moment when you choose to listen to what is going on "behind," you will be rewarded by real activity, not just mechanical strumming. It is as though solo and tutti both managed to be foreground and background at the same time.

The theme that brings the first big change of character (and also of key and of mode, from minor to major) is deliciously scored. The violin has made a graceful landing on its lowest G after a descent of more than three octaves, and it is over that quiet, sustained, and solitary sound of the G that the clarinet (with another clarinet and a pair of flutes) introduces the new tune. The presentation is immediately reversed, with the violin playing the melody and the four winds accompanying. Either way, the combination of wind quar-tet with a single string instrument is wonderfully fresh. In the recapitulation, Mendelssohn will be able to offer us the pleasure of a subtle coloristic differ-entiation when the violin's sustained note is not the open-string G but a vibrant E.

The cadenza in the first movement is famous. One might wish that Joachim and others, setting to work on the Beethoven and Brahms concertos, had taken to heart the lesson in Mendelssohn's tact and punctuality. The big surprise, however, is in where the cadenza occurs. In Classical practice, the cadenza comes at the joint of recapitulation and coda, so that it really is a cadence, a brilliant expansion of the last big harmonic settling of the move-ment. Mendelssohn places it instead at the other crucial harmonic juncture, the arrival of the recapitulation, the return to the home key after the pere-grinations of the development. He prepares this homecoming subtly, allowing himself some delicate anticipations of what it will be like to be in E again, and managing this maneuver as a gradual subsidence of wonderful breadth and serenity: it must be the first cadenza since the Brandenburg Concerto No. 5 not arrived at by way of orchestral bluster.

On the doorstep of home, the orchestra stops and defers to the soloist. But the exit from the cadenza is as much of a surprise as the entrance into it was. After some rhetorical gestures based on trills and stretches, the soloist embarks on a series of arpeggios about which Mendelssohn in his letter to David worried they might be too tiring. Obviously they are preparatory in character, but when what they have prepared duly occurs, namely the un-ambiguous arrival in E minor and the return of the opening theme, the ar-peggios do not cease; rather, they continue and in continuing add a new and crackling surface to the familiar melody. Mendelssohn always enjoyed making this most obvious place in a composition, the Big Return, a bit unobvious, often by having the bass and the melody arrive a little out of phase, but none of his many ingenious solutions is wittier and more captivating than this most charming overlap.[5]

A couple of years earlier, in his *Scotch* Symphony, Mendelssohn experimented with the idea of going from movement to movement without a break, something he may well have picked up from the first version of Schumann's Symphony in D minor. Here Mendelssohn takes the plan a step further, not merely eliminating the pauses between movements but actually constructing links. Writing in 1921, D. F. Tovey, who had been going to concerts for forty years, complained that he had never heard "the most remarkable stroke of genius in this most popular of violin concertos." He was referring to the way in which the Andante mysteriously emerges from the brilliant close of the first movement, a passage always in his experience drowned out by applause.

The last *fortissimo* chord of E minor is cut off by all instruments save a single bassoon, who holds on to a B for a long time before—still alone—moving up a half-step to C. In turn, flute, violas, second violins, first violins, and cellos imitate this half-step motion, and so we slip gently into the new key, C major. Even the fact that this is done by a series of half-steps is important and characteristic. Throughout the first movement, Mendelssohn's harmony has been singularly chaste, colorful chromatic progressions (that is to say, those based on half-steps) used sparingly. Specifically, chromatic basses of any prominence occur only at critical structural junctures—the end of the development, the end of the recapitulation, the end of the coda. The effect of the half-steps here is doubly telling because of Mendelssohn's reserve up to this point. And when the solo melody comes in after this suspenseful preparation, it too begins with a rising half-step (and on a pair—E-F—not used in the introduction).

This could be one of Mendelssohn's songs (with or without words). It is a sweet and lovely melody of surprising extension, beautifully harmonized and scored. Listen to the effect, for example, of the woodwinds in the few measures (fourteen out of forty-three) in which they participate. The middle section, back in minor, brings an upsurge of passion. Then the first melody returns, set still more beautifully than before, with the accompanying instruments unable to forget the emotional tremors of the movement's central section.

Between the Andante and the finale, Mendelssohn places another kind of bridge, a tiny and wistful intermezzo, just fourteen measures long and

---

[5]David is very much present in this cadenza in that what ended up in the published score is a slightly simpler version: evidently he did find the original tiring or otherwise inconvenient. A performance I heard Stephanie Chase give in 1995 of Mendelssohn's original, with its denser four-part arpeggios, was no doubt more taxing but also more powerful and brilliant. Mendelssohn told David that the arpeggios "must begin immediately in tempo and continue that way until the tutti entrance."

having something of the character as well as the function of a recitative. Strings alone accompany the solo violin, which sets off nicely the touch of fanfare that starts the finale. This is sparkling and busy music whose gait allows room for swinging, broad, thoroughly Mendelssohnian tunes as well as for the dazzling sixteenth-notes of the solo part. The pace is not altogether easy to gauge. It is not *presto delirando*, although some famous violinists have been led into temptation by their own technical prowess to take it so fast that some passages have sounded like the pitchless key-clackings so often found in the avant-garde flute pieces of the 1960s. Here, too, Mendelssohn delights in the witty play of foreground and background, and so steers the Concerto to its close in a festivity of high spirits and with a wonderful sense of "go."

# Wolfgang Amadè Mozart

Joannes Chrisostomus Wolfgang Gottlieb Mozart, who began to call himself Wolfgango Amadeo about 1770 and Wolfgang Amadè in 1777—but who never used Amadeus except in jest—was born in Salzburg, Austria, on 27 January 1756 and died in Vienna on 5 December 1791.

The identifying K numbers refer to the chronological thematic catalogue of Mozart's works published in 1862 by Ludwig, Ritter von Köchel, an Austrian botanist, mineralogist, and music bibliographer. Köchel was an amateur at musicology (a term not yet known during his lifetime), as he was at botany and mineralogy, but his Mozart catalogue was a model and set the standard for the composer catalogues that followed his. The Köchel catalogue has been revised several times in light of new knowledge. Sometimes a K number appears with a second number in parentheses right after it: for example, K. 361(370a). In such a listing, the first number is Köchel's original, the second the one to be found in one of the more recent editions of the catalogue.

## Concerto in A major for Clarinet and Orchestra, K. 622

*Allegro*
*Adagio*
*Rondo: Allegro*

Mozart wrote a concerto for the clarinetist Anton Stadler between the end of September and mid-November 1791, and presumably Stadler performed that work in Vienna soon after. The concerto does not, however, survive in the form in which Mozart wrote it, and it is generally heard now in an adaptation of unknown authorship dating from about 1800. Mozart makes no room for cadenzas in this Concerto.


**Solo clarinet, two flutes, two bassoons, two horns, and strings.**


Anton Stadler gets a generally bad press in the Mozart literature. "Dissolute" is an adjective frequently applied, and one of Mozart's sniffier relatives, his sister-in-law Sophie Haibel, counted Stadler among the composer's "false friends, secret bloodsuckers, and worthless persons who served only to amuse him at the table and intercourse with whom injured his reputation." We know little about Stadler's life, neither where he was born nor when he and his younger brother Johann, also a clarinetist, came to Vienna. Köchel tells us that Stadler was fifty-nine when he died in June 1817. Both Stadlers were in the orchestra of Prince Galitzin, the Russian ambassador in Vienna, whose grandson would become one of Beethoven's last and most important patrons.

Stadler's first known contact with Mozart was in March 1784, when he took part in a concert whose major work was the big Wind Serenade in B-flat, K. 361(370a). Like Mozart, he was a Freemason, though they belonged to different lodges. Mozart liked him, particularly as a companion for those pleasures of the table (including the gambling table) of which Mozart's widow, her second husband, and her sister were so disapproving. Mozart even lent Stadler 500 gulden without security. It was a debt that went unpaid.[1]

But Stadler's artistry has never been in dispute. Here is a rhapsody from the pen of Johann Friedrich Schink, a Prussian-born critic of theater and opera who lived in Austria from 1780: "My thanks to you, noble Virtuoso! Never have I heard the like to what you contrive with your instrument. Never should I have imagined that a clarinet might be capable of imitating the human voice as deceptively-faithfully as it was imitated by you. Verily, your instrument has so soft and lovely a tone that none who has a heart can resist it, and I, dear Virtuoso, have a heart. Let me thank you!"[2]

Still more telling is the testimony of what Mozart wrote for Stadler: this concerto; the Quintet with strings, K. 581, of almost equal loveliness; perhaps

---

[1]That was a considerable bundle, more than Mozart's normal commission fee for an opera and nearly two-thirds his annual salary as an imperial court musician. Mozart may have won the sum gambling, Stadler borrowing it quickly before it got turned back into chips.

[2]Otto Erich Deutsch, *Mozart: A Documentary Biography*, transl. Eric Blom, Peter Brunscombe, and Jeremy Noble (Stanford: Stanford University Press, 1965).

the rich and subtle Trio in E-flat with viola and piano, K. 498; certainly the obbligatos in two of the arias in *La clemenza di Tito*, Sesto's "Parto, parto" and Vitellia's "Non più di fiori." (Mozart had taken Stadler along for the opera's premiere in Prague in September 1791 and reported home with delight that his friend had received ovations for his playing.) It is also likely that the late addition of clarinet parts to the Symphony No. 40 in G minor was undertaken to please the Stadlers.

Mozart had written for the clarinet as early as 1771, when it was just beginning to be established as a normal part of the orchestra, but his real discovery of its character came about in the 1780s. The soft edge of its tone, the vocal possibilities that Schink noted in Stadler's playing, its virtuosic potential in matters of flexibility and range all made it an ideal voice for Mozart's fantasy and musical thought. At that time, however, the low register of this relatively new instrument was deemed colorless as well as a bit uncertain in pitch.

Stadler was intent on correcting those deficiencies, and he also wished to extend the range further downward. He therefore built, or had built for him, clarinets that added four centimeters at the bottom, encompassing the low A on the bass staff for the bass clarinet and the corresponding B-flat for the instrument in that key. It is for one of Stadler's stretch models that Mozart wrote the Quintet, the brilliant obbligato to "Parto, parto," and the Concerto.

The trouble is that Mozart's autograph manuscripts of the Quintet and Concerto do not survive, and our earliest sources for the Concerto are three printed editions published by Sieber (Paris, possibly as early as 1799), André (Offenbach, 1801), and Breitkopf & Härtel (Leipzig, 1801 or 1802). In each of these the Concerto has been shrunk, so to speak, to accommodate the compass of an ordinary clarinet in A, for the Stadler extension did not catch on.

The anonymous reviewer of the Breitkopf edition in the March 1802 issue of the *Allgemeine musikalische Zeitung* was informed about the situation and may well have seen Mozart's original score. (Very likely it was the journal's editor himself, Johann Friedrich Rochlitz, one of the most astute critics in the history of the profession.) He writes that, given how rare instruments with the extension are "so far," he understands the publisher's decision from the commercial point of view; nonetheless, he wishes Breitkopf might have given both versions, with the adaptation in small notes, and adds that "the Concerto has not exactly gained from the changes." In the standard version, Mozart's melodic curves and dramatic plunges often have to be hobbled and compromised by the need to eliminate the low notes he built into them. The Concerto is beautiful, no matter what, but with the full gamut restored it is more beautiful.

Since 1948 several scholars, notably George Dazeley, Jiři Kratochvíl,

Milan Kostohryz, and Ernst Hess, have taken an interest in what is now, following Kratochvíl's lead, generally called the basset clarinet. (Stadler had no special name for the instrument.) Some builders, editors, and players—Eric Hoeprich, Colin Lawson, and Antony Pay are notable among the latter—have carried their conclusions into the real world of practical music-making, and these speculative reconstructions of Mozart's lost original tend to support the contentions of the *Allgemeine musikalische Zeitung*'s critic.

The history of Mozart's Concerto is both complicated and clarified by the existence of an autograph fragment, 199 measures long, of a concerto in G for basset horn with an orchestra of flutes, horns, and strings.[3] This fragment, K. 621b, whose date we do not know precisely but which most scholars assume to be 1791, closely corresponds to a little more than half the first movement of the Clarinet Concerto as we know it; from it, moreover, we can infer what the solo clarinet part looked like before the arrangers got their hands on it. Just why and when Mozart abandoned his basset horn score and switched to Stadler's basset clarinet is yet another pair of questions to which we have no answer. Trying to sort out the chronology of the Concerto, we see that Mozart returned in mid-September 1791 to Vienna from Prague, where he had introduced *La clemenza di Tito* and conducted some performances of *Don Giovanni*, Stadler remaining behind to play some more opera performances and give a concert of his own on 6 October; that he entered *The Magic Flute* in his catalogue as complete on 28 September and conducted its first performance on the 30th; that in a letter to his wife, who had gone to take the waters at Baden, he reported on 7–8 October that he was scoring "Stadler's Rondo," that is to say, the finale of the Concerto. It was the last major work he completed, with only the *Little Masonic Cantata*, K. 623, and the fragments of the Requiem to follow. He conducted the cantata on 18 November, went ill to bed two days later, and died on 5 December at one o'clock in the morning.

Given the vagueness of the reports and the peculiarities of eighteenth-century medical terminology, we cannot tell for sure what Mozart died of: biographers have offered us everything from Bright's disease to acute rheumatic fever (now assumed to be the most likely cause) to a broken heart. German writers like to refer to the Mozart of 1791 as *todgeweiht* or *vom Tode gezeichnet*, dedicated to death or marked by the stigmata of death, but that is sentimental rubbish. He went through patches of severe depression in 1791, but it was also a year of what we might well call Mozartian energy, one that

---

[3]The basset horn is a gently mournful relative of the clarinet, with a range down to the F at the bottom of the bass staff. Mozart was fond of it and used it to beautiful effect in his Requiem; it still shows up as late as a number of scores by Richard Strauss and in the Violin Concerto by Roger Sessions.

began with the composition and performance of his Piano Concerto in B-flat, K. 595; in which he wrote *The Magic Flute* and completed *La clemenza di Tito* (a work whose chronology is a bit uncertain); and in which the smaller works include such marvels as the *Ave verum corpus*, K. 618 and the F-minor *Fantasy for a Mechanical Clock*, K. 608, best known now in a transcription for piano duet. And if in the later 1780s he had fallen out of favor with the easily distracted Viennese, in *The Magic Flute* he had come up with the greatest hit of his life.

There is a recognizable Mozart-in-A-major mood, softly lit, more intimate than festive, serene rather than impassioned, the sense of physical energy somewhat muted, the music often starting with a theme that descends from the fifth note of the scale, E: the first movements of the Clarinet Concerto, the Clarinet Quintet, and the Piano Concerto, K. 488, exemplify it. In the Clarinet Concerto, Mozart soon reveals that there is more to the first theme than innocence, that it lends itself to closely worked polyphonic elaboration. Some of these excursions echo the gravely glorious music Mozart put into the chorale prelude for the two men in armor in *The Magic Flute*. The clarinet introduces new ideas that move the expressive range in the direction of a certain gentle melancholy. The sheer sound of this movement is of transcendent beauty: never had Mozart used flutes so delicately in an orchestra, and often he gives the sonority an airy lightness by building on a foundation of cellos without basses. After the rich adventures of the exposition and development, the recapitulation is tight.

The slow movement is an Adagio, rare in Mozart and always a sign of special seriousness. Its second idea, a five-note descent, is so simple that you are amazed each time at what Mozart makes of it, particularly in its fragrant harmonizations. This movement, whose beauty is of a truly ineffable sort, begins in calm but grows to admit Mozart's tribute to Stadler's virtuosity and vocality, and its arpeggios rise into quiet and deeply affecting ecstasy.

In the Rondo that brings the Concerto to its close, Mozart shows once again how simple beginnings may lead to unexpected riches. One of the most remarkable of these is the eloquent theme in minor that constitutes its third main thematic group. Toward the end, Mozart stops our breath with heartbreaking brief silences. Describing this movement, H. C. Robbins Landon invokes a phrase from *The Winter's Tale*: "[The] heart dances, but not for joy."

# Concerto No. 3 in E-flat major for Horn and Orchestra, K. 447

*Allegro*
*Romance: Larghetto*
*Allegro*

The date of this work is not known. It used to be given as 1783, but studies both of Mozart's handwriting in the manuscript and of the paper itself have led scholars to conclude that 1787 or 1788 would be more accurate. The puzzle that attends this redating is the omission of this Concerto from the catalogue of his works that Mozart began keeping in February 1784, an omission that 1783 as the date of composition would of course explain. Nothing is known about the first performance, nor did Mozart leave any cadenzas.

**Solo horn, two clarinets, two bassoons, and strings.**

The numbering of Mozart's horn concertos is a mess. The first one he completed, in May 1783, was K. 417 in E-flat, which is usually known as No. 2. Next came K. 495, also in E-flat, dated June 1786, and usually listed as No. 4. Then comes the present work, K. 447, called No. 3. As for the so-called No. 1, in D major, K. 412(386b), Mozart wrote two movements of it somewhere between 1786 and 1788, and in 1791 began a finale which he never finished. From March 1781 there is also an unattached Rondo in E-flat, K. 371.

The music in Mozart's concertos often has a quality of transposed opera and, like most of Mozart's operatic roles and concert arias, these works are, to borrow from dance parlance, "made on" particular performers—often, in the piano concertos, Mozart himself. The voice and personality behind the horn concertos are those of Joseph Leutgeb, whose name Mozart spelled Leitgeb and which, with his Austrian accent, he would have pronounced that way, too. The relatively little known Quintet for Horn with Violin, Two Violas, and Cello, K. 407(386c), was also written for Leutgeb.

Leutgeb was a virtuoso who had been principal horn in Salzburg during Mozart's young years. By 1770 he was doing considerable solo work, enjoying exceptional success in Paris, where the *Mercure de France* praised his ability "to sing an adagio as perfectly as the most mellow, interesting, and accurate voice." In February 1773 he joined Wolfgang and Leopold Mozart on part of their Italian tour. In 1777 he moved to Vienna where, in addition to keeping up his musical activities, he ran a cheese store.[4] He retired from playing about 1792 and died in 1811. A certain bratty vein of Mozart's humor emerges in the manuscripts destined for Leutgeb, which contain such remarks as "a sheep could trill like that," and in one of which he sets a trap for the soloist by marking his part *Adagio* while the orchestra has *Allegro*, but "Leitgeb the ass, ox, and fool," as the dedication of one the concertos has it, was an unswervingly loyal friend.

More to the point, Leutgeb was an artist. Playing the French horn is not easy now; in Mozart's and Leutgeb's day it was even riskier. Valves came in around 1820, but until then, players had available only those sixteen pitches that were part of the natural overtone series (nine of them bunched together in the highest of the instrument's three octaves, and not perfectly in tune), plus some other notes that could be produced by inserting the hand in the bell one-fourth, half, or three-quarters of the way. The trouble was that this hand-stopping altered the tone, making it in various degrees nasal, muffled, or snarly. This meant that to play a continuous melody required unremitting vigilance and uncanny finesse. It is no wonder that Mozart's concertos for the horn are much shorter than those for other instruments.

Mozart's horn concertos offer many delights to the listener as well as challenges to the soloist. One of the most enchanting pages is the rollicking finale of K. 495, which the English comedy team of Flanders and Swann turned into a vocal tour de force in *At the Drop of a Hat*. K. 447 is the most poetic of the concertos as well as the one whose sound is the most special, for here alone Mozart departs from the oboe-horn combination of the other works to give us instead the velvety background of clarinets and bassoons. For so compressed a work, an astonishing variety of musical characters passes before us. In his boldest flight of poetry, not to mention his utter faith in Leutgeb's artistry, Mozart begins his development in a dreamily remote D-flat major, making his way back to the home key by way of a succession of magic modulations we would find remarkable if we came across it in one of his most inventive piano concertos.

The middle movement, which Mozart labels *Romance*, is in A-flat major, a key he ventures into rarely and one that always sets him to musing. The serene melody of the Romance stages an unexpected reappearance when it turns up—in quick tempo—as one of the episodes in the artful hunt-music finale (a device Mahler would charmingly imitate in his Fifth Symphony).

---

[4]Leutgeb was not the only associate of Mozart's to venture into the grocery business. Lorenzo da Ponte, who wrote the librettos of *Figaro's Wedding*, *Don Giovanni*, and *Così fan tutte*, emigrated to New York in 1805 and for a while ran a *salumeria* in Morristown, New Jersey; however, to quote *The New Grove Dictionary of Music and Musicians*, "not being equal to the business practices of the New World," he went into teaching, eventually becoming the first professor of Italian language and literature at King's College (later Columbia University).

## Mozart's Piano Concertos

> Did you know that Mozart wrote *twenty* concertos for the piano and that nine
> of them are masterpieces? Yet nobody plays them. Why? Because they are too
> hard, Deppe says, and Lebert, the head of the Stuttgardt conservatory, told me
> the same thing at Weimar. I remember that the musical critic of the *Atlantic
> Monthly* remarked that "we should regard Mozart's passages and cadenzas as
> child's play now-a-days." *Child's play*, indeed! That critic, whoever it is, "had
> better go to school again," as C. always says.[5]

That is the spirited Miss Amy Fay on 12 February 1874, writing to her
family in Cambridge, Massachusetts, from Berlin, where, as one said in those
days, she had gone for the improvement of her taste and the perfection of
her technique. (Her teacher, Ludwig Deppe, had just assigned her the Mozart
Concerto for Two Pianos.) Half a century later, Mozart's concertos were
hardly better known. Their present ubiquity is the fruit of the persistence of
a few artists, notably Artur Schnabel and Edwin Fischer; also, one should by
no means underestimate the contribution of Donald Francis Tovey.[6]

Mozart's first piano concertos are not original compositions, but arrangements for piano and orchestra of sonata movements by Carl Philipp Emanuel
Bach, Johann Christian Bach, and Johann Schobert, plus a few now deeply
obscure composers. These pieces date from Mozart's twelfth through sixteenth years, and it may be that his father assigned these tasks to him. Mozart's first real concerto is the one in D major, K. 175, which he wrote just
before he turned eighteen, and it is an impressive work indeed. In 1776 there
followed two agreeable, lightweight works, K. 238 and K. 246; three if you
count the Concerto for Three Pianos, K. 242. From this time there is also a
Concerto for Two Pianos, K. 365, and it is a real charmer. The big concerto
he wrote at the beginning of 1777 for the French pianist Mlle. Jeunehomme,
K. 271, represents a further, and huge, step into maturity.

Mozart moved from Salzburg to Vienna in March 1781, set to work
composing *The Abduction from the Seraglio,* and quickly found himself immensely in demand in the capital. In what Friedrich Blume calls the composer's "first creative ecstasy" after his liberation from the provincialism and
wretched working conditions of Salzburg, Mozart composed three piano con-

---

[5]*Music-Study in Germany, from the Home Correspondence of Amy Fay,* ed. Mrs. Fay Peirce (New York:
Macmillan, 1896), p. 303.
[6]Tovey, who also studied with Deppe for a time, played many of Mozart's concertos with the Reid
Orchestra at the University of Edinburgh, but he made still more impact with the program notes he
wrote for those performances, which, along with his major essay, "The Classical Concerto," he
published in 1936 as Vol. 3 of *Essays in Musical Analysis* (Oxford: Oxford University Press).

certos for the 1782–1783 season in Vienna. The earliest of the three is the lyric one in A major, K. 414(385p), a most neatly cut jewel that has always enjoyed the most consistent public favor, more than its chamber-musical neighbor in F major, K. 413(387a) or the brilliant, ambitious, and somewhat eccentric essay in C major, K. 415(387b).

None of these three is quite as grand in scale as K. 271. For Mozart this was a time of change. He was writing for a public of whose taste he was not certain (and which, in three or four years, would confirm his darker suspicions), but at the same time he was eager to expand the possibilities of the concerto, a genre in which his brilliance as a pianist and his flair for the presentational made him especially at home. Among other things, then, these first Viennese concertos taken together are a crucial step in adapting, in learning, in stretching: without K. 415 there could be no K. 467 or K. 503, without K. 414 no K. 488. (By a curious coincidence—which is almost certainly no coincidence at all—the sketches for the later A-major Concerto, K. 488, are on the back of the sheet on which Mozart wrote the cadenzas for this earlier one.) "They are a happy medium," Mozart wrote to his father about his first Viennese concertos, "between too hard and too easy—very brilliant, pleasing to the ear, natural, without lapsing into vapidity. There are passages here and there from which connoisseurs alone can derive satisfaction, but they are written so that the non-connoisseurs cannot fail to be pleased even if they don't know why." And even if we did not know it from his letters, the music would tell us Mozart was having a wonderful time.

Mozart's popularity reached its crest in 1784 and 1785. On 3 March 1784 he wrote to his father that he had given twenty-two concerts in thirty-eight days, adding, "I don't think that in this way I can possibly get out of practice." From this popularity grew the astonishing run of piano concertos that Mozart wrote in those years—twelve of them between February 1784 (K. 449 in E flat) and December 1786 (K. 503 in C major), nine of them for performance by himself at his own concerts.[7] He had already played the piano in public when he was still too short to reach the pedals without having wooden blocks attached to them. What happened later tells an equally vivid story of the dip in Mozart's fortunes: in the not-quite-six remaining years of his life, he wrote just two more piano concertos, one for a journey to Frankfurt, the other for an appearance as supporting artist in a Vienna concert by somebody else.

The twelve richly worked, poignant, witty, and effervescent concertos of 1784–1786 amount to a series of masterpieces to delight the mind, charm and seduce the ear, and pierce the heart. More than two hundred years later, they remain the ideal realization of what might be accomplished in the genre.

---

[7] I have sometimes wondered which nine of the eighteen concertos from K. 271 (1777) to K. 595 (1791) Deppe admitted as masterpieces.

Part of what made them so was Mozart's discovery in 1782 of the music of Handel and of Johann Sebastian Bach, the father of Johann Christian Bach, whose music he had known and loved since childhood. We could think this way: He learned how to integrate elements from the music of both generation of Bachs, folding into Johann Christian's *galant* manner Johann Sebastian's wonderfully rich and involved polyphonic textures. This made possible such miracles as the development sections of many of his concerto first movements, that in K. 503 being the most breathtaking example, and in other realms, the first movement of the *Prague* Symphony, the famous finale of the *Jupiter*, and of course his great operatic finales. This is the foundation and the essence of what we now call the Classical style.

It did not make everyone happy; inevitably there were those who wanted their music to be less complex, less demanding on their attention. In 1782, after the premiere of *The Abduction from the Seraglio*, Emperor Joseph II lodged his famous complaint, "Too many notes, dear Mozart, too many notes." His Majesty was ahead of his subjects by several years, but by 1787 or so, much of the Viennese musical public was inclined to think of Mozart as too complicated. Replicating a phenomenon the world has witnessed thousands of times, they resented the idol they themselves had created, and were ready for the next sensation. They found a pretty good one ten years later in the young Beethoven, and in 1820, when Mozart would have been in his sixties and at the height of his powers, they discovered a sensation to end all sensations, Gioachino Rossini.

All this helps to account for the departure of the *Coronation* from the manner of the great run of Mozart's piano concertos since K. 449 to K. 503. Trying to meet what he took to be the taste of his Viennese audience, Mozart made this work less complex than its predecessors and wrote music meant more to please and charm than to stimulate the mind and stir the emotions. This work enjoyed enormous popularity during the nineteenth century when the public thought of Mozart chiefly as a purveyor of Rococo charm, albeit allowing that he had made occasional excursions into the proto-Romantic vein (*Don Giovanni*, the D-minor Piano Concerto); "expression" was added to music later, by Beethoven. For this view, the elegant *Coronation* Concerto is the quintessential Mozart. It is typical for this situation that when the composer, pianist, and conductor Carl Reinecke published a small book in 1891 advocating the revival of Mozart's piano concertos, he drew all his examples from the *Coronation*.

The final concerto, K. 595, is another matter, a gently, heartbreakingly resigned work in which Mozart composed to please himself and, as Stravinsky put it, "the Ideal Other." In those final years, Prague took Mozart up with limitless generosity and enthusiasm, but at home he had lost his public, his patrons, his students, and his earning power. Of course he tried desperately until the end to regain his hold on Vienna, and the success of *The Magic*

*Flute* with a new audience, one that lived in a world of popular rather than high culture, was promising; however, death came before Mozart could complete this reversal.

## Concerto No. 9 in E-flat major for Piano and Orchestra, K. 271

> *Allegro*
> *Andantino*
> *Rondo: Presto—Menuetto: Cantabile—Presto*

Mozart completed this concerto in January 1777 for a touring French pianist, Mlle. Jeunehomme, whose name that liberated speller writes as "jenomé" or "jenomy" and which his father, Leopold Mozart, turns into "genommi." Presumably Mlle. J. played the first performance, although we do not know where or when. Mozart included cadenzas for all three movements in his autograph. In February 1783 he sent his sister newly composed *Eingänge*, or cadenzalike flourishes to introduce solo passages.

**Solo piano, two oboes, two horns, and strings.**

After Mozart's preceding piano concertos—the dashing display of ingenuity in K. 175 (December 1773) and the charms of K. 238 in B-flat major and K. 246 in C major (January and April 1776 respectively)—this work is an immense leap forward in ambition and achievement alike. It leaves us most curious about "*die jenomy*," whose playing or personality or perhaps whose reputation so stimulated the twenty-one-year-old composer. But to no avail. She passed through Salzburg and through musical history for just a moment in January 1777, leaving her indiscriminately spelled name forever attached to the work in which Mozart, so to speak, became Mozart. Then she vanished from view. Mozart himself played "her" concerto at a private concert in Munich on 4 October 1777, and from his having sent his new *Eingänge* to his sister Nannerl in 1783, we know that it continued to engage his attention.

The scoring is modest. Only pairs of oboes and horns join the strings, something remembered always with surprise because the impression the work leaves is so firmly that of a big concerto. (It is, in fact, Mozart's longest.) But Mozart uses these restricted resources remarkably: the horn gets to play a melody in unison with the piano, and more than once Mozart explores the uncommon sonority of the keyboard joined only by the two oboes.

The orchestra's opening flourish is a formal call to attention. The piano's response is a delicious impertinence. Normal concerto etiquette, after all, obliges the soloist to wait until the conclusion of an extended tutti. And having thumbed her nose at convention once, the pianist does not hesitate to do it again by interrupting the formal—very formal—close of the tutti with a long and impatient trill on the dominant. With the piano's penchant for playing at unexpected times established, the whole issue of who plays when becomes the subject of continuing jokes and surprises. The second theme to appear is an elegant melody whose sweet beginning makes the passion of its continuation an always amazing surprise. (This is the melody the horn gets to play in the recapitulation.) In the development, Mozart finds unexpected and ingenious use for the phrase with which the piano so cheekily interrupted the orchestra's pompous beginning. When the cadenza comes at the end of the movement, Mozart adds even more intensity to the continuation of the second theme.

Now, in the Andantino, Mozart presents a scene from some sober operatic tragedy. Strings are muted, violins proceed by close imitation, and the music that prepares the singer's entrance makes its cadence on the formal full close of an *opera seria* recitative. The aria is impassioned and complex, the C minor of its beginning soothed from time to time by a gentler music in E-flat major, but the gestures that dominate the discourse are those of recitative, now pathetic, now stern. Mlle. Jeunehomme would have enjoyed the grandiose gesture that introduces the cadenza, a moment usually assigned to the orchestra alone. The cadenza itself is an extraordinary moment of rhetoric, and as the trills rise over chromatic harmonies, Mozart even directs that the playing be *agitato*, one of the exceedingly rare appearances of the word in a score before the nineteenth century. Mutes come off for the powerful close.

The finale begins in unbuttoned virtuosity, and we might once again infer that Mlle. Jeunehomme was an especially elegant executant of trills. One of the bravura sweeps down the keyboard and up again leads to the opening of a door into a world of whose existence we had not expected to be reminded: we hear a minuet, music of a new character, in a new meter and in a new key. Mozart outdoes himself both in his melodic embellishments—so exquisitely Mozartian in their confluence of invention and control, of pathos and grace—and in the piquant scoring as each strain of piano solo is repeated with orchestral accompaniment (first violins and the lowest strings pizzicato, but the violins with far more notes; the middle voices sustained, second violins singing ardently but with their tone veiled by mutes). Most astonishing is the poignant postlude to the minuet. This dissolves into another cadenza, whence the Presto emerges again to send the music to its runaway close, but not before Mozart has found time to ring one more change on his trill joke.

# Concerto No. 11 in F major for Piano and Orchestra, K. 413(387a)

*Allegro*
*Larghetto*
*Tempo di Menuetto*

Mozart composed this Concerto at the end of 1782—it was advertised in the *Wiener Zeitung* of 15 January 1783 as available for sale—but we do not know when he first played it. He left cadenzas for the work.

**Solo piano, two oboes, two bassoons, two horns, and strings. In a letter to the Parisian publisher Sieber, Mozart said of this concerto and its neighbors in A major and C major that they could be performed "with full orchestra, or with oboes and horns, or merely *a quattro,*" i.e., with string quartet. This is not literally untrue, but it should be read as marketing copy rather than as artistic conviction.**

In this delicately inventive chamber-musical Concerto, the first surprise is the meter: this is one of only three piano concerto first-movements by Mozart in 3/4. The themes are brief and perhaps a touch impersonal, but there are many of them, they never lack charm, and Mozart deploys them with delightful ingenuity. As Cuthbert Girdlestone puts it in his celebrated study *Mozart and His Piano Concertos,* "If the heart of the work represents the collective soul of [Mozart's] listeners rather than his own, originality is not lacking in the form." Details of phrases are constantly recombined in unexpected ways, and some of the themes have a certain teasing cousinship so that one is not always immediately sure whether a melody is actually familiar or a newly arrived member of the family.

A moment one always waits for with special anticipation is the first solo entrance, and Mozart manages it here with singular charm, with surprising material, and rhythmically in a surprising place. In the development, the music becomes first unexpectedly dark and pathos-laden, then more virtuosic than before. The recapitulation begins with a witty reshuffling as the piano's entrance moves to the front of the line, ahead of the movement's "real" opening. Mozart's cadenza is startlingly assertive for its demure surroundings; discovered in 1921 in Salzburg, it survives only in a manuscript in the hand of Leopold Mozart. For the brief fourteen bars after the cadenza, Mozart reserves both something new and, at the very close, another flash of wit.

The Larghetto will remind some listeners—and all pianists—of the wonderful Adagio in the popular F-major Piano Sonata, K. 332. What is immediately astonishing in this *sotto voce* song is the irregularity of the phrase lengths. The embellishments are inventive and lovely. This is not music of great passion, and in no obvious sense does much "happen" in these pages; this is music for the pianist to bring to life, a grand challenge from Mozart the composer to Mozart the pianist (and his successors).

Here is one of those Mozart concertos that get better and better as you go from movement to movement. This rondo finale is in minuet tempo, like something by Johann Christian Bach or in a piece of chamber music, but in the very first phrase the suspensions between violins (the seconds only, to begin with) and violas, and the scales in the cellos and basses create a richness of texture that announce immediately that this music means to be more than sweet and smooth. As he is in the first movement, Mozart is lavish with ideas, full of surprises in the ways he moves his building blocks about, but never losing sight of that naturalness he mentions in his letter to his father. And only here and in the companion piece in C major does he end a piano concerto *piano-pianissimo*.

## Concerto No. 12 in A major for Piano and Orchestra, K. 414(385p)

*Allegro*
*Andante*
*Allegretto*

Mozart probably composed this Concerto in the fall of 1782 and introduced it in Vienna that winter. He left two cadenzas for each of the three movements. I would guess that Beethoven remembered the Andante's second cadenza when he wrote the slow movement of his own Piano Concerto No. 2.

**Solo piano, two oboes, two horns, and strings. The first advertisement of publication (*Wiener Zeitung*, 15 January 1783) states that the work can also be performed "*a quattro*, that is to say, with two violins, viola, and cello."**

This Concerto begins with one of those passages Mozart proudly described to his father as working so well both for connoisseurs and amateurs, even if the amateurs didn't know why. We first hear a neat eight-measure phrase, one, however, that has a special character, thanks to the dissonance of the violas' B and G-sharp against the A in the cellos and basses, as well as to the syncopations in the second half of the phrase that inject a note of urgency the sweet urbanity of the first half had not led us to expect. These eight measures done, Mozart repeats the phrase. More precisely, he repeats its first measures and then moves to new ground: a gently running passage for strings (violins in octaves begin and are imitated first by the violas, then by the cellos and basses) and then the first *forte*, scale fragments alternately in violins and violas, to which the winds add snappy punctuations. Enjoy this extension, for you will not hear it again.

But let us linger for a moment on the first half of the opening phrase. At its repetition it is subtly—and very beautifully—transformed by the addition of two sustained chords in the oboes and horns. That in itself is lovely. What makes it special is the timing. The obvious point at which to introduce a new color is right when the second statement of the melody begins. Mozart, however, begins by repeating the melody just as it was before, and only in the *second* measure of the restatement do the wind instruments add their gentle stab. Now there is something to make connoisseurs smile.

The orchestra proposes two more themes and so, in due course, does the piano. The last of these new ideas—surprisingly—begins the development, which is therefore not so much development as excursion. This theme is in major at first; soon, however, Mozart darkens it into minor and intensifies the repeated notes after the octave leap. In its new form it becomes the subject of an impassioned conversation between piano and orchestra, and the development/excursion ends on the highest pitch of intensity attained thus far. The recapitulation is—for Mozart—unusually regular.

The Andante begins with a solemnity we do not often find in Mozart's concertos. This touching, hymnlike melody is actually a quotation from the overture that Johann Christian Bach contributed to Baldassare Galuppi's opera *La calamità de' cuori* (The Calamity of Hearts), which had its premiere in London on 7 February 1763 and was seen by Mozart when he lived in the English capital as a small boy in 1764–1765. Johann Christian Bach had died on New Year's Day 1782. "A pity for the whole world of music," wrote Mozart, who mourned him with a special sense of loss, indebtedness, and personal affection. As an eight-year-old in London, Mozart had played for George III, accompanied Queen Charlotte, and given public concerts, but no musical experience delighted him more than his meetings with Bach, the master setting the boy on his lap while they improvised at the harpsichord, sometimes taking alternate measures, or perhaps with Mozart completing a fugue that Bach had begun.

But beyond these personal memories, what Mozart had learned from "the London Bach," so persuasive a model of elegance, sweetness, and accomplished vocal style, formed his musical language. Here Mozart erects a musical *tombeau* for his mentor and friend, making Bach's theme a bit richer in harmony and scoring (those wonderful bass octaves in the piano!), as well as subtly giving the melody itself a more serious mien. What immediately follows is Mozart's own melody from the concerto's opening page, but transformed—in tears and in mourning, as it were.

It may be that the Rondo in A major, K. 386, left unfinished by Mozart but completed more than once by other hands, is a rejected attempt at a finale for this work. The final rondo, relaxed in gait, partakes of a certain *galant* innocence characteristic of J. C. Bach. It is predominantly bright in mood, with hardly a shadow of minor harmony, though Mozart achieves some fine effects with startling deceptive cadences. Near the end, when the movement resumes after the cadenza, there are two strange and wistful halts. Did Schubert remember those when he composed the finale of his great A-major Piano Sonata, D. 959? And is it going too far to wonder whether these hesitations are part of Mozart's farewell to Johann Christian Bach?

## Concerto No. 13 in C major for Piano and Orchestra, K. 415(387b)

*Allegro*
*Andante*
*Allegro*

Mozart wrote this Concerto in the winter of 1782–1783 and introduced it at the Burgtheater, Vienna, on 23 March 1783. He left cadenzas for the work.

**Solo piano, two oboes, two bassoons, two horns, two trumpets, timpani, and strings.**

Several of Mozart's concertos open with a figure in dotted rhythm, sometimes characterized as "military," similar to the one that starts this brilliant and ambitious concerto. None, however, does it quite like this, in a single part, unaccompanied, for all the world as though beginning a fugue, a tease that the subsequent entries of the second violins and then of the lower strings do nothing to dispel.

With a quick and deliciously asymmetrical buildup, Mozart makes his way to the first *forte* of the full orchestra. Ideas, all full of vigor, all carefully impersonal, succeed each other rapidly. One of these, the tripping eighth-notes of violas and violins after the first cadence, will never reappear.[8] Another may sound familiar even to newcomers to this Concerto because forty years later Beethoven used it to build his *Consecration of the House* Overture, undoubtedly thinking of it as a Handelian cliché rather than as a quotation from Mozart. Probably Mozart thought of it that way, too, for 1782 had been the year of his great and stimulating immersion in the music of Handel and J. S. Bach.

When the piano enters, it is with something much more harmless, nor is the solo deflected by the orchestra's quiet suggestion that *its* opening idea is really more interesting. Mozart is delightedly fascinated by the challenge of finding new ways of dividing material between solo and orchestra. Here they talk past each other, the orchestra proposing material to be "worked," the piano responding with charm, sixteenth-notes, and one exquisite lyric melody. And when we remember that it was Mozart himself at the keyboard in 1783, we catch on to something else, namely that it is for the soloist to infuse charm with wit, to find the harmonic energy and melodic contour in those scales and arpeggios that look so neutral on the page, and gently to pierce our hearts with that lovely tune.

The Andante is, more than anything, demure. It is also an opportunity for a pianist to demonstrate both concentration as well as something that would have especially mattered to an eighteenth-century audience: taste in the projection of sustained melody. Here, somewhat by exception, Mozart wrote out in full the embellishments that so lavishly adorn the melody.

In the finale, Mozart's invention is at its zenith. As they were in the Andante, solo and orchestra are in agreement about what they ought to do. They are at the beginning, anyway, with the orchestra happily seconding and extending the piano's jaunty tune. But the cadence that brings this phase to a halt is rather more dramatic than we expect, and what emerges from the suspenseful silence is an Adagio in C minor! Hardly less surprising than its appearance in the first place is its brevity: fifteen bars and it is over. There is a second exposition of the initial material, leading to varied, delightful, and beautifully scored excursions, and the Adagio, heightened now by luxuriant ornamentation and a more colorful orchestral backdrop, returns to introduce the final appearance of the main theme.

How serious is all that? These Adagios are not expansive lyric interludes like the minuets (more or less) that so tenderly halt the finales of the great concertos in E-flat, K. 271 and K. 482; neither are they grand building blocks of the sort that occasionally appear in Haydn's finales. They seem simply to be mysterious visitors from some other affective world, opening the door, looking in, and quietly withdrawing. At the same time, they serve notice that composers are beginning to be on the lookout for ways to give more

---

[8]The neighboring A-major Concerto, K. 414, also has a theme that appears once and once only.

weight to finales. Mozart himself takes the decisive step in the last movement of his last symphony, the *Jupiter* of August 1788, and with Beethoven's *Eroica* the process became irreversible. The theme's last return, in any event, leads to a delicious dénouement. It is, surely, the funniest close to any concerto of Mozart's.

## Concerto No. 14 in E-flat major for Piano and Orchestra, K. 449

> *Allegro vivace*
> *Andantino*
> *Allegro ma non troppo*

Mozart wrote this Concerto for his pupil Barbara von Ployer. On 9 February 1784, he began to keep a catalogue of his compositions, initiating that enterprise by entering this work. Probably this was the concerto Mozart played in Vienna on 17 March that year. Whatever the work was on that occasion, Mozart reported to his father that it won "extraordinary applause." This concerto was played at the Ployer house in Döbling, outside Vienna, on 23 March that year, though whether by student or teacher is not clear. Mozart left cadenzas for it.

**Solo piano, two oboes, two horns, and strings. The wind parts are optional, but the Concerto is impoverished without them.**

This concerto begins the amazing series of twelve piano concertos Mozart wrote in 1784–1786, the years when his popularity in Vienna was at its crest. Mozart wrote this concerto and the one in G major, K. 453, for his student Barbara von Ployer. Babette, as she was called, was a gifted and evidently delightful young woman whose father, Privy Councillor Gottfried Ignaz von Ployer, held responsible positions in several ministries—everything from Education and Justice to Mint and Mines—and who also had business connections with Salzburg. Mozart was much attached to Babette, to whom Haydn also dedicated one of his strongest piano pieces, the F-minor Variations of 1793.

The Allegro vivace is one of only three piano-concerto first movements by Mozart in triple meter. Its scale is as modest as its sonority—this is the shortest of Mozart's mature concertos—but the temper of the music is anything other than bland: here is music that is peppery in spirit, often abrupt in gesture, full of surprises in strategy and detail.

The manner of the Andantino is gentle, but this is music of affecting depth of feeling. This movement is also distinguished for its lovely scoring detail and for the lavish embellishments in the piano part.[9] Perhaps if Mozart had been writing for himself rather than for a student, even one so gifted as Babette, he would have improvised the embellishments rather than writing them out.

It is, however, the finale that is the most striking part of K. 449. As I noted in the essay on K. 415, Mozart at this time was interested in giving more weight and substance to his concerto finales, and it is a problem to which he finds many fascinating solutions: the elaborate minuet interludes in K. 271 and K. 482, the *opera buffa* finale-within-a-finale in his other concerto for Babette, K. 453, the profusion of counterpoint in K. 459 are among the most radical examples. In this Concerto, too, Mozart achieves a piquant enlivening of the texture by means of polyphony, beginning at once with the first eight bars in the two groups of violins. (These should be on opposite sides of the stage, not with the seconds tucked behind the firsts.) The *Allegro ma non troppo* tempo—full of energy but measured and articulated in a delightfully prickly sort of way—is itself as unusual as anything in the whole Concerto, and it is slow enough to allow room for brilliant elaboration. Not least, one should mention the remarkable sense of unity in this finale, a movement in which everything seems to be witty expansion from a single point of departure.

## Concerto No. 15 in B-flat major for Piano and Orchestra, K. 450

> *Allegro*
> *Andante*
> *Allegro*

Mozart entered this Concerto into his own catalogue on 15 March 1784 and gave the first performance on the 24th of that month at the Trattnerhof in Vienna. He left cadenzas for the work.

---

[9] A small and possibly illuminating curiosity: Mozart absentmindedly marked the bass part *Andante*, which is slightly quicker than Andantino.

Solo piano, flute (in the finale only), two oboes, two bassoons, two horns, and strings.

The E-flat Concerto, K. 449, precedes this one by only seven weeks, but Mozart himself took pains to point out that, with its chamber-musical format and demeanor, that was another sort of animal. This B-flat Concerto, he told his father in a letter on 26 May 1784, "is the first I have done in this manner," by which he meant work on a new level of ambition, compositional brilliance, and keyboard virtuosity. He was also able to report that in performance it had "pleased extraordinarily." Writing about this concerto and the next one, K. 451 in D major, he said: "I consider them both as concertos to make one sweat—in difficulty the one in B-flat is ahead of the one in D." Most pianists would concur, and many regard this as the most difficult of all of Mozart's concertos.

The orchestra here is small; nonetheless, the writing, though intimate, is especially fragrant in sonority and harmony. The opening is plain and fancy together. Plain in the I-could-have-thought-of-that tune, cut with such economy from so few notes, and in its wholesome tonic-and-dominant harmonies; fancy in the notion of starting with chattering woodwinds almost alone, and in the piquant edge produced by the pairs of double-reed instruments in thirds and an octave apart. The violins have quite another sort of speech: darting arpeggios as against the demure little steps of the oboes and bassoons. For winds and strings to behave independently is characteristic of this Concerto.

In less than half a minute, Mozart works up to his first tutti in *forte*; cunningly he steers the two winds and strings so that they come together to constitute an orchestra. A second, gently syncopated theme is first played by the strings, and when the oboe and bassoon repeat it, the violins hang garlands on it. The orchestral exposition ends with another dialogue, but one that reverses the original roles of winds and strings, the winds now playing the arpeggios. And how subtly Mozart manages this. We hear the arpeggio horn call

Ex. 1

twice, in two different scorings (oboes and horns an octave apart; then horns and bassoons an octave apart, but with the horns on top). The sweet answer

Ex. 2

appears four times in four different scorings (violins; violins again, but an octave lower; violins with a bassoon an octave lower; the violin-bassoon combination with an oboe an octave above the violins).[10]

And now it is time for the long-awaited appearance of the soloist—for that first audience in 1784 Mozart himself, the most sought after and admired musician in Vienna. This moment is managed with a flourish. The courtly bow suggested by the piano's first phrase heightens the sense of anticipation. It is pure gesture, and the only statement is "Here I am."

Then the pianist resumes the real business of the Concerto, going both to the music of the winds and the strings for his material. Next he introduces a new theme, a fascinatingly ambiguous one whose beginning is full of pathos and in minor but which almost immediately makes a turn back into major. It suffices, though, to make very personal something that had seemed to start out with the intention of being no more than delightfully friendly. The darkness of this melody is heightened in the recapitulation, as indeed it is altogether a tendency in this movement for the play of compositional invention and wit to become constantly more elaborate and more overt. The development begins innocently by echoing the cadential figures that close the exposition, but soon Mozart enters a darker world in which steady triplets on the piano both accompany and spur on the triste conversations of woodwinds and strings. In the recapitulation, Mozart ingeniously reshuffles all this material.

In several letters during the spring and summer of 1784, Mozart keeps promising to send the cadenzas along to his father and sister, and apologizing that he is too busy to write them out. He did eventually send them, and presumably they represent his recollection, perhaps an improved recollection, of what he had improvised at the premiere. They continue and then wrap

---

[10]Another Mozartian subtlety: the wind figure begins and ends with slurs and is staccato in the middle; the violin figure, which in fact serves to unite the two groups, begins staccato and puts the slurred pairs of notes in the middle and at the end.

up the movement so perfectly that to use them is virtually an artistic imperative.

The second movement is a theme with two variations, an interruption, and a coda. Writing to Salzburg in June 1784, Mozart stresses that the middle movements of all the concertos he has recently sent are Andantes, not Adagios. His choice of time signature, 3/8 rather than 3/4, would also have told an eighteenth-century musician that the pulse of this second movement must not be too slow. Nonetheless, the eighth-notes of Mozart's theme, one both hymnic and tender, need space because later they will be divided into eight sixty-fourth-notes each.

The two halves of the theme are first played by the strings; each is then repeated, already varied, by the piano. Mozart retains this design for the first variation, although he has the piano add an active and eloquent accompaniment. In the second variation he mixes things up more, inventing a less predictable mode of conversation between piano and orchestra. He also works miracles of sonority with the simplest of means: it is as though pizzicato had been invented expressly for these pages. This second variation is dramatically interrupted just before its completion, and a spacious coda, gently melancholic, brings the music to its hushed close.

In this Andante the pianist must show what a fine chamber-music player he is: his tasks as accompanist and subtle conversational partner require sensitive listening. In the finale, he again steps into the foreground as open-tempered soloist. The main theme is a graceful version of a hunting-horn theme of the kind also found in the finales of the horn concertos as well as the one in the E-flat Piano Concerto, K. 482. The harmonic adventures here surprise, and for this movement, too, Mozart has provided a superb cadenza, brilliant, impulsive, and integrating. The coda with its conspiratorial strings is one of Mozart's most enchanting inventions in his translated *opera buffa* vein; the eight-measure exchange between piano and winds just before the coda was a late and inspired insert.[11]

---

[11]Inspired not only because it is delightful in itself, but because, with its contrast between the piano's arpeggio fanfare and the winds' conjunct reply, it takes us back to the conversations in the first movement. The roles—who says what—have been redistributed yet again.

# Concerto No. 16 in D major for Piano and Orchestra, K. 451

*Allegro assai*
*[Andante]*
*Allegro di molto*

Mozart entered this Concerto into his catalogue on 22 March 1784 and gave the first performance in Vienna nine days later, on 31 March. He left a cadenza for the first movement.

**Solo piano, flute, two oboes, two bassoons, two horns, two trumpets, timpani, and strings.**

This is a concerto we hear too rarely. Its immediate neighbors, K. 450 and K. 453, both begin with lyric gestures—in the latter work one that is highly individual as well—which immediately and unmistakably set the tone for the remarkable events to come. The D-major Concerto, on the other hand, begins with a cliché, a dotted "military" rhythm, and this robust and familiar simplicity has deceived too many critics into characterizing this piece as being one of essentially superficial brilliance.[12] Virtuosity is conpsicuous here, and this is certainly one of those rare works by Mozart in which he does not expose any human vulnerability: wonderful chromatic harmonies do occur, but their purpose is color, not pathos.

Several of Mozart's concertos have a marchlike beginning on the order of the one we get here, but this is the only one that starts *forte* and in full trumpet-and-drums splendor, the others all being more inclined toward the conspiratorial. This is, in fact, the first time Mozart used trumpets and drums in a concerto. But nothing here is as simple as it seems. The call to attention is followed by a major scale that ascends through two octaves. What an out-of-the-ordinary scale it is, though, with its alternation of long notes and short, its *forte* interjections, and its accelerating rhythms (it takes seven measures to traverse the first octave, but only two and a half for the second). What goes up must come down, and, neatly, the climbing scale is balanced by a descending one. For the trip down, however, Mozart introduces a new

---

[12]Actually the opening of K. 453 puts it rhythmically into the "military" family as well, but the melodic and harmonic twists of the phrase are so idiosyncratic that they distract us from recognizing that family relationship.

rhythm, a texture enriched by imitations, and an ingenious way of dividing the scale among all the strings plus both bassoons.

This turns out to be Mozart's way throughout the Concerto—the constant turning of the familiar into the unexpected. It is as though Mozart had set himself the task of treating in the most subjective manner possible materials that were themselves completely impersonal and part of the common stock of musical language.

Here is music rich in subtleties and surprises: the first quiet passage, which appears for a moment to be a new theme in the dominant, but whose function turns out to be quite different; the passage that follows, a stalking bass under syncopated violins and violas, leading to an amazing outburst of chromatic harmony; the soft question and its cadential tag at the end of the opening tutti, and the astonishing role that this music will play later in the movement; the three bars for piano alone just before the syncopations come back in the second part of the exposition, a passage that for me is the most sheerly surprising—in the Haydnesque sense—four or five seconds of music in all of Mozart. Altogether, this movement is one of Mozart's most dazzling achievements.

The second movement is a rondo with more than a touch of romance in its languorous principal theme and pathos-filled episodes. Mozart's sister, Nannerl, once referred to it as an Adagio, but her brother was quick to set her straight: it is an Andante, though in fact he forgot to mark the tempo in his manuscript. Nannerl also objected to the bareness of the episode in C major that occurs after the main theme's second appearance. Here Mozart acknowledged that she was right, that something was missing, and he sent her an embellished variant of the passage. In performance he would of course have taken care of clothing the proper passage by improvising ornaments. This afterthought, which survives and which is customarily played, gives us valuable information—albeit controversial in its interpretation—about the relation of what Mozart wrote down to what he played or expected others to play.

The finale starts out in a light-hearted manner that does not lead us to expect the seriousness and complexity of what comes later. The 2/4 meter is frequently enlivened with eighth-note triplets, a rhythmic development that finds its fulfillment at the end of the movement when, after the cadenza, the music resumes in 3/8, to remain in that meter to the end.

## Concerto No. 17 in G major for Piano and Orchestra, K. 453

*Allegro*
*Andante*
*Alegretto—Finale: Presto*

Mozart completed this Concerto on or by 10 April 1784, the date he entered it into his own catalogue of his works. The first performance of which we have certain record is the one given on 13 June that year by Mozart's student Barbara Ployer at her father's house; it is likely, however, that K. 453 was what Mozart played at his Kärntnerthor Theater concert in the presence of Emperor Joseph II on 29 April. The Kärntnerthor Theater concert also featured the premiere of the Sonata in B-flat for Piano and Violin, K. 454, which Mozart played with the young Italian virtuosa Regina Strinasacchi. At the concert *chez* Ployer, Mozart was at the keyboard for the first performances of his Quintet for Piano and Winds, K. 452, and of the Sonata for Two Pianos, K. 448, Barbara Ployer being his partner in the latter. Mozart left cadenzas for this work.

**Solo piano, flute, two oboes, two bassoons, two horns, and strings.**

On 27 May 1784 Mozart paid 34 kreuzer, roughly $10 in today's money, for a starling that could whistle the beginning of the finale of his G-major Piano Concerto—or at least something very close to it. Mozart jotted down the musical notation in his account book with the comment *"Das war schön!"*, even though the bird insisted on a fermata at the end of the first full measure and on sharping the G's in the next bar:

Ex. 1

Ex. 2

The starling

Understandably, the editor of the sixth edition of the Köchel catalogue
wonders where the starling got his education—not, that is, who taught him
K. 453 incorrectly, but who taught it to him at all. Barbara von Ployer's
performance on 13 June occurred more than two weeks after Mozart acquired
the starling.[13] The bird (who died and was buried with full honors in the
Mozarts' garden on 4 June 1787, the occasion being commemorated with a
poem by the composer) seems to provide evidence that the otherwise-
unidentified concerto that Mozart played at a concert given before the Emperor in the Kärntnerthor Theater on 29 April 1784 was indeed the brand-
new G-major.

The concertos of the miraculous spring of 1784 are vividly differentiated.
K. 449, seemingly so modest but in fact all enterprise, wit, and virtuosic
demands, is a like a trick box with a false bottom. K. 450 is intimate and
warm but technically the most difficult of them all. K. 451, with bright D-
major trumpets and drums, is smart and dapper, though anything other than
coolly formal. K. 453 is music in which that most characteristically Mozartian
mixture of gaiety and melancholy is especially delicate.

You need wait no longer than the fourth measure for that ambiguity to
show up: the F-natural in the violins says it all. The comments in that measure from the flute and the oboe are no less surprising, and these turns are
the more telling because the marchlike theme, so spruce, in every way suggests "normal" music. Mozart likes to erase the traces of "indiscretions" such
as that F-natural so as to create in us a feeling of "Wait—did I really hear
that?" And that is what he does here: no more F-naturals, no more disturbing
shadows. At least not for a while. For the next thirty measures or so, the
orchestral exposition, keeping the promise of its first three measures, moves
along in high good humor, even including a good bassoon joke.

That joke turns into a classic instance of Mozartian ambiguity. The
bassoon can't stop playing the little fanfare with which the orchestra ends
the first large paragraph of the exposition, but the flute sees the possibility of
pathos and beauty in the bassoon's delighted self-absorption, and together
the two instruments gently shift the music into a sweetly shaded place, to a
melody full of sighs and exquisitely harmonized. And, I should add, F natural
is readmitted. A deceptive cadence drops the music into the remoteness of

[13]For more on Barbara von Ployer, see the essay on K. 449.

E-flat major, the effect of this shift being the greater because nothing comparably abrupt has happened thus far. Again we encounter one of Mozart's "erasures": with only a fleeting, wistful shadow here and there, this exposition is completed smilingly. Mozart's own entrance—or Babette von Ployer's—is prepared.

The piano assumes the privilege of contributing a new theme on the way to the formal cadence with the bassoon joke, and of course a whole new vocabulary based on solo-orchestra dialogue is now available. The dramatic deceptive cadence, we learn, was more than a local event: its impact, if not its detail, is re-experienced to powerful effect at the beginning of the development. Shadows, "millions of strange shadows," darken and color this movement, though it ends in brightness.

Now, to begin the Andante, Mozart reverses the harmonic process with which he began the first movement. There F-*naturals* had unexpectedly darkened the G-major beginning. This time Mozart starts plainly enough in C major, but within a few seconds, certainly before we have had a chance to register a sense of harmonic "place," piquant and startling F-*sharps* cast doubt. It is as though the C-major harmony of the first measure were just a subsidiary event in what is really to be a movement in G major. The opening phrase— an asymmetrical one of five measures—makes a cadence on G, and, further to blur any certainty we might feel, Mozart follows it with an unmeasured silence. Only after the music resumes with an exquisite choreography for intertwined woodwinds do we feel sure that what we first heard—C major— was right after all.

The orchestral music—emphatically not an introduction but substance—at the beginning of this Andante is long and uncommonly filled with adventure and event. Indeed, throughout this movement the orchestra is almost disturbingly assertive. The piano entrance is normal, that is, it corresponds to the opening bars of orchestral music; what follows the unmeasured silence, however, is a powerful departure indeed. Harmonic leaps of the kind we experienced at the first movement's dramatic deceptive cadence are central to the vocabulary of this concerto. The unmeasured silence will generate some manner of surprise at each recurrence. From moment to wonderful moment, this tender Andante, so vocal, so full of pathos, is one of the most richly inspired pages in all of Mozart.

And so we come to what the starling sang. The emotional weight here is slighter, but the musical inspiration is no less amazing. There are five variations. In the theme and the first variation each half is repeated exactly, but in the other four variations the repeats themselves are varied, too. Humor, lyricism, and pathos all come to the fore. Most amazing, though, is what happens after this set of formal variations has run its delightful course. Mozart ratchets the speed up from allegretto to presto and begins what he labels the "Finale." No passage shows more clearly what is meant when we call Mozart's piano concertos "transposed opera." This operatic "finale-within-a-finale" accounts for half the movement, and it is Mozart at his greatest and funniest.[14] And how it makes one long for audiences who have not forgotten how to laugh—or even smile!

## Concerto No. 18 in B-flat major for Piano and Orchestra, K. 456

> *Allegro vivace*
> *Andante un poco sostenuto*
> *Allegro vivace*

Mozart completed this Concerto on 30 September 1784, but nothing is known about its first performance. He left two different cadenzas for the first movement and one for the finale.

**Solo piano, flute, two oboes, two bassoons, two horns, and strings.**

Among Mozart's piano concertos, K. 456, understated and subtle wonder that it is, has never been an obvious favorite with pianists or their audiences. Its performance, then, is always a special occasion, one that leaves delighted listeners with that "Where have you been all my life?" question on their lips.

On 13 February 1785, Mozart took part in a concert given in the presence of Emperor Joseph II at the Vienna Burgtheater by the soprano Luisa Laschi, soon to be the Countess in the first *Figaro* and Zerlina in the first Viennese production of *Don Giovanni*.[15] Leopold Mozart, just arrived for a ten-week visit to his son, reported home to his daughter that Wolfgang had played "a magnificent concerto which he had written for Paradis," adding that he was so overcome "by the pleasure of hearing the interplay of the instruments so clearly that tears came into my eyes for sheer delight."

---

[14]Beethoven knew Mozart's piano concertos, played some of them, and composed a set of cadenzas for one of them, the D minor, K. 466, that have become virtually a standard feature in that work. I should think that his huge and humorous tail-wagging-the-dog codas to the finales of the Second and Eighth Symphonies owe something to K. 453. Schoenberg's Opus 31 is another example of a set of variations with a large multisectional finale, as is his later Theme and Variations in G minor, Opus 43.

[15]A reminder of how ideas of voice types change over time. Today a Zerlina might eventually graduate to the Countess, but when did a soprano last have both roles in her current repertory?

Leopold had good reason to be emotional. He had arrived from Munich on Friday the 11th; had heard his son play the D-minor Concerto, K. 466, at a concert at the Mehlgrube Casino the same night (this, remember, was his first encounter with a mature Mozart concerto); and had, on Saturday, heard Wolfgang's three newest string quartets, K. 458, 464, and 465, at a private party at whose end Haydn had said to him that Mozart was "the greatest composer known to [him], personally or by reputation." And now, on Sunday, there was this B-flat Concerto.

Mozart's great nineteenth-century biographer, Otto Jahn, was the first to establish that this concerto was the one "for Paradis." Maria Theresia von Paradis was a Vienna composer, pianist, organist, and singer, twenty-five years old in 1784, and blind since the age of three. She had been excellently taught by Antonio Salieri and Abbé Vogler, among others, and she was a determined woman who let nothing stand in the way of her musical ambitions. In later years, she devoted much of her energy to a music school she had founded in Vienna in 1808. She died in 1824.

Late in the summer of 1783, Paradis set out on a tour to London and Paris, stopping en route to call on the Mozarts at Salzburg. (Wolfgang had moved to Vienna in March 1781, but he and his wife were in Salzburg at this time on a four-month visit.) It was probably on that occasion that Paradis asked Mozart for a concerto and that he promised her one. She was in Paris from March 1784 until the end of October, giving fourteen concerts as pianist and singer, and Mozart's concerto, completed on 30 September—at least, entered into his catalogue on that date—would have reached her in time for one of her last appearances at the Concert Spirituel, the most important concert series in the French capital.

This is an intimate piece without trumpets and drums; it does, however, begin with that marchlike figure we encounter in several of Mozart's concertos. We hear it first played by strings, and we can immediately get a taste of one of Mozart's delightful textural ingenuities when he has the winds repeat the sentence, but this time with strings putting in little three-note bridges where there had been silences before. Although the gestures are mostly demure, shocks of various intensities are administered. At the first orchestral *forte,* for example, everyone is tripped in their swinging-forward motion when the first phrase is stopped after three measures instead of being allowed to complete itself in the 2 + 2 = 4 pattern we expect. A little later, when the orchestra draws up to a halt on the dominant, obviously with the intention of presenting a new theme, what follows this half-measure of silence is a strangely dark and remote chord, E-flat minor, delivered by the strings with a kind of cushioned shudder. Considerable mystery—and much B-flat minor—prevails before the oboes finally introduce a new theme, one, by the way, of singular innocence. The scoring for winds is delicious, particularly the gently curved lines for flute and bassoons two octaves apart (a very *Figaro*-flavored sonority, this): no wonder Leopold was delighted. These are characteristic of the pleasures that this Concerto, and especially its first movement, offers—quiet rewards to the attentive and keen-eared listener and often drawing on the play with the delicate balance between major and minor.

The Andante responds fully to all of the first movement's urgings in the direction of the darker mode. This movement is a set of variations, but one that goes far beyond the decorative tradition associated with variation movements. Mozart gives us five variations and a considerable coda. The theme is built in two sections, each to be repeated, but beginning with Variation 2, Mozart writes out these repeats and varies *them,* so that the five variations actually turn out to offer nine different transformations of the theme. Here, too, Mozart plays with the ambiguities of major and minor, although in this instance it is the major mode that is the fascinatingly disturbing intruder. Most wonderful of all is the coda, introduced by notes longer than any we have heard so far, and layered so as to create the most poignant dissonances. The hushed near-stopping of motion is created not only by the long notes but also by the way the harmony is suddenly made to stand still on a long dominant pedal.

The finale is quick, varied, gratifyingly brilliant for the pianist, and again full of surprises. Most of these surprises are soft-spoken; one that is not is the leap into a shockingly remote B minor. There the piano delivers an impassioned arioso, and the boldness of this harmonic and rhetorical departure is emphasized by a metrical division that sets the piano's new 2/4 meter in rhythmic dissonance against the orchestra's continuing 6/8. This passage is so powerful and so startling that it is always an amazement to be reminded how brief it is—just eight measures for the arioso. The original key of B-flat major returns, as does the uncomplicated 6/8 meter, and the movement ends with a breezy display of wit and jollity.

## Concerto No. 19 in F major for Piano and Orchestra, K. 459

*Allegro*
*Allegretto*
*Allegro assai*

Mozart entered this Concerto into his catalogue on 11 December 1784. The date of the first performance is not known, though it is likely to have occurred at one of the six subscription concerts Mozart gave in Vienna between 11 February and 18 March 1785. He left cadenzas for this work.

Solo piano, flute, two oboes, two bassoons, two horns, and strings. Mozart's catalogue entry also lists two trumpets and timpani; there are, however, no parts for these instruments. Either they are lost or Mozart made an absent-minded slip.


This Concerto is the last of the miraculous harvest of 1784, a singularly flavorful piece in which the slightly tart sound of the woodwind group is prominent. Like its three immediate predecessors, K. 459 starts with a dotted marchlike theme. K. 451 in D major, which begins with trumpets and drums, makes the most of the martial possibilities of this rhythm; K. 453 in G major, which begins with violins alone and puts a trill on the second beat, offers a lyric variant of the idea; in K. 456, Mozart wittily stops the phrase when it has barely begun. In K. 459, the issue was long confused by the fact that the older printed scores got the time signature wrong, indicating four beats per measure rather than Mozart's two. In four, you do indeed get the martial effect you read about in most commentaries (and which is quite legitimately present in K. 451), even though it gives the impression of an innocent sort of militia; in two, the music, as Alfred Brendel puts it in his essay "A Mozart Player Gives Himself Advice," moves "dancingly and in whole bars."

This first movement is fond of symmetry and four-measure phrases, and inclined to repeat things, but right away we are reminded that a repetition in Mozart is rarely literal. Mozart presents new ideas in remarkable profusion—a beautifully curved lyric one, another in staccato with suddenly loud "Scotch snaps" on the downbeats, a third with slightly sinister offbeat stabs in the low strings and woodwinds, another where *forte* horns and strings complete a thought begun by *piano* woodwinds descending through chains of thirds and in which you can't be quite sure where the downbeat is. And more. The language is that of understated high comedy. The swirling triplets that we hear in the woodwinds just after the passage with the stabs will have insistent consequences throughout the movement.

The soloist enters with something we know, the opening march figure, yet everything is different. The scoring is fresh, and before long, new themes, witty and graceful, are introduced, one by the piano, another by the orchestra. The development is brief, but it brings the first serious explorations of minor keys. The retransition to the recapitulation sounds like a simple affair when described—six measures of the opening dance/march in dialogue between winds and strings—but the harmonies, after the leisurely pages just before, are suddenly so condensed and driving that these few seconds of music make you sit up like nothing else in this movement. In the recapitulation, Mozart works miracles by inventing fresh detail and setting familiar ideas into new sequences. The cadenza is one of Mozart's best, continuing the musical thought when the orchestra bows out, perfectly combining the functions of sharp commentary, display, and expanded final cadence.

This is one of those Mozart concertos in which each movement is more original and special than the one before. After the first Allegro, we get neither a slow aria nor a set of variations but an Allegretto in 6/8. It is of a pastoral turn to begin with, but as it proceeds it assumes surprising force and is darkened by equally unexpected shadows. In other respects, too, this is music delightfully wanting in innocence. The first phrase is an odd five measures long, with every move and extension a revelation. Major and minor mix fascinatingly, and virtually every repetition turns out to be a variation. There are also patches of canonic writing, Mozart of course being consummately graceful in the way he wears his technical skill, that *Compositionswissenschaft* that Haydn so admired in him. The rising woodwind scales in the last half-minute anticipate the nocturnal magic in Count Almaviva's dangerously moonlit garden.

The third movement, proceeding from artlessness to outbursts of learning and crazy energy, all coupled to some of Mozart's most effervescent piano writing, is the most astonishing of the three. Charles Rosen describes it as "a complex synthesis of fugue, sonata-rondo finale, and opera buffa style. The weightiest and the lightest forms of music are fused here in a work of unimaginable brilliance and gaiety." If I cannot quite bring myself to go along with Rosen in calling this "the greatest of all Mozart's concerto finales," it is not because I value this one too little but because there are a few others—K. 466, K. 482, K. 503, none, to be sure, as ingenious as K. 459—that I love as much.

When Mozart composed this Concerto, it had been two years since his encounter with the music of J. S. Bach and Handel had changed his life. Well schooled as he was, he had always been good at counterpoint but, like most of his contemporaries, he thought of canons and fugues as belonging to the classroom or, at best, the church. Now he suddenly saw how the polyphonic style could also be the stuff of real life. He saw what an instrument of architectural strength and of expression it could be, and more, he began to imagine how he might integrate the learned style of the masters of the High Baroque with the *galant* manner he had grown up with. That synthesis, which made possible the marvels of the concertos, symphonies, chamber works, and operas of the last ten years of his life, is the heart of the Classical style. Here is a constantly surprising, funny, captivating, altogether brilliant example.

The piano, with each of its eight-measure phrases echoed by the orchestra, begins with an anapestic theme that is pure *opera buffa*. It took two hundred years for someone to notice—it was the American musicologist and conductor Joshua Rifkin—that the theme is also a bow to a friend and colleague, being a variant of one in the finale of Haydn's Symphony No. 78 in

C minor (1782).[16] The astonishing response to this opening paragraph is a tutti that is nearly three times as long and which, furthermore, starts out with music that sounds as though it comes from the middle of a fugue. (Middle, because the successive entrances of the voices are overlapped more tightly than would be the case at the beginning of a fugue.) Before it is done, this tutti finds its way back to the anapests of the first theme, which it tosses about amusingly, alludes grandly to the fugue subject, and gets rounded off with an idea full of repeated notes to which Mozart would return almost seven years later in the "PapapapapapagenoPapapapapapagena" duet in *The Magic Flute*.

For now, the task is to bring the disparate elements—the *opera buffa* theme and the fugato—into harmony, and we want to remember that they would have sounded much more disparate to an audience in 1785 than to one in 1998. In a sense, Mozart relives in this one movement the challenge the last couple of years had offered him. Here is this wonderful thing called fugue; how do I put it together with my native musical language? Between jaunts in *buffa*-land, the fugato returns twice, the first time as a grand and highly energized development section, and it also plays a role in the cadenza. Meanwhile, the modes of synthesis become ever more ingenious and witty, and they are combined with some of Mozart's most virtuosic passages for the piano. The stuttering lovers have the last word.

## Concerto No. 20 in D minor for Piano and Orchestra, K. 466

*Allegro*
*Romance*
*Rondo: Allegro assai*

Mozart entered this Concerto into his catalogue on 10 February 1785 and was the soloist at the first performance at the Mehlgrube Casino in Vienna the very next day. A letter of Leopold Mozart's suggests that Wolfgang wrote out cadenzas for this concerto, but they do not survive.

**Solo piano, one flute, two oboes, two bassoons, two horns, two trumpets, timpani, and strings.**

---

[16]When he composed this Concerto, Mozart had just finished the fourth of the six string quartets he was to dedicate to Haydn, who was therefore much on his mind at this time. Haydn's symphony begins with an angular, very "Baroque" theme, and Mozart would return to something like it a year and a half later in his own piano concerto in the same key, K. 491.

Leopold Mozart, just arrived in Vienna from Munich by way of Salzburg in February 1785, sent his daughter, Nannerl, news of her famous younger brother in the capital: "[I heard] *an excellent new piano concerto by Wolfgang*, on which the copyist was still at work when we got here, and your brother didn't even have time to play through the rondo because he had to oversee the copying operation."

K. 466 is one of only two Mozart concertos in minor, and of the two it is the stormier. It is no surprise that the young Beethoven made a stunning impression as an interpreter of this work, and the pair of superbly intelligent and powerfully expressive cadenzas that he wrote for it are still played more often than any others. During the nineteenth century, when Mozart was often dismissed as a gifted forerunner of Beethoven's, this work was one of the very few Mozart piano concertos to hold a firm place in the repertory.[17]

It shows its temper instantly in an opening that is all atmosphere and gesture—no theme. Violins and violas throb in agitated syncopations. Their energy is concentrated on the rhythm, and the pitches change little at first; meanwhile, the low strings anticipate the beats with upward scurries of quick notes. A general crescendo of activity—the bass notes occur twice in each measure instead of just once, the violin melody becomes more active (that is, more like a melody), all the lines push toward higher registers—and the full orchestra enters with flashes of lightning to illuminate the scene.

Most of what follows in the next two minutes is informed more by pathos than by rage, the most affecting moment of all being reserved for the first entrance—with an almost new melody over an already familiar accompaniment—of the solo piano. Now the witty and serious play of conversation, the exchange of ideas and materials, can begin, and the pianist has the opportunity to ravish with the plangency of simulated song and to dazzle with the mettlesome traversal of brilliant passagework. (With delight, Leopold told Nannerl about a performance in March 1786 when Heinrich Marchand was the pianist and Haydn the page-turner, because that put Haydn in a position really to appreciate "the artful composition and interweaving, as well as the difficulty of the Concerto.") The tempests eventually recede in a *pianissimo* fascinatingly seasoned with the distant thud of drums and the curiously and hauntingly hollow low tones of the trumpets.

The second movement, after this, is by intention mild. Mozart gives no tempo indication, though any pianist in his day would have known at a glance what to do; neither does his designation *Romance* denote a specific form as much as it suggests a certain atmosphere of serene songfulness. An

---

[17]The other popular one was its temperamental opposite, the *Coronation*, K. 537, the most nearly Rococo of Mozart's concertos. Brahms, during his piano virtuoso years in the 1860s, played the G-major, K. 453, A-major, K. 488, and C-minor, K. 491 as often as he could and also persuaded Clara Schumann to take K. 491 into her repertory.

interlude brings back the minor mode of the first movement and something of its storms, but this music is far more regular and to that degree less agitating. Once again we hear from Leopold Mozart, this time writing to Nannerl in January 1786: "I am sending you one concerto, the slow movement is a Romance, the tempo, so that the theme doesn't come out too flabby, to be taken at the quickest speed at which you can manage the noisy part with the fast triplets that show up on the third page and which really need to be practiced." With all its formality, Mozart's gradual application of the brakes as he approaches the return of his Romance melody is one of his most masterly strokes of rhythmic invention.

The piano launches the finale, a feast of irregularities, ambiguities, surprises, and subtle allusions to the first movement. Its most enchanting feature is the woodwind tune that is first heard harmonically a bit off center, in F major; next in a delicious variant whose attempt to be serious about being in D minor is subverted by the coquettish intrusion of F-sharps and B-naturals from the world of D major; and again after the cadenza, now firmly in major and on the home keynote of D, made more delightful by perky remarks from the trumpet, and determined to lead the ebullient rush to the final double bar.

## Concerto No. 21 in C major for Piano and Orchestra, K. 467

*[Allegro maestoso]*
*Andante*
*Allegro vivace assai*

Mozart dates the autograph of this Concerto "nel febraio 1785," but did not enter it into the catalogue he kept of his own works until 9 March 1785, the day before the first performance, which took place at the Burgtheater in Vienna with the composer as soloist. There are no cadenzas by Mozart.

**Solo piano, flute, two oboes, two bassoons, two horns, two trumpets, timpani, and strings.**

The first page poses a puzzle. What is the tempo of the first movement? The autograph gives no indication at all. Though fairly rare this late in the eighteenth century, this is not an isolated case: the autograph of the C-minor Piano Concerto, K. 491, has no tempo heading for any of its three movements. And from the days of Baroque music to Stravinsky (in the work that typifies his most neo-Baroque mood, the *Dumbarton Oaks* Concerto), composers have, besides sometimes specifying nothing at all, occasionally headed movements *Tempo giusto*, which really means no more than "the right tempo." What, then, do you do? You look at the way the harmonies move, you check the prevailing note values, you know the language, and in most instances you know pretty much what the tempo should be.

Now when, a few weeks after drawing the final double bar in the autograph, Mozart entered this Concerto into his own catalogue of his works, he gave the tempo of the first movement as *Allegro maestoso*. Many printed editions follow Mozart's "Verzeichnüß" and indicate *Allegro maestoso*. Most pianists, however, have not been convinced and, whether through intuition, study, or a combination of the two, they tend to go for a relatively brisk, unmajestic Allegro; in fact, one eminent Mozart interpreter for years avoided taking this Concerto into his repertory because he could not reconcile the *Allegro maestoso* in the score with what he felt to be the character of this movement.

But we need to consider that Mozart's catalogue entry is not only later than his autograph manuscript, it's late enough to make it likely that the Concerto had already been rehearsed in preparation for the next day's premiere. And even if there was only one rehearsal, and that on the day of the premiere itself, by 9 March the work would have been not just something in Mozart's imagining ear but something in his fingers, something he had been practicing and whose performance details had taken on a certain concreteness. In sum, there is good reason to give *Allegro maestoso* serious consideration, strange (literally) though that character and its concomitant tempo may be to most of us.

K. 467 is a big piece in Mozart's festive trumpets-and-drums vein. The opening illustrates the tempo problem: the bare, stalking octaves of the first four measures invite *maestoso*, but it is much more difficult to make the lyric phrase that follows convincing at the weightier tempo. The orchestral exposition offers one finesse after another, in color and texture no less than in the unfolding of events.

And always there is the crucial question: When will the pianist enter, and how? And remember that it was for the acclaimed Mozart himself that the Viennese crowded the Burgtheater in 1785. The orchestra concludes with due ceremony, but instead of the piano entrance we are waiting for, we hear the oboe carry the music forward with a new idea. Bassoon and flute second their colleague's notion, and when the piano does come in, it happens almost by the way, and neither when nor how we expect. The movement is full of brilliant passagework, but always as an organic part of the piece, all harmonic bite, with the tensions in those bold dissonances vigorously pushing the music forward. The interests of virtuosity and of symphonic discourse are one, which is ideally what you want in a concerto.

In the Andante—which Bo Widerberg brutalized and made a film star in *Elvira Madigan* in 1967—the pianist aspires to be a great singer, great in virtuosity and taste alike.[18] The orchestra sets the scene for this nobly impassioned aria. Over a troubled accompaniment we hear one of the world's astounding melodies, each phrase a new surprise in the direction it takes or in the amount of breath that is drawn. The opening orchestral melody is twenty-one measures long, articulated 3 + 3 + 2 + 2 / 8 + 3; the piano's version is twelve measures long, articulated 3 + 3 + 2 + 4. Woodwinds add their voices, discreetly at first, then more intensely, and in a crescendo of poignant dissonance. Once present, the piano plays for all but two measures—two incredible measures—and the orchestra is never silent. It is a uniquely concentrated and sustained utterance that Mozart makes in this poignant setting of an imaginary poem.

Not the least of the miracles in this rich and subtle concerto is that Mozart finds for it a finale at a level of spiritual and intellectual energy worthy of what we has preceded it. Here is music of crackling brilliance, not unshadowed, but informed by a captivating sense of momentum and exuberantly inventive humor.

## Concerto No. 22 in E-flat major for Piano and Orchestra, K. 482

> *Allegro*
> *Andante*
> *Rondo: Allegro—Andantino cantabile—Allegro*

Mozart entered this Concerto into his catalogue on 16 December 1785 and introduced it on the 23d of that month in Vienna as an entr'acte at a performance of the oratorio *Esther* by Karl Ditters von Dittersdorf. Antonio Salieri conducted the oratorio and perhaps the concerto as well. Mozart left no cadenzas.

---

[18]In *New Choices in Natural Healing*, ed. Bill Gottlieb (Emmaus, Pa: Rodale Press, 1995), Don G. Campbell, director of the Institute for Music, Health, and Education in Boulder, Colorado, is cited as recommending listening to "Mozart's C Major Piano Concerto, performed by Elvira Madigan" as therapy for memory problems.

Solo piano, flute, two clarinets, two bassoons, two horns, two trumpets, timpani, and strings.


This Concerto, written in the middle of Mozart's work on *Figaro,* is the
third of three he composed in 1785. In his classic 1939 monograph on
Mozart's piano concertos, Cuthbert Girdlestone writes that "combining
grace and majesty . . . this one is the queenliest" of these works. Both
grand and gentle, it offers remarkable contrast to its two immediate predecessors, the D-minor, K. 466, and the C-major, K. 467, both of them
hyper-inventive and audaciously personal. K. 482 and the lovely A-major
Concerto, K. 488, which followed two and a half months later, are a soft
interlude in the series. With the C-minor Concerto, K. 491 (March
1786) and the magnificent C-major, K. 503 (December 1786), Mozart returned to a denser, more symphonic manner of composition and to a
higher level of emotional intensity.

Mozart begins here with a formula we find often in his pieces in E-flat:
a firm, fanfarelike phrase and a quiet response. This is another of his
trumpets-and-drums concertos, although in this key the sonority of these
instruments is more mellow than brilliant. Mozart, being Mozart, of course
makes something remarkable even of these conventional fanfares—for example, the sudden *fortissimo* in the middle of the second measure in the
*Sinfonia concertante* for violin and viola, or here the odd three-bar phrase
lengths. The truly personal note in this opening, however, comes in the
answer, which consists of a series of softly dissonant suspensions in two horns
with the two bassoons in unison providing a bass. The harmonies outlined
by that bass are not extraordinary; the specific articulation and presentation,
on the other hand, are altogether individual and delightful.

Statement and answer are repeated, only this time the horn suspensions
are given a sound never before heard in a Mozart concerto, that of clarinets,
still novel in the middle 1780s, and a timbre for whose round softness Mozart
had a special weakness. Everything is now an octave higher than before, and
so Mozart can assign the bass role to quintessentially non-bass instruments,
namely, to violins. In twenty seconds of music, Mozart has set the stage
for us.

It is lavishly endowed with lyric themes, this Allegro, and it brings its
share of surprises. One of the most notable of these is the piano's outburst in
B-flat minor, as impassioned as it is sudden. The development is conceived
simply—sequences of arpeggios in the orchestra, accompanied by scales on
the piano—but the harmonic voyages achieved in these passages make for
exciting listening. The recapitulation is exceptionally non-automatic and
inventive in the reshuffling of materials.

At the first performance, the audience demanded (and got) an encore of the Andante. It is a most wonderful movement, the richest and most deeply expressive of Mozart's minor-key variation slow movements. Muted strings play its lamenting theme, long and irregular, all broken lines, sighs, and grieving silences. We hear three variations on this paragraph, the first two for piano alone or with a quiet accompaniment of strings, the third an astounding dialogue that engages the whole orchestra (save trumpets and drums, which are silent throughout this movement). But Mozart puts an independent episode on either side of Variation 2, the first for winds alone, the second a string-accompanied duet for flute and bassoon. The last variation, which is more expansive than the theme and the first two variations, spills into a coda that, for pathos and sheer magic of harmony, surpasses everything we have yet heard. Here Mozart anticipates Schubert in the way he makes the turn into major the most heart-piercing moment of all. This Andante is the Concerto's true center, sensuous, shadowed, deeply moving, surprising and complex, yet utterly clear.

From there Mozart heads into a 6/8 hunting finale on a theme that is a slightly more formal, less capricious variant of the corresponding one in the B-flat Concerto, K. 450. Like the finale of the earlier great Concerto in E-flat, K. 271 (January 1777), this movement, after some preparatory lowering of the lights, is interrupted by a slower interlude in 3/4, though not so specifically minuetlike this time nor as rich in pathos. This harks back to the textures of the Andante, beginning with wind music that comes from the world of serenades and also looks ahead to the perfumes of Fiordiligi's and Dorabella's garden, and alternating these fragrant sounds with the union of piano and strings.

The formality and simplicity of the principal theme allow Mozart room for subtle alterations of shape and harmony at its various returns. Even beyond that, the pianist is given many opportunities to be inventive. In the Allegro portions of the finale there are several instances where Mozart wrote shorthand rather than completely realized piano figuration, passages where the soloist is asked to meet the challenge of putting flesh on the bones and color on the skin, and the minuet, too, begs for embellishment. Here is a glorious opportunity for the pianist who has both education and imagination (and who is not shy about occasionally borrowing and perhaps improving on a colleague's idea). The whole movement is a feast of gentle wit, the best of all the jokes—and it is a wistful one—being saved for the very end.

## Concerto No. 23 in A major for Piano and Orchestra, K. 488

*Allegro*
*Adagio*
*Allegro assai*

Mozart entered this Concerto into his catalogue on 2 March 1786 and presumably played it in Vienna soon after. His autograph includes a cadenza for the first movement.

**Solo piano, flute, two clarinets, two bassoons, two horns, and strings.**

*Figaro* was the big project in the spring of 1786 and it was ready for performance on 1 May, but Mozart repeatedly interrupted himself, dashing off his one-act *The Impresario* for a party at the imperial palace at Schönbrunn as well as writing three piano concertos that year, presumably for his own use.

With his final piano concerto, K. 595 in B-flat, this one is the most chamber-musical of his mature works in the genre. It is gently spoken and, at least until the finale, shows little ambition by way of pianistic brilliance. Lyric and softly moonlit—as the garden scene in *Figaro* might be, were there no sexual menace in it—it shares something in atmosphere with later works in the same key, the great Violin Sonata, K. 526, the Clarinet Quintet, and the Clarinet Concerto.

The first movement, music of lovely and touching gallantry, is the essence of Mozartian reticence and *dolcezza*.[19] Its second chord, darkened by an unexpected G-natural in the second violins, already suggests the sadness that will cast fleeting shadows throughout the Concerto and altogether dominate its slow movement. The two main themes are related more than they are contrasted, and part of what is both fascinating and delightful is the way Mozart scores them. He begins both with strings alone. He continues the first with an answering phrase just for winds, punctuated twice by forceful string chords, and that leads to the first passage for full orchestra. But now that the sound of winds has been introduced and established, Mozart can proceed

---

[19]Most pianists play the first movement at a rather gentle tempo; some indeed are downright droopy. But in a recording of a 1946 concert performance, Artur Schnabel is brisk and sparkling, thus shedding quite a different light on the character of the music. What he does is not at all incompatible with what is in the score.

more subtly. In the new theme, a bassoon joins the violins nine measures into the melody and, as though encouraged by that, the flute appears in mid-phrase, softly adding its sound to the texture, with horns and clarinets arriving just in time to reinforce the cadence. When the same melody appears about a minute and a half later, the piano, having started it off, is happy to retire and leave it to the violins and bassoon and flute who had invented it in the first place, but it cannot after all refrain from doubling the descending scales with quiet broken octaves, adding yet another unobtrusively achieved, perfectly gauged touch of fresh color.

The beginning of the development is spliced neatly into the end of the exposition; much of the development itself is concerned with the wistful seven-measure tag with which the strings conclude the exposition. The real activity is in the woodwinds, and the piano accompanies with bright figurations. The recapitulation brings new distribution of material between solo and orchestra. After the cadenza comes a buoyant coda whose close is tongue-in-cheek matter-of-fact.

Slow movements in minor keys are surprisingly uncommon in Mozart, master of melancholy in music, and this one is in fact the last he writes. An Adagio marking is rare, too, and this movement is an altogether special transformation of the lilting siciliano style. The orchestra's first phrase harks back to "Wer ein Liebchen hat gefunden" (He Who Has Found a Sweetheart), Osmin's animadversions in *The Abduction from the Seraglio* on the proper treatment of women, but nothing in the inner life of that grouchy, fig-picking harem steward could ever have motivated the exquisite dissonances brought about here by the bassoon's imitation of clarinet and violins. A second theme is more chromatic and thus still more moody than the first. Upon its return, the first is extended by one of the great deceptive cadences in the literature.

Throughout, Mozart the pianist imagines himself as the ideal opera singer. Near the end, he writes a miraculous and especially operatic passage, the strings playing simple broken chords, part pizzicato, part arco, over which the piano declaims a noble and passionate melody notable for its range: two and a half octaves, at one point traversed in a single leap. Pianists differ about what to do here, some simply playing the notes in the score, others filling the gaps (in time and space) with embellishments of their own. I am not doctrinaire on this point. Our knowledge of eighteenth-century practice suggests that Mozart might well have taken the latter way, and I am delighted and moved by the elegant and expressive way Alfred Brendel sees the spare writing as an invitation to invention; on the other hand, I am no less captivated when Schnabel creates a line of tremendous tensile strength using only the few written notes.

After the restraint of the first movement and the melancholia of the second, Mozart gives us a finale of enchanting high spirits. It keeps the pianist very busy in music that comes close to perpetual motion and in which there is plenty to engage our ear, now so alert to the delicacy and overflowing invention with which Mozart uses those few and quiet instruments.

## Concerto No. 24 in C minor for Piano and Orchestra, K. 491

*Allegro*
*Larghetto*
*Allegretto*

Mozart entered the C-minor Concerto into his own catalogue on 24 March 1786 and introduced it at the Burgtheater, Vienna, ten days later, on 3 April. The tempo indications are those Mozart marked in his catalogue; his autograph manuscript has none. No cadenzas by Mozart survive.

**Solo piano, one flute, two oboes, two clarinets, two bassoons, two horns, two trumpets, timpani, and strings.**

This piece comes in the middle of Mozart's work on *Figaro's Wedding*, which he finished about a month later. *Figaro* is both one of the most effervescent and one of the least frivolous of comedies. Very little of it is in minor, and, to repeat an observation made by many a critic and historian, it is as though Mozart had a certain quota of music in minor that had to be given vent. This Concerto, one of only two by Mozart in that darker mode, sets determinedly about this task—so, at least, its powerful opening tutti suggests.

It is a gripping start: seven measures of octaves whose bleakness is accentuated rather than alleviated by the mordant intervention of oboes and clarinets with an infusion of harmony. The theme, moreover, touches all twelve notes of the chromatic scale, a restless traversal of the known world in not quite a quarter of a minute. (The German composer Giselher Klebe actually used this opening as a twelve-tone series in his Symphony of 1953.) Another unusual feature is the triple meter, which we find in only one other first movement of a Mozart concerto, that of the one in E-flat, K. 449.

The piano responds with pathos to the dark defiance of the opening tutti. It very much tends, in fact, to go its own way, and that way includes much of what Glenn Gould called "caressing" E-flat major. In one of his first concertos for Vienna, the excitingly adventurous and too little known C major, K. 415, Mozart experimented boldly with the dissociation of solo and tutti; in K. 491—and what a distance Mozart had traveled in just three years—we hear exactly what he was striving for. In the recapitulation, when his seemingly disparate materials are richly combined for the first time, we fully sense the force of his strategy. There is, furthermore, integration of yet another kind: uniquely in this Mozart concerto, the pianist plays through the closing tutti.

The Larghetto's opening melody is of extreme simplicity. Or, given the range of nearly two octaves in just four bars, should one say "seems" rather than "is"? Try to sing it. There are two contrasting episodes initiated by the winds alone, with the coda beautifully pulling all the elements together. A lovely and subtle detail: during the course of the movement, Mozart offers three rhythmic variants of the opening measure.

The finale is a march with six variations plus an elaborate coda. Each variation after the first has differentiated repeats so you get two for the price of one. Variation 6, which begins as a conversation between oboe and bassoon, moves into C *major*, a key virtually untouched so far. Some in the audience at the first performance would have heard Mozart's other piano concerto in minor, the D-minor, K. 466, when he played it the year before. Perhaps this moment recalled to them the delightful "happy ending" with the perky trumpet in the earlier piece. But Mozart means no such thing here, and the penumbra of all those E-flats and D-flats from the world of the minor mode returns to darken the music until its last chord. "Ah, we shall never be able to do anything like this," sighed Beethoven when he attended a rehearsal of this Concerto. Brahms was one who thought Beethoven's C-minor Concerto "much less significant and weaker" than Mozart's. And indeed, not even Beethoven could "do anything like this," nor anyone else.

## Concerto No. 25 in C major for Piano and Orchestra, K. 503

> *Allegro maestoso*
> *Andante*
> *[Allegretto]*

Mozart completed this Concerto on 4 December 1786 and played it in Vienna later that month. He left no cadenzas.

**Solo piano, two flutes, two oboes, two bassoons, two horns, two trumpets, and strings.**

This Concerto, less operatic and more symphonic than its predecessors and imbued with even greater compositional richness, is one of Mozart's big trumpets-and-drums concertos, and its first chords acquaint us with its grandly festive sonorous possibilities. But even so formal an exordium becomes a personal statement in Mozart's hands—"cliché becomes event," as Adorno says about Mahler—and across the seventh measure there falls for a moment the shadow of the minor mode. And when the formal proclamations are done, the music does indeed take off in C minor. Such harmonic—and expressive—ambiguities inform this entire movement. Mozart always liked those shadows: new here are the *unmodulated* transitions from major to minor and back again, the forceful definition of the chiaroscuro.

Strong as its impact is, this C-minor phase with all its chromaticisms lasts just eight measures; then the music gets going on its proper C-major path. Functionally, this is festive noise. In almost any other composer's concerto, or even in some earlier ones by Mozart, it would be no more than that; here, however, Mozart again makes something special of an ordinary task, inventing a complex texture involving two distinct ideas (the leaping octaves and fifths in the violins and low strings, seconded by flute and brass, and the more conjunct writing for the middle strings, oboes, and bassoons), imitations between low and high strings, and, as he approaches the cadences, brilliant scales for the second violins.

The music arrives at an emphatic cadence on G major. Following Donald Francis Tovey, I distinguish between *on* and *in* G major. *On* G major means that, while this is clearly a G-major cadence, the context is still C major; *in* G major would mean that we have really changed key from C to G. But it is too soon for that. In a Classical concerto, the exposition of material proceeds in two parts, the first without and the second with the soloist. The first part stays in the home key, and only in the second part does the music undertake a serious voyage to some other harmonic area.

The full orchestra celebrates this cadence by reiterating G eight times. This is the rhythm of that reiteration:

Ex. 1

It is played twice (to make up the eight G's). Then the violins pick up the da-da-da-DAH rhythm and turn it into the start of a new theme, a march, one that often reminds people of the as yet unwritten *Marseillaise*. Seemingly harmless, this is an amazing passage. First of all, the march starts in C minor. Almost immediately it shifts to E-flat major. Then it goes back to C minor, and only after that does it continue in C major. The scoring is wonderful: first, strings with languorous woodwinds, then crisp wind-band writing with trumpets and drums, all *piano*. After another round of formal cadences, the violins continue with a more lyric melody, and so the music arrives at the close of this chapter. The da-da-da-DAH rhythm of Example 1 is almost constantly present in the main material or the accompaniment.[20]

This is already a lot of event, and we haven't even heard the pianist yet. The first solo entrance in this Concerto is one of Mozart's subtlest and most gently winsome. We expect the piano to come in when the orchestra's assertive cadences are done, and probably to enter in the grand manner of the movement's opening measures. Instead, after a silence, the strings propose a different, quieter cadence. That gentleness elicits a response from the soloist, one that could almost be described as a written-out, accompanied cadenza, a quasi-improvisatory passage that leads back to the grand opening chords, again played by the orchestra.

For the moment, the piano is content to comment and decorate, adding scales and arpeggios as the second exposition repeats—more or less—the course of the first one. But at the moment where the orchestra had previously introduced the march, the piano now plays a quiet new theme of its own. The common ground with the march is something very subtle: it is in E-flat major, thus corresponding to the most surprising detail of the march. Further sparkling keyboard work finally propels the exposition to its real destination, the dominant, G major, and there the piano proposes yet another new and sweetly lyric theme. (For one poignant half-bar, it is touched by the shadow of the minor mode.) Now things become more active, the piano bows out on a long trill, and the orchestra alone concludes the exposition with the assertive cadences that culminate in the da-da-da-DAH rhythm of Example 1.

The greatest marvel of all in this movement is the development. The piano picks up Example 1, but quietly, and on a different note, B. Using that B as a triple upbeat, it can now play the quasi-*Marseillaise* march in E minor. As the phrase ends on E, the oboes and bassoons suddenly understand that they can join this game. In their turn picking up Example 1 on E, they can send the march into A minor. This bald description does not begin to convey the beauty of all the detail with which Mozart invests these events. What follows is brief but dense. The harmonic range

---

[20]Beethoven learned a lot from Mozart's concertos and was open in his admiration of them. The march theme in K. 503 left its mark on the first movement of Beethoven's Concerto No. 1, also in C major, sketched just nine or ten years later.

is breathtaking, and Mozart enriches the texture with an incredible intricacy of canonic writing. At first, the piano withdraws, as though to listen in amazement. It returns, ready to propose new ideas and new directions, but then settles back and turns into an accompanist who listens to the woodwinds carry out what she has imagined. How keenly one senses Mozart's own presence at the keyboard here.

The recapitulation is no less inventive. Its most remarkable stroke is what Mozart now does with the tiny hint of minor in what was the second of the solo piano themes in the exposition: upon its return, this shadow grows beyond all expectation, like the genie released from the bottle. And, as the movement nears its end, even what happens in the brief five pages after the cadenza is full of surprise.

The Andante is not one of Mozart's purple slow movements like, for example, the Andante of K. 467 or the poignant Adagio of K. 488. To call it austere would be going too far, but subdued it is, also formal and a little mysterious at the same time, like a knot garden by moonlight. A remarkable musical feature is the uncommonly wide span from its slowest notes (the dotted half-note in measure 2) to its fastest (the flute run six measures later). The ratio is 1:24. Much of the piano writing appears to allow room for added embellishments, though pianists today disagree whether the immense leaps in a passage such as

Ex. 2

are moments of tension best left as written or invitations to invention and brilliance. (K. 488 poses the same choice.)

For the finale, Mozart adapts a gavotte from his then five-year-old opera *Idomeneo*. As he does at the beginning of the first movement, Mozart takes us into C minor startlingly soon. Here, too, the counterpoint astonishes with its richness. Neither in the gavotte's courtly and witty measures nor in various episodes that follow is there anything to prepare us for the epiphanic moment when the piano, accompanied by cellos and basses alone (a sound that occurs nowhere else in Mozart), begins a smiling and melancholy song that is continued by the oboe, the flute, and the bassoon, and which the cellos cannot resist joining. This is never finished. As though he could not bear simply to bring this miraculous passage to formal closure and go on to something else,

Mozart makes it dissolve and grow into a music whose sumptuous texture and whose poignancy and passion amaze us. This is the favorite page in this Concerto of every musician I know. From that ecstasy of joy and pain, Mozart brings us back to earth by leading us back to his gavotte—the oboe staying intent on pathos longer than his colleagues do—and thence into a brilliant close, exuberantly inventive to the last double bar.

## Concerto No. 26 in D major for Piano and Orchestra, K. 537, *Coronation*

*Allegro*
*[Larghetto]*
*[Allegretto]*

This Concerto is dated 24 February 1788 in Mozart's own catalogue. Mozart played it at the Royal Saxon Court at Dresden on 14 April 1789 and again in Frankfurt on 15 October 1790 at the festivities surrounding the coronation of Emperor Leopold II—hence its name. Not only did Mozart leave no cadenza, much of the piano part is indicated in shorthand and requires a lot of filling out by the soloist.

**Solo piano, flute, two oboes, two bassoons, two horns, two trumpets, timpani, and strings.**

In the nineteenth century, the *Coronation* was one of the most popular of all of Mozart's concertos. Today, having learned to rejoice in the emotional and compositional richness of the great concertos from K. 449 to K. 503, we tend to be rather snooty about K. 537, and it has not been much in favor in the second half of the twentieth century. This is unfair, first, because it is a beautiful concerto, and second, because we have not really been able to know it properly. Mozart, writing the score strictly for his own use, could make do with a sort of shorthand in which, for example, accompaniments might be no more than minimally sketched. If you look at the autograph, which is in the Morgan Library in New York, you see that the part for the pianist's left hand is virtually unwritten. The first edition, published by André in 1794, perpetuated this sketchy and incomplete version of the piece, and the editors of the complete Mozart edition published by Breitkopf & Härtel in the nineteenth century, who should have known better, did the same thing. In other words, when Mozart played this Concerto in Dresden and Frankfurt, it did not sound as bare and primitive as it does when one follows one of the André-based prints exactly. Nor of course should it. More recently, pianists have begun to catch on, preparing their own editions that fill in the blanks, thus bringing the texture of the work in line with what we expect of Mozart in 1788, the year of his last three symphonies.

Here is a trumpets-and-drums concerto in bright D major, although, presumably in the hope of increasing performance opportunities, Mozart marks all the winds and timpani as *ad libitum*. Availing oneself of this permission would of course make a wretched effect. Although one meets more regularities and symmetries here than in most of Mozart's music of the 1780s—and this is the main thing I meant by "less complex"—it is pleasing to discover that even on the very first page Mozart cannot help himself and follows his first pair of "rhymed" four-bar phrases with a phrase of five measures, yielding an initial sentence of thirteen bars. And throughout, his sense for colorful harmony is very much alive.

The middle movement is a "romance," cousin to those in the D-minor Concerto, K. 466, and *Eine kleine Nachtmusik* (and, more remotely, to the middle movement of K. 451). It is marked *Larghetto*, but in a hand other than Mozart's. Moreover, André and most of his successors changed Mozart's time signature of ¢ to c with, as Alfred Brendel has remarked, "painful results." Brendel further comments that this movement, "far from trying to plumb mysterious depths, is self-sufficient in its graceful charm. Its sweetness is present without contrast . . . the first eight bars, already consisting of two almost identical phrases, reappear unvaried four times during the course of the piece. Hardly another movement by Mozart gives the player so much opportunity for improvisatory figuration, and needs it so badly to come alive."[21]

The rondo finale is simple in design as well in choice of material, but it too is replete with happy detail. Again, Mozart could not help being Mozart.

[21]Alfred Brendel, liner note to Philips recording 411468-D.

## Concerto No. 27 in B-flat major for Piano and Orchestra, K. 595

*Allegro*
*Larghetto*
*Allegro*

This work is dated 5 January 1791, and Mozart himself introduced it in Vienna on 4 March that year at a concert put on by the clarinetist Joseph Bähr. He left cadenzas for the first and third movements.

**Solo piano, flute, two oboes, two bassoons, two horns, and strings.**

When the year 1791 began, Mozart's career seemed to be halted, his financial affairs were in disarray, and he was sunk in a serious depression. That most bubbly of correspondents wrote to his wife: "If people could see into my heart I'd almost have to be ashamed—everything is cold for me—ice cold." And, a few months later: "I can't explain to you how I feel, there's a kind of emptiness—it just hurts me—a kind of longing that is never stilled, therefore never stops—it just goes on and on—no, it grows from day to day."[22]

The composer and pianist who not so many years earlier had scarcely been able to keep up with public demand for compositions and concerts now paid the rent by writing music for ballroom dances and as background for waxworks. He no longer gave concerts of his own, and we owe the existence of this, his last piano concerto, to Joseph Bähr (or Beer), a clarinet virtuoso in the service of the tsar of Russia. Bähr thought to invite Mozart, who was an acquaintance from Paris days in the 1770s, and Mozart's sister-in-law, Aloysia Lange, the ice-queen soprano Mozart had once hoped to marry, to participate in an evening of music at Jahn's Hall, Vienna, on Friday evening, 4 March 1791. It turned out to be Mozart's final appearance in concert. Toward the end of the year—his last—the huge success of *The Magic Flute* brought, too late, an upturn in his fortunes, but even that success would have been compromised in the eyes of some because it took place not in the Burgtheater, with its elegant ambience and audience, but in a suburban musical comedy house. And when Mozart died at the beginning of December, he was engaged in a job of ghostwriting for a young nobleman who wanted to pass off a well-written Requiem as a composition of his own.

[22]Volker Braunbehrens, *Mozart in Wien* (Munich: Piper, 1986).

Like Mozart's earlier concertos in B-flat, K. 450 and 456, both of 1784, K. 595 is subtly lyrical and almost chamber-musical in its coloration. It partakes as well of a certain simplicity that is characteristic of Mozart's late pieces and that is most famously embodied in much of *The Magic Flute* and the sublime motet *Ave verum corpus*. An unanswerable question: Do these works presage a new style period for Mozart, one for which there was no time?

Right away, the Concerto offers a surprise. Normally a piece by Mozart begins with its first phrase, as it were, whether that is a rhetorical flourish or a lyric melody. Here he sets the music gently into motion with a measure of murmuring accompaniment, and only when tempo, key, and atmosphere have been thus "neutrally" set do the first violins begin to project a melody against this background.[23]

The melody brings its own subtleties and surprises. The first is its punctuation (or interruption?) by little five-note flourishes for woodwinds and horns; you could leave them out, splice the phrases of the melody together, and get something perfectly coherent. Another is the foreshortening of the melody as it unfolds: four measures plus three, plus three again. When, after a brief spray of *forte*, Mozart presents a new melody, he also reveals the point—or one of the points—of the wind interruptions of the first theme. Here, too, the violins carry the melody, with wind instruments taking over between phrases; this time, however, the wind interventions are in no sense interruptions but essential links from one violin phrase to the next. It is a lovely play of the same and not the same. Moreover, when Mozart at last introduces the piano, he continues his game with colors, for he now has the strings play the flourishes that cut into the piano's melody.

The development is quietly astonishing. What Mozart conjures with is the opening theme and its interrupting wind flourishes. But even before we get to that, the entry into this new chapter of the movement is breathstopping. The final cadences of the exposition are left unfinished, but Mozart uses an entirely formulaic four-note phrase to move the music into new—disturbingly new—territory.[24] In a few seconds, we have been taken from the safety of F major to the terra incognita of B minor, and it is in that remote

---

[23]The other work by Mozart to begin with an accompaniment alone is the Symphony No. 40 in G minor; there the atmosphere is agitated rather than serene. In the nineteenth century this becomes a favorite way of beginning pieces—for example, Beethoven's *Moonlight* Sonata, Schubert's A-minor Quartet, the Mendelssohn Violin Concerto, all the Bruckner symphonies—and it continues to appear in such twentieth-century works as Bartók's Violin Concerto No. 2.

[24]Worth hearing: Benjamin Britten's conducting of this transition on his 1970 recording with Clifford Curzon and the English Chamber Orchestra. There is awe in those four-note phrases. Perhaps only a fellow-composer could have been so deeply struck by this moment and found the courage to bring it out so vividly. There comes to mind the story of Richard Strauss saying he would have given his complete works to have composed the music that introduces the trio of the masked visitors in the ballroom scene of *Don Giovanni*. The passage in question is two measures long, consists of twelve notes, unharmonized, and looks like pure formula on the page.

place, where we seem to be without landmarks, that the piano proposes revisiting the opening theme. The piano's phrase is duly followed by the flourish we expect—in the strings this time, with woodwinds offering a closing tag—but the notes are skewed so that we are propelled into C major, and there the piano tries again. From B minor to C major is another dizzying leap: like Puck, Mozart could put a girdle round about the earth in forty minutes. These explorations continue, focusing more and more on the melodic rather than the flourish, and it is all a marvel of harmonic boldness, of fertile and witty invention that goes into the decisions about who plays what, in the ease of the counterpoint, and at last in the casual perfection of timing with which the transition into the recapitulation is arranged.

The Larghetto—and it is not Adagio but Larghetto, and in cut time, therefore not exceedingly slow—is of radiant simplicity. The mood is melancholic (but never sentimental); the sense is that of all passion spent. Toward the close comes an utterly desolate minute in which flute, first violins, and piano join in playing the elegiac melody, virtually without accompaniment. What mourning there is here.

The item that Mozart entered into his own catalogue of his works immediately after this Concerto—it was nine days later, on 14 January—was a set of three songs. The first of these is called *Sehnsucht nach dem Frühling* (Longing for Spring); in Germany it soon took on folk-song status. Its melody is a close cousin to the one that begins this concerto's finale. Notably, though, this movement fails to keep its promise of simplicity: invention and variety of presentation are prodigious. As for the world of feeling brought to life in this music, one could not say it better than in the words from *The Winter's Tale* that H. C. Robbins Landon cites in connection with Mozart's Clarinet Concerto: "[The] heart dances, but not for joy."

## Mozart's Violin Concertos

Mozart the performer means most of all Mozart the pianist, and he was probably the greatest of his time. But he was no mean violinist, either. On 4 October 1777, for example, he took part in a private concert in Munich, playing not only a couple of piano concertos but also the demanding violin solo part in the B-flat-major Divertimento, K. 287(271h), and playing, as he wrote to his father, "as though I were the greatest violinist in all of Europe. They all opened their eyes."

Bragging? Yes, of course. Exaggerating? Almost surely not. Mozart had a sober sense of his gifts and accomplishments. He was, moreover, writing to the most knowledgeable and exigent connoisseur of string-playing alive: Leopold Mozart, himself a first-rate violinist, a prolific and able composer, and an outstanding musician all around. Like J. J. Quantz's treatise on flute-playing (1752) and C. P. E. Bach's on keyboard performance (1753–1762), Leopold's *Essay on the Fundamental Principles of Violin-Playing*, which made its appearance the same year as baby Wolfgang, goes far beyond the immediate promise of its title to touch on many points of aesthetics and technique from a broad perspective. Its publication affirmed Leopold Mozart's standing as one of Europe's premier musical minds, and like the books of Quantz and Bach, it is one of our most important keys to eighteenth-century music-making.

Leopold Mozart was also not extravagant when it came to praising his son. When, therefore, he writes, "You yourself do not know how well you play the violin . . . when you play with energy and with your whole heart and soul, yes indeed, just as though you were the first violinist in all of Europe," or when he suggests in connection with a proposed tour that Wolfgang would do well to introduce himself with a violin concerto, these are not just the words of a proud, let alone indulgent, papa.

Wolfgang began to play the violin right at the beginning of his career, which is to say when he was six, and he was just seven when he made his public debut playing a concerto—we do not know whose—at a birthday celebration for Archbishop Sigismund von Schrattenbach of Salzburg. (His ten-year-old sister played a harpsichord concerto on the same occasion.) Playing the violin was his meal ticket during the galley years of working for another archbishop of Salzburg, Count Hieronymus Colloredo, something of a violinist himself but, from Mozart's perspective, a patron of unsurpassed boorishness. In justice one should point out that Mozart, with his constant requests for extended leaves of absence, was not an easy employee. This unhappy relationship came to a violent end on 8 June 1781, when Count Arco, the archbishop's chief steward, literally kicked Mozart down the stairs of Colloredo's Vienna *palais*. One of the ways Mozart celebrated his liberation from Colloredo was to give up the violin. When he played chamber music with friends he took the viola part, and the inventory of his possessions at his death shows that he no longer even owned a violin.

We cannot be absolutely sure that Mozart wrote any or all of his five concertos for himself, but it is probable. A name that often comes up in connection with these works is that of Colloredo's Neapolitan concertmaster, Antonio Brunetti. Almost certainly, Brunetti played these pieces later, and Mozart wrote some pieces for him, but since he only joined the Salzburg establishment in March 1776, he cannot have been the original recipient of the concertos. Leopold Mozart refers in a letter to "the concerto you wrote for Kolb," presumably Franz Xaver Kolb, another Salzburg violinist and a friend of the Mozart family.[25]

---

[25]The Kolb issue is not easy to disentangle. In the index of Deutsch's *Mozart: A Documentary Biography*, we find both Franz Xaver and Andrä Kolb, with the latter's strange given name followed by a

On the question of the dates of composition of these works, I quote Neal Zaslaw in *The Compleat Mozart*:

> It has long been thought that Mozart wrote all five of his violin concertos within a space of eight months from April 14 to December 20, 1775, in accordance with the dates written by the composer on the original manuscripts. Recently, however, the German musicologist Wolfgang Plath has shown that on all five manuscripts the last two digits of the date have been tampered with: it appears that all were changed to read *1780* at some point, and then changed back to *1773* later. Judging from the evidence of handwriting and water marks, Plath argues that 1775 is probably correct for the last four concertos, but that the first concerto probably originally bore a date of 1773.[26]

Mozart's five violin concertos show a remarkable progression, from the agreeable but seldom played K. 207 and 211 to the more familiar K. 216, 218, and 219. For that matter, there is a fair amount of difference between the first two pieces in quality and confidence. Plath's redating, if correct, would help explain that.

In addition to the canonical five, three other "Mozart violin concertos" still ghost about. Two of them, K. 268 and K. 271a, *may* contain some material from projects Mozart abandoned, but they are certainly not *by* Mozart as they stand. K. 294a, the so-called *Adelaide*, is an out-and-out forgery by the French violist and viola d'amore player, Henri Casadesus (1879–1947), who also composed a "Handel" Viola Concerto in B minor that used to be much played.[27] *Adelaide* has pretty much disappeared from the scene, though the recording by the eighteen-year-old Yehudi Menuhin with Pierre Monteux is still available. K. 268 and K. 271a were in the repertory of violinists such as Thibaud, David Oistrakh, Menuhin, Szeryng, and Grumiaux, all active before World War II, but more recently they have also been played and

---

question mark. Franz Xaver was a professional, Andrä an amateur musician. It is not, however, clear from the text which Kolb did what. The English Mozart scholar Stanley Sadie endorses the candidacy of Andrä as the one for whom Mozart wrote a concerto, but in *The Compleat Mozart*, his American colleague Neal Zaslaw confidently identifies the Kolb in question as Franz Xaver. *The Mozart Compendium*, edited by H. C. Robbins Landon, lists a Joachim Kolb in the index, but the name does not occur on the page indicated.

[26] *The Compleat Mozart: A Guide to the Musical Works of Wolfgang Amadeus Mozart*, ed. Neal Zaslaw with William Cowdery (New York: Mozart Bicentennial at Lincoln Center and W. W. Norton, 1990).

The original manuscripts of the first four concertos are in the Jagiellonian Library in Krakow, Poland, that of the fifth in the Library of Congress. All five autographs as well as those of the Adagio in E major, K. 261, and the Rondo in B-flat major, K. 261a, are published in facsimile by Raven Press, New York. It is, however, somewhere between difficult and impossible to see the details of these tamperings in the facsimile.

[27] The orchestration of the *Adelaide* Concerto is by Paul Hindemith, no less. The Hindemith scholar Giselher Schubert comments: "He wanted this forgery, which of course he instantly recognized as such, to sound as 'authentic' as possible (so as to annoy the 'specialists')."

recorded by, among others, Kantorow, Suk, Lin, Zehetmair, and Zimmermann.

## Concerto No. 3 in G major for Violin and Orchestra, K. 216

> *Allegro*
> *Adagio*
> *Rondeau: Allegro—Andante—Allegretto—Allegro*

The G-major Violin Concerto is dated 12 September 1775, but for more on the question of the date, see the introductory note on Mozart's violin concertos. Nothing is known about its first performance, though it is safe to assume that it took place soon after the work was completed and probably with Mozart as soloist. Mozart left no cadenzas.

**Solo violin, two flutes, two oboes, two horns, and strings.**

In this Concerto, Mozart gives us a first movement of delightfully buoyant energy. At the beginning, he is recycling music he had written a few months before: an aria from *Il rè pastore*, a serenata that was performed at Salzburg on 23 April 1775. The development section is based on a new and crackling theme.

The miraculous second movement is a real Adagio, something relatively rare in Mozart, and this is one of those touching pages to which Cuthbert Girdlestone, in his masterly study of Mozart's piano concertos, has given the designation "dream andantes." The sound of muted strings, the slightly troubled triplets in the inner voices, the plucked basses, the delicate comments and punctuations of the wind instruments instantly cast a poetic spell. The flutes, by the way, are used only in this movement: presumably the Salzburg wind players doubled on flute and oboe. Here too the development, though brief, is of striking harmonic breadth.

Mozart gets quirky in the finales of these concertos. What starts out here as a simple and rustic rondo is interrupted by a double episode in contrasting duple meter, the first part a grave gavotte in G minor, the second a jolly country dance. In both Leopold and Wolfgang Mozart's letters there is occasional reference to a *Strassburger* Violin Concerto. This second tune has been identified by the musicologist Dénes Bartha as a folk melody known in the eighteenth century as "The Strassburger." No words have come down with the tune, so we do not know the reason for the name, but clearly this is the *Strassburger* Concerto. After this double episode, the original material returns, but whimsy and surprise reign to the very last gesture.

## Concerto No. 4 in D major for Violin and Orchestra, K. 218

> *Allegro*
> *Andante cantabile*
> *Rondeau: Andante grazioso—Allegro ma non troppo*

This Concerto is dated October 1775, but see the introductory note on the Mozart violin concertos. No details are known about its early performance history. There are no cadenzas by Mozart.

**Solo violin, two oboes, two horns, and strings.**

The first movement begins in the eighteenth century's most charming martial manner. Soon, however, this gives way to a beautifully rounded lyric idea, and all the way through, Mozart enjoys—and invites us to enjoy with him— the contrast between the two worlds, the swaggering and the yielding. The Andante cantabile is all generous songfulness, and it abounds in quiet orchestral detail to reward the attentive listener.

As in all of Mozart's violin concertos, the finale is delightfully individual. It is built upon a double thematic unit in two tempos and two different meters: Andante grazioso in 2/4 and Allegro ma non troppo in 6/8, the latter a kind of gigue. (The Allegro is a variant of the second movement's main theme.) The Andante is stable, but Mozart ingeniously finds a new direction for the Allegro to move off into each time it comes back. The movement is interrupted by a rustic tune of very different character, musettelike and with a drone accompaniment. Mozart liked it well enough to bring it back a year later in one of his contredanses, K. 269b.

# Concerto No. 5 in A major for Violin and Orchestra, K. 219

*Allegro aperto*
*Adagio*
*Rondeau: Tempo di Menuetto—Allegro—Tempo di Menuetto*

The A-major Violin Concerto is dated "Salisburgo li 20 decembre 1775." Nothing is known about its first performance, though it is safe to assume that it took place soon after the work was completed and probably with Mozart as soloist. Mozart left no cadenzas.

**Solo violin, two oboes, two horns, and strings.**

A-major is always a special key for Mozart. It is the farthest he ventures out toward the sharp side of the harmonic spectrum—there are single movements in E but no large-scale works, and there are none in B, F-sharp, or C-sharp—and the music for which he chooses this key often partakes of a special and moonlit luminosity. Here he marks the first movement *Allegro aperto*, a direction used apparently only by him and only in eight other places. A nonstandard term, it appears in no reference work of Mozart's time, and one must try to infer from the music itself what Mozart meant by an "open" allegro. In his extraordinarily interesting book *The Tempo Indications of Mozart*, Jean-Pierre Marty notes that all the vocal pieces marked *Allegro aperto* are "hymns to hope, to joy, to love, to nature and to happiness" or liturgical songs of praise. That certainly tells us something, and it even fits with an idea I had before I had read Marty that the first movement of this Concerto asks for a certain Beechamesque swagger.[28]

Mozart, or whoever the soloist was, would have played along with the first violins in the orchestra at the beginning, and the audience would have waited for him to detach himself and take off in solo flight. The first solo entrance in a concerto was often, for Mozart, an occasion for wit and ingenuity. Here he gives us a double surprise. The solo violin enters adagio, with murmuring strings and delicately accented wind chords that look ahead to the farewell trio in *Così fan tutte*. It is a lovely example of Mozart's A-major

---

[28]*The Oxford Companion to Music* offers "broad in style" as a meaning for *aperto*, but the editor, Dr. Percy A. Scholes, cites no authority. Other modern reference books shy away from the question altogether.

moonlight. Then, at the resumption of the quick tempo, he adds a brand new violin tune to the energetic zigzag arpeggios of the original orchestral beginning. More adventures lie ahead. Mozart finds new ways of using the charmingly casual arpeggios with which the orchestra's exposition ends. The solo violin introduces new themes among which the first, an elegantly impassioned declamation in C-sharp minor, is especially impressive. The movement ends with a final appearance of the little upward flick across a chord of A major.

The second movement is a real Adagio, which is relatively rare in Mozart, and its soft wave patterns recall the poetic adagio surprise of the solo entrance in the first movement. Here is music close to what Cuthbert Girdlestone called "dream andantes," perfectly exemplified by the slow movement of the G-major Violin Concerto, K. 216. This Adagio is also one of Mozart's rare voyages into E major.[29] Mozart knows that the opening theme invites canonic imitation, but wishing to keep this movement simple, he reserves this for a single moment, the recapitulation, where the second violins, followed by the firsts, anticipate the re-entrance of the solo player. Because this touch of textural complexity is so different from anything else we have heard in this movement, the effect is truly magical. Brunetti found this Adagio "too studied," which strikes us as an odd criticism; in any event, it has been proposed and often repeated that the single E-major Adagio, K. 261, is the substitute slow movement that Mozart obligingly wrote for him.

The finales of Mozart's violin concertos are not brilliant virtuosic closes like those of the piano concertos. This one begins as an ever-so-slightly coquettish minuet, but its courtly gestures are interrupted by piquant country dance music. This episode long ago earned the concerto the nickname *Turkish*, but this vigorous music is in fact Hungarian. "Turkish," to the Austrians, was a loose but handy designation for something hailing from east of Salzburg or even Vienna. Here Mozart also quotes himself, for the jagged theme that most recalls the zigzags of the first movement comes from the eighth movement of *Le gelosie del seraglio*, a ballet he sketched in 1772 for insertion into his opera *Lucio Silla*. (It was not the only time he tranferred dance music to one of his concertos: the finale of the C-major Piano Concerto, K. 503, is an adaptation of the gavotte from his *Idomeneo* ballet music.) Here Mozart introduces a (literally) striking orchestral detail, instructing the cellos and basses to play with the wooden stick of the bow rather than the hair. This in-

[29]In his other A-major concertos, both for piano, Mozart chooses D major for the slow movement of one (K. 414(385p) and F-sharp minor for the tragic Adagio of the other (K. 488). D major is also his choice for the slow movements of the Symphony No. 29, the String Quartet, K.4 64, and the great Violin Sonata, K. 526.

struction got lost, or was possibly suppressed by editors with more "taste" than was good for them, and did not make its way into print until the 1960s.[30] The movement returns to the minuet music, sweetly recast, and making a graceful exit with a variant of the A-major arpeggio we came to know so well in the first movement.

## *Sinfonia concertante*, in E-flat major for Violin, Viola, and Orchestra, K. 364(320d)

> *Allegro maestoso*
> *Andante*
> *Presto*

Mozart probably wrote this work in the summer of 1779. We have no information about its early performance history. The first performance in America, on 8 April 1865, by Theodore Thomas as violinist and conductor and with the violist George Matzka, is worth recalling for the review in the *New York Times*, whose critic wrote: "On the whole we would prefer death to a repetition of this production. The wearisome scale passages on the little fiddle repeated *ad nauseam* on the bigger one were simply maddening." Mozart includes cadenzas in the score.

**Solo violin, solo viola, two oboes, two horns, and strings, the latter including two sections of violas.**

In 1778–1779, Mozart became intensely interested in the possibilities of concertos with more than one solo instrument. Earlier, in May 1774, he had written what he called a Concertone, literally "a big concerto," for two solo violins and an almost equally prominent oboe part (C major, K. 187e), but now there suddenly appeared a whole run of such works. More precisely, we have three completed works—two that were abandoned part way through, and one puzzle. The completed ones are the Concerto for Flute and Harp, K. 297c, of April 1778, agreeably Rococo but a bit perfunctory; the delightful Concerto for Two Pianos, K. 316a, written in the early part of April 1779; and the present work. In November 1778 he be-

---

[30]As Donald Tovey remarked about the "Turkish" part of this finale and the objections to it of some critics, "Turks will be Turks and tasters will be tasters."

gan a concerto in D for piano and violin, K. 315f, and in the summer or early fall of 1779 started an A-major *Sinfonia concertante* for violin, viola, and cello, but abandoned both scores because the concerts for which they were intended were canceled.[31] The puzzle is the *Sinfonia concertante* in E-flat for four wind instruments, K. 297b, whose genesis cannot be properly established and which has not come down to us in any form that can be authenticated as being by Mozart.

In the middle of this frustrating package of plans, experiments, and accomplishments, the *Sinfonia concertante* for violin and viola stands out as one of Mozart's most seductively rich works and surely as the finest of his string concertos. Excellent violinist though he was, when he played chamber music he liked best to take up the viola. He enjoyed being in the middle of the texture, besides which there is surely an affinity between the viola's dark and somehow pent-up sonority and the element of melancholy that tends to invade even the most festive of Mozart's compositions. The viola is *the* Mozartian sound par excellence. Mozart's chamber music attains its highest point in those quintets where he adds a second viola to the standard string quartet.

Here, in this *Sinfonia concertante*—the title suggests a symphony that behaves like a concerto—he stresses that characteristic color by dividing the violas into two sections. As for the two solo instruments, Mozart is more interested in the distinction of color than in the difference of range.[32] He sends the viola clear up to the high E-flat above the treble staff, an altitude it never comes near approaching in his chamber music. To allow the viola to be more penetrating, Mozart writes the part not in E-flat but in D, a more sonorous and brilliant key for the instrument because it takes better advantage of the open strings and their overtones, asking the player to tune the instrument up a semitone so that what is played in D will actually sound in E-flat. Most violists shudder at the thought of thus playing the part on a retuned instrument and in the "wrong" key and simply play it in E-flat. Hindemith was one of the few modern violists who always played the part in D.

Indeed, everything about the sheer sound of the *Sinfonia concertante* attests to the richness of Mozart's aural fantasy: the piquant wind writing, the delightful and serenadelike pizzicatos in the orchestra, the subtle interaction of solo and orchestral strings beginning with the very first emergence of the two soloists from the tutti, and, not least, the way so sumptuous and varied a sonority is drawn from so modest a complement.

The splendid and majestic first movement is followed by an operatic

[31]Robert Levin has prepared completions of both these movements.
[32]One hears something similar when he writes for a first and second soprano, as, for example, in the C-minor Mass or *Così fan tutte*.

Andante of deep pathos: one can almost hear the Italian words as the two singers vie in passionate protestation. In *Symphonie Concertante*, the ballet he created in 1947 for Tanaquil LeClercq and Maria Tallchief, George Balanchine rendered these conversations visible, the gay and spirited ones of the first and last movements no less than the darkly impassioned ones of the Andante. The way this Andante begins is a glorious instance of how Mozart can surprise us by opening doors whose very existence we never suspected. The music begins with regular questions and answers, but the third time—I always think of Tamino finding the right door—something opens, the barriers come down, formality and symmetry are gone, and we witness and share in raw pain.

The finale, after that, is all high spirits and virtuosic brilliance.

# Carl Nielsen

Carl August Nielsen was born at Sortelung near Nørre Lyndelse on Funen, Denmark, on 9 June 1865 and died in Copenhagen on 3 October 1931. The FS numbers refer to the chronological catalogue of Nielsen's works by Dan Fog and Torben Schousboe.

Nielsen's first instrument was the woodpile behind the house, where he discovered that logs, when struck, yielded different pitches according to their thickness and length. From the woodpile he progressed to the violin, which his father, a housepainter, played, and from there to the piano, an instrument he first encountered at an aunt's house when he was six. At fourteen he became an army bandsman, and a kindly older musician introduced him to the central classics of European music: Mozart, Beethoven, and eventually Bach. At nineteen Nielsen was admitted to the Copenhagen Conservatory, supporting himself as a violinist. For most of his life, he depended financially on his playing and conducting.

Nielsen became a prolific composer, the most important his country had produced, certainly since the death of Dietrich Buxtehude in 1707. Over the years, his catalogue came to include six symphonies; concertos for clarinet, flute, and violin; two operas, *Saul and David* and *Maskerade*; a Wind Quintet; and other chamber music, powerful piano and organ pieces, choral works, and strikingly beautiful songs.

In 1922 Nielsen developed angina pectoris, and with it came depression, intellectual disorientation, and loss of energy. But he returned to life, frail though he now was and wracked by heart attacks. His Symphony No. 4 (1916) had been a celebration of "the Inextinguishable . . . the elemental Will of Life," those forces of regeneration that would prevail even after "the devastation of the world through fire, flood, volcanoes, etc," and Nielsen's last ten years showed that he could live that principle as well as write a great symphony about it. He died at sixty-six, hardworking to the end. His funeral was a great public event, like Verdi's, but it would not be until after World War II that his music, so unlike any other in sound and personality, came to be known abroad.

There is a world of difference between Nielsen's first concerto for violin (1911), a work whose first and second movements are full of momentum and flavor but whose leisurely finale tends to disappoint in public performance (it is just fine on recordings), and the ones for flute (1926) and clarinet (1928). By 1916 and the great Fourth Symphony, *The Inextinguishable*, Nielsen had turned from a strong, assured, and skillful composer with a distinctive voice into a tone poet and musical dramatist in the grip of singular and astonishing fantasies. His works from the 1920s can be full of rage (the gun battle of the timpani in *The Inextinguishable* is an anticipation of this), and they mean to disturb. Nielsen would have understood Dylan Thomas's "Do not go gentle into that good night" very well.

Nielsen found the concerto a congenial arena for expressing his growing fascination with conversation and confrontation, with "scenario." In his later music, he also takes immense delight in experiment and risk, as well as making more room for humor. We can hear these things in his Flute and Clarinet concertos. Nielsen's major works from the 1920s are not the failures to relive or reproduce earlier successes that some of their first critics took them for, but new, private, bold, quirky voyages of discovery.

## Concerto for Clarinet and Orchestra, FS 129

*Allegretto un poco—Poco adagio—Allegro non troppo—Adagio—Allegro vivace*

Nielsen completed this Clarinet Concerto, his last work for orchestra, on 15 August 1928. Aage Oxenvad, for whom he had written it, gave the first performance in Copenhagen on 2 October 1928 with the composer conducting.

**Solo clarinet, two bassoons, two horns, snare drum, and strings.**

This concerto, of which it is hardly too much to say that it is a piece for an actor who happens to play the clarinet wonderfully, is altogether more mysterious than the Flute Concerto comedy.[1] The music begins with cellos and basses playing a stalking theme which seems—for five seconds, anyway—to be innocently and firmly settled in F major, but which is full of odd, slanty turns that make the harmony veer off into strange places. (There are no voices other than those of these low strings in octaves, and so "harmony" means "implied harmony.") As usual in Nielsen's mature music, rivalry between key centers is an important component of the drama.

The bassoon comes in with the same theme beginning on the dominant, C, and—aha!—this is going to be a fugue. The clarinet appears to follow suit, but it has not been in the game for more than two measures when it creates a disturbance with a little scale, up and down. Three measures later comes more of a distraction, with another scale up and an arpeggio down, which elicits an agitated chatter of protest from the violins and bassoons; undeterred, however, the clarinet becomes still more rambunctious in its bid for independence. This is predictive of the alternations between unruly behavior and attempts at restoring law and order that keep occurring in this Concerto. It is a piece for a soloist and a conductor who live comfortably with non sequiturs.

As the solo clarinet continues to flex its virtuoso soloist muscles, the horns, then bassoons, then strings try *fortississimo* to restore some decorum. Instead, they unleash a new demon: the snare drum. The drum cannot quite decide whether its purpose is actually to disrupt the proceedings or merely to insist on joining the play group even though uninvited. What is sure is that from here on, threatening or playful, insistently in the foreground or a background rattle, the snare drum will be a constant presence. A clarinet cadenza, sufficiently assertive to quiet the snare drum, takes us into the recapitulation. As though maddened by a tarantula bite, the music gets faster and faster, but recovers enough to revert to the original tempo, if not to the original innocent mood.

The Concerto observes no breaks between movements, and now the music flows into the Poco Adagio. This begins with a lyric horn solo, accompanied by the two bassoons, after which the clarinet continues and develops what the horn has begun. All of a sudden the mood changes: the music jolts forward as the strings begin and for quite a time maintain a jumpy and quite undignified gait. It is as though they had been given the same "drop that made the old woman go hippety-hop" in the old English folk song about Oliver Cromwell. The clarinet, however, is intent on showing that it is quite unaffected by this, and rides across the agitation with a wingèd melody, delivered expressively and with sovereign poise.

---

[1] In *Carl Nielsen: Symphonist* (New York: Taplinger, 1979) Robert Simpson points out that Aage Oxenvad was a darker and generally more complicated character than Holger Gilbert-Jespersen, for whom Nielsen wrote his Flute Concerto.

The slow movement returns briefly to its opening and then, by way of another short cadenza, finds its way into the third movement, Allegro non troppo. In character this is something between a scherzo and a fairly relaxed intermezzo. The clarinet becomes very engaged in a testy exchange with the snare drum, and it is not entirely easy for the orchestra to make itself heard in a reminder that this is supposed to be a concerto. The movement resumes, with the snare drum, though *pianissimo*, insistently present. For a moment it even drives the strings to take up percussion in a passage where rapidly re-peated loud harmonics sound like a demented glockenspiel.

Yet another cadenza and another return to a very slow tempo form the bridge into the finale, which is based on a tune of amusing faux-naïveté. Interruptions are still the order of the day, the strangest of them being a tiny episode—blink and you've missed it—in a Spanish dance hall. After one more touch of Adagio comes the coda. The basses settle on F while the tempo—not the beat, but the tempo as measured in the spacing of events—becomes slower and slower. Strings, *pianissimo* and softer, play a series of calming chords; the bass descends from F to a lower F by way of notes that discreetly remind us there might—just might—still be a possibility of distur-bance; the clarinet holds a long F; there is one more tap on the snare drum; and we are done, tiptoeing to the door and turning out the light after a spooky bedtime story.

## Concerto for Flute and Orchestra, FS 119

*Allegro moderato*
*Allegretto—Adagio ma non troppo—Allegretto—Tempo di marcia*

Nielsen wrote his Flute Concerto in 1926 for Holger Gilbert-Jespersen, who, twenty days after the completion of the score, gave the first performance on 21 October that year, in Paris at an all-Nielsen concert conducted by the composer's son-in-law, Emil Telmányi. Right afterwards, Nielsen revised the ending and, again with Gilbert-Jespersen, introduced this final version in Oslo on 9 November 1926.

**Solo flute, two oboes, two clarinets, two bassoons, two horns, bass trombone, timpani, and strings.**

The flutist Timothy Day once remarked in an interview that the great music for his instrument was not to be found in the concertos or other solo repertory but in the orchestral literature. He was, by and large, quite right. But there are a few exceptions, and the Nielsen Flute Concerto is not merely the finest example of the genre but in every way a marvelously winning, altogether personal piece.

In 1922 Nielsen wrote a Wind Quintet, the finest work in that problematic genre, for the Danish Wind Quintet. Their playing of it was everything he could have hoped for and more, and he decided to give each of the players, all them friends of his, a present of a solo concerto. But this was the time Nielsen's health took a dramatic turn for the worse. When the vital juices began to flow again, the composition of his Symphony No. 6 was his most urgent concern; only after that was achieved, in December 1925, did he feel free to turn his attention to the concerto project. He began with this Flute Concerto, but as things turned out, he was able to compose only one more of the projected pieces, the one for clarinet.

A musician hearing only the energetic sixteenth-notes for high strings and woodwinds with which the Flute Concerto begins would say that we are in D minor, although the C-naturals (instead of C-sharps) give the music a certain modal tinge. But the bass note that underpins this passage so firmly, so definitely, is an E-flat! In other words, the questions of where we are harmonically and where we mean to be are raised immediately. In this dissonant conflict the flute sides with D, even though the first music that sounds like a theme rather than an introductory flourish is in fact in E-flat minor.

Not that the music stays there; rather, Nielsen touches down at many places and in rapid succession. One stop of which he makes a great deal is E major, remote indeed from the magnetic fields of either D or E-flat, but given special prominence at the dynamic climax of the development and also as the site of a melody whose breadth and tranquillity are not just especially lovely but strikingly different from the surrounding music. The movement eventually settles in G-flat major, which is handily rationalized as the relative major of E-flat minor, but which in this context produces an effect that is anything other than settled or "at home." Clearly the end of the first movement is no more than a break in mid-business. With this harmonic restlessness goes a corresponding inclination to shift tempo and character often and sometimes abruptly. This is a movement full of cadenzas and conversations, the clarinet (and to a lesser extent the bass trombone) showing a particular tendency to push themselves into prominence.

Like the first movement, the second begins in two places, as it were, the gruffly spluttering opening by the orchestral strings (*fortissimo* but muted) being "corrected" by the *grazioso* approach of the solo flute. Again Nielsen presents us with mercurial changes of mood and of course an enormous harmonic range. The instrument most prone to offer to turn this into a double concerto is the bass trombone: this Great Trombone Joke had a special private significance in that Gilbert-Jespersen was a French-trained flutist of exceptional delicacy of tone and manner. And, in a nicely ironic touch, it is the coarsely self-centered, unnoticing trombone who finds in the harmonic maze the secret door to where the quest leads, that E major that was so magically illuminated in the first movement, and it is there that this Concerto finds its sweetly whimsical conclusion.

# George Perle

George Perle was born in Bayonne, New Jersey, on 6 May 1915 and lives in New York City and Richmond, Massachusetts.

## Concerto No. 1 for Piano and Orchestra

*Allegro*
*Scherzo*
*Adagio*
*Allegro*

Through the generosity of Mrs. Paul L. Wattis, this Concerto was commissioned for Richard Goode by the San Francisco Symphony. The commission was to honor Herbert Blomstedt, then the orchestra's music director. Perle completed the composition on 20 May 1990 and finished the orchestration that fall. The first performance was given on 24 January 1991 by Richard Goode with David Zinman conducting the San Francisco Symphony.

Solo piano, four flutes (fourth doubling piccolo), three oboes and English horn, four clarinets (fourth doubling bass clarinet), four bassoons (fourth doubling contrabassoon), four horns, four trumpets (with straight mutes, Harmon mutes, stem removed, cup mute, and Whispa mute), three trombones and bass trombones (with straight and cup mutes), tuba, harp, xylophone, marimba, tam-tam, large and small triangles, crash cymbals, suspended cymbal, snare drum, celesta, chimes, and strings. This could be one for *The Guinness Book of Records*, at least I don't know of another piano concerto with such a large orchestra.

In one of his 1989 lectures as Ernest Bloch Professor of Music at the University of California at Berkeley—these have been published under the title *The Listening Composer*—George Perle told the story of getting a phone call in 1985 from a television producer who asked him to give a talk to commemorate the 100th anniversary of the birth of Alban Berg. Perle did not say this in his lecture, but he was the obvious choice insofar as he is, no contest, the leading Berg scholar in the United States, perhaps in the world. He had, however, to decline the invitation because of a concert of his own music that same night. "But," said the astonished voice at the other end of the telephone, "you're not the same George Perle who composes, are you?"

He is, and with his multiple careers as composer, theorist, musicologist, and teacher, he has long been one of America's most eminent and versatile musical citizens. Berg's music, and particularly the complicated issues surrounding the third act of *Lulu*, not quite complete when Berg died and subjected to a performance ban by his widow, became a cause for Perle. For years, beginning in the 1960s and continuing into the early 1980s, he devoted enormous amounts of time and energy to the campaign for the release of Act 3 of *Lulu* and to the writing not only of many articles but also of his two-volume study, *The Operas of Alban Berg*.

For years, then, he was more in view as a writer of words than as a writer of notes. But with the two books on *Wozzeck* and *Lulu* put safely to bed and published by the University of California Press in 1980 and 1984, George Perle once again became the George Perle who composes, full time. As he approached and then entered his seventies, he was also able to retire from full-time university work—he had been at the University of Louisville, the University of California at Davis, and Queens College in New York—and he found himself more than ever in demand as a composer, receiving many commissions and being awarded handsome prizes, including a Pulitzer for one of his wind quintets, as well as a MacArthur Foundation grant, which is an intellectual's or artist's equivalent of going platinum. This did not displease him, and as for the composing itself, it went, as Beethoven remarked of one of his late string quartets, with not less imagination than before.

In the 1930s Perle was one of the first American musicians to be drawn to the music of Schoenberg, Webern, and Berg. Not only did Perle make practical and historical findings of prime importance—besides doing the research that led to the completion of a performance edition of Act 3 of *Lulu*, he discovered the secret scenario behind Berg's *Lyric Suite* (see the essay on Berg's Violin Concerto)—but he also, led by this interest of his, made significant original developments in music theory, notably the concept of what he has called "twelve-tone tonality," which is also the title of the book in which he expounds his idea. In a profile of Perle he wrote for the February 1991 program book of the San Francisco Symphony, Laurence Rothe describes this as

> a still-evolving system of compositional rules and guidelines Perle has *deduced* over the years: by writing music, certainly; but also by analyzing the work of Schoenberg, Berg, Webern, Bartók, Stravinsky, Scriabin, Debussy: all in an attempt to give composers today the kinds of tools available to the great tonal composers—Bach, Mozart, Haydn, Beethoven, Schubert, Brahms—an attempt to embrace the history of the art in an all-encompassing way and to compose a music that does not break with, but rather continues the great tradition of Western music.

The idea of *deducing*, which Rothe is careful to emphasize in his essay, is characteristic of Perle's approach to music. Start from the music! When Perle was a small boy living in Chicago, an older cousin, Esther, newly arrived from Russia, came to live with the family. George's father, a housepainter, had saved enough money to buy a piano for Esther to practice on. Nearly seventy years later, Perle recalled the experience of hearing her play the F-minor Étude from Chopin's *Trois Nouvelles Études* as "so intense, so startling, as to induce a traumatic change of consciousness." That afternoon George Perle the composer was born. He told the story to Rothe: "Nobody told me what composition was. I just knew that was my connection with music, not sitting there playing the piano. I didn't know where this music came from. Yet when I heard that first piece I identified with the *source* of the music, not with my cousin's playing."

To begin with, he did not know what "source," a concept he had of course not formulated, meant. But puzzling over the question, puzzling over the relationship between Chopin, Cousin Esther, and himself as listener, was the beginning of a lifelong quest for *conscious* understanding. Speaking to Rothe, he recalled getting a rave review from a critic who famously hated Schoenberg and other twelve-tone music but who praised Perle for having composed a good piece despite having done it according to some sort of system. "Why didn't he consider the possibility that the music makes sense *because* of what I'm doing? Which is the case. I have a language that permits progressions, and cadences, and keys. I can think in a systematic way about music. That's what you can do when you have a language—as with Mozart, Brahms, Palestrina, Schubert."

Perle served the San Francisco Symphony as composer-in-residence from 1989 to 1991; the Piano Concerto No. 1, however, is a work that the orchestra had commissioned before that appointment. I was the person who, in 1988, had the privilege and pleasure to make the first exploratory telephone call to Perle about this project, and I still remember his instant excitement at the prospect. He loved writing for piano, he said, and was also happy at the thought of composing his first full-scale concerto. He had already written a Concertino for Piano, Winds, and Timpani (1979) and a Serenade for Piano and Chamber Orchestra (1983); in addition he had composed some fresh and winning works for solo piano, including two books of brilliant Études (1973–1976 and 1984) and a warmly ruminative Ballade (1981). The Piano Concerto No. 1 was the culmination of Perle's imaginative delight with the piano—for the moment. It was followed in 1992 by his Piano Concerto No. 2, written for and premiered by Michael Boriskin.

In the Concerto No. 1, Perle has given us a four-movement work, one that feels large yet compact at the same time. (The playing time is about that of a Mozart concerto.) It steps out with pizzicato strings at a brisk tempo. The first pitches you hear outline a diminished seventh chord (F-sharp/A/C/E-flat), and this same idea, though patterned differently, is also the one that sets Perle's next work, the Sinfonietta II (1990), in motion. In both works this ascent is answered by a corresponding descent that introduces new colors and a new rhythmic picture. The continuations from this point, both immediately and long-range, are quite different in the two works, but clearly the Haydnesque or Bachian economy of this procedure pleased Perle.[1]

In the Piano Concerto, the descent I mentioned is precipitate, with hurrying clarinets and a landing on a strongly accented wind chord. When the violas and cellos pick up that chord, the piano makes its first entrance in a scurry of sparkling sixteenth-notes. This leads to an expanded version of this orchestra-solo dialogue, and that expansion conveys a sense of the scale, the breadth of this first movement, which will in fact turn out to constitute nearly half the concerto. Perle has a strong Classical leaning, something that is particularly obvious in his two Sinfoniettas, both of which are avowed *hommages* to the eighteenth century, but one senses his taste for transparency, for lightness and air everywhere in his later music. Even if the idea of a four-movement concerto first brings Brahms to mind, this throwing of the center of gravity forward, with a big first movement and shorter movements to follow, is very Classical indeed.

[1]Schoenberg wrote that one of the things he learned from Bach was "the art of producing everything from one thing." If you listen to the aria "Ach, bleibe doch" in the Ascension cantata *Lobet Gott in seinen Reichen*, BWV 11, and then to the Agnus Dei in the B-minor Mass, you can hear how Bach used the same beginning to start two entirely different pieces.

The first piano entrance, though it sounds brilliant, is not especially difficult. But just wait. Apart from several oases of writing for the two hands in unison, the technical demands in the concerto become more and more exacting, especially in the matter of accurate marksmanship at high velocity, combined always with some restraint, even delicacy. Perle—and this is another Classicism—is not a loud composer: *fortissimo* is rare—the more telling therefore when it does occur—and the plea for *delicato* occurs more than once.

The evolution of the piano writing is also the physical correlative of the evolution of the compositional thought, which also grows more complex as the movement unfolds and fresh ideas, or fresh variants of familiar ones, are introduced. A special feature of this movement is the way Perle articulates events by setting them in distinct tempos. There is always, however, a clear relationship between one tempo and the next, some common unit of pulse binding them together.

Silences are another manifestation of Perle's liking for air and breathing space, and a major silence precedes the appearance of a new and strikingly different theme. Clarinets (and what a pleasure to have four of them for this spot) and muted strings set up a softly rocking motion, charming in its rhythmic unpredictability as well as in the flavor of its seductive harmonies. Over this the piano begins a quiet but impassioned declamation, speech almost from the world of Falla's *Nights in the Gardens of Spain*. Once again, the two hands are in octaves, a sonority that is a characteristic feature of the Concerto.

This passage builds magnificently, but eventually leads back to quiet and to the first rat-tat of sixteenths we heard the piano play. Everything returns in due course, but nothing returns literally: all is development, variation, invention, play. The first word is also the last. When the movement began, the English horn caught the rising string pizzicatos at the top, its sustained F-sharp making a thin but firm bridge of sound between ascent and descent. Now, at the end, the same thing starts to happen, only there is no descent. More precisely, there is just the hint of one. The English horn plays its long F-sharp alone, then—still alone—it flips down to E-flat for just a second. The movement is over.

Next comes the "extra" movement, a scherzo—humorous, dancelike, simple in design, rich in detail, very short.

The marvelous Adagio begins with a long piano solo, another impassioned declamation and intensely rhetorical, though held for the most part to a quiet dynamic level. This is the most powerfully expressive music in the concerto. When the orchestra enters, it does so in the form of a woodwind quartet (English horn, two clarinets, and bass clarinet) that echoes—and inevitably varies—the piano's phrases. The orchestral writing throughout this movement is exceptionally beautiful, and it is almost entirely conceived as a series of chamber ensembles—the woodwind quartet already mentioned, a sextet of bassoons and horns, a string quartet, a clarinet quartet, a bassoon quartet, a flute quartet. These ensembles engage in various sorts of conversations with the piano. It is here that we clearly understand Perle's purpose in using so large an orchestra, not to make noise, but to allow for the possibility of rich chords in a single color.[2] The piano has the pensive last word.

The finale is brilliant, and here, too, Perle plays ingeniously and fascinatingly with differentiated but related speeds. For example, the five beats of the third and fourth measures take exactly the same amount of time as the six beats of the first and second measures. As is often his way, Perle knits the work together by reminding us of its beginnings, its sources, as he approaches the end. As for that end, it is firecrackers going off, explosive and delightful.

[2]This is also the reason for the extravagantly large orchestra in the original versions of two early-twentieth-century classics, Schoenberg's *Five Pieces*, Opus 16, and Webern's *Six Pieces*, Opus 6. The real—and sad—loss in the revised and unquestionably more "affordable" version is that of those rich one-color combinations.

# Sergei Prokofiev

Sergei Sergeievich Prokofiev was born in Sontsovka (now Krasnoye), Government of Ekaterinoslav (Dniepropetrovsk) in Ukraine. The date, according to his birth certificate, was 27 April 1891, although he himself always gave it as 23 April. He died in Nikolina Gora near Moscow on 5 March 1953, not quite an hour before Stalin.

Prokofiev was a much-cosseted boy who was raised as an only child because his two sisters had died before he was born. He began composing at five, and before he was out of his teens he had written four operas, two symphonies, and a stack of piano music. His mother, a cultivated player, was his first piano teacher, and in 1902 the composer Reinhold Glière was brought into the household as musical tutor to the eleven-year-old Sergei Sergeievich.

At thirteen Prokofiev was admitted to the Saint Petersburg Conservatory. He gave Rimsky-Korsakov and Liadov a hard time in their classes and did poorly in them. Happily, he found friends to keep his musical spirits alive, most significantly two fellow students—the composer Nikolai Miaskovsky and the critic Boris Asafiev—and two teachers, the pianist Anna Esipova, who after a bloody battle of wills instilled discipline into the boy and was crucially responsible for turning him into a remarkable pianist, and the composer and conductor Nikolai Tcherepnin, who of all the people at the Conservatory was most informed about and in sympathy with the newest musical developments. Prokofiev's exit from the conservatory in 1914 was grand: he won the Rubinstein Prize, the highest honor available to a pianist, for the performance of his own Concerto No. 1, completed and already performed in Moscow two years before. All the members of the jury, headed by Alexander Glazunov, the director, received copies of the score specially printed and bound for the occasion.

Prokofiev left Russia in the aftermath of the Revolution. He first came to America, then tried living in the Bavarian village of Ettal, and finally, in the early fall of 1923, settled in Paris. His return to his homeland was a slow process, beginning with a visit in 1927 and concluding when he and his family settled in Moscow in 1936. The success particularly of *Romeo and Juliet* and the Fifth Symphony made him a hero in his old/new country, but it did not protect him from brutal bullying at the hands of the Central Committee of the Soviet Party and Commissar Andrei Zhdanov in the last years of his life. He died a discouraged and broken man, worn out by several years of heart troubles, and just too soon to be able to rejoice in the news of Joseph Stalin's death.

## Concerto No. 2 in G minor for Piano and Orchestra, Opus 16

*Andantino—Allegretto—Andantino*
*Scherzo: Vivace*
*Intermezzo: Allegro moderato*
*Finale: Allegro tempestoso*

Prokofiev began the Piano Concerto No. 2 in the winter of 1912–1913, completing it in April 1913, while still a student at the Saint Petersburg Conservatory. With A. P. Aslanov conducting, he introduced it on 5 September 1913 at the Vauxhall at Pavlovsk, the imperial park outside the Russian capital. This version was lost in a fire during the 1917 Revolution. Prokofiev reconstructed the work from his sketches and reintroduced it on 8 May 1924 in Paris, Serge Koussevitzky conducting. Prokofiev dedicated the score *in memoriam* Max Schmidthof, a fellow-student of his at the Saint Petersburg Conservatory who committed suicide in April 1913. He also dedicated his Second and Fourth piano sonatas to his friend's memory.

**Solo piano, two flutes, two oboes, two clarinets, two bassoons, four horns, two trumpets, three trombones, bass tuba, timpani, snare drum, tenor drum, bass drum, cymbals, and strings.**

In its original form, one in which it scandalized rather more people than it delighted, this Concerto is the work of a young man just moving into his twenties. We have no way of knowing how close the surviving version comes to what Prokofiev played at Pavlovsk for the Russian Musical Society and in Rome, where one critic—in 1915!—expressed disappointment that the composer was "not a new Stravinsky, tart and interesting." Prokofiev himself certainly wished it understood that in creating the 1924 version he had taken advantage of everything he had learned in a rich and eventful decade: "It was so completely rewritten," he wrote to friends in Moscow, "that it might almost be considered No. 4," the famous No. 3 having appeared in 1921. A few who remembered the early performances suggested that Prokofiev exaggerated, but the matter is past settling.

Only a couple of months separate Prokofiev's completion of his First Piano Concerto and the beginning of the Second, but it sounds like a long journey from those orotund D-flat-major chords that open the First to the assorted pricklinesses of its successor. Prokofiev definitely meant to make the new Concerto quite different: "The charges of surface brilliance and a certain 'soccer' quality in the First led me to strive for greater depth of content in the Second." That he achieved his aim—certainly attaining far greater variety and range—is not in doubt, but he did not do it by giving up that "certain 'soccer' quality": Prokofiev's Second is one of the most challenging of all concertos to the pianist-as-athlete.

The premiere at Pavlovsk, the critic Viacheslav Karatigin reported, "left listeners frozen with fright, hair standing on end. . . . The public hissed. This means nothing. Ten years from now it will atone for last night's catcalls by unanimously applauding a new composer with a European reputation." Karatigin's colleagues were not so sympathetic, and Prokofiev's biographer Israel Nestiev quotes their expressions of outrage: "a Babel of insane sounds heaped upon one another without rhyme or reason" (Yuri Kurdiumov in *Peterburgsky Listok*), "a cacophony of sounds that has nothing in common with civilized music. . . . One might think [the cadenzas] were created by capriciously emptying an inkwell on the page" (N. Bernstein in *Peterburgskaya Gazeta*), and "Prokofiev has outdone Scriabin, the 'man of reason and illumination' " (an anonymous writer in *Novoye Vremya*).

The *Petersburgskaya Gazeta* also ran an account signed "Non-Critic":

> The debut of the piano cubist and futurist has excited universal interest. On the train to Pavlovsk one heard on all sides, "Prokofiev, Prokofiev, Prokofiev." . . . On the platform appears a youth with the face of a Peterschule student.[1] He seats himself at the piano and begins to strike the keyboard with a sharp, dry touch. He seems either to be dusting or testing the keys. The audience is bewildered. Some are indignant. One couple stands up and runs toward the exit. "Such music is enough to drive you crazy!" "What is he doing? Making

---

[1]The Peterschule was the most fashionable boys' school in Saint Petersburg.

fun of us?" . . . The most daring members of the audience hiss. Here and there seats become empty. Finally the young artist ends his concerto with a mercilessly discordant combination of brasses. The audience is scandalized. Most of them hiss. Prokofiev bows defiantly and plays an encore. . . . On all sides there are exclamations: "To the devil with all this futurist music! We came here to enjoy ourselves. The cats at home can make better music than this!"[2]

The Concerto did not much please its Paris audience in 1924 either. (Meanwhile, one wonders, where had the events of 1917 dispersed the 1913 audience?) Later, Prokofiev noted wryly that his practicing had maddened his neighbor, who had taken to building bookshelves so that the piano would come as a relief after the hammering. The new Prokofiev baby also got more than its normal quota of hours in the park during this time. Prokofiev hardly ever played the Second Concerto again and on his international tours made his fortune with the brilliant but less taxing Third. In the Soviet Union Maria Yudina scored an enormous success in 1938 with the by-then totally unfamiliar Second, but even there it did not take and hold a firm place in the repertory until after the war. Internationally it was rediscovered in the late sixties and early seventies by Vladimir Ashkenazy and Malcolm Frager, after which it began to make its way at least to the edge of the standard repertory.

Prokofiev begins gently with two measures of orchestral stage-setting, leading to two more measures of piano vamp until the appearance of the first theme, a melody of surprising extensions. Trying to put this melody together with Non-Critic's bit in the *Peterburgskaya Gazeta* about dusting the keys, we wonder whether the beginning was really so different in the 1913 version, whether the reporter was put off by Prokofiev's *sec* tone and manner (documented on his enchanting recording of the Third Concerto, the *Visions fugitives*, and some other solo pieces), or whether we have simply run into one more instance of inaccurate writing about music. Prokofiev wants a certain "speaking" quality in the performance at this point, for he has marked the theme *narrante*. A contrasting theme introduces an element of caprice and a new repertory of colors. Most of the development and even much of the recapitulation take the form of a huge cadenza, maybe the hugest in any concerto. (The instruction to the pianist at the climax is *colossale*.) The orchestral continuation is likewise larger than life, but then a modest restatement of the opening melody brings the movement to a quiet close.

The scherzo is a tour de force of perpetual motion, of non-stop sixteenth-notes for the soloist. "Intermezzo," at least in the piano repertory, tends to suggest a rather contained sort of music, but this one is fierce: Sviatoslav Richter said that to him it evoked "a dragon devouring its young." There is something here of the grinding harshness of the *Scythian* Suite of 1915, and

[2]Harlow Robinson, *Sergei Prokofiev* (New York: Viking, 1987).

it is a model for those sinister marches that rage their way through the pages of Shostakovich. Prokofiev's inventiveness in piano figuration is remarkable.

In a sense, the second and third movements are both intermezzi in that they are on a far smaller scale than the first movement and the finale. The last movement reverts to the expansive manner of the first and also has a cadenza as its focal point. The entry into this cadenza is one of Prokofiev's wittiest strokes in the work. This movement brings together the Scythian wildness of the Intermezzo and the touching, rather Mussorgskian narrative lyricism of the first movement's Andantino. That the harmonic boldnesses of the last pages—simultaneous G-minor and A-major triads, or A-flat combined with D minor or E minor—left some of the vacationers at Pavlovsk with their hair standing on end, one need not doubt.

## Concerto No. 3 in C major for Piano and Orchestra, Opus 26

> *Andante—Allegro*
> *Theme (Andantino) with Variations*
> *Allegro ma non troppo*

The theme of this Concerto's second movement was the first part to be composed, in 1913. Prokofiev spent some time on this score in the winter of 1916–1917, but it was not until the summer of 1921 that he completed it. He introduced the work on 16 December 1921 with Frederick Stock conducting the Chicago Symphony.

**Solo piano, two flutes (second doubling piccolo), two oboes, two clarinets, two bassoons, four horns, two trumpets, three trombones, timpani, bass drum, castanets, tambourine, cymbals, and strings.**

Prospects in Russia did not look promising to Prokofiev as he surveyed what happened there in the months following the October Revolution. He had formed a friendship with the conductor Serge Koussevitzky, who would become as devoted and effective an advocate in western Europe and America as he already was in Russia, and who was also his first publisher. He persuaded Koussevitzky to give him a substantial advance, raised more money through concerts (he conducted the premiere of the *Classical* Symphony at one of these), and, having talked an official into issuing a passport with no expiration date, he took off for America in March 1918. He did it by heading east, via the Trans-Siberian Railway to Vladivostok, then by ship to Tokyo, where he gave some concerts, and finally across the Pacific.

In San Francisco the immigration authorities took him for a Bolshevik spy and did not treat him kindly, and so, with few dollars but carrying a hefty package of scores, he got on a train to New York as soon as he could. There he gave a piano recital that won him a reputation as a sort of musical *fauve*, recorded a few piano rolls, and whiled away many hours at the Russian Chess Club.

At a concert in Petrograd, Prokofiev had met Cyrus McCormick, president of the International Harvester Company (his father had invented the first mechanical reaper). Prokofiev liked machines; McCormick, who liked modern music, had given the young composer his card, and, with expansive American bonhomie, had said, "Look me up if you're ever in Chicago." On that basis, Prokofiev took off for the midwest.

There things began to look up: Frederick Stock programmed the *Scythian Suite* with the Chicago Symphony, and Cleofonte Campanini, the Chicago Opera's music director, undertook to produce *The Love for Three Oranges*, whose march would years later become the theme music for *The FBI in Peace and War*. Campanini's death in 1919 delayed the production of the opera, but within a two-week period in December 1921 Prokofiev took bows both as conductor of *The Love for Three Oranges* and as the brilliant pianist in his new Concerto.

He was skeptical about the genuineness of Chicago's enthusiasm, however. It was chauvinism, he figured: "I was the composer whose opera we are going to produce."[3] He was confirmed in his skepticism when, not many weeks later, New York, with no chauvinistic or possessive interest in him, detested both works: "It was as though a pack of dogs had broken loose and were tearing my trousers to shreds." Prokofiev headed back to Europe. Yet the Third Concerto became his own favored calling card in his guest appearances in Europe and America, and it has brought roaring acclaim to countless pianists since. In June 1932 Prokofiev recorded the Concerto with Piero Coppola and the London Symphony: next to his, most other performances sound lazy.

The concerto begins with music Prokofiev invented in his frustrated attempt to get it done in 1916: a melody, deeply Russian, for a single clarinet. Violins continue it. Almost immediately, the tempo shifts to something much faster, with scrubbing sixteenths for the strings, and leading to a seemingly new theme that turns out in fact to be a variant of the first clarinet melody. Piano

[3]Produce at a cost of $250,000, he might have added. The 1921–1922 Chicago Opera season—the new director was Mary Garden, Debussy's first Mélisande—ended with a deficit of $1 million. These were 1921 gold-standard dollars: such sums were unheard of in the music world of that time.

and orchestra give it a vigorous workout, after which the piano paves the way to another idea, half lyric, half mocking. The oboe presents this, with pizzicato accompaniment, this too being carried forward in all sorts of ways. In the recapitulation, the original clarinet melody is transformed into something quite grand, after which the remainder of the movement is an exciting indulgence in keyboard virtuosity.

Flute and clarinet begin the second movement, a stalking march whose tune Prokofiev had jotted down in 1913. This is followed by five variations. The first, set in motion by a piano glissando and a single, ironic pop at the bottom of the keyboard, is a pseudo-sentimental gloss on the theme. The second and third variations move at a faster tempo, the former with muted brass and rushing keyboard figurations, the latter a chord study that reminds me of the big cadenza in Rachmaninoff's Concerto No. 3. Variation 4, a melancholic contemplation of the theme, returns to the original Andantino tempo. The final variation, back in a faster tempo (Allegro giusto), begins in a *scherzando* mode, then becomes almost violently energetic. Prokofiev ends the movement with a beautiful coda in which the orchestra plays the theme while the piano adds some strangely distanced chatter. And that he tops with an enigmatic little cadence.

Bassoons begin the finale, another Prokofiev stalking theme, angular, humorous. But as in the first movement, this mood is not with us long, and both piano and orchestra embark on a new, breathlessly whirling music. The dominant idea, however, turns out to be an expansive, singing theme, as-signed to oboe and clarinet. The piano objects that this does not suit the Concerto's prevalent mood, and the final impression is one of caustic humor (Prokofiev's own phrase) and fiery virtuosity.

## Concerto No. 1 in D major for Violin and Orchestra, Opus 19

> *Andantino*
> *Scherzo vivacissimo*
> *Moderato*

Prokofiev began a concertino for violin in 1915 but soon abandoned the project in order to concentrate on his Dostoyevsky opera *The Gambler*, returning to what became his Violin Concerto No. 1 in the summer of 1917. The first performance was given on 18 October 1923 at one of the Concerts Koussevitzky in Paris, with Marcel Darrieux, the concertmaster of Koussevitzky's orchestra, as soloist. Leading the first performance of his own Octet for Winds, Stravinsky made his debut as conductor on the same program.

The first performance of Prokofiev's Concerto in the Soviet Union is worth mentioning, for it was given just three days after the Paris premiere by two extraordinary nineteen-year-olds, Nathan Milstein and Vladimir Horowitz, the latter playing the orchestra part on the piano. ("I feel that if you have a great pianist like Horowitz playing with you, you don't need an orchestra!" wrote Milstein in his memoirs, *From Russia to the West*.) Milstein and Horowitz introduced Karol Szymanowski's Concerto No. 1 in the Soviet Union on the same occasion.

**Solo violin, two flutes (second doubling piccolo), two oboes, two clarinets, two bassoons, four horns, two trumpets, tuba, timpani, tambourine, military drum, harp, and strings.**

Nineteen-seventeen cannot have been an easy year for a Russian composer to concentrate on his work. A series of strikes, anti-war marches, and the refusal of soldiers to fire on the demonstrators led, step by step, to revolution and the abdication of the tsar; Lenin arrived at Petrograd's Finland Station after ten years of exile; the Black Sea fleet mutinied; the big cities experienced terrible food shortages; the Kerensky government was overthrown in the October Revolution (which actually took place on 7 November according to the Western calendar) and Lenin became Chairman of the Council of People's Commissars; and an armistice with Germany was signed at Brest-Litovsk. Nonetheless, 1917 was Prokofiev's most richly productive year, in which he composed the Violin Concerto No. 1, the *Classical* Symphony, the Third and Fourth Piano Sonatas, and the *Visions fugitives* for piano; began the ambitious and in many ways remarkable cantata on Chaldean texts, *Seven, They Are Seven*; and worked on his Piano Concerto No. 3.

The belated premiere of the Violin Concerto No. 1 in Paris was not a great success. First of all, it had been difficult to find a soloist. Back in 1917 the plan had been for the superb Polish violinist Pawel Kochański, then teaching in Petrograd, to give the premiere, but by 1923 he and Prokofiev had lost touch. Milstein was still in Russia. Huberman refused even to look at the score. Darrieux, Koussevitzky's Paris concertmaster, was a solid musician and an able violinist, but he lacked the spark to make a convincing case for the piece. Its real career began the following year, when Joseph Szigeti played it in Prague with Fritz Reiner; that incomparable Hungarian violinist subsequently carried it all over Europe and America, was the first to play it with orchestra in the Soviet Union, and was politely persistent with English Columbia executives until they allowed him to make the first recording of it, with Sir Thomas Beecham in 1935.

But even beyond whatever hindrance to acceptance the Darrieux-

Koussevitzky performance might have created, the work itself was not likely to please *tout Paris* just then. Audiences there, and particularly those for the Concerts Koussevitzky, wanted their modern music to carry a certain shock value. (The failure ten years earlier of *Le Sacre du printemps* is a famous moment in Parisian musical history, but that was a *dance* failure, not a *music* failure; the first concert performance of *Le Sacre* under Monteux was a huge success a few months later.) Paris welcomed the Prokofiev of the spiky *Buffoon* and the savage *Scythian* Suite (the latter, let's face it, quite a successful go at capitalizing on the *Sacre* sensation); the Violin Concerto was simply too Romantic. The composer Georges Auric brought out the most wounding adjective in his vocabulary: Mendelssohnian. Ironically and not altogether surprisingly, Prokofiev had the opposite experience when he returned to Russia for the first time: they loved the Violin Concerto, but *The Buffoon* and the *Scythian* Suite did not please.

Prokofiev remarks that his "lyric line"—and he cites the opening of the First Violin Concerto as an instance—was "not noticed until late. For a long time I was given no credit for any lyric gift whatever, and for want of encouragement it developed slowly. But as time went on I gave more and more attention to this aspect of my work."[4]

What the violin plays in the first moments of this concerto is ravishing lyric invention indeed, rhythmically afloat, unpredictable in its unfolding. *Sognando*—dreaming—is the direction in the violin part. The melody is also beautifully accompanied by a soft aureole of string sound; a few woodwinds and the second violins shyly offer to add a little counterpoint. Prokofiev in the 1930s and beyond was no less likely to find such a melody; the difference is that by then he was no longer inclined to make such delicate settings for his gems.

More and more the offers of counterpoint are taken up, more and more the action moves into the orchestra while the violin accompanies and comments. Then, over a stubborn cello figure, comes a new theme which is different in every respect: key (C rather than D), meter (4/4 instead of 6/8), and atmosphere. Now the instruction to the violinist is *narrante*. David Oistrakh, who when he first played the Concerto for Prokofiev as a boy in Odessa was publicly shamed by being told he was doing it all wrong but later became one of the composer's favorite interpreters of it, recounted that Prokofiev had said of this section, "Play it as though you're trying to convince someone of something." The music gathers momentum and the solo part becomes ever more virtuosic. A brief passage for the violin alone opens the way for shimmering tremolandos like those with which the movement began, and what one might call this textural recapitulation introduces at last the return of the

[4]Robinson, op. cit.

wonderful first melody, a little slower this time, played by the flute, with harp and solo violin adding delectable filigree. The last word is the flute's, a quiet run of sixty-fourth-notes curling upward like a twist of scented smoke.

Szigeti writes in his memoirs, *With Strings Attached*, that at first sight this concerto fascinated him "by its mixture of fairy-tale naïveté and daring savagery in lay-out and texture." We have experienced that juxtaposition within the first movement; now it is extended in that the second movement, a scherzo marked *vivacissimo*, represents the "savage" element as against the generally more lyrical first and third movements. The music, full of contrast, is by turns amusing, naughty, for a while even malevolent, athletic, and always violinistically ingenious and brilliant. It seems to be over in a moment.

Against a tick-tock of clarinet and strings, the bassoon proposes the first melody of the finale and does it rather in the manner of "As I was saying . . .". The violin extends, varies, adds conversational remarks. In the second theme, too, the solo violin is often commentator more than protagonist. Most of the music is generously lyrical and the orchestral textures become ever more elaborate. As the pace becomes calmer, the melody that opened the first movement returns. Now it belongs both to the soloist and to the orchestra's first violins, the soloist playing it an octave higher and as a chain of trills. The glowing orchestral texture is studded with fragments of material from the third movement. The close is dreamy and at peace. As at the close of the first movement, the flute is the last character to slip from the stage.

## Concerto No. 2 in G minor for Violin and Orchestra, Opus 63

*Allegro moderato*
*Andante assai—Più animato—Tempo I—Allegretto—Tempo I*
*Allegro ben marcato*

Prokofiev composed this Concerto in 1935 for the French violinist Robert Soëtens; at the same time he was working on his ballet score *Romeo and Juliet*. The Violin Concerto No. 2 was Prokofiev's last western European commission, and he noted that "the principal theme of the first movement was written in Paris, the first theme of the second movement in Voronezh, the orchestration completed in Baku, while the first performance was given in

Madrid." Soëtens was the soloist, Enrique Fernández Arbós conducted, and the date was 1 December 1935.[5]

**Solo violin, two flutes, two oboes, two clarinets, two bassoons, two horns, two trumpets, castanets, triangle, snare drum, cymbals, bass drum, and strings.**

By 1935 Prokofiev was tiring of the restless existence that is reflected in his account of the genesis of this concerto. He would continue to travel as conductor and pianist until the outbreak of war in 1939, but a yearning to settle—and to settle in his homeland—had been growing stronger. He had left Russia in March 1918 and returned for the first time in 1927. His repatriation by degrees continued in 1933, when he gave concerts in Russia and was asked to score the film *Lieutenant Kijé*. His visits became more and more frequent, and in 1936, he, his wife, and their two children took an apartment in Moscow. One of his first projects was a modest work for a children's theater there: he called it *Peter and the Wolf*.

Assessment of Prokofiev was long muddied by politics. Soviet critics maintained that he had lost himself during his long sojourn in the West and that he found what he had lost only when he came home. Conversely, Western writers tended to deplore Prokofiev's decision to go back, many implying that the demands of Socialist Realist aesthetics ruined him as an artist.

There are different Prokofievs. People who find their ideal Prokofiev in *Romeo and Juliet* may well find *The Fiery Angel* unpleasantly scratchy. One can also understand that those whose favorite Prokofiev is the Symphony No. 2 might be disappointed in the famous Fifth. More of his sharp-edged and fairly dissonant music, which he himself might, with Stravinskian self-irony, have joined his critics in calling brittle and "heartless," comes from his earlier years; most of his music that is more mellifluous in style, painted with a broader brush, and less inclined to humor comes from his later years in the Soviet Union, when he can even seem downright self-conscious in his concern not to rub the wrong way. There is little of the lushness of *Romeo and Juliet* and *War and Peace* in his early work and almost none of the sharpness of *The Buffoon*, *Visions fugitives*, or *Suggestion diabolique* in his post-1936 music. But the lyric melody that opens the Violin Concerto No. 1 came to Prokofiev in 1915 and was not rejected by him in Paris; the Sixth and Seventh symphonies are not exactly mushy. He himself recognized in his life work four "basic lines,"

---

[5]Prokofiev had met Soëtens in Paris in 1932 when he was one of the players in the premiere of his Sonata for Two Violins. Soëtens's partner on that occasion was Samuel Dushkin, the violinist for whom Stravinsky had recently composed his Violin Concerto.

which he called classical, modern, motoric, and lyrical. All are present all the time, although of course in different balances. The Violin Concerto No. 2 is a work in which these characteristics live together convincingly.

The violinist begins the Concerto alone, playing a slightly elaborated G-minor chord, ruminating on this very simple matter for eight measures. At first, the ear tells us that the music is in 5/4, but after only two times through a five-beat phrase, the line settles into a regular 4/4 meter. (The notation on the page is in 4/4 all along.) At the end of the eighth measure, the violin arrives on F-sharp, the leading tone of G minor, and with the obvious intention of moving on to G. It is at this point that the orchestra enters. It reads the F-sharp not as the leading tone of G minor but as the dominant of B minor, and so it is in this remote new key that it enters, repeating the violin's theme. It is the kind of harmonic shift Prokofiev was fond of all his life. The orchestral sound—just muted violas and basses, two octaves apart—is austere. Prokofiev had first thought of writing a "concert sonata," and although the work became more concertolike than he had at first imagined, the mood is often intimate in a way that suggests he had not entirely let go of his initial idea. It is a versatile theme, and very soon Prokofiev lets us hear it as a canon with the violin trailing the cellos and basses by half a measure.

After further play with fragments of this theme, the music slows slightly for a new melody, one so sweetly lyric that we could almost imagine a page from one of the *Romeo and Juliet* notebooks had found its way into the sketches for the Concerto. Not long before beginning work on this score, Prokofiev, sincerely but also with a canny sense for what was wanted in the Soviet Union, had issued a manifesto proclaiming that "what we need is great music." (No losing points there.) The sine qua non of great music, he went on to declare, was that it be "melodious [and] that the melody must be simple and comprehensible, without being repetitive or trivial. . . . We must seek a new simplicity." This quasi-*Romeo* theme here is like a textbook demonstration of what he meant. This melody and the first idea provide Prokofiev with all the material he requires for this movement: his harmonic energy, at its strongest here, and his inventive violin writing carry him brilliantly to the end.

Prokofiev gently sets the second movement in motion with a simple arpeggiated accompaniment in triplets. (The classic example is the opening of Beethoven's *Moonlight* Sonata.) Prokofiev liked the effect well enough to bring it back, again to beautiful effect, at the start of the Adagio of his Fifth Symphony. Here, as the pizzicato triplets continue, the solo violin enters with one of Prokofiev's most inspired melodies. The slight sense of rhythmic dissonance produced by the way its duplets are set against the orchestra's triplets gives it just the right amount of edge. This and the *Romeo* theme in the first movement are indeed examples of a manner one would not have found in Prokofiev's music before the 1930s. (What would Georges Auric, who condemned the Concerto No. 1 as "Mendelssohnian," have said?) Here Prokofiev gives us another of his characteristic harmonic shifts when, at the conclusion of the violin's first long clause, he lifts the music and puts it down in B major—but *pianissimo, dolcissimo,* and with the strings muted.

At the close of the paragraph, Prokofiev brings in a slightly faster interlude. The accompaniment is stripped down, and we hear a constant succession of rapid triplets, some in repeated notes, some as mordents, and a few arpeggiated. The principal melody returns, now with the accompaniment enriched and culminating in a magically scored passage in which the solo violin scurries like a dragonfly on a pond. A second interlude, also faster than the main tempo, offers an effective combination of highly energized melodic writing both for orchestra and solo with busy figurations. When the first theme returns, the orchestral violins get to play the melody, which is what they must have been yearning to do all this time. The soloist adds a high-flying descant. The very brief coda, with muted cellos, horns, and clarinets reminding us of the melody's opening, is especially lovely.

After these dreams, the finale jolts us into a rude awakening. This is dance music, and I would guess that Prokofiev added the castanets and other suggestions of Spanish flavoring because he knew that the Concerto would first be played in Madrid. Here Prokofiev indulges his appetite for dissonance and fierce accent, so firmly kept in check in the first two movements. The closing pages are marked *tumultuoso.* There is a story that once, when Prokofiev played his Third Piano Concerto with Serge Koussevitzky, he assured his partner, easily thrown by odd rhythms, "Let the Maestro be calm. This is not Stravinsky—there are no complicated meters, no dirty tricks." Conducting the American premiere of the Violin Concerto No. 2 with Heifetz in 1937, Koussevitzky must have sweated.

# Sergei Rachmaninoff

Sergei Vasilievich Rachmaninoff was born at Semyonovo, district of Starorusky, Russia, on 1 April 1873 and died in Beverly Hills, California, on 28 March 1943.

## Piano Concerto No. 2 in C minor, Opus 18

*Moderato*
*Adagio sostenuto*
*Allegro scherzando*

Using some material that goes back to the early 1890s, Rachmaninoff wrote the second and third movements of this Concerto in the fall of 1900 and performed them in Moscow on 15 December that year; his teacher and first cousin, Alexander Siloti, conducted. Rachmaninoff completed the first movement on 4 May 1901 and was soloist at the first complete performance on 9 November that year, again in Moscow and again with Siloti on the podium. The score is dedicated to Dr. Nikolai Dahl.

**Solo piano, two flutes, two oboes, two clarinets, two bassoons, four horns, two trumpets, three trombones, tuba, timpani, bass drum, cymbals, and strings.**

Ten years come between the first version of Rachmaninoff's First Piano Concerto and the completion of his Second—ten difficult but finally fulfilling years. Having come of age with the achievement of the First Concerto and the tone poem *Prince Rostislav* in 1891, Rachmaninoff wrote prolifically until 1895—the two *Trios élégiaques*, the opera *Aleko*, the tone poem *The Rock*, the Suite No. 1 for Two Pianos, several sets of songs, that C-sharp-minor Prelude whose outlandish popularity was to be a source of gloom and frustration to him all his life, and the Symphony No. 1. This last work was completed in September 1895 and introduced by Alexander Glazunov at a concert in Saint Petersburg in March 1897.

Glazunov was a good composer and so uncommonly decent a man that one hates to speak ill of him, but he does seem to have been a terrible conductor, and on this occasion he wrought disaster. Rachmaninoff hid on a staircase, his fists pressed against his ears, so appalling was the cacophony. It was certainly not the only time in the history of music that the critics, like the lay public, were unable to distinguish between an awful performance and an awful piece. César Cui wrote an oft-quoted review: "If there were a conservatory in Hell, if one of its gifted students were given the assignment of writing a program symphony on the Seven Plagues of Egypt, if he were to write a symphony just like Mr. Rachmaninoff's, he would have carried out his task brilliantly and given acute delight to the inhabitants of Hell."[1]

Rachmaninoff, always clear-sighted about his own music, must have known how strong and original a piece his symphony was; in 1908 he thought of bringing it out again with some revisions, but in 1917 he wrote to the critic Boris Asafiev that he would show it to no one and make sure in his will that it would remain forever hidden.[2] Obviously he was aware how much Glazunov's performance had been at fault, and he also knew how much the situation was exacerbated by musico-political currents that inflamed the blood-lust of Saint Petersburg critics when confronted with the work of a Muscovite. Nonetheless, always and easily subject to depression, Rachmaninoff almost immediately found himself unable to face the sight of blank manuscript paper. He kept busy, chiefly as principal conductor of the newly founded Moscow Private Russian Opera, also with the occasional concert. But he grew more and more despondent. The longer his composer's voice was silent, the worse he felt; the worse he felt, the more impossible the idea of composing. Family and friends suggested one remedy after another. Probably the worst proposal was that he visit Tolstoy. Rachmaninoff went twice

[1]Geoffrey Norris, *Rakhmaninov* (London: J. M. Dent & Sons, Ltd., 1976).
[2]After Rachmaninoff's death there came to light first a two-piano transcription of the Symphony No. 1, then a set of orchestral parts, and so the symphony had a second premiere in Moscow in 1945.

to call on that rude and egotistical kvetch, once by himself and once with Fyodor Chaliapin, and found himself obliged to listen to homilies on the lines of "You must work. Do you think I am pleased with myself? Work. I work every day." After Chaliapin and Rachmaninoff had performed one of the latter's songs for him, Tolstoy offered: "Tell me, do you really think anybody needs such music? I must tell you how much I dislike it. . . . Beethoven is nonsense. Pushkin and Lermontov as well."

At the head of the first page of Rachmaninoff's Second Piano Concerto stands the simple dedication, "À Monsieur N. Dahl." Monsieur Dahl was actually Dr. Nikolai Dahl, an internist who had followed with keen attention the work Jean-Martin Charcot was doing with hypnosis at the Salpêtrière Hospital in Paris. He was a friend of Rachmaninoff's cousins, the Satins—it was in that branch of the family that Rachmaninoff would find his bride, Natalia Alexandrovna—and he had successfully cured Rachmaninoff's aunt Varvara Arkadyevna of a psychosomatic ailment. Dahl was also an excellent violist and cellist, and the founder of his own string quartet. Rachmaninoff began daily visits to him in January 1900. The first aim was to improve Rachmaninoff's sleep and appetite. The larger goal was to enable him to compose a piano concerto: he had promised one to Alexander Goldenweiser in 1898, he had also promised the London Philharmonic Society that he would return with a new concerto in the 1899–1900 season, and he had accomplished nothing.

Dr. Dahl's treatment, a nicely gauged mixture of hypnotic suggestion ("You will begin your concerto . . . you will work with great ease . . . the concerto will be excellent . . .") and cultured conversation, did the trick. Almost immediately Rachmaninoff felt better and looked better. By April he was confident and well enough to accompany Chaliapin to Yalta, where they visited Chekhov and the gifted composer Vasily Kalinnikov (who would die of tuberculosis at thirty-five a few weeks later). Rachmaninoff and Chaliapin continued to Italy, where the great bass was to make his debut at La Scala in Boito's *Mefistofele*.

In July Rachmaninoff, "bored without Russians and Russia," went home, bringing back with him an *a cappella* chorus, *Pantalei the Healer*; a love duet for his opera *Francesca da Rimini*; preliminary sketches for his Suite No. 2 for Two Pianos; and sketches in quite an advanced state for the new piano concerto. Two movements, the second and third, were finished that fall, and plans were made to present them in December at a benefit concert for the Ladies' Charity Prison Committee. Rachmaninoff was to play and his cousin and former teacher, Alexander Siloti, would conduct. One imagines that when Rachmaninoff came down with a cold the day before the concert, Dr. Dahl was too humane to say he had done it on purpose. One of the innumerable cousins filled him to the gills with mulled wine, thus happening on yet another way of disabling that delicate six-foot-four organism, but in the event, in spite of Glazunov, Cui, Tolstoy, and the cold-curing cousin, everything went off brilliantly.

Next, Rachmaninoff attended to his new two-piano suite, which he completed in April 1901; then, with pleasure and with the speed Dr. Dahl had predicted, he added the first movement to his concerto.[3] One gets the impression that he had kept the score of Tchaikovsky's First Piano Concerto at hand while working on the second and third movements of his own concerto, or perhaps the music was simply at the surface of his memory, but when it came to the first movement he was ready to declare independence.[4] Five days before the premiere of the complete Concerto that November, Rachmaninoff suffered a moment of panic and was convinced he had produced a totally incompetent piece of work, but the wild acclaim he enjoyed at the concert convinced him otherwise. In the immediate months ahead lay the composition of his Cello Sonata, the cantata *Spring*, and the twelve songs of Opus 21 (including the famous *Lilacs* and *How Fair This Place*), as well as the beginning of a happy marriage.

More happened in Dr. Dahl's study than the dissolving of a specific block. Stravinsky, with little liking, described the change in Rachmaninoff at this time as one from watercolors to oils, from a very young composer to a very old one. One could tell the story another way and say that the crisis of 1897 and its aftermath and resolution had released Rachmaninoff's full powers as a composer. It is ironic that the single pre-crisis work to convey a sense of those powers is the one that precipitated the crisis, the Symphony No. 1. For Robert Simpson, one of the most deeply understanding writers on music and himself an admirable composer, it is not only the best of Rachmaninoff's three symphonies, but "a symphony that might well come to be regarded as the strongest by a Russian since Tchaikovsky." Simpson mourns the disappearance from Rachmaninoff's work after this of "a genuinely tragic and heroic expression that stands far above the pathos of his later music." One reads these words with sympathy as well as with the awareness that we cannot "know" whether between 1897 and 1900 Rachmaninoff found himself or lost himself. Certainly he acted as though something positive had

[3]An event that must have been moving to those who witnessed it is recounted by Sergei Bertensson and Jay Leyda in their biography of Rachmaninoff: "In 1928 [Dr. Dahl] was playing viola in the orchestra of the American University of Beirut in Lebanon. After a performance of [Rachmaninoff's Second Piano Concerto] with Arkadie Kouguell as soloist and conductor, the audience, informed of the dedication and of Dr. Dahl's presence, would not be content until Dahl rose from his seat and bowed."

[4]Rachmaninoff had known Tchaikovsky since boyhood because the older composer was a frequent visitor to the hothouse for pianists—Scriabin and Josef Lhévinne as well as Rachmaninoff—maintained by Nikolai Sergeievich Zverev; Rachmaninoff did not, however, add the famous B-flat-minor Concerto to his repertory until December 1911.

happened, and during the next decade and a half he composed with ease, invention, technical fluency, and the confidence of an artist at one with his language and style.[5]

An especially appealing quality in the Second Piano Concerto and something new in Rachmaninoff's music is a sense of effortlessness in its unfolding, which is surely related to the confidence he had gained in Dr. Dahl's deep leather armchair and, more broadly, from the growing feeling that he was after all built to survive. He begins magnificently, and with sounds by now so familiar that we come perilously close to taking them for granted and to not paying them much heed: a series of piano chords in crescendo, each based on the tolling of the lowest F on the keyboard, and, through the gathering of harmonic tension and dynamic force, constituting a powerful springboard for the move to the home chord of C minor.

Once there, the strings with clarinet initiate a plain but intensely expressive melody, which the piano accompanies with sonorous broken chords. Prokofiev writes that "someone once said (rather venomously) of [Rachmaninoff's] melodies that they were mostly written for a voice with a very small range. And yet he managed to fit amazingly beautiful themes into that small range; for example, in the Second Concerto." Here is an instance. That narrowness of gamut contributes to our sense that this music is profoundly and unmistakably Russian, compare, for example, Stravinsky's melodies, both the borrowed and the original ones, in Le Sacre du printemps and Symphonies of Wind Instruments.

The piano's role as accompanist is also worth noting. Rachmaninoff liked playing accompaniments and he liked making them interesting to play. In none of the works for piano and orchestra is the pianist so often an ensemble partner and so rarely a spotlight-hogging soloist as in the first movement of the Second Concerto. Rachmaninoff composed at the piano, and one gets a vivid sense of the fresh, ingenious, ever-varied figurations—whether they are subsidiary, as in the songs and concertos, or themselves the nub of the matter, as in many of the Preludes and Études-Tableaux—being invented directly in and by the fingers.

To come back to the first movement of this Concerto: the initial impulse plays itself out in one grand, tightly organized paragraph, to which Rachmaninoff appends two small afterthoughts, a bit of scurrying for the piano

[5]While Simpson's essay on the First Symphony in the compilation The Symphony he edited for Penguin Books in 1967 is supposed to be a survey of all three Rachmaninoff symphonies, nine-tenths of it is about No. 1. The essay continues to bother one with its questions. If "tragic and heroic" expression were never again dominant components in Rachmaninoff's music, neither was pathos an inevitable presence—consider most of the brilliant and even rather speculative Études-Tableaux, the Rhapsody on a Theme of Paganini, much of the Third Symphony, and the Symphonic Dances. Nor should one forget Rachmaninoff's own fiercely rugged, boldly limned, tough, anti-pathetic playing even of his own most pathos-drenched music.

and a quite formal set of cadential chords. It is only then that the orchestra falls silent and the pianist steps forward as a vocal soloist in the grand Romantic manner (this singer, too, has a range of only an octave plus a semitone). It all sounds so natural and cohesive and assured, this combination of energy and something like neutrality, and it makes such an effective preparation for this vocal moment, that it is hard to imagine that this had Rachmaninoff deeply worried just before the premiere. He had sent the score to Nikita Morozov, a conservatory classmate, and Morozov had evidently responded with some reservations, eliciting this from Rachmaninoff:

> You are right, Nikita Semionovich! I've just played over the first movement of my concerto and only now has it suddenly become clear to me that the transition from the first theme to the second is not good, that in this form the first theme is no more than an introduction, and that when I begin the second theme no fool would believe it to be a second theme: everybody will think this is the beginning of the concerto. I consider the whole movement ruined, and from this minute it has become positively hideous to me. I'm simply in despair! And why did you pester me with your analysis five days before the performance?!![6]

But there is no substitute for experiencing the effect of a work in public performance, and at his triumphant Moscow Philharmonic concert Rachmaninoff was persuaded that his design in fact worked just as he thought it would when he first imagined it and wrote it down.

Rachmaninoff places the second movement in E major, a key quite remote from C minor. This is precisely the key relationship we find between the first and second movements of both Beethoven's Piano Concerto No. 3 and the Brahms First Symphony, but familiarity has softened its pungency. Beethoven and Brahms obviously enjoyed the jolt, as did Haydn in comparable situations; Rachmaninoff—with C. P. E. Bach, Mendelssohn, and Dvořák as models—preferred to construct a mitigating bridge passage.[7] The four bars for muted strings in which he gently sets the music down in E major are singularly lovely. In the first movement, he had brought the orchestra in only at the point of arrival in the real key; here he reverses the procedure, and the entrance of the piano is saved for the first E-major chord. As for the delicately syncopated arpeggios with which the piano introduces itself, they are taken from a *Romance* for piano six-hands that Rachmaninoff had composed in the fall of 1891 for yet another set of cousins, the sisters Natalia, Ludmila, and Vera Skalon.

---

[6]Norris, op. cit.

[7]I doubt Rachmaninoff was familiar with C. P. E. Bach's music other than the *Solfeggietto*, but he certainly knew Mendelssohn's Violin Concerto and probably the Symphony *From the New World* as well, even though that work was only seven years old in 1900.

Again, the pianist begins as accompanist, briefly to the flute, at greater length to the clarinet. Through the movement, the relationship between piano and orchestra is imagined and realized with great delicacy. There is something captivating to the way the piano shyly inserts just six notes of melody between the first two phrases of the clarinet. Later in the movement these roles are reversed, and it is the orchestra that shyly makes itself heard between phrases of piano cantilena. It brings to mind Chaliapin's moving tribute: "I shall remember Rachmaninoff's cold hands. I shall remember him accompanying me. . . . When he plays for me I can truly say, not that 'I'm singing' but 'we're singing.' "

A quicker interlude functions as a token scherzo, an idea Rachmaninoff would develop more fully in the Concerto No. 3 and the Third Symphony. This interlude spills into a splash of cadenza, and perhaps no detail in the Concerto is more lovely than the appearance for just five notes of a pair of flutes to ease the music back into the softly swaying arpeggios of the Skalon *Romance*.

Rachmaninoff makes another bridge from the Adagio to the finale, beginning with distant, conspiratorial march music in E major, then working his way around to the doorstep of C minor and to the piano's grandly assertive entrance. The march music is now determined and vigorous; for contrast, Rachmaninoff finds the ultimate archetype of his big tunes, the one that Buddy Kaye and Ted Mossman turned into *Full Moon and Empty Arms*, which the young Sinatra recorded so sweetly. It all moves to a rattling bring-down-the-house conclusion, and when one remembers the biographical background to this Concerto it is pleasing to see that the last tempo mark is *risoluto*.

## Piano Concerto No. 3 in D minor, Opus 30

> *Allegro ma non tanto*
> *Intermezzo: Adagio*
> *Finale: Alla breve—Scherzando—Tempo I*

Rachmaninoff composed this Concerto for his first North American tour in 1909 and introduced the work on 28 November that year with the New York Symphony, Walter Damrosch conducting. Rachmaninoff dedicated the score to the pianist he regarded as the greatest of his time, his slightly younger contemporary Josef Hofmann; Hofmann, however, never played the work—perhaps, it has been suggested, because his small hands made it uncomfortable for him.

**Solo piano, two flutes, two oboes, two clarinets, two bassoons, four horns, two trumpets, three trombones, tuba, timpani, bass drum, cymbals, snare drum, and strings.**

In October 1906 Rachmaninoff moved from Moscow to Dresden with his wife and their daughter, Irina. He was a busy pianist and conductor—he had just concluded two years as principal conductor at the Bolshoi Opera—and like all composers who have consuming careers as performers, he longed for time just to write. The purpose of the move to Dresden was to take himself out of circulation, and he chose the beautiful Saxon capital because he and his wife had become fond of it on their honeymoon four years earlier. Among the works he wrote there or during summer visits to the family estate at Oneg were this concerto; the Symphony No. 2; *The Isle of the Dead* (after the Böcklin painting in the Dresden State Gallery); and the Piano Sonata No. 1. Offers to play and conduct kept coming in and they were by no means all to be denied. Rachmaninoff decided to accept an invitation to visit the United States, not without anguish: "My hands tremble," he wrote to a friend. "You . . . could not possibly understand what tortures I live through when I realize that this question has to be decided by me and by me alone."

Rachmaninoff made his American debut at a recital at Smith College in Northampton, Massachusetts, on 4 November 1909. Next he went to Philadelphia to conduct the first American performance of his Second Symphony, initiating a long and happy relationship with what would soon become a great orchestra, and a few weeks later he introduced his new Concerto with Walter Damrosch and the New York Symphony. Soon after, he played it again, and to his much greater satisfaction, with the New York Philharmonic under Gustav Mahler, another conductor struggling to find time to compose.

Rachmaninoff invented arresting beginnings for all his works for piano and orchestra. In the First and Fourth Concertos he was aggressive, outright combative. The Second emerges from a series of groping, tolling chords. As much as these are the essence of all that is Romantic, so is the prickly, skeletal start of the *Rhapsody on a Theme of Paganini* wittily anti-Romantic.

In the first measures of the Third Concerto we find a quality we do not usually associate with Rachmaninoff: simplicity. For two measures, clarinet, bassoon, horn, timpani, and muted strings set up a pulse against which the piano sings—or is it speaks?—a long and quiet melody, the two hands in octaves as in a Schubert piano duet. It is a lovely inspiration, that melody unfolding in subtle variation, just a few notes being continually redisposed rhythmically. Once only, to the extent of a single eighth-note, does the melody exceed the range of an octave; most of it stays within a fifth. (See also my essay on the Concerto No. 2.) Rachmaninoff told the musicologist Joseph Yasser that the theme had come to him "ready-made" and had in effect "written itself," an impression and observation given new meaning by Yasser's later discovery of a close relationship to a Russian liturgical chant, *The Tomb, O Savior, Soldiers Guarding.*

The accompaniment cost Rachmaninoff considerable trouble. He was thinking, he told Yasser, of the piano singing the melody "as a singer would sing it, and [finding] a suitable orchestral accompaniment, or rather, one that would not muffle this singing." What he found invites, for precision and delicacy, comparison with the workmanship in Mozart's concertos. The accompaniment does indeed let the singing through, but even while exquisitely tactful in its recessiveness, it is absolutely specific—a real and characterful invention, the fragmentary utterances of the violins now anticipating, now echoing the pianist's song, the woodwinds sometimes and with utmost gentleness reinforcing the bass or joining the piano in a few notes of its melody. (Around the same time and with his own "nervous" sense of detail, Mahler was inventing similar not-quite-doublings of voice by instruments in *Das Lied von der Erde.*)

Such a conjunction of integration and contrast is characteristic of this Concerto. The second theme, for example, is first adumbrated as a kind of twitch in a few wind instruments behind delicate pianistic passagework before its formal arrival is announced by a mini-cadenza and an expansive preparatory gesture in the orchestra. When it does at last appear, Rachmaninoff presents it in two strikingly different guises: first as a dialogue between orchestra and piano, feline and staccato, then as a lyric melody, legato and *espressivo*, to which bassoon and horn add their *dolce* comments.[8]

The further progress of the movement abounds in felicities and ingenuities, sharply imagined and elegantly executed. The development begins with the surprise of a return to the movement's opening, including the two preludial measures for the orchestra. The alteration of a single note in the piano's melody is like the throwing of a switch that diverts the music downward into a strange key whence the development proper can take off. In another brilliant stroke, a huge cadenza, shedding still more fresh light on by now familiar material, assumes the rights and function of a recapitulation. But what is going on when—after a thunderous climax; after the touching intervention, one by one, of flute, oboe, clarinet, and horn; after spacious subsidence—the opening music appears yet again? Is it explicit recapitulation after the implicit recapitulation of the cadenza? No, the leisurely singing of the melody leads with extraordinary compressions and encapsulations to a

---

[8]The composer's own tiger-spring playing of the piano's answer to the orchestra on his 1939 recording embodies—as much as nine chords can—the essence of Rachmaninoff the pianist.

final page in which fragments of themes ghost by in a startling amalgam of epigram and dream.

"Intermezzo" is a curiously shy designation for a movement as expansive as this Adagio, though we shall discover that it is in fact all upbeat to a still more expansive Finale. But the Intermezzo itself is all adventure and event, not least the piano's disruptive entrance, which so determinedly wrenches the music away to new and distant harmonic ground. What ensues is a series of variations, broken up by a feather-light waltz that perhaps represents Rachmaninoff's remembrance of a similar interruption in the slow movement of Tchaikovsky's Concerto No. 1. The clarinet-and-bassoon melody of the waltz is close cousin to the Concerto's principal theme, and if one could scrutinize the piano's dizzying figuration through a time-retarding device, one could detect that it, too, is made of diminutions of the same material.

When the Intermezzo yields to the explosive start of the Finale, we again find ourselves caught up in a torrent of virtuosity and invention. Here, too, the second theme gets a double presentation, first in harmonic outline, solidly packed piano chords against drumming strings, then—in a contrasting key, even—as a beautifully scored, impassioned melody for the piano. After that, Rachmaninoff gives us the surprise of a series of variations on what pretends to be a new idea but is in fact an amalgam of the first movement's second theme and the beginning of the finale.

In the course of this episode—remarkable for existing in the first place, for the singular brilliance of its piano style, and for being almost entirely anchored to the chord of E-flat—the Concerto's opening melody makes an unobtrusive, slightly varied appearance in violas and cellos. That it is once again varied is characteristic, for the idea of repetition as instant variation has been implicit since the first unfolding of that opening melody. Now this idea has become an important tool at Rachmaninoff's disposal as he faces the task of integrating a work laid out on an uncommonly large scale, but doing so without sacrificing diversity or forward thrust. His evocations of earlier material are imaginative and structural achievements on a level far above the naïve quotation-mongering of, say, César Franck or even Dvořák.

Rachmaninoff was anxious to put his best foot forward in America. His Second Concerto had already been played in New York by Raoul Pugno, Tina Lerner, and Ossip Gabrilowitsch, and Rachmaninoff wanted his new work to convey a clear sense of his growing powers as composer and pianist. It is easy to misread the Third Concerto as an attempt to consolidate by imitation the success of the Second. Of course they have features in common: the coruscating, dense, yet always lucid piano style, a certain melancholy to the song, a extroverted rhetorical stance, the apotheosized ending (taken over from Grieg's Concerto, which Rachmaninoff liked), even the final YUM-pa-ta-TUM cadential formula that is as good as a signature. But the differences are even more important, and they are essentially matters of ambition and scope: the procedures that hold this work together are far beyond the capabilities of the composer of the C-minor Concerto eight years earlier.

Also, much more is asked of the pianist. The Third Concerto makes immense demands on stamina, the orchestral passages that frame the Intermezzo being the soloist's only moments of respite. I have not yet met a pianist who agrees with Rachmaninoff's own assessment that the Third Concerto is "more comfortable" than the Second. As in the Second Concerto, Rachmaninoff sees the soloist not merely as someone who can sing soulfully and thunder imposingly, but as an alert, flexible, responsive musician who knows how to listen, blend, and accompany. And even in this non–prima-donna role the challenge is greater here than in the Second Concerto.[9]

Two points of about performance practice remain to be mentioned. Like the Symphony No. 2, this Concerto has a confusing history of composer-authorized cuts. Rachmaninoff played the Concerto complete in its first round of performances, and he was still doing so when he returned to America in 1919. But by 1935 he was making one cut in each of the work's three movements—they are marked with his initials in blue crayon in the score of the Boston Symphony's library (and probably elsewhere)—and when he recorded the Concerto in December 1939 and February 1940 he made a second cut in the finale. The cut near the beginning of the finale was a disastrous idea of Rachmaninoff's in that it eliminates the first statement of one of the movement's main themes. Most pianists used to make these cuts, but more recently there has been an inclination to give the work complete.

Rachmaninoff wrote two alternative cadenzas for the first movement. One begins by treating the material in a scherzando manner, gradually building to a climax of massive chords; the second, which is both longer and harder, starts right away with an onslaught of such chords. Rachmaninoff played only the former, and it used to be rare indeed that one heard the latter. It appears on a 1940 broadcast by Walter Gieseking with Willem Mengelberg and the Amsterdam Concertgebouw Orchestra, but I am sure I never heard the longer cadenza until Van Cliburn played it in his many and widely noticed performances after winning the International Tchaikovsky Competition in 1958. It certainly offers an extraordinary opportunity for the right pianist—Cliburn, for example, with his huge hands and bronzen sound.

---

[9]In the winter of 1996-1997, this concerto came in for a lot of new attention thanks to *Shine*, an interesting, often powerful film based on the harrowing life of David Helfgott, an Australian pianist who showed promise in his youth but whose playing, by the time the film propelled him into prominence, was embarrassingly substandard. Learning and performing the Rachmaninoff Third Concerto is a major element of the story—it is even given the role of precipitating Helfgott's mental breakdown—and the point is made repeatedly that as a technical and expressive challenge to the pianist, this work is at the summit of the repertory. But there is no quantifiable measure of difficulty by which the undeniably difficult "Rach 3" is the most difficult piece in the world. And there are many respects in which, as Rachmaninoff would have been the first to agree, concertos by Mozart, Beethoven, and Brahms demand more.

As you can hear on the RCA recording of his Carnegie Hall performances, he played it fantastically well and so, perhaps not fortunately, began a vogue for it. For considerations of both variety and scale, there is, however, much to be said for the "little" cadenza the composer himself preferred.

## *Rhapsody on a Theme of Paganini,* for Piano and Orchestra, Opus 43

Rachmaninoff wrote the *Rhapsody on a Theme of Paganini* between 3 July and 18 August 1934. The first performance was given on 7 November 1934 in Baltimore, Maryland, with the composer as soloist and Leopold Stokowski conducting the Philadelphia Orchestra.

**Solo piano, two flutes and piccolo, two oboes and English horn, two clarinets, two bassoons, four horns, two trumpets, three trombones, tuba, timpani, snare drum, triangle, cymbals, bass drum, glockenspiel, harp, and strings.**

Audiences everywhere instantly took to the *Rhapsody on a Theme of Paganini,* and it quickly became an indispensable repertory piece. Among connoisseurs and professionals it is probably the most admired of Rachmaninoff's works. It embodies his late style at its brilliant and witty best, it has one of the world's irresistible melodies, and it gives the audiences the satisfaction of watching a pianist work very hard and with obviously rewarding results. Moreover, variation form, which is what we have here, though disguised by the title *Rhapsody,* is an unobtrusively effective corset, useful because control of large designs had never been the most highly developed among Rachmaninoff's remarkable gifts. The composition of the *Variations on a Theme by Corelli* three years earlier had no doubt been profitable preparation for the *Rhapsody.*[10]

   Turning to Paganini's Caprice No. 24, Rachmaninoff was following in

[10]The theme of the *Corelli Variations* is not actually by Arcangelo Corelli: it is *La Folia,* a succession of harmonies in wide circulation as the basis of variations in the seventeenth and eighteenth centuries, but most familiar through a particularly brilliant movement in Corelli's Violin Sonata, Opus 5, no. 12. It is interesting that Rachmaninoff, who had written variations on a Chopin Prelude in 1902–1903, turned to violin music for the themes of the two variation sets of his later years. The *Corelli Variations,* although rejected by their first listeners and still not on the hit parade, are first-rate Rachmaninoff, an introspective and hardly less ingenious counterpart to the *Paganini Rhapsody.* As is not surprising for someone whose business was virtuosity, Rachmaninoff was fascinated by the figure of Paganini. He was delighted when Michel Fokine came to him with a proposal to make a Paganini ballet on the *Rhapsody* and even wrote a scenario himself. *Paganini* had its premiere in London in 1939.

the footsteps of Schumann, Liszt, and, more particularly, Brahms. I make the distinction because Brahms's two books of variations are original reflections on the theme, even though they make occasional allusions to Paganini's own variations (as do Rachmaninoff's as well), while Schumann's and Liszt's studies are not so much independent pieces as pianistic expansions of Paganini's Caprice.[11]

About 1805, while part of the musical household of Princess Elisa Baciocchi, just installed by her brother Napoleon Bonaparte as ruler of the former Republic of Lucca, Paganini codified his evolving technical resources in a set of twenty-four caprices for unaccompanied violin. He published them as his Opus 1, but not until 1820. The Caprice No. 24 is a set of eleven variations plus a fifteen-measure "finale" on the now-so-familiar leaping theme with its striking contours and simple, easily grasped harmonic scaffolding.

Ex. 1

Rachmaninoff begins with an introduction, which is followed by Variation 1 (marked *precedente*), the theme itself, Variations 2 through 24, and the coda. What is this about? Rachmaninoff takes the second half of the first measure as his launching pad and, beginning *in medias res*, uses it over eight measures to build up excitement and suspense. Then comes Variation 1— on a theme not yet heard. It is a skeleton, appropriate enough for an evocation of the cadaverously thin Paganini, and Rachmaninoff draws it for us by sounding only the first note of each of Paganini's measures (he also changes Paganini's F and E in the sixth and eighth measures to D and C). As this variation nears its close it begins to assume a hint of flesh. Very likely Rachmaninoff got the idea of variations before a theme from the finale of Beethoven's *Eroica*.

The theme proper, when it appears, is assigned—again with a nice sense of the appropriate—to the violins, while the virtuoso pianist, the translated

[11]Further virtuosic and delightful responses to Paganini's provocative Caprice have come along since Rachmaninoff's *Rhapsody*, among them Witold Lutoslawski's *Variations for Two Pianos* (1941—arranged rather less effectively for piano and orchestra in 1978), Boris Blacher's *Orchestral Variations* (1947), and George Rochberg's *Fifty Caprice-Variations for Solo Violin* (1970).

Paganini, as it were, accompanies with the skeleton. (Here are sixteen measures of a Rachmaninoff concerto that anyone can play!) As in Variation 1, the last measures add new activity, looking ahead a bit to what is to come, a technique Rachmaninoff uses with some consistency throughout the *Rhapsody*. Unlike Brahms, he has no notion of sticking to the phrase structure and measure count of the theme.

I, in turn, have no notion of writing a variation-by-variation description. Taking the *Rhapsody* by chapters, this is what we hear: The first five variations are increasingly excited, after which the sixth is more relaxed and even allows time for a couple of mini-cadenzas. Variation 7, rather slower, introduces a new theme, the Dies irae from the Gregorian Mass for the Dead, a melody that haunts so much Romantic music from the Berlioz *Symphonie fantastique* and which Rachmaninoff was particularly fond of quoting. While the piano plays the Dies irae, the orchestra sticks with Paganini, cellos and bassoons being chastened by the funeral atmosphere, violins being irrepressibly and slyly frivolous. The Dies irae, though always a secondary idea in the scheme of the piece, remains very much a presence. Through Variation 10, Rachmaninoff is particularly concerned to explore everything that is sinister about Paganini and the Dies irae; his imagination and skill in orchestration play a large role here.

Using Variation 11 as a loose, cadenzalike transition, Rachmaninoff begins a new phase in Variation 12, which is in a demure minuet tempo. The basic allegro is soon resumed, but this chapter is rounded off with another variation (No. 16) in a gentler tempo and scored almost as chamber music. Variation 17 is another transition, but a strange and dark one, with little suggestion of Paganini. The travail of this mysterious exploration—it is like making your way, hands along the wall, through a dark cave—is rewarded when the music emerges into the soft moonlight of D-flat major and the inspired melody that Rachmaninoff found by inverting Paganini's theme. "This one," he said, "is for my agent."

Ex. 2

Actually Variation 18 is three variations in one, for Rachmaninoff gives us three different continuations of a single beginning, the scoring getting warmer as he goes. He has moved far from where he started, in mood and also in key. The harmonic relationship of Variation 18 to the *Rhapsody* as a whole is like that of the Adagio of Rachmaninoff's Piano Concerto No. 2 to its first movement—and, for that matter, like the slow movements of Beethoven's Piano Concerto No. 3 and Brahms's Symphony No. 1 in their contexts. How do you leave such a dream? Rachmaninoff in his concerto and Brahms in his symphony do it by gentle transition, Brahms's being wonderfully subtle as well; Beethoven does it with a joke. Here Rachmaninoff chooses Beethoven's example. The orchestra wakes the dreamer—and the rapt audience—with a snappy reminder that our proper business is to be vivacious and in A minor (it is a characteristic touch of wit that the actual wake-up call is a chord of A major), and the piano responds at once with a bravura variation, quasi-pizzicato, and close to Paganini's own Variation 9 with its dazzling left-hand pizzicatos.

Rachmaninoff's Variation 19 begins the final chapter, saturated in Paganiniana and spooky Dies irae atmosphere. At the summit of a hectic climax, one with palpable touches of Broadway, the pianist launches into a brief cadenza with thundering octaves. Somehow this has managed to position itself in A-flat major, and, upon resuming with Variation 23, the piano is amused to pretend that it really believes this to be the right key. The orchestra is not amused at all, but it takes two firm interventions to get things back on the proper harmonic course. The two final variations work up tremendous excitement; the mischievous coda, all two measures of it, is another stroke of delicious wit.

# Maurice Ravel

Joseph-Maurice Ravel was born in Ciboure near Saint-Jean-de-
Luz, Basses-Pyrénées, on 7 March 1875 and died in Paris on 28
December 1937.

## Concerto in G major for Piano and Orchestra

*Allegramente*
*Adagio assai*
*Presto*

According to the critic Gustave Samazeuilh, some of the music of the first and third movements of this Concerto originated about 1914 in an unfinished score for piano and orchestra titled *Zaspiak bat* (Basque for "the seven are one"). Ravel originally intended to play the Concerto itself on his 1928 American tour, but as things turned out, he only began work on the score in 1929. The next plan was for him to give the premiere in March 1931 with Willem Mengelberg and the Amsterdam Concertgebouw Orchestra, but the project was delayed when Ravel received and immediately got to work on a commission to write a concerto for piano left-hand for the Austrian one-armed pianist, Paul Wittgenstein. Only after that was accomplished in 1930 did Ravel return to "his" concerto, completing it on 14 November 1931. As late as the end of October of that year, he still planned to play the Concerto himself, and he practiced both it and Czerny études to the point of exhaustion; however, when the score was virtually complete, he decided that in view of his poor and worsening health—"The concerto is nearly finished and I am not far from being so myself," he wrote to Henri Rabaud—it would be safer if he conducted and turned the solo role over to Marguerite Long, the pianist who had given the first performance of his *Tombeau de Couperin* in 1919. Long also received the dedication of the score. The premiere took place at the Salle Pleyel in Paris on 14 January 1932 at a concert of the Lamoureux Orchestra, and it was followed in the next four months by performances in more than twenty cities, among them Brussels, Vienna, Prague, London, Warsaw, Berlin, Amsterdam, and Budapest, as well as by a recording for Columbia with Long as soloist.

**Solo piano, piccolo, flute, oboe, English horn, B-flat and E-flat clarinets, two bassoons, two horns, trumpet, trombone, timpani, triangle, snare drum, cymbals, bass drum, tam-tam, wood block, whip, harp, and strings.**

As work on this Concerto neared completion in the summer of 1931, Ravel gave this statement to the critic M. D. Calvocoressi for publication in the London *Daily Telegraph*:

> Planning the two piano concertos simultaneously was an interesting experience. The one in which I shall appear as the interpreter is a concerto in the truest sense of the word: I mean that it is written very much in the same spirit as those of Mozart and Saint-Saëns. The music of a concerto should, in my opinion, be lighthearted and brilliant, and not aim at profundity or at dramatic effects. It has been said of certain classics that their concertos were written not "for" but "against" the piano.[1] I heartily agree. I had intended to title this concerto "Divertissement." Then it occurred to me that there was no need to do so because the title "Concerto" should be sufficiently clear. [2]

It is an odd paragraph. For one thing, only a Frenchman could come up with so bizarre a coupling as "Mozart and Saint-Saëns." But stranger still is the notion Ravel expresses here of what the specific gravity of a concerto should be, strange not only because we hear Mozart as profound *as well as* lighthearted and brilliant (and in that we differ from most listeners in 1931),

---

[1]It sounds as though Ravel had his anecdotes confused and was half-remembering the distinction Hans von Bülow made between the *violin* concertos of Bruch ("for") and Brahms ("against").
[2]Arbie Orenstein, *Ravel, Man and Musician* (New York: Columbia University Press, 1975).

nor because we bristle at the implied rejection of at least some of Beethoven's concertos and those of Brahms, but because Ravel himself, in his Concerto for the Left Hand (which he does go on to concede is "very different"), has given us a work that is dark, fiercely dramatic, and perhaps even profound.

It is another occasion, I suppose, for learning the lesson that while we should always read composers' letters, memoirs, program notes, and so on, we need to be circumspect about evaluating them. And Maurice Ravel, we might remember, was a man fascinated by masks. He was born in Basque country, just a couple of miles from the Spanish border, and his mother, Marie Delouart, was Basque. Ravel himself lived in Paris from the time that he entered the Conservatoire as a fourteen-year-old student but, like Antaeus, the giant son of Poseidon who derived his strength from touching his mother, the Earth, he never ceased to feel the need to renew himself by returning to his native soil. And his Basque heritage formed his personality: he was not, he insisted, cold and unemotional, "but I am Basque, and while the Basques feel deeply they seldom show it, and then only to a very few." It is no wonder that in his statement to Calvocoressi he chose to underplay the roiling emotional content of his Left-Hand Concerto.

Pierre-Joseph Ravel, the composer's father, was a deeply musical engineer who contributed significantly to the development of the two-stroke internal combustion motor fondly remembered by 1960s Saab owners. Maurice, his eldest son, became a musician enchanted by elegantly functioning machines. He was charming, shy, dandified, and of the most delicate build: Marguerite Long recalled how once, on their concerto tour, he forgot to pack his patent-leather shoes and how difficult it was to find any in his size.[3] A lifelong bachelor not known to have had any close personal attachment, Ravel loved children: *Mother Goose* and, even more, his operatic collaboration with Colette, *L'Enfant et les sortilèges* (The Child and the Magic Spell), are miraculously perceptive and loving masterpieces for and about children.

The prelude to his other opera, *L'Heure espagnole* (Spanish Time), depicts a clockmaker's shop and is a delicious love letter to devices with moving parts that whir and tick and buzz and clack. Children, moreover, could almost always melt Ravel's reserve, and for Mimie and Jean Godebski, the two for whom he wrote the original piano duet version of *Mother Goose* (although it turned out they were not up to playing it), their honorary uncle, hardly taller than themselves, invented stories, constructed astonishing and minuscule toys, and, when away, sent a stream of funny postcards. The musicologist Stephen Parkany has pointed out that Ravel's G-major Concerto also begins

[3]In Thomas Mann's *Doctor Faustus* there is a character, one who passes across the stage for just a moment, so delicately built and equilibrated that even as an adult he chose a pediatrician as his personal physician.

like some wondrous contraption in a toy shop: "To start it up, a percussionist releases the wound-up spring of the whip"—or, as we more often call it in America, the slapstick.

The piano is there, right from the beginning, contributing to the bitonal (shades of *Petrushka*) buzz against which the piccolo cheerfully whistles the first, jaunty tune. After a while, the piano comes to the fore with a languid theme that reminds us that the first intention behind this work had been to charm American audiences. Like many "classical" musicians at that time, Ravel was smitten with what he knew of jazz, which meant mostly the somewhat sweetened and watered-down translations of it that had made their way to Paris. He had alluded to it with wonderful wit in *L'Enfant et les sortilèges*, and diverse blue twists, some of them quite specifically reminiscent of Gershwin's *Rhapsody in Blue*, are seductively prominent in the first movement of the G-major Concerto. Spanish flavoring comes in as well: the master of the *Rapsodie espagnole*, *L'Heure espagnole*, and *Boléro* had probably lifted some of the Concerto from *Zaspiak bat*, a rhapsody to his Basque homeland. Toward the end, the harp subtly suggests that a cadenza might be in order, an idea the piano embraces with enthusiasm, after which the music moves swiftly to a conclusion end both bright and firm.

The Adagio is the reason we not only delight in this concerto but truly love it. The piano, alone, spins out a long, long melody over a kind of slow waltz bass that manages to be incredibly gentle even while it moves in constant cross-rhythm against the song in the right hand. When this melody is rounded off, a flute and then other woodwinds softly make their presence known. Eventually the English horn steps forward to sing the serene melody, while the piano decorates it with fanciful garlands. At some early stage, Ravel had told Marguerite Long that the Concerto would end softly, with trills. He changed his mind about that, but at least the idea of expressive trills stayed live in his mind, as we can hear in this Adagio and, for that matter, in the quiet part of the first-movement cadenza.

Ravel composed this music, as he put it, "with the assistance" of the slow movement of Mozart's Clarinet Quintet. Although the two pieces share a wondrous stillness as they begin, the connection is not obvious; there is nothing that approaches actual quotation. But you can hear how Ravel picked up a thing or two about deceptive cadences (his flute entrance and the harmonic diversion just before Mozart's first long paragraph comes to its close), about unexpected duetting (piano and English horn in Ravel, clarinet and violin in Mozart), and about the lovely effect of wreathing a slow melody in quicker notes. What surprises us is to learn that Ravel's Adagio, which sounds so spontaneous and has so natural a flow, cost him endless trouble: he squeezed it out, he said, painfully, a bar or two at a time, and it came as close as any project he ever undertook to carrying him to the edge of despair.

The brief and irresistible finale, which was encored at many stops on that first tour in 1932 as indeed it has often been since then, completely lives up to Ravel's "lighthearted and brilliant" concerto ideal. Variously, Ravel alludes to the first movement. The piano figurations at the beginning are similar, although the pianist has now abandoned any notion of being an accompanist or chamber-music partner and is unmistakably out front in the most soloistic manner possible. Here, too, wind solos speak in beguiling foreign accents, which is to say in foreign keys: there are startling trombone smears and there is a particularly demanding virtuoso bit for the bassoon. A whip crack carries our minds back to the Concerto's opening sound, and the final bang is colored by the same bass drum thump that ended the first movement.

## Concerto for Piano Left-Hand and Orchestra

Ravel wrote this Concerto in 1929–1930 on commission from Paul Wittgenstein, who gave the first performance with Robert Heger and the Vienna Symphony on 5 January 1932. The score is dedicated to Wittgenstein.

**Solo piano, three flutes (third doubling piccolo), two oboes and English horn, two clarinets with E-flat and bass clarinets, two bassoons and contrabassoon, four horns, three trumpets, three trombones, tuba, timpani, triangle, snare drum, cymbals, bass drum, wood block, tam-tam, harp, and strings.**

If life had gone well for Paul Wittgenstein, we would probably never have heard of him; as it is, he is a perpetual footnote in the history of twentieth-century piano music. He was the seventh of eight formidably gifted children in the affluent and musical household of a Viennese steel manufacturer; the youngest of the eight was the famous Ludwig, author of the *Tractatus Logico-Philosophicus* and the *Philosophical Investigations*, himself a good clarinetist and a virtuoso whistler. Paul studied piano with Theodor Leschetizky, the teacher of Paderewski, Gabrilowitsch, Friedman, Schnabel, and Moiseiwitsch, among others, and he made a successful debut in 1913. Serving in the Austrian army on the Russian front, he had his right arm shot off in the first months of the 1914–1918 War. After spending time as a prisoner of war in Siberia, he was repatriated in 1916 and bravely set about reconstructing his musical life. Allan Janik and Stephen Toulmin write in *Wittgenstein's Vienna* (Simon & Schuster, 1973): "The determination and discipline so required of him, as well as his steadfast and single-minded devotion to perfection of technique,

were integral elements in the heritage of stern Protestant morality characteristic of the world-view which Karl Wittgenstein transmitted to his entire
family."[4]

Paul Wittgenstein had learned much about courage in the face of ad-
versity from a family friend who was also his theory teacher: the composer,
organist, and pianist Josef Labor, who had been blind since childhood. Wittgenstein's money enabled him to commission more than a dozen works for
piano left-hand, some with orchestra, some in chamber-music combinations,
and a few for solo piano. Beginning in 1923, he successfully approached
Labor, Hindemith, Franz Schmidt, Korngold, Strauss, Ravel, Prokofiev, and
Britten, as well as such minor figures as Rudolf Braun (another Labor student, and also blind), Sergei Eduardovich Bortkiewicz, Hans Gál, and Ernest
Walker.

Ravel's Concerto is a masterpiece that quickly became standard repertory; Prokofiev's Piano Concerto No. 4 is a sparkling work, too little known;
Britten's *Diversions* is a witty composition worth more attention than it gets;
Gary Graffman has made a strong case for the overripe Korngold Concerto;
Strauss's *Parergon zur Symphonia domestica* and *Panathenäenzug* are complicated and interesting tours de force, worth reconsideration and (probably)
revival; and the music of the Austrian post-Romantic Franz Schmidt has its
devoted aficionados, of whom I am one (I especially recommend the delightful *Concertante Variations on a Theme by Beethoven*).

But Wittgenstein hardly enjoyed the fruits of his efforts. He disliked
many of the works he got; Prokofiev's Concerto went particularly against his
Viennese grain, and he never played it. (But he paid promptly, always.) Not
long before he died in 1961, Wittgenstein admitted that of all "his" pieces,
he had felt truly close only to Schmidt's; these he played whenever there was
an opportunity, which was nearly never after his emigration to the United
States in 1938. He came to regard the Ravel Concerto as "a great work," but
only after some time and a quarrel with the composer. (Wittgenstein's persistence in going to composers such as Hindemith, Prokofiev, and Britten,
whose works he would be virtually guaranteed not to find "sympathisch," is
psychologically fascinating.)

There is another issue. A piece for left hand alone is a tour de force by
definition, and it tends to arouse in composers the desire to astound, especially when they are witty spirits like Britten, Hindemith, Prokofiev, and
Ravel. Britten and Prokofiev were also exceptional pianists. (The "astounding" element is almost totally absent from Schmidt's Wittgenstein pieces.)
The question is, did Wittgenstein, for all the hard work to which Janik and
Toulmin attest, have the technique to play "his" pieces comfortably, or at

---

[4]Reading on, however, you learn that Karl Wittgenstein's three eldest sons committed suicide, two
of them in direct response to their father's rigidity.

all? His two recordings of the Ravel Concerto sound labored in contrast, say, to Alfred Cortot's, which is sometimes messy but always commanding; my only experience of hearing Wittgenstein in concert—it was a performance of one of the Schmidt quintets in New York—was painful, but that was late in his life and probably an unfair basis for judgment.[5]

"In der Beschränkung zeigt sich erst der Meister" (Only under restrictions does the master reveal himself). The words are Goethe's, and sententious Germans are fond of quoting them when you protest a bad piano, an inadequate stage, or an abject library. But Ravel was in fact an artist whose mastery was stimulated by circumscriptions. (Stravinsky and Britten are two others who come to mind.) We hear it in a work as popular as *Boléro* or in one as relatively little known as the superb Sonata for Violin and Cello. No wonder, then, that Ravel was enchanted by the challenge presented him in the fall of 1929, when Paul Wittgenstein asked him for a piano concerto for the left hand alone—sufficiently enchanted to interrupt work on a concerto he was writing for his own use.

Wittgenstein's first encounter with Ravel's Concerto was unhappy. Ravel struggled through the piano part for him with both hands, then played the orchestral part separately. "I wasn't overwhelmed by the composition," said Wittgenstein many years later. "It always takes me a while to grow into a difficult work. I suppose Ravel was disappointed, and I was sorry, but I had never learned to pretend." He enormously offended Ravel by proposing a number of changes, and it was because the two men were unable to come to terms that the premiere took place in Vienna instead of Paris. Marguerite Long, the pianist who gave the premiere of Ravel's two-handed G-major concerto, proved an effective peacemaker, and when Wittgenstein finally brought the Left-Hand Concerto to Paris in 1933, with Ravel conducting the Orchestre Symphonique, the occasion was a triumph for composer and pianist.

In my essay on Ravel's G-major Concerto, I quote part of a statement the composer made about his two piano concertos, in which he maintains that a concerto should "be light-hearted and brilliant, and not aim at profundity or at dramatic effects," and suggests that the G-major Concerto fits that description. He then goes on to concede that the Concerto for Left Hand is "very different. It contains many jazz elements, and the writing is not so light. In a work of this kind, it is essential to give the impression of a

---

[5]Technique is not just a quantitative thing that would allow you to establish that one pianist commands 922 Horowitz units but another only 741. Different kinds of music call for different kinds of finger, hand, and arm action, or for different kinds of body/mind interplay. A superb pianist who has the considerable technical equipment and the stamina it takes to play the Brahms Second Concerto—still as difficult as piano music gets—can be confounded by the opening of Ravel's *Ondine*. Or vice versa. It is possible to imagine that a two-handed Wittgenstein, free to choose his repertory, might have been a fine player of Mozart, Beethoven, Schubert, Schumann, and Brahms.

texture no thinner than that of a part written for both hands. For the same reason, I resorted to a style that is much nearer to that of the more solemn kind of traditional concerto."

Reviewing the Left-Hand Concerto in *La Revue musicale*, Henry Prunières regretted that "the author of *Daphnis*" had so seldom chosen "to let us observe what he was guarding in his heart instead of encouraging the legend that his brain alone invented these admirable sonorous phantasmagorias. From the opening measures, we are plunged into a world into which Ravel has but rarely led us." Perhaps at the end of the 1990s we are more inclined than our counterparts in the first half of this century to look for what is dark and thus to be more conscious of Ravel's sinister side, the side he explored in "Le Gibet" and "Scarbo" in *Gaspard de la nuit*, in *La Valse*, in the Sonata for Violin and Cello, in the second of the *Chansons madécasses* ("Aoua!"), and which is by no means absent from *L'Enfant et les sortilèges* and *Boléro*. With his entire oeuvre in view, we are ready to hear this Concerto as a singularly impressive distillation of the dark Ravel. Discussing this work, Ravel's student Claude Roland-Manuel spoke of its "caractère panique."[6]

As Prunières points out, Ravel establishes the climate in the opening measures. Cellos and basses create a distant thundercloud against which the contrabassoon plays a solemn theme. Low horns enter with a melody whose metrical dislocations first suggest those "jazz elements" which Ravel mentioned. The suspense of waiting for the soloist to begin playing is a traditional component of the concerto experience. Ravel produces that suspense not only with a crescendo cunningly built over thirty-two slow measures, but also by means of the harmony. The dissonance is resolved in two stages: The first, murky chord, set upon an E in the bass, is a dominant to the great arpeggio splash on A with which the piano at last asserts its presence, and the grand A-chord in turn moves to the Concerto's real keynote, D.

In a piece for left hand alone, we have the additional suspense that grows from the question "How in the world is this going to work?" Ravel had prepared thoroughly for his task. Arbie Orenstein, his biographer, lists the music he studied: "the *Six Études pour la main gauche* by Saint-Saëns, Godowsky's transcriptions for the left hand of Chopin's *Études*, and works by Czerny (*École de la main gauche*, Opus 399, and *24 Études pour la main gauche*, Opus 718), Alkan (´Etude, Opus 76, no. 1), and Scriabin (Prelude and Nocturne, Opus 9)." So not to worry.

Ravel, in a manner altogether characteristic of that fascinating, games-playing, mask-wearing personality, made his one-handed concerto as three-handed as he could, creating massive sonorities at which one might well

---

[6]In an inspired bit of program-planning, John Nelson once paired this Concerto with Mahler's cataclysmic Sixth Symphony.

marvel if they were produced in the ordinary way by two hands.[7] The piano's *grande entrée* begins with a leap that spans five octaves and is capped by a glissando from the bottom A on the keyboard to the top D.

To the ideas already presented, Ravel adds an expressive melody for the piano and a crackling scherzo that is punctuated by clattering cascades of parallel triads. The deployment of these ideas in what is surely the shortest concerto in the standard repertory is simple, concentrated, and correspondingly powerful. The color, gray and glare, is distinctive; the scoring is remarkably inventive, even for Ravel. A passage in the scherzo for flutes, plucked violins and violas, harp, and piano offers an example of Ravel's delight in mimicry, for it is the harp that plays a one-finger piano tune, while the piano plays harp music. Ravel saves for the cadenza his most eye-popping device of a soprano and tenor duet with an accompaniment in brilliant thirty-second-notes sweeping between the two voices. One more fierce orchestral crescendo and a four-second reminder of the scherzo bring this music to a brusquely furious end.

---

[7] Leschetizky's transcription for the left hand alone of the sextet from *Lucia di Lammermoor* actually requires three staves for its notation. Ravel stops just short of that.

# Max Reger

Johann Baptist Joseph Maximilian Reger was born at Brand in the Upper Palatinate, Bavaria, on 19 March 1873 and died in Leipzig on 11 May 1916.

## Concerto in F minor for Piano and Orchestra, Opus 114

*Allegro moderato*
*Largo con gran espressione*
*Allegretto con spirito*

Reger began work on his Piano Concerto at the beginning of June 1910. By the 30th of that month, the first movement was already being typeset and the second movement was complete in draft. The second movement was fully written out by 5 July, ready to go to the printer three days later. On 13 July the finale was "half finished," had "prospered enormously" by the next day, and was completely finished on the 16th. Frieda Kwast-Hodapp, to whom the score is dedicated, gave the first performance on 15 December 1910 with the Leipzig Gewandhaus Orchestra under Arthur Nikisch. There had been a public dress rehearsal the day before.

**Solo piano, two flutes, two oboes, two clarinets, two bassoons, four horns, two trumpets, timpani, and strings.**

*"You will sweat, sweat! Why do you play such stuff?"*
Reger to Frieda Kwast-Hodapp, 21 June 1910

Max Reger died of a heart attack in a Leipzig hotel room in the early morning hours of 11 May 1916. He had spent the evening with Karl Straube, the organist at Saint Thomas's Church and later its Kantor and thus successor, at eight removes, to Johann Sebastian Bach. They had talked about Bach, a passion they shared, and Reger had told stories of his recently completed concert tour of Holland. He was just forty-three, but he had crammed his life chock-a-block. His catalogue is prodigious, and the works in it are for the most part "difficult" and not the sort one thinks of as written quickly. In addition, he maintained a full career—meaning over 100 concerts a year— as pianist and conductor. His principal teachers had been Adalbert Lindner, the organist in his home town of Weiden in Bavaria, and then Hugo Riemann, best remembered as a musicologist but also a considerable theorist and pedagogue. He lived in Munich; in Leipzig, where he taught at the university and privately (George Szell was among his pupils); in Meiningen, where he led the Court Orchestra, made famous by Hans von Bülow (whose assistant was the twenty-year-old Richard Strauss) and Fritz Steinbach; and finally in Jena, where he went in hopes of peace and quiet.

Reger falls in the middle of that twenty-five-year span in which Mahler, Wolf, MacDowell, Delius, Debussy, Strauss, Nielsen, Sibelius, Busoni, Pfitzner, Vaughan Williams, Scriabin, Rachmaninoff, Schoenberg, Holst, Ives, Ravel, Ruggles, Falla, Bloch, Bartók, Stravinsky, Webern, Varèse, and Berg were born. Insofar as he never desired to upset the existing order, he belongs at the conservative end of that amazing spectrum. Like most of his contemporaries, he was, however, in the thrall of a rapidly modulating post-*Tristan* chromatic language and, within the bounds of tonality, he translated his fascination into a series of extraordinarily original, personal compositions. To accompany Reger on one of his harmonic voyages can be like a ride on the world's wildest roller-coaster, but the structure is safe and the track sure. Still, nothing that has happened in harmony since the beginning of this century makes his music any less challenging and new.

Reger learned some of his chromatic harmony from Bach, but what he got from Bach that was even more influential on his style was an unshakable belief in the structural and rhetorical power of polyphony.[1] In Reger's music there is likely to be a lot going on at any one moment. To this "maximalism,"

---

[1] Reger's delight in Bach has provided pleasure for three generations of pianists, amateur and professional, for he made hard but wonderfully playable piano duet arrangements of the Brandenburg Concertos. That was long before those works had attained their present staggering popularity, a process set in motion in the second half of the 1930s by the performances and recordings led by Reger's disciple, the great violinist and quartet leader Adolf Busch.

if I may be forgiven a pun I saw only after I had written it, there is added a Brahmsian appetite for rich sonority, with much weight in the lower and lower-middle registers. Music of exceptionally dense texture and facture is not apt to be immediately popular: J. S. Bach and Brahms furnish examples before Reger; Schoenberg and Sessions do so after him. It was not easy for Reger to establish himself in his early years, though by 1910, the year of the Piano Concerto, honors, which he unabashedly appreciated were coming his way and his music was getting to be widely performed in Germany. Holland was also friendly to his music, just as it was—uniquely—to Mahler's at this time. Reger's concert calendar sometimes makes amazing reading: his String Quartet, Opus 109, had its premiere in Barmen on the same evening that the Piano Concerto was introduced in Leipzig; two days before, his Piano Quartet, Opus 113, was given its first performance in Cologne, with three other major works being heard that evening in Leipzig, Munich, and Strasbourg (then German and Straßburg).

An honor that particularly delighted Reger, not least because it surprised him, was an honorary M.D. from the medical school of the University of Berlin. That day—it was about half way between the completion of his Piano Concerto and the first performance—he wrote to his friend Reinhold Anschütz, "If my medical practice grows to the size of my musical practice I really will work myself to death."[2] More often than not this was not a joking matter. A month earlier he had told his future biographer, the musicologist and conductor Fritz Stein, that the coming season threatened to be "dreadful—I am enormously, superhumanly busy." A month before that he had written to Frieda Kwast-Hodapp, who had invited the Regers to visit in Berlin: "I must work, I can't come. My work is all so urgent. I'll have rest only when I'm dead.—Your old beleaguered Reger."

A devoted husband, excommunicated for marrying a Lutheran and a loving father to the two daughters he and his wife adopted, Reger was a big man with a big hunger for music, work, friendship, food, beer (given up along with all other alcohol in 1912). His catalogue is astounding, the more so when one adds to the labor of composition his enormous activity as an extraordinary organist, powerful and versatile pianist (for years he was in effect chamber-music pianist-in-residence to the Leipzig Gewandhaus), impressive and revealing, if unconventional, conductor, and hard-working teacher. When he died in that Leipzig hotel room, newspaper in his hands, spectacles on his nose, page proofs of his newest choral work on the table, he had literally worked himself to death. Susanne Popp, editor of his correspondence with Stein, calls it "suicide in installments."

In 1896 Reger planned a piano concerto for Eugen d'Albert, the first

[2]Extracts from Reger's letters from *Max Reger: Briefe eines deutschen Meisters*, ed. Else von Hase-Koehler (Leipzig: Koehler & Amelang, 1928).

performer of international reputation to recognize his gift, but this project did not get beyond the sketch stage. He came to orchestral composition relatively late, when he was in his thirties, and wrote his first concerto for the violinist Henri Marteau in 1907–1908. About that time he met Frieda Kwast-Hodapp, then still in her twenties and recently married to her former teacher, the Dutch pianist and teacher James Kwast. Reger had immense admiration and affection for this young artist whom he addressed in letters as "Colleague in Apollo," "Passacaglia prima," "Clarinet Sonata," "Piano Sonata," "Piano Concerto," "Pitiable One (because you have to play this unspeakable concerto)," "Cadenzaless One," "Courageous in the Lord," and "Capitalist" (when an all-Reger concert had yielded an unexpected surplus and he was able to send her an extra 70 marks). She in turn remained devoted to his work as performer and teacher all her life (she died in 1949).

Reger's accounts to his friends tell us that Kwast-Hodapp was a splendid advocate for the Concerto, which she was later able to play on several occasions with the composer on the podium. There was warm applause from most of the audience, enough for Reger to be called to the stage twice; the reviews were, as usual, hostile. (The Leipzig *Tageblatt* called it "another miscarriage issuing from the inbreeding that chokes the Regerian muse.") Reger, as usual, was not surprised and not notably disturbed. He was of course pleased when a month later he was able to report to Duke George II of Saxe-Meiningen that "my 'feared' Piano Concerto had great success in Jena," but more typically he wrote, also to the duke, an ideal patron who loved and understood music and did not use it only for his social adornment: "My Piano Concerto will continue not to be understood for some years. Its musical language is too severe[3] and serious. It is, so to speak, the complement to the Brahms D-minor Concerto, and the public first has to get used to it." (The Brahms D-minor failed disastrously at its first performance, was still regarded as difficult and esoteric music when Reger wrote these lines in 1912, and did not become a pianists' "success" piece until a long way into this century.)

Reger's reference to Brahms's First Concerto is no surprise. He adored Brahms and performed his chamber and orchestral music as often as he could, and when we become acquainted with the design of Reger's Concerto—a massive opening Allegro, a very slow Adagio with religious connotations, and a finale as light as was compatible with the composer's temperament—we find in fact something quite akin to Brahms's early, rugged, and problematic masterpiece.

The music begins imposingly. Against the background of a drum roll with support from the basses, winds sing out a phrase of intense pathos that is continued and completed by the strings in a great downward plunge. Ex-

---

[3] Reger writes "*herb*," which carries a wide range of meanings, including austere, harsh, bitter, sharp, dry (as for a wine).

tensions of this idea rise to a climax, then subside. A moment of suspense
and then the piano enters with thunderous double octaves. The effect is that
of a cadenza, and Reger here is surely indebted to the second solo entrance
in Brahms's Concerto No. 2. In the middle of this cadenza something more
firmly thematic is adumbrated, whose rising fourths will play a crucial role in
the concerto. The agitation increases, followed by release in a new and tranquil theme. In the development these themes will exchange characters, the
first becoming more gentle and dreamy, the second almost fiercely grandiose.
The taut concentration of the recapitulation is balanced by a coda which is
not only expansive—there is much energy to "ground"—but brings the surprise of a new theme. Its steady quarter-notes, decorated by lovely pianistic
filigree, suggest a chorale; it actually quotes briefly a favorite German Christmas hymn with words and tune by Martin Luther, *Vom Himmel hoch* (From
Heaven Above). This seems to promise a serene close, but demonic trills and
clangorous octaves disrupt the atmosphere. The anguished opening phrases
of the concerto reappear, and the movement ends *marcatissimo* and triple
*forte*. Frau Kwast-Hodapp had hoped for a cadenza in this movement, but
Reger explained that the coda was too tautly wound to allow for such an
excursion.

The promise of the chorale phrase is redeemed in the Largo, a movement
that stands high among the great musical achievements of the miraculous
years just before the 1914–1918 War. (I would make the same claim for the
slow movement of Reger's Violin Concerto.) The music moves extremely
slowly and begins in utmost quiet, with the piano alone. The first chord,
though voiced differently and completely different in expressive effect, is the
same as the piano's opening chord in the first movement. After the piano's
dream-rapt melody the woodwinds enter, and then strings. What they play
too suggests the hymnbook. This Largo is saturated in the chorale style, but
the beloved melodies are hinted at, touched on, rather than fully sounded.
*Vom Himmel hoch* is part of this material, and so are *Nun ruhen alle Wälder*
(Now the Woods are All at Rest) (also known as *O Welt, ich muß dich lassen*
[O World, Now I Must Leave You] and Hans Leo Hassler's *Wenn ich einmal
soll scheiden* [When Some Day I Must Depart]), known as the Passion Chorale
from Bach's repeated use of it in the *Passion According to Saint Matthew*.

While Reger was fairly indifferent to the value judgments that critics
made about his music, he was unbounded in his contempt when "those asses"
could not hear these melodies. Another element is of a very different nature,
and that is an agitated reminiscence of the first movement, particularly the
demonic chains of trills. Most touchingly, Reger brings these sublime pages
to a close with an allusion to one of the most poetic of all concerto movements, the Andante of Beethoven's Fourth.

The Largo is Reger's vision of heaven. The finale, mystery swept away,
returns us to earth. As suggested earlier, the robust finale of Brahms's First

Concerto makes a good point of reference. Reger even manages a humorous gloss on his model when he inserts a delightful parody of a fugal episode. It is a confidently wrought movement, lighter in weight than its two predecessors, which is of course a perfectly normal arrangement for a concerto, and it brings this grand, demanding, indrawing, engaging work to a spirited close.

# Camille Saint-Saëns

Charles Camille Saint-Saëns was born in Paris on 9 October 1835 and died in Algiers on 16 December 1921.

The dates amaze: he was born the year of *Lucia di Lammermoor, I puritani,* and Schumann's *Carnaval;* when he died, Alban Berg's *Wozzeck* was nearly finished. *The Pickwick Papers* and *The Waste Land* were written within his lifetime. The entire life spans of Mahler and Debussy, of Grieg, Bizet, Dvořák, Musorgsky, and Tchaikovsky were encompassed within his own. He was born in the reign of Louis-Philippe; when he died, France was a republic, and the final curtain had fallen for the Russian, Austro-Hungarian, and German empires (the last of which had been founded when he was thirty-five). France had had steam railways for only three years when he was born, but he lived long enough to know that Captain Alcock and Lieutenant Brown of the Royal Flying Corps had flown from Newfoundland to Ireland in sixteen hours.

Across his life there lay the shadow of his two children's early deaths and the mystery of his wife's sudden desertion in 1881 (she lived until 1950!). Perhaps still darker, though no one was close enough to him to say for sure, was a certain discontent with the place assigned him in the musical landscape. He was applauded and honored, and, like Voltaire and Stalin, he was celebrated in statuary during his lifetime; still, some measure of recognition for which he yearned eluded him. The playwright and actor Sacha Guitry summed it up in a famous nasty remark: "If Monsieur Camille Saint-Saëns was determinedly wedded to *la Gloire,* I have a notion that she deceived him with Monsieur Debussy." And while Monsieur Saint-Saëns could be a cordial, helpful senior colleague to such juniors as Casella, Falla, Enescu, and Paderewski, he was venomous when it came to musicians whom his intelligence identified with certainty as threats to his life and thought: Musorgsky, Debussy, Stravinsky.

He seemed, for the most part, to make his way imperturbably through his many years, deploring excess in politics and art but not deeply affected by a changing world in which (in his own words) he yielded music "as an apple tree yields apples"; taught; conducted; played the piano and the organ; prepared transcriptions; worked on the scholarly edition of the works of Rameau; wrote articles and books about archaeology, astronomy, philosophy, botany, biology, Roman drama, and the history of the postage stamp, as well as about music; and traveled with zest.

We would have a hard time working out a chronology for his music on the basis of stylistic evidence alone. "This young man knows everything," said Berlioz, "but he lacks inexperience." We are apt to be a little down on him for the combination of fluency and emotional detachment that informs so much of his music. But that does seem to be how he meant to write. Alfred Cortot begins the chapter on Saint-Saëns in his *La Musique française de piano* with a bundle of quotations by the composer: "Beware of all exaggeration"; "For me, art is, above all, form"; "The search for originality is fatal for art"; "The artist who is not perfectly satisfied by elegant line, harmonious colors, a beautiful sequence of chords, does not understand art"; and—famously— "Art has the right to descend into the abyss, to insinuate itself into the secret folds of dark and distressed souls. This right is not a duty."

Saint-Saëns resembles Mendelssohn in being awesomely elegant in his command of craft, immensely likable when he aims to please, not always convincing when he aims for more. He is, as well, the victim of a cultural prejudice that causes us to take him not quite seriously because he is not German. He composed abundantly—the opus numbers go past 160—and one would hardly know where to look for a musician or a scholar who is acquainted with all of his music. His ample catalogue includes works that are in one way or another of genuine importance to us, as serious as his opera *Samson et Dalila*, whose most profane bits are the most attractive, and also the fiery Symphony No. 3; as sheerly charming as *The Carnival of the Animals*, a private joke not intended for publication (he would be horrified to know it has become the prime foundation of his fame); or the sparkling Piano Concerto No. 2. Cellists find his A-minor Concerto indispensable, as do violinists his Concerto in B minor and the Introduction and Rondo capriccioso. His two-piano *Variations on a Theme by Beethoven* are brilliant. And among the works whose positions in the repertory are more tenuous, the D-minor Violin Sonata and the symphonic poems *Le Rouet d'Omphale*, *Phaëton*, and *La Jeunesse d'Hercule* always astonish us with their vitality, not to forget *Danse macabre*, unjustly exiled to the Pops.

Berlioz also said that Saint-Saëns was as formidable a musical mechanism as he had ever encountered. Evidence of prodigious gifts came in early. At two, as Saint-Saëns recalled, he was listening with precocious connoisseurship to creaking doors, striking clocks, and particularly "the symphony of the kettle . . . [waiting with] passionate curiosity for its first murmurs, its slow crescendo so full of surprises, and the appearance of a microscopic oboe whose sound rose little by little until the water had reached a boiling point." At three he could find his way about the keyboard, and at four years and seven months he played the piano part of one of Beethoven's violin sonatas at a private concert. On 6 May 1846 in the Salle Pleyel in Paris—he was now ten and a half—he made his formal debut, playing concertos by Mozart and Beethoven, as well as solos by Bach, Handel, Hummel, and Kalkbrenner, and offering to play as an encore any Beethoven sonata requested, from memory of course. His widowed mother and his great-aunt did not, however, exploit him as a prodigy, and the next years were devoted to study, not just of music but of humanistic and scientific disciplines as well. He became a grand presence on the French musical scene, and at least in the Symphony No. 3 he both aspired to and reached the heights.

Charles Gounod was in the audience when Saint-Saëns introduced the Third Symphony in Paris in January 1887, eight months after its wildly successful premiere in London, and announced, as the composer left the stage, "There goes the French Beethoven!" No doubt that was quickly reported to Saint-Saëns, and he must have loved it. The Third Symphony is one of Saint-Saëns's most resolute moves in his courtship of *la Gloire,* and this aspect of the piece may be the one we are least likely to be convinced by. As the Beethoven Tenth, it simply doesn't make it. Nonetheless, it is a piece one can love as one can love the glorious Romantic hokum of Saint-Saëns's slightly older contemporary Gustave Doré, especially his illustrations for *The Inferno* and the Bible. That comparison does insufficient justice to Saint-Saëns's structural intelligence, though, and perhaps one wants to go back a century and invoke Piranesi's *Prisons,* with their compelling sense of drama, grandeur, and romance, to say nothing of their dazzling technical mastery.

Camille Saint-Saëns was a witty man. Even if we had only *The Carnival of the Animals* to tell us, we would know that. I do not believe, though, that Camille Saint-Saëns was, to his mind, an admissible subject for humor. Had he been a touch more easygoing about himself, he might with justice have claimed what the very old Richard Strauss said in 1947: "I may not be a first-class composer, but I *am* a first-class second-class composer."

The pianist Saint-Saëns had in mind while penning the coruscating measures of his piano concertos was of course his remarkable self. He had detractors who found his performances dry, clean to a fault; even Cortot, who took his music extremely seriously and played it superbly, used such words as "pasteurized" and "aseptic" when he described his playing. But let me close this introduction with the words of an admirer, a most perceptive one, Marcel Proust, who has left us an eloquent, not to say perfumed, description of Saint-Saëns at the piano:[1]

---

[1] One of the many theories about the haunting "little phrase" in Vinteuil's Violin Sonata in À *la recherche du temps perdu* is that it comes from Saint-Saëns's Violin Sonata No. 1 in A minor. Saint-

[It] was truly beautiful. . . . There were none of those *pianissimi* that make you feel as though you must faint if they go on any longer and which are cut off just in time by a reviving *forte*; none of those arpeggios that titillate every nerve in your body; none of those *fortissimi* that shatter your arms and legs as though you had flung yourself headfirst into the breakers, of those writhings, that tossing of the head and shaking of the locks, all of which adulterate the purity of music with the sensuality of dance. . . . Saint-Saëns had no trace of any of that in his playing. But it was regal. . . . [A great actor's] gestures and voice are decanted with such delicacy, with both gold and dross so finely filtered, that we are left with the impression of pure water through which we can see perfectly. Saint-Saëns's playing has attained just that purity and transparency. We see Mozart's concerto not through a stained-glass window or the by glow of footlights, but, as it were, through air separating us from our table or from a friend, an air so pure that we do not notice it. . . .

The moment Saint-Saëns took his seat, like any student at the Conservatoire, and played the Mozart concerto with such simplicity, there was not one of those strokes of inspiration in the C-minor Symphony, not one of the sad strains of *Henry VIII*, not one of the beautiful choruses in *Samson et Dalila*, not one of the inventive Bach transcriptions that was not there, surrounding the musician with a choir as impressive as the choir of the Muses themselves, smiling upon the genius they cherished like a sacred fire in his soul, and filling ours with delight, enthusiasm, and respect.[2]

# Concerto No. 2 in G minor for Piano and Orchestra, Opus 22

*Andante sostenuto*
*Allegro scherzando*
*Presto*

Saint-Saëns composed his Piano Concerto No. 2 in 1868 and gave the first performance at a Concert Populaire in Paris on 13 December that year, with Anton Rubinstein conducting.

**Solo piano, two flutes, two oboes, two clarinets, two bassoons, two horns, two trumpets, timpani, and strings.**

---

Saëns's association with Proust and with Proust's friend, the composer Reynaldo Hahn, is behind the thought that Saint-Saëns may have been homosexual, which in turn could shed light on the mysterious departure of his wife.

[2]Marcel Proust, *Essais et articles* (Paris: Bibliothèque de la Pléiade, Gallimard, 1971).

This Concerto, in which the worlds of Bach's organ loft and the cabaret meet so equitably, is the earliest work by Saint-Saëns that we commonly hear, although by the time of its premiere, the impression made by his Symphony No. 1 had been consolidated by the Trio in F, and Pablo de Sarasate had played his First Violin Concerto. The composition of the G-minor Piano Concerto came about because in 1868 the great Anton Rubinstein had given a cycle of eight concerto evenings in Paris with the thirty-two-year-old Saint-Saëns as conductor. As the project neared its conclusion, Rubinstein remarked that for all the times he had appeared in Paris as pianist, he had never conducted there: he would like to lead an orchestral concert before returning to Russia, and it would give him special pleasure to have Saint-Saëns as piano soloist.

Saint-Saëns later described the contrast between Rubinstein and himself: "He athletic, tireless, colossal in physical stature as well as in talent, myself fragile, pale, and a bit consumptive, we were a pair analogous to the one exhibited earlier in the persons of Liszt and Chopin." In three weeks Saint-Saëns produced the Concerto, discovering that while he had no trouble getting the piece written, he had budgeted too little time for practicing it. The performance was not as finished as he would have hoped, but he noted that it went well anyway and that the scherzo pleased especially. Alfred Cortot, in the highly appreciative chapter on Saint-Saëns in his *La Musique française de piano*, remarks a bit more ruthlessly that, except for the scherzo, "the work did not make a great impression" and that the composer played it "*faiblement.*"

In one of his more censorious moments, Saint-Saëns stated that to prefer Gounod's *Ave Maria* "meditation" on Bach's C-major Prelude to the Prelude unadorned was prima facie evidence of bad taste. In the first movement of his G-minor Concerto, Saint-Saëns expressed his admiration for Bach's abstract preluding manner in other terms. The pianist discovers the keyboard, and we in turn discover the pianist's fluency and strength. The piano writing with its flying octaves has been touched by Liszt—an influence on Saint-Saëns always—and the general effect of this splendid exordium is not unlike that of one of Liszt's Bach transcriptions.

Next we can discover the pianist's sense of humor. The little vamp for kettledrums with which the scherzo begins must have surprised and delighted the Parisians (a hundred years earlier, they might have applauded the way they applauded the surprise beginning of the finale of Mozart's *Paris* Symphony), and they probably went home whistling the dapper tune that begins in lower strings and bassoons over the piano's oom-pe-dees. The finale perhaps shows that the deadline was drawing near, but what writer would wish to be unsympathetic to that plight? Saint-Saëns was not, at any rate, stingy with the glitter, and the Concerto's close anticipates the popping of corks at the post-concert party.

# Concerto No. 4 in C minor for Piano and Orchestra, Opus 44

*Allegro moderato—Andante*
*Allegro vivace—Andante—Allegro*

Saint-Saëns composed his Piano Concerto No. 4 in 1875 and was the soloist at the first performance, which took place in Paris on 31 October that year, with Édouard Colonne conducting. The work is dedicated to the Austrian pianist Anton Door.

**Two flutes, two oboes, two clarinets, two bassoons, two horns, two trumpets, three trombones, timpani, and strings.**

The composer of the C-minor Concerto was a man of forty at the height of his powers: *Samson et Dalila*, the impressive oratorio *Le Déluge*, and the *Variations on a Theme of Beethoven* are contemporary to this work. Liszt had long ago become a strong influence on him and would remain so: Saint-Saëns knew the B-minor Piano Sonata and the tone poems thoroughly and had absorbed Liszt's technique of thematic metamorphosis.[3] (The name of Schubert seems not to figure in the Saint-Saëns biographies, and I do not know whether he played or otherwise knew the *Wanderer* Fantasy, that crucial source work for Liszt.) Saint-Saëns had little interest in the rhetorical and expressive possibilities of such transformations; what fascinated him was their implication for compositional economy, for elegance of facture. Particularly in this Fourth Piano Concerto and again, eleven years later, in the grand Third Symphony (dedicated to Liszt), Saint-Saëns, bringing to bear on the matter all of his intellect, imagination, and what Alfred Cortot calls his "*lucide volonté*," wrought quasi-Lisztian structures of remarkable originality and power.

The C-minor Concerto is in two movements, of which the first is in two parts and the second in three. It begins with a two-limbed theme, symmetrical (eight plus eight measures) and dominated by a three-note figure (with a short pause between the two notes), whch is in fact the first thing we hear. The orchestral strings play the first eight measures, *sec*, and the piano responds with a more buttery variant; the same thing happens with the second eight measures. In other words, the theme itself already contains a variation. The contrast between orchestra and solo sets a pattern for this

[3]For more about symphonic metamorphosis, see the essay on Liszt's Piano Concerto No. 2.

Concerto: the orchestra proposes and the piano elaborates, subjectively and often quite showily.

After the theme come two variations, each again including its own internal variant, and introducing an ever-expanding vocabulary of harmony, texture, and figuration. (Alfred Cortot, whose 1935 recording of this Concerto, in spite of some messy moments, is one of the glory moments in the history of the phonograph, reports that Saint-Saëns had exhorted him to "*jouer le solo comme une rôle,*" to play the solo like a part in a play.) Variation 2 is never concluded; rather, it dissolves into a slower movement, shifting into a major key (A-flat) at the same time. This begins as pure texture and figuration, but before long, a chorale melody emerges in the voices of wood-winds.

The piano responds with a new, meditative music, delicately harmonized and subtly poised in its rhythm: it is one of the rare poignant and personal utterances Saint-Saëns permits himself. At the height of a great crescendo, the piano proclaims the chorale with utmost majesty of sound, after which this movement, first traversing a passage of filigree, arrives at a close of touching simplicity.

Cortot writes that intuition had always led him to make an *attacca* into the second movement, to press forward just as soon as the string players could remove their mutes, and that when he acquired the manuscript of this Concerto—he was a great and famous collector—he was delighted to discover the instruction "*enchaîner*" at the end of the first movement. (This instruction did not make its way into the printed score.) Cortot liked the *attacca* because of the surprise produced by the sudden irruption of the scherzo after "*la conclusion extasiée*" of the Andante; of course it also draws attention to the unity of the Concerto.

The scherzo in fact begins with piano figurations—a descending four-note group and a triplet rhythm, both in ringing octaves—that we have heard before: to be precise, at the point where Variation 2 in the first movement turns into the bridge to the Andante. And the first time the orchestra has anything to offer in the scherzo other than the oom-pahs that tactfully second the piano's octaves, runs in double thirds, and flying arpeggios, it is the theme of the first movement, infected now and transformed by the giddiness emanating from the solo part. An underground conspiracy to replace the prevailing 2/4 meter with 6/8 takes hold in the trio, a captivating canter in which the orchestra ingeniously accents single notes of the piano tune. This, by the way, is the only theme in the second movement that is not derived from the first movement.

After the scherzo makes its expected return, the music again slows down. Unlike the previous Andante, this is more of an interlude than a full-fledged movement; it is, however, based on components of the first Andante, on the chorale as well as on the piano's meditative response. A grand pile-up of broken octaves culminates in a reverberant trill, against which horns and trumpets proclaim the first phrase of the chorale, now in martial dress (but also in 3/4 time). The piano picks it up, and that begins the pianistically inventive and brilliantly exuberant finale.

# Arnold Schoenberg

Arnold Franz Walter Schönberg, who spelled his name
Schoenberg after settling in the United States in 1934, was
born in Vienna on 13 September 1874 and died in Brentwood,
a suburb of Los Angeles, on 13 July 1951.

*My works are twelve-tone compositions, not twelve tone compositions.*
*Schoenberg to Rudolf Kolisch, 27 July 1932*

Like all of Schoenberg's main works from 1923 on, the Piano Concerto and the Violin Concerto are composed with the twelve-tone
(or twelve-note) technique, or, to use Schoenberg's own terminology,
both more precise and more awkward, "method of composing with twelve
notes related only to one another." Schoenberg himself suggested that the
presence of this method was a criterion for determining whether a work is
one of his main ones—obviously, though, referring only to the post-1923
pieces.

The method, anticipated in parts of the *Five Pieces for Piano*, Opus 23,
and the *Serenade*, Opus 24 (both completed in 1923), then fully explored
and consistently used in the *Suite for Piano*, Opus 25 (also 1923) and the
Wind Quintet, Opus 26 (1924), involves referring all of the pitches to a
particular ordering of the twelve notes of the chromatic scale. This ordering
is generally called the row or, more learnedly, the series or set. This is what
Schoenberg means by "related only to one another"—distinct, that is, from
all being related to one keynote or tonic. Every row has its own particular
properties or characteristics. The sequence of minor and major triads spelled
out by the row in Alban Berg's Violin Concerto is an example, and the

composer exploits these properties—he needs them, if you will—in working out his composition. His choice of ordering, therefore, is personal, not arbitrary.

Composing in this way does not determine a sound or a style. Schoenberg does not sound like Berg, and neither one sounds like Webern or Sessions or Dallapiccola or Babbitt. Webern already was Webern and sounded like Webern before his first twelve-tone pieces, and Stravinsky continued to sound like Stravinsky after he began to use this way of inventing music.

## Concerto for Piano and Orchestra, Opus 42

> *Andante*
> *Molto Allegro*
> *Adagio*
> *Giocoso (moderato)*

Schoenberg began to sketch his Piano Concerto in July 1942 and completed the score on 30 December that year. The first performance was given on 6 February 1944 by Edward Steuermann with Leopold Stokowski conducting the NBC Symphony. Because of his insistence on championing this work, Stokowski was offered no further engagements at NBC. The year before in Los Angeles, with Leonard Stein at the second piano, Steuermann had given a private performance for Schoenberg and friends.

**Solo piano, two flutes (second doubling piccolo), two oboes, two clarinets, two bassoons, four horns, two trumpets, three trombones, tuba, timpani, bells, gong, cymbal, xylophone, bass drum, snare drum, and strings.**

In *The Memoirs of an Amnesiac*, his second book of reminiscences and whatnot, the composer, pianist, radio entertainer, and occasional actor Oscar Levant recalls how, after achieving "a certain fame and notoriety," he asked Arnold Schoenberg, who had been his composition teacher off and on for three years and with whom, in an edgy sort of way, he was on rather friendly terms, to write him "a slight piano piece." Levant gave him a payment and reports that Schoenberg was delighted.

His account continues:

When I returned to New York there was correspondence and suddenly this small piece burned feverishly in Schoenberg's mind and he decided to write a piano concerto. He sent me some early sketches and it is possible that in the main row of tones my name or initials were involved. However, I wasn't prepared for a piano concerto and in the meantime Hans [sic] Eisler assumed the role of negotiator for Schoenberg. Among other things, the fee grew to a vast sum for which, as the dedicatee, I was promised immortality.[1]

The "vast sum" was $1,000, quite considerable then; it was the amount Elizabeth Sprague Coolidge had paid Schoenberg for each of his last two string quartets. But it was for personal more than financial reasons that Levant came to find the venture oppressive, and he withdrew from it. Almost all of Levant's orchestral engagements involved the music of his friend Gershwin, and it is as about as hard to imagine the New York Philharmonic engaging Levant, not the most refined of pianists, for the Schoenberg Concerto as it is to imagine him playing it.

There is, however, a Levantine postscript to the story. At a meeting with Schoenberg several years later, Levant "in a spasm of good will said, 'I owe you some money.' [Schoenberg] nodded agreement and I gave him a check. He was very cheerful about the whole thing. I didn't really owe him any money—it was just an excuse to ameliorate the old situation."[2] In fact, the commission fee was paid by Henry Clay Shriver, a well-to-do student of Gerald Strang, a composer who had been one of Schoenberg's teaching assistants at the University of California at Los Angeles.

A row, as well as being a matrix—or, as the composer John Adams has put it, the genetic code of the piece—may also be a theme in the familiar sense of the word. It is that in Schoenberg's Piano Concerto. The first thing you hear is the piano alone playing a lyric melody in a gentle waltz tempo. It begins with a phrase of eight measures, a nicely symmetrical twice-four. In the eighth measure, the orchestra inserts a soft, three-note punctuation mark. The piano melody up to this point is a statement of the row:

Ex. 1 (melody, mm.1-8)

[1]Oscar Levant, The Memoirs of an Amnesiac (New York: G. P. Putnam's Sons, 1965).
[2]Levant, op. cit.

Everything that happens thereafter is an outgrowth of the patterns of intervals those pitches define. By the way, I find no trace of Oscar Levant's name. The Schoenberg circle did go in for a certain amount of musical cryptography, but this work does not seem to be an example, at least not in its finished form.

But back to the music. The opening piano melody is expansive, and characteristically, it is generated by self-variation; that is, its continuing phrases consist of the same line or sequence of pitches as before, but first in retrograde inversion (with each downward step of the original replaced by an upward one of the same distance, and vice versa, *and* with the order of the notes reversed), then in plain retrograde, and finally in plain inversion. This is as orderly as can be, and it is in fact the procedure that generates the melody, but what Schoenberg would have wanted is for you to delight in the easy and natural-sounding unfolding of the melody. Or to put it another way, Schoenberg, like Bach, Haydn, Beethoven, or Brahms, would have wanted you simply to feel the satisfying result of his way of unifying material.

Characteristic, too, is the placement in that melody of the first orchestral punctuation mark to which I referred earlier. Piano concertos that begin with unaccompanied solo instruments are rare—no doubt because of the daunting precedent of the Beethoven Fourth—and the listener is likely to anticipate the first orchestral entrance with special attention. The first orchestral entrance here, as we have already noted, is strategically placed at a structurally vital point, namely, the close of the explicit statement of the musical shape that will be the source for the entire work. As the piano melody expands, orchestral punctuations occur more frequently. They also become a little less reticent, even to the point that for four measures the clarinet plays the melody along with the piano. The sonorous delicacy, however, of the first three-note punctuation—clarinet, violas, and cellos only—is typical of the orchestral writing throughout the Piano Concerto, as indeed it is of Schoenberg's music generally.

As for the further course of the first movement, Schoenberg outlined it in a handwritten note in the holograph near the end of the piano melody: "repeated in orchestra, piano adds a countermelody, this countermelody is repeated in orchestra, piano adds a second countermelody, all three together." In other words, it is a theme with variations. Apropos Schoenberg's glosses, there is an amusing one, all but one word in English, at measure 117, about two-thirds through the first movement: "13 mal [times] 9 = 117!!! It cost two days to find out, what wrong. A great error in construction at measure $13 \times 9 = 117$." Need one add that Schoenberg was desperately superstitious about the number 13?

The Concerto is laid out in four movements, to be played without pause. The lyric first movement is followed by an energetic, even aggressive, scherzo. Then comes a great Adagio, passionate, urgent, and rhetorical, which includes both a cadenza for the piano and the one extended passage in the work for the orchestra alone. Finally, there is a rondo, marked *giocoso*, humorous without always being good-humored, and whose central episode is a set of three variations on the theme of the Adagio. The opening waltz also makes a grand return, and the close of the concerto is emphatic and all but in C major.

In an explanatory note, Schoenberg paraphrased into English the events of his piano concerto in terms that perhaps seem a bit quaint, but which, in their concern for meaning, are not altogether surprising from a composer who, in his own metaphor, was less concerned with the Chinese philosopher's speaking Chinese than with wanting to know what he says:

> Life was so easy
> Suddendly [sic] hatred broke out (Presto)
> A grave situation was created (Adagio)
> But life goes on (Rondo)

This was long assumed to be have been a translation into words for Levant's benefit, but as Walter Bailey's fascinating study *Programmatic Elements in the Works of Schoenberg* makes clear, this program was in the composer's mind from the beginning. In his text *Fundamentals of Musical Composition,* Schoenberg advised his students and readers that even in the most modest exercise, "the student should never fail to keep in mind a special character. A poem, a story, a play or a moving picture may provide the stimulus to express definite moods."[3] In a lecture titled "Heart and Brain in Music" that he gave at the University of Chicago in 1946, Schoenberg began with Balzac's description of a man in his *Seraphita,* part of the *Comédie humaine:* "He was of medium height, as is the case with almost all men who tower above the rest.[4] His chest and his shoulders were broad and his neck was short, like that of all men whose heart is in the domain of the head." It was always Schoenberg's ideal that heart and head, fantasy and structure, should be inseparable allies, and that is something always to remember about him and his music.

---

[3]Very much worth knowing is one of Schoenberg's greatest—and smallest—pieces, *Music to Accompany a Film Scene,* Opus 34 (1929-30), whose three brief sections are titled "Threatening Danger," "Fear," "Catastrophe."
[4]Schoenberg himself was five feet, two inches tall.

# Concerto for Violin and Orchestra, Opus 36

*Poco Allegro*
*Andante grazioso*
*Allegro*

Schoenberg completed his Violin Concerto on 23 September 1936. It was published in 1939 and first performed on 6 December 1940 by Louis Krasner with Leopold Stokowski conducting the Philadelphia Orchestra. Schoenberg dedicated the score to his former pupil Anton Webern.

**Solo violin, three flutes (third doubling piccolo), three oboes, two clarinets with E-flat clarinet and bass clarinet, four bassoons, four horns, three trumpets, three trombones, tuba, timpani, xylophone, glockenspiel, tambourine, military drum, snare drum, tamtam, cymbals, triangle, bass drum, and strings.**

Schoenberg left Berlin on 17 May 1933. Hitler had become chancellor on 30 January, and on 1 March the composer Max von Schillings began the *Entjudung*—literally, the de-Jewing—of the Prussian Academy of Arts, whose president he was and where Schoenberg, succeeding Ferruccio Busoni, had taught since 1925. Schoenberg first went to Paris, where he formally rejoined the Jewish faith which he had left in 1898 to become a Protestant (Marc Chagall was one of the witnesses at the ceremony). On the last day of October he arrived in Boston, where he taught at the Malkin Conservatory and commuted to New York for other teaching assignments. Asthma sufferer that he was, he soon saw that one more Boston winter would kill him, and what the weather didn't accomplish the trains to New York, which he described as resembling crematoria on wheels, would. Declining offers from the Juilliard School and Chicago, he moved to Los Angeles in October 1934. There he taught privately and at the University of Southern California, the following year switching to the University of California at Los Angeles, where he stayed until his forced retirement when he reached the age of seventy in 1944. He never went back to Europe. He toyed with the idea of returning for his seventy-fifth birthday celebrations, but by then he was too ill. In 1949 Vienna, whose smug and arch-conservative musical establishment had hated and rejected his work, bestowed the freedom of the city on him now that his music seemed to be safe.

    In the summer of 1936, Schoenberg and his wife and their four-year-old daughter Nuria moved into a newly built house in Brentwood, where he was

to live the rest of his life. (Two sons were born in 1937 and 1941.) Schoenberg also began to compose again after a considerable hiatus; his last work
had been the Suite in G for String Orchestra, completed in December 1934.
Just before that had come his Cello Concerto and a Concerto for String
Quartet and Orchestra. Both are reworkings of eighteenth-century pieces, a
keyboard concerto by Georg Matthias Monn and a Handel concerto grosso.
These are pretty radical reworkings; nonetheless, as reworkings rather than
original compositions, they are in a sense part of Schoenberg's fallow period.
At the same time, both of them being concertos and dauntingly demanding
virtuoso ones at that, we can also think of them as preparatory warmups for
the Violin Concerto. At any rate, Schoenberg's first California pieces were
the Fourth String Quartet and the Violin Concerto, completed on 26 July
and 23 September 1936 respectively. He had worked on both scores simultaneously and, as always, he had worked quickly. His life was full of unfinished
projects, some of them gnawed-over for decades, but when he was *in vena* he
wrote with Mozartian facility and speed.

Although Otto Klemperer, then conductor of the Los Angeles Philharmonic, made noises about introducing the Violin Concerto in Los Angeles,
London, and Moscow in the 1937–1938 season, no performance materialized
until Stokowski, more or less over the dead bodies of the Philadelphia Orchestra's board and management, conducted the premiere in 1940.[5] The soloist was Louis Krasner, the Russian-born American violinist who had commissioned Alban Berg's Violin Concerto and was also the first to play the
Sessions Concerto with a professional orchestra.

Even now, performances of the Schoenberg Concerto are rare, though,
happily, some of the best of the younger violinists have taken it into their
repertory. It is formidably difficult, musically and technically, and early in its
history Schoenberg reinforced that reputation when he said that it would
require a new and special brand of fiddler with six fingers on the left hand.[6]

I don't know what it feels like to play Schoenberg's Concerto; I do know
that it sounds beautiful and very much like a concerto *for* rather than *against*
the violin (as was said of Brahms's Concerto). I also know that when it is

---

[5]Stokowski himself paid Krasner's fee. The conductor's insistence on programming the premiere of
Schoenberg's Piano Concerto with the NBC Symphony in 1944 cost him further engagements with
that orchestra.

[6]Schoenberg took violin lessons as a boy but does not seem to have gained great proficiency. In his
early twenties, as he told the story (in English) many years later, he "procured a large viola furnished
with zither strings, which produced the pitch and compass of a cello. This instrument . . . knowing
no better, I played by using the fingering of the viola. Soon thereafter I purchased a cello, and this
I also played with the same fingering with which I had played the violin, viola, and the (as I called
it) violincello. This went on quite a time, until [my friend Oskar] Adler had been told by a real
cellist that the fingering on the cello is quite different. The rest I had to find out myself." *Schoenberg,
Berg, Webern—The String Quartets, a Documentary Study*, ed. Ursula von Rauchhaupt (Hamburg,
Deutsche Grammophon Gesellschaft m.b.H, 1971).

commandingly and elegantly played—and I remember especially Joseph Silverstein's performances with the Boston Symphony under Erich Leinsdorf in 1965 and Seiji Ozawa in 1974, Zvi Zeitlin's with Leonard Bernstein and the New York Philharmonic in 1967, Christian Teztlaff's with Christoph von Dohnányi and the Cleveland Orchestra in 1988, and Viktoria Mullova's with Kazuyoshi Akiyama and the San Francisco Symphony in 1990—audiences like it.

Let us start at the surface, with the sound. The instrumentation is big, much bigger in fact that in most concertos somewhat idiosyncratic in distribution, but still within the framework of the "normal." Schoenberg's writing for this orchestra is, however, very special indeed. One of his choices here (but not only here) is to avoid octave doublings, meaning that if, for example, middle C occurs in a chord, there will be no lower or higher C in the same chord. This gives to each single sound and to each simultaneous stack of sounds a striking sharpness and singularity of profile.

This also presents the composer with a new challenge. In conventional scoring, most instruments are engaged in just such doublings much of the time. How then do you deploy an orchestra when there are no octave doublings? Schoenberg, indebting himself to Mahler, treats his large orchestra as a kaleidoscope in which you can find constantly varying chamber combinations, but with his limitless fantasy and dazzling technique, he creates a completely original style that is unmistakably full-orchestral at the same time.

This is also where some of the special challenges for the violinist come in. In any concerto the soloist needs to know what is going on in the orchestra, but no concerto offers a more richly varied, quickly changing—kaleidoscopic, in fact—series of relationships with the orchestra. It goes far beyond the ordinary both in the complexity of what is to be known and in the necessity of knowing it. What is required—and at an extreme level of concentration—is a chamber-musical sense of what is going on in every voice and of the harmonic, rhythmic, and melodic context of every musical event.

What beautiful things the kaleidoscope shows us: the solo violin beginning alone, low on the G-string, with darker echoes and comments from two groups of cellos; then the delicately imagined, carefully plotted entries of other instruments, one bassoon, violas (replacing the top line of cellos), bass clarinet and the other bassoons, basses, oboe (retiring the other winds) the orchestral violins (at which point the solo violin becomes an accompanist), and so forth; the fine texture at the beginning of the second movement, with the solo violin high and bright (but *piano*), accompanied by flute, bass clarinet, and muted cellos; in a different mood, the quartet in the finale for two bassoons with violin in double-stops.

And the percussion: nothing in the first movement except a single passage for xylophone and the miraculous entrance of the timpani for just four *piano/pianissimo* beats at the final cadence. (But how imaginative Schoenberg is at getting other instruments to function as pseudo-percussion!) The second movement has only timpani—ten notes in *pianissimo*. But in the finale which is marchlike and akin to the Israelites' triumphant "Almighty, thou art stronger than Egypt's gods" in *Moses und Aron* Schoenberg unleashes everything (except the timpani). There is the giddy place where snare drum and military drum begin a tattoo together with low strings beaten with the bows' wooden backs; the passage to which this tattoo leads, a quasi-cadenza accompanied by military drum and cymbal; and the sudden NOW!, setting off the brief coda and marked by an explosion of cymbals and bass drum (the latter saved for this moment).

All this is brilliant, and exuberantly so, but it is not there for its own coloristic, decorative sake. Everything is rigorously functional in this Concerto, which Joseph Silverstein has called "one of the great classical works, spare and precise." Schoenberg uses colors primarily in order to bring the right things into focus at the right times. This is also the reason the "orchestration" of the solo violin part is unprecedented in its complexity, its profusion of multiple stops, pizzicatos, tremolandos, and harmonics, all deployed to clarify the material and to separate the simultaneous currents of compositional activity. Everything that Schoenberg demands by way of virtuosity, individual and collective, is organic. The famous difficulty of this Concerto goes beyond the lack of that no-doubt-so-useful sixth finger on the left hand; Schoenberg might equally well have said that here is music for a musician with an extra ear and a few thousand more gray cells.

Apropos the conjunction of architecture and the virtuoso tradition, a word about cadenzas. I don't know another concerto so dominated by them. (Elgar's Violin Concerto comes to mind at once, and it is in its last-movement cadenza that that great work touches deepest mysteries, but there it is a question of one huge cadenza, while Schoenberg has riddled this whole piece with such interventions, great and small.) With their dazzling technical display, they appear to provide points of intellectual repose as well as loosenings of form and texture. That is true but also illusory, insofar as the cadenzas also function as large formal summaries, places where structural threads are gathered and where the music is, in a sense, at its most concentrated—another example of the delightful complexity of Schoenberg's imagination.

As in most of Schoenberg's major works from the middle 1920s on, all the melodic and harmonic material is generated from a single source idea, a particular way of ordering the twelve notes of our chromatic scale that defines, in John Adams's useful and appealing metaphor, the genetic code for the work. Semitones or halfsteps are prominent in that ordering—semitones proper like the A/B-flat with which the solo violin begins the Concerto (and which are immediately echoed in the cellos); semitones stretched into ninths by going, for example, not to the B-flat right next to the A but to the one an octave higher; or semitones inverted into sevenths, going from A to the B-flat below.

Ex. 1

These are intervals of enormous expressive potential, and they dominate the Concerto. The opening of the second movement affords an especially lovely example: a four-note chord is attacked, not quite synchronously, by muted cellos, then flute and bass clarinet, then solo violin. (The chord itself is made of a seventh and a ninth interlocked—in other words, of variants of semitones.) One by one the orchestral instruments, reticent accompanists, resolve their notes downward by half-steps, but the violin, with mixed passion and grace, swoops down a major seventh.

Ex. 2

Quite traditionally, Schoenberg has cast his concerto in three move-ments, of which the first offers the greatest diversity in rhythm, sonority, and mood. Then comes a quasi-slow movement a delicate song without words to begin with, but with excursions both toward more impassioned utterance and into something more of a scherzando character. After that comes the march finale, a rondo with a memory. Like some of Mozart's concerto finales, it turns out, in spite of a certain simplicity of language and style, to be the most generously and wittily inventive movement of the three.

# William Schuman

William Howard Schuman was born on 4 August 1910 in New York and died there on 15 February 1992.

## Concerto for Violin and Orchestra

*Allegro risoluto—Molto tranquillo—Tempo primo—Cadenza—
    Agitato, fervente*
*Introduzione (Adagio—Quasi cadenza)—Presto leggiero—Allegretto—
    Adagietto,*
*poco a poco accelerando al Allegro vivo*

Schuman composed his Violin Concerto on commission from Samuel Dushkin, for whom Stravinsky had written his Violin Concerto
and *Duo Concertant*, and whose "deeply perceptive musical insight"
is acknowledged in the original version of the present score. Schuman began
the Concerto in the spring of 1946, interrupted it in order to compose *Night
Journey*, a dance score for Martha Graham, and completed it on 13 July 1947.
The plan was for Dushkin to give the first performance with Serge Koussevitzky and the Boston Symphony. For reasons not now retrievable, Koussevitzky did not schedule the Concerto in his two remaining Boston seasons;
in the event, then, it was not Dushkin who gave the first performance but
Isaac Stern, and with Charles Munch conducting the Boston Symphony. The

date was 10 February 1950.¹ Subsequently, Schuman revised the concerto extensively, and Isaac Stern introduced the new version on 24 February 1956 at an American Music Festival celebrating the fiftieth anniversary of the Juilliard School of Music, whose president Schuman was at that time. Jean Morel conducted the Juilliard Orchestra. In its third and final version, the work was reintroduced at the Aspen Festival on 9 August 1959 by Roman Totenberg with Izler Solomon conducting.

**Solo violin, three flutes (third doubling piccolo), two oboes (second *ad libitum*) and English horn, three clarinets (third *ad libitum*) and bass clarinet, two bassoons (second *ad libitum*) and contrabassoon, four horns, three trumpets, three trombones, timpani, snare drum (with and without snares), suspended cymbal, bass drum, crash cymbals, chimes, and strings.**

On several occasions William Schuman turned with striking originality and strong effect to the concerto, beginning with a work for piano and chamber orchestra in 1942, continuing with the three versions of the Violin Concerto and the beautiful *Song of Orpheus* for cello and orchestra. Twice Schuman interestingly combined instrumental concerto soloists with singing: the delightful *Concerto on Old English Rounds*, Schuman's largest work in this genre, is a piece for viola with women's chorus and orchestra, and *The Young Dead Soldiers*, based on a text by Archibald MacLeish, is in effect a double concerto for soprano and French horn. Schuman's last concertante work is the set of *Three Colloquies* for French Horn and Orchestra, composed in 1979.

The Violin Concerto was well received at its premiere in 1950. I suppose a tape must exist of that performance, but I have never heard it. It is easy, though, to imagine how suited the temperament of the twenty-nine-year-old Isaac Stern and the fiery Munch would have been to the projection of what the composer described as his "very Romantic" concerto. Only Schuman himself was dissatisfied with the piece: "Munch loved it and praised it highly; Stern liked it; it was successful with the audience. But I wasn't happy with it. I didn't like the three-movement structure and I didn't like the second movement."² He withdrew the score, but the composition of the String Quartet No. 4, his baseball opera *The Mighty Casey*, a score for Martha Graham called *Voyage for a Theater*, a remarkable piano cycle titled *Voyage*, and *Cre-*

---

¹My colleague Richard Freed, program annotator for the National Symphony, Washington, D.C., points out that Schuman's Concerto "repeats a frequently observed phenomenon . . . in having been composed for a soloist who never performed it." Among the violin concertos Freed cites are those by Schumann and Dvořák for Joseph Joachim, Tchaikovsky's for Yosif Kotek, and Barber's for Iso Briselli.

²Cited in liner note on Rovert McDuffie's EMI/Angel recording, DS37341.

*dendum*, an orchestral work commissioned by the State Department for UNESCO, as well as the sheer demands of life such as, for example, the addition of a Dance Division at Juilliard, intervened before there was time or occasion to revise it.

The principal issue in the two revisions of 1956 and 1959 was "How many movements?" Originally there were three, the most familiar design for concertos. The first corresponded pretty much to the present first movement, the third rather less closely to the present finale from *Presto leggiero* up to the coda. The middle movement that Schuman did not like was an Interlude (*Andantino*). He finally settled on a two-movement design something like the one that had worked so well for his Third Symphony. He described it as "two big chunks of music, two big symphonic movements, each self-contained but inter-dependent." He added the grandiloquent coda in the first revision and the Adagio Introduction to the second movement in his final recension. One thing that was never at issue was the violin writing. "I can feel it on the violin," said Schuman, himself quite a skilled fiddler in his young years, and the solo part, while difficult, is brilliant in effect and thoroughly rewarding.

Most of the composers who began to call themselves "Romantic" or "Neoromantic" in the 1980s are in wimpy retreat. When William Schuman described himself as "an unabashed Romantic," as he liked to do, he was thinking of the real Romantics—exploring artists full of fervor and fire. The way the Violin Concerto begins—charges into action, one wants to say—leaves no doubt about the composer's temper and conviction. *Risoluto*, the adjective that qualifies this Allegro, is a good Schuman word: characteristically, his music is determined and tough.

The solo violin, enjoined to play "with full, broad strokes of the bow," gets things going with a splendidly ample melody. Impressive in itself, it is also a rich seedbed for subsequent ideas and developments. So, for that matter, is the accompaniment, sharp, irregularly placed chords for real and imitation percussion (snare drum played with wire brushes, plus bass clarinet, bassoon, muted horns, and strings struck with the wooden backs of the bow). The violin melody not only traces handsome curves; it also moves rhythmically in that Schuman constantly finds new patterns for the divisions of measures (two half-notes, a half and two quarters, four quarters, eight eighths phrased with the beat or syncopated across it, triplets, and so forth). This melody, constantly renewing and varying itself and briefly assumed by the cellos, unfolds for a good two minutes and a half, during which the accompaniment also becomes more and more involved.

A long tutti begins with wild energy but calms down into a more lyrical music. This prepares the way for a glorious new solo opportunity, this one *molto tranquillo* in character. The violin is muted here, the accompaniment is for divided and muted strings, playing slow chords. The solo evolves into duets with clarinet and flute. A bridge that sounds like improvisation takes us back to the first tempo and to yet more transformations of the opening melody. The violin part becomes more virtuosic, this aspect then being allowed ample play in a real cadenza. This begins by concentrating on brilliance and ends in a reflective manner. What emerges next is the closing section of the movement, *agitato*, *fervente*, swift-moving, mercurial, bringing still more new thoughts about the opening material, rhythmically exciting, and charging to a bravura finish.

The second movement opens with a proclamatory introduction in slow tempo. The forceful writing for brass and strings is underlined by a pugnacious timpani solo. The violin's response is to wax more lyrical than ever: taking the three timpani pitches—E, F-sharp, B—as a point of departure, it offers a new melody, broad and quiet. The orchestra grows silent and, still at a slow tempo, the soloist plays a quasi-cadenza. Twice its mood is jolted by single measures of *presto*. These interruptions are harbingers of the next "real" movement to come, a snappy (*presto leggiero*) fugue for strings on a jagged subject.[3] The fugue yields to new and often playful variants of earlier ideas. An *allegretto* features clever, in fact outright funny dialogue between the solo violinist and his colleagues in the orchestra.

A dramatic and sonorous passage for orchestra leads to a lyric *Adagietto* in which the violin's thoughts again turn to the first movement. Gradually the music speeds up. Then, contrary to the usual Romantic concerto ethos in which The One vanquishes The Many, the solo violin is engulfed in an overpowering close for the full orchestra.[4]

[3]The earliest example I can recall of such an impatient incursion of the coming movement into the present one occurs in the transition from the introduction into the first movement proper of Beethoven's B-flat major String Quartet, Opus 130. At the beginning of the finale of the *Hammerklavier* Sonata, Opus 106, Beethoven does the converse; that is, ghosts of one movement persist while the next is trying to get going. Listen also to wonderfully witty variants of this idea in Mahler's Symphony No. 5, Debussy's *Ibéria*, Elgar's Cello Concerto, and Elliott Carter's String Quartet No. 1.

[4]In this coda, added in 1956, Schuman revisits the close of his own *Credendum*, written the year before. As for the surprising solo-tutti situation in these last pages, the question occurs to me whether Schuman was impressed by and was emulating the similar close of Bernstein's quasi–piano concerto, *The Age of Anxiety*, first performed in 1949.

# Robert Schumann

Robert Schumann was born in Zwickau, Saxony, on 8 June 1810 and died, insane, at Endenich, near Bonn, on 29 July 1856. Some reference works give him a middle name, Alexander, but that is a fiction.

## Concerto in A minor for Cello and Orchestra, Opus 129

*Not too fast*
*Slow*
*Very lively*

Schumann composed his Cello Concerto, which he listed in his own catalogue as a *"Concertstück"* for cello and orchestra, between 10 and 24 October 1850, but the first performance was posthumous, given by Ludwig Ebert at the Leipzig Conservatory on 9 June 1860 at a concert in honor of the composer's fiftieth birthday. In 1966 Dmitri Shostakovich arranged this work as a violin concerto; in 1986 a similar transcription by Schumann himself, presumably made for Joseph Joachim, came to light among the Joachim papers at the Prussian State Library, Berlin.

Solo cello, two flutes, two oboes, two clarinets, two bassoons, two horns, two trumpets, timpani, and strings.

On 1 September 1850 the Schumanns—Robert, Clara, and six children—moved to Düsseldorf after six unhappy years in Dresden, a city of which Clara, always quick to be judgmental, said, "Everything seems so antiquated here. Not a single intelligent person can be seen on the street; they all look like Philistines! Musicians one doesn't see at all." Actually, Dresden was a lively musical center, not least because of Wagner's presence there until 1849, but the Schumanns found it personally and artistically stultifying. The fact that the Royal Saxon Opera declined to stage Schumann's *Genoveva* rankled, no doubt. Schumann had a good friend in the conductor and composer Ferdinand Hiller, and when Hiller had left Dresden for Düsseldorf in 1847, he had recommended that Schumann succeed him as conductor of the Dresden Liedertafel. Three years later, when Hiller was ready to move again, this time just a few miles upriver to Cologne, he once again proposed Schumann as his successor, and on 31 March 1850 Schumann formally accepted his appointment as Düsseldorf's municipal music director.

Düsseldorf had a reputation as a conductor-eating town (why was Hiller so eager to move on to Cologne?), but Schumann badly wanted an orchestra of his own and he was willing to give Düsseldorf a try. He arrived at his new Rhineland home in high spirits, and the Düsseldorfers did everything they could to make their new music director feel welcome, unleashing an exhausting round of speeches, serenades, celebratory concerts, banquets, and balls. But contentment was brief. Clara worried about social standards, especially "the breezy, unconstrained conduct of the women, who at times surely transgress the barriers of femininity and decency. . . . Marital life is more in the easy-going French style." (All she could do about the women was to avoid them.) Both Robert and Clara were distressed by the noisiness of their first apartment, although a Rhine excursion at the end of the month and a move to quieter quarters helped.

Through all this turmoil, Schumann's creative energies were not to be suppressed: in just fifteen October days he composed his Cello Concerto, and in what remained of 1850 and in 1851 he wrote the *Rhenish* Symphony, revised his D-minor Symphony into what he considered its definitive form (Symphony No. 4), and wrote two violin sonatas, the *Märchenbilder* for viola and piano, two substantial cantatas, and several overtures on literary themes. The Cello Concerto—and this always comes as a surprise—is the first important one since the beautiful examples by Boccherini from the 1780s.[1]

---

[1] I don't know whether Schumann was familiar with any of Boccherini's music: there is no mention of it in his collected prose writings. Schumann had nothing good to say of the music of Bernhard Heinrich Romberg (1767–1841), whose cello concertos enjoyed a certain vogue. On the other hand, Beethoven's Triple Concerto, in which the cello soloist is very much *primus inter pares*, is likely to have been a source of inspiration to him: Beethoven's glorious Largo, especially, points toward the world of Schumann. Schumann himself played the cello a bit, and in 1832, when problems with his

The day Schumann finished the Cello Concerto he conducted the first of his ten subscription concerts; Clara was his soloist in Mendelssohn's G-minor Piano Concerto, and, except that Robert was miffed because she got more attention than he did, it went well. Nonetheless, it soon became inescapably clear that Schumann was unequal to his new position, and in October 1852 he was asked to resign. The matter was smoothed over temporarily, but a year later he had conducted his last concert in Düsseldorf. Always subject to depression, Schumann threw himself into the Rhine on 27 February 1854. This suicide attempt was not his first. He was rescued and committed into Dr. Richarz's hospital at Endenich, where he died two and a half years later.

Clara Schumann was delighted by the Cello Concerto. "It pleases me very much and seems to me to be written in true violoncello style," she noted in her diary on 16 November 1850. The following October she wrote: "I have played Robert's Violoncello Concerto through again, thus giving myself a truly musical and happy hour. The romantic quality, the vivacity, the freshness and humor, also the highly interesting interweaving of violoncello and orchestra are indeed wholly ravishing, and what euphony and deep feeling one finds in all the melodic passages!" Robert, on the other hand, seems to have had reservations: he canceled plans for a performance in the spring of 1852 and he did not send it to Breitkopf & Härtel, his Leipzig publisher, until 1854.

Here we encounter the experimental side of Schumann's temperament. He had several times shown interest in finding ways to connect the parts of a multi-movement composition: the twenty-one sections of *Carnaval*, for example, are based on two related four-note cells; the movements of the Symphony No. 4 are to be played without break and are thematically related; and the first movement of the Piano Concerto is a series of explorations of one three-note idea.

In the Cello Concerto, each movement is linked to the next, and the middle one, even while it blooms in gloriously expressive song, has something of the character of a bridge or an intermezzo.[2] The Concerto begins with three solemn chords for woodwinds with pizzicato strings. Their immediate purpose is to usher in the solo cello's impassioned melody, but we soon discover that they have more than a local function, appearing at many of the Concerto's important junctures and especially pervading the slow movement.

---

right hand made it impossible for him to continue playing the piano, he consoled himself for a time by returning to the cello, which he had studied briefly as a boy.

[2]Here Schumann took a leaf from Beethoven's book. In many of Beethoven's compositions in the first decade of the nineteenth century, the middle movements have something of this bridge character: for example, those in the Triple Concerto and the *Waldstein* and *Appassionata* Sonatas.

They are not, by the way, static and unalterable; rather, Schumann constant-ly finds new harmonies, rhythms, and colors for them, although they are always and instantly recognizable. And to make the bridge from the slow movement to the finale, Schumann turns the cello theme itself into a grip-ping recitative, fascinatingly shared by soloist and orchestra in a moment both tender and full of pain.

Like the Piano Concerto, Schumann's Cello Concerto has no opening tutti, only a brief but striking gesture that introduces the soloist right away. That gesture is the one I have already mentioned, the three rising chords for woodwinds, each accented by pizzicato strings. Quiet though this is, it sug-gests the opening of a theater curtain, and the performer who stands revealed is an inspired singer who gives us an expansive and constantly developing—that is, non-repeating—melody. Here is Schumann at his most personal, his most poignantly vulnerable. Only when this lyric utterance is done does the orchestra ground the music with a vigorous and impassioned paragraph. Clearly, though, Schumann means this to be the cellist's day, and the soloist returns with another lyric and exploring song, one of great range and full of wide intervals. A brilliant passage in triplets ends the exposition. The de-velopment is a kind of contest between virtuoso display and lyricism, and the chugging triplets are constantly interrupted—almost rebuked, it seems—by reappearances of parts of the opening melody in ever more distant and mysterious keys.

After the recapitulation, the opening wind chords return, now heard from a deeply strange harmonic perspective. This time, the cello responds not with its first melody, but with a brief transition that gently sets the music down in F major. The slow movement has begun, and Schumann gives us a new melody, one full of melancholy downward curves. Like a chorus of sym-pathetic mourners, woodwinds echo the ends of the phrases. The passage reminds us that Tchaikovsky was one of the great Schumann-lovers. The accompaniment is notable, for along with neutral pizzicato chords we hear a soft countermelody played by another solo cello. A solo cello had appeared in the slow movement of the Piano Concerto that Clara Schumann (then Clara Wieck) had composed as a girl of sixteen and in whose orchestration Robert had had a hand; he himself used the same effect, and most wonder-fully, in the Lento of his own Violin Concerto of 1853. Brahms, one of Schumann's heirs, raised the voice of the cello to even greater prominence in the Andante of his Piano Concerto No. 2, and Tchaikovsky virtually turned the slow movement of *his* Piano Concerto No. 2 into a trio with cello and violin.

After the urgent recitative that forms the bridge into the finale, Schu-mann gives us a more swift-moving music than any we have yet heard in the piece. Unfortunately, it is likely to sound not brilliant but just damnably difficult. Schumann relies much on sequences, and it takes a special mix of planning and spontaneity to bring out the energy in this music. (The 1953 Prades Festival recording by Casals and Ormandy shows wonderfully what can be done.) The drooping two-note phrases from the slow movement are often heard in the background.

Schumann moves into the coda by way of an accompanied cadenza, an inspiration to Elgar and probably also to Schoenberg and Walton in their violin concertos. Many famous cellists, among them Casals, Piatigorsky, and Starker, all of whom should have known better, have struck out thirty-two measures of Schumann's music at this point and substituted grandly rhetorical unaccompanied cadenzas of their own. But Schumann was right, he really was: in the last moments of this finale, which is so difficult to move purposefully forward, it is important not to bring everything to a halt but to keep the momentum going, as Schumann does with his in-tempo cadenza. When he emerges from this episode, one of the Concerto's most original and effective, Schumann shifts metric gears, going from 2/4 into a still peppier 6/8, a device Brahms found worth imitating, and often.

## Concerto in A minor for Piano and Orchestra, Opus 54

> *Allegro affettuoso*
> *Intermezzo: Andantino grazioso*
> *Allegro vivace*

That is how the movements are marked in the score and how they are usually given; Schumann, however, wished them to be listed in concert programs as follows:

> Allegro affettuoso
> Andantino and Rondo

Between 4 and 20 May 1841, Schumann composed a Concert Fantasy for Piano and Orchestra, and on 13 August that year, Clara Schumann, eight and a half months pregnant, played it through twice at a closed rehearsal of the Leipzig Gewandhaus Orchestra with Felix Mendelssohn conducting. Four years later, the Fantasy, in somewhat different form, became the first movement of Schumann's Piano Concerto. He began that transformation in late May 1845, completing the second movement on 16 July and the finale on 31 July. Clara Schumann was the soloist at the first performance, which was given in Dresden on 4 December 1845; the conductor was Ferdinand Hiller, to whom the work is dedicated. The Fantasy in its original form was not heard again until the summer of 1967, when Malcolm Frager played it at a reading rehearsal with the Berkshire Music Center Orchestra at Tanglewood, Erich Leinsdorf conducting. The following summer, also at Tanglewood but with the Boston Symphony, Frager and Leinsdorf gave the Fantasy its first public performance, this time using it as the first movement of the Piano Concerto. Frager was a fervent champion of the original version of the first movement and played it whenever he could persuade a conductor to let him do so.

**Solo piano, two flutes, two oboes, two clarinets, two bassoons, two horns, two trumpets, timpani, and strings.**

"And are you a musician, too?" they used to ask Robert Schumann when he went along on his wife's concert tours. Clara Schumann, née Wieck, was a celebrated keyboard artist from her youth, and she was renowned through her long life (1819–1896) for her musical intelligence, taste, sensibility, warm communicativeness, and truly uncommon ear for pianistic euphony. She was a gifted and skilled composer, and Brahms, who was profoundly attached to her when he was in his early twenties and she in her middle thirties—and indeed all his life, though eventually at a less dangerous temperature—never ceased to value her musical judgment.[3]

Their marriage, though in most ways extraordinarily happy, was difficult, what with Robert's psychic fragility and Clara's demanding and conflicting roles as an artist, an artist's wife, and a mother who bore eight children in fourteen years. Their courtship was difficult as well. Clara's father, Friedrich Wieck, was a celebrated piano pedagogue, and when Schumann was an unwilling and easily distracted law student at the University of Leipzig in 1828, he took lessons from him.[4] Clara was then just nine, but she was already beginning to give concerts. Immediately there was mutual liking between the gifted girl and the moody, piano-playing law student. Soon Schumann left for a year at the University of Heidelberg, where he found law school no more congenial than he had at Leipzig. When he returned to Leipzig in 1830, it was to live in the Wieck household and, finally with his widowed mother's blessing, to prepare himself to become a musician.

Quickly there was distress on practically every front. Schumann quar-

---

[3]Some questions about the connection between Brahms and Clara Schumann will and need never be answered. For more on the subject, see my essay on the Brahms First Piano Concerto.
[4]On his way to Leipzig for the first time, Schumann had, characteristically, made a huge detour, first to Bayreuth to see the home of Jean Paul, the patron saint of German literary Romanticism, then to Munich to call on Heine, whose poems would inspire some of his greatest songs.

reled not only with Friedrich Wieck about the course his training ought to take, but also with Heinrich Dorn, the theory teacher to whom he had gone against Wieck's advice. Deaths in his family affected Schumann deeply, he suffered his first attacks of depression, and his devotion to cigars and champagne jeopardized his health. Through the unwise use of some sort of mechanical contraption for strengthening the middle fingers of his right hand, he did so much physical damage that he had to give up any thought of a career as a pianist.[5]

Then Clara Wieck fell in love with him. In a few years he would reciprocate that feeling, passionately, but here too he made a considerable detour, becoming involved with Ernestine von Fricken, another of Friedrich Wieck's pupils. (Ernestine was the illegitimate daughter of Baron Ignaz von Fricken, the composer of the beautiful and solemn theme on which Schumann based his *Symphonic Études*.) After that affair was broken off, Schumann, in what may only have been a cruel tease of Clara, put out the word that he was thinking of marrying someone else. When, finally, he was ready to return Clara's love, Wieck did everything in his power to separate the two, even invoking the law. Meanwhile, Clara encouraged Robert's advances but refused to marry him without financial security and her father's permission.

These were years, for Robert, of anger, despair, heavy drinking, lawsuits, and fantastic fertility in composition. Most of his greatest piano works— *Davidsbündlertänze*, *Carnaval*, the F-sharp-minor Sonata, the *Phantasiestücke*, the *Symphonic Études*, the F-minor Sonata, *Scenes from Childhood*, *Kreisleriana*, the C-major Fantasy, *Humoreske*, the G-minor Sonata, the *Novelletten*, and *Faschingsschwank aus Wien* among them—come from this time. Schumann had also founded what would long be an influential magazine, the *Neue Leipziger Zeitschrift für Musik*, later *Neue Zeitschrift für Musik*, and had begun his distinguished career as a writer about music. He had formed friendships with Chopin, Mendelssohn, and Ignaz Moscheles. And finally, in 1840, the various legal, psychological, and financial obstacles were overcome and Robert and Clara were able to marry. That became Schumann's great song year: the Heine and Eichendorff *Liederkreise*, *Myrthen*, the songs on texts by Justinus Kerner, *Frauenliebe und -leben*, and *Dichterliebe* are among the songs— 136 in all—that bear that date.

Clara Schumann was ambitious for her thirty-year-old husband and urged him to conquer the world of orchestral music as well. He had actually ventured into that territory a few times, making starts on four piano concertos and writing a rather jejune symphony in G minor, but he had not yet met

[5]Just what happened to disable Schumann's hand is a disputatious business. The story about the mechanical device is the classic one; however, various revisionist theories circulate: for example, that the partial paralysis of his hand was caused by mercury poisoning, the unfortunate by-product of a cure for syphilis, or that the ailment was psychosomatic, resulting from his guilt about masturbating.

with success. He now went ahead and produced a superb Concert Fantasy with Orchestra for Clara as well as writing two symphonies: the first version of the D-minor (now known almost exclusively in its revised form of 1851 and listed as No. 4) and the *Spring*. He could interest neither publishers nor orchestras in the one-movement Concert Fantasy, and so he expanded it into a full-length three-movement concerto. In doing so he revised the original Fantasy, making choices, as almost always he was apt to do whenever he had second thoughts, in the direction of safety and conventionality. One can only guess whether the revisions of the Concert Fantasy and those of the *Davidsbündlertänze* and *Kreisleriana* reflect Schumann's own musical convictions or responses to the urgings of the more conservative Clara.[6]

In 1839 Robert had written to Clara: "Concerning concertos, I've already said to you they are hybrids of symphony, concerto, and big sonata. I see that I can't write a concerto for virtuosi and have to think of something else." He did. Now, in June 1845, while the metamorphosis of the Concert Fantasy was in progress, Clara Schumann noted in her diary how delighted she was at last to be getting "a big bravura piece" out of Robert (she meant one with orchestra), and to us, even if it is not dazzling by Liszt-Tchaikovsky-Rachmaninoff standards, the Schumann Concerto is a satisfying occasion for pianistic display. (Of course it is very much more than that.) On the other hand, compared to the concertos by Thalberg, Pixis, and Herz that Clara had played as a young prodigy, Schumann's Concerto, considered strictly as bravura stuff, is tame by comparison.[7]

Schumann's "something else" was noticed—first of all, of course, by Clara, who wrote in her and Robert's marriage diary that in the Fantasy "the piano is interwoven with the orchestra in the most delicate way—one can't imagine the one without the other." Most of the chroniclers of the first public performances, along with noticing how effective an advocate Clara was for the Concerto, were also attuned to the idea that something new—and very pleasing—was happening in this work. Many of them noted as well—and how much all pianists will appreciate this—that because of this "interweaving," the Concerto needs an exceptionally attentive and sensitive conductor.

---

[6]It is not easy to get a fix on Clara's feelings about Robert's music. I get the impression that as an artist she was more down-to-earth than imaginative (as she was certainly a down-to-earth woman), that she was not at ease with the darker and more fantastical sides of her husband's musical personality, and that her championing of his work, a championing that was somewhat cautious at least until after his death, was founded more on loyalty and personal love than on deep artistic identification.

[7]Under Robert's influence, Clara's recital programs changed after her marriage: the showpieces began to drop away and there was a greater presence of "solid" repertory such as Beethoven sonatas and even the occasional piece by Robert Schumann. In this sense, Clara Schumann influenced the next generation of pianists, players such as Anton Rubinstein, von Bülow, Tausig, and her own contemporary, Charles Hallé, much as Artur Schnabel changed ideas about program-building in the second quarter of the twentieth century.

F.W.M., who reviewed the first performance in Leipzig on New Year's Day 1846 for the *Neue Zeitschrift für Musik,* noted that the many interchanges between solo and orchestra made the first movement harder to grasp at first hearing than the other two. One thing that strikes us about this first movement—but perhaps only in a very good performance—is how mercurial it is, how frequent, rapid, and sometimes radical its mood-swings are. Or, to put it another way, how Schumannesque it is.

The opening is as dramatic as can be. The orchestra fires the starting gun, a single eighth-note E, and the piano moves out of the blocks with a powerful cascade of fully voiced chords.[8] Not only is the cascade itself dramatic, so is the contrast between it and the wistful oboe tune it introduces and which the piano immediately repeats. In 1868 the twenty-five-year-old Grieg, then a student at Leipzig, had heard Clara Schumann play her husband's concerto and recalled this very precisely when it came time for him to write his own Piano Concerto in the same key.

Schumann, like many composers before him and quite a few since (see, for example, my essay on the Berg Violin Concerto) was fond of encoding names in musical notation. Bearing in mind that what we call B-natural the Germans call H, you can see that the first four notes of the oboe theme could be taken to spell Chiara, or CHiArA, using those letters that have musical counterparts (C/B/A/A) in this Italian version of Clara's name, a version that occurs in Schumann's fanciful prose writings and, in its affectionate diminutive of Chiarina, in his *Carnaval.*

Whether or not Schumann intended it as Chiara, this oboe theme dominates the entire movement. It turns up in C major at the point where one might expect a new theme, but this time the clarinet adds a different and impassioned continuation. (In the Fantasy, the clarinet had descending arpeggios that competed with the four-octave descending arpeggio in the pianist's left hand.) Then Chiara is transformed into a tender exchange of intimacies between the piano and the clarinet, with sympathetic but *pianissimo* nods of agreement from the violins—in the remote and mellow key of A-flat major. This is the most poetic and magical moment in the concerto and, not least, a lovely tribute to Clara's singing tone. And finally, after the sweeping cadenza, part recitative, part a Robert Schumann translation of Bachian polyphony, part flying chords that even Thalberg and Liszt would have had to practice hard, it becomes a quick march, all pungent off-beat accents and suppressed excitement, and which ends the movement gloriously.

[8]In the 1841 Fantasy, the piano begins by itself, and the orchestra inserts a quick punctuation mark between its second and third chords. It is a wonderfully dramatic idea, but as good as impossible to execute unless the conductor gives an empty downbeat before the piano's first chord, which then spoils the dramatic surprise. I imagine Clara Schumann and Mendelssohn made this unhappy discovery at their reading rehearsal and that this is why Schumann changed the opening.

The Viennese critic Eduard Hanslick perceptively heard this movement as "a reduced depiction" of a full concerto, with the A-flat episode standing for the slow movement and the cadenza and march for the finale.

Those are the components or, if you like, *the* component in diverse guises, but it is Schumann's way of composing with this material that turns it into wonderful music. One has to evoke the two personalities he invented to be his mouthpieces in his writings about music and who in the *Davids-bündlertänze* and *Carnaval* actually speak in music itself: enthusiastic, hyperbolic Florestan and meditative, inward Eusebius. Schumann sweeps the listener from mood to mood, from soapbox to pillow, and the pianist is now the most dramatic of protagonists and now the most sensitive of accompanists. (Rachmaninoff, that hardly reticent piano animal, learned a lot from this soloist-as-accompanist idea.) And Chiara, if it is she, is the firm frame that holds it all together. If it is indeed Chiara-Clara, it is also a picture of the Schumanns' life together, for it was she who represented order, organization, the frame.

Now the climate shifts. The first movement's impulsive fantasia style gives way to the slower but far-from-slow middle movement of a type invented by Beethoven, small in scale, and an introduction or transition to a much bigger finale. In tone of voice, though, this movement—which does, after all, admit to being an Intermezzo—is pure Schumann. (One of the first critics heard it as *"echt Mozart"* style, which seems most odd to us; on the other hand, if we recall the extent to which listeners at that time were inclined to hear Mozart as Rococo, it becomes less surprising.) It begins and ends with demure conversation between piano and orchestra, but in the middle, Schumann gives us an episode in which the strings sing a passionate song that is both frank in expression and touchingly contained in sound. Or it should be: conductors too easily succumb to the temptation of cranking the heat all the way up and in their excitement (not about Schumann, but about themselves and their cello sections) so stretch the upbeats that the music gets twisted into triple meter.

The principal idea of the first movement now reappears to effect the transition into the finale. (Schumann has his eye just a bit on Beethoven's Concerto No. 5.) This movement, which really *is* in triple meter, is robust and joyous but not heavy. In the middle, Schumann puts a theme that sounds as though it is in triple meter at half the tempo, but writes it in the original meter so that it becomes a minefield of syncopations and displaced accents. It is a famous conductor trap, and Mendelssohn had great difficulty with it at the first Leipzig performance. Schumann celebrates the close of his Concerto in a buoyant waltz.

POSTSCRIPT: Two of Schumann's shorter pieces for piano and orchestra are well worth knowing and seeking out, and seeking out is what it will take, for they do not get played much. The first is the Introduction and Allegro Appassionato in G major, Opus 92, which Schumann composed in 1849 and which Clara Schumann introduced at the Leipzig Gewandhaus on 14 February 1850. Its opening is as beautiful a page as Schumann ever wrote. To an accompaniment of richly scored piano arpeggios with solo cello, a clarinet begins an ardent melody. A horn takes over from the clarinet, and meanwhile the orchestral texture becomes richer through a gradual accretion of strings, begun by the entry of divided violas. The transition into the Allegro—solo piano conversing with strings—is exquisite. The Allegro is exuberant, but it is the Introduction that makes magic.

The other work is the Introduction and Allegro in D minor, Opus 134, written in the last week of August 1853 and also introduced by Clara Schumann, in Utrecht on 26 November that year. Schumann dedicated this score to Brahms, who loved it and played it often. Rudolf Serkin was a champion of it and left a beautiful recording. This is sterner stuff than Opus 92. It begins with a solemn conversation between the piano and pizzicato strings, a passage whose material—and whose effects—permeates the entire work. This piece has one of those remarkable Schumann cadenzas, comparable to those in the Piano Concerto, the Cello Concerto, and the little-known Violin Fantasy, Opus 131, that are brilliantly integrated into the flow and whose weight almost give them the significance of an extra development section.

## Concerto in D minor for Violin and Orchestra

*In powerful motion, but not too fast*
*Slow*
*Lively, but not fast*

On 21 September 1853 Schumann noted in his journal of events and expenses that he had begun "a piece for violin." The entry for 1 October reads: "The Violin Concerto is finished. A visit from Brahms (a genius)." Two days later Schumann reports that the Concerto is "completely orchestrated." In January 1854 Robert and Clara Schumann visited Hanover, where Joseph Joachim, the violinist Schumann had in mind when he wrote the work, had put a week-long Schumann festival together. Among other things, Joachim performed the C-major Fantasy, Opus 131, that week and played through the Concerto at a reading rehearsal with his orchestra. The latter was an unsatisfying experience: Joachim was unprepared and his arm was tired from conducting. On 17 November 1854 he wrote to Schumann, by then an inmate of the insane asylum at Endenich, that he now knew the Concerto better than on that previous occasion when "I did it such injustice," and offered to come and play it for him. Joachim did in fact visit Schumann twice at En-denich but did not play for him, and Schumann, who died on 29 July 1856, never heard the work again.

Joachim played the Concerto privately with Clara Schumann on 15 September 1855 by way of a rather strange celebration of her fifteenth wed-ding anniversary, and he seems occasionally to have played at least parts of it for such colleagues as his quartet partner Carl Halir and the composer Max Bruch, but he never gave a public performance of the work. After that, the Concerto in effect vanished from the scene for eighty years, Clara Schumann, Joachim, and Brahms all agreeing that the work, which they considered weak and a tragic example of the decline of the composer's creative powers, should not be published. Even though he contributed to several of the great nineteenth-century complete editions with remarkable editorial and musi-cological astuteness (Chopin, Couperin, Handel, Mozart, Schubert, Schu-mann), Brahms did not approve of complete editions, believing that, while everything should be available in libraries for scholars, for "amateurs and young artists . . . to stuff their rooms and brains with all 'Complete Works' " would "confuse their judgment."

The first performance was finally given on 26 November 1937, when Georg Kulenkampff played the Concerto with Hans Schmidt-Isserstedt and the Berlin Philharmonic. At Kulenkampff's request, Paul Hindemith had thoroughly rewritten the solo part; I do not know whether the cuts in the first-movement tutti were made at the concert or only on the recording pro-duced by Telefunken a month later. Ten days later, on 6 December, Yehudi Menuhin played the work as Schumann had written it (although with piano reduction) at a recital in Carnegie Hall, New York; on the 23rd of that month he gave the Concerto its first real performance at a concert of the Saint Louis Symphony, Vladimir Golschmann conducting.

**Solo violin, two flutes, two oboes, two clarinets, two bassoons, two horns, two trumpets, timpani, and strings.**

Jelly d'Arányi was one of the most fascinating violin personalities in the first half of the twentieth century. She was born in 1893, the great-niece of Joseph Joachim and the younger sister of another interesting violinist, Adila Fachiri. Like so many other Hungarian violin virtuosos, including Fachiri, Joseph Szigeti, Zoltán Székely, Sándor Végh, André Gertler, and Tibor Varga, d'Arányi studied with Jenö Hubay, himself a Joachim pupil. She gave many concerts with Bartók, who wrote his two violin sonatas for her; Ravel com-posed *Tzigane* for her after she had entertained him with Gypsy melodies far into the night as postlude to a private musicale. In 1913 she settled in England, where she became immensely popular. Holst, Vaughan Williams, and Ethel Smyth wrote concertos for her, and she played in chamber ensembles with such musicians as Fanny Davies, Guilhermina Suggia, Felix Salmond, and Myra Hess. Her recordings, which unfortunately do not include her Bartók and Ravel pieces, show her to have been an sensitive, interesting, rather impulsive performer.

D'Arányi was a spiritualist, and in 1933 she announced she had been in contact with her famous great-uncle: he had told her about a violin concerto by Robert Schumann of whose existence no one was aware, and he urged her to find and perform it. It is true that very few people knew of Schumann's unpublished and unperformed Violin Concerto, but its existence was no secret: it is mentioned in Wilhelm Joseph von Wasielewski's big Schumann biography (1871) and in Andreas Moser's life of Joachim (1900), and the manuscript score itself was in the Prussian State Library in Berlin. It had been bequeathed to that institution by Joachim, although with the stipulation that it not be published until 1956, one hundred years after Schumann's death.

Joachim did not reveal to d'Arányi why he had neglected to tell her about this masterpiece while he was still alive (she was fourteen and already with Hubay at the Budapest Academy when he left this sphere) rather than, as Lawrence Gilman put it in his 1938 program note for the New York Philharmonic-Symphony, "waiting to communicate with her . . . by the somewhat laborious route of the spiritistic grapevine." Neither did Joachim explain his change of heart about the quality of the Concerto. After all, writing sorrowfully about it to Andreas Moser in 1898, he had used such phrases as "mental lassitude," "bewildering passages," "morbid brooding," "drabness," "tiresome repetitions," "unaccustomed and ineffective effort."

But d'Arányi's tale had the desired effect, one that probably would not have been achieved by an article in a musicological journal: suddenly a lot of people were interested in the Schumann Violin Concerto. Willy Strecker, one of the directors of the influential publishing house B. Schott Söhne, threw himself into the cause and, in 1937, together with d'Arányi, persuaded Joachim's son to permit the Prussian State Library to release the Concerto for publication and performance.[9]

D'Arányi would have been the logical choice for the first performance: she was a brilliant player; she was connected to Joachim, who was himself so intimately connected to the Concerto; and she was, however strangely, responsible for the exhumation of the work. Strecker, however, opted for the more famous Yehudi Menuhin, and sent him the score. Menuhin responded

---

[9]The Schumanns' youngest daughter, Eugenie, then about to turn eighty-six, protested the publication of the score of the Violin Concerto in 1937 as well as its performance later that year.

enthusiastically, and arrangements were set in motion for a premiere in the violinist's home town of San Francisco.

It was at this point that politics took over. The Reichsmusikkammer, the official authority on all musical matters in Germany, decided that a first performance in America by a Jewish violinist and with a Jewish conductor, Pierre Monteux, was unacceptable. D'Arányi would also have been disqualified as a Jew. The honor thus fell to Georg Kulenkampff, a solid player who had become Germany's ranking violinist by default after the great Adolf Busch had left the country in 1933 in disgust at the Nazi regime. The premiere was explicitly politicized in that it was scheduled as part of the Reichskulturkammer's national conference in Berlin. A month later, in December 1937, Menuhin gave the American premiere and indeed the first performance of Schumann's own text, without the extensive rewriting of the solo part that Kulenkampff had requested from his friend Paul Hindemith; with Sir Adrian Boult conducting, d'Arányi gave the first performance in England in February 1938.[10]

Both Kulenkampff and Menuhin found several occasions to repeat the concerto, and both were able to record it immediately, the former with his partners at the premiere, the latter with the New York Philharmonic-Symphony, although with John Barbirolli replacing Georges Enescu, who had conducted the first New York performances in January 1938. The Kulenkampff recording preserves a curiosity that would otherwise have vanished from public view, namely Hindemith's revision of the solo part.[11] Hindemith invented new figurations, transposed passages up an octave for better audibility, added trills for extra intensity, changed articulations, and the like. It is as excellently done as one would expect from a musician of Hindemith's compositional and violinistic expertise (he had been concertmaster of the Frankfurt Opera at nineteen and was one of the most important violists of his time), and, no question, the solo stands out effectively from the orchestra. But Hindemith's violin patterns are clichés of nineteenth-century virtuoso string-writing; we are suddenly brought close to Tchaikovsky and Bruch, and Schumann's Concerto loses freshness thereby. (See footnote 7 in my essay on the Stravinsky Violin Concerto.)[12]

[10]It speaks volumes about American attitudes to Germany in 1937 that none of this is mentioned in the program notes for the first American performances by the Saint Louis Symphony, the Philadelphia Orchestra, and the New York Philharmonic-Symphony.

[11]The 1994 Teldec CD with Kulenkampff's recording preserves another historical curiosity as well: a 1935 recording of the Mendelssohn Concerto, also by Kulenkampff with Schmidt-Isserstedt and the Berlin Philharmonic. That is a remarkably late date for a Mendelssohn recording to have been made in Nazi Germany, and it may well have been the last until after the war.

[12]The most awkward technical feature of the Violin Concerto comes from Schumann's fondness for wide-ranging arpeggios. These lie comfortably under a pianist's fingers, but they can be diabolical on a string instrument. Violinists who have had to prepare the scherzo of Schumann's Second Symphony

What would have moved Hindemith, who was a champion of late Schumann and who frequently expressed contempt for arrangers, to undertake this project? First and most obviously, he was undoubtedly glad to do a favor for Kulenkampff, a colleague and friend. Beyond that, a good answer comes (in a personal communication) from the Hindemith scholar Giselher Schubert:

> Hindemith never spoke about this matter. I suspect that he did it for reasons we cannot go along with: he wanted the solo part to sound "competent," "professional," "brilliant," "conventionally virtuosic," in order to save it from the then current and generally accepted judgment that this was the work of a sick, burnt-out composer who did not know how to write for the violin. Probably he also thought that his name as editor would help to promote this controversial work. In the event, his name was omitted because it had become "intolerable" in Nazi Germany.

But let us return to the second half of the nineteenth century. Clara Schumann, Joseph Joachim, and Johannes Brahms were formidable personalities and formidable musical brains. They were, all three, sincerely devoted to Robert Schumann and to his memory, although there is much to suggest that Clara did not always understand her husband or, to put it less harshly, that she was not ideally suited by temperament to follow his mind on all its fantastical journeys.

One wants to think twice before dismissing the professional judgment of such musicians as Clara Schumann, Joachim, and Brahms, but one also needs to ask whether their professional judgment was not colored by personal feelings. Clara's and Brahms's relationships with Schumann were complicated; Clara, moreover, was what the Germans call a "Besserwisser," one who always knows better. And Joachim, as he grew older, became more and more of an imperious eminence. Today it is clear that this distinguished troika was wrongheaded in their evaluation of the Violin Concerto and high-handed in their decision to suppress it, especially Joachim, who survived longest and had the manuscript in his possession.

The three created a critical tradition in which a phrase like "all this music is that of a tired mind" (from Joan Chissell's widely read Schumann biography for the Master Musicians series) makes its way onto the page all too easily in a discussion of Schumann's late works. Some years ago, when I had to write program notes on some of Schumann's late chamber pieces, I discovered that the fattest book on Schumann then readily available in English (and actually *Robert Schumann: The Man and His Music*, edited by Alan

---

for orchestra auditions (where it is a regular feature) and cellists who have struggled to learn the finale of his Cello Concerto know this well.

Walker, is useful as well as fat), did not mention any of the works in question; neither, except for a mere listing, did the twenty-three-page Schumann article in *The New Grove Dictionary of Music and Musicians*.[13]

Schumann's compositions with opus numbers in three figures—and if the Violin Concerto had one it would be in the 140s—still need defending. No question, there are weak and distracted pieces among these later works, although there is not always agreement as to which ones they are; it is wrong, however, to hear most of what he wrote from the middle 1840s on as clouded by a growing intellectual and artistic uncertainty foreshadowing the mental collapse that led to his suicide attempt and hospitalization in 1854. In fact, 1849, when he completed his opera *Genoveva*, the music for Byron's *Manfred*, the *Requiem for Mignon*, the *Waldscenen* for piano, and some of his most original chamber duos, was a banner year by any standards, and 1851, the year of the G-minor Piano Trio, the final version of the Symphony No. 4, several interesting overtures, the first two violin sonatas, the *Märchenbilder* for viola and piano, and some excellent songs, was a fine moment too. W. W. Cobbett was so distressed by Richard Aldrich's negative evaluation of the later works in his Schumann article for Cobbett's *Cyclopaedic Survey of Chamber Music* (1929) that he commissioned an additional amending essay from the pianist (and Clara Schumann pupil) Fanny Davies. Today, such musicians as the oboist and composer Heinz Holliger and the cellist Steven Isserlis are ardent champions of late Schumann, and it is gratifying to watch the much-maligned Violin Concerto finally enter the repertory.

The Concerto starts magnificently with a theme that begins quietly, quickly reaches *forte*, and strides powerfully through a thirty-two-measure paragraph. The sound is somber: this music is part of a D-minor family that includes Mozart's Piano Concerto, K. 466, the String Quartet, K. 421, and the opening of *Don Giovanni*; the first movement of the Beethoven Ninth; Schumann's own Fourth Symphony and *Faust* Overture; and, later, the First Piano Concerto and the third movement of *A German Requiem* of Johannes Brahms, the young visitor who appeared unannounced the day Schumann began this score. The grand opening paragraph comes to an end when it sinks into the softness of the relative major, F, where there begins a lyric theme, *dolce*, of which even Joachim spoke affectionately. This is with us only briefly: its twelfth measure is already a return to the stern material of the opening, which swiftly leads to the entrance of the solo. This economy and concentration— "classical," if you like—are characteristic of the best of late Schumann.

When we hear the first theme played by the solo violin in three- and four-note chords, we hear another connection—with Bach's great D-minor

---

[13]I must add, though, that Alfred Nieman's brief discussion of the Violin Concerto in the Walker symposium mentioned above is sympathetic.

Chaconne. Both in the development and the recapitulation, this material is treated with fantasy and vigor; the entrance into the recapitulation is managed with panache. When the lyric theme returns in D major, it is embedded in figurations of the kind Kulenkampff obviously could not bear. But even if the patterns are unaccustomed for the hand, they can sound effective and individual, as you can hear in the playing of the young Menuhin or, more recently, of Joshua Bell. It is a splendidly assertive statement of "Robert Schumann was here."

The slow movement also begins in somber colors: strings (with divided cellos) plus horns and bassoons. Half the cellos, *pianissimo*, play a restlessly syncopated music, something part-way between melody and figuration. To that, beginning at the end of the fourth measure, the solo violin adds a slow and lyric melody.[14] Schumann makes the syncopated cello music and the violin descant into a subdued dialogue in which the syncopated idea, though remaining ever hushed, comes to dominate the discourse more and more. It makes its way into the solo violin part, it functions equally well as accompaniment and principal material, it yields beautiful bridges and transitions. Toward the end, the violin melody reappears in minor: it is a deeply moving transformation. This slow movement is the most intimate moment in Schumann's music with orchestra, and it reminds me of the lines by Friedrich Schlegel that Schumann put at the head of his Piano Fantasy: "Through all the tones in this colorful earthly dream, there sounds one soft tone for him who listens in secret."

The syncopated cello theme urges a speeding-up that carries us into the finale. At the reading in Hanover, Schumann and Joachim came up with and delighted in the fantasy of Tadeusz Kościuszko, the freedom fighter who also participated in the American Revolution, and John III Sobieski, the seventeenth-century king of Poland, leading a polonaise: "So stately!" Schu-

---

[14]During the night of 17 February 1854, ten days before he jumped into the Rhine in the last of his suicide attempts, Schumann wrote down a melody—he said it had been dictated to him by angels—whose opening bar is the same as that of the concerto's slow movement. The resemblance led Hans Gál into an unfavorable comparison of the Concerto's "short phrase of six bars, aimlessly meandering" with "its final shape . . . [which] has the large breadth of Schumann's finest inventions, a widely spaced, perfectly conclusive tune of twenty bars." This is an all too common example of tendentious Schumann criticism. First of all, the beautiful melody Schumann got from the angels is no more the "final shape" of the Concerto theme than, say, the Agnus Dei of Bach's B-minor Mass is the final shape of the aria *"Ach, bleibe doch"* in the *Ascension Oratorio*, or the Lacrymosa in the Verdi Requiem is the final shape of the duet "Qui me rendra ce mort" in *Don Carlos*: Bach's Agnus Dei, Verdi's Lacrymosa, and Schumann's angelic melody are new inventions, each growing from the same thematic seed as some earlier work. Second, in the Violin Concerto, Schumann clearly did not intend to write a "perfectly conclusive tune"; rather, he wanted precisely the open-ended, quasi-improvisatory melodic commentary that he in fact wrote. By printing the beginning of the Concerto melody without any indication of what is happening in the orchestra—in other words, with no context—Gál does indeed make it look shapeless and "aimlessly meandering," but that is not at all the impression it makes when we hear it with the orchestra.

mann's marking is *Lively, but not fast,* his metronome mark is slow (63 for the quarter), and the polonaise was a majestic dance. Still, Schumann's tempo is hard to bring off. Gidon Kremer and Nikolaus Harnoncourt give it a try on their 1994 recording, but the playing and conducting are so stiff that one also ends up unpersuaded about the tempos. I think the jury is still out on this particular tempo question. It is an engaging movement, this finale, gracious as well as spunky, and it is more than engaging when the syncopated cello theme from the slow movement returns to cast a shadow over the festivities. As for the repetitions about which Joachim complained, the violinist must take them as invitations to exercise his or her fantasy in color and inflection.

## *Concertstück,* for Four Horns and Orchestra, Opus 86

> *Lively*
> *Romance: Fairly slow, but not dragging*
> *Very lively*

Schumann began this work on 18 February 1849 and completed it three weeks later, on 11 March. On 15 October that year it was played in a private reading with piano by Messrs. Lewy, Schitterlan, Eisner, and Hübler, the horn quartet of the Dresden Court Orchestra; the first public performance was given in Leipzig on 25 February 1850 by Messrs. Pohle, Jehnichen, Leichsenring, and Wilke, the horn quartet of the Gewandhaus Orchestra, with Julius Rietz conducting. Simultaneously with the appearance of the original score in the fall of 1851, the Hamburg publisher Schuberth brought out a transcription of this work for piano and orchestra. Marc Andreae, editor of a score of the piano version published by C. F. Peters in 1986, thinks it probable that Schumann himself was responsible for this transcription, "which in its independence goes beyond a mere arrangement." If it was not Schumann himself, Andreae believes the only plausible candidates for authorship of the piano version to be Clara Schumann or Carl Reinecke.

**Four solo horns, two flutes and piccolo, two oboes, two clarinets, two bassoons, two natural horns *ad libitum,* two trumpets, three trombones, timpani, and strings.**

Here is a showpiece for a new instrument—as though Elliott Carter or John Adams or Aaron Kernis were to write a concerto for the digital sampler. The French horn was of course not new itself in 1849; new were the valves that for the first time allowed a player access to all the notes of the chromatic scale with dependable production and evenness of tone. Horn players and instrument builders were experimenting with valves as early as 1814, and the story of the invention, resistances, and gradual acceptance of them as told in such books as R. Morley-Pegge's *The French Horn* and Barry Tuckwell's *Horn* makes fascinating reading.

It was about mid-century when the valve horn began clearly to replace the hand horn. Schumann was living in Dresden at that time, and the other famous composer in the city was Richard Wagner, then working on *Lohengrin*, in its own way a landmark in the triumphal progress of the valve horn. Schumann and Wagner had no great admiration or liking for each other, but their paths crossed frequently enough. Did they ever talk about their frustrations with the hand horn and the liberation that the valve horn promised? Certainly they were at one in their regard for Joseph-Rudolph Lewy, principal horn of the orchestra that is now called the Dresden Staatskapelle, which Wagner conducted regularly both in concert and at the opera and which Schumann hoped would play his *Concertstück* for Four Horns.[15]

Lewy, born in Nancy, France, but active first in Vienna, then in Dresden from 1837 on, had studied with his older brother Edouard-Constantin, who as an early valve-horn owner had been the first to play the famous fourth-horn solo in the slow movement of Beethoven's Ninth Symphony. It was for Joseph-Rudolph that Schubert wrote his song with horn obbligato *Auf dem Strom*. He was a poetic performer, reputedly the first to get his section to play the quartet at the beginning of Weber's *Freischütz* Overture sweetly rather than as a pompous blare. He was fascinated with extending the technical possibilities of the horn, and around 1850 he published a book of études, two of which involve the playing of chords on the instrument, something that would still be regarded as an avant-garde experiment a hundred years later. Schumann's *Concertstück* asks for a Lewy-like blend of poetry and confident virtuosity. At the same time, one gets a sense of Schumann's nervousness: several of the high-flying passages for the first two horns are doubled in other instruments. I am not in general a fan of messing with Schumann's orchestration and am glad that nowadays, as opposed to the earlier part of the twentieth century, you get to hear his symphonies as he wrote them, unre-

[15]The other horn connection in Schumann's life was through the family of the Leipzig composer and pianist Ludwig Schuncke, who died in 1834 just before his twenty-fourth birthday and whom Schumann admired immensely. Schuncke's father, four uncles, and one cousin were horn players, some of international renown.

touched by conductors; here, however, is an instance where some wielding of the blue pencil would only do good.

Schumann's interest in the valve horn was manifested in a number of pieces in 1849, notably the Adagio and Allegro for Horn and Piano, Opus 70, and also his *Hunting Songs* for men's chorus with horn quartet, Opus 137. He was excessively modest in calling his composition for horn quartet and orchestra a *Concertstück* (Concert Piece) rather than a concerto: *Concertstück*, as for example in Weber's delightful work for piano and orchestra, or *Pièce de concert* usually implies something smaller and lighter than a full-dress concerto and often a piece in just one movement. Schumann's *Concertstück* for horns is relatively brief, about eighteen minutes—lip fatigue is, after all, a serious consideration—but it is in three distinct movements and comes across with the force of a real concerto.

Schumann starts with two orchestral chords that seem to come harmonically out of nowhere. This dramatic gesture introduces a fanfare whose rising triplets will be a pervasive feature of the first part of the work. It is a fiery beginning, and the temperature hardly drops during the energetic and brilliant first movement, which, its brevity notwithstanding, is one of Schumann's most ambitious and elaborate. Even the lyric phrases move with tremendous energy and sweep.

This movement comes to a full close, but Schumann wants the music to continue without a separating pause. He calls this slow movement a Romance, warns us that it must not drag, and writes a beautifully lyric and serene piece rather in the manner of the identically titled movement in the Fourth Symphony. Here the horn players are allowed to be singers rather than acrobats. Trumpet signals awaken us from this romantic dream and, definitely without break this time, Schumann moves into the finale. Midway, he makes room for a flowing passage to be played "with great expression," but overall, this movement is quick in pace, buoyant in spirit, and full of daring and bravura for the solo quartet.

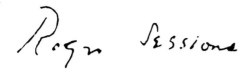

# Roger Sessions

Roger Huntington Sessions was born in Brooklyn, New York, on 28 December 1896 and died in Princeton, New Jersey, on 16 March 1985.

## Concerto in B minor for Violin and Orchestra

*Largo e tranquillo, con grande espressione*
*Scherzo: Allegro*
*Romanza: Andante*
*Molto vivace e sempre con fuoco*

Sessions began the first movement of his Violin Concerto in 1930 in Rome, continuing the following year at Lutjenberg, a resort on the Baltic Sea, and in Berlin and Hamburg. He wrote the second and third movements over the next two years, for the most part in Berlin, though he finished the third movement in Massachusetts. Sessions wrote the finale in San Francisco in the summer of 1935 and the score is dated "San Francisco, Calif., August 1935"; however, the orchestration was not completed until the fall of that year, in New York. When Sessions began the Violin Concerto, vague plans were made for the first performance to be given in 1931 or 1932 by Max Strub, concertmaster of the Berlin Philharmonic, with Otto Klemperer conducting (Strub also assisted Sessions with violinistic details during his stays in Berlin). The composition, however, took very much longer, and the formal premiere was scheduled for January 1937 with Albert Spalding as soloist and Serge Koussevitzky conducting the Boston Symphony. (There was a reading at the New School for Social Research, New York, in 1935 by the violinist Serge Kotlarsky with the composer at the piano). The Boston performances were first postponed because Spalding was not ready and then canceled because he wished to make changes the composer could not accept. (As of the summer of 1997, the Boston Symphony has still not played the work.) In the event, the Concerto was not heard until 8 January 1940, when Robert Gross played it with the Illinois Symphony under Izler Solomon. The first performance by a professional orchestra was given in November 1947, when Louis Krasner was soloist with Dimitri Mitropoulos and the Minneapolis Symphony. Sessions dedicated the Concerto to his first wife, Barbara.

**Solo violin, three flutes (second doubling piccolo, third doubling alto flute), two oboes and English horn (second oboe also doubling English horn), clarinet in E flat (doubling clarinet in B flat), clarinet in A, basset horn (also doubling clarinet in A), bass clarinet, two bassoons and contrabassoon, four horns, two trumpets, two trombones (tenor and bass), timpani, triangle, snare drum, tambourine, cymbals, violas, cellos, and basses.**

This work is part of the amazing crop of violin concertos that appeared in the 1930s, from Stravinsky's in 1931 to Barber's, Britten's, Hindemith's, Piston's First, and Walton's, all of the Class of 1939. When Sessions completed this score, he was known chiefly as the composer of incidental music to Andreyev's *The Black Maskers*, the concert suite drawn from that score being the first work to make a reputation for him. Koussevitzky had introduced the Symphony No. 1 with some success in Boston, and there was an impressive piano sonata. Sessions himself had recently returned from seven years in Europe, where he had watched the rise of Fascism in Italy and of the Nazis in Germany, and he was now working to reestablish himself in his own depression-beleaguered country.

Sessions had studied with Archibald Davison and Edward Burlingame Hill at Harvard (which he entered at fourteen), and then, because outbreak of war interfered with a plan to go to Ravel in Paris, with Horatio Parker at Yale. As an instructor at Smith College, feeling he knew too little, he continued his education through books by Cherubini and d'Indy, and after that, by going to Ernest Bloch, then director of the Cleveland Institute of Music. It was a critical decision, and all his life, Sessions referred to his first lesson with Bloch, spent analyzing the first bars of Beethoven's First Piano Sonata, as "about the most important thing in my whole musical education."

Sessions spent much of the 1920s and 1930s in Europe, and there his distinctive style began to take shape. Like so many of his contemporaries, he felt the impact of Stravinsky, but Sessions was always himself, writing a music stockier than Stravinsky's and, as John Harbison has pointed out, with a "total lack of Stravinskian irony and distance."

This Stravinskian surface eventually disappeared, but even while it was still present, as it is in the Violin Concerto, elements from another, more German tradition—long-breathed melody broad gestures, polyphony—were becoming ever more prominent. The Concerto is full of detail—the voicing of a chord, a turn of harmony, a melodic figuration—that will remind us of Stravinsky as will its sheer, exuberant athleticism. This strain has, however, been crossed with the Romantic, always noble diction of Brahms and with Sebastian Bach's sinuously winding melodies. Bach's melos fascinated Stravinsky in his Violin Concerto too; the difference is that Sessions also takes over Bach's love for entwining these lines in elegantly elaborate contrapuntal tracery.

Whatever Sessions composed, from *The Black Maskers* to the last work he completed, a Concerto for Orchestra for the Boston Symphony, is possessed of electrifying energy, both physical and intellectual. This energy produces a densely active music in which hardly anything is neutral, one where even accompaniment figures become so specific as to take on an assertive life of their own. The music throws events at you at a tremendous rate, and, to quote Harbison again, it is all "abundance and sublime willfulness." It is also profoundly traditional in the tensions and releases of its arching melodies, in its commitment to "the long line," in its expressive and ethical intent, its address to what Sessions called the "energies which animate our psychic life."

The Piano Sonata No. 1 (1927–1930), the Violin Concerto, the String Quartet No. 1 (1936), and *Pages from a Diary* (piano pieces from 1937–1939, renamed *From My Diary* by the publisher, to the composer's annoyance) are important way stations in the development of Sessions's musical language: the strands of polyphony grow ever more independent, the bass becomes more bass-ic, the treble moves higher, the harmony is more chromatic. Individual movements often recapitulate this development as they progress from comparative simplicity to greater complexity.

"It covers space and time and history," said Sessions of his Violin Concerto toward the end of his life. He meant the time of gestation and composition, and also the four-year delay of the premiere, the seven-year wait after that for performance by a major orchestra, the further twelve years before the work was heard in New York.[1] All this was frustrating and painful, especially for a composer who worked slowly and had a small catalogue.

---

[1] Dimitri Mitropoulos, for whom the work was "one of the greatest achievements in American composition" and who thought of Sessions as "the only one who could compete with the rest of the

The rumor of the Concerto's unplayability was further damaging, and it still persists, particularly among violinists who have never looked at the score. In the midst of his troubles with Albert Spalding, Sessions asked his friend, the composer Alfredo Casella, for advice about what he might to do reduce the Concerto's difficulties. Nothing, said Casella: "*È nato difficile*" (it was born difficult). Casella meant that the difficulties, the enormous demands on the player's skill, are organic, like the difficulties of the Brahms and Elgar and Schoenberg concertos, not pyrotechnics as in Paganini or Wieniawski. One would not, however, wish to underestimate what Sessions takes for granted by way of easy technical command. The violinist Jorja Fleezanis, also stressing that the violinistic challenges are an inseparable part of Sessions's musical thought, put it this way: "Yes, it's difficult if you don't like fourths and sevenths. What it takes is virtuosity of the ear more than of the fingers."

The Concerto presents a luxuriant wealth of detail within a simple frame-work. There are four movements—slow, fast, slow fast, a scheme familiar from Bach sonatas and Handel concertos though rarely met in a classical, Romantic, or modern solo concerto. The first movement, *Largo e tranquillo, con grande espressione*, starts with a quietly assured call to attention by trombone and trumpet. Each of its three sections begins with this call, which leads first to an expansively lyric violin melody, richly accompanied, the second time to Bachian music in fastflowing notes, and the third time to a cadenza Sessions described as an "improvisation in the spirit of the movement." The movement ends quietly in a way Sessions was fond of, the strands withdrawing from the top down, until only the bass is left. This is also the moment to draw attention to the orchestral colors: to set the solo in higher relief Sessions omits violins (a touch both Stravinskian and Brahmsian, as in the Symphony of Psalms but also Brahms's A-major Serenade and the first movement of *A German Requiem*). At the same time he makes much of some of the less common and darker woodwinds such as the alto flute, basset horn, bass clarinet, and contrabassoon.

Percussion is heard for the first time in the scherzo whose trio (*più tranquillo*) provides one of the rare occasions for the soloist to catch her breath. Sessions described the Romanza as "just a song in three verses." The violin is the principal singer, gently seconded by various members of the clarinet family. The accompaniment is a little more elaborate in each successive stan-

---

great," was responsible for the Minneapolis performance in 1947, but when he wished to present it at the New York Philharmonic with Tossy Spivakovksy as soloist, Arthur Judson, the orchestra's manager, forbade the performance. Spivakovsky was soloist when the Philharmonic under Leonard Bernstein finally gave the Concerto in 1959; by then Judson was gone. Stories like this, including accounts of the many occasions when "controversial" music (including, at that time, Mahler's) could not be included on the Philharmonic's Sunday matinees, which were nationally broadcast, merit a proper study. See also my essays on Schoenberg's Violin and Piano concertos.

za. This is a short movement indeed, and it soon spills into the vertiginous finale, a tarantella, that frenzied dance of victims of the dread tarantula. Two waltz episodes sardonic and reminiscent of the dance hall music in Berg's *Wozzeck*, briefly interrupt the wild intensity that is this movement's predominant mood, but the Concerto ends in a dizzy burst of speed.

# Dmitri Shostakovich

Dmitri Dmitrievich Shostakovich was born in Saint Petersburg on 25 September 1906 and died in Moscow on 9 August 1975.

## Concerto No. 1 for Cello and Orchestra, Opus 107

*Allegretto*
*Moderato*
*Cadenza*
*Allegro con moto*

Shostakovich wrote this Concerto in 1959. Mstislav Rostropovich received his copy on 2 August, learned and memorized the work in four days, played it for the composer at his dacha on 6 August with the pianist Alexander Dedyukhin, and gave the first performance on 4 October, with Yevgeny Mravinsky conducting the Leningrad Philharmonic. The concerto is dedicated to Rostropovich.

**Solo cello, two flutes and piccolo, two oboes, two clarinets, two bassoons and contrabassoon, horn, timpani, celesta, and strings.**

The Cello Concerto No. 1—Shostakovich wrote another, also for Rostropovich, in 1966—comes from one of the calmer periods in this much-buffeted composer's life. Khrushchev's de-Stalinization campaign was in full swing; it

even included a statement to the effect that the late Great Leader and Teacher had been excessively subjective in his views on art. The catalogue of
Shostakovich's works for any given year does not, however, necessarily reflect
such vicissitudes. Especially by comparison with the 1940s, Shostakovich was
writing relatively little during the fifties, and in the three years preceding the
composition of the Cello Concerto No. 1, the only works of major ambition
and stature are the String Quartet No. 6 and the Symphony No. 11, *The Year
1905*.

Even though Shostakovich was free from harassment in 1959, the Cello Concerto is a work that feeds on grim memories. The first movement is marked
*Allegretto*, a friendly direction in most composers' music, but more often than
not ominous in Shostakovich. The first theme, whose first four notes dominate the movement, is questioning and nervous. The second theme is a fiercely contained melody of great tensile strength. Something the two ideas have
in common is the obsessive anapests (two short notes and one long) behind
them in the orchestra. The meter is irregular, and the colors are predominantly dark, with Shostakovich making strikingly effective use of the contrabassoon's subterranean rumble. When the sound is not dark it tends to go
to the other extreme of shrillness. This is a scarily relentless movement,
uncompromisingly so right up to its brutally abrupt end.[1]

The direction *Moderato* for the second movement is a little deceptive,
too, in that the metronome mark of 66 to the quarter indicates a distinctly
slow tempo. Strings, and then the horn, sing an expressive, pliant melody,
one based on Jewish folk song. The mood is reminiscent of the Idiot's wailing
lament in *Boris Godunov*. The cello replies with sterner stuff, even changing
the meter from three to four in its tune. A new and more declamatory idea
becomes the means for building a climax. When the lament returns, the
orchestral violins accompany it with creeping eighth-notes, tired and dispir-
ited, that Shostakovich borrowed from the second song of Mahler's *Lied von
der Erde*.

The reprise dissolves into an enormous written-out cadenza, which
Shostakovich actually presents and numbers as a separate movement. It explores further the ideas of the Moderato. Three times it leads to a series of
punctuations in pizzicato whose rhythm recalls the first movement's four-
note motto. Then it gradually builds up speed and reveals itself as a bridge
to the finale.

The last movement brings the fastest music we have heard in the Concerto thus far. The violently obsessive character of the first movement once

---

[1]The official analysis in the magazine *Sovietskaya Kultura* by the critic Lev Ginsburg interpreted this
cadence as representing "a firm will to find an answer," presumably to the question posed by the
cello in the first measure.

again makes itself felt, and, as the music approaches its ferocious close, the Concerto's opening theme returns. Rostropovich has pointed out that the sharp timpani blows toward the end are a detail, one among many, that show the influence of Prokofiev's *Symphonie-Concertante* for Cello and Orchestra, a work Shostakovich "loved passionately." According to the account in *Sovietskaya Kultura*, the ferocious closing pages of Shostakovich's Concerto depict "the will to live, victory in the struggle for happiness." But Shostakovich had quite different things in mind: a five-note phrase that the strings play just after the start of the finale comes from Stalin's favorite song, a sentimental ditty called *Suliko*. Shostakovich transforms it from sweet to crazed and, repeating it maddeningly, sends it up without mercy. Only fragments of the song are heard so that not even Rostropovich spotted the allusion right away: even six years after Stalin's death one could not be too careful.[2]

## Concerto No. 1 in C minor for Piano and Orchestra, Opus 35

*Allegretto—Allegro vivace—Allegretto—Allegro—Moderato*
*Lento*
*Moderato*
*Allegro con brio*

Shostakovich composed this work, originally titled "Concerto for Piano with the Accompaniment of String Orchestra and Trumpet," between 6 March and 20 July 1933. He himself was the soloist at the first performance, which took place on 15 October 1933 with the Leningrad Philharmonic under Yevgeny Mravinsky, with Alexander Schmidt playing the solo trumpet part.

**Solo piano, trumpet, and strings.**

As a conservatory student in Leningrad, Shostakovich was not sure whether his destiny lay in composing or playing the piano. He pursued what we would call a double major, and he was enough of a pianist to have included Beethoven's fearsomely difficult *Hammerklavier* Sonata in his graduation recital. Later, he played Prokofiev's Concerto No. 1, no easy task either. The success

[2]I am grateful to Lynn Harrell, who told me about the *Suliko* quotation, having himself had it pointed out by Rostropovich. Since then, the story has been recounted fully in Elizabeth Wilson's *Shostakovich: A Life Remembered* (Princeton, N.J.: Princeton University Press, 1994).

of his Symphony No. 1, also a graduation exercise but introduced with much éclat by the Leningrad Philharmonic when he was only twenty, gave Shostakovich the confidence to choose composition as his real métier, a confidence bolstered still further when such conductors as Bruno Walter and Leopold Stokowski introduced that brilliant work in western Europe and America. For a time, Shostakovich kept up his piano-playing: for one thing, he helped pay the family's rent with the money he earned accompanying silent films. Gradually, though, performance receded from the center of his concerns, and when he gave his last solo recital in 1930, he assumed he was done with it for good.

But 1930 was also the year that Shostakovich's Gogol opera *The Nose* achieved great success. People were curious to see the twenty-four-year-old composer, and inquiries about possible concert appearances increased. He began to practice the piano again and began to write music for himself to play; first, in 1932, the Preludes, Opus 34, for solo piano, then, the year after, the Concerto No. 1. The even greater success in 1934 of his opera *Lady Macbeth of Mtsensk* put him more in demand than ever. Ironically, *Lady Macbeth* was also his downfall: Stalin saw it in Moscow in January 1936 and was enraged by it, sight and sound. The consequence was two attacks in *Pravda*, the beginning, in that bloody decade in the Soviet Union, Shostakovich recalled later, of "the bitterness that has colored my life gray." The Fifth Symphony, introduced in 1937, made him *persona grata* again, but this was not, for him, the last cycle of degradation and rehabilitation.

The experience increased Shostakovich's nervousness, and that markedly decreased his appetite for giving concerts: shy, withdrawn, ironic, he was never really a performance animal anyway. Until 1966, when tremors in his arms made playing in public impossible, he did continue to give occasional performances, mostly of his chamber music with piano, but the next time he wrote a piano concerto, in 1957, it was a graduation present for his nineteen-year-old son Maxim.[3] Shostakovich's rhythmically incisive, crisply objective playing is well documented on recordings, which include performances, in many instances more than one, of the Piano Trio No. 2, the Piano Quintet, the Cello Sonata (with Rostropovich), several solo pieces, and both concertos.

The Concerto No. 1 begins with two quick scales for the piano, one down and one up, behind which the muted trumpet plays a micro-fanfare of its own. The piano then sings an extended and grave melody, one that begins

---

[3]The score of the Second Concerto in the complete Shostakovich edition published in 1982 by the State Music Publishing House in Moscow gives the date of the first performance, but does not mention Maxim Shostakovich, who, having emigrated to the United States in 1981, had become a non-person in his native country.

with what sounds like an allusion to Beethoven's *Appassionata*: that idea is not totally far-fetched in that the style of the Concerto more than once appears to make reference to Classical models. The texture is spare, the piano part proceeding much of the time either in bare octaves or, at most, in two-part counterpoint. After a while, the tempo is increased and the movement reveals its comedic intentions. The trumpet reappears playing music much like the famous and satiric polka in Shostakovich's *Age of Gold* ballet. With violins and piano dividing the task, the opening melody returns, and it is this theme—played on the piano with a few very low trumpet notes in the background—that brings the movement to its moody close.

The strings are muted as the second movement begins its melancholy: this is not just *triste* but *tristissimo*. Or, to borrow a Debussian turn of phrase, one might call this Lento "la plus que triste." Slowly the piano insinuates itself into the action. The music ascends to a forceful and intense climax. When it resumes its initial course, it is the muted trumpet, unheard for a long time and almost forgotten, that assumes the role of principal singer.[4] High cellos make a final, poignant plea, after which the piano lifts the music to its ethereal close.

Listening to this Concerto with no knowledge of how the composer has divided it into sections, we would probably take what follows as the intro-duction to the finale; Shostakovich, however, designates it as a separate movement. It begins with a Bachian prelude for the piano alone—a remi-niscence perhaps of the way the finale of the *Hammerklavier* Sonata begins?—which is interrupted by a melody, *molto espressivo*, for the violins. A briefer spell of preluding then carries us into the finale itself. Some of its music is taken over from music Shostakovich had contributed in 1929 to a Leningrad production of *Poor Columbus*, an opera by the German composer Erwin Dres-sel.[5] The finale is infectious comedy, and at least one of its jokes—the emer-gence of the long piano solo just before the conclusion—is one that Haydn or Beethoven might not have been embarrassed to sign. At the very end it is the trumpet that runs away with the show.

---

[4]In *Shostakovich: A Life Remembered* Elizabeth Wilson writes that, while Shostakovich had initially tailored the trumpet part in this Concerto to the brilliant style of the Leningrad Philharmonic's solo trumpet, Alexander Schmidt, he later came to prefer the more lyric playing of the Moscow Philhar-monic's Leonid Yuriev.

[5]This sounds like an improbable sort of procedure, and indeed by 1929 it was one that had long died out. In the eighteenth century, though, the *pasticcio*, an opera to which several composers contributed or added music, was not uncommon. Many Mozart arias, for example, came into being as additions to operas by other composers.

# Violin Concerto No. 1 in A minor, Opus 99

*Nocturne: Moderato*
*Scherzo: Allegro*
*Passacaglia: Andante*
*Burlesque: Allegro con brio—Presto*

Shostakovich composed his Violin Concerto No. 1 in 1947–1948, giving it the opus number 77; however, he kept the work to himself until 1955, when he released it for publication and performance, and recatalogued it as Opus 99. In an interview with Elizabeth Wilson, editor of *Shostakovich: A Life Remembered*, Mstislav Rostropovich blames the "shameful and cowardly" David Oistrakh for this seven-year delay; no other account of this matter or of anything else pertaining to Shostakovich's relationship to Oistrakh substantiates this accusation. In his *Music and Musical Life in Soviet Russia*, Boris Schwarz writes: "Whether the Concerto underwent any changes during the seven-year span between composition and première is not known." Schwarz also states that "the composer later indicated that he wanted the Concerto to be numbered Op. 77, in keeping with the time of its composition (1947–1948), rather than of its publication (1956)." This request has been pretty consistently ignored. Shostakovich dedicated the score to David Oistrakh, who gave the first performance on 9 October 1955 with Yevgeny Mravinsky and the Leningrad Philharmonic. Long before this, both Shostakovich and Oistrakh had played the work privately for their students.

**Solo violin, two flutes and piccolo (doubling third flute), two oboes and English horn (doubling third oboe), two clarinets and bass clarinet (doubling third clarinet), two bassoons and contrabassoon (doubling third bassoon), four horns, tuba, timpani, tam-tam, tambourine, xylophone, celesta, two harps, and strings.**

Joseph Stalin died on 5 March 1953, less than twenty-four hours after word went out that he had suffered a stroke a couple of days earlier. He had become Secretary General of the Communist party's Central Committee in 1922, and there were millions in the Soviet Union who could not remember a time when he had not been dictator. As the novelist and journalist Ilya Ehrenburg wrote, "We had long lost sight of the fact that [he] was mortal."

Prokofiev died the same day, about an hour before Stalin. Boris Schwarz reports in his book that the April issue of *Sovietskaya Muzyka*, the official music journal, carried Stalin's obituary on page 1 and Prokofiev's on page

117. I don't know how his senior colleague's death affected Shostakovich; I imagine, though, that the news of Stalin's demise brought a momentary and secret smile to his thin, down-turned lips.

Shostakovich began work on the Symphony No. 10 a few weeks after Stalin's death, and it was ready in time for performance at the end of the year. The next major project was to go through the 1947–1948 Violin Concerto, give it its new, up-to-date opus number, and arrange for its publication and first performance. Shostakovich's later wish to revert to the original opus number was neither whim nor musicological pedantry: it was important to him to make the point that the Concerto went back to an earlier time and thus, wordlessly, to remind people why it had lain in his desk drawer so long.[6]

Oistrakh, always a good friend to living composers, accepted the dedication, gave the premiere, made the first recording, and introduced the work in western Europe on a Leningrad Philharmonic tour. With Dimitri Mitropoulos and the New York Philharmonic-Symphony, Oistrakh also gave the first performances in America. After the Soviet critics, lacking clear direction from the official opinion-makers, were non-committal or out-and-out silent about the concerto, Oistrakh championed it verbally in an article in *Sovietskaya Muzyka*.

The Concerto No. 1 is a big, four-movement work that takes about thirty-five minutes. It is difficult—Oistrakh noted that it "does not fall easily into one's hands"—and its first and third movements ask exceptional interpretive and organizational skill from the violinist and the conductor.

The first movement, titled Nocturne, begins with the orchestra's low strings setting key (A minor), pace (*moderato*), and atmosphere (dark, brooding). When the soloist enters, his first notes suggest that he is going to offer an elaboration of the orchestra's theme, but this happens on so stretched a scale that we can hardly think of it as a simple variation; rather, it is as though the orchestra had merely suggested a way of beginning, and what the violin now unfolds is a new melody of immense span. It constantly refers back to the orchestra's introduction and is in fact spacious enough to cite that introduction in its entirety. The bassoon briefly joins the violin in counterpoint, and its contribution is occasionally seconded by other instruments; essentially, though, this is an aria for the soloist, and the orchestra knows its place. There is one *passionato* outburst for the violin; for the most part, though, the solo is meditative and quiet, though by no means always at peace.

---

[6]With one exception, every score, concert program, and recording I have seen calls the concerto Opus 99. The exception is the Intaglio CD of a 1972 concert performance in London by David Oistrakh with the New Philharmonia conducted by Maksim Shostakovich. The composer was present at that event, and I assume that he, his son, and Oistrakh were able to persuade the New Philharmonia to list the work as Opus 77 and that Intaglio simply took that number over from the concert program. The commercial recording made five days later for EMI has the usual Opus 99.

Dominated by the wondrous subterranean vibrations of the contrabassoon, a group of woodwinds caps the long first stanza with a brief interlude. When the violin enters again, very high, it is muted and *pianissimo*. The harp, playing harmonics, and the celesta add their bell tones. The violin line breaks each beat into triplets, in which the orchestral strings join. The music rises to a great crest with double stops and biting dissonance, then returns to the mood of the opening. The triplets remain as an essential part of the vocabulary until harp and celesta show the way to the ethereal close.

The Scherzo is almost a study for its counterpart in the Symphony No. 10 (1953), that savage movement about which Shostakovich is supposed to have said that it was a portrait of Stalin. Woodwinds begin, with the violin adding sharp and unlovely accents. After a contrasting section with the character of an unruly, vodka-fueled country dance, the movement returns to an even more wildly energized version of the fiercely sardonic opening music.

In this scherzo Shostakovich spells out his own initials in musical notation, He does this by using the German transliteration of his name (Schostakowitsch) and German notation, where E-flat is called "es" and B-natural is called H. Thus the sequence D/E-flat/C/B spells DSCH.

Ex. 1

This imprinting of his own presence is a device that Shostakovich used several times in his later works. It would not have met with approval in 1948: cult of personality was permitted only to Stalin. This movement is where Shostakovich did it first; the most prominent later occurrences are in the Symphony No. 10, the String Quartet No. 8, and the last symphony, No. 15.

The essential thing for Shostakovich is the characteristic shape of the four-note motif rather than the specific D/E-flat/C/B pitches; in fact, in the Violin Concerto it always appears transposed rather than at its actual pitch. Not quite a minute and a half into the scherzo of the Violin Concerto, the woodwinds blast out DSCH so that it is impossible to miss, but the four-note pattern is present in a different permutation right at the beginning of the movement: the first four notes of the theme, transposed up from B-flat minor to C minor, would spell CDSH. (This happens also to be the form in which Shostakovich introduces the motto in the Tenth Symphony.)

About that woodwind yell of DSCH: you may have noticed in the instrumentation list that the orchestra includes neither trumpets nor trombones. This is surprising in a "big" piece like this concerto, and especially in one by Shostakovich, who was very much a trumpets-and-trombones composer. What the sound of this work conspicuously—and of course deliberately—lacks is the easy brilliance of trumpets. And trombones, though they add weight, also have a keen, bright edge to their tone. The Concerto's dominant sound, after solo violin, is that of woodwinds, used as a choir, in unisons and octaves (often with a typically Shostakovich grittiness of sound), or, as in the DSCH yell, as surrogate trumpets. The special sound world Shostakovich has invented here, sometimes blunted, sometimes strained, contributes potently to the expressive effect.

For that matter, almost anyone, seeing a piano reduction of the third movement would suppose the fanfares at the beginning to be trumpet music. It is actually the horns who play these fanfares, another instance where the composer imposes a certain matte quality on the sound. This movement, the Concerto's powerful center of gravity, is a passacaglia, a series of variations over a repeated bass. It is the part of the Concerto Shostakovich was working on during the worst phases of the 1948 hearings at which he, Prokofiev, Khachaturian, and others were brutally bullied by Andrei Zhdanov, the commissar in charge of ideological and cultural affairs. The composer Mikhail Meyerovich reported that Shostakovich had shown him the "exact spot" he had arrived at when Zhdanov's condemnation of him was published: "The violin played [sixteenth-notes] before and after it. There was no change evident in the music."

Like his friend Britten, but arriving at the idea independently, Shostakovich found the passacaglia with its stubborn reiterations to be a marvelous device for creating slow movements of great mass and power. The Piano Trio No. 2, the Symphony No. 8, and the Second, Third, Sixth, and Tenth String Quartets include stirring movements of this type; the Prelude No. 12 in G-sharp minor of the Twenty-Four Preludes and Fugues is a strong example closely contemporary to the Concerto.

The bass here is long—seventeen measures of Andante—beginning and ending on the keynote, F.

Ex. 2

Here is an outline of what happens:

*Variation 1:* Low strings play the bass, horns add stern fanfares, timpani support both lines. (In most passacaglias the composer introduces the bass by itself, but here Shostakovich in effect starts with the first variation.)

*Variation 2:* English horn, clarinets, and bassoons play a chorale while bassoon and tuba take the bass.

*Variation 3:* The bass is in low strings again and the solo violin, after its first minutes of respite in the Concerto, enters with an expressive counterpoint.

*Variation 4:* The bass stays in the low strings, English horn and bassoon repeat what the violin played in the previous variation, and the solo violin continues its meditation.

*Variation 5:* A solo horn plays the bass, the violin becomes more passionate and forceful, low strings add a new counterpoint, woodwinds bring back their chorale.

*Variation 6:* All the horns, tuba, and pizzicato low strings play the bass, the violin adding increasingly impassioned commentary in triplets.

*Variation 7:* With a rich string accompaniment, the solo violin plays the passacaglia bass in *fortissimo* octaves.

*Variation 8:* The bass goes back to bassoon and tuba, the violin adding a song, *molto espressivo*, on its lowest string.

*Variation 9:* Timpani and pizzicato low strings take the bass, the violin recalls the horn fanfares of the first variation.

With timpani, cellos, and basses on a long-sustained F, the music dissolves. The violin plays wide-ranging arpeggios and, as the orchestra falls silent, begins an immense cadenza. This is the bridge to the finale. In 1959 Shostakovich would do exactly the same thing in his Cello Concerto No. 1, but there he actually called the cadenza a separate movement. He could equally well have done so here. This is an extraordinary passage, as brilliant architecturally as it is violinistically.[7] The cadenza begins with music derived from the passacaglia's fanfares; then, as speed and intensity build—and Oistrakh remarked that pacing was everything here, so that one would not "run out of breath"—ideas from the first two movements recur as well.

Originally, the violin flew from the scales in fifths and octaves at the end of the cadenza directly into the last movement; however, Oistrakh begged for just enough respite to allow him time to wipe his brow, and Shostakovich, humorously embarrassed not to have thought of this himself, redesigned the beginning of the finale so that it starts with twenty seconds of tutti. The Burlesque-Finale itself is a torrentially virtuosic movement in Shostakovich's most athletic style in which the passacaglia theme makes a striking return.

---

[7]Again there is a striking parallel with Britten, specifically with his Violin Concerto, where a large-scale cadenza fulfills the same function. It is very unlikely that Shostakovich could have known Britten's concerto in 1947.

# Jean Sibelius

Sibelius was born at Tavastehus (Hämeenlinna), Finland, then
an autonomous grand duchy in the Russian Empire, on 8 December 1865 and died at Järvenpää, Finland, on 20 September
1957.

## Concerto in D minor for Violin and Orchestra, Opus 47

*Allegro moderato*
*Adagio di molto*
*Allegro ma non troppo*

Sibelius began his Violin Concerto in September 1902, completed
the work in short score—that is, with the orchestration worked out
but not written down in detail—in the fall of 1903, and finished the
full score around New Year's, 1904. The first performance was given at Helsingfors (Helsinki) on 8 February 1904, with Victor Nováček as soloist and
the composer conducting the Helsingfors Philharmonic. Sibelius withdrew
the work for revision, a task he accomplished in June 1905. In its new and
present form, the work had its premiere in Berlin on 19 October 1905, with
Karl Halir as soloist and Richard Strauss on the podium.

Solo violin, two flutes, two oboes, two clarinets, two bassoons, four horns, two
trumpets, three trombones, timpani, and strings.

In no violin concerto is the soloist's first note—delicately dissonant and off the beat—more beautiful. It made Sibelius happy, too: in September 1902 he wrote to his wife Aino—and this was the first mention of the work— that he had just had "a marvelous opening idea." But after that inspired start, the history of the piece was troubled. Sibelius, drinking heavily and virtually living at Kamp's and König's restaurants in Helsingfors, was lim- itlessly inventive when it came to finding ways of running from work in progress. He behaved outrageously to Willy Burmester, the German virtu- oso who had been concertmaster in Helsingfors for a while in the 1890s, admired Sibelius and was ambitious on his behalf, stirred him up to write a violin concerto, and of course hoped to give the first performance. Sibelius sent the score to Burmester—"Wonderful! Masterly! Only once before have I spoken in such terms to a composer, and that was when Tchaikov- sky showed me his concerto"—and let word get about that he would ded- icate the work to him. Meanwhile, Sibelius was also pushing for a premiere at a date when Burmester was not free or, at best, would not have had enough time to learn a piece that in its original form was even more tech- nically demanding than it is now.

Victor Nováček—not to be confused with the better-known Ottokar Nováček (to whom he was not related)—was a violin teacher with no rep- utation as a performer. That he would fail with this concerto was a fore- gone conclusion, yet that was the plan the self-destructive and, in this in- stance, also sadistic Sibelius chose. After the near-disastrous premiere, Burmester offered his services again for a series of performances in October 1904—"All of my twenty-five years' stage experience, my artistry and in- sight will be at the service of this work. . . . I shall play the concerto in Helsingfors in such a way that the city will be at your feet"—only to find himself passed over again, this time in favor of Karl Halir, concertmaster in Berlin, a former member of the Joachim Quartet, and the leader of a quar- tet of his own. Burmester never played the work, and the dedication finally went to yet another musician, Ferenc von Vecsey, a Hungarian violinist born in 1893, who, in his prodigy days, was one of the Concerto's earliest champions.

From Bach to Bartók, many of the great keyboard concertos have been written by composers for themselves. Rather more of the famous violin con- certos have been written for others to play. Sibelius wrote his for a kind of ghostly self. He was a failed violinist. He had begun lessons late, at fourteen, but then "the violin took me by storm, and for the next ten years it was my dearest wish, my overriding ambition, to become a great virtuoso." In fact, aside from the double handicap of his late start and the provincial level of even the best teaching available in Finland, he had neither the physical coordination nor the temperament for such a career. In 1890–1891, when he was in Vienna studying composition with Robert Fuchs and Karl Goldmark, he played in the conservatory orchestra (its intonation gave him head-aches), and on 9 January 1891 he auditioned for the Philharmonic. "When he got back to his room," we read in Erik Tawaststjerna's biography, "Sibelius broke down and wept. Afterwards he sat at the piano and began to practice scales." With that, he gave up, although a diary entry in 1915 records a dream of being twelve and a virtuoso. His Violin Concerto is, in any event, imbued both with his feeling for the instrument and the pain of his farewell to his "dearest wish" and "overriding ambition."

Sibelius assigns a role of unprecedented importance to his first-movement cadenza, which in fact takes the place and function of the development section. The original 1903–1904 version has two large cadenzas in the first movement, the familiar one that survives and another, near the end, that is full of echoes of the solo Bach pieces to which Sibelius the aspiring violinist never advanced.[1]

What leads up to that big cadenza is a sequence of ideas that begins with the sensitive, dreamy melody that introduces the voice of the soloist. This leads to what we might call a mini-cadenza, starting with a flurry of sixteenth-notes marked *veloce*. (In the original version, the sixteenths are strictly in tempo and backed, to fine and tense effect, by a soft drum tattoo.) From this solo passage there emerges a declamatory statement upon which Sibelius's personal voice is ineluctable—an impassioned, super-violinistic recitation in sixths and octaves. What follows is a long tutti that slowly subsides from furious march music to wistful pastoral to darkness. It is out of this darkness that the development/cadenza erupts, an occasion for sovereign virtuosity, brilliantly, fancifully, and economically composed.

Whether comparing his own Concerto with Brahms's, which he heard in Berlin in January 1905, or, many years later, with the Prokofiev D-major, Sibelius set store by having composed a soloistic concerto rather than a symphonic one. It seems an odd point for him to have been insistent about for so long. True, there is none of the close-knit dialogue characteristic of the great concertos of Mozart[2], Beethoven, and Brahms: Sibelius opposes rather than meshes solo and orchestra, or casts the orchestra as accompanist. But while it is true that the Sibelius is one of the really smashing virtuoso con-

---

[1]In 1905 Sibelius forbade further performances of the original version of the Violin Concerto; in 1990, however, the composer's family gave permission for the violinist Leonidas Kavakos to make a recording. This is not the place to discuss Sibelius's revisions in detail, though I shall mention one or two points en route. I can summarize their effect by saying that Sibelius usefully tightened the form of the first and third movements, that he suppressed his previous urge to keep the soloist busy all the time and at all costs, and that he got rid of a lot of conventional, rather frivolous (though undeniably effective) violin figuration. There are a few things one is sorry to lose, but there is no question that Sibelius achieved what I take to have been his aim, namely, a more consistent work, one less liable to interruption or distraction by bravura display, one more precise, noble, and serious.
[2]This would be the Mozart of the piano concertos, not of the early, lovely, and quite simply composed violin concertos.

certos, it would be a mistake to associate it with the merely virtuosic tradition represented by the concertos of, say, Tchaikovsky and Bruch, to say nothing of Paganini, Vieuxtemps, Wieniawski, and others of that ilk. Sibelius's first movement, with its bold sequence of highly diverse ideas, its quest for the unity behind them, its daring substitute for a conventional development, its recapitulation that continues to explore, rearrange, and develop, its wedding of violinistic brilliance to compositional purposes, is one in which the breath of the symphonist—one who was to become perhaps the greatest symphonist after Brahms—is not to be mistaken.

The second and third movements are less ambitious as structures, but that does not keep the Adagio from being one of the most moving pages Sibelius ever achieved. Between its introductory measures and main theme there is a fascinating disparity. Clarinets and oboes in pairs suggest an idea of rather tentative mien, one also in which something survives of Sibelius's early passion for Wagner. This is a gentle beginning, leading to the entry of the solo violin with a melody of vast breadth. *Sonoro ed espressivo*, it speaks in accents we know well and that touch us deeply. The world and the gestures evoked are the world and the gestures of Beethoven, particularly those of the Cavatina in the B-flat major String Quartet, Opus 130. Sibelius never found—perhaps never sought—such a melody again: this, too, is farewell. Very lovely, later in the movement, is the imagination for orchestral sound that has Sibelius accompany the melody (now in clarinet and bassoon) with scales, all *pianissimo*, broken octaves moving up in the violin, and with a soft rain of slowly descending scales in flutes and quiet strings. Three measures from the end, the original version has a tiny and strange ghost of a cadenza, beautiful but wrong.

"Evidently a polonaise for polar bears," said D. F. Tovey of the finale—a remark it seems no program note writer can resist quoting. The charmingly aggressive main theme was an old one, going back to a string quartet from 1890. The enlivening accompaniment

Ex. 1

 etc.

in the timpani against

Ex. 2

in the strings is one of the fruits of revision: originally it was all as in Example 1. As the movement goes on, the rhythm becomes more and more giddily inventive, especially in the matter of the recklessly against-the-beat bravura embellishment the soloist fires across the themes. It builds to a drama that reminds us how much Sibelius enjoyed Dvořák's D-minor Symphony when he heard Hans von Bülow conduct it in Berlin in 1890, and it ends in utmost and syncopated brilliance.

# Richard Strauss

Richard Georg Strauss was born in Munich, Bavaria, on 11 June 1864 and died in Garmisch, Germany, on 8 September 1949.

## *Burleske,* in D minor for Piano and Orchestra

The *Burleske* was originally composed in 1885, but only attained its final form in 1890. Eugen d'Albert, to whom Strauss later dedicated the work, was the soloist at the first performance, which the composer conducted and which took place at Eisenach on 21 June 1890 at a convention of the General German Music Association. Strauss conducted the premiere of *Death and Transfiguration* at the same concert.

**Solo piano, two flutes and piccolo, two oboes, two clarinets, two bassoons, four horns, two trumpets, timpani, and strings.**

Dear Papa,
So—I arrived here in good shape on Monday afternoon and find the town small, to be sure, but pretty. The environs are delightful. Yesterday morning I called on Herr von Bülow, who was very gracious and already returned my visit today. The first concert is on the 11th: all Beethoven. . . . The second, at which I begin with the Mozart concerto, then conduct my symphony, then a Beethoven symphony, is scheduled for the 18th. On the 15th—imagine my pleasure—Brahms is coming to rehearse his Fourth Symphony for the first time.

The first rehearsal starts tomorrow at 9. This morning I went to see the Duke, who was very gracious.[1]


That is the twenty-one-year-old Richard Strauss on 30 September 1885 in a filial report to his father, Franz Strauss, solo horn at the Munich Court Opera and professor at the Academy of Music in that city. The small but pretty town where Richard had just arrived and where so much activity awaited him was Meiningen, capital of the tiny principality of Saxe-Meiningen, about a hundred miles east-northeast of Frankfurt. Little though it was, the population then being about 10,000, Meiningen was a lively center for theater and music, and the orchestra, conducted since 1880 by the brilliant Hans von Bülow, was one of Europe's most renowned ensembles.

Strauss had come to know von Bülow in 1883. At nineteen he was already the experienced author of, among other things, a string quartet, a symphony, sonatas for piano and for cello, concertos for violin and horn, and a wind serenade. The Serenade, in Strauss's own later estimation, was "nothing more than a decent conservatory exercise"; nonetheless, von Bülow took it on tour with his Meiningen players, and it was at a concert in Berlin that the fledgling composer met the waspish and celebrated conductor and pianist, then fifty-three.[2]

That was not all. Von Bülow asked for another such serenade, which Strauss duly delivered in the summer of 1884. Silence. But then von Bülow appeared in Munich for three concerts with the Meiningen Orchestra and, in Strauss's words,


surprised me with the news that he had decided on an extra matinee after the third concert, at which, along with Rheinberger's *Wallenstein* Symphony, my Serenade would be performed—and I was supposed to conduct! I asked when I might have a rehearsal, whereupon von Bülow answered brusquely: "No rehearsals, the orchestra is already overworked." With a sigh I submitted and, without ever having held a baton in my hand before, I got through the performance with great success, von Bülow of course having prepared it well.[3]


Von Bülow was interested in the young man. He had known his father well from the days when he had conducted the first performances of *Tristan* and *Meistersinger* in Munich, and the two musicians, alike in their prickliness as well as in their sovereign artistry, had gone through many a nasty verbal

[1]Richard Strauss, *Briefe an die Eltern, 1882-1906*, ed. Willi Schuh (Zurich: Atlantis Verlag, 1954).
[2]Conductors, wind players, and audiences still take pleasure in the brief and charming Serenade, Opus 7.
[3]Strauss, op. cit.

exchange.[4] Now, early in 1885, von Bülow began to make discreet inquiry about Richard's availability "to rehearse the chorus and conduct the orchestra at Meiningen during my absence [on concert tours] . . . gratis, on an interim basis, for the sake of his training, as interne."

Strauss, who had no illusions about his inexperience, leaped at the chance to be von Bülow's assistant. Correspondence went back and forth, the essential support of Princess Marie of Meiningen, herself an excellent pianist, was secured, and on 9 July 1885, Strauss received a contract effective 1 October. For Strauss's first concert, von Bülow assigned him a double role as conductor of his own Symphony in F minor, whose first performance had been given in New York by Theodore Thomas the previous December, and as soloist in Mozart's Piano Concerto in C minor, K. 491. After the first movement of the Mozart, von Bülow told Strauss: "If you didn't have it in you to be something better, you could even make it as a pianist."

Strauss's apprenticeship took an unexpected course in that von Bülow resigned and departed for Saint Petersburg in December, leaving his young assistant in sole charge for four months. At the end of that period, Strauss preferred for various reasons to accept an appointment as third conductor at the Munich Court Opera, where his father still played incomparably all those Wagner solos he so passionately detested, but the Meiningen experience was the beginning of his long career as a conductor regarded by many as the greatest Mozart interpreter of his time.[5] A quarter of a century later he wrote about von Bülow: "For anyone who ever heard him play Beethoven or conduct Wagner, who attended one of his piano lessons or observed him in orchestral rehearsal, he inevitably became the model of all the shining virtues of a performing artist, and his touching sympathy for me, his influence on the development of my artistic abilities, were decisive factors in my career."[6]

Strauss's duties in Meiningen left him little time for composition, yet he sought to honor his mentor with the offering of a scherzo for piano and orchestra. But von Bülow indignantly rejected the work as unpianistic and certainly impossible for a pianist with as small a hand as his (Strauss says that von Bülow could barely reach an octave), and he let the composer know that he had no intention of knocking himself out practicing such stuff. Strauss tried it himself. He was a good pianist but not *that* good, and his attempt to play and conduct at the same time brought discouraging results. "Sheer nonsense," he grumbled and put the score away.

[4]Franz Strauss loathed Wagner's music. Von Bülow was devoted to it, but had broken off contact with Wagner himself after his wife had left him to go and live with the Great Man. Wagner's and Cosima von Bülow's first child, Isolde, was born the day von Bülow conducted the first orchestra rehearsal of *Tristan und Isolde*.

[5]Strauss's recordings of Mozart symphonies, several of which have recently been reissued, do not bear this out, but then he was never happy in the recording studio.

[6]Richard Strauss, *Betrachtungen und Erinnerungen*, ed. Willi Schuh (Zurich: Atlantis Verlag, 1949).

His friend Eugen d'Albert found out about its existence. Just one month older than Strauss and already a famous virtuoso, he was also a good composer and well disposed toward new music and literature: Grieg, Humperdinck, Reger, Pfitzner, von Reznicek, Gerhart Hauptmann, and Hermann Hesse were among his friends. D'Albert persuaded Strauss to have another go at his scherzo. Strauss did so and renamed it *Burleske*, after which the two young men, both just turned twenty-six, introduced it at Eisenach with considerable éclat. (When d'Albert took the *Burleske* to Berlin seven months later, the man on the podium was Hans von Bülow.) For a time, Strauss continued to harbor reservations about the piece and refused publication for another four years, but eventually the need for money prevailed. In later life he became fond of it and, with Alfred Blumen as soloist, it was one of the works—*Don Juan* and the *Symphonia domestica* were the others—on the last full concert he ever conducted. That was with the Philharmonia in London in September 1947.[7]

As appropriately as Scherzo or *Burleske*, Strauss could also have called this piece a Concert Waltz for Piano and Orchestra. It is not *precisely* a waltz, but who cares, and certainly the waltz mood is more prevalent than any other. I should guess that Strauss's pleasure in waltzes was nourished by sharing the name of the composers of the *Radetzky* March, *Tales from the Vienna Woods*, and *Village Swallows from Austria*. (They were not related; in fact, Dr. Richard spelled his name Strauss while his Viennese predecessors wrote theirs Strauß.) Richard Strauss loved waltzes and was good at composing them. *Burleske* brings us his first waltzing music; the melancholy "memorial waltz" of 1945, *München*, was his last. We hear relatively little straightforward dance music in *Burleske*, but we do get a lot of the slightly soured, faintly offbeat waltzing of the kind one finds in such odd pieces as Busoni's *Tanzwalzer* and Otto Klemperer's *Lustiger Walzer*. Within Strauss's own work, *Burleske*'s three-quarter-time music is closer to the somewhat abstract *München* than to the "realistic" waltzes in *Der Rosencavalier* or to the song *Schlechtes Wetter* (Bad Weather).[8] What is clear is that a pianist who cannot play waltzes seductively cannot make a go of *Burleske*.

The first idea that came to Strauss is the first one we hear, the four bars for timpani, unaccompanied. He was pleased with that and wrote it out in full in a letter to his father. There is no denying that the shadow of Brahms falls across this work, but in the shapes of the themes, almost all of them related to the witty drum exordium and its continuation in woodwinds and strings, and particularly in the sound of the orchestra, we taste a piquant

---

[7]It was at a rehearsal for this concert that Strauss made the delightful and perceptive remark, "I may not be a first-class composer, but I *am* a first-class second-class composer."

[8]The published score of Strauss's great comedy spells the title *Rosenkavalier*; Strauss himself, however, preferred and always used the more old-fashioned spelling with a *c*, and I follow him in that.

something that is already very much Strauss's own. The sonata-form devel-opment of these ideas is perhaps conscientious to a fault—or to put it more directly, Strauss's recapitulation as written makes the piece too long by about three minutes—but we also meet plenty of invention, humor, and seductive sensuality. Near the end, the pianist gets a rewarding cadenza. Strauss was always good at endings, and the coda of *Burleske* is a winner!

## Concerto No. 1 in E-flat major for Horn and Orchestra, Opus 11

*Allegro*
*Andante*
*Allegro*

Strauss wrote this Concerto in 1882–1883. With the composer at the piano, Bruno Hoyer played the work in Munich shortly after its completion; the first performance with orchestra was given on 4 March 1885 by Gustav Lein-hos with Hans von Bülow conducting the Meiningen Orchestra, in which Leinhos was principal horn. The score is dedicated to yet another hornist, Oscar Franz. The title is a puzzle: Strauss specifies a Waldhorn, that is, a valveless natural horn, but the Concerto cannot be played on that instru-ment.

**Solo horn, two flutes, two oboes, two clarinets, two bassoons, two horns, two trumpets, timpani, and strings.**

All of us can summon up some sort of very early musical memories; there must also have been musical noises around us that we no longer recall spe-cifically and consciously, but that did penetrate and make a difference. For the infant Strauss, diapered, swaddled, and secure in his parents' comfortable and, one imagines, overstuffed apartment at the corner of Sonnenstrasse and Schwanthalerstrasse in Munich, the most persistent feature of the aural decor would have been the sound of his father practicing the French horn.

Franz Joseph Strauss, forty-two years old when his son was born, was principal horn at the Munich Court Orchestra for forty-nine years, retiring in 1891. He not only was a player of formidable technique and stamina—his proud son tells us that at sixty-eight he could still play an uncut *Siegfried* flawlessly, albeit leaving the famous call in Act 2 to his assistant—but was universally admired as an inspired artist of impeccable taste. Connoisseurs looked forward for weeks to the great solos in the *Eroica* and the Ninth Symphony, *Freischütz*, *Oberon*, and *A Midsummer Night's Dream*.

Like most of the conductors who had to deal with Franz Strauss, Richard found Papa something of a terror, recalling him as being as "vehement, irascible, tyrannical" as his mother, Josephine Strauss, a member of the Pschorr brewery clan, was soft-spoken and gentle. Franz Strauss had no tolerance for slack rhythm and unsteady tempos: "How often he would yell at me, 'You rush like a Jew.' But I learned good music-making from him the countless times I had to accompany him in Mozart's beautiful horn concertos and Beethoven's Horn Sonata."[9]

Franz Strauss also inculcated something of his own obdurate musical conservativism into his son. Franz himself would have been happy if music had stopped with the Viennese Classics, Weber, and Mendelssohn: he loathed the Wagner operas in which he played so angelically, and he was not even minimally polite to Wagner himself or to Hans von Bülow, Hermann Levi, and the others who conducted Wagner's music at the Court Opera. "Strauss is a detestable fellow," said Wagner, "but when he plays the horn you can't be angry with him."

Richard Strauss made little of *Tannhäuser*, *Lohengrin*, and *Siegfried* when he saw them as a boy, but at seventeen, having barely arrived at Brahms by way of Mendelssohn, Chopin, and Schumann, he defied his father's orders and secretly studied the score of *Tristan*. More than sixty years later he recalled how he had "positively wolfed it down as though in a trance," but he had not yet internalized it so that it influenced his own compositions. Full and final conversion came in 1885 through his friendship with Alexander Ritter, a violinist at Meiningen, where Strauss was then conducting. Ritter was a passionate Wagnerian who set himself the task of turning the young man toward "the music of the future." As for Franz Strauss, he enjoyed his son's success, but not the music that brought that success. "It's like having your pants full of June bugs," Franz Strauss wrote to his by-then very famous son about the *Symphonia domestica*; at least, by dying in 1905, he was spared *Salome*.

Along with great care about rhythm, tempo, and Classical style in his own distinguished career as a conductor, a piece of his patrimony that Richard Strauss carried with him through his long life was a love for the French horn. That love continues across more than six decades, through *Don Juan*, *Death and Transfiguration*, *Till Eulenspiegel*, *Ein Heldenleben*, the *Symphonia domestica*, and *Der Rosencavalier*, on to *Capriccio*, the Second Horn Concerto, and the *Four Last Songs*.

The Concerto No. 1 was not Strauss's first paternally inspired compo-

---

[9] Richard Strauss, *Betrachtungen und Erinnerungen*, ed. Willi Schuh (Zurich: Atlantis Verlag, 1949).

sition: at fourteen, he had written a set of variations for horn as well as a song, *Ein Alphorn hör' ich schallen* (I Hear an Alpine Horn Sounding) with what Norman Del Mar describes as a "fiendishly difficult" obbligato. Both were offerings to "his dear Papa," but the dedication of the concerto went to Oscar Franz, a highly regarded virtuoso and teacher. (There are no doubt biographers who would want to make something of Strauss's choice of a dedicatee who shared half his father's name.) In the event, Oscar Franz never played the work and neither did Franz Strauss, at least not in public; the senior Strauss did, however, read it at home several times with his son at the piano, and both Richard and his sister Johanna well recalled the old man's complaints that there were too many high notes. Gustav Leinhos, who gave the premiere with the Meiningen Orchestra, of which he was a member, had been chosen to lead the horn group at the first Bayreuth Festival, and was described by Richard Strauss as "colossally secure" in the high register.

When you hear the Concerto No. 1, it is obvious that this work precedes the young composer's seduction into the Wagnerian world. Indeed, except for the figure near the beginning that leaps up a ninth and then comes tumbling down through a dominant seventh chord, we might well call it pre-Straussian. But make no mistake, it is a charming and totally surefooted work.

Strauss casts it in the traditional three movements. The opening is arresting—and startling—for after just one tonic chord in the orchestra, the soloist asserts his presence in a fanfare, *energico*. Only then does Strauss move on to a tutti, though it is a brief one. When the horn returns, it is with a new, lyric, and gracious theme that allows itself the luxury of spreading over thirty-six measures. By contrast, the next horn entrance is dramatic, *fortissimo*, and in minor; after another lyric episode, it leads to some airy virtuoso display.

The slow movement follows without a break, the transition managed with impressive skill. The orchestra seizes our attention with an outburst Strauss marks *patetico*, after which the pace relaxes and the harmony slides into the penumbra of A-flat minor. Here, too, the melodies are sweet and their orchestral setting exquisite. Among other things, Strauss transforms a vigorous horn call from the first movement into a delicate accompaniment for the violins.

Unlike the first movement, the second comes to a full close, but even so, Strauss wants to proceed into the third without a major stop. He starts this finale with one of those "hunting" themes in 6/8 that we know so well from Mozart's concertos (including a few for piano as well as those for horn), but that is just the beginning of a richly varied movement. Right away we hear that the finale's first theme is a transformation of the fanfare with which the Concerto began. One of the things Ritter showed Strauss was "thematic metamorphosis," the technique Liszt had used in his tone poems—and which he had learned from Schubert's *Wanderer* Fantasy—that involves getting a single theme to yield many new ones, keeping the notes of the original one but changing their character through alterations of tempo, rhythm, harmony, and so on. But Strauss, as we can hear in this Concerto, had already found his own way to this idea. As though to make sure we don't miss the point, he actually quotes the first-movement fanfare in its original form. Toward the end there is a great darkening and slowing down, but finally, adding the direction *con bravura*, he lets things rip, and the close makes a fine effect.

## Concerto No. 2 in E-flat major for Horn and Orchestra

*Allegro*
*Andante con moto*
*Rondo: Allegro molto*

Strauss composed this Concerto in 1941–1942, completing it on 28 November 1942. The first performance was given at the Salzburg Festival on 11 August 1943 by Gottfried von Freiberg with Karl Böhm conducting the Vienna Philharmonic, in which von Freiberg was principal horn. The dedication is "to the memory of my father."

**Solo horn, two flutes, two oboes, two clarinets, two bassoons, two horns, two trumpets, timpani, and strings.**

Nearly sixty years separate Strauss's two horn concertos, a period longer than Beethoven's entire life span. The composer of the First Concerto was a teenager just beginning to make a noise in the world; the Second came from the pen of a man who, at seventy-eight, was the best-known living composer of classical music. A half dozen of his tone poems had been standard concert fare since the turn of the century, three of his operas were in the repertory of every major house in Europe and the Americas, singers everywhere cultivated his lieder. As a conductor, he had been a major figure in Munich, Berlin, and Vienna, as well as at the festivals of Salzburg and Bayreuth. He was rich, famous, deeply sad, and disillusioned. He had allowed himself to be co-opted as a reluctant and rather ineffectual collaborator with the Nazi regime he despised and which he felt did not sufficiently appreciate him; his rationale was that if he did not, for example, take the chairmanship of the Reichsmusikkammer, the government agency that oversaw all musical affairs, the position would go to a Nazi who could do real damage. Witness to decades of mostly depressing history, he had seen the slow disintegration of the world in which he had grown up and prospered and whose values he understood and cared about. He described the destruction of the Munich Opera in 1943 by Allied bombs as "the greatest catastrophe" of his life, one for which there could be "no consolation and, in my old age, no hope." (Remembering what else had happened in the previous ten years, one does not type these words easily.)

Strauss in the 1940s seemed to be more a historical figure than a living composer. He was still writing—he had never stopped—but his fame rested on music dating from before World War I. His more recent operas had been given with the best singers and conductors, but no work of his after *Der Rosencavalier*, first produced in 1911, had really caught on. At mid-century it was a truism that Richard Strauss was washed up and had been for decades, that he had outlived himself.

In the years since his death, that judgment has been revised, much as comparable verdicts on late Puccini, Debussy, and Rachmaninoff have been reconsidered. True, none of the later operas is a box office magnet like *Rosencavalier*, but no one now avers that *Ariadne auf Naxos*, *Die Frau ohne Schatten*, *Arabella*, and *Capriccio* are feeble efforts by a composer in decline; indeed, they all have a large public that loves them. The *Four Last Songs* have become so ubiquitous that some years ago I heard a conductor famous as a Strauss specialist refer to them as *Wirtshausmusik*—tavern music.[10]

Those songs, poignant in expression, sumptuous in sound, and a glorious opportunity for the soprano who can manage them, did more than any other work to get people to reconsider late Strauss—they and that dark masterpiece *Metamorphosen*, which seems almost to have been designed not to be popular. The Second Horn Concerto, the Oboe Concerto (1945), and the gentle Duet-Concertino for Clarinet and Bassoon (1947) have been belated beneficiaries of this revisionist assessment. If the Second Horn Concerto remains the least known of these pieces, that is so in part because it is insanely difficult, in part because if a hornist wants to play a Strauss concerto, No. 1, while anything but easy, is, with its simple nineteenth-century "pre-Straussian" language, more accessible and less of a challenge for the conductor and orchestra.

The French horn was practically part of Strauss's genetic makeup, something I touch on in my essay on the First Concerto. Like his love affair with the soprano voice, his attachment to that most Romantic of instruments was for life. Both loves, I should add, were accompanied and nourished by pro-

---

[10]There is actually a fifth "last song," *Malven* (Mallows), dated 23 November 1948. Strauss had written it as a last gesture of affection and gratitude to the soprano Maria Jeritza, a great Salome, Octavian, Ariadne, Empress, and Helen. Jeritza kept the precious manuscript to herself, and it only came to light in 1986 when her papers were auctioned by Sotheby's in New York.

found understanding for the Beloved. On 3 August 1941, Strauss completed his last opera, *Capriccio*. The simple but unforgettably scored dominant and tonic chords at its deliciously melancholic, ambiguous, teasing curtain-fall are each preceded by a quizzical five-note phrase for the solo horn: these gestures stay in the memory longer and with more sweet pain than any vocal phrase in the opera.

That was Strauss's farewell to the stage—"*Capriccio* was meant to be the end," he wrote five years later to Clemens Krauss, the librettist of that beguiling *jeu d'esprit*—but it is as though something about those last sounds of the French horn would not let him go. Strauss was not yet done with his father's instrument, the instrument whose music must have been some of the first he ever heard. At any rate, about a year after completing *Capriccio* he wrote to Viorica Ursuleac, the soprano who had taken the leading role in that opera (and who was Krauss's wife), that he had just "completed a little horn concerto whose third movement—a rondo in 6/8—has come out especially well."

It is a spirited work, this Second Horn Concerto, beautifully made, full of the joy of inventing, slightly longer than its predecessor and much harder. I called the First Concerto "pre-Straussian"; this one is all Strauss, and unmistakably so. Again, Strauss cast the work in the classic three-movement form. The first movement is a fairly broad Allegro. The solo horn begins it alone with what starts out as a simple flourish on the tonic chord, but already by the third measure the music has started on its harmonic adventures. Strauss had called *Capriccio* a "Conversation Piece in Music." That could almost be a designation for the Second Horn Concerto as well. The texture is transparent and chamber-musical like that of the *Capriccio* orchestra, and the instruments keep up a stream of cordial, witty, sometimes surprising conversation, the solo horn duetting at moments with the clarinet, a solo violin, the oboe, and even the orchestra's principal horn.

As he had done in his 1883 Concerto, Strauss links the first two movements: near the end of the Allegro, the opening flourish appears in the orchestra, but *tranquillo*, and then the music slides into a dreamy A-flat major. The softly lilting melody, which the orchestra presents at leisure before the solo horn takes it up, is one of Strauss's loveliest. There is a brief contrasting section, slightly quicker and in faraway D major, after which Strauss returns to a lovingly enriched variant of the opening.

Strauss had every reason to be happy with his finale, a sunny and playful movement and a feast of risky bravura. His use of the orchestral horns is especially felicitous and amusing. Just before the end, the timpani join in for the first time and help to propel the music to its buoyant conclusion.

# Concerto for Oboe and Small Orchestra

*Allegro moderato—Andante—Vivace—Allegro*

Strauss completed his Oboe Concerto on 25 October 1945, slightly revising the ending on 1 February 1948. The first performance was given on 26 February 1946 by Marcel Saillet with the Concerto's dedicatees, the Zurich Tonhalle Orchestra and Dr. Volkmar Andreae (whose name is misspelled by the publisher in the study score).

**Solo oboe, two flutes, English horn, two clarinets, two bassoons, two horns, and strings.**

Late in life, Strauss rediscovered the charms of absolute, that is, nonprogrammatic, music for instruments. In 1870—the year his father played principal horn in the premiere of *Die Walküre*—he had begun his seventy-eight-year career as a composer with a *Tailor's Polka* for piano, and from the days of his young manhood we have a number of attractive pieces that still get an occasional airing today, among them a wind serenade, a cello sonata, a violin concerto, the Horn Concerto No. 1, the F-minor Symphony, the *Burleske* for Piano and Orchestra, and the Violin Sonata. With *Aus Italien* in 1886, he began a flirtation with illustrative music, soon taking a more decisive step in that direction with *Macbeth*.

From then until 1903, the year of the *Symphonia domestica*, the orchestral tone poem was Strauss's principal concern; with *Salome*, finished and performed in 1905, he completed the shift to what he thought of as his real métier, that of opera composer. There is of course some overlap: with *Guntram* (1894) and *Feuersnot* (1901) he had already made forays into the operatic world, and *An Alpine Symphony* (1915) is a grand postscript to the series of tone poems. But except for the *Alpine Symphony* and the two quasi-concertos for the one-armed pianist Paul Wittgenstein, *Parergon zur Symphonia domestica* (1924) and *Panathenäenzug* (1927), years went by without a significant piece of instrumental music from Strauss's pen.[11] Indeed, he complained that the prospect of writing a piece of music unattached to a poetic

---

[11] The *Parergon* and the *Panathenäenzug* await revival. Since as recently as twenty years ago it seemed completely unlikely one would ever hear *An Alpine Symphony* in concert, to say nothing of its becoming one of the great conductor success pieces like *Pictures at an Exhibition*, there is perhaps hope for the two Wittgenstein pieces as well. D. F. Tovey was a champion of both and included his notes on them in his *Essays in Musical Analysis*.

or dramatic plan suggested no ideas to him; listening to such works as the *Festliches Praeludium*, composed in 1913 for the inauguration of a new concert hall in Vienna, or the *Festmusik*, written in 1940 to celebrate the 2,600th anniversary of the Japanese imperial dynasty, one is obliged to concede that he may have been right. When Strauss was in his late seventies all this changed. As always, he was motivated by practical considerations The regime he had neither endorsed nor repudiated had pressed the self-destruct button, and prospects for opera were not good: theaters were going up in flames or collapsing as rubble, musicians and technical personnel were absorbed into the armed forces, and in 1944 such theatrical establishments as were still functioning were shut down as part of an attempt to alleviate the fuel crisis.

Having completed his last opera, *Capriccio*, in 1941, Strauss next wrote his Second Horn Concerto, continuing on his new path with two substantial works for wind ensemble (they are titled *From an Invalid's Workshop* and *Cheerful Workshop*), the wondrous *Metamorphosen* for Twenty-three Solo Strings, this Oboe Concerto, and the Duet-Concertino for Clarinet and Bassoon with Strings and Harp. The *Four Last Songs* and *Metamorphosen*, an agonized meditation on a theme revealed on the last page as that of the *Eroica* Funeral March, are the rich and deep gatherings of that remarkable *Spätlese*; the other works are more by way of divertissements. Strauss called these his "wrist exercises." However it came about, through some loving-kindness the old man found the strength and the concentration to present to the world one more bundle of masterpieces, major and minor, and, even at their most lightweight, music of elegance and purity.

Among the music-loving American soldiers stationed in Bavaria whose curiosity was aroused by the Garmisch villa with the nameplate "Dr. Richard Strauss" on the gate was Alfred Mann, who would later become one of our most distinguished musicologists and teachers as well as an enlivening conductor of Baroque music. As a refugee from the Third Reich, Mann was fluent in German and thus particularly welcomed when he called to pay his respects. He was invited to return, and on several later visits brought along a younger friend, John de Lancie, who had joined the army as a bandsman but was later transferred to the Office of Strategic Services. Though only twenty-one when he was drafted, de Lancie had already been Fritz Reiner's principal oboe in the Pittsburgh Symphony; in 1954 he went on to succeed his teacher, the great Marcel Tabuteau, as principal oboist of the Philadelphia Orchestra, and in 1977 he was appointed successor to Rudolf Serkin as director of his alma mater, the Curtis Institute of Music.

"During one of my visits with Strauss," de Lancie recalled some years ago,

> I asked him if, in view of the numerous beautiful, lyric solos for oboe in almost all his works, he had ever considered writing a concerto for oboe. He answered

"NO," and there was no more conversation on the subject. He later told a fellow musician friend of mine (Alfred Mann . . . ) that the idea had taken root as a result of that remark. He subsequently, in numerous interviews and letters, spoke of this concerto in reference to my visits with him, and I have a letter from him inviting me to the first performance in Zurich. . . . After my return to America and civilian life in 1946, I corresponded with the family. I received a letter from the editor of Boosey [& Hawkes, Strauss's English publisher] informing me of a request from Strauss that I should be offered the first performance in America. . . .

That was not to be: the first American performance was given in 1948 on a broadcast by Mitchell Miller and the Columbia Concert Orchestra under Daniel Saidenberg. Strauss's autograph score is headed "Oboe Concerto 1945/suggested by an American soldier/oboist from Chicago"; nonetheless, until he recorded it in 1988, de Lancie had only a single opportunity to perform "his" concerto, and that was with Eugene Ormandy and the Philadelphia Orchestra at Interlochen, Michigan, in the summer of 1964.[12]

Oboists of course long for opportunities to play this work, but they also tend to go pale when you say the words "Strauss Concerto." Most particularly this response has to do with the opening, where, after two twitches from the cellos, the oboe has a solo of fifty-seven measures in a fairly leisurely tempo and with not so much as a single sixteenth-rest. John de Lancie has published and recorded what William Bennett, the San Francisco Symphony's solo oboe, describes as essentially a student edition with an aim to easing this technical obstacle. The de Lancie edition provides occasional interjections of flute, clarinet, and horn so as to give the oboist some places to breathe. Bennett comments: "One of the challenges of the Strauss Concerto is that the oboe voice is a constant ingredient and requires an air supply that Strauss might have imagined easily available following his experiments with the Vienna Philharmonic and the compressed-air hoses he recommends for his *Alpine Symphony*."

Specifically, for sustaining very long wind chords Strauss urges Bernhard Samuels's aerophone, or aerophor, described in the tenth edition of *The Oxford Companion to Music* as "a device patented in 1912 to help wind instrument players. A small bellows, worked by one foot, communicated by means of a tube with a corner of the mouth of the player, leaving him free to carry on his normal breathing processes through his nose whilst his mouth is supplied with the air required for his instrument by means of the bellows." To-

---

[12]Eric Van Tassel suggests in the notes to John de Lancie's recording that perhaps Strauss had never heard of Pittsburgh, but his and Pauline Strauss's American tour in 1904 had included two concerts in that city, an orchestral program and a lieder recital. More likely, it was a simple memory slip on the part of the eighty-one-year-old composer. De Lancie's account of the Concerto's genesis is quoted in the liner notes to his recording (RCA).

day's wind players wax derisive at the thought of using a mechanical aid of this sort. They have also become increasingly adept at circular breathing, that is, simultaneous inhalation and exhalation. *The New Grove Dictionary of Musical Instruments* explains that "this is done by using the cheeks as a reservoir for the air to be exhaled while the player inhales into the lungs through his nose."

Having conquered the technical difficulty of endless breath supply, the oboist finds a melodic line that is sinuous and lovely, thoroughly vocal in manner: the oboe seems to be a kind of *seconda donna*, somewhere between serious or semi-serious heroine and soubrette. If you are occasionally reminded of the *Symphonia domestica* or *Ariadne auf Naxos* it is probably because Strauss wanted you to be; there are also moments when the concerto seems like a study for the *Four Last Songs*, particularly *Beim Schlafengehen*. The orchestral framework is delightfully detailed as well as managed with admirable (and necessary) discretion and tact.

The cello twitch that starts the music rolling turns out to be a pervasive feature of the first movement; it is also a bit of common ground between that movement and the gentle Andante. Here, too, Strauss begins with a cruel endurance challenge, an unbroken cantilena thirty-three measures long. The Andante spills into an elaborate cadenza with orchestral punctuation, which in turn leads directly into a spirited rondo, gracefully nostalgic for the eighteenth century. By way of another, shorter cadenza, Strauss moves into an expansive coda. The tempo of this Allegro is actually slower than that of the preceding Vivace; however, the leisurely beats allow for subdivision into very fast notes so that the effect of the close is nicely brilliant.[13]

---

[13]Strauss's 1948 revision of the Concerto consisted of slightly reshuffling the internal order of the first eighteen measures and expanding the coda from seventeen measures to twenty-nine. He did it ingeniously; nonetheless, I find myself wishing he had left the coda alone. Boosey and Hawkes published the original version minus the nervous 1948 redundancies (only with piano reduction, never as a study score), but they have long since withdrawn this edition, which is now nearly impossible to find. The first recording of the Concerto, made in 1946 by the great Leon Goossens, of course gives the original ending, and so does John de Lancie's.

*Igor Stravinsky signature*

# Igor Stravinsky

Igor Fedorovich Stravinsky was born on 18 June 1882 in Ora-
nienbaum, now Lomonosov in the Northwest Saint Petersburg
Region of the Russian Republic, and died in New York on 6
April 1971.

## Capriccio for Piano and Orchestra

*Presto—Doppio movimento*
*Andante rapsodico*
*Allegro capriccioso ma in tempo giusto*

Stravinsky began the Capriccio in December 1928, completing the
three movements on 26 October, 13 September, and 9 November
1929 respectively. The first performance, for which the composer was
at the piano and Ernest Ansermet conducted the Paris Symphony Orchestra,
was given at the Salle Pleyel, Paris, on 6 December 1929. In 1949 Stravinsky
revised the work to correct some misprints and omissions in the 1929 score.

**Solo piano, plus a concertino group of strings (violin, viola, cello, and bass)
and a ripieno group of two flutes and piccolo, two oboes and English horn, two
clarinets and bass clarinet, two bassoons, four horns, two trumpets, three trombones, tuba, timpani, and strings.**

The Capriccio came into being because of Stravinsky's success as soloist in his own Piano Concerto four years earlier. (He had engagements with more than thirty orchestras in the first five years of that work's existence.) Both to give himself a change and in the hope of getting return dates where he had already played the Concerto, he decided to add one more work for piano and orchestra to his catalogue. Even before he had finished what was then the work in progress (*The Fairy's Kiss*, his magical dance score for Ida Rubinstein, based on themes by Tchaikovsky), he began the Capriccio, starting with what would become its finale.

In his 1936 autobiography, Stravinsky wrote that he took the title Capriccio from the early-seventeenth-century composer and theorist Praetorius, who "regarded it as a synonym of the *fantasia*, which was a free form made up of *fugato* instrumental passages." This sounds like a bid for scholarly respectability concocted for Stravinsky by his friend Walter Nouvel, the ghost-writer of the *Chroniques de ma vie*: I have a hard time believing that Stravinsky was really up on Praetorius's *Syntagma musicum*. But Paul Griffiths makes sense when he writes: "The title seems to have less to do with ancient precedent than with a taste for piquantly unassuming descriptions (Serenade, Divertimento), and also with a wish to avoid the form 'Piano Concerto no. 2.' Stravinsky's titling of his symphonies, chamber concertos and string quartets similarly avoided any implication of a series, and therefore of development. All his works carry an implicit 'no. 1' tag."[1] Stravinsky's final work for piano and orchestra, composed 1958–1959, is titled *Movements for Piano and Orchestra*.

The Capriccio begins with what sounds like a slow introduction, although the score-reader can see that the first tempo marking is Presto. Stravinsky gives us three forceful measures of trills in the piano, all on E, together with rapid scales in the orchestra. Both the trills and the scales end with an F, whose effect is to give a wittily dissonant edge to what is happening. This triple outburst is followed by a bang and a silence. Each of these three trill-and-scale combinations is in fact a whole Presto measure, but they could just as well be single beats of one measure in a very slow tempo. To this the orchestra responds with four measures of genuinely slow music for string quartet and solo woodwinds, quiet and harmonically bare. The process is repeated, with a new harmonic underpinning; then the feeling of introduction, of anticipation, is over, and the first movement really gets going.

It is a playful cousin of the Piano Concerto's first movement. There is plenty of motoric sixteenth-note motion, but it is often broken up by bits of fast scales. A special feature of the Capriccio is the appearance of rapid repeated notes, reminiscent, as the composer was the first to point out, of the sound of the cymbalom, the Hungarian dulcimer that Stravinsky had used

[1]Paul Griffiths, *Stravinsky* (New York: G. Schirmer, 1993).

to brilliant effect in *Renard*. In this first movement, and again in the third, we are constantly teased and delighted by phrases that sound as if they come from music-hall tunes. Griffiths remarks about this aspect of the Capriccio: "From this point Stravinsky could have become Poulenc." The energy of the music begins to subside, an effect achieved because the harmony stops moving, becoming more and more fixed on G and B-flat. Then the introduction returns, the trills and scales now based on D, which confirms the strong implications of G minor set up by those G's and B-flats, and this time the second slow section for the orchestra expands into a very spacious settling into that key. As the harmonies wind down, the piano supplies staccato G's in the bass, each one of which brings a response of B-flat from the orchestra.

Without a break, Stravinsky goes on into the second movement. The piano writing is notably brilliant, fanciful, and original in sound; the interplay between solo and orchestra is extraordinarily rich and tight: Ezra Pound notes that "the piano and orchestra are as two shells of a walnut." The music certainly lives up to what is promised in the marking *rapsodico*, and this aspect culminates in an extraordinary cadenza, again very suggestive of cymbalom style. Stravinsky described it as "a kind of Rumanian restaurant music."

As Stravinsky begins the finale, he again simulates the effect of a slow introduction by his use of silences and long notes within a quick tempo. Once more, playfulness is the order of the day, and at moments the humor becomes so broad that it comes close to that of Shostakovich's *Age of Gold* polka (a comparison that would have infuriated Stravinsky). Just before the end, the comic potential of the trumpet as sentimentalist is explored, and the Capriccio arrives at its final cadence with a nonchalant laugh.

## Concerto for Piano and Wind Instruments

*Largo—Allegro*
*Largo*
*Allegro*

Stravinsky began his Piano Concerto in the summer of 1923 and completed it on 21 April 1924. (The score misprints this date as 21 August 1924.) Virtually all performances today follow Stravinsky's revised edition of 1950. The work was introduced on 22 May 1924 at the Paris Opéra at one of the Concerts Koussevitzky: the composer was the soloist and Serge Koussevitzky conducted. This formal premiere was preceded a week earlier, on 15 May, by two performances on two pianos for which Stravinsky was joined by Jean Wiéner, a public one at the Salle Gaveau and a private one at the house of the Princesse de Polignac, the composer giving a talk about the new work before each one.

**Solo piano, two flutes and piccolo, two oboes and English horn, two clarinets, two bassoons (second doubling contrabassoon), four horns, four trumpets, three trombones, tuba, timpani, and string basses.** Stravinsky explained his unusual choice of instrumentation: "The short, crisp dance character of the Toccata [the first movement], engendered by the percussion of the piano, led to the idea that a wind ensemble would suit the piano better than any other combination. In contrast to the percussiveness of the piano, the winds prolong the piano's sound as well as providing the human element of respiration."

For Stravinsky, the early 1920s was a time of intense interest in the piano. He finally found the festive four-pianos-and-percussion solution to the vexing problem of how to score *Les Noces*; he concocted for Arthur Rubinstein one of the most diabolically demanding of piano solos, the *Three Movements of Petrushka*; and he composed this Piano Concerto, the Piano Sonata, and the Serenade in A. Though not unskilled, Stravinsky had not played the piano much in public. Now Serge Koussevitzky, who had encouraged Stravinsky to take up the baton for the first time for the premiere of the Octet in October 1923, persuaded him to polish up his keyboard skills and appear as soloist in his new Concerto.[2] This Stravinsky did; indeed, during the next five years he played the Concerto more than forty times with more than thirty orchestras. Playing the piano—in the concerto or its "sequel," the Capriccio (1929), in solo pieces, as partner to the violinist Samuel Dushkin in the *Duo Concertant* and in various arrangements, and with his son Soulima in the Concerto for Two Pianos—would account for a fair portion of Stravinsky's income until the late 1930s.

The idea of "back to the eighteenth century," one aspect of the anti-Romantic revolt that seemed necessary to many composers after World War I, comes up constantly in early discussions of the Piano Concerto. This is not surprising: Stravinsky himself conceded that a feature like the slow introduction in dotted rhythms could be read as, indeed was intended as, a "conscious stylistic reference." It is hard—or impossible—to hear certain figurations without being put in mind of Bach,[3] but the real compositional matter is in the intervals and the harmonies they generate, and in the rhythms; the

---

[2]In his entertaining but unreliable memoirs, Arthur Rubinstein takes credit for suggesting to Stravinsky that he take up conducting and piano-playing as a source of income.
[3]The first movement of Bartók's Piano Concerto No. 2, composed 1930–1931, has even more startlingly Bachian passages.

ear that has imagined those intervals and harmonies and rhythms is always and unmistakably Stravinsky's. To say that about the Piano Concerto or any other work of his is perhaps sheer banality now that we have learned to hear what Elliott Carter called those "Stravinsky notes" in each of his pieces from *Petrushka* to the 1966 *Requiem Canticles*, but it is not so long since Stravinsky's development as a composer was regarded not as a development at all but as a series of shocking *volte-faces* indicative of a deplorable lack of cultural and moral center.

Stravinsky kept the performance rights of the Concerto to himself for a number a years. He wanted the engagements, of course, and in the 1920s he was a hot item on the market, as he would not be again until he had attained Grand Old Man status in the late 1950s. At the same time, he urgently desired to avoid having "incompetent or Romantic hands begin to 'interpret' [the Concerto] before undiscriminating audiences."[4]

It was also of the greatest importance to Stravinsky always to have an extremely articulate piano with a clear bass "and above all not velvety." Stravinsky's piano writing is a "fixing" of his own playing, a fair bit of which is preserved on recordings, as surely as Bartók's and Copland's piano writing was a portrait of their playing. And, we must presume, the same thing is true of Brahms, Liszt, Chopin, Beethoven, and Mozart. Elliott Carter, who first heard Stravinsky's "electricity-filled" playing at a private audition of *Perséphone* in 1934, recalls:

> What impressed me most, aside from the quality of the music itself, was the very telling quality of attack he gave to piano notes, embodying often in just one sound the very quality so characteristic of his music—incisive but not brutal, rhythmically highly controlled yet filled with intensity so that each note was made to seem weighty and important. Every time I heard him play . . . the strong impression of highly individualized, usually detached notes filled with extraordinary dynamism caught my attention immediately—and this was true in soft passages as well as loud.[5]

Stravinsky begins his Concerto without piano: all of the grand introduction, which the composer characterized as a "processional," is for orchestra alone. Then the Allegro explodes into being, a moment that brings a change of lighting as much as a change of pace. Now, for the rest of the first movement, save for one brief moment when the flute proffers a melody of its

---

[4]Stravinsky had much to say, then and later, about incompetents, "Romantics," and "interpreters." Roger Sessions, who heard Stravinsky play the Piano Concerto in Philadelphia with Fritz Reiner in February 1925, many years later remembered with wicked delight that while giving his crisp and wittily inflected performance, "in slow passages he looked at the ceiling just like all pianists, and afterwards, when he bowed, he put his hand over his heart."

[5]Elliott Carter, *Igor Stravinsky, 1882-1971*, in *The Writings of Elliott Carter*, ed. Kurt and Else Stone (Bloomington: University of Indiana Press, 1977).

own, the orchestra turns accompanist, adding color, weight, accent, and, just as Stravinsky described, prolonging the piano's staccato attacks. This movement is a toccata, concentrated, brilliant, full of metrical dislocations. Bach is a forceful presence here, especially the violinistic figurations that are so prominent in Bach's Keyboard Concerto in D minor, which was almost certainly a transcription of a lost violin concerto.[6]

The Largo is of immense gravity and sonorous weight. It was Stravinsky's second essay at the movement: he lost the manuscript pages of his first try, found himself unable to recall anything of what he had done, and so began again on a new tack. (His memory failure carried over into the first performance: at the end of the first movement he suddenly had no idea of what came next, and Koussevitzky had to come to the rescue by singing the first bars to him.) The piano plays a solemn melody, supported by dense chords in both hands, which the trumpet continues. Twice the movement breaks for a cadenza—these, too, are very Bachian indeed—each with orchestral "encouragement"; between these two flourishes comes a passage of faster melodies for the orchestra, chiefly oboe and horn, with the piano accompanying. The return to the slow music is brief, but this close is one of Stravinsky's most beautiful pages. Dare one say warm and melancholy?

The Largo's final cadence, now speeded up fivefold, serves as the opening propulsive gesture of the finale. This is another toccata, interrupted for a few bars just before the end by a recollection of the "processional" introduction.

## Concerto in D for Violin and Orchestra

*Toccata*
*Aria I*
*Aria II*
*Capriccio*

The first two movements of Stravinsky's Violin Concerto are dated 20 May 1931 in the manuscript, the third is dated 10 June, and the fourth is undated. The full orchestral score was completed on 25 September 1931, and the first performance took place on 23 October that year with Samuel Dushkin as soloist and the composer conducting the Berlin Radio Orchestra. There is

[6]See my essay on Bach's D-minor Concerto. Richard Taruskin discusses Stravinsky's leaning on Bach in a lively and characteristically contentious essay, "The Pastness of the Presence and the Presence of the Past," in *Authenticity and Early Music*, ed. Nicholas Kenyon (Oxford: Oxford University Press, 1988).

no dedication as such, but the published score is prefaced by a note in French by the composer (reproduced in his handwriting), acknowledging his "reconnaissance profonde" and his "grande admiration" for Dushkin and the high artistic value of his playing.

**Two flutes and piccolo, two oboes and English horn, two clarinets and E-flat clarinet, three bassoons (third doubling contrabassoon), four horns, three trumpets, three trombones, tuba, timpani, bass drum, and strings (eight first and eight second violins, six violas, four cellos, and four basses).**

The idea that Stravinsky should write a violin concerto was born in the minds of Willy Strecker, head of the German publishing house of Schott & Sons (an agent for Serge Koussevitzky's Édition Russe de Musique, which had handled most of Stravinsky's work since *Petrushka*), and Samuel Dushkin, a Polish-born violinist who lived in Paris. Strecker agreed to put the matter to Stravinsky. The composer was reluctant at first, being suspicious of virtuosos in general. (A few years later, Louis Krasner would encounter the same resistance when he approached Alban Berg about writing a violin concerto.) Stravinsky also had doubts about his ability to write something both brilliant and practicable for the violin, an instrument with which he did not feel at home, but Strecker assured him that Dushkin, a cultivated musician as well as an accomplished instrumentalist, would be available to offer advice.[7] Dushkin, for his part, was taken with the idea that he might be Stravinsky's collaborator as Ferdinand David had been Mendelssohn's and Joseph Joachim Brahms's. (Unlike Mendelssohn, Brahms, and most of the non-violinist composers who received help from a violinist, Stravinsky acknowledges his collaborator's contribution in the published score.)

At any rate, a meeting was arranged at the Streckers' villa in Wiesbaden. The composer and the violinist liked each other, and work was under way as soon as Stravinsky's concert schedule allowed. The two men met at various times in Paris, at the Stravinsky house just outside Nice, and at Voreppe, a village near Grenoble, where Stravinsky wrote the finale while Dushkin learned the first three movements.

Describing their work together, Dushkin wrote that his "function was to advise Stravinsky how his ideas could best be adapted to the exigencies of the violin as a concert display instrument":

[7]Many years later, Hindemith assured Stravinsky that he was better off coming to the violin as a foreigner, so to speak: that way he was not in danger of having experienced violin-playing fingers suggest cliché figurations.

At various intervals he would show me what he had just written, sometimes a page, sometimes only a few lines, sometimes half a movement. Then we discussed whatever suggestions I was able to make. Whenever he accepted one of my suggestions, even a simple change such as extending the range of the violin by stretching the phrase to the octave below and the octave above, Stravinsky would insist on altering the very foundations correspondingly. He behaved like an architect who if asked to change a room on the third floor had to go down to the foundation to keep the proportions of the whole structure.[8]

The collaboration prospered, leading to many concerts and recitals together, to Stravinsky's writing the *Duo Concertant* immediately after the concerto, and to Dushkin's making arrangements for violin and piano of several Stravinsky pieces. The friendship prospered, too, and lasted until Stravinsky's death. Dushkin died in New York in 1976. He had introduced Stravinsky's Concerto in nearly a dozen cities on both sides of the Atlantic, and in 1932 he had made the first recording of it.

Dushkin also recalled that at lunch one day in a Paris restaurant, Stravinsky

took out a piece of paper and wrote down this chord

Ex. 1

and asked me if it could be played. I had never seen a chord with such an enormous stretch, from the E to the top A, and I said "No." Stravinsky said sadly, *"Quel dommage."* After I got home, I tried it, and, to my astonishment, I found that in that register, the stretch of the eleventh was relatively easy to play, and the sound fascinated me. I telephoned Stravinsky at once to tell him that it could be done. When the concerto was finished, more than six months later, I understood his disappointment when I first said "No." This chord, in a different dress, begins each of the four movements. Stravinsky himself calls it his "passport" to that concerto.[9]

To begin with, then, the passport, plus three further upbeating chords for the soloist with plucked cellos and basses, opens the way to a bright

[8]Samuel Dushkin, *Working With Stravinsky*, in *Igor Stravinsky*, ed. Edwin Corle (New York: Duell, Sloan and Pearce, 1949).
[9]Dushkin, op. cit.

Toccata. It is marchlike at first, but extra and elided beats constantly and deliciously subvert the tread that the trumpets, so neatly supported by horns and bassoons, seem to want to establish. Actually it turns out that the trumpets are not so serious on this issue of steadiness either. For instance, how many repeated eighth-notes follow the initial four-note turn? Is the turn itself an upbeat or a downbeat? And once the oboes pick up on the idea a few bars later, how long are their downward scales? Here, too, it seems that the question of upbeats and downbeats remains unsettled. Characteristically, Stravinsky presents material that partakes of all the clichés of stability in the most mercurial way possible. Nothing, when it comes back, is ever quite the same, and in that connection, too, it is worth quoting Dushkin's memoir once again:

> I was particularly struck by the fact that he did not use music paper for his first sketches. He uses a book with plain white pages. On these blank sheets he draws the five staff lines according to his needs of the moment with a diminutive roller made especially for him. Some staves are longer, others shorter, sometimes just one line, sometimes several lines, so that when the page is finished, it looks like a strangely designed drawing, and each page looks different from the preceding page.[10]

However much Stravinsky leaned on Dushkin for help with the violin part, the orchestral sound and the whole concept of how to use solo and orchestra together are unmistakably, wittily, triumphantly Stravinsky's own. The orchestra is actually not so very small (though the number of strings is kept down), but the work sounds as though scored for brilliant chamber orchestra. There are very few measures for anything like the full band, and those that do occur mostly involve short chords for accent and punctuation. The violin soloist, moreover, finds himself constantly in the role of chamber musician, duet partner, and even accompanist. In no aspect of composition is Stravinsky's flair for making fresh presentations of what we expect to be familiar statements more dazzlingly evident in this Concerto than in matters of color and texture.

The two Arias in the middle of the Concerto are in sharp contrast to each other as well as to the bright, eighteenth-centuryish D-major poppings and bubblings of the outer movements. Aria I, like the Toccata, begins with the "passport" chord plus three more chords of upbeat. This time the gesture leads to music that is actually faster than that of the first movement (116 to the quarter-note as against 96). The spirit is that of sublimely elegant salon music, but the middle section surprises us by extending the idiom to the point of embracing a kind of gentle gravity especially characteristic of *Apollo*

---

[10]Dushkin, op. cit.

(or *Apollon Musagètes*, as it was first called), Stravinsky's ballet score of 1927–1928.

Aria II is the Concerto's slow movement, a latter-day view of an expressively embellished Bach Adagio. Charles Rosen has called Stravinsky the greatest melodist among twentieth-century composers; this Aria is eloquent support for such a claim. If the "passport" chord was a long and poignant sigh at the beginning of Aria II (though with a Stravinskian cutting edge), at the start of the Capriccio-finale the soloist touches the sound for no more than one-fourth of a second. It is a springboard from which dazzling D-major scales are launched, themselves leading to further amusements and delights, including the charming outrage of the concertmaster's offer to compete with the soloist in agility and fleetness.

# Piotr Ilyich Tchaikovsky

Piotr Ilyich Tchaikovsky was born on 7 May 1840 at Votkinsk in the district of Viatka, Russia (now in the Udmurt Republic), some 700 miles east-northeast of Moscow, and died in Saint Petersburg on 6 November 1893.

## Concerto No. 1 in B-flat minor for Piano and Orchestra, Opus 23

*Allegro non troppo e molto maestoso—Allegro con spirito*
*Andantino semplice—Prestissimo—Tempo I*
*Allegro con fuoco*

Tchaikovsky composed his Piano Concerto No. 1 in November and December 1874, completing the orchestration on 21 February 1875. He made some revisions in 1876 and 1889. Hans von Bülow gave the first performance at the Music Hall in Boston on 25 October 1875, B. J. Lang conducting. The orchestra was a freelance group, though largely corresponding to that of the Harvard Musical Association. The Boston Symphony Orchestra was founded six years later, and at various concerts in 1883 and 1885, B. J. Lang, the conductor of the premiere, was the first pianist to play the concerto with the new orchestra.

Solo piano, two flutes, two oboes, two clarinets, two bassoons, four horns, two trumpets, three trombones, timpani, and strings.

Nicolai Gregorievich Rubinstein, who Tchaikovsky hoped would be the first
to play his Piano Concerto No. 1, was born in Moscow in 1835, trained in
law as well as music, and was director of the Moscow Conservatory from its
founding in 1866 until his death in 1881. If not generally so highly esteemed
a pianist as his famous older brother Anton, who was also a composer of
merit and had been Tchaikovsky's teacher, Nicolai was thought the better
conductor and teacher. The list of Tchaikovsky premieres he led between
1866 and 1880—the first four symphonies, *Eugene Onegin*, *Romeo and Juliet*,
*Marche slav*, *Francesca da Rimini*, the Suite No. 1, *Capriccio italien*, and the
*Variations on a Rococo Theme*—tells its own story of the closeness of the two
men, but their encounter of the B-flat-minor Concerto was a disaster. A
famous disaster, and Tchaikovsky, telling the story three years after the event
in a letter to his patron, Nadezhda Filaretovna von Meck, still trembles with
hurt and rage. He writes from San Remo on 2 February 1878:

> In December 1874 I had written a piano concerto. As I am not a pianist, it
> was necessary to consult some virtuoso as to what might be ineffective, im-
> practicable, and ungrateful in my writing. I needed a severe but at the same
> time friendly critic to point out just these external blemishes. Without going
> into details, I must mention that some inner voice warned me against the
> choice of Nicolai Rubinstein as a judge of the pianistic side of my composition;
> however, since he was not only the best pianist in Moscow but also a first-rate
> all-round musician, and, knowing how deeply offended he would be if he heard
> that I had taken my concerto to someone else, I decided to ask him to hear
> the work and give me his opinion on the solo part.
>
> It was Christmas Eve 1874. We were invited to Albrecht's house,[1] and
> Rubinstein proposed that before going over there we should meet in one of
> the Conservatory classrooms to go through the concerto. I arrived with my
> manuscript, and Rubinstein and Hubert came soon after.[2] The latter is a wor-
> thy, intelligent man, but with no inclination to assert himself; moreover, he is
> exceedingly garrulous and needs a long string of words just to say "yes" or "no."
> He is incapable of giving his opinion in any decisive form and generally lets
> himself be pulled over to the strongest side. I must add, however, that this is
> not cowardice on his part but mere want of character.
>
> I played the first movement. Not a single word, not a single comment! If
> you knew how stupid and intolerable the situation of a man is who cooks and
> sets a meal before a friend, a meal the friend then proceeds to eat—in silence!
> Oh for one word, for friendly abuse even, but for God's sake, one word of
> sympathy, even if it is not praise! But Rubinstein was preparing his thunderbolt,
> and Hubert was waiting to see what would happen so that he could decide

---

[1] Evgeny Karlovich Albrecht was a violinist on the faculty of the Moscow Conservatory.
[2] Nicolai Albertovich Hubert, whom Tchaikovsky had known since his student days, was a teacher
of theory and a critic, Rubinstein's housemate, and eventually his successor as director of the Conservatory.

which way to go. I did not want judgment on the artistic value of the piece: what I needed was comment on pianistic questions. R's silence was eloquent. "My dear friend," he seemed to be saying, "how can I speak about details when the whole thing is so repellent?" I summoned all my patience and played through to the end. Still silence. I stood up and asked, "Well?"

Then a torrent poured from Nicolai Gregorievich's mouth, gentle to begin with, but growing more and more into the sound and fury of *Jupiter Tonans*. My concerto, it turned out, was worthless and unplayable—passages so frag-mented, so clumsy, so badly written as to be beyond rescue—the music itself was bad, vulgar—here and there I had stolen from other composers—only two or three pages were worth preserving—the rest must be thrown out or com-pletely rewritten. "Here, for instance, this—now what's all that?" (caricaturing my music on the piano). "And this? How could anyone . . ." etc., etc. But the chief thing I can't reproduce: the *tone* in which all this was uttered.

An independent witness in the room might have concluded that I was a maniac, an untalented, senseless hack who had come to submit his rubbish to an eminent musician. Having noted my obstinate silence, Hubert was aston-ished and shocked that a man who had already written a great many works and had given a composition course at the Conservatory should be the victim of such a telling off, that such a contemptuous judgment—without appeal—should be pronounced over him, a judgment such as one would hardly pro-nounce over a student with minimal talent who had been careless about his homework, and then he began to explain N. G.'s judgment, not disputing it in the least, but softening a bit what His Excellency had expressed with too little ceremony.

I was not just astounded but outraged by the whole scene. I am no longer a boy trying his hand at composition and I no longer need lessons from anyone, especially when they are offered so harshly and in such a spirit of hostility. I need and shall always need friendly criticism, but this was nothing like it, with not a trace of friendliness to the whole proceedings. This was censure, indis-criminate, and deliberately designed to hurt me to the quick. I left the room without a word and went upstairs: in my agitation and rage I could not have said a thing. Presently R. joined me and, seeing how upset I was, asked me into one of the other rooms. There he repeated that my concerto was impossible, pointed out many places where it would have to be completely revised, and said that if within a limited time I reworked the concerto according to his demands, then he would do me the honor of playing this thing of mine at his concert. "*I shall not alter a single note*," I replied. "*I shall publish the work exactly as it stands!*" And this I did.[3]

For the moment, anyway. In 1876 Tchaikovsky gratefully accepted some suggestions about the piano writing—the very thing he had hoped Rubin-stein could provide—from Edward Dannreuther, the English pianist, writer,

[3]Modest Tchaikovsky, *Life and Letters of Tchaikovsky,* ed. and transl. Rosa Newmarch (London: John Lane The Bodley Head, 1906), translation amended.

and Wagner exegete, who had just given the London premiere. In 1889 Tchaikovsky put out a revised edition, and that is what we almost always hear today. It brings many changes of detail as well as two major alterations so striking that even a fairly casual listener notices them. I shall comment on these, their nature and their merits, in context. The 1875 version has its champions among pianists: Malcolm Frager was one, Lazar Berman and Jerome Lowenthal are others.[4]

A few years later, Tchaikovsky had a similar collision with Leopold Auer over his Violin Concerto, but the two stories had parallel happy endings; that is, both Rubinstein and Auer came around to their respective concertos, learned them, enjoyed success with them, and taught them to their pupils. With Sergei Taneiev as soloist, Rubinstein even conducted the Moscow premiere of the concerto less than a year after the Christmas Eve massacre. Taneiev, Alexander Siloti, and Emil von Sauer, who were all Rubinstein students, together with Hans von Bülow, Vassily Sapelnikov, and Adele aus der Hohe (who played the Concerto with Tchaikovsky both at the opening of Carnegie Hall as well as at the last concert he ever conducted), constituted the generation of pianists that established the work as indispensable.

But after the row with Rubinstein, the premiere took place far from home, in Boston's Music Hall (now the Orpheum Theater on Washington Street). Hans Guido von Bülow, ten years older than Tchaikovsky, had a distinguished double career as pianist and conductor. He had been particularly associated with the Wagnerian movement, had led the premieres of *Tristan* and *Meistersinger,* and would later become an important interpreter of Brahms and give the young Richard Strauss his first boost up the career ladder. His young wife, Cosima, the daughter of Franz Liszt and the Countess Marie d'Agoult, had by degrees left him for Wagner during the second half of the 1860s; much embittered, he left the concert stage for some years. In 1872, safely divorced, he resumed his career and in March 1874 gave a recital at the Bolshoi Theater in Moscow. Tchaikovsky was stirred by the combination of intellect and passion in von Bülow's playing; von Bülow, in turn, liked Tchaikovsky's music and soon after took the opportunity of smuggling in a good word for him in an article on Glinka's *A Life for the Tsar:*

> At the present moment we know but one other who, like Glinka, strives and aspires, and whose works—although they have not yet attained full maturity—give complete assurance that such maturity will not fail to come. I refer to the young Professor of Composition at the Moscow Conservatory—Tchaikovsky.

[4]Berman's recording with Yuri Temirkanov and the Berlin Radio Symphony (Koch Schwann) is of the 1875/1879 version, but his earlier one with von Karajan and the Berlin Philharmonic (Deutsche Grammophon) is of the standard 1889 edition. The 1992 Dover score of Tchaikovsky's piano concertos gives the 1879 version of No. 1 as it appears in the complete Tchaikovsky edition issued by the State Music Publishing House, Moscow, 1955, with the footnotes translated into English.

A beautiful string quartet of his has won its way in several German cities. Many other works by him merit equal recognition—his piano compositions, two symphonies, and an uncommonly interesting *Romeo and Juliet* Overture, which commends itself by its originality and luxuriant melodic flow. Thanks to his many-sidedness, this composer will not run the danger of being neglected abroad as Glinka was.[5]

In the autograph of Tchaikovsky's Concerto the inscription to Rubinstein is scratched out, just as Beethoven's to Napoleon was in the manuscript of the *Eroica*, and von Bülow was happy to accept the dedication in Rubinstein's stead. He set about making arrangements to introduce the "Grand Concerto (Op.23) in B flat," as the program had it, at the fifth of a series of concerts he gave in Boston. The audience was informed that "the above grand composition of Tschaikowsky, the most eminent Russian *maestro* of the present day, completed last April and dedicated by its author to Hans von Bülow, has NEVER BEEN PERFORMED, the composer himself never having enjoyed an audition of his masterpiece. To Boston is reserved the honor of its initial representation and the opportunity to impress the first verdict on a work of surpassing musical interest."

Von Bülow sent the composer a telegram announcing the triumphant reception of the Concerto, and Tchaikovsky spent most of his available cash, of which he had very little just then, on a cordial return message. Von Bülow consolidated his success by repeating the Concerto at his matinée five days later, and upon his return to Europe he introduced it as expeditiously as possible in London and other musical centers.[6] The Boston concert was a strenuous one for von Bülow, who also played Beethoven's *Moonlight* Sonata and Liszt's version with orchestra of Schubert's *Wanderer* Fantasy. (There were also overtures by Spohr and Beethoven, and Mendelssohn's *Wedding March* to finish up with.) I do wonder, though, what it all sounded like with B. J. Lang's little orchestra with its four first violins!

The opening of the Concerto is magnificent. All four horns in unison three times proclaim a four-note motif, which the rest of the orchestra punctuates with a series of chords whose further function it is to swing the music around from B-flat minor, where it begins, to grand D-flat major, something it takes them just five bars to accomplish. Actually, "punctuate" hardly does the effect of these chords justice: "say 'yeah!' " and "cheer on" is more like it. When everybody lands on D-flat, the piano enters with a series of massive chords that go crashing up across more than six octaves of the keyboard in each measure. These chords are the accompaniment of a memorable string

[5]Hans von Bülow: *Briefe und Schriften*, ed. Marie von Bülow (Leipzig: Breitkopf & Härtel, 1908).
[6]It is less well known that in February 1885 von Bülow was responsible for another Tchaikovsky premiere when he conducted the Orchestral Suite No. 3 in Saint Petersburg.

melody, and readers of sufficient antiquity will remember that this theme flourished in 1941 and for a while thereafter as a Freddy Martin pop song: the title was *Tonight We Love*, and the meter was stretched on the rack from three beats in each measure to four.

The crashing piano chords were new in the 1889 edition; the previous versions had arpeggiated piano chords of narrower range. And here, I must say, I am totally in favor of the 1889 revision. The effect is splendid, it is even exciting to watch, and it makes much more of Tchaikovsky's bold idea of having the first solo entrance be an accompaniment—but what an accompaniment! I still remember how frustrated I was when I first heard this concerto as a boy on the unsurpassed Rubinstein (Arthur, no relation to Nicolai and Anton) recording with Barbirolli because this great tune in the introduction never comes back. Soloists' narcissism often leads them to refer to everything that precedes their first entrance as an "introduction." People speak, for instance, of the opening moments of the Brahms Piano Concerto No. 2, that musing dialogue of horn and piano, as an "introduction." But that is not an introduction, it is an organic part of the movement. In the Tchaikovsky, however, we have a true introduction, extraneous to the main part of the movement. It is common enough for an introduction to share no material with the rest of the movement; what is uncommon is for a composer to more or less throw away such a grand invention as this tune. I think I have become used to it, but it still seems odd to me.

The introduction dies away on a series of softly glowing brass chords, then the Allegro begins with a hopping theme in the piano. If in *Tonight We Love* Tchaikovsky was a lender, albeit a posthumous one, here he is a borrower, for the hopping theme is a Ukrainian folk song traditionally sung by blind beggars. Tchaikovsky goes on to add more lyric themes to the mix, including one, introduced by woodwinds and quickly taken up and expanded by the piano, of delicious melancholy. There is a huge cadenza, and besides that plenty of opportunities for pianistic fireworks, notably big passages in flying double octaves.

The middle movement begins with a sweet song for the flute, soon repeated (with a difference of one note) by the piano, and exquisitely scored on each of its appearances. I have always wondered why the flute's third note is F and the piano's B-flat; moreover, the flute's version of the melody never reappears. It cannot be a mistake that went uncorrected through the three editions published in Tchaikovsky's lifetime and the various performances he conducted and heard, yet it is not enough of a difference to make a significant point. Perhaps he could not make up his mind between the two versions and wanted to give both an airing.[7] This movement has an enchanting scherzolike interlude, something akin to a waltz at about triple speed (Allegro vivace

[7]There is a similar discrepancy in Act I of *The Sleeping Beauty*.

assai in the earlier versions, Prestissimo in the final one). Here, too, Tchaikovsky was borrowing, this time from a cabaret song, *Il faut s'amuser, danser et rire*, from the repertory of Désirée Artôt, a Belgian soprano who has the distinction of being the only woman to whom he responded sexually. Tchaikovsky actually proposed to her in 1869 and was distressed when, without a prior word to him, she suddenly married the Spanish baritone Mariano Padilla y Ramos. Here we can tie two threads of this story together, for it was Nicolai Rubinstein who brought Tchaikovsky the news of Artôt's defection.

The finale is based on a highly energized theme—in triple meter but always with a strong accent on the second beat—and this, too, is a Ukrainian folk song. For contrast, Tchaikovsky introduces a broadly lyric theme. The first time he brings it in he gives it an extra charge by stretching its first note; at the end of the movement, after one final orgy of octaves, he makes a kind of apotheosis out of it in the manner so effectively emulated by Rachmaninoff in his Second and Third Concertos.

It is in this movement that we find the other major revision: this takes the form of a cut, measures 109–24 being replaced by a four-measure splice. Here I would vote for the original, longer version, for the sixteen dropped measures are a quirkily engaging continuation of a new rhythmic pattern of alternating short and very short notes that has just begun. And finally, a change that is not so major but nonetheless noticeable: later editions—it is not clear from the Moscow 1955 score whether this refers to the Tchaikovsky's 1889 version or to editions after his death—indicate a sudden slowing of tempo (*sostenuto molto*) when the "hopping" rhythm settles into a series of scales. I have never heard a conductor manage to make this spot sound anything other than exceedingly awkward and jolty. Staying with the main tempo (Allegro con fuoco) requires very fleet playing from the strings, woodwind, and piano, but reverting to the original with no tempo change would be a real musical improvement.

## Concerto No. 2 in G major for Piano and Orchestra, Opus 44

> *Allegro brillante e molto vivace*
> *Andante non troppo*
> *Allegro con fuoco*

Tchaikovsky began his Piano Concerto No. 2 on 22 October 1879, finished the sketches for the first movement on 1 November, and by 15 December had the entire work "ready in rough," as he put it to his patron, Nadezhda von Meck. He began the orchestration in February 1880 and completed the score on 10 May that year. Like the Piano Concerto No. 1, it had its first performance in America: the soloist was Madeleine Schiller, the conductor Theodore Thomas, the orchestra the New York Philharmonic, and the date 12 November 1881. The dedication is to Nicolai Rubinstein.

**Solo piano, two flutes, two oboes, two clarinets, two bassoons, four horns, two trumpets, timpani, and strings, with important solos for violin and cello in the second movement.**

When I wrote the original version of this essay in 1987, I began: "I would guess that nine out of ten people at this concert are hearing [this work] for the first time and that many of the remaining ten per cent encountered it first as the score for Balanchine's *Ballet Impérial*." (It strikes me now that "nine out of ten" was probably a low estimate.) Tchaikovsky's Piano Concerto No. 1 is one of the most popular of his works, if not even the most popular of all concertos. It got off to a horrendous start, however, when Nicolai Rubinstein, who Tchaikovsky hoped would be the first to play it, reviled it to the composer's face. A little more than four years later, Rubinstein had become an ardent champion of that Concerto, playing it himself and teaching it to his students, and Tchaikovsky was ready not only to compose a new concerto but to submit it to Rubinstein for criticism. Unlike Rachmaninoff, his successor in the dynasty of Russian composers, who had been stopped cold by the failure of his First Symphony, Tchaikovsky did not even need psychotherapy in order to keep going after this shattering experience.

   This time Rubinstein was nervous. He had been asked to convey his comments to his student Sergei Taneiev, who was also a former composition student of Tchaikovsky's and a friend, but his criticisms, and Taneiev's, were voiced only after the Concerto had been published and performed. Tchaikovsky's response, as his biographer David Brown puts it, was "tartly grateful": "I regret that those persons to whom [the concerto] was entrusted two years ago for critical scrutiny didn't indicate this failing [of excessive length] at the proper time. In this they would have been doing me a great service—one perhaps even greater than the superb performance of the Concerto in its present, so imperfect form. All the same—*merci, merci, merci!*"[8] Taneiev gave the first good performance in Russia of the First Concerto with Rubinstein conducting (there had been an unsatisfactory one by Gustav Kross and Eduard Nápravník three weeks earlier) and also introduced the Concerto No. 2 in Russia, this time with Rubinstein's brother Anton on the podium.

[8]David Brown: *Tchaikovsky: The Years of Wandering 1878–1885* (New York: W. W. Norton, 1986).

Tchaikovsky himself seems to have made some cuts in the occasional performances of the Second Concerto he conducted, and another of his students, Alexander Siloti (Rachmaninoff's cousin), prepared a *Nouvelle Édition revue et diminuée d'après les indications de l'auteur*. David Brown writes that Tchaikovsky's own cuts were "probably" of measures 319–42 in the first movement and 247–81 and 310–27 in the second, but gives no reason for his speculation. Except possibly for what Brown tentatively identifies as Tchaikovsky's own cuts, Siloti's "*d'après*" is bold poetic license, and the composer objected strenuously. As in the case of Wilhelm Fitzenhagen's recomposition of the *Variations on a Rococo Theme*, the actions of Tchaikovsky's publisher, P. I. Jürgenson, were equivocal. Jürgenson urged the composer to hold his ground; eventually, however—and during Tchaikovsky's lifetime— he brought out Siloti's "diminution," which became the basis for almost all performances and recordings (and for *Ballet Impérial*), until Tchaikovsky's original was republished in 1949.

Cuts almost never solve problems of design; they merely shorten the time you have to live with them. Also, Siloti's revision of Tchaikovsky's keyboard style coarsens the texture—for example, the replacing of fluid runs for the two hands in octaves by *martellato* octaves in both hands (of which Tchaikovsky provided enough of his own). As with Bruckner, a master's possible miscalculations are more interesting than a fixer's fixings, and pianists are more and more coming round to playing this Concerto as Tchaikovsky composed it.[9]

Tchaikovsky may not have explicitly believed that the devil finds work for idle hands to do, but lack of work certainly did make him nervous. He spent the fall of 1879 at his sister Alexandra's country place at Kamenka, going through the exacting but tedious labor of proofreading his Suite No. 1 for Orchestra. He helped pitch hay and joined the family in sewing bees, reporting to his brother Anatol that he had "hemmed and monogrammed a handkerchief." But it was not enough. On 22 October he wrote to Anatol's twin, Modest:

> These last days I've begun to observe in myself things that at first I didn't understand. I felt a certain vague dissatisfaction with myself, a disturbingly frequent and virtually irresistible desire to sleep, a certain emptiness, and finally *boredom*. There were times when I simply didn't know what to do with myself. Yesterday it at last became clear to me what the problem was. I had to get going on something: I find myself absolutely incapable of living long without

---

[9]The editor of the 1949 version, published by the Bruckner-Verlag, Wiesbaden, was Fritz Oeser, a musicologist notorious for his dreadful edition of *Carmen*, in which, in a frenzy of anti-cutting, he restored everything Bizet had been careful to take out during the later stages of composition and the rehearsals for the premiere.

work. Today I began to create something, and my *boredom* vanished as if by magic.[10]

The "something" was the Piano Concerto No. 2. He enjoyed himself, writing to Madame von Meck that the new score "began to grow and to display characteristic features. I work with pleasure and am also trying to curb the habitual haste that has so often been damaging to my efforts." Tchaikovsky's work sheets accompanied him to Berlin, Paris, and Rome, but it was at Kamenka, where he had begun the score, that he finished it.

The premiere in New York was not a great success. The *New York Times* declared that "it cannot be said that the concerto possesses any great merit," and after a performance in Boston two months later, the *Gazette* called it "dry, groping, and wearisome." William Apthorp reviewed a performance by the Harvard Musical Association. Making sure of having an escape hatch that would allow him, wearing his other hat, to eventually write a program note for the Boston Symphony, he harrumphed in the *Evening Transcript*: "Were we to say that all of it that did not sound horrible and outrageous sounded cheap, vulgar, and meretricious, we should be merely recording a first impression." In Russia, Taneiev's performance, part of the Moscow Exposition of Industry and Arts, brought the audience to its feet, but there, too, the critics were reserved. Opinions about the Second Concerto have been widely divergent, but the work has always had its champions, a few of whom have probably taken their stand just because the First Concerto—less calculated yet in some respects more sure—is so consumingly popular.

Tchaikovsky begins with a thundering march whose odd scansion gives it a nice twist. The orchestra plays it, then the piano repeats it with enthusiastic encouragement from the crowd. It does not take long for the extrovert G-major exuberance to disappear, for the flute gives it a melancholy turn, which then leads to the piano's next solo—nervously fluttering, thin-skinned music. Both the initial march and the piano solo are, in their contrasting ways, instantly suggestive of Schumann, a composer Tchaikovsky learned to love in his student days and whose voice ghosted through his music, always unexpectedly, all his life.

A dramatic change of key, heralded by a string tremolo that immediately carries us into *Eugene Onegin* and Tatiana's painful, sleepless night, brings new, lyric material. The development is most originally arranged, consisting of two extended passages for orchestra, the first harmonically static, the second powerfully propelling the music from dark minor-mode caverns to D major and the doorstep of the home key of G. Each of these episodes is

[10]M. Tchaikovsky, op. cit.

followed by a huge cadenza for the piano. Some years later, while working on his Concert Fantasia, Opus 56, Tchaikovsky remarked that he disliked the sound of piano and orchestra together: in the Concerto No. 2 he certainly went to some extreme lengths to segregate them. The piano writing in this work is far more demanding even than that in the First Concerto, both in range of keyboard vocabulary and in sheer taxing athleticism and endurance. The recapitulation is a drastically tightened revisiting of the materials of the exposition; the coda is brilliant and brief.

The second movement starts with one of those unprepared dissonances that struck terror into the hearts of nineteenth-century harmony teachers. This is the first in a series of shifting string chords through which Tchaikovsky makes his way to his new key of D major. The approach is completed by a solo violin—and how extraordinarily startled the first audiences must have been when they heard the violin move on into an extended and beautiful song all by itself. The song begins like a variation on Gounod's *Méditation sur le I^er Prélude de piano de S. Bach*, better known as his *Ave Maria*, wildly popular ever since its publication in 1873 and something Tchaikovsky cannot have escaped knowing.

The violin's twenty-seven-measure paragraph completed, a solo cello continues the thought, with the violin adding a descant for a further twenty-one bars. It is as though Tchaikovsky had forgotten he was writing a *piano* concerto. At last, the piano plays its own version of the soulful melody—and *there* is a challenge: for the seated percussion virtuoso to compete with colleagues on real singing instruments! After an agitated middle section, a cadenza for violin and cello leads to the return of the first melody, sung now by the violin and accompanied by cello and piano. Eventually the violin and cello decently retire, leaving the piano and orchestra—and the scoring here is magical—to bring the Andante to its atmospheric close. No feature of this work has been more controversial than Tchaikovsky's strange and daring move to offer us fifteen minutes of a triple concerto in the middle.[11] It is a strange thing, to have the dancers—and the music does among other things suggest *Swan Lake*—suddenly appear, only to disappear again without a trace, but these pages are undoubtedly Tchaikovsky's loveliest in this score and indeed some of his most beautiful altogether.

After the grand formal adventures of the first two movements, the third is as simple in design as it is straightforward in tone. Its spirit is that of high-stepping country dance, and piano virtuosity continues to be demanded in a big way right to the whirling end.

---

[11] The producers of the 1986 EMI recording by Barry Douglas with Rudolf Barshai and the Bournemouth Symphony actually engaged two prominent soloists—Nigel Kennedy and Steven Isserlis—to play in the second movement.

# Concerto in D major for Violin and Orchestra, Opus 35

*Allegro moderato—Moderato assai*
*Canzonetta: Andante*
*Finale: Allegro vivacissimo*

Tchaikovsky began work on his Violin Concerto at Clarens, Switzerland, in March 1878, and completed the score on 11 April that year. Leopold Auer, to whom he had intended to dedicate the concerto, rejected it, and the first performance was given by Adolf Brodsky at a Vienna Philharmonic concert conducted by Hans Richter on 4 December 1881. Tchaikovsky had been in Vienna on his way from Kiev to Venice just three weeks earlier, but seems to have had no idea that this long-delayed premiere was pending. The question of the dedication is discussed in the article by Auer quoted below.

**Solo violin, two flutes, two oboes, two clarinets, two bassoons, four horns, two trumpets, timpani, and strings.**

Tchaikovsky's Violin Concerto is as indispensable to violinists as his B-flat-minor Piano Concerto is to the keyboard lions—actually even more so, inasmuch as violinists have a smaller repertory to choose from. Both works got off to dismaying starts. The Piano Concerto, completed early in 1875, was turned down by Nicolai Rubinstein in the most brutal terms and had to travel to faraway Boston for its premiere at the hands of Hans von Bülow. Three years later, the painful episode repeated itself when the Violin Concerto's dedicatee, Leopold Auer, the concertmaster of the Imperial Orchestra in Saint Petersburg, declined to play it.

But the first of the three violinists who figured in the Concerto's early history was Yosif Yosifovich Kotek, one of Tchaikovsky's composition students. Kotek, twenty-two years old in 1878 when Tchaikovsky composed the Concerto, was described by the composer's brother Modest as a "good-looking young man, warm-hearted, enthusiastic, and a gifted virtuoso." He was a witness at Tchaikovsky's wedding and a confidant during its catastrophic aftermath; possibly he was Tchaikovsky's lover for a time. He was the first in the series of musicians employed by Tchaikovsky's patron, Nadezhda von Meck, and it was in fact he who established contact between the composer and that wealthy and secretive lady. He gave Tchaikovsky advice on violinistic matters, learned the piece page by page as Tchaikovsky wrote it, and, according to the composer's testimony, knew it so well "that he could have given a performance." In the event, he never did so: when an opportunity arose early in 1882, he passed it up, to Tchaikovsky's disgust; by then, however, he was more of a teacher than a public performer. He died in 1883.

From the beginning, Tchaikovsky had intended to have the Concerto played by Leopold Auer, who had come from Hungary to Saint Petersburg ten years earlier to take up his post with the Imperial Orchestra and to teach at the newly founded Conservatory. Here is the story as Auer told it to the New York magazine, *Musical Courier,* writing from Saint Petersburg on 12 January 1912:

> When Tchaikovsky came to me one evening, about thirty years ago [actually thirty-four], and presented me with a roll of music, great was my astonishment on finding that this proved to be the Violin Concerto, dedicated to me, completed, and already in print.[12] My first feeling was one of gratitude for this proof of his sympathy toward me, which honored me as an artist. On closer acquaintance with the composition, I regretted that the great composer had not shown it to me before committing it to print. Much unpleasantness might then have been spared us both. . . .
>
> Warmly as I had championed the symphonic works of the young composer (who was not at that time universally recognized), I could not feel the same enthusiasm for the Violin Concerto, with the exception of the first movement; still less could I place it on the same level as his strictly orchestral compositions. I am still of the same opinion. My delay in bringing the concerto before the public was partly due to this doubt in my mind as to its intrinsic worth, and partly that I found it would be necessary, for purely technical reasons, to make some slight alterations in the passages of the solo part. This delicate and difficult task I subsequently undertook, and re-edited the violin solo part, and it is this edition which has been played by me, and also by all my pupils, up to the present day. It is incorrect to state that I had declared the concerto in its original form unplayable. What I did say was that some of the passages were not suited to the character of the instrument, and that, however perfectly rendered, they would not sound as well as the composer had imagined. From this purely aesthetic point of view only I found some of it impracticable, and for this reason I re-edited the solo part.
>
> Tchaikovsky, hurt at my delay in playing the concerto in public and quite rightly too (I have often deeply regretted it, and before his death received absolution from him), now proceeded to have a second edition published, and dedicated the concerto this time to Adolf Brodsky, who brought it out in Vienna, where it met with much adverse criticism, especially from Hanslick. The only explanation I can give of the orchestral score still bearing my name is that when the original publisher, Jürgenson, of Moscow, to suit the composer, republished the concerto, he brought out the piano score in the new edition,

---

[12]The printed edition that was issued by P. I. Jürgenson (Moscow) in 1878 was of the reduction for violin and piano; the orchestral score came out in 1888.

but waited to republish the orchestral score until the first edition of it should be exhausted. This is the only way I can solve the problem of the double dedication.

. . . The concerto has made its way in the world, and after all, that is the most important thing. It is impossible to please everybody.

Auer's account in his autobiography, *My Long Life in Music*, differs in tone and in a few details. He mentions that Tchaikovsky had played the concerto for him at the piano (a "somewhat awkward" rendering) and cites two places in the work that struck him immediately, "the lyric beauty of the second theme in the first movement, and the charm of the sorrowfully inflected second movement." He sounds altogether less defensive, less patronizing, and there is no hint of suppressed pleasure in the account of the bad reception of the concerto in Vienna; indeed, he writes that Hanslick's comment that "the last movement was redolent of vodka . . . did credit neither to his good judgment nor to his reputation as a critic."[13]

Nicolai Rubinstein had eventually come round in the matter of the Piano Concerto; Auer not only became a celebrated exponent of the Violin Concerto himself but, as he pointed out, taught it to his remarkable progeny: Heifetz, Elman, Zimbalist, Seidel, Parlow, Milstein, Dushkin, Shumsky, and others. The "absolution" to which he refers in the *Musical Courier* article must have come in the last years of the composer's life, because in 1888 Tchaikovsky not only was still resentful about Auer's actions a decade earlier but also believed him to be intriguing against the work by, for example, dissuading the French violinist Émile Sauret from taking it into his repertory. As for Auer's editorial emendations, they are unnecessary, strictly speaking, but they do not amount to a betrayal.[14] Just the same, his initial rejection of the work was a nuisance at the beginning: his verdict, Tchaikovsky observed, "coming from such an authority . . . had the effect of casting this unfortunate child of my imagination into the limbo of the hopelessly forgotten." And hence the premiere in a far-off and unsympathetic venue.[15]

Adolf Brodsky, who turned thirty in 1881, the year he introduced the Tchaikovsky Concerto, was of Russian birth but trained chiefly in Vienna. He became an important quartet leader (there is now an English quartet named for him), served as concertmaster of the New York Symphony and

[13]Leopold Auer, *My Long Life in Music* (New York: Frederick A. Stokes, 1923).
[14]Certain changes that have become habitual among violinists—taking the theme of the Canzonetta up an octave upon its restatement and some cuts in the last movement—do not appear in Auer's printed edition but do seem to have been taught by him.
[15]Auer's recordings of the *Mélodie* from Tchaikovsky's *Souvenir d'un lieu cher* and a Brahms *Hungarian Dance* give us some picture of his strong technical command (he made them on his seventy-fifth birthday!) and peppy temperament. According to Stravinsky, Auer used to brag that he would deliberately play passages in octaves very slightly out of tune; otherwise, he claimed, no one would know he was playing octaves, so clean was his intonation.

the Hallé Orchestra in Manchester, England, and eventually settled in Manchester as director of the Royal College of Music. (In England he changed the spelling of his first name to Adolph.) He had already tried to place Tchaikovsky's concerto with the orchestras of Pasdeloup and Colonne in Paris before he managed to persuade Richter and the Vienna Philharmonic to take it on. The performance must have been awful. Brodsky himself was prepared, but Richter had not allowed enough rehearsal time, and most of the little there was went into correcting mistakes in the parts. The orchestra, in terror, accompanied everything *pianissimo*. Brodsky was warmly applauded, but the piece itself was hissed.

What is best remembered about that premiere is the Eduard Hanslick review in the *Neue freie Presse* to which Auer refers:

> The Russian composer Tchaikovsky is surely no ordinary talent, but rather, an inflated one, obsessed with posturing as a man of genius, and lacking all discrimination and taste. . . . The same can be said for his new, long, and ambitious Violin Concerto. For a while it proceeds soberly, musically, and not mindlessly, but soon vulgarity gains the upper hand and dominates until the end of the first movement. The violin is no longer played: it is tugged about, torn, beaten black and blue. . . . The Adagio is well on the way to reconciling us and winning us over when, all too soon, it breaks off to make way for a finale that transports us to the brutal and wretched jollity of a Russian church festival. We see a host of gross and savage faces, hear crude curses, and smell the booze. In the course of a discussion of obscene illustrations, Friedrich Vischer [the nineteenth-century aesthetician] once maintained that there were pictures whose stink one could see. Tchaikovsky's Violin Concerto confronts us for the first time with the hideous idea that there may be musical compositions whose stink one can hear.[16]

But, as Auer said, it is impossible to please everybody. Tchaikovsky does, however, please us right away with a gracious melody, minimally accompanied, for the violins of the orchestra. Indeed, we had better enjoy it now because he will not bring it back. (He does the same tease with the big *Tonight We Love* tune at the beginning of the First Piano Concerto.) But as early as the ninth measure, a few instruments abruptly change the subject and build up suspense with a quiet dominant pedal. The violins at once get into the spirit of this unexpected turn, and they have no difficulty running over those few woodwinds who are still nostalgic about the opening melody. And thus the soloist's entrance is effectively prepared. What the solo plays at first is in fact the orchestral violins' response to the dominant pedal, but set squarely

[16]Eduard Hanslick, *Music Criticisms 1850-1900*, ed. and transl. Henry Pleasants (Baltimore: Penguin Books, 1963).

into the harmonic firmament and turned into a "real" theme. Later, Tchai-kovsky introduces a new and lyric theme for the solo violin, the one Auer liked so much, quiet but *con molto espressione*. The transitional passages provide the occasion for the fireworks that endear the Concerto to violinists and audiences. The cadenza is Tchaikovsky's own, and it adds interesting new thoughts on the themes as well as providing further technical alarums and excursions.

At the first run-through in April 1878 by Kotek and the composer, everybody, Tchaikovsky included, sensed that the slow movement was not quite right. Tchaikovsky quickly composed a replacement in the form of the present tender Canzonetta and found a new home for the original Andante as the *Méditation* that opens the three-movement suite *Souvenir d'un lieu cher*. The Canzonetta is lovely indeed, both in its melodic inspiration and in its delicately placed, beautifully detailed accompaniment.

Perhaps with his eye on the corresponding place in Beethoven's Violin Concerto, Tchaikovsky invents a dramatic crossing into the finale, though unlike Beethoven he writes his own transitional cadenza. So far we have met the violin as a singer and as an instrument that allows brilliant and rapid voyages across a great range. Now Tchaikovsky presents it to us with the memory of its folk heritage intact. We can read Hanslick again and recognize what so offended him. To us, the finale sounds like a distinctly urban, cultured genre picture of country life, but one can imagine that in the context of 1880s Vienna it might have struck some delicate noses as distinctly uncivilized. And, although Tchaikovsky couldn't please Dr. Hanslick, he has no trouble at all winning us over.

## Variations on a Rococo Theme, for Cello and Orchestra, Opus 33

Tchaikovsky composed these Variations in December 1876, and Wilhelm Fitzenhagen, to whom the score is dedicated and who is in fact responsible for much of the work in the form in which we almost invariably hear it today, gave the first performance in Moscow on 30 December 1877 with Nicolai Rubinstein conducting. That was probably the last performance of the work as Tchaikovsky wrote it until 1941, when it was played in Moscow without Fitzenhagen's by-then standard emendations. Of that, more below.

**Solo cello, two flutes, two oboes, two clarinets, two bassoons, two horns, and strings.**

Listening to this charmer, we would not guess that Tchaikovsky wrote it in a state of grievous depression. *Vakula the Smith,* one of the operas he wrote between his Fourth and Fifth symphonies, had just enjoyed what he called a "brilliant failure" at the Maryinsky Theater in Saint Petersburg; Sergei Taneiev had reported from Paris that Jules-Étienne Pasdeloup had "shamefully bungled" *Romeo and Juliet* and that the work had not pleased; and he learned that not only had Hans Richter had no success with *Romeo* in Vienna either, but that the feared Eduard Hanslick had written one of his most abusive reviews. All this happened within two weeks at the beginning of December 1876. But Tchaikovsky was learning to escape depression through work; even though ill, he pursued a project begun a couple of months earlier (and to be abandoned soon after), an opera based on *Othello,* and rapidly composed the *Rococo Variations.*

He intended them for the twenty-eight-year-old Wilhelm Karl Friedrich Fitzenhagen, since 1870 principal cellist of the Orchestra of the Imperial Russian Music Society in Moscow and professor at the conservatory there. Fitzenhagen intervened considerably in the shaping of "his" piece, enough so that we really ought to bill it as Tchaikovsky-Fitzenhagen when it is played in the standard edition. Much of the detail in the solo part is his and was actually entered by him into Tchaikovsky's autograph, but more important, he dropped one entire variation and changed the order of the others, a procedure that then necessitated some further cut and splices.[17]

Tchaikovsky did not explain to his publisher, P. I. Jürgenson, that he had asked Fitzenhagen to go through the *Variations,* and so Jürgenson wrote to him: "Horrible Fitzenhagen insists on changing your cello piece. He wants to 'cello' it up and claims you gave him permission. Good God! *Tchaikovsky revu et corrigé par Fitzenhagen!*" But in one of those fits of insecurity about his work, particularly about questions of form, that possessed him from time to time, Tchaikovsky yielded authority to his German-trained friend and acquiesced in the publication of the work as recomposed by Fitzenhagen—with piano in 1878 and in full score eleven years later. Anatol Brandukov, one of Fitzenhagen's students, once asked Tchaikovsky whether he planned to do anything about restoring his own ideas. It was clear the question irritated the composer. "Oh, the hell with it!" he replied. "Let it stay the way it is." Moreover—and this is truly puzzling—in 1887 Tchaikovsky made sure to

[17]Perhaps it is no coincidence that Fitzenhagen was a student of the unscrupulous Friedrich Grützmacher, the cellist who scrambled together bits and pieces of various Boccherini concertos, reorchestrating them elaborately and passing the result off as "Boccherini's Concerto in B-flat." I do not know when Grützmacher concocted that piece, which is still current under that fraudulent title—it was not published until 1895 (after Fitzenhagen's death)—but clearly he was not a teacher from whom to learn artistic ethics.

send his next piece for cello and orchestra, the *Pezzo capriccioso*, Opus 62, to Fitzenhagen for vetting.[18]

It leaves those who prefer Tchaikovsky to Fitzenhagen little firm ground to stand on. Tchaikovsky's original is better than Fitzenhagen's revision, and it is not difficult to argue that point, but aside from the inertia of cellists who have learned the *Variations* à la Fitzenhagen, there is a serious obstacle in that no one, as of the late 1990s, has published the performance materials of the original. The Russian complete edition of Tchaikovsky includes a score of the unretouched *Variations*, but the State Publishing House has never made orchestral parts or a piano reduction for study purposes available. Cellists who want to play what Tchaikovsky really wrote need to go to a lot of bother and expense. Only a handful have done so.

Tchaikovsky's piece consists of an introduction, theme, eight variations, and a coda. He keeps all the variations in 2/4 together, with the somewhat slower (Andante) D-minor variation coming in the middle of the series; the one variation in a much slower tempo (Andante sostenuto), different meter (3/4), and more remote key (C major) is placed in the traditional spot for such an excursion, which is just before the finale.

In the following table, the left-hand column shows Tchaikovsky's order, while the one on the right shows where each section occurs in the standard edition (keys and time signatures are the same, as are tempo marks unless otherwise indicated):

**Tchaikovsky**
Introduction: Moderato assai quasi
   Andante—A major—2/4
Theme: Moderato semplice—A major
   —2/4
Var. 1: Tempo della thema [*sic*]—
   A major—2/4
Var. 2: Tempo della thema—A major—
   2/4
Var. 3: Andante—D minor—2/4
Var. 4: Allegro vivo—A major—2/4
Var. 5: Andante grazioso—A major—
   2/4
Var. 6: Allegro moderato—A major—
   2/4
Var. 7: Andante sostenuto—C major—
   3/4
Var. 8 and Coda: Allegro moderato
   con anima—A major—2/4

**Fitzenhagen**
Introduction (Moderato quasi
   Andante)
Theme (Moderato semplice)
Var. 1 (tempo del tema)
Var. 2
Var. 6
Var. 7
Var. 4
Var. 5
Var. 3
Coda (35 mm. cut)

[18]Perhaps Tchaikovsky liked Fitzenhagen's version of the *Variations* but was unable to say so outright.

Other than the outcome itself, we have no clue as to what exactly was in Fitzenhagen's mind. Perhaps his point of departure was the idea that the melancholy D-minor Variation (Tchaikovsky's Variation 3) should assume the place of honor near the end of the series; he therefore substituted it for the slow C-major Variation (Tchaikovsky's No. 7), moving the sections before and after it (a recitative-cadenza and Tchaikovsky's Variation 4) along with it. But this created two problems. Variations 4 and 8 are too much alike to make good neighbors, and so Fitzenhagen simply deleted No. 8, a charmingly balletic and cellistically brilliant episode, going straight from Variation 4 into the coda. Variation 8 is too delightful to lose. Fitzenhagen also had to find a spot for the displaced Variation 7, and this he simply moved forward into the one vacated by Variation 3. The trouble with this is that the C-major Variation, so different from its surroundings as well as so weighty, now comes much too soon and its effect is disruptive rather than climactic as Tchaikovsky had intended in his own exquisite design. (This had always bothered me about the piece long before I had ever heard of Fitzenhagen.) By the same token, the D-minor Variation is, relatively, a weak climax.[19]

What is beyond dispute (other than that Fitzenhagen's Italian is better than Tchaikovsky's) is that Fitzenhagen himself enjoyed immense success with this grateful, gracious, and charming piece whenever he played it, as have most of his successors. Liszt's reaction at the Wiesbaden Festival in 1879 gave cellist and composer particular pleasure: "At last, music again," the elderly master had sighed.

The theme, so far as we know, is Tchaikovsky's own. Nothing here can be mistaken for anything genuinely Rococo, not the little tune itself, nor what Tchaikovsky builds upon it, whether it trips along like the cygnets and toys of *Swan Lake* and *The Nutcracker* or, as in the glorious C-major Variation, indulges itself in luscious melancholia. These Variations are one of Tchaikovsky's most warmhearted declarations of love to what he perceived as the lost innocence of the eighteenth century.

---

[19]If you are clever about programming your CD player, you can take a conventional recording of the *Rococo Variations* and go at least some way toward restoring the original order.

*William Walton*

# William Walton

William Turner Walton, knighted by King George VI in 1951, was born in Oldham, Lancashire, on 29 March 1902 and died at Ischia, Italy, on 8 March 1983.

At wide intervals Walton wrote three string concertos, each for an eminent virtuoso: in 1929 the Viola Concerto for Lionel Tertis, ten years later the Violin Concerto for Heifetz, and seventeen years after that the Cello Concerto for Piatigorsky. The twenty-seven-year-old composer of the Viola Concerto, which is both the finest example of its genre and an important landmark on Walton's journey to maturity, was already famous—or notorious—thanks to *Façade*, the recitation to his dazzlingly apt chamber-musical accompaniment of Edith Sitwell's crackling and nostalgic poems, heard in 1923 by a London audience part delighted and part scandalized. *Façade* had already had a number of private performances in 1922, and a string quartet, which has not survived in the repertory, made Walton's name known to professionals internationally when it was selected as one of three works to represent England at the first festival of the International Society for Contemporary Music at Salzburg in 1923.

Walton learned music from his father, a teacher of singing. He went on to Christ Church Cathedral School at Oxford and from there to the university. His academic career was a disaster, but the libraries at Oxford provided the chance to read many scores, and he formed important friendships, particularly with literary people such as Ronald Firbank and the three Sitwells. But, as Walton's first biographer, Frank Howes, put it, "the Oxford connexion was ratified many years later by the conferment of an honorary D.MUS. in 1942 and an honorary Studentship of Christ Church." As a musician he was essentially self-taught.

The English critic David Cox has observed that "Walton began like a seventh member of *Les Six*. The style was marked 'continental,' pointed with wit and satire, bursting with exuberance. Nothing folksy." But the Andante of the *Sinfonia concertante* for Orchestra with Piano Obbligato (1927) introduces a new tone of voice, a new color and sentiment, and what Walton found there he pursued and splendidly fulfilled in the Viola Concerto. His big-screen oratorio *Belshazzar's Feast* (1931), for which Osbert Sitwell had drawn a libretto from the psalms and the book of Daniel, is Walton's most popular work; in the Symphony No. 1, finished after much travail in 1935, he attained a level of ambition, concentration, and sheer human energy for which he seems rarely to have tried again. By the time Walton had completed that score, Walton had also started to write film scores. His first was *Escape Me Never*, an Elisabeth Bergner weepie; the most famous of his later ones were *Major Barbara* and Laurence Olivier's Shakespeare films, *As You Like It*, *Henry V*, *Hamlet*, and *Richard III*.

## Concerto for Cello and Orchestra

> *Moderato*
> *Allegro appassionato*
> *Tema con improvvisazioni*

On 10 August 1955 Walton wrote to his friend Roy Douglas that he had "got the Vlc. Con. under way but that is only just. Rather a good opening." This had come about because Gregor Piatigorsky, who liked the Violin Concerto Walton had written for Piatigorsky's friend Heifetz, had offered the composer a commission, using his English accompanist Ivor Newton as an intermediary. In February 1956 Walton began concentrated work on the Cello Concerto, and at the same time started his *Johannesburg Festival* Overture, commissioned by the city of Johannesburg for its seventieth anniversary. He completed the Overture in May and the Concerto in October of that year. Piatigorsky gave the first performance of the Concerto on 25 January 1957 with Charles Munch and the Boston Symphony Orchestra. Walton composed three new endings, the last in December 1974: that story is told in the essay below.

**Solo cello, two flutes (second doubling piccolo), two oboes (second doubling English horn), two clarinets (second doubling bass clarinet), two bassoons and contrabassoon, four horns, two trumpets, three trombones, tuba, timpani, vi-**

braphone, suspended cymbal, bass drum, xylophone, snare drum, tambourine, celesta, harp, and strings.

Walton wrote no major orchestral work between the Violin Concerto, completed in June 1939, and the Cello Concerto. His big project of those years was his Chaucer opera, *Troilus and Cressida,* which occupied him between 1947 and 1954; along with that went a host of special projects and occasional scores, of which the score for Olivier's *Henry V* film is the most famous, and which also included such tasks as a Te Deum for the coronation of Queen Elizabeth II, and arrangements of the British and American national anthems for a Philharmonia tour of the United States. The Cello Concerto, Walton's first major composition after *Troilus,* is the most eloquent of the fairly sparse series of orchestral works that followed this opera.

At almost the last moment, Piatigorsky wrote that he was not happy about the way the Concerto ended, and that Heifetz wasn't either. Piatigorsky had specified that "the ending should be brilliant and the coda fairly long; all the existing concertos end abruptly, even the Dvořák." He certainly had not gotten what he had asked for, but he played Walton's original, quiet ending anyway. Three times Walton wrote a new close, but himself withdrew the first two of these. The third, from December 1974, was intended for Piatigorsky to play at his comeback concert in London in June 1975 after a long illness and absence from the concert stage. Piatigorsky liked that revision, but his cancer never went into remission enough to allow him to return to public performance, and in fact Walton's 1974 version has never been performed.

In his Cello Concerto, Walton once again returned to the design he had used in his two earlier string concertos: a slow-to-medium first movement, a scherzo, and a finale with reminiscences of the first movement. Walton begins here with a softly dissonant chord: C major, blurred by E-flat and A-flat, shades from the darker world of C minor. Several instruments, including harp and vibraphone, sound the chord all at once; woodwinds and pizzicato violins lay it out in gently moving eighth-notes; and the solo cello, which enters in the third measure, translates those notes into the horizontal and spins from them an inspired and spacious melody. What makes the melody beautiful is its wide-ranging contour and also its internal rhythmic variety; the little drum figure just after the beginning is especially striking. A contrasting theme, sung by the cello against a spare accompaniment and with the occasional sympathetic comment from this or that woodwind instrument, is more conjunct. These themes and the major-minor ambiguity proposed in the first chord dominate this lyric movement.

The scherzo is full of surprises in harmony and motion; the solo part is full of sixteenth-note patterns that will remind some listeners (and all cellists) of the corresponding movement in Elgar's Concerto. The movement ends with a delightful throwaway cadence.

Both these movements are preparatory to the finale, which Walton titles *Tema con improvvisazioni*. In his *Improvisations on an Impromptu by Benjamin Britten*, which Walton composed for the San Francisco Symphony in 1968–1969, he also fancies designating as improvisations what most composers would call variations. The finale of the Cello Concerto shares another feature both with the *Britten Improvisations* and the somewhat earlier *Variations on a Theme by Hindemith*, and that is a predilection for working with long themes.[1] The theme in the Cello Concerto is Walton's own, and it is an expansive melody, all tensile strength, and in slow tempo.

For the first improvisation, the melody is transformed—simplified really, and strangely accented—in a setting of piquant coloration (woodwinds, with strings either plucked or bowed at the bridge so as to produce a bony sound, with stopped horns and an ensemble of vibraphone, xylophone, celesta, and harp), against which the cello plays scale figurations in repeated notes. The next improvisation is for cello alone, in quick triple meter, varied in dynamics, range, and modes of attack, and marked *risoluto . . . brioso, con bravura*. Then comes a vigorous variation without the soloist, and this is in fact the first passage in the entire Concerto for the full orchestra *fortissimo*. After this summit of volume and speed there is a turning back in the form of another variation for the cello alone, more cadenzalike than the previous one (Walton marks it *rapsodicamente*) and built on even more dramatic contrasts. This quasi-cadenza concludes in a chain of trills, under which the orchestra steals in for the meditative epilogue, which is based on material from the first and third movements.

## Concerto for Viola and Orchestra

*Andante comodo*
*Vivo, con molto preciso*
*Allegro moderato*

Walton wrote his Viola Concerto in 1928–1929. Paul Hindemith was the soloist at the first performance, which was given in London on 3 October 1929, with the composer conducting the Queen's Hall Orchestra. A prefatory note in the printed score tells us that "in 1962 the composer rescored the

---

[1] The Britten theme comes from his Piano Concerto, the Hindemith theme from his Cello Concerto (also written for Piatigorsky).

work for a smaller orchestra, using double instead of triple woodwind, omitting one trumpet and tuba, and adding a harp. . . . The composer strongly
prefers [the revised version]."[2] This revision was actually undertaken in 1961,
not 1962; the first performance of the new version was given on 18 January
1962 by John Coulling, with Sir Malcolm Sargent conducting the London
Philharmonic.

**Revised version: Solo viola, two flutes (second doubling piccolo), two oboes
(second doubling English horn), two clarinets (second doubling bass clarinet),
two bassoons, four horns, two trumpets, three trombones, timpani, harp, and
strings. Walton distinguishes between passages when all the strings are to play
and those when the sections are to be reduced to 8-6-6-4-4.**

It was Sir Thomas Beecham, Walton's fellow-Lancastrian, who encouraged
Walton to write a viola concerto for Lionel Tertis. In 1929 Tertis and Paul
Hindemith were the two most celebrated violists in the world. Through his
tenacity as well as his artistry, Tertis, who was born in 1876 (on the same
day as Casals, whose partner in concert he often was) and who lived until
1975, did more than anyone else to establish the viola as a solo instrument,
fighting tremendous prejudice all the way; he titled his memoirs *Cinderella
No More*. Hindemith, who was just eight years older than Walton, gave the
occasional solo performance, but he was better known as a chamber player
(as a member of the Amar Quartet and of a string trio with Szymon Goldberg
and Emanuel Feuermann) and as a performer on the viola d'amore. He was
also a pianist, conductor, and teacher, and of course he was best known as a
composer, thought of by many people at the time as a scandalous modernist.

    For some reason, Tertis was irritated by the arrival of Walton's unsolic-
ited concerto—I suspect he did not approve of *Façade* and the whole Sitwell-
Firbank circle—and he sent it back by return mail. Walton wrote later that
this "depressed me a good deal as virtuoso violists were scarce," but

---

[2]Apropos revisions—on the two recordings of the Concerto made by William Primrose, one with
Walton conducting, the other conducted by Sir Malcolm Sargent but in Walton's presence, portions
of the solo part have been rewritten, especially in the second movement. In *Playing the Viola*, a
valuable book of conversations between Primrose and David Dalton (Oxford University Press, 1988),
Primrose says: "Keenly aware of the reputation the viola had gained as a nasty, growling, and grunting
instrument . . . I was ever on the lookout for ways of offsetting this presumption. Among other devices
I used was . . . to play rapid, virtuosic passages an octave higher . . . in order to avoid the unseemly
scrubbing that so often resulted from placement on the lower two strings." Primrose goes on to tell
that Walton never indicated that he minded this, that his own inquiry to Walton yielded no clear
answer, and that it was only after another player had asked Walton what he thought about Primrose's
transpositions that the composer indicated that he definitely preferred to hear the music just as he
had written it.

Edward Clark, who performed heroic tasks on behalf of new works during the years he was in charge of music at the BBC, suggested going to Hindemith. Walton had met Hindemith at the 1923 Festival of the International Society for Contemporary Music and was rather in awe of his slightly senior and very much more famous and established colleague. Walton was also embarrassed because he realized there was a lot of Hindemith in his Viola Concerto; nonetheless, through Clark's good offices, Hindemith agreed to give the Concerto its first airing. The Hindemith-Walton friendship flourished until Hindemith's death in 1963. Tertis, to his credit, came to the premiere, was delighted by the piece, learned it, and performed it at the ISCM Festival at Liège in 1930 and many times thereafter until his retirement in 1936.

The Concerto is in three movements, with a not-very-slow slow movement placed first. With a little help from a couple of woodwinds, muted violas and violins establish a flowing 9/8 motion, and almost at once the solo viola expands these hints into a broad and expressive melody. I don't know whether Walton attended the first English performance by Szigeti and Ansermet of Prokofiev's Violin Concerto No. 1 in 1925, but it would be surprising if he had not. This opening melody is close cousin to the one with which Prokofiev's Concerto begins, and for that matter the general layout of Walton's Concerto—quasi-slow movement, scherzo, and allegro finale with dreamy epilogue—precisely mirrors that of his colleague's masterpiece.[3]

This opening melody is beautifully spun out, Walton's sense of dialogue between the viola and various orchestral solo instruments being particularly lovely. Several times woodwinds punctuate the flow with a three-note phrase whose special feature is the juxtaposition of major and minor chords, to distinctly piquant effect. These "false relations," as they are called, were characteristic of English music in the sixteenth and seventeenth centuries.

A second theme, delicately accompanied by trombone chords with bassoon, harp, and plucked low strings, is also lyric in character, but its rhythm—alternating measures of 3/4 and 4/4, combining to make 7/4—gives it a character markedly different from that of the opening music. The development becomes increasingly athletic, the *martellato* triple-stops just before the soloist briefly exits the scene being another touch borrowed from Prokofiev. This disappearance of the solo viola is brief; soon, however, a much longer orchestral passage introduces the recapitulation, which is about as compressed as is compatible with clarity. The oboe now gets the first theme, while the viola hangs triplet garlands on it. The movement ends with the viola meditating upon the major-minor false relations.

The scherzo, whose prevailing fourths are very Hindemithy, is fairly

[3]Prokofiev, Hindemith, and Walton trod parallel paths from youthful styles characterized by sharp edges and a fondness for satire to a preference for a more mellifluous musical language.

brief, but it covers a lot of territory with rambunctious energy. For readers of Italian, the tempo and character direction, *Vivo, con molto preciso*, is quite as bad as it looks: "Lively, with very precise." I assume that the older Walton, the elective Ischian, chose out of a combination of nostalgia and humor to retain this reminder of his linguistically callow youth.

The scherzo began with rising fourths, F-sharp/B/E; the finale begins with the same three notes deployed as rising fifths, E/B/F-sharp. The instrument is a bassoon, the mood humorous and *sec*. The theme takes quite a lot of space, the bassoon version being followed by one for solo viola, and that by another for the woodwinds and lower strings. The next idea is more lyrical, and the prevalence of parallel sixths for the viola is reminiscent of the first movement, where that sound played a large role. The contours, as well, are drawn from material in the Andante. Walton is beginning to gather things together.

As in the first movement, the development is extensive, the recapitulation compressed. And here is where the finale takes an unexpected course. What we imagine to be the beginning of the coda turns out to be a whole new development section that culminates in by far the longest tutti in the entire Concerto. When this subsides, bass clarinet and harp, back in the home key of A major, offer to recapitulate the bassoon theme with the stalking fifths one more time, but their music is moved into the background by the still, small voice of the solo viola, *pianissimo* but *molto espressivo*, singing the Concerto's very first melody. The last music of all is another meditation on the false relations, but with the conflicting notes heard simultaneously rather than consecutively, the viola holding a C-sharp/A double stop while the harp and the lower strings softly sound repeated chords of A minor. The finale has made a voyage from something like frivolity to nostalgia and gentle melancholy.

## Concerto for Violin and Orchestra

> *Andante tranquillo*
> *Presto capriccioso alla napolitana*
> *Vivace*

Urged by the violist William Primrose, Jascha Heifetz commissioned this Concerto in 1936. Film scores and other projects kept Walton from getting to the Violin Concerto before 1938; in the spring of 1939, he visited America so as, in the words of his biographer Frank Howes, "to incorporate into the solo part Heifetz's own suggestions for presenting the substance of the music in the most effective light that violin technique could cast upon it." Walton then completed the score in New York on 2 June 1939, and Heifetz gave the first performance on 7 December that year, with Artur Rodzinski and the Cleveland Orchestra. In 1941 Walton revised the work, and the first performance of the new version was given on 17 January 1944 in Wolverhampton, England, by Henry Holst with Malcolm Sargent and the Liverpool Philharmonic.

**Solo violin, two flutes (second doubling piccolo), two oboes (second doubling English horn), two clarinets, two bassoons, four horns, two trumpets, three trombones, timpani, snare drum, cymbals, tambourine, xylophone, harp, and strings.**

In his Violin Concerto, Walton returned to the formal design he had used in his Viola Concerto and which he would again find useful in his Cello Concerto: a first movement in a slow-to-medium tempo and of considerable gravity, a scherzo, and a finale with contemplative episodes looking back to the first movement.

What we hear first, a seesawing figure for the clarinet, is definitely background; nonetheless, Walton invents a rhythmic pattern for those few notes (and for their continuation by the violas and eventually the second violins) that gives them a clear sense of character. The first theme proper appears almost immediately; it is actually a double theme, one melody for the solo violin, another for bassoon with half the cellos.

The double melody immediately introduces us to the expressive world, intimate and intense at the same time, in which the Concerto lives. Yearning rising sevenths, a characteristic feature of Walton's vocabulary, are prominent in both lines. Gradually the soloist comes to dominate the proceedings, withdrawing only to allow the orchestra to present a second theme. The scoring is notably rich, the harmonic angle is unexpected (E-flat minor after the B minor, which is "home" in the Concerto), and the melody itself takes as its point of departure a four-note phrase (E/F-sharp/A/G) from the bassoon line in the first theme. Sevenths are still prominent, but now more in the harmony than in the melodic lines. Walton is orthodox in his super-clear layout of themes, unorthodox and fresh in his harmonic strategy, thoughtful about every matter affecting overall coherence, and generous in melodic invention.

The exposition comes to an end with a definite feeling of closure; the development starts with the winds declaiming a powerfully distended version of the opening violin melody, while the strings provide an agitated hubbub of sixteenth-notes. That melody is in fact the subject of the whole excited first part of the development. A short cadenza functions as a caesura, after

which the development concerns itself at length with the second theme—
at such length, in fact, that Walton leaves it out of the recapitulation. That
section, which arrives after a tense buildup, consists of the return of the
opening double theme, but varied in detail and with the roles redistributed
so that the flute sings the original violin melody, while the solo violin takes
on the music that formerly belonged to the bassoon and cellos. The seesaw
accompaniment is now in muted violins, moving later to a wonderful combination of harp, timpani, and bassoon. It is also a little slower than before.
At the end, low strings and bassoon find just a moment in which to allude
to the second theme, a gesture that elicits sympathetic response from the
English horn just before the final, quiet bars.

The second movement is a brilliant scherzo: "Quite gaga, I must say,
and of doubtful propriety after the 1st movement," Walton wrote to his
publisher, Hubert Foss. There is much flying passagework for the soloist; it
seems Walton had a hard time making it difficult enough to please Heifetz,
and not just egged on by the violinist but responding to specific suggestions,
he constantly invents variations of color, dynamics, bow-stroke, and even of
actual notes. A slinky tune in parallel sixths brings momentary relief from
all this busyness; silky and a bit coy, it is a perfect fixing of one aspect of the
unmistakable Heifetz style. The trio also brings a moment of repose: Walton
labels it *Canzonetta*, and it begins as a horn solo harmonized with charming
obliqueness. Much of this *alla napolitana* movement was written in Walton's
future home, Italy, for which he had early developed an affinity under the
guidance of the Sitwells.

Walton begins the finale with a stalking theme in the cellos and basses,
soon joined by bassoons; the violin soloist quickly discovers how to change
its character while keeping its contour. By way of contrast, violins and high
woodwinds present a nervously jumping theme, but this proves to be merely
an episode on the way to the formal second theme, a lush and expansive
violin tune that shows the Romantic Walton at his best. (It of course abounds
in sevenths.) But little patience is shown for such reveries, at least for now,
and the development erupts briskly. As in the first movement, there is a short
cadenza partway through, which seems, whether intentionally or not, to
quote a famous Heifetz specialty, the Tchaikovsky Concerto.

Again, Walton rings attractive changes on a familiar formal design. This
time he begins the recapitulation with the second theme, freshly distributed
between orchestra and soloist, and scored with soft gorgeousness. Then comes
the stalking first theme, and for the spot where, if it had not already occurred,
we would normally expect the return of the Romantic second theme, Walton
reserves a lovely expansion of the horizon: the return in a new and beautiful
voicing of the soloist's melody from the very beginning of the Concerto. That
quietness now sinks into the still deeper quietness—deeper because harmonically so static—of an accompanied cadenza, lovingly modeled on the dream-

cadenza in the third movement of Elgar's Violin Concerto. Walton invites us to review where we have been this half hour, and like Elgar, he actually uses the word *sognando*—dreaming. Then the stalking theme, entering softly and with deliberation, returns us to reality, so that a coda in march style may bring the Concerto to a suitably brilliant conclusion.

# Bernd Alois Zimmermann

Bernd Alois Zimmermann was born on 20 March 1918 at Bliesheim near Cologne, Germany, and died by his own hand at Großkönigsdorf, also in the Cologne region, on 10 August 1970.

## *Nobody Knows de Trouble I See,* for Trumpet and Orchestra

Zimmermann composed this work in 1954 on commission from the Northwest German Radio (now North German Radio), Hamburg. It was first performed in Hamburg, on 11 October 1955. The soloist was Adolf Scherbaum, and Ernest Bour conducted the Orchestra of the North German Radio. The score is dedicated to Ernest Frice.

**Solo trumpet, flute (doubling piccolo), oboe (doubling English horn), jazz clarinet, three alto saxophones, tenor saxophone, baritone saxophone, bassoon, horn, three jazz trumpets, jazz trombone, tuba, timpani, tam-tam, vibraphone, small cymbal, snare drum, wood block, high-hat cymbal, long drum, large and small bongos, temple block, large and small tom-toms, crash cymbals, xylophone, guitar, harp, piano (doubling Hammond organ, or xylophone if the Hammond organ is not available), and strings.**

The face that looks out at us from my favorite photograph of the composer is friendly, sad, not without humor, a trifle quizzical. One is acutely aware of the shadows, and these are echoed in the dark patches that remain in the grizzled, thick, brush-cut hair and beard. Bernd Alois Zimmermann, Bazi to his friends, described himself as a typically Rhenish mixture of Dionysus and monk. All who remember him speak of his vitality, wit, and charm, but his life, dislocated by the war, with its wretched prelude and postlude, ended in despair. Through it all, he became a great composer. Entering Zimmermann's *Requiem for a Young Poet*, a bulletin on the state of the world mid-century and which he himself called a " 'Lingual' . . . based on texts by various poets and on reports and accounts," can leave you shattered. *Die Soldaten* (The Soldiers) has been hailed as the most important opera since *Wozzeck* so often that the accolade has virtually turned into a cliché.

Zimmermann went to a boarding school at a Salvatorian monastery at Steinfeld in the Eifel mountains south of Cologne. There he learned to love books and pictures, and he wrote and painted all his life. (The range of reference in his essays—from the Bible to Twiggy—is staggering.) Music lessons were offered only to older boys and as a reward for high grades, but since Zimmermann was a good student he was allowed organ lessons at sixteen. When the Nazis shut the monastery down in 1935, he was transferred to a state Catholic high school in Cologne (now named for Konrad Adenauer, its most famous alumnus). At twenty-one, finally realizing how much music had become a central passion, he gave up his plan to be a classics scholar and enrolled at the Cologne Conservatory.

Drafted when the war began, Zimmermann worked for an officer with a subversive taste for non-German music who sent him to Paris to buy scores of Stravinsky and Milhaud, amazing eye- and ear-openers for the very civilian young soldier. Years later, he wrote to a friend that he had never shot at a living being. He managed the occasional lesson with Heinrich Lemacher, Germany's leading Catholic church composer, and with Philipp Jarnach, a Busoni pupil, but his professional education was really deferred until after the war, when he was able to study with Wolfgang Fortner and René Leibowitz as well as enroll in the International Summer Courses in New Music, that exciting breeding ground for the postwar avant-garde, when they began at Darmstadt in 1946.

Meanwhile, Zimmermann found work as an arranger at the Cologne Radio, gradually being offered more interesting assignments for radio, film, and stage. These jobs gave him scope to realize an idea he had imagined in boyhood: musical collage. For example, in a William Saroyan play he added scraps of Schumann and Duke Ellington to a boogie-woogie of his own he had made from electronically manipulated sounds of hammering.

Zimmermann liked quotations, not so much for their allusive and evocative value as for their ability to obliterate the distinction between past, present, and future. "The most distant compositional achievements in musical history can be the most closely linked," he wrote in his essay "On Productive Discontent." The marriage in *Nobody Knows de Trouble I See* of (more or less) Schoenbergian twelve-note technique to an African-American spiritual is an example right at hand.

Zimmermann's boyhood reading of Saint Augustine had aligned him with those philosophers who believe that a human being's—or human-kind's—advance through time and even the flow of time itself are illusory. His later reading of Joyce, Pound, and the diaries of Paul Klee supported his belief and also suggested ways of turning his idea of "the spherical nature of time" into music. A composer, he said, must come to terms with time, for in a musical composition time is, so to speak, "overcome" and brought to a standstill, and it was this overcoming of time that gave Zimmermann his most acute pleasure in composing. Collage and quotation were means by which he sought to turn these ideas into vividly direct experiences for his listeners. The pieces in which Zimmermann's lifework culminates, *Die Soldaten* and *Requiem for a Young Poet*, are the ones in which his collage is richest.

German musicians had a lot of catching up to do after the twelve years of the Thousand-Year Reich, which had cut them off from Stravinsky, Schoenberg, Webern, Berg, and Bartók, to name just a few who had changed the face of music in the first half of the twentieth century. Zimmermann, fast heading for thirty, called himself "the oldest of the young generation," but he was the worst possible age. Orff (born 1895), Egk (1901), Blacher (1903), and Hartmann (1905) were old enough to have formed clearly defined artistic personalities and to have established themselves before the war; Henze (born 1926) and Stockhausen (1928) were young enough not to have had their education interrupted and to be counted after the war as interesting, "emerging" newcomers.

Zimmermann wrote music of high density, demanding much of his performers and hoping for much from his listeners. It was too "modern" to be quickly accessible like the work of Orff and Egk, nor did it tickle fans of the sort of avant-garde that screams "novelty." And the angel who bestows the gift for self-promotion had passed Zimmermann by at his baptism. That, as some of his great seniors such as Schoenberg, Sessions, and Dallapiccola could have told him, is not the road to "success." Zimmermann knew that anyway. His music, he wrote apropos *Die Soldaten*, did not "seek contact with the audience—that comes about another way."

He observed that the word *obstinacy* (*Widerborstigkeit*) stuck to him like a trademark. But, he wrote,

> Obstinacy will inevitably appear where unshakable convictions about what is right and sound in compositional choices and the consequences of those convictions make themselves felt, and an uncompromising attitude toward composition is probably not easily combined with social flexibility. And since I am between schools and tendencies and have steadfastly maintained this independence, naturally I find myself always between two stools. Thereby I at least fulfill Ezra Pound's postulate to the effect that between two stools is the only

legitimate place for an artist, but there's not much success or "success" to be won that way.[1]

In 1969 Zimmermann completed his *Requiem for a Young Poet*, dedicated to three writers who had committed suicide: Vladimir Mayakovsky (in 1930, at thirty-six), Sergei Yesenin (in 1925, at thirty), and Konrad Bayer (in 1964, at thirty-one). As the critic Marion Rothärmel puts it, Zimmermann compresses half a century of European history into an hour's music, superimposing on the liturgical Requiem text words in seven languages by, among others, Pope John XXIII, Joyce, Hitler, Wittgenstein, Churchill, Aeschylos, Schwitters, Mao, Camus, and the Beatles.

The two works that followed the *Requiem for a Young Poet* were a delicate orchestral *pianissimo* called *Stille und Umkehr* (Silence and Reversal), written for the celebrations in Nuremberg of the 500th birthday of Albrecht Dürer, and *Ich wandte mich und sahe an alles Unrecht, das geschah unter der Sonne* (So I returned, and Considered All the Oppressions that Are Done under the Sun), a powerful, deeply pessimistic "ecclesiastical action" on words from Ecclesiastes and the Grand Inquisitor scene in *The Brothers Karamazov*.

A few months before Zimmermann's death, the television director Horst Bienek had asked him to write a film score. Zimmermann's terse reply indicating that he was "no longer available" came on a postcard with a photograph of Cesare Pavese (a suicide in 1950, shortly before his forty-second birthday); printed on the card were the first words of a famous Pavese poem, *Verrà la morte* (Death Will Come). Zimmermann completed *Ich wandte mich* on 5 August 1970. Five days later he took his life.

Zimmermann's final action was long prepared. Dallapiccola called the life of a composer "la scuola della pazienza" (the school of patience). Zimmermann had run out of *pazienza* and succumbed to depression, which he had once called "discontent's quiet sister." He had spoken of "an insidious illness" and had been in despair over having to miss the premiere of his *Requiem* in December 1969 because of illness. He had never recovered from the death of his daughter Barbara at the end of 1963. Perhaps, as Harry Halbreich suggests in his essay "Requiem for a Suicide," Zimmermann had also suffered a religious crisis. As a boy he must have read in Augustine's *De civitate Dei* about "the will of a good God that good things should be"; it is easy to believe that he no longer knew how to reconcile this with "all the oppressions that are done under the sun."

Not all of Zimmermann's work is apocalyptic; central to his instrumental work, for example, is a group of seven concertos, virtuoso pieces which all, even when preponderantly serious, as *Nobody Knows de Trouble I See* surely is, relish that sportive element that has been so essential to the concerto

---

[1]Bernd Alois Zimmermann, *Intervall und Zeit*, ed. Chr. Bitter (Mainz: B. Schotts Söhne, 1974).

tradition. The earliest of these is the Violin Concerto of 1950, the last the Cello Concerto *en forme de pas de trois* of 1966. The others are for oboe, cello, trumpet, two pianos, and viola, *Nobody Knows de Trouble I See* being the fourth in the series. Zimmermann said that he composed it in response to the "racial madness" (*Rassenwahn*) he saw all around him.

Some of Zimmermann's compositions continue a musical thought from an earlier piece: in this instance, the twelve-note series is the same as the one on which he had based his Oboe Concerto two years earlier. It is a series that leans toward C minor, and in *Nobody Knows de Trouble I See* Zimmermann makes a happy marriage between the tune of the spiritual and a volatile accompaniment whose rich harmonic language ranges from the extremely simple to the densely dissonant. The accompaniment is sometimes an un-complicated, supportive background, but it can also be incredibly alive with flashes of light. Zimmermann remarked that three ways of composing—the chorale-prelude, free variations, and what he called concert jazz—constitute the motor of the work.

Over a dark, distant-sounding accompaniment, a trombone suggests at least the possibility of the existence of melody. The solo trumpet picks up the hint and begins a rhapsodic declamation. Soon the tempo speeds up, and the trumpet continues its now-impassioned melody against a dark ostinato in piano, harp, and timpani. A cadenza with orchestral punctuation inter-rupts this, and then an alto saxophone gives out the first clear evocation of the spiritual named in the title. The solo trumpet responds by jolting the music into a much faster tempo, playing now with enormous brilliance, and leading to a powerful climax. The music has become propulsive, moving forward with huge physical energy, and this provides the background for the solo trumpet at last to play the spiritual—*molto espressivo* and with continuous vibrato, Zimmermann directs. At this point he also writes the text into the trumpet part.

When the orchestra stops for a moment, the trumpet introduces a new idea based on a dotted rhythm, and this dominates the next phase of the piece. The solo is now more virtuosic than ever. Then everything subsides and seems to stop. The trumpet takes advantage of this by playing a fantas-tical, high-flying version of the spiritual. After one more short cadenza, the soloist offers a final variation on the tune, this one slow and in a low register, and the music ends quietly, peacefully, not without sadness.